THREE CENTURIES OF
TRAVEL WRITING BY
MUSLIM WOMEN

THREE CENTURIES OF TRAVEL WRITING BY MUSLIM WOMEN

—≈—

Siobhan Lambert-Hurley, Daniel Majchrowicz, and Sunil Sharma, editors

INDIANA UNIVERSITY PRESS

This book is a publication of

Indiana University Press
Office of Scholarly Publishing
Herman B Wells Library 350
1320 East 10th Street
Bloomington, Indiana 47405 USA

iupress.org

Manufactured in the United States of America

First printing 2022

Cataloging information is available from the Library of Congress.

ISBN 978-0-253-06204-8 (hardback)
ISBN 978-0-253-06239-0 (paperback)
ISBN 978-0-253-06205-5 (ebook)

پر لکھاں کتاباں شعر بناواں جد تک زندگی پاواں

تے لکھ گلہ جے کرن گلوئی ہر گز نہ پچھتاواں

دنیا وچ اولاد نہ میری لگا شوق حقانی

لوکاں نام اولادوں رہے میری رہی ایہہ نشانی

نال کتاباں نام رہے میرا تیک قیامت جاری

روزِ حشر بھی ہر سختی تھیں امن رکھے رب باری

نور بیگم، مظاہر نور

I will write books and compose poetry for as long as I live;

No matter how much they gossip and reproach me, I will never regret it.

I have no offspring in this world, but I do have this divine calling;

People are remembered by their children, but my legacy shall be this!

May I be remembered, through my writing, until the Day of Judgment,

And on that day, may God shield me from every hardship.

—Nur Begum, *Manifestations of Celestial Light*

CONTENTS

ACKNOWLEDGMENTS

A BOOK OF THIS TYPE is, inevitably, a truly collaborative venture.

Funding for the research was generously provided by a three-year project grant from the Leverhulme Trust in the United Kingdom (2015–18). Siobhan Lambert-Hurley also benefited from a visiting post in the Department of History at the University of British Columbia in Vancouver, Canada (2017). Daniel Majchrowicz benefited from the support of funding from Northwestern University in completing research on travel writing in early Urdu periodicals.

The core team of Siobhan Lambert-Hurley, Daniel Majchrowicz, and Sunil Sharma collected most of the research materials. However, we were supported by an advisory committee made up of regional specialists. Our thanks to Hülya Adak, Asiya Alam, Margot Badran, Marilyn Booth, Roberta Micallef, and Nawar al-Hassan Golley for their invaluable contributions and advice. Sylvia Vatuk inspired us early on by sharing a text from Hyderabad. C. Ceyhun Arslan and Greg Halaby offered additional expertise on Arabic texts. For their guidance on Southeast Asian materials, we thank Sylvia Tiwon, Megan Hewitt, John Roosa, Tineke Hellwig, and Eric Tagliacozzo. Margaret Litvin, Marianne Kemp, Eileen Kane, Masha Kirasirova, and Maximilian Drephal provided important aid in our search for Central Asian texts. Nurten Kilic-Schubel later filled a gap there. Later on, Andrew Amstutz also drew our attention to a unique text from Sindh, as did Hans Harder to a text in Bengali. Although some of the original travel accounts have been republished, far more emerged from private and archival collections in the United States, the United Kingdom, Germany, Egypt, Turkey, Iran, Uzbekistan, Pakistan, India, Indonesia, and Australia. We are particularly grateful to the Jhander Library in Mailsi, Pakistan, for sharing with us several accounts in Urdu and Punjabi.

While in progress, parts of our material were presented to a number of academic forums before engaged and thought-provoking audiences. A first opportunity was a panel entitled "'As Seen by a Woman': Reading Travel Writing from Muslim South Asia" at the Annual Conference on South Asia, University of Wisconsin at Madison, October 20–22, 2016. A second was a panel entitled "Veiled Voyagers: Muslim Women Travelers from Asia and the Middle East" at the Seventeenth Berkshire Conference on the History of Women, Genders and Sexualities, Hofstra University, New York, June 1–4, 2017. We also disseminated the research in numerous individual presentations and benefited from the feedback we received. For example, Lambert-Hurley presented at the Fourth European Congress on World and Global History; the "Gendered Lives Research Group" at Loughborough University; and the Institute of Modern Languages Research, University of London. Majchrowicz delivered papers at LUMS University in Lahore, Habib University in Karachi, Buffalo University, the University of Punjab in Lahore, Gadjah Mada University in Yogyakarta, Northwestern University, and the University of Chicago. Sharma spoke at the University of Kashmir, State University of New York at Binghamton, and Yale University.

We also undertook public engagement activities to reach a wider audience. Of particular note was a collaboration with Dead Earnest Theatre in Sheffield to produce an immersive theater experience based on the project's research materials. "Veiled Voyagers—A Mahfil" has so far been staged at Festival of the Mind (September 28–29, 2018) and the Migration Matters Festival (June 16–17, 2019) in Sheffield. It was also translated into a radio play for the virtual program of Britain's inaugural South Asian Heritage Month in August 2020 (available on YouTube here: https://youtu.be/DpPNXi9Yvug). The lively Q&A sessions at the end of these performances alerted us to what a general audience found significant in our historical materials and thus helped to structure the introduction here. We mark our debt to the wonderful and ever calm Charlie Barnes, who directed the productions, and the amazing cast of actresses, musicians, and dancers who brought the women in this book to life. Lambert-Hurley and Majchrowicz also benefited enormously from presenting the book's materials at two public events in Pakistan in November 2018, namely "Meet the Author: An Anthology of Muslim Women Travelers" at the Faiz International Festival, Lahore, November 16–18, 2018, and "Veiled Voyagers: A Workshop on Muslim Women Travel Writers from Asia and the Middle East," British Council Library, Karachi, November 20, 2018. Our thanks especially to Moneeza Hashmi at FIF and Gayle Franklin at the British Council for their kind invitations, generous hospitality, and careful organization. Early in the project, Lambert-Hurley also prepared a journalistic piece drawing on these materials, "Indian Students at

British Universities Is a Tradition We Should Cherish and Protect," for *The Conversation*, December 16, 2016. It drew useful feedback when it was republished in several Indian outlets, plus *The Independent* in the United Kingdom.

As a published work, there were many individual contributions to the collective output of specific chapters. The attributions in the first note of each chapter recognize the main players involved in preparing them for publication—those who composed introductions, completed fresh academic translations, and assembled annotations and further reading. In an insufficient attempt at scholarly recognition, we list the broader contributions as follows.

Siobhan Lambert-Hurley prepared the introductions, extracts, and annotations for the chapters on Halide Édib, Huda Shaarawi, Iqbalunnisa Hussain, Safia Jabir Ali, Sayyida Salamah bint Said/Emily Ruete, Selma Ekrem, Shareefah Hamid Ali, Sultan Jahan Begum, Zainab Cobbold, Zaib-un-nissa Hamidullah, and Zeyneb Hanoum. Amiruddin Jabir Ali kindly provided access to a typewritten transcript of the speech by his mother, Safia Jabir Ali, in his home in Mumbai in 2006. The extracts by Huda Shaarawi are from a published translation by Margot Badran, *Harem Years: The Memoirs of an Egyptian Feminist* (London: Virago, 1986). Our thanks to the Feminist Press for permission to use this material. Some of the extracts by Sayyida Salamah bint Said/Emily Ruete are from *An Arabian Princess Between Two Worlds: Memoirs, Letters Home, Sequels to the Memoirs, Syrian Customs and Usages* (Leiden: Brill, 1992). We are grateful to the publisher for their permission to reproduce this material. Our gratitude to Zaib-un-nissa Hamidullah's daughter Yasmine Ahmed and grandson Akbar Shahid Ahmed for permission to use extracts from *Sixty Days in America* (Karachi: Mirror Publications, 1956). Generously, they also commented on this chapter, as did Arif Zaman on the chapter on his grandmother, Iqbalunnisa Hussain.

Daniel Majchrowicz prepared the introductions, translations, and annotations for the chapters on Begum Inam Habibullah, Begum Hasrat Mohani, Begum Sarbuland Jung, Rahil Begum Shervaniya, Sughra Humayun Mirza, Ummat al-Ghani, Muhammadi Begum, and Qaisari Begum, all of which were originally written in Urdu. He also translated and introduced the Punjabi text by Nur Begum. All these chapters benefited from the support of many generous individuals in Pakistan. We are grateful to Mavra Azeemi for her input for the chapters on Muhammadi Begum, Begum Habibullah, Nur Begum, and Raheel Shervaniya. We also owe a debt of gratitude to Zehra Masrur Ahmad for allowing us access to Muhammadi Begum's diary, and for her careful revisions to both that chapter and the one on Qaisari Begum. We likewise thank the late Dr. Asif Farrukhi and Ameem Lutfi for facilitating this scholarly exchange and providing their own input and assistance. We also express our deep gratitude to

Muneeza Shamsie for her invaluable assistance in preparing the chapter on her grandmother, Begum Inam Habibullah. The novelist Kamila Shamsie was the first to use some of this material on her great-grandmother for the public Weinrebe Lecture on "Writing Women: The Fourth Generation" at the University of Oxford (January 24, 2018). Some of the material for the chapter on Begum Hasrat Mohani comes from *Worlds of Knowledge in Women's Travel Writing* (Boston: Ilex, 2022). We are grateful to the Ilex Foundation for allowing us to reproduce this material. We also thank Sylvia Vatuk for her kind assistance with the chapter on Ummat al-Ghani Nur al-Nisa. Not only did she draw our attention to this travel account, but she also discussed her research on this author's family, led us to additional sources, and carefully read through early drafts of the chapter. Ali Aftab Saeed, Saad Sultan, Ameem Lutfi, Arafat Razzaque, Salwa Nur, David Boyk, Mariam Chughtai, Dr. Abdurrashid, and Katherine Merriman provided helpful feedback and resources to complete these chapters, and we are grateful to them all. Finally, we thank Sharmain Siddiqui for helping us to gather information on the history of travel writing in Urdu periodicals.

Sunil Sharma prepared the translations from Persian for the chapters on Jahanara, the widow of Mirza Khalil, Mehrmah Khanom, Hajjiyeh Khanom Alaviya Kermani, Sakineh Soltan Khanom Esfahani Kuchak, Sediqeh Dowlatabadi, and Shams Pahlavi. Siobhan Lambert-Hurley prepared the introductions and annotations for all these chapters with input from Sharma. Lambert-Hurley prepared the introduction but worked with Sharma to prepare the extracts and annotations for the chapter on Taj al-Saltanah from a published translation: Taj al-Saltana, *Crowning Anguish: Memoirs of a Persian Princess from the Harem to Modernity, 1884–1914*, translated by Anna Vanzan and Amin Neshati and edited by Abbas Amanat (Washington, DC: Mage, 2003). We are grateful to the publisher for giving permission for these extracts to be included here. Houchang Chehabi at Boston University played a vital role in commenting on all the Iranian material.

Sunil Sharma prepared the translations from Urdu for the chapters on Atiya Fyzee and Nazli Begum; Siobhan Lambert-Hurley prepared the introductions and annotations. The material on Atiya Fyzee was prepared originally for their coauthored book, *Atiya's Journeys: A Muslim Woman from Colonial Bombay to Edwardian Britain* (Delhi: Oxford University Press, 2010). The material on Nazli Begum will be expanded for a forthcoming book.

Daniel Majchrowicz prepared the translations from Urdu for the chapters on Nawab Sikandar Begum and Maimoona Sultan; Siobhan Lambert-Hurley prepared the introductions and annotations.

Asiya Alam prepared the translations from Urdu with input from Daniel Majchrowicz and worked with Siobhan Lambert-Hurley to prepare the introductions and annotations for the chapters on Shaista Suhrawardy and Sughra Sabzwaria.

Andrew Amstutz prepared the introduction and translations from Urdu for the chapter on Mahmuda Rizvia.

C. Ceyhun Arslan and Greg Halaby prepared the introduction and translation from Arabic for the chapter on Amina Said. Siobhan Lambert-Hurley added material on the All-India Women's Conference and the Indian context to the introduction and annotations.

David Boyk prepared the introductions and translations from Urdu for the chapters on Mehr al-Nisa and Fatima Begum.

Megan Hewitt prepared the introductions and translations from Indonesian for the chapters on Suharti Suwarto and Nyonya Aulia-Salim, with input from Siobhan Lambert-Hurley and Daniel Majchrowicz based on texts supplied by Majchrowicz. Hewitt worked with Lambert-Hurley to prepare the introduction and extracts for the chapter on Herawati Diah.

Nurten Kilic-Schubel prepared the introductions, translations from Chaghatai Turki and Persian, and annotations for the chapter on Dilshad.

Roberta Micallef prepared the introduction and translation from Turkish for the chapter on Şükûfe Nihal Başar. She worked with Siobhan Lambert-Hurley to prepare the introduction, extracts, and annotations for the chapter on Melek Hanım.

Hans Harder prepared the introduction and translation from Bengali for the chapter on Rokeya Sakhawat Hossain.

Many of our translators produced longer extracts than are printed here for inclusion as supplementary material on an accompanying website, Accessing Muslim Lives (http://www.accessingmuslimlives.org). This website was originally crafted by Siobhan Lambert-Hurley and Marilyn Booth with Dark Text Productions. However, it was reenvisioned and recreated during the course of this project under the lead of Daniel Majchrowicz with the assistance of Robert Ward at Notne Digital. This new website was funded in part by our grant from the Leverhulme Trust. A significant additional contribution came in the form of an Arts Enterprise grant from the Faculty of Arts and Humanities at the University of Sheffield.

Finally, these acknowledgments could not be complete without expressing our gratitude to everyone at Indiana University Press for their enthusiasm, patience, and professionalism. Our two anonymous reviewers also provided detailed and challenging comments that enhanced this final draft. We thank Ishan Mehandru for his hard work in creating the index, no small task for a book of this size.

A NOTE ON TRANSLATION, TRANSLITERATION, AND SYNTAX

THE ORIGINAL MATERIALS IN THIS collection appeared in many different languages, including Arabic, Persian, Turkish, Chaghatai Turki, Urdu, Punjabi, Bengali, Indonesian, German, and English. A special effort has been made to make the translations as clear and comprehensible as possible for contemporary readers. As such, some of the literal quality of the originals may have been sacrificed for accessibility. Given the impossibility of precise transliteration across so many languages, a system that is relatively consistent but intuitive for native American English speakers has been adopted. Generally, we have omitted diacritical marks from the text with the exception of the *'ain* (') and the *hamza* (')—unless they appear in an English title or have been omitted in a standardized form (e.g., Amina Said, inshallah, Huda Shaarawi). The Persian-language *izafah* connector is denoted by *-i* (as in *safar-i hajj*) or *-e* in some cases; where it occurs after a vowel, it is sometimes replaced by *-yi* or *-ye*. The Arabic definite article *al-* is typically left in this form (rather than as it would be pronounced) for parity across languages. Place names are given according to English spellings, usually in terms of how they were used at the time (hence, Bombay appears more often than Mumbai). Foreign words adopted in English are never italicized (hajj, purdah, burqa) and spelled according to convention (begum, paan). Unassimilated foreign words are denoted by italics, unless they are used frequently (ziyarah, Eid, namaz). For ease of reading, we have corrected punctuation, capitalization, spelling errors, and certain anachronisms in texts reprinted from English.

THREE CENTURIES OF
TRAVEL WRITING BY
MUSLIM WOMEN

INTRODUCTION

Muslim Women, Travel Writing, and Cultures of Mobility

SIOBHAN LAMBERT-HURLEY AND
DANIEL MAJCHROWICZ

ON THE FACE OF IT, the premise of this volume is simple: a comparative study of travel narratives by Muslim women who traveled the world before the "jet age" transformed modern mobility. Yet in our contemporary moment, the very juxtaposition of these terms—Muslim, women, travel, mobility—instantly raises a number of questions. These may relate to practices of veiling, the need for male guardians, or perhaps restricted access to halal foods. Many of these suppositions are grounded in colonial or Orientalist notions about Muslim women and their life-worlds. No matter our background, we are all liable to make assumptions like these because the historical record about women's lives and their mobility in these contexts is weak at best. Only the specialist really has access to material that might tell us what it meant to travel as a Muslim woman from seventeenth-century Iran, nineteenth-century Turkey, or early twentieth-century India. Even those who live in Muslim societies today—whether Lahore or London—will perforce make assumptions about gendered mobility in centuries and decades past. The ubiquity of these assumptions is neatly captured in the interaction between one traveler in this volume, Sediqeh Dowlatabadi, and an immigration officer on her arrival in France in 1926 who reportedly said to her, "I can't believe that I am facing a Muslim and Iranian woman. Now tell me, with whom have you come all the way here? I mean, who has brought you? ... A Muslim Iranian woman has travelled alone from Tehran to France! How did your government permit you to leave? Where did you get this passport?"[1] In short, this is an unfamiliar history for most.

We express our sincere thanks to our collaborator and dear friend, Sunil Sharma, for his close reading of the draft introduction and fascinating suggestions for additions.

The present book will belie many of these assumptions, even as it affirms or inflects others. The accounts here date from the seventeenth to the middle of the twentieth century, spanning the arrival of the earliest extant travel accounts by Muslim women to the transformative arrival of the jet engine on transatlantic commercial routes in 1958. They were composed originally in ten different languages. The authors are all women, but their roster is diverse, taking in queens, reformers, pilgrims, Sufis, wives, converts, captives, flâneurs, litterateurs, and provocateurs. They hailed from Asia, the Middle East, Africa, and Europe, and their destinations were as varied as their points of origin: this volume will take the reader from Java to Alabama, from London to Mecca. Most of them identified as Muslim, and their writing engages meaningfully with that identification, whether from a religious or social perspective. They typically showed a distinctive concern for the lives of women at home and abroad, often with an eye to improving their own societies based on best practices encountered elsewhere. They are likewise united by their conscious decision to leave a record of their travels and to reflect on their experiences, typically for the benefit of other readers. It is this willingness to travel, combined with an inclination toward introspection and a desire for communal engagement or social and political change—and not simply their identity as Muslim women alone—that brings them together.

The kaleidoscopic array of their dispositions, cultural backgrounds, and perspectives necessarily nuances how we understand Islam and cultures of mobility. This study ruptures the seemingly bounded, transparent categories mentioned above to force deeper interrogation and reflection. With each successive chapter, readers will ask themselves again and again: What *does* it mean to speak of the Muslim woman? To what extent is that category meaningful across the centuries and regions from which these women hailed? Islam, of course, is not a monolith.[2] Neither is gender, or the concept of womanhood, any more fixed.[3] How, then, can we speak with any consequence of the experience of travel as a Muslim woman? Invoking travel as a concept is itself fraught, for even that category is historically and culturally determined.[4] These questions are taken up in more detail in the two sections that follow, the first by considering the relationship between travel writing and women, and the second by tracing Muslim women's participation within localized cultures of travel.

We hasten to note that these questions about Muslim women and travel are not only contemporary concerns. In fact, they are raised repeatedly by the women studied here. These travelers, too, sought to explore the multiple and contrasting ways that Muslim women lived and traveled throughout the world and across the centuries. Leaving home necessarily meant meeting other women, Muslim or otherwise, from a range of cultural backgrounds. Particularly for authors of the

nineteenth and twentieth centuries, the novel experiences mediated by travel allowed them to examine their own ideas of womanhood and to reconcile the idea
of a single Muslim community, or *ummah*, with its immense variety. We focus on
these meetings and mediations in the chapters that follow, joining these authors
on their terrestrial and intellectual journeys. We find, as did they, that there is
no single perspective or experience that inheres to Muslim women. Rather, the
positionality of every person is determined not only by gender or creed but also
often, and often principally, by other factors that include cultural background,
race, class, political outlook, and of course individuality.

This journey into the pasts of Muslim mobility leads through terrain that
is almost entirely new. Tragically, few Muslim women travelers have been the
subject of academic study or popular regard. Indeed, there is a glaring lack of
knowledge about the experiences of travel for women from much of what is now
called the Global South. A vast majority of the texts here are being translated
into English for the first time. Most are lost even to the literary traditions out
of which they grew. Such is the state of neglect that in a few cases, only a single
copy remains, sometimes found in obscure and inaccessible locations that were
brought to light only after years of research. The works excerpted, translated,
and studied in this volume thus represent a bounty of newly discovered writing
on social interactions between women across cultural and linguistic boundaries. Their obscurity is not due to their irrelevance or lack of quality: these new
sources for confronting and reconceptualizing gendered histories of mobility in
Muslim societies will provide insights for scholars, students, and other readers
interested in these wider debates. A more detailed interrogation of this material's
broader significance to history and literature in terms of reorienting the global
is contained in the final section of this introduction.

Travel writing can be read in many ways. Many of the voyagers in this volume
wished to convey to their readers an accurate description of the destinations
they visited and the places through which they passed. This intention makes
their writing a valuable source for historians, especially those interested in distinct locations and moments in the past. But our objective in introducing them
now goes beyond that. We principally hope to gain insight into the authors
themselves—their ideas of self, community, culture, service, foreignness, and
familiarity. The text in each chapter is essentially a form of autobiography as the
authors, intentionally or otherwise, construct an image of themselves—one that
is often set against the backdrop of an unfamiliar locale. For this reason, this
volume is primarily a study of the self.[5] It is simultaneously a study of interaction, community, belonging, and alterity. In general, the accounts included in
this volume take a greater interest in human than physical geography. More than

the terrain, the authors record their observations of others while traveling, allowing us in turn to reflect on the contingent and historical nature of sociality. They interacted constantly with people from a range of social classes and diverse religious and cultural backgrounds. For some, the novel circumstances meant that the rules of sociality were altered or abrogated, even as others seem to have remained well within the bounds that ruled their everyday lives. Some women found their own ideas of community and Islamic practice challenged. For others, travel provided more affirmation than abrogation. Finally, then, this study is a meditation on the inherent diversity of Islam. There are so many experiences, and so few of them overlap, that their mere juxtaposition is a potent reminder that this category is as limiting and as it is enabling.

But before proceeding, a word on this book's unique form. Individual authors and their writing are the focus of each short chapter, and thus we reference them by name throughout this introduction.[6] Each chapter opens with meticulously researched biographical data, literary and historical context, and textual analysis. These descriptions are themselves a major intervention, for most of the women have never been written about before and are otherwise unknown. Meanwhile, images let readers envisage our authors on the move.[7] The main body of each chapter presents selected extracts from travel narratives in English translation or, occasionally, the original English. To facilitate engagement, extracts are sometimes divided into subsections with titles indicative as to their content. Generally, these subtitles have been inserted by us as editors unless otherwise noted as original. These subtitles may interrupt the flow of text, but their value in highlighting themes or guiding the reader should be evident. Annotations identify terms and figures not familiar to a general audience—though to avoid a staccato of repetitive footnotes, commonly used foreign terms are defined in a comprehensive glossary. Each chapter concludes with a concise list of further reading. This includes the original texts from which extracts have been translated or reprinted, as well as complementary writings, biographical or literary studies, and contextual materials. In most cases, there are links to our project website, Accessing Muslim Lives (https://www.accessingmuslimlives.org), where interested readers may find supplementary materials in digital form, including additional translations, original texts, and visual sources.

To emphasize thematic trends, chapters are grouped into four main parts reflecting the different motivations to travel identified by the authors. The book begins with "travel as pilgrimage" on the basis that religious pilgrimage was the longest, most consistent, and best accepted type of travel by women. Although there is a dizzying range of pilgrimage practices within Islam, it is visits to Mecca (known as *hajj* or *'umrah*), Medina, and the Shiite holy sites of Iraq and Iran (*ziyarah*) that are most frequently recorded. Part II then turns to what emerged as a primary impetus to women's mobility in the nineteenth century: "travel as emancipation and politics." The range of political impulses here is wide: feminist in its broadest interpretation, but also nationalist, internationalist, and even communist. The earliest authors in this section traveled as individuals, but by the twentieth century, many were on governmental assignment or part of official delegations. The early twentieth century also saw Muslim women going abroad for formal and informal learning, including training programs, university courses, and educational schemes, at first to Europe and later to the United States. This development is captured in part III on "travel as education." Finally, part IV addresses "travel for obligation and pleasure." This section reflects that from the earliest author to the latest, travel for women was also about their commitments to family: those who accompanied fathers, brothers, and husbands as they journeyed into exile, for work or study, or as recreation.

Studies of travel writing often take a regional approach in terms of where travelers went to or where they came from. We prefer a thematic form of organization as it allows comparison between authors and regions. The short introduction to each part underlines this comparative element by highlighting overall arguments and trends, including the parallels and divergences between chapters and the relationships linking authors. The chapters within each part are then broadly organized chronologically to underscore the development of genre over time.[8] The first section, on "travel as pilgrimage," thus begins with a seventeenth-century hajj narrative in Persian verse authored by a woman known only as "the widow of Mirza Khalil." Later texts in prose and poetry from Qajar Iran and British India then grapple with how to write that most quintessentially Muslim journey in the "Age of Empire." One unexpected observation that emerges from this thematic structuring is that travel writing has peculiar regional specificities: we discovered no Arab or Southeast Asian narratives on pilgrimage from before 1950, whereas all of the Ottoman and Turkish texts we unearthed fell into part II on politics. Of course, to group materials as we do here is not straightforward; women often had multiple motivations to travel. Certainly, the hajj has historically been an opportunity for politics as much as piety. Motivations might also be public and private all at once, with the result that texts could have fit easily into multiple categories. Shaista Suhrawardy Ikramullah, for instance, lived in Britain in the 1930s as the wife of an Indian civil servant, but she also studied for a PhD during that time. Because her available writings focus on the former experience, she is included in part IV on obligation, rather than part III on education. And yet as the next section indicates, grouping texts has actually proved one of the easier tasks on this book's route to completion.

TRAVEL WRITING AND WOMEN

Among the greatest challenges for this study was to simply break ground in what was otherwise a terra incognita. There are many reasons for the failure to preserve women's narratives. For one, the written word has not always been the primary mode through which narratives have circulated. In some periods and regions, oral culture has been dominant; in other cultures, access to literacy has been the preserve of men.[9] What is more, it appears that the tendency to view this work as "women's literature," and therefore not relevant to "general interest," has led to a lack of preservation. Thus it is likely that much literature has been destroyed or will require significant efforts to be recuperated.[10] Meanwhile, travel and its literature, despite being a subject of enduring fascination, have long been associated with bravado and masculinity.[11] It was not until the final decades of the twentieth century that the contributions of women began even to be recognized as serious travel writing. This process began in the 1980s and 1990s as feminist scholars turned toward producing anthologies and studies of these narratives.[12] These efforts not only wrote women back into the history of the genre but also undertook pioneering work to think with increasing precision about how our construction of the genre is gendered. That said, though a wealth of studies now exist *on* European women travelers in "the Orient," only a handful have appeared on the women *from* those same regions. In short, the "feminist turn" in travel studies has largely left non-European women behind. Muslim women have been particularly excluded, though this imbalance is gradually being addressed by a coterie of dedicated scholars.[13]

In writing Muslim women back into a history of travel, we must expand our archive while also following and furthering the theoretical innovations made already in the study of European travel writing, particularly in interrogating the exclusions and biases of terminology and categories of analysis. A particular concern regards form: How does narration and recording vary across cultures and time? What restrictions and possibilities have determined how women tell their stories within their own life-worlds? To seek out travel writing as defined by a European understanding of that genre is inherently exclusionary. Once we have expanded and sensitized our metric to account for local literary practice, a second step is to use theoretical insights to reassess world literatures and find where travel narratives may be hiding in plain sight—perhaps in a collection of love lyrics that may relate to a journey—but are not flagged as such. The range of "Muslim literatures" is vast and, in some cases, little known. Might there yet be travel accounts lurking in the abundant but understudied *'Ajami* literature (West African languages written in the Arabic script) of sub-Saharan western Africa?

Or in the diverse linguistic and cultural space of Central Asia? This volume is just a first step, intended to lay the ground for that future study.

Attentiveness to localized approaches are needed, for travel writing is a notoriously amorphous genre located at the interstices of a multiplicity of forms: autobiography, history, fiction, and others. Its indeterminateness has long bedeviled the scholars who grapple with its contours, unable to say with much conviction or agreement just what constitutes it. What does it mean to travel? How is one to speak or write about it? Mobility is certainly as universal a human trait as any, but narratives of and ideas about it vary greatly across cultures and time, and even within a single, supposedly homogenous context. Many of the pieces included in this study—which include magazine articles, speeches, diary entries, poems, and book excerpts—would, until very recently, not have been properly considered to be travel writing at all. By the same token, the majority of the women who wrote these pieces—a woman accompanying her husband on a diplomatic mission, for instance—have not always been considered true "travelers."[14] The inherent unconventionality of this volume offers us a starting point from which to unpack these terms and understand how they have been historically determined and gendered.

Women have long been so excluded from being considered serious travelers or travel writers that most readers will likely struggle to think of a single such figure from any historical or literary tradition. What is more, those that may come to mind will surely be Western women considered oddities, outliers, or quite simply masculine. As Debbie Lisle has observed, "It is still the case that women must overcome their 'natural' limitations as women and become 'extraordinary' in order to be manly enough to travel and write books about it."[15] Muslim women travelers are rarely accorded even this limited recognition but are instead twice neglected: for being insufficiently masculine, and the Orientalist assumption that they belong to a religious or cultural background that demands meekness. Rather than ask whether or not the women here are "travelers," or whether their writing constitutes "travel writing" proper, the more compelling and telling question is: How have our ideas about travel and methodologies for the study of travel and travel writing neglected the experiences and voices non-European women, particularly Muslim women?

Travel is not a neutral concept, a simple word referring to the act of going from point A to point B. Likewise, a traveler is not merely a person who traverses that same line. Like all concepts, words like *travel* and *traveler* are deeply embedded in the cultural contexts that employ them. Our lives are filled with all forms of mobility, but not all mobility constitutes travel. What does count is culturally and historically determined. The voyages of Magellan or Lewis and

Clark are surely considered travel, yet others who traversed similar paths have not been equally acknowledged. Think, for example, of the men and women, the Sacagaweas, who guided or accompanied them as they went about "discovering" new lands.[16] The honorific title *traveler* likewise is rarely extended to enslaved Africans on the Middle Passage, Eritreans traversing the Sahara en route to Europe, migrant Filipino workers seeking temporary employment in Dubai, or those who travel with a spouse on assignment. These men and women are often given labels such as migrants, temporary workers, staff, guides, but rarely are they called travelers.[17]

Even today, the category of travel remains gendered, stratified, and above all closely linked with a European history of exploration, upper-class recreation, and colonial expansion.[18] As the anthropologist James Clifford writes, "I struggle, never quite successfully, to free the related term 'travel' from a history of European, literary, male, bourgeois, scientific, heroic, recreational, meanings and practices."[19] In short, travel has remained the province of elites, or aspirants toward it. Over time, the concept became closely linked to lofty ideals that obscured the link between money and travel. Thus, even as anyone might attempt to become a traveler, the ideal of "good," proper, praiseworthy travel remained predetermined by idealistic concepts such as independence, free will, sturdiness, and initiative. These are the very qualities that have been denied to women, the colonized, and the impoverished in discourse and practice alike. When Muslim women were already considered by Euro-American society to be living the very antithesis of free lives (as they continue to be by some today), it was almost natural to exclude them from the hallowed category of the traveler, defined as it was by the unencumbered expression of a supposedly independent, inquisitive spirit. As Nyonya Aulia-Salim, one of the Indonesian authors here, observed astutely in 1954 after traveling to the United States, "It's often forgotten that many wives suffer the same misery as their husbands while traveling. . . . They are no less brave in opposing danger and persevering in the face of misery. Would there be victory if they were not just as fully committed in the struggle? Now, only the civil servants are awarded!"[20]

For many, whether they live in "the West" or even in a predominantly Muslim context, the historical Muslim woman is an imprisoned figure, not an itinerant, curious traveler. For many years now, there have been significant efforts to reject these exclusionary ideas of oppressed women, located as they are at the very heart of imperialist discourses, to offer up more sensitive and sympathetic models.[21] The most recent efforts have come partly in response to a wave of xenophobic and neocolonial discourses that present Muslim women as a monolithic instance of religiously-based misogynistic oppression in the service of new imperialist projects.[22] But for all this, these associations persist. Moreover, where allowances *are* made for the freedom of Muslim women, the credit for their "liberation" is often laid at the feet of "the West" itself. There is little space in this type of discourse for women, or even for Muslims of any gender, to be regarded as true "travelers," particularly those born after the age of the great Islamic empires. Indeed, Ibn Battuta, subject of a handful of popular books and an IMAX documentary, is perhaps the most recent Muslim traveler to be celebrated globally, and he traveled in the fourteenth century CE. Most nonspecialist readers will struggle to name anyone more recent than him.

Unfortunately, few of the pieces here disrupt the pervasive association between travel and privilege, particularly with regard to class and wealth. Several of the authors were royalty, occasionally in possession of immense power and resources (Jahanara Begum, Sikandar Begum, Melek Hanım, Zeyneb Hanoum, Nazli Begum). Others hailed from influential and frequently moneyed families (Atiya Fyzee, Shareefah Hamid Ali, Begum Sarbuland Jang). Only a few came from more "modest" backgrounds (Dilshad, Nur Begum, Suharti Suwarto), though even these women were privileged by dint of their access to literacy and the possibility of writing about their experiences. In colonial India, for instance, female literacy was recorded at less than 1 percent in 1901. By 1947, around the end of the period under consideration in this book, that figure had risen to a mere 8 percent.[23] By comparison, in early communist Uzbekistan, literacy was around 5–10 percent in cities but just 1 percent in rural areas in the 1920s.[24] As explored in the next section, women who may have been from less influential backgrounds were travelers themselves, but unfortunately their voices have not been preserved.

Just as the concept of travel is entangled in a range of associations that link it to European, masculine practices, so too are many reigning assumptions about what constitutes travel writing. This concern has guided us to abandon the usage of terms such as *travelogue*, with its historical associations and genre claims, to the more general *travel writing*. In most of the linguistic and cultural contexts under study here, the travel account was not a prominent or coherent genre.[25] Even where it was, the ability of women to publish cohesive, first-person prose narratives in book form (as we typically expect of travelogues) was circumscribed. In turning away from the term *travelogue*, we not only eschew its association with colonial epistemologies but also acknowledge that narratives often occur in a variety of forms that are often gendered (much as they have been in a Euro-American context).[26] Women chose the format of their writing by balancing the forms available to them against considerations of their objective.[27] In some cases, this might mean writing anonymously, avoiding the first person, writing letters to an imaginary female interlocutor, or even rejecting prose altogether.

This is also a reflection of the reigning literary aesthetics of the cultures that produced these accounts. Many of the travel accounts here are accordingly "unconventional" only to the English reader. Undoubtedly, many of the authors do meet our expectations of what we instinctively consider a travelogue, and they saw themselves as participating in that genre (Sikandar Begum, Halide Édib, Zainab Cobbold, Amina Said, and Nyonya Aulia-Salim, among others). Other accounts are less intuitive. Several are excerpted from autobiographical writings and were not intended as standalone travel accounts (Salamah bint Said/Emily Ruete, Qaisari Begum, Huda Shaarawi). Still others are private diary entries or letters that were never intended to be published (Muhammadi Begum, Begum Hasrat Mohani) and thus can be more intimate because they were drafted away from a public gaze. A few are magazine articles (Rokeya Sakhawat Hossain, Sughra Sabzwaria, Shaista Suhrawardy Ikramullah, Shams Pahlavi). Two of the accounts here were written entirely in rhyming couplets (the widow of Mirza Khalil, Nur Begum) in keeping with the popular literary genres. Several were initially intended for circulation exclusively among family members (Begum Sarbuland Jang, Ummat al-Ghani Nur al-Nisa), and two come from public lectures (Safia Jabir Ali, Iqbalunnisa Hussain). Some appear to be political treatises more than standard travel writing (Zeyneb Hanoum, Melek Hanım, Suharti Suwarto).

Historically, travel writing has hewed toward an informative, rather than an experiential, mode. Indeed, in Islamic contexts travel literature once played this very role in the development of various sciences, physical and intellectual.[28] From this perspective, a set of letters exchanged between mother and daughter would not have been considered worthy of the categorization, much less publication. Yet the purposes of writing about travel have shifted over time, and those purposes vary across culture, class, and gender. A fascinating example of this comes from Begum Sarbuland Jang, who wrote a deeply personal account of her journey through the Middle East and Europe. Her account was only published twenty years later, after her husband's death. Her husband, in contrast, published a number of accounts of the same journey almost immediately. They are not at all personal but are rather filled with topographical observations and notes on distances. The radically different trajectories of writing of a single trip by a husband and wife exemplify these gendered distinctions. Travel writing had other itineraries too: recording one's journey may, for instance, also be considered a devotional act. In nineteenth- and twentieth-century India, accounts of the hajj and other pilgrimages allowed readers and listeners to become fellow travelers on a journey that may otherwise be unrealizable while also allowing the author to accrue religious merit (*thawab/savab*) or to announce their changed social or spiritual status.[29]

Another common purpose was to stake out positions on matters political or social. To what extent should women participate in the public sphere? Did women of "the Orient" require saving (Zeyneb Hanoum)? These and many more debates were explored in travel accounts with varying degrees of polemic. Others were not concerned with gender and instead threw themselves into a hornet's nest of issues surrounding colonialism (Muhammadi Begum), Pan-Islamism (Fatima Begum), contemporary calamities like the demise of the Ottoman Empire and the Islamic Caliphate (Sughra Humayun Mirza), the Palestinian crisis (Amina Said), or the contributions of communism (Suharti Suwarto). Still others adopt an anthropological tone, detailing practices encountered abroad and frequently weighing in on their relative merits and limitations (for instance, on childcare in Iraq, as discussed by Begum Hasrat Mohani, or Sikandar Begum's assessment of Arab women).

All of these examples point to the inherently global nature of Muslim travel writing. Indeed, it has always been global. The genre first appeared in Islamic literatures not in the so-called Islamic heartland of Iraq, Syria, or Arabia, but at the far fringe of the known world—the Maghrib, Andalusia, and Persia—though none of its known writers were women.[30] However, travel writing was not a prominent genre in any premodern Islamic language, with the sole exception of early modern Safavid and Mughal verse travel narratives, which flourished particularly in the *masnavi* form.[31] This broad lack counterintuitively butts up against the understanding that travel itself has been crucial to the spread of Islam and indeed to its intellectual evolution. The most convincing and sustained attempt to account for the relationship between travel and Islam (and, in passing, the role of travel writing in that development) is to be found in Haouri Touati's *Islam et Voyage au Moyen Age*.[32] Focusing on a period between the eighth and twelfth centuries, Touati argues that travel first emerged as the solution to a logistical problem Muslim intellectuals faced as Islam rapidly expanded. Initially, information about the Prophet Muhammad and his era were conveyed exclusively in oral form. However, as the Islamic world expanded, those who possessed reliable information became diffused across a vast, continuously unfurling empire. Thus, for the researcher or aspiring scholar to become well-rounded in his knowledge, he had to travel widely to learn from these sources. At the same time, geographers traveled to familiarize themselves with Islam's new domains. Meanwhile, Sufis took to travel to deepen "their mysterious knowledge of reality." Ultimately, it was travelers themselves who formulated the idea of an entity that could be called the Islamic world (*dar al-Islam*). Yet even as countless intellectual works were produced thanks to the use of travel as a methodology, travel writing itself was late to make its appearance. Even then, its efflorescence, if it can be called that, was a relatively short-lived crescendo. From the tenth until the fourteenth century, a number of well-known travel accounts appeared, with the *Rihla* of Ibn Battuta perhaps representing the zenith of the medieval Arabic travel account. From the fourteenth until perhaps the nineteenth century, Touati shows that travel writing became increasingly negligible in the Arabic-speaking regions of the Middle East.

Yet this was not the end of Islamic travel writing. The genre instead reappeared in regions where other languages were dominant. Between the fifteenth and eighteenth centuries, the most influential works of travel belonged to the three great empires of that era: the Ottoman Empire centered in today's Turkey, the Safavid Empire in Iran, and the Mughal Empire in India. Touati's thesis does not apply to the travel writing of this era: travelers were not motivated by a desire to formulate an Islamic world so much as they were working within the imperial contexts that hosted them. It was an "age of exploration," one that would parallel an emergent tradition of travel writing in Europe. Despite this, it is difficult to make the claim that travel writing was a fixture of Islamic literatures in this period. Sanjay Subrahmanyam and Muzaffar Alam have argued for the existence of a corpus of travel writing from this period, but one is still hard-pressed to escape the conclusion that the genre was never fully formed, other than in the Persian poetic tradition (exemplified by the chapter on the widow of Mirza Khalil).[33] Despite patchy or intermittent production, several works were nevertheless landmarks of their time, including the monumental (and never fully translated) *Siyahatname* of Evliya Celebi.[34]

All of this would rapidly change in the latter half of the nineteenth century when the production of travel writing, including by women, suddenly appeared across the Muslim world. A number of causes may be attributed to this, including the advent of affordable printing, increased literacy, and, as we see in the next section, revolutionary changes in access to efficient and affordable transport. This was also not coincidentally the era of high imperialism and colonial influence. New regimes of knowledge, conceptions of geography, and literary styles were being introduced in colonies with large Muslim populations. Travel writing, including by women, had already become a major genre in Europe at this time—indeed, it was *the* quintessential genre of colonial literature.[35] This popularity and pervasiveness contributed to its spread in the colonized world and among uncolonized empires that wished to emulate, or perhaps better translate, Europe's recent successes.[36] Ironically, just as Europeans began to write extensively about the women of "the Orient," those same women began to compose their own accounts of Europe and other regions.

In fact, one of the first Muslim women to write a travel account in the colonial era was herself at least partially of European descent: Melek Hanım was the granddaughter of a French officer in the Ottoman Empire who converted to Islam and married a Circassian woman. Melek Hanım would eventually leave Istanbul for Europe, where her two memoirs were welcomed by audiences hungry for "true" accounts of "the harem." In this, Melek Hanım's account participated in a booming industry of European travel accounts that sought to offer readers ever more "authentic" (and often salacious) descriptions of life as a woman in the Ottoman Empire.[37] Where earlier authors had only been able to describe their experiences as visitors, Melek and, in 1913, her fellow Ottoman Zeyneb Hanoum offered European readers a firsthand experience as members of a harem. Their accounts were not always found to be entirely convincing, though readers eager for this type of affirmative material consumed it avidly. In terms of European accounts, the two sisters would later be followed later by the far less sensationalized account of a convert, Lady Evelyn Zainab Cobbold, who wrote an account of her pilgrimage to Mecca in 1934.[38] These accounts show how travel literature by Muslim women could even attain transnational circulation. Zainab Cobbold, for instance, was quickly translated into Urdu to offer a "guiding light" for "wayward Muslims" in India.[39] The book appears to have found a wide and avid readership. Indeed, travel writing by European converts was of great interest to Indian readers in particular, as exemplified by a translation of an account of a visit to India's religious sites by a woman identified only as "a German Muslim Woman."[40]

Unsurprisingly, the great majority of travel writing was produced in Islamic societies outside of Europe, though as indicated already, it was anything but equal across geographic, linguistic regions, or social backgrounds. We note that very little material seems to have been produced by women in Arabic-speaking Middle East and North Africa. As travel writing by Muslim men is first found here as early as the last centuries of the first millennium, it might be expected that this is where we would identify similar writing by women. Alas, works in Arabic appear to be almost nonexistent before the twentieth century, with two of the earliest known accounts being Huda Shaarawi's memoir, *Mudhakkirrati*, from the 1940s, followed by reformer and feminist Amina Said's 1946 travel account *Mushahadat fi'l-Hind (Observations from India)*.[41]

A similar situation inheres at the opposite end of the Islamic world. Southeast Asia, despite boasting one of the most populous Muslim regions on earth, seems to have very few instances of travel writing by women. As in Arabic-speaking regions, these start to appear only in the late 1930s, 1940s and 1950s. Perhaps a reflection of Indonesia's location near the Pacific (and the time period when travel writing emerged there), two of the three accounts are of travel to the United States (Herawati Diah, Nyonya Aulia-Salim), whereas a third, overtly political piece is written by a group of women on a sponsored trip to view technical and social advances taking place in the Soviet Union (Suharti Suwarto). Sub-Saharan Africa is even more poorly represented in the selections here. From the entire continent, there is only the late-nineteenth-century account of Sayyida Salamah bint Said, later known as Emily Ruete, whose father belonged to the ruling class of the Omani Empire and who bore the title Sultan of Zanzibar. To date, no accounts have come to light in the many Muslim civilizations of West Africa (though as indicated already, this is a region whose literature is tragically understudied).

Iran and India, in contrast, have a far more evident history of women's travel writing. It is in Persian, a language with a vast and varied literary history, that we find the earliest instances of women writing about their travels, including two contemporaneous authors from the seventeenth century. The first is the anonymous writer from Iran already introduced, and the other is the well-known Mughal princess Jahanara (1614–81). Yet these two authors are more of a happy anomaly than heralds of a new tradition. Pending further research and discovery, it appears that there are no other instances of travel writing that predate the late nineteenth century, when women writers suddenly spring to life. Indeed, most of the pieces here were written between the 1870s and 1950s. Though it is likely that works of travel from many regions and languages have yet to come to light, it is certain that three languages have been far more productive than any others: Turkish, Persian, and Urdu.[42] Turkish and Persian in particular were long affiliated with major empires and were used transregionally for quotidian communication and intellectual exchange. Yet women's writing—by Christians, Hindus, and Bahais, as well as Muslims—appears in those languages only after those empires had largely faded. In short, for all that travel has been intertwined with Islam, the history of Muslim women's travel writing has been largely a modern affair.[43]

These points raise the question of readership and audience. Who were the works studied here actually intended for? One such category has already emerged, namely European audiences interested in Muslim perspectives, particularly those that would fuel Orientalist fantasies. More typical, though, was for literature to be consumed in the places whence its author hailed. Many authors here wrote for their own societies and did not imagine a gendered audience: men and women alike might be expected to read their accounts, and they were published accordingly. In other cases, particularly in India, women published for an audience imagined to comprise their "sisters"—an exclusively female readership, in other words, though these materials were undoubtedly consumed avidly by men too. For a variety of reasons, other women opted not to publish at all but instead circulated their writing through more exclusive channels: in courtly circles, in family newspapers, or by passing a single copy from family to family. It was in the nineteenth century that women began to participate more extensively in literary spaces, composing novels, poetry, memoirs, and travel writing.[44] As the readership varies widely according to the context of the writer, the question is explored further in the introduction to each chapter.

MUSLIM WOMEN IN CULTURES OF TRAVEL

If travel writing has been limited historically in many Muslim contexts, travel has certainly not. The history of Islam is filled with mobility as its adherents crisscrossed the globe on their adventures and errands. It is often forgotten that women too were riding, sailing, and walking these same paths. At the level of doctrine, Islam itself may be seen to offer all Muslims, male and female, the motivation and opportunity to travel. No single word in Arabic corresponds to the Christian concept of pilgrimage with its more recent metaphorical connotations. Instead, we typically find the terms ziyarah/ziyarat, 'umrah or hajj, all of which refer to fixed journeys. Ziyarah, which literally means *visitation*, incorporates journeys to sacred shrines and tombs of all sorts. 'Umrah refers specifically to visits to Mecca that may occur at any time of the year. In contrast, undertaking the hajj, or pilgrimage to Mecca, is considered a "pillar" of Islam for those who have the means: one must undertake this scripted journey on a specific date in the annual lunar calendar at least once in a lifetime, if it can be afforded.[45] Beyond this, Muslim travelers often cite a more general Quranic exhortation to "travel the earth."[46] Islam also encourages travel for education: *rihla* or *talab al-'ilm*. The celebrated Arab historian Ibn Khaldun (1332–1406) wrote, "Travelling in search of knowledge is absolutely essential for the acquisition of useful learning."[47] The Prophet himself encouraged travel for knowledge: "Those who go out in search of knowledge will be in the path of God until they return."[48] The Qur'an might even inspire travel for the purpose of migration: the *hijra* from an "abode of war" (*dar al-harb*) to an "abode of peace" (*dar al-Islam*).[49] However, how Muslims in different times and places experienced this Islamic doctrine was incumbent on a wide range of factors.

Muslim travel is most often associated with the hajj, but economic limitations meant that throughout history, most Muslims did not fulfill this obligation. Exact numbers are hard to gauge before the modern era. Nevertheless, even at the time of our first account (by the widow of Mirza Khalil) in the very late seventeenth century, the hajj was a monumental enterprise. The main hajj caravans departed from Cairo, Damascus, and India, but there were also numerous smaller ones from Yemen, southern Persia, and elsewhere. Cairo was the collection point for Egypt, North Africa, and some from West Africa, while Damascus took from Syria, Turkey, and parts of Persia.[50] Most Muslims from Africa and West Asia would travel overland, though some Africans from the Sudan south and west would cross the Red Sea by boat. Predictably, most South, Southeast, and East Asian Muslims also came by boat, usually on the final leg, on ships from Surat sponsored by an Indian ruler.[51] Some leaving from India might also go overland, meeting pilgrims from Central Asia before joining one of the bigger hajj caravans.[52] An estimate of two hundred thousand pilgrims has been advanced as the annual total in the eighteenth century. Of these, around forty thousand are thought to have come via Damascus, perhaps thirty or forty thousand from Cairo, and around fifteen thousand from India.[53]

Pilgrimage is always shaped by politics, and as indicated already, the hajj is no exception. The role of political factors in the hajj experience is apparent in the drop in numbers that occurred after the eighteenth century, as the relative stability afforded by Ottoman suzerainty across much of the Middle East and North Africa gave way to the more tumultuous nineteenth and twentieth centuries. Of course, there were political perils before that time: the widow of Mirza Khalil points to the challenge of traveling from predominantly Shiite Safavid lands to Sunni Ottoman territories. The expansion of Wahhabi influence across the Arabian peninsula, typified by an opposition to many elements of customary hajj practice, also acted as a major curb. Hajj caravans were interrupted for several years after the sack of Mecca in 1803, which witnessed the destruction of many historical sites and shrines that were deemed idolatrous—actions that were both political and ideological, since shrines were sources of immense power and wealth.[54] Even when they restarted, the Damascus caravan was reduced to fewer than ten thousand pilgrims and, later in the nineteenth century, to fewer than one thousand.[55] The hajj caravans and especially boat traffic from India were disrupted again by the First World War and the linked Hashemite uprising in Arabia.[56] Once the Hijaz was seized by Ibn Saud's forces in 1925, the Wahhabis' more puritanical Islam triumphed over Mecca. Zainab Cobbold and Nur Begum, who both traveled in 1933, point to the iconoclasm and subterfuge generated by this regime. Despite objections, they simultaneously highlight its implications for pilgrim safety: the hajj is purported to have become safer under the Saudi regime than it had ever been under the sharifs of Mecca who had stewarded the holy cities from the tenth century.[57]

With just one exception, all the pilgrimage narratives included in this collection date from the early 1860s to the late 1930s. The most precise data for this period comes from India, departure point for ten out of fourteen of our hajj authors, thanks to the regulating instincts of the British Raj. Using official sources, William R. Roff sets the figure at five to seven thousand Indian pilgrims per year in the mid-nineteenth century, rising to at least ten thousand by the 1880s.[58] Once hajj committees were set up in Bombay and Karachi in 1908 and Calcutta in 1913, surveillance increased, with the effect that the numbers became even more precise: 36,089 pilgrims sailed from three Indian ports in the bumper year of 1927.[59] Meanwhile, in Southeast Asia, pilgrim numbers from the Dutch East Indies were approximately double, and in British Malaya at least half of those who came from India.[60] While the largest numbers of Indian pilgrims (but not pilgrim-authors) came from Bengal and Punjab, yearly variations were attributed to "failure or success of the agricultural season."[61] This points to the comparative poverty of the "average Indian pilgrim" that, certainly during the 1930s depression, made the hajj nearly impossible. It is no wonder that total numbers of hajj pilgrims dropped to an all-time low of around twenty thousand in 1933.[62] This precarity is rarely on display in the autobiographical accounts in this volume; as specified already, not all of the women here were rich by any means, but few of them were living harvest to harvest.

The available data also points to important gender distinctions: around 20 percent of Indian pilgrims were female in the 1920s.[63] It is commonly held that a woman cannot perform the hajj without an appropriate male companion (or *mahram*). Yet it is clear from historical sources that sometimes women went on hajj when their menfolk did not. In Ibn Jubayr's *Rihla*, he writes while in Mecca that an officer had been sent to the regions north of Syria each of the previous eight years to escort various *khanums,* or princesses, for their hajj. These were women of note and wealth: one of them traveled with one hundred camels' worth of belongings and contributed to the improvement of the road and public works en route.[64] A more famous case from the Mughal period relates to the emperor Akbar's court. In 1575, a large group of women set out on a seven-year hajj initiated, organized, and led by elder women of the harem. Among the party were many "chief ladies" of the court: the emperor's aunt Gulbadan; his wife Salima Sultan Begum; two cousins, Gulizar Begum and Hajji Begum (whose name suggests she had already undertaken the pilgrimage); another aunt, Sultanam; and more. Inevitably, they were accompanied by a large number of female attendants, servants, and singers. Akbar himself is said to have walked a short distance from Agra with the hajj caravan, dressed in the pilgrim's garb (ihram), but then to have gone no further.[65] Other women went on hajj multiple times, including several in this collection.[66]

Clearly, the interpretation and experience of Islamic doctrine on hajj varied widely. Practice and belief were impacted by regional affiliation and sectarian difference. Several travelers included in part I on "travel as pilgrimage"—including all those from Iran and some from India—identified as Shia. For Shias, ziyarat to the shrines was a particularly important aspect of religious practice alongside the obligatory hajj pilgrimage.[67] To visit the 'atabat, namely, the shrine cities of Karbala, Najaf, and Kazimayn—as described here by Mehrmah Khanom, Hajjiyeh Khanom Alaviya Kermani, and Sakineh Soltan Khanom Esfahani Kuchak—could thus have a value and a meaning for Shias comparable to a sojourn in Mecca and Medina in inspiring travel. Many nineteenth-century Iranian travelers followed the model of the Qajar ruler Naser al-Din Shah, a prolific traveler who visited the shrines in Iraq and wrote a narrative about his pilgrimage. These sites were also sometimes meaningful for travelers with other sectarian affiliations; Begum Hasrat Mohani, a Sunni, describes them with great reverence. Historians have similarly noted how a visit to a local shrine or spiritual master, like Princess Jahanara meeting Mulla Shah, was one of the main reasons for travel before the modern era (much as it continues to be for many pious pilgrims in India, Pakistan, and elsewhere).[68] It may be that for many women especially, visiting a Sufi shrine for a more personal and intimate experience of the divine had greater resonance than the hajj's prescribed process. Certainly, many female authors here, like their male counterparts, describe the emotional experience of visiting the Prophet's tomb in Medina with greater fervor than they did their hajj pilgrimage. Likewise, the founder of the reformist Tablighi Jama'at, Muhammad Ilyas, suggested that tabligh, or proselytization—necessarily requiring travel in most contexts—could be "as important as, if not more important than" the hajj itself.[69]

Rihla, like hajj, points to the contingency of Islamic doctrine. The celebrated medieval Muslim travelers Ibn Jubayr and Ibn Battuta may have titled their travel narratives Rihla as an indication of their inspiration to seek knowledge.[70] But after their era, the emphasis on "travel for knowledge" receded until the nineteenth century, when it appeared again, particularly in conjunction with the advent of colonialism in the Indian subcontinent. A British colonial regime that envisaged travel as good for a "superstitious" and "backwards" Indian polity made travel writing a mandatory component of colonial education. Inculcated from childhood into an idea of "travel for pleasure and enlightenment," Indian Muslims began to popularize an old phrase: safar vasila-i zafar, or "travel is the means to victory/success."[71] Illustrative of this trend within this collection is

Sultan Jahan Begum, who included this very phrase in the introduction to her 1909 pilgrimage narrative. Skipping over any notion of travel as "hell" (*safar surat-i saqar*), she evoked as her inspiration Ibn Jubayr and Ibn Battuta, whose writings had recently been republished in an Urdu translation.[72]

The high noon of European imperialism saw many other transformations when it came to travel. Technological innovations enabled a "specific phase" of globalization summed up by James L Gelvin and Nile Green as "an age of steam and print."[73] Signified by their descriptor is the prime role of these technologies in facilitating "intensified and accelerated interactions" in Islamic regions between 1850 and 1930—in other words, the period in which over half of the travelers featured in this collection lived and wrote. Faster and cheaper continental and intercontinental travel became possible with the adaptation of James Watt's steam engine to propel ships and trains. Though the first steamship made the passage from Britain to India in 1825, it was not until around 1880 that further modifications—in the form of the screw propeller, iron plating, and the compound engine—made larger, more efficient steamships possible.[74] This transportation miracle inspired reflection by many of the authors here, who traversed the Indian Ocean, the Persian Gulf, the Red Sea, the Suez Canal, the Mediterranean, and the Pacific Ocean with P&O and other carriers. Hajjiyeh Khanom Alaviya Kermani was perhaps most verbose on the vitality of ocean travel and trade, but many others documented the workings, setup, and activities aboard ship.[75] The specific experience of traveling by steamship during the First and Second World Wars was even captured by Huda Shaarawi, Shaista Suhrawardy Ikramullah, and Shams Pahlavi.[76] Hailing from the agricultural and landlocked region of Punjab, Nur Begum was most astonished by the steamship's power and how it seemed to float on the sea "like a ball of cotton."

The railways followed a similar course to the steamship. The first "practical railroad" was built in 1825 too, but it took until the early twentieth century before the rail network had truly global scale—with around one million kilometers (or 620,000 miles) of track by the First World War. Around 4,000 kilometers (2485 miles) of this track were in Egypt, and another 6,000 kilometers (3700 miles) were in the rest of the Ottoman Empire.[77] India, however, provides the most staggering statistics. Appreciating rail's potential for moving troops and goods quickly, the British invested in Asia's first rail network with a maiden commercial journey undertaken in 1853 in India. By 1890, British India had 25,495 kilometers of track that doubled by 1920–21, making it the world's fourth largest network.[78] Curiously, only some of the Indian travelers here, like Qaisari Begum, recorded their journeys by rail or road to Bombay and other ports when narrating intercontinental travel, perhaps due to the regularity of this experience for many. In contrast, a trip on the luxurious Orient Express, connecting Paris and Istanbul from 1883, warranted suitable amazement from Nazli Begum of Janjira and Maimoona Sultan.[79] Equally wondrous was the Tube in London to Atiya Fyzee and Safia Jabir Ali and the subway in New York to Selma Ekrem and Herawati Diah. For other women in this collection, railway journeys across Britain, Europe, the Middle East, and the United States were more an occasion to reflect on the people met and the places observed.

By the 1930s, other transportation technologies—specifically, the automobile and the airplane—enabled another new phase in global travel and globalization. Though "production" automobiles had been around since the late nineteenth century, their development peaked in the early 1930s with more efficient boiler and engine designs.[80] The impact these cars had on the hajj is documented by Zainab Cobbold, Fatima Begum, and Qaisari Begum. Suddenly, a journey that had taken many months or even years could be reduced to weeks. Along with being one of the first to make the pilgrimage by car, Zainab Cobbold was also the first of the authors here to record air travel when she "engaged" a seat on a small "air liner" to hasten her return from Marseilles to Croydon Aerodrome in 1933.[81] Commercial air travel to and from Asia had been available from the 1920s, but its exclusivity and cost meant it was still only accessible to some of the latest travelers in this collection, including Shareefah Hamid Ali, Nyonya Aulia-Salim, Mehr al-Nisa, and Zaib-un-nissa Hamidullah going to the United States and Suharti Suwarto en route to the Soviet Union. Those who toured the United States from the 1930s to the 1950s reflected the flourishing automobile culture in North America at that time by responding most enthusiastically to the opportunity to travel by car: Herawati Diah and Zaib-un-nissa Hamidullah cruised coast to coast.[82]

Alongside these technological innovations, the imperial system opened up particular opportunities for Muslims to experience global travel and migration. A British colonial passport, for instance, could facilitate certain (though certainly not all) journeys around the empire.[83] Scholarly work on imperial shipping and transportation has pointed to the pivotal role played by "native" seafarers, or lascars, of whom the majority were Muslim due to their willingness to "cross the black waters."[84] Most hailed from British India, but others were Chinese, Malay, Sinhalese, Arab, and East African. These maritime laborers were employed from the seventeenth century, but their numbers reached a height in 1914 when as many as fifty-two thousand lascars were employed on British shipping vessels alone.[85] European armies offered another employment opportunity abroad due to colonial recruitment practices in, for example, French Algeria, British India, and the Dutch East Indies. Censored letters, as preserved in war files, offer a unique insight into the experiences of 1.45 million Indian soldiers on the Western Front and in East Africa, Egypt, and Mesopotamia during the First World War alone.[86] Less prestigious still was the indenture system that expanded after slavery's demise within the British Empire in 1833. Of around 1.5 million "coolies" carried from the Indian subcontinent to Mauritius, British Guiana, Natal, Trinidad, and elsewhere, 10–20 percent were Muslim.[87] Other imperial routes to Muslim mobility included domestic and civil service, commerce, diplomacy, contract labor, and education.[88]

Of these opportunities, the first two of being a lascar or joining a colonial army were not, on the whole, open to Muslim (or any) women. Yet playing a role in war was not impossible: Noor Inayat Khan operated as a secret agent in France during the First World War.[89] Large numbers of poorer Muslim women traveled for other employment. From the eighteenth century onward, there are written and visual records of female servants and nursemaids, or ayahs, who traveled to Europe with their colonial masters. Between 1792 and 1856, the second largest group of bonded servants leaving Britain for India (at 30 percent of the total) was those with identifiably Muslim names—and of those, half were women.[90] When dismissed, some of these female servants married in Britain or returned to India with outgoing British families, but enough were unable to secure a husband or livelihood to justify the setup of various ayahs' homes for the destitute in London from 1825.[91] Indenture, in contrast, was primarily male to start but saw growing numbers of women recruited by the government of India from the 1850s as part of its policy of "settling" Indian labor.[92] Different locations had a different gender balance at different times, but a statutory fix of "a minimum of 40 women to every 100 men per shipment" in 1868 meant the proportion of women remained fairly high (at just under 30 percent of the total) until the system was disbanded in 1917.[93]

The more elite women represented in this collection were thus far from the only Muslim women traveling before the mid-twentieth century. Nevertheless, their own family histories do exemplify some of the broader trends of global Muslim mobility in the colonial era. For example, Emily Ruete's lineage as the daughter of a Circassian slave married to the sultan of Zanzibar points to the role of slavery and marriage in moving Muslim women around the Middle East, Africa, and beyond. Another four authors in this collection, sisters Atiya Fyzee and Nazli Begum of Janjira, cousin Safia Jabir Ali, and niece Shareefah Hamid Ali, belonged to a prominent merchant family from Bombay, the renowned Tyabji clan, which had business interests throughout Europe, the Middle East, and Asia by the late nineteenth century. Hence, Atiya and Nazli were actually born in Istanbul, where their father was a respected merchant known at the sultan's court.[94] At the time of her travels, Safia resided in Burma where her husband, Jabir, and his brother Sálim traded in hardware and invested in mining.[95] Jabir and Shareefah's father, Abbas, were also part of the large cohort of colonial subjects who studied in the imperial metropole to gain necessary qualifications or prestige.[96] Shareefah's mother, Amina, in contrast, traveled as part of a princely entourage from Baroda when she visited Britain in 1893–94.[97] Many other authors had parents who also traveled for formal education or administrative service.

Unfortunately, the majority of historic travelers—often illiterate and sometimes living in precarious circumstances—did not leave written accounts from which we may gauge their experiences. This collection is thus a rare source from which to extrapolate the specifics of Muslim women's travel before the contemporary era. Not only can we gain access into female authors' own experiences and perspectives, but we also frequently encounter, through them, poorer women travelers who did not leave a record of their own. Undoubtedly, there is often a gulf of class or understanding between these workaday travelers and their privileged interlocutors. But the materials collected here still offer a unique opportunity to read between the lines of literary accounts and access a clearer picture of what this travel might look like. With female spaces largely inaccessible to men, this book sources offer particularly unusual insight. Rahil Begum Shervaniya, for instance, writes at length (if with teeth-gnashing derision) about the daily practices of women aboard her pilgrimage ship. We find her regularly sitting with women, transcribing (and then ridiculing) their banter.[98] Similarly, Begum Hasrat Mohani laments her experiences in the women's carriage of a train.[99] Nur Begum shows us how crowds of women responded to taking a group shower while in quarantine, and Suharti Suwarto records how everyday women lived in Russia.

We have seen already that a primary assumption about Muslim women's travel may relate to the requirement for a close male relative, or mahram. Many authors here did travel with fathers, husbands, brothers, or sons. Qaisari Begum evoked this requirement explicitly and yet demonstrated the flexibility of the idea. She first suggested that should a nephew accompany her to Bombay, that would effectively meet the condition. Yet she was plagued by doubt. During this time, she had a vision of herself traveling with a powerful but unknown figure. It was only when she reached Bombay that she understood what this dream had meant: "In this trip, and indeed in every trip, a woman is required to have a *mahram* with her. In Bombay, ʿAbid ʿAli sahib shared with me the good news that [my spiritual advisor] *Hazrat Pir* Jamaʿat ʿAli Shah sahib would be traveling on the same ship as me. My heart was elated, and I suddenly remembered my dream from that night. . . . My heart was brimming with gratitude that [God] resolved the issue of a male companion himself."[100] Unable to organize a blood relative as a travel companion, Qaisari Begum still managed to legitimize her journey. Another example from this volume is Hajjiyeh Khanom Alaviya Kermani, who evoked rulings by Shiite jurists to justify traveling in the protection of close friends rather than with an immediate male relative.

Others report traveling entirely alone: Safia Jabir Ali from Bombay to meet her husband in post–First World War Britain, Sediqeh Dowlatabadi from Tehran in 1923 to study at the Sorbonne in Paris, Selma Ekrem from "Stamboul" to New York in 1924 on the promise of work, Muhammadi Begum with her infant child from Bonn to Oxford in the mid-1930s, and Herawati Diah en route to study at Barnard College in New York in 1937. Diah noted the benefits of welfare organizations like Travelers Aid in assisting women who traveled independently across the United States.[101] Other authors may have accompanied male relatives abroad but, finding the latter engaged with work or study, spent their days sightseeing alone or pursuing their own work or interests.[102] A few who claimed to travel "all alone"—from the wife of Mirza Khalil in the late seventeenth century to Lady Evelyn Zainab Cobbold in the 1930s—were in reality supported by slaves and servants. Nur Begum, also traveling on hajj in the 1930s, was unique in claiming to travel alone until the final pages of her account, when she finally recognized her husband's presence; it was as though he hardly mattered at all.

A second assumption may relate to the detrimental effect of veiling practices, or purdah, on Muslim women's experience of travel. Bengali author and educationalist Rokeya Sakhawat Hossain writes in her chapter here about a joyous trip to Kurseong in the eastern Himalaya in 1904, but she later sought to advertise the perils of purdah when it came to travel. She did so in a series entitled "Abarodhbasini" (The Secluded Ones) for a Bengali periodical, the *Monthly Mohammadi*, in 1929. Most brutal was "report fourteen," in which Rokeya recorded how a distant aunt of her husband stumbled over her burqa while changing trains at a railway junction and fell onto the track: "The Begum's body was smashed—her burqa torn. A whole station-full of men witnessed this horrible accident—yet none of them was permitted to assist her. Finally, her mangled body was taken to a luggage shed. Her maid wailed piteously. After eleven hours of unspeakable agony she died. What a gruesome way to die!"[103] Thankfully, none of the authors included in this collection faced this kind of tragedy, but many from colonial India especially used their written accounts to reflect on the additional challenge of traveling in purdah. Notable examples are Sughra Humayun Mirza and Fatima Begum, who both used their travelogues to express their objection to the severity of Indian practice (though, it must be noted, not the practice altogether).

The latter noted the difficult circumstances for less privileged female travelers on the sea journey from Bombay to Jeddah: "below decks," it was an "absolute prison" thanks to the "purdah upon purdah," which meant there was "no room even to take a breath."[104]

Another circumstance that proved problematic for veiled voyagers was medical quarantine. Throughout the nineteenth century, the hajj pilgrimage was plagued by cholera in particular—though also by malaria, smallpox, dengue fever, and dysentery—with the worst epidemic turning global in 1893 (an experience once again familiar as another pandemic, COVID-19, compelled Saudi authorities to heavily discourage the hajj in 2020 and limit it to those already vaccinated in 2021). The colonial response was to set up quarantine stations on the sea and land routes to Mecca, with the most important being that on the island of Kamran off the Yemeni coast. During a mandatory ten-to-fifteen-day stay, pilgrims experienced "cleansing" at disinfection stations and isolation if sick in an attempt to control the spread of communicable diseases.[105] Male pilgrims were often highly critical of quarantine in their hajj narratives, describing it as a "curse on their life"—not least because they were charged with maintaining women's honor in impossible circumstances.[106] Quarantining women was deemed serious enough by authorities to warrant a special regulation in 1897 detailing how to search female passengers who otherwise may be hidden from officers by protective male relatives.[107] From women's own accounts, we get a sense of their specific grievances. The long list compiled by Rahil Begum Shervaniya included the following: the mandatory bath was required even when one was ill, the female attendants were "ill-bred and rude," pilgrims had to strip bare in front of a crowd, the towels provided were not of sufficient size to cover one's "private areas," women were manhandled into the shower, and there were no purdah arrangements in the quarantine accommodation. As she summarized, "Such a calamity can only be compared to Judgment Day."[108] It is no wonder that more elite travelers like Nawab Sultan Jahan Begum invested so much correspondence in convincing the British government to exempt them and their female companions entirely.[109]

Other authors were more accepting of the special arrangements of purdah travel, identifying veiling as a means to remain comfortable and safe while moving around freely. Qaisari Begum, for instance, recorded how, on her 1936 hajj, a service existed at Nampally Station in Hyderabad by which *pardah-nashin* travelers could be transported from the women's waiting room to the women-only train car in a curtained "station rickshaw." A problem arose only when she attempted to board the train in her burqa, at which point her way was blocked physically by two irate European women obviously not keen on sharing their accommodation with a veiled Indian woman. Later in her journey, on the road to Medina, the men in her party stopped at a caravanserai to get some rest, and the women were left to sleep in the car, presumably to maintain purdah. Clearly this arrangement was quite natural to Qaisari Begum, because her only observation was that it was good to be able to "stretch out" in the men's absence.[110] Donning a burqa, charshaf, chador, yashmak, or simple headscarf to maintain modesty while out and about was so usual for many of these female authors that they did not deem it necessary even to mention as a feature of their travel experience unless they were consciously performing their piety for a conservative audience back home.[111] For others, travel was an opportunity to think about purdah and how best to practice it, as seen in the above quote from Fatima Begum. Veiling could offer female travelers anonymity and an opportunity to avoid unwanted gazes and interactions. Segregation also allowed them to interact with other women freely without the presence of husbands or other menfolk.

Of course, not all the women in this collection practiced veiling or seclusion in the same way, whether at home or abroad. A good number, particularly toward the end of our timescale, did not veil at all. Others took a kind of vacation from purdah by which as soon as they boarded a steamship, customary practices ceased. A useful example here is Nazli Begum of Janjira, who, as the wife of Indian princely ruler, observed "strict seclusion" at home so as not to make herself a "target of censure" but moved in mixed company in London and Paris.[112] Begum Inam Habibullah also experimented with living outside purdah while in Britain in the early 1920s, only to decide that she would not continue it upon her own return to India. For those experiencing life outside seclusion for the first time while abroad, the sensation could be exhilarating—or very frightening. Despite the wide span of time and distance and the different audiences addressed, it is worth contrasting here the testimonies of Zeyneb Hanoum arriving in Europe from the Ottoman Empire in 1906 with that of Nyonya Aulia-Salim visiting the United States from Indonesia in the 1950s. Whereas the former reveled (perhaps for the benefit of a European readership) in being able to look through a window with "neither lattice-work nor iron bars," the latter found it difficult to walk the streets alone after a highly cloistered childhood. As Nyonya Aulia-Salim put it so poignantly, "Previously confined by custom, now from fear. It is a cruelty like no other!"[113]

Another common question for travelers then, as now, was what to wear abroad in terms of everyday dress. Many male travelers fulfilled the expectation to wear "cuff and collar" while touring, working, or studying in Europe or North America no matter their place of origin, but women's habits were more complex. Most of the Turkish, Arab, and later Iranian authors here, as well as the Indonesian student Herawati Diah, reported wearing "European costume" (or its American equivalent), or they appeared in images in the same. South Asian women, in contrast, typically continued to wear the same type of clothes that they did at home, most often a highly decorative sari draped over a full- or half-sleeved blouse. This may have reflected personal comfort but also a nationalist discourse in which women functioned as emblems of cultural identity.[114] Clearly, their usual attire was not always practical in colder climes and had to be augmented with woolens, gloves, cloaks, and "good walking shoes."[115] It also attracted a good deal of attention to which some women responded with glee, whereas others recoiled.[116] That dress was a contentious issue signifying broader cultural capitulation can be seen in the vicious rebukes issued to those "desi" women who adopted "Western" styles—"like the crow that fancies itself a swan," as Muhammadi Begum put it.[117] A notable exception was nurse Mehr al-Nisa, who, in order to continue her work in an Ohio hospital in the early 1950s, adapted to skirts and blouses according to the axiom "When in Rome . . ."[118]

For Muslim women with families, their children's comfort and well-being proved another travel challenge. The concerns may be practical, often in ways familiar to any parent today: how to carry luggage while holding a child's hand or carrying a baby, how to bathe children regularly in accommodation without facilities, how to breastfeed or relieve oneself on a train when traveling with an infant, or how to reach a mountaintop shrine when little legs could not manage.[119] They could also be cultural and religious. With three boys at boarding school in England, Begum Inam Habibullah worried that her sons would lose their first language and culture. Would they still be able to speak Urdu? Would they remember to say their prayers? Would their religious beliefs remain intact? For those women who spent extended periods abroad, there was also the question of how to maintain a home in foreign climes. Taking into account their elite status, it is perhaps not surprising that some authors struggled without the domestic servants—including cleaners, cooks, ayahs, gardeners, and washers—to which they may have been accustomed at home. Others upturned racial hierarchies by employing local help, like Shaista Suhrawardy Ikramullah with her Swedish nurse and English nanny to care for her three children while she studied for a PhD in London in the late 1930s.[120] Finding familiar food and ingredients for a meal redolent of home was also a recurrent theme.[121]

In closing this section, we observe that evoking "the Muslim woman" in our current political climate too often conjures images of black veils and shrouded faces: the hijab becomes a symbol of clipped horizons and curtailed movement. Against this, historical evidence highlights the contingency of how Muslim women actually participated in cultures of travel before the jet age. Islam itself may facilitate travel for pilgrimage, education, and migration, but how that doctrine is interpreted remains highly variable and inflected by social positioning, location, nationality, and individual circumstance. Just as Muslim women travelers had to negotiate cultural expectations and local patriarchies, so they shared experiences along the way with other women, their coreligionists, and many others—including us. For contemporary readers, some observations made by these authors will expose the distance of time and place: how cultures of travel were impacted by changing technologies, political systems, economic realities, and social mores. Others may feel oddly familiar. Who has not felt the shock of alien environs, the fun (and disgust) of trying new foods, the longing to see distant family and friends, the comforts of home, or the frustration of not being able to understand a foreign tongue? The chapters will remind some readers of the travel and migration experiences of their own mothers and grandmothers. Keeping in mind the specific historical contexts in which our authors traveled and wrote is thus key to appreciating this material and, with it, Islam's diversity—but it should not shroud our common humanity.

REORIENTING THE GLOBAL

This book is intended to be accessible to undergraduates and general readers while also offering new insights to scholars and specialists. Indeed, an underlying purpose of this project from its conception has been to integrate gendered subjectivities into a deepened understanding of our global past. In recent years, global history as a subdiscipline has come under fire not just for being "out of step" with a present in which "nationalism is the antidote"—think Trump, Brexit, Modi, Erdoğan, Le Pen, and Bolsonaro—but also for inaugurating what Jeremy Adelman calls "its own segregation."[122] The first segregation he identifies is language. As he writes with suitable provocation, "It is hard not to conclude that global history is another Anglospheric invention to integrate the Other into a cosmopolitan narrative on our terms, in our tongues."[123] English has become "globish," he observes, taking foreign language learning into further decline. A collection of English translations of the sort one finds in this volume will not stem this tide, but it still makes available to global, international, and imperial histories a type of historical source rarely employed in their service. If the average historian with globalizing ambitions for their scholarship cannot gain access to original sources in, for example, Turkish, Persian, or Urdu, this collection at least opens their eyes to what they are missing.

In making this point, we do recognize the risks inherent to translation. Translation is one of the most prominent tools for intercultural communication, but it is also among the most dangerous. Translators do not simply transfer language and ideas from one language to its equivalent in another; they wield immense power to shape how a text is perceived, to make it anew.[124] In an anthology such as this, the selection of excerpts from a text is another site of negotiation and power because only a fraction of an author's thoughts makes it onto the page. The politics of translation and selection have had an especially checkered past when it comes to the representation of Muslims in European languages—as colonialists and Orientalists sought to shape perceptions of the religion, often as intolerant or rigidly legalistic.[125] This book addresses these issues in a number of ways. First, the translations remain faithful to the original in intention and style, but in a language that is as clear and comprehensive as possible for a general reader. Rather than seek misleading equivalences for specific terms, a glossary introduces readers to the concepts used by the translated authors. Every excerpt is also carefully contextualized in the introduction to the text so the reader may judge their meaning for themselves. Citations to the original sources and the provision of some original text on the project website bring further transparency. Collectively, the translations here adopt a wide range of attitudes and viewpoints, thus underlining the complexity and diversity of Muslim thought. We hope these considerations will evade the inherent risks of translation and selection and bring otherwise inaccessible voices directly into the conversation.

And even if available only in the form of translated or original extracts, what these sources reveal can be game-changing. A second "segregation" identified by Adelman relates to the "do-good storytelling" that he claims underpins the global history project. By emphasizing our "cosmopolitan commonness"—what we share, how we connect—it sets those in motion apart, in his view, from those left behind: those who did not travel, but instead stayed "at home."[126] In fact, these categories are far from dichotomous. As our sources show, connecting need not mean sharing; being in motion can still herald exclusion. We may consider as an example the accounts of hajj in the first part of this collection. The pilgrimage to Mecca is often depicted as the quintessential reflection of Muslim solidarity: regardless of nation and color, all pilgrims, rich and poor, male and female, young and old, don the pure white ihram to pray on equal footing before the holy Kaaba.[127] The sheer joy that this encounter can kindle infuses Qaisari Begum's account: the women from Egypt, Palestine, Syria, and Yemen that she encountered may be unique from her description, but they are indistinguishable in their devotion. For Nur Begum, even the reviled quarantine was an occasion for harmony and rapture: those women from "all over" could laugh and play as they bathed together.

For other women travelers, the "commonness" never came. One of the great ironies to emerge from Dale F. Eickelman and James Piscatori's seminal edited collection on Muslims traveling to other parts of the Muslim world was the "difference" they experienced. Pilgrims may have gone on hajj expecting to be enveloped by the "spiritual unity of the *umma*," but more often than not, they found their "consciousness of locality and difference" amplified.[128] Through women's eyes, our accounts suggest, the sense of difference related most often to other women. Sikandar Begum may have expressed disapproval for most people and places that she encountered in the Hijaz, but it was Arabian women who garnered her greatest wrath. Faced with their physicality, language, cultural practices, and religiosity, her identity as an *Indian* Muslim was only confirmed.[129] Not so for Rahil Begum Shervaniya, who spurned pilgrims from other parts of India—Bengalis and Biharis especially—even more than her Arab fellow travelers. In sharp contrast to Nur Begum, her quarantine descended into accusations and quarrel. Even those on a conscious quest for Islamic sisterhood, like Begum Sarbuland Jang, could find themselves overwhelmed by cultural and linguistic difference. In the end, she was reduced to performing Muslim unity before an audience of Englishwomen.[130]

Those women who traveled from colonized territories to Europe reacted with equal ambivalence to the connections facilitated by motion. Connection could inspire friendship, as Atiya Fyzee found among her fellow students at Maria Grey Training College in London in 1906–7.[131] The strict binaries between "West" and "non-West," colonizer and colonized, might thus be blurred, as Leela Gandhi has explored, by "affective communities" forged at the heart and height of empire.[132] Nevertheless, existing scholarship focused on Indian male students in Britain in the high colonial period has highlighted the racial abuse and ostracism faced by this group perceived to be a political, economic, and sexual threat.[133] For elite women, curiosity seemed more the norm. We may point to the "chubby little children" described so charmingly by Safia Jabir Ali as gifting her flowers at Rosyth tramway station or parading past "merely to look" at London Zoo. In a parallel to the Indian and Colonial Exhibition opened to "rave review" in London in 1886, Safia and her party were turned into a "spectacle of empire": "as if we were also a part of the Zoo for them!"[134] The small number of elite Indian women in Britain, their perceived lack of threat, and the exoticism exuded by their customary dress seems to have made British society more receptive to their presence.

Of course, British curiosity was not always received with equanimity, as Begum Inam Habibullah indicates. Who would not feel uncomfortable being part of the "Indian party" that came under the watchful gaze of an entire restaurant?

Her accompanying complaints about British cuisine point in turn to the cultural entrenchment—as opposed to vaunted open-mindedness—that could result from travel.[135] Muhammadi Begum may have enjoyed a wide social circle while living and studying in Oxford in the 1930s, but still she was inspired by her sometimes lonely existence to relinquish any sense of commonality with the proclamation: "It is true, after all, the West is the West and the East is the East!"[136] A lengthy stay in early twentieth-century Europe or North America only convinced many female travelers, including Zeyneb Hanoum from Turkey, Sultan Jahan Begum from India, and Herawati Diah from Indonesia, that "Western" culture and society could not live up to its billing. "The *mirage* of the West," as Zeyneb Hanoum called it, pertained most obviously for these women to the "freedom" of women—which they equated with women's suffrage and professional careers.[137] Woe betide those Muslim countries, like Turkey, where women turned their backs—as Maimoona Sultan and Begum Sarbuland Jang both observed—on Islamic morality in favor of European mores.

Being female could also prove key to how those in motion might still be left behind—sometimes physically, sometimes metaphorically. We may think here of another hajji, Sakineh Soltan Khanom Esfahani Kuchak. On the road to Mecca in 1900, her party split: half went to Damascus, and half went to Aleppo. Her greatest desire to visit the shrine of a female saint, Hazrat Zainab, in Damascus seemed to have been spurned purposefully by her brother, inspiring an astute observation: "Whatever a man is and whatever a woman is, the poor woman is the man's slave."[138] A few years later in a very different part of the world, Maimoona Sultan's possibilities for experiencing Britain and continental Europe were curtailed by the limits of purdah, or women's seclusion, as practiced in India. She traveled and even wrote about her travels, yet much of what she observed was secondhand through family or newspapers as she remained behind from public outings in hotels or rented homes. Taj al-Saltanah, in contrast, never fulfilled her desire to travel from Iran to Europe despite traveling widely within Qajar territories. Yet her mind remained open always to the possibilities of exchange and connection, particularly when it came to women's rights. In other words, those in motion could experience commonness, or not, just as much as those left behind—but either way, the phenomenon was most often gendered.

What these few examples also point to is the complex renegotiation of global geographies required by these travel writings. The recurrent Victorian metaphor of the "voyage out"—implying a one-way traffic between imperial "core" and colonial "periphery"—has much to answer for here. Too often in the course of this project, we were faced with the assumption that in undertaking a project on "women travelers," we must be studying those British women in particular who traveled to "the colonies." Their experiences have, as we have seen already, been captured in a wealth of academic studies, as well as popular anthologies with such charming titles as *Memsahibs Abroad* and *Unsuitable for Ladies*.[139] The requirement to counter such deeply entrenched notions is encapsulated by Michael Fisher's title for his monumental study of Indian travelers to Britain before 1857, *Counterflows to Colonialism*.[140] To trace the convoluted paths of Muslim women travelers is to disrupt one of the primary assumptions of Eurocentrism: that people and knowledge and ideas radiate outward from "the West" to the rest.[141] We may think of Selma Ekrem as just one example, moving from Turkey to Palestine, back to Turkey, to Greece (twice), and then ultimately to the United States.

The pieces here also challenge us to rethink what constitutes domestic and international travel. Most of them reflect travel to distant regions: Indians in Mecca, Indonesians in the United States, Egyptians in India, Turks in Finland, Iranians in South Africa. A few of the authors here, though, reflect on travel much closer to home—for instance, Princess Jahanara's summering in the Kashmir Valley, Taj al-Saltanah's peregrinations within the bounds of Qajar Iran, or Rokeya Sakhawat Hossain venturing from Calcutta to Kurseong in the eastern Himalaya. Of particular note are those South Asian travelers who regularly wrote about their visits to other parts of India.[142] These journeys often took them from a British-run presidency to a semi-independent "princely state," or vice versa, and areas with different currencies, languages, and cultural practices. Often authors would include descriptions of neighboring "countries" within India alongside the narrative of their intercontinental journeys. The patent unfamiliarity of, say, Bombay to the Punjabi Nur Begum helps us to remember that present-day national boundaries were often more imaginary than real for earlier travelers. At the same time, a visit to Iraq or Britain from India could mean remaining within the British Empire when understandings of "imperial citizenship" were being formulated by colonizers and colonized alike.[143]

Also inherent to this material is a challenge to any notion of the global subsumed within a British imperial frame. The somewhat disagreeable term *British world* has been seized upon in the last twenty years or so by a whole score of imperial historians eager to recast the broad reach of the British Empire in such a way so as to jump on the global bandwagon.[144] An effect has been the firming up of notions of the British Empire's exceptionality to the point that it is conceived, in the words of Antoinette Burton, as "a static, fully accomplished, or (worse yet) teleologically hegemonic phenomenon untouched by the threat of competition or the spectre of native resistance from within."[145] One imagines that in her worst-case scenario, she envisions Niall Ferguson's contentions in his bestselling *Empire* (first published in 2003 and reprinted ever since) as captured by its subtitle: *How Britain Made the Modern World*.[146] Those scholars employing a biographical approach to global history—as we do here—tend to fall into similar traps whereby "global lives" are, far more often than not, Britons operating within the British Empire.[147] Early modernists have been more successful at using individuals, albeit mostly male, to tell "connected histories" outside this frame, but there are some notable exceptions among modernists too. Take Seema Alavi, who, in her study of five Indian Muslim men connected to Ottoman territories, puts a "spotlight on the interstices" between empires traversed by "British subjects (rather than Britons)."[148]

The implications of the materials here for individual fields of study within global and international history are also highly significant. Clearly it is not possible to survey all scholarly repercussions within a comparatively short introduction, but it is worth flagging up a highlight or two. Let us turn our attention first to human rights historiography. This literature has tended to portray the Universal Declaration of Human Rights (UDHR), adopted by the United Nations in 1948, as a "Western project" imposed by male leaders on women and "postcolonial subjects." Recent rereadings have sought to reinterpret the UDHR as a document "rooted in conflicting cultural narratives, rather than stemming from a Western hegemonic consensus"—but even then, the role of women delegates, advisors, and consultants from Asia, Africa, and Latin America is often underplayed.[149] Chapter 23 features extracts from a travel narrative written by Indian feminist Shareefah Hamid Ali in 1947 while a delegate to the Commission on the Status of Women (CSW). Formed as a committee under the Commission of Human Rights, the CSW was charged with ensuring women's rights were duly considered in the drafting of the UDHR. This frank account underlining an Indian female delegate's involvement and contributions may not be found in the United Nations Archives in Geneva usually frequented by historians of international organizations; neither has it been republished before now beyond the local women's journal *Roshni*, in which it first appeared at the time.

By emphasizing circulation over movement from A to B, our sources also unsettle some of the basic categories of migration studies. Evidently, travel, as emphasized in this collection, can represent a different impulse to migration. And yet by broadening our source base in the way detailed in the first full section, we illuminate the overlap and nexus captured by the "new mobilities paradigm" so often positioned within the social sciences.[150] Once in movement, many of our subjects just kept moving. The example of Selma Ekrem has been noted already, but perhaps even more apposite is that of Sayyida Salamah bint

Said, later known as Emily Ruete. Nineteen years after migrating from Zanzibar to Germany (during which time she traveled extensively within Europe), she returned "home" twice, only to leave again for a multidecade stay in the Levant before finally returning to Germany.[151] Those who traveled for education may never have intended to stay at their destination, yet they often lived there for long enough that it started to feel like a home (see part II). The shift in historiography from large-scale analyses of mass migration based on quantitative data to a focus on lived experiences is also supported by these accounts. Oral interviews may be used in a contemporary context to highlight the plurality of migrants' experiences by gender, age, religion, and nationality, among other factors.[152] But for the longer past, narratives of the type here are crucial not just for what they tell about the narrator but also about the narrated. This collection thus reinforces the contributions already and still to be made by arts and humanities scholars to understanding mobilities in terms of "how movement is enacted, felt, perceived, expressed, metered, choreographed, appreciated and desired."[153]

There are also important implications here for thinking about global or world literature, particularly in terms of Eurocentric approaches to the travel of knowledge and ideas. Consider Franco Moretti's highly influential model that, drawing on Immanuel Wallerstein's "world-system" theory, purports there to be a single literary map on which only three literary spaces exist in hierarchy to one another: the core, the periphery, and the semiperiphery. When Moretti first expounded this theory, his map was underpinned by a diffusionist model according to which the novel spread from the European "core" to the non-European "periphery."[154] Later iterations of his argument make a distinction between a pre-eighteenth-century world in which "local" literary cultures existed and a later era of European cultural and economic domination in which a "stunning amount of sameness" prevailed.[155] In Francesca Orsini's critique, this approach to world literature has the effect of "making nine-tenths of the map (and its literature) drop off the map entirely"—or at best, "appear hopelessly 'peripheral.'"[156] Orsini's call to take a "multilingual approach" that keeps "both local and cosmopolitan perspectives in view" may be borne out by this book—if we keep in mind that exclusions may be not simply the work of Eurocentric models but also gendered imbalances within the linguistic traditions producing the travel writing featured here.

We point in this section to just a few of the possibilities for how this book may *reorient* the global—though with an attentiveness to gender and sexuality not necessarily envisaged by the term's most famous proponent, Gunder Frank.[157] As to how this collection is actually used by scholars, university teachers, students, and the general public, we await to see. Certainly, the potentials for the undergraduate classroom are as significant as those highlighted here for global historiography and world literature. In Antoinette Burton's *A Primer for Teaching World History*, she flags the importance of "centering connectivity," using women and gender to "make hypervisible" systems of power and "thinking world history from below."[158] Clearly, the materials in this collection could, when designing a syllabus for "World History 101," invigorate all of those quests. Particular chapters could also be embedded into specific history courses on a wide variety of time periods and themes—from Muslim empires and European colonialism to British multiculturalism and US immigration—as part of the transformation required to "decolonize history." Some critics of this movement have posited that perspectives on race and gender are "not relevant to certain subject matter"—like US foreign policy, for instance—or that a "less Eurocentric history" means expunging certain favored topics (the Tudors and the English Civil War are common examples in the United Kingdom) from our curriculum.[159] But we hold that it is only through incorporating the kinds of perspectives inherent to this volume into broader historical study that we can critically reflect on the privileging and marginalization of certain voices while bringing the past to bear on our contemporary debates about globalization, migration, and decolonization.

Chapters from this book have already found their way into the syllabi of courses in Islamic studies. This field has increasingly turned away from an emphasis on Islam as an "object" or "category" with a prescriptive theological doctrine and instead toward an engagement with "the historical and human phenomenon that is Islam in its plenitude and complexity of meaning."[160] Despite this, classes on gender and Islam continue to draw largely on a set of normative texts, supplemented by modern ethnographies and contemporary writing, perhaps in part because so little material is available in English. This book will allow instructors to bring historical depth to their syllabus and create the possibility for comparative analysis that is culturally and temporally diverse. One might use these texts to read contemporary Iranian pilgrimage against practices from Qajar or Safavid periods, or compare those experiences to those of Indians. Yet these texts should not be used simply to reject essentializing approaches to Islam and to remind ourselves that there are "multiple Islams." Rather, reading them should help us remain acutely aware of how class, race, empire, gender, and creed interact and are determinate of Islamic history. These elements are crucial because "countering essentialism demands *engagement* with history" to overcome the consequences to the study of Islam from the "discriminatory and racialized governing practices of European empires [which] collectivized the political struggles and destinies of societies where Muslims lived."[161]

At the same time, those who teach literature, particularly comparative literature, will find in these pages the opportunity to reflect on the ways individual literary traditions have approached the expression of a single theme, travel. These chapters show how travel literature was a gendered practice in a range of Islamic societies, much as it was in Europe. Although travel writing by women from Euro-America is almost always treated separately from that by women from the "Global South," we hope that this material will offer an opportunity to read across gendered literary traditions for their similarities as much as for their differences. Indian writing on Europe could be fruitfully paired with the vast body of European writing on India, for instance. This collection offers students and scholars alike the opportunity to reflect on just what constitutes travel writing in a global context and how our methodologies and assumptions about the genre shape which texts we engage with and which we do not. These pieces will surely facilitate discussion on the question of just what it means to be a traveler. Although all of the authors included here are Muslim women, that is but one potential conceptual lens. They are also, and perhaps primarily, scholars, politicians, and reformers.

In closing, we invite you, the reader, to become their fellow travelers if only for a moment and join them on their peregrinations and explorations—of themselves, of others, and of the world in which we all live.

NOTES

1. See chapter 27.
2. Shahab Ahmed, *What Is Islam: The Importance of Being Islamic* (Princeton, NJ: Princeton University Press, 2017).
3. Judith Butler, *Gender Trouble: Feminism and the Subversion of Identity* (New York: Routledge, 1990).
4. James Clifford, *Routes: Travel and Translation in the Late Twentieth Century* (Cambridge, MA: Harvard University Press, 1997).
5. This work thus builds on our other work in this area, notably, Siobhan Lambert-Hurley's *Elusive Lives: Gender, Autobiography and the Self in Muslim South Asia* (Redwood City, CA: Stanford University Press, 2018) and Daniel Majchrowicz's *The World in Words: Travel Writing and the Global Imagination in Muslim South Asia* (forthcoming).
6. To follow up these references, please see individual chapters. We direct readers to specific chapters only when including direct quotations.
7. Even when published, women's accounts rarely included photographs or images, which were typically expensive. For this reason, most of the images used in this book come from external sources accessed through our research. Just a few are reproduced from the original travel accounts. In some cases, we have included images of the texts themselves.

8.   Some readers may wish that this chronological element was emphasized further by the inclusion of a date in the chapter titles. We made a conscious decision not to include a precise date on the basis that it was unclear which date was most pertinent: The date(s) of travel? The date(s) of writing? The date of first publication? The date of a more widely circulated reprint? However, relevant dates are indicated immediately in the first line or lines of the introductory text.

9.   See, for instance, Lila Abu-Lughod, *Veiled Sentiments: Honor and Poetry in Bedouin Society* (Berkeley: University of California Press, 1986).

10.   As we go to press, we continue to make discoveries of new texts. As interest in the field grows, more are sure to follow.

11.   Sara Mills, *Discourses of Difference: An Analysis of Women's Travel Writing and Colonialism* (London: Routledge, 1991), 111–13.

12.   Some examples are Mills, *Discourses of Difference*; Indira Ghose, *Women Travellers in Colonial India: The Power of the Female Gaze* (Delhi: Oxford University Press, 1998); Mary Russell, *The Blessings of a Good Thick Skirt: Women Travellers and Their World* (London: Collins, 1986).

13.   Some classic studies of women travelers from India are Inderpal Grewal, *Home and Harem: Nation, Gender, Empire, and the Cultures of Travel* (London: Leicester University Press, 1996); Antoinette Burton, *Dwelling in the Archive: Women Writing House, Home, and History in Late Colonial India* (New Delhi: Oxford University Press, 2003); Meera Kosambi, *Pandita Ramabai's American Encounter: The Peoples of the United States (1883)* (Bloomington: Indiana University Press, 2003). Our previous work on Muslim women travelers is also pertinent here: Siobhan Lambert-Hurley, "Out of India: The Journeys of the Begam of Bhopal, 1901–1930," *Women's Studies International Forum* 21, no. 3 (June 1998): 263–76; Siobhan Lambert-Hurley, ed., *A Princess's Pilgrimage: Nawab Sikandar Begum's A Pilgrimage to Mecca* (New Delhi: Women Unlimited, 2007); Siobhan Lambert-Hurley and Sunil Sharma, *Atiya's Journeys: A Muslim Woman from Colonial Bombay to Edwardian Britain* (Delhi: Oxford University Press, 2010); Daniel Majchrowicz, "Malika Begum's *Mehfil*: Retrieving the Lost Legacy of Women's Travel Writing in Urdu," *South Asia: Journal of South Asian Studies* 43 (October 2020): 860–78; Majchrowicz, *The World in Words*. For Iran, see Amineh Mahallati, "Memoirs of Iranian Women Travelers to Mecca," *Iranian Studies* 44 (2011): 831–49; Piotr Bachtin, "Women's Writing in Action: On Female-Authored Hajj Narratives in Qajar Iran," *Iranian Studies* 54 (2020): 67–93. For Turkey, see Reina Lewis, *Rethinking Orientalism: Women, Travel, and the Ottoman Harem* (London: I. B. Tauris, 2004). Work on the Arab Middle East and Southeast Asia is more scant.

14.   The issue of women travelers as "the exception" in a European context is taken up early on. See for example Clifford, *Routes*, 105. For more on a South Asian context, see Majchrowicz, "Malika Begum's *Mehfil*."

15.   Debbie Lisle, *The Global Politics of Contemporary Travel Writing* (Cambridge, UK: Cambridge University Press, 2012), 97.

16.   Sacagawea was a Shoshone woman who was kidnapped by a rival tribe and then sold into marriage with a trapper from Quebec. She was subsequently made to serve as guide and interpreter for Lewis and Clark in their expedition of the American West. It is likely that her presence was critical to their success. Most guides like her are never recognized. When they are, they are still rarely accorded full status as "travelers."

17. Clifford, *Routes*, 107.

18. See, among others, Dean MacCannell, *The Tourist: A New Theory of the Leisure Class* (Berkeley: University of California Press, 2013), and Johannes Fabian, "Time, Narration, and the Exploration of Central Africa," *Narrative* 9, no. 1 (January 1, 2001): 3–20.

19. Clifford, *Routes*, 106.

20. See chapter 45.

21. Edward W. Said, *Orientalism* (New York: Vintage, 2003).

22. Lila Abu-Lughod, "Do Muslim Women Really Need Saving? Anthropological Reflections on Cultural Relativism and Its Others," *American Anthropologist* 104, no. 3 (September 1, 2002): 783–90; Lara Deeb, *Enchanted Modern: Gender and Public Piety in Shi'i Lebanon* (Princeton, NJ: Princeton University Press, 2006).

23. Lambert-Hurley, *Elusive Lives*, 57.

24. Marianne Kamp, *The New Women in Uzbekistan: Islam, Modernity, and Unveiling under Communism* (Seattle: University of Washington Press, 2006), 222.

25. Barbara Daly Metcalf, "The Pilgrimage Remembered: South Asian Accounts of the Hajj," in *Muslim Travellers: Pilgrimage, Migration, and the Religious Imagination*, ed. Dale F. Eickelman and James P. Piscatori (Berkeley: University of California Press, 1990), 86.

26. Lisle, *Global Politics of Contemporary Travel Writing*, 97.

27. Majchrowicz, "Malika Begum's *Mehfil*."

28. Houari Touati, *Islam and Travel in the Middle Ages* (Chicago, IL: University of Chicago Press, 2010); Fabian, "Time, Narration, and the Exploration of Central Africa."

29. Majchrowicz, *The World in Words*.

30. Abderrahmane El Moudden, "The Ambivalence of Rihla: Community Integration and Self-Definition in Moroccan Travel Accounts, 1300–1800," in *Muslim Travellers*, 69–84.

31. Sunil Sharma, *Mughal Arcadia: Persian Literature in an Indian Court* (Cambridge, MA: Harvard University Press, 2017).

32. Touati, *Islam and Travel in the Middle Ages*.

33. Muzaffar Alam and Sanjay Subrahmanyam, *Indo-Persian Travels in the Age of Discoveries, 1400–1800* (Cambridge, UK: Cambridge University Press, 2007).

34. Evliya Çelebi, *An Ottoman Traveller: Selections from the Book of Travels of Evliya Çelebi* (London: Eland, 2011).

35. Mary Louise Pratt, *Imperial Eyes: Travel Writing and Transculturation* (New York: Routledge, 2008).

36. Majchrowicz, *The World in Words*.

37. Lewis, *Rethinking Orientalism*, 13.

38. Another author worthy of note here is Isabelle Eberhardt, of Swiss descent, who, after moving to Algeria in 1897, converted to Islam and adopted the name Si Mahmoud Saadi. See her compelling "cult classic," *Dans l'ombre chaude de l'Islam* (Paris: Charpentier, 1921), translated from the original French and republished as *In the Shadow of Islam* (London: Peter Owen, 2003).

39. Evelyn Zainab Cobbold, *Lady Evelyn Cobbold Zainab ka safarnamah-i Haramain* (Hyderabad: Idarah-i Adabiyat-i Urdu, 1939).

40. Khwaja Mu'in al-Din Ahmad Makrani, trans., "Jama' Masjid Gulbarga—Ek Musulman Jarman khatun ke shauq-i siyahat ka natija," *Saheli* 6, no. 1–2 (1929): 76–77.

41. Only in the final stages of the project were our attentions drawn to the remarkable fifteenth-century poet and scholar 'Ā'ishah al-Bā'unīyyah of Damascus, who described

her experiences as a pilgrim in Mecca. See Th. Emil Homerin, "Living Love: The Mystical Writings of ʿĀʾishah al-Bāʿunīyyah (d. 922/1516)," *Mamluk Studies Review* 7 (2003): 211–34, esp. 219. We were also unable to include a mid-twentieth-century ʿumrah pilgrimage by the professor, scholar, and political commentator Bint al-Shati, who, like the other Arabic-language authors in this volume, was committed to the emancipation of women in the Middle East. See Richard van Leeuwen, "In the 'Land of Wonders': Bint al-Shāṭi''s Pilgrimage," in *Muslim Women's Pilgrimage to Mecca and Beyond*, ed. Marjo Buitelaar, Manja Stephan-Emmrich, and Viola Thimm (London: Routledge, 2020). We are grateful to Marilyn Booth, Margot Badran, Ceyhun Arsalan, and Greg Halaby for their efforts, however unsuccessful, to find other material in Arabic.

42.   Our observations here are corroborated by Roberta Micallef and Sunil Sharma, eds., *On the Wonders of Land and Sea: Persianate Travel Writing* (Boston: Ilex, 2013).

43.   This observation complements Metcalf's description of hajj narrative from South Asia as a "modern phenomenon." See her "The Pilgrimage Remembered," 87, 101. We should also note that this lack of women's voices is not specific to travel literature: "Although women surely partook of Persian literature, they represent a minority voice that is often hard to identify . . . women are a regrettably minor presence in Persian literature of the fifteenth to eighteenth centuries." Alam and Subrahmanyam, *Indo-Persian Travels in the Age of Discoveries*, 24.

44.   Lambert-Hurley, *Elusive Lives*, 3.

45.   Quran 3:96–97.

46.   Quran 6:11.

47.   Quoted in Tim Mackintosh-Smith, ed., foreword to *The Travels of Ibn Battutah* (London: Picador, 2002), x.

48.   Al-Tirmizi, *Sunan*, 39:2. See Sam Gellens, "The Search for Knowledge in Medieval Muslim Societies: A Comparative Approach," in *Muslim Travellers*, 50–68.

49.   Ian Richard Netton, ed., *Golden Roads: Migration, Pilgrimage and Travel in Medieval and Modern Islam* (Richmond: Curzon, 1993), part I: "Hijra." Notably, part II is on hajj and part III is on rihla. On a modern migration defined as hijra, see Kemal H. Karpat, "The *Hijra* from Russia and the Balkans: The Process of Self-definition in the Late Ottoman State," in *Muslim Travellers*, 131–52.

50.   Qaisari Begum in particular offers a fascinating description of the grand entrances of these various caravans into Mecca in her description of a pilgrimage in the 1930s. See chapter 13.

51.   On pilgrimage ships from India, see A. Jan Qaisar, "From Port to Port: Life on Indian Ships in the Sixteenth and Seventeenth Centuries," in *India and the Indian Ocean, 1500–1800*, ed. Ashin Das Gupta and M. N. Pearson (Delhi: Oxford University Press, 1987), 331–49.

52.   For this summary of the early modern hajj, we draw on Micheal N. Pearson, *Pilgrimage to Mecca: The Indian Experience 1500–1800* (Princeton, NJ: Markus Wiener, 1996), ch. 2. Pearson in turn draws on a much wider set of literature on Africa, the Middle East, and South Asia. On the Southeast Asian hajj, also see Eric Tagliacozzo, *The Longest Journey: Southeast Asians and the Pilgrimage to Mecca* (New York: Oxford University Press, 2013). On the Central Asian hajj, see Eileen Kane, *Russian Hajj: Empire and the Muslim Pilgrimage to Mecca* (Ithaca, NY: Cornell University Press, 2015).

53.   Russel King, "The Pilgrimage to Mecca: Some Geographical and Historical Aspects," *Erdkunde* 26 (1972): 65–66; Pearson, *Pilgrimage*, 53, 57.

54. Pearson, *Pilgrimage*, 45.

55. King, "Pilgrimage," 65–66.

56. Sugata Bose, *A Hundred Horizons: The Indian Ocean in the Age of Global Empire* (Ranikhet: Permanent Black, 2006), 206.

57. Michael Wolfe, ed., *One Thousand Roads to Mecca* (New York: Grove, 1997), 408. On the sharif of Mecca's shortcomings, also see Sikandar Begum's chapter in this volume.

58. William R. Roff, "Sanitation and Security: The Imperial Powers and the Nineteenth Century Hajj," *Arabian Studies* 6 (1982): 145, 148.

59. Bose, *Hundred Horizons*, 204. Bose draws his material from the "Haj Pilgrimage Report, 1927," file no, 448-N, 1926, and "Haj Enquiry Committee Report," file no. 97-N, 1930, Foreign and Political Department, National Archives of India.

60. Bose, *Hundred Horizons*, 204. For a more detailed comparison with Malaya, see Mary Byrne McDonnell, "Patterns of Muslim Pilgrimage from Malaysia, 1885–1995," in *Muslim Travellers*, 11. Unfortunately, comparative data has not been identified for Qajar Iran from where two more of our pilgrim authors embarked.

61. Bose, *Hundred Horizons*, 204.

62. William Facey and Miranda Taylor, introduction to *Pilgrimage to Mecca*, by Lady Evelyn Cobbold (London: Arabian, 2008), 34.

63. Bose, *Hundred Horizons*, 204.

64. R. J. C. Broadhurst, trans., *The Travels of Ibn Jubayr* (New Delhi: Goodword, 2016), 189–90.

65. Annette S. Beveridge, introduction to *The History of Humâyûn (Humâyûn-nâmâ)*, by Gul-Badan Begam (1902; 3rd reprint, Delhi: Low Price, 1996), 69–76. Also see Ruby Lal, *Domesticity and Power in the Early Mughal World* (Cambridge, UK: Cambridge University Press, 2005), 66–67.

66. Some examples include Begum Sarbuland Jang (who, according to the sources here, went on hajj in 1909 and 1934), Begum Hasrat Mohani (who went on four consecutive annual trips in the 1930s), and Herawati Diah (who undertook the 'umrah, or minor pilgrimage, four times after her 1976 hajj). On Herawati Diah's experience, see Herawati Diah, *An Endless Journey: Reflections of an Indonesian Journalist*, trans. Heather Waugh (Jakarta: Equinox, 2005).

67. Carl W. Ernst, *Following Muhammad: Rethinking Islam in the Contemporary World* (New South Wales: Accessible, 2010), 172.

68. Kumkum Chatterjee, "Discovering India: Travel, History and Identity in Late Nineteenth- and Early Twentieth-Century India," in *Invoking the Past: The Uses of History in South Asia*, ed. Daud Ali (New Delhi: Oxford University Press, 1999), 192–227; Ernst, *Following Muhammad*, 175–77.

69. Dale F. Eickelman and James Piscatori, "Social Theory in the Study of Muslim Societies," in *Muslim Travellers*, 8.

70. For a development of this point, see Methal R. Mohammed-Marzouk, "Knowledge, Culture, and Positionality: Analysis of Three Medieval Muslim Travel Accounts," *Cross-Cultural Communication* 8, no. 6 (2010): 1–10. For a full study of travel and travel writing in the medieval period, see Touati, *Islam and Travel in the Middle Ages*.

71. Daniel Majchrowicz, "Travel, Travel Writing and the 'Means to Victory' in Modern South Asia" (PhD diss., Harvard University, 2015), 6, 8–9.

72. Sultan Jahan Begum, *Rauzat al-riyahin* (Bhopal: Sultania, 1909), 4, 6–7.

73. James L. Gelvin and Nile Green, eds., *Global Muslims in the Age of Steam and Print* (Berkeley: University of California Press, 2014). On how these technologies impacted experiences of the hajj in particular, see Nile Green, "The Hajj as Its Own Undoing: Infrastructure and Integration on the Muslim Journey to Mecca," *Past and Present* 226, no. 1 (February 2015): 193–226.

74. Gelvin and Green, *Global Muslims*, 6.

75. For examples, see the writings of Emily Ruete, Atiya Fyzee, Nazli Begum of Janjira, Safia Jabir Ali, Rahil Begum Shervaniya, Begum Hasrat Mohani, Iqbalunnisa Hussain, Nur Begum, Zainab Cobbold, Qaisari Begum, Mahmooda Rizvia, and Herawati Diah. Not all of the passages on sea travel are included in the extracts here, but the further reading to each chapter should act as a signpost.

76. Shaista Suhrawardy Ikramullah's description of wartime sea travel is available as supplementary material to this collection at https://accessingmuslimlives.org/travel /shaista2/.

77. Gelvin and Green, *Global Muslims*, 6–7.

78. Judith Brown, *Global South Asians: Introducing the Modern Diaspora* (Cambridge, UK: Cambridge University Press, 2006), 15.

79. Nazli Begum of Janjira, *Sair-i Yurap* (Lahore: Union Steam Press, n.d.), entry for August 19, 1908; Maimoona Sultan, Shah Bano Begum, *A Trip to Europe*, trans. Mrs. G. Baksh (Calcutta: Thacker, Spink & Co., 1914), 103.

80. See Erik Eckermann, *World History of the Automobile* (Warrendale, PA: SAE International, 2001).

81. Lady Evelyn Zainab Cobbold, *A Pilgrimage to Mecca* (London: John Murray, 1934), 262–63.

82. See Herawati Diah's account dated June 13, 1938, in *Doenia Kita* 2, no. 2 (December 1938), 25, and the many chapters on cars and car culture in Zaib-un-nissa Hamidullah's *Sixty Days in America* (Karachi: Mirror Publications, 1956), including ch. 7, "Let Us Buy a Car"; ch. 13, "Talking of Cars"; and ch. 14, "Travelling by Road."

83. On the emergence and operation of the passport regime in the British Empire, see Radhika Mongia, "Race, Nationality, Mobility: A History of the Passport," *Public Culture* 11, no. 3 (Fall 1999): 527–56; Radhika Singha, "The Great War and a 'Proper' Passport for the Colony: Border-Crossing in British India, c. 1882–1922," *Indian Economic and Social History Review* 50, no. 3 (2013): 289–315.

84. The reference here is to caste prohibitions within Hinduism against crossing the seas around India.

85. Gopalan Balachandran, *Globalising Labour: Indian Seafarers and World Shipping, c. 1870–1945* (Oxford: Oxford University Press, 2012), 36. Also see Michael H. Fisher, "Working across the Seas Indian Maritime Labourers in India, Britain, and in Between, 1600–1857," *International Review of Social History* 51 (2006): 21–45.

86. David Omissi, *Indian Voices of the Great War: Soldiers' Letters, 1914–18* (New York: MacMillan, 1999); David Omissi, "Europe through Indian Eyes: Indian Soldiers Encounter England and France, 1914–18," *English Historical Review* 122 (2007): 371–96.

87. Brown, *Global South Asians*, 30–31.

88. For an overview from the Indian context, see Brown, *Global South Asians*, 34–39.

89. For a brief summary of her life, see Elizabeth Dearnley, "Musician, Author, Princess, Spy: Noor Inayat Khan," accessed July 19, 2019, https://london.ac.uk/news-and-opinion

/leading-women/musician-author-princess-spy-noor-inayat-khan. Ghulam Fatima Shaikh, from the colonial Indian province of Sindh, also narrated later how she accompanied her husband, Shaikh Shamsuddin, a medical doctor, to Turkey to assist "the sick and the wounded" during the First World War under the auspices of the Hilal-i Ahmar, or Red Crescent, organization. *Footprints in Time: Reminiscences of a Sindhi Matriarch*, trans. Rasheeda Husain (Karachi: Oxford University Press, 2011), 30–31.

90.   Michael H. Fisher, *Counterflows to Colonialism: Indian Travellers and Settlers in Britain 1600–1857* (Delhi: Permanent Black, 2004), 222–23.

91.   On ayahs in Britain, see Olivia Robinson, "Travelling Ayahs of the Nineteenth and Twentieth Centuries: Global Networks and Mobilization of Agency," *History Workshop Journal* 86 (Autumn 2018): 44–66; Satyasikha Chakraborty, "'Nurses on Our Ocean Highways': The Precarious Metropolitan Lives of Colonial South Asian Ayahs," *Journal of Women's History* 32 (2020): 37–64.

92.   Samita Sen, "Wrecking Homes, Making Families: Women's Recruitment and Indentured Labour Migration from India," in *Routledge Handbook of the South Asian Diaspora*, ed. Joya Chatterji and David Washbrook (London: Routledge, 2013), 96–109. For the story of a Muslim female laborer in Mauritius, see Satyendra Peerthum, "Daughter of Indentured Labour," *Mauritius Times*, November 7, 2016, http://www.mauritiustimes.com /mt/satyendra-peerthum-15/.

93.   Brown, *Global South Asians*, 31. On "coolie" women in different locations, see Gaiutra Bahadur, *Coolie Woman: The Odyssey of Indenture* (London: Hurst, 2013) (on Guiana); Jo Beall, "Women under Indenture in Colonial Natal, 1860–1911," in *South Asians Overseas: Migration and Ethnicity*, ed. C. Clarke, C. Peach, and S. Vertovec (Cambridge, UK: Cambridge University Press, 1990), ch. 2; Brij V. Lal, *Chalo Jahaji on a Journey Through Indenture in Fiji* (Acton: Australian National University, 2000), ch. 6, "Kunti's Cry"; Marina Carter, *Lakshmi's Legacy: The Testimonies of Indian Women in 19th Century Mauritius* (Stanley, Rose Hill: Editions de l' Océan Indien, 1994); Arunima Datta, *Fleeting Agencies: A Social History of Indian Coolie Women in British Malaya* (Cambridge, UK: Cambridge University Press, 2020).

94.   On this connection, see Lambert-Hurley and Sharma, *Atiya's Journeys*, 18–20.

95.   On these business interests, see Sálim Ali, *Fall of the Sparrow* (Delhi: Oxford University Press, 1985), ch. 3, "Burma 1914–17," and ch. 5, "Memories of Burma."

96.   For numbers of Indian students in Britain, see Shompa Lahiri, *Indians in Britain: Anglo-Indian Encounters, Race and Identity, 1880–1930* (London: Frank Cass, 2000), 5.

97.   On her travels, see Lambert-Hurley, *Elusive Lives*, 163.

98.   See, as example, a translated extract provided as supplementary material to this collection here: https://accessingmuslimlives.org/travel/rahil/.

99.   See Daniel Majchrowicz, "Begum Hasrat Mohani's Journey to Iraq," in *Worlds of Knowledge in Women's Travel Writing*, ed. James Uden (Boston: Ilex, 2022).

100.   See chapter 13.

101.   Herawati Diah, "Amerikaansche Brieven II," *Doenia Kita* 1, no. 3 (January 1938): 18.

102.   Examples to consider here are Safia Jabir Ali, Muhammadi Begum, Mehr al-Nisa, and Nyonya Aulia-Salim.

103.   Rokeya Sakhawat Hossain, *Sultana's Dream and Selections from the Secluded Ones*, ed. and trans. Roushan Jahan (New York: Feminist, 1988), 27. Another well-known feminist

author from India, Rashid Jahan, wrote at least two "travel stories" that highlighted the difficulties of wearing a burqa while traveling. See Priyamvada Gopal, *Literary Radicalism in India: Gender, Nation and the Transition to Independence* (London: Routledge, 2005), 39–60.

104. See chapter 12.

105. There is an extensive literature on hajj and the regulation of disease. As an example, see Eric Tagliacozzo, "Hajj in the Time of Cholera: Pilgrim Ships and Contagion from Southeast Asia to the Red Sea," in *Global Muslims*, 103–20; Saurabh Mishra, *Pilgrimage, Pestilence, and Politics: The Haj from the Indian Subcontinent, 1860–1920* (New Delhi: Oxford University Press, 2011); Elena I. Campbell, "The 'Pilgrim Question': Regulating the Hajj in Late Imperial Russia," *Canadian Slavonic Papers* 56, no. 3–4 (2014): 239–68; Roff, "Sanitation and Security."

106. Majchrowicz, "Travel, Travel Writing and the 'Means to Victory' in Modern South Asia," 21–23.

107. Tagliacozzo, "Hajj in the Time of Cholera," 114.

108. See the chapter on Rahil Begum Shervaniya. A fuller translation of her experience— worthy reading for its frank and ironic tone—is available as supplementary material to this collection here: https://accessingmuslimlives.org/travel/rahil/.

109. This correspondence is preserved in Sultan Jahan Begum, *The Story of a Pilgrimage to Hijaz* (Calcutta: Thacker, Spink & Co., 1909).

110. This extract is available as supplementary material to this collection here: https://accessingmuslimlives.org/travel/life/.

111. Atiya Fyzee offers the best example of the latter in her entry for November 10, 1906.

112. Nazli, *Sair-i Yurap*, 57–58.

113. See chapters 18 and 45.

114. Useful for gaining this comparative perspective is Sanjay Seth, "Nationalism, Modernity and the 'Woman Question' in India and China," *Journal of Asian Studies* 72, no. 2 (May 2013): 273–97.

115. Lambert-Hurley and Sharma, *Atiya's Journeys*, 151. Also see Muhammadi Begum's entry for January 3, 1935.

116. These responses are discussed in more detail in the final section.

117. See chapter 30.

118. See chapter 32.

119. For examples, see chapters 30 and 42.

120. Shaista Suhrawardy Ikramullah, *From Purdah to Parliament* (Karachi: Oxford University Press, 1998), 81.

121. This point is developed in Siobhan Lambert-Hurley, "'Human or Not, Everyone Has Their Own Habits and Tastes': Food, Identity and Difference in Muslim South Asia," *Global Food History* (forthcoming).

122. Jeremy Adelman, "What Is Global History Now?" *Aeon*, March 2, 2017, https://aeon.co/essays/is-global-history-still-possible-or-has-it-had-its-moment. On global history as a specific field or practice, see Sebastian Conrad, *What Is Global History?* (Princeton, NJ: Princeton University Press, 2016). The introduction is available here: http://assets.press.princeton.edu/chapters/s10748.pdf.

123. Adelman, "What Is Global History Now?"

124. See Susan Bassnett, *Translation Studies*, 4th ed. (London: Routledge, 2014); Lawrence Venuti, ed., *The Translation Studies Reader*, 4th ed. (Abingdon, UK: Routledge, 2021).

125. Manan Ahmed Asif, *The Loss of Hindustan: The Invention of India* (Cambridge, MA: Harvard University Press, 2020); Said, *Orientalism*.

126. In responding to this charge here, we join other critics—for example, Richard Drayton and David Motadel, "Discussion: The Futures of Global History," *Journal of Global History* 13, no. 1 (2018): 1–21.

127. As example, Sultan Jahan Begum and Ummat al-Ghani Nur al-Nisa both quoted the Quranic adage that "all believers are brothers" (49:10)—apparently without questioning its gendered formulation.

128. Eickelman and Piscatori, *Muslim Travellers*, xii–xv.

129. For a development of this point, see Lambert-Hurley, *A Princess's Pilgrimage*, xli–li.

130. See Majchrowicz, *The World in Words*, esp. ch. 5.

131. For a development of this theme, see Lambert-Hurley and Sharma, *Atiya's Journeys*, 91.

132. Leela Gandhi, *Affective Communities: Anticolonial Thought, Fin-de-Siècle Radicalism, and the Politics of Friendship* (Durham, NC: Duke University Press, 2006).

133. See Lahiri, *Indians in Britain*, 72–76; A. Martin Wainwright, *'The Better Class' of Indians: Social Rank, Imperial Identity and South Asians in Britain, 1858–1914* (Manchester: Manchester University Press, 2008), ch. 8, "Assimilation and Ostracism in Education." For a fictive account, see Sajjad Zaheer, *A Night in London*, trans. Bilal Hashmi (Noida: HarperPerennial, 2011 reprint).

134. See chapter 40. On this exhibition, see Antoinette Burton, "Making a Spectacle of Empire: Indian Travellers in *Fin-de-Siècle London*," *History Workshop* 46 (1996): 127.

135. For a development of this point, see Lambert-Hurley, "'Human or Not.'"

136. See chapter 30.

137. See chapter 18.

138. See chapter 5.

139. For examples from this vast literature, see note 13. The two anthologies mentioned are Jane Robinson, *Unsuitable for Ladies: An Anthology of Women Travellers* (Oxford: Oxford University Press, 2001); Indira Ghose, *Memsahibs Abroad: Writings by Women Travellers in Nineteenth Century India* (Delhi: Oxford University Press, 1998). Another is Mary Morris and Larry O'Connor, eds., *The Virago Book of Women Travellers* (London: Virago, 2004). Also pertinent was a special exhibition entitled "Off the Beaten Track: Three Centuries of Women Travellers" at the National Portrait Gallery in London in 2004—only twelve women who traveled *to* Britain.

140. Fisher, *Counterflows to Colonialism*. Another example focused more explicitly on Muslims is Claire Chambers, *Britain through Muslim Eyes: Literary Representations, 1780–1988* (London: PalgraveMacmillan, 2015).

141. For a more explicit statement of this Eurocentric assumption, see J. M. Blaut, *Eight Eurocentric Historians* (New York: Guildford, 2000). "The main form of interaction between Europe and non-Europe is the outward diffusion of progressive innovations (ideas, things, settlers—in aggregate, civilisation) from Europe to non-Europe" (7).

142. Other texts we might have included, as example, are Zehra Fyzee's *Mazamin* (Agra: Mufid-i 'Am, 1921) and Sughra Humayun Mirza's *Sair-i Bhopal o Bengal* (1914) and *Roznamchah-i safar-i Bhopal* (Hyderabad: al-Nisa Monthly, 1924), which narrate travels within the borders of the British Indian empire.

143. See Sukanya Banerjee, *Becoming Imperial Citizens: Indians in the Late-Victorian Empire* (Durham, NC: Duke University Press, 2010).

144. Surveying and critiquing this body of literature is Rachel K. Bright and Andrew R. Dilley, "After the British World," *Historical Journal* 60, no. 2 (June 2017): 547–68.

145. Antoinette Burton, "Getting Outside the Global: Repositioning British Imperialism in World History," in *Empire in Question: Reading, Writing, and Teaching British Imperialism* (Durham, NC: Duke University Press, 2011), 279. "Native" would be better in quotation marks.

146. Niall Ferguson, *Empire: How Britain Made the Modern World* (New York: Allen Lane, 2003).

147. An illustrative example is Miles Ogburn, *Global Lives: Britain and the World 1550–1800* (Cambridge, UK: Cambridge University Press, 2008).

148. Seema Alavi, *Muslim Cosmopolitanism in the Age of Empire* (Cambridge, MA: Harvard University Press, 2015), 12–13. "Connected histories" is a phrase attributed to Sanjay Subrahmanyam and put into practice in a book with Muzaffar Alam that was inspirational to our own study: *Indo-Persian Travels in the Age of Discoveries, 1400–1800*. Also galvanizing to our efforts were Natalie Zemon Davis, *Trickster Travels: The Search for Leo Africanus* (London: Faber and Faber, 2007); Julia A. Clancy-Smith, *Mediterraneans: North Africa and Europe in an Age of Migration, c. 1800–1900* (Los Angeles: University of California Press, 2011); Eric Tagliacozzo, *Secret Traders, Porous Borders: Smuggling and States along a Southeast Asian Frontier, 1865–1915* (New Haven, CT: Yale University Press, 2009).

149. Rebecca Adami, "On Subalternity and Representation: Female and Postcolonial Subjects Claiming Universal Human Rights in 1948," *Journal of Research on Women and Gender* 6 (2015): 56–66. Thanks to MA student Sammi-Beth Clarke at the University of Sheffield for conversations linked to her dissertation on "How Women from the Global South Shaped Human Rights," which enabled this point to be developed.

150. See, for example, Mimi Sheller and John Urry, "Mobilizing the New Mobilities Paradigm," *Applied Mobilities* 1 (2016): 10–25.

151. See chapter 36.

152. For an example, see Nando Sigona, "The Politics of Refugee Voices: Representations, Narratives, and Memories," in *The Oxford Handbook of Refugee and Forced Migration Studies*, ed. Elena Fiddian-Qasmiyeh, Gil Loescher, Katy Long, and Nando Sigona (Oxford: Oxford University Press, 2014), 369–82.

153. Peter Merriman and Lynne Pearce, "Mobility and the Humanities," *Mobilities* 12, no. 4 (2017): 493–508.

154. Franco Moretti, "More Conjectures," *New Left Review* 23 (2003): 73–81.

155. Franco Moretti, "Evolution, World Systems, *Weltliteratur*," *Review: Frank Braudel Center* 28, no. 3 (2005): 227–28.

156. Francesca Orsini, "The Multilingual Local in World Literature," *Comparative Literature* 67, no. 4 (2015): 345–46. Italics in original.

157. Andre Gunder Frank, *ReOrient: Global Economy in the Asian Age* (Berkeley: University of California Press, 1998). For Frank's clearest omission of gender as a theme for global history, see Frank, "A Plea for World System History," *Journal of World History* 2, no. 1 (1991): 1–28. A key statement on the importance of "recovering women and gender in world history" was Tony Ballantyne and Antoinette Burton, eds., *Bodies in Contact: Rethinking Colonial Encounters in World History* (Durham, NC: Duke University Press, 2005), 13.

158. Antoinette Burton, *A Primer for Teaching World History: Ten Design Principles* (Durham, NC: Duke University Press, 2012), ch. 2–4.

159. There is a huge literature now on "decolonizing history" or "decolonizing the curriculum" in the popular and academic press, but we quote here from James Muldoon, "Academics: It's Time to Get Behind Decolonising the Curriculum," *The Guardian*, March 20, 2019, https://www.theguardian.com/education/2019/mar/20/academics-its-time-to-get-behind-decolonising-the-curriculum; "Do We Need to Decolonise History? And, if so, How?" *History Extra*, March 25, 2019, https://www.historyextra.com/period/modern/decolonise-history-curriculum-education-how-meghan-markle-black-study/.

160. Ahmed, *What Is Islam*, 5.

161. Cemil Aydin, *The Idea of the Muslim World: A Global Intellectual History* (Cambridge, MA: Harvard University Press, 2019), 228. Emphasis added.

PART I

TRAVEL AS PILGRIMAGE

PILGRIMAGE CONSTITUTES ONE OF THE central rituals of Muslim religious practice. By far the most recognized destination of Muslim pilgrimage is the holy Kaaba, which lies at the center of the city of Mecca in present-day Saudi Arabia. Pilgrims visiting the city throughout the year may perform the ʿumrah, or lesser pilgrimage. The greater pilgrimage, or hajj, however, takes place only once a year according to the Hijri calendar. Although the hajj may constitute a requirement of the faith, for many it is a pilgrimage to the neighboring city of Medina (once called Yathrib, but today known simply as the City of the Prophet, or Medina), where the Prophet Muhammad is buried, that evokes the most emotion. These two cities are the subject of most pilgrimage travel writing by Muslims. Historically, travelers' descriptions of the hajj have appeared formal and ritualized. Accounts of Medina, in contrast, are more likely to be filled with emotion, a reflection of the intense devotion that many pilgrims around the world feel for the Prophet. At the same time, some authors included here do not reflect on their devotion or personal experience at all.

The chapters in this section also reflect that there are more centers of religious devotion than the famous Holy Cities. Iraq and Iran in particular are host to a range of shrines and pilgrimage sites, particularly those related to Shia Islam. Yet again, our authors defy expectations in that Shia and Sunni travelers alike have written about their visits to these sacred sites. Less represented in the following chapters are more regional pilgrimage centers. Across the Muslim world, shrines were, and remain, popular sites of visitation. South Asian women travelers were especially likely to visit these sites in India. These journeys were less likely to be recorded, perhaps due to their relative familiarity, though they are nevertheless a prominent part of pilgrimage writing, particularly in Urdu. Due to this volume's focus on interactions across linguistic and cultural barriers, these travels featured less prominently here.

Devotion is not the only reason that pilgrimage travel accounts are so prominent among Muslim women's travel writing. Its ubiquity, indicated in this section's length, is also a reflection that for many women, religion was one of the few avenues available for travel. Many Muslim men would have only traveled rarely in their lives for religious purposes, but women were far less likely to leave the home to pursue an education, a vocation, or political objectives (although, as the other sections of this book show, women were nevertheless active in these realms as well). As a religiously sanctioned and even mandatory practice, pilgrimage allowed women a way to leave the home and undertake risks or expenditures that might otherwise have been hard to justify. Readers will note that many of these travelers had to overcome significant social barriers to undertake their journeys, but, according to their own accounts, they persisted due to the spiritual importance of the undertaking. Despite the many styles of narration and the varied focus of the following chapters, the reader cannot help but be impressed by these women's tenacity, whether in overcoming a lack of travel companions or complicated logistics.

THE WIDOW OF MIRZA KHALIL

A Bereaved Wife Seeks Solace

INTRODUCTION

Almost nothing is known about the author of the first known hajj narrative by a woman, written in Persian, beyond her description as a "lady of Esfahan." According to the text's scribe, she was the widow of a Safavid official, Mirza Khalil, who was a secretary (*raqamnavis*) in the elite bureaucracy of this early modern Iranian polity. He is said to have penned royal decrees in the financial department of the chief administrative office (*diwan-i a'la*) for the last Safavid king, Shah Sultan Husayn (1694–1722). The scribe also introduced the author as "the Bilqis and Khadijah of the age." This reference to two Muslim female exemplars—the queen of Sheba and the Prophet's first wife—suggests the author's education and status. Though a resident in the capital city Esfahan, she appears to have belonged to a literary family from Urdubad in present-day Azerbaijan. Certainly, she was privileged enough to afford what was a very expensive and dangerous trip to the Hijaz in the late seventeenth century. Her age at the time of pilgrimage is unknown, but we may assume middle maturity on the basis that, from her own account, she left children behind yet was still young enough to be courted (if unsuccessfully) on the journey. As a mother, a widow, and a pilgrim, she seems to have moved fairly freely, meeting and conversing with men and women of different social standings with notable ease.

The opening section of the widow's travel narrative, included here in the first extract, provides the context for her journey: how she undertook the hajj pilgrimage to recover from the recent death of her husband. As she wrote in response

The translation was prepared by Sunil Sharma. The introduction and annotations were prepared by Siobhan Lambert-Hurley with input from Sunil Sharma.

to her grief, "I saw no recourse other than travel." This passage also implied that she was a lone traveler when she set out on her journey given that none of her relatives would accompany her. But oblique references to fellow travelers later on indicate that she was probably accompanied by at least one slave or some servants. The trip lasted seven months. According to her own description, the route she took was through northwestern Iran into Ottoman lands. After a brief stop at her husband's tomb just outside Esfahan, also described in the first extract, the widow headed through mountainous terrain and prairie highlands toward the Caucasus, taking in Qom, Qazvin, and Tabriz before stopping for over three weeks in Urdubad. As noted in the second extract, she was received here by her relatives, among whom was a dear friend from Esfahan. The particular terms of affection used for this woman, a "beloved" friend with whom she was reunited after thirty years, suggest the possibility of a homoerotic relationship.

From Nakhchivan (now in Azerbaijan), she joined an Iranian hajj caravan. The third extract details how this grouping was necessitated by the threat of bandits along the route. Upon the widow's entry into territory controlled by the neighboring Ottoman Empire, her journey took a somewhat dramatic turn. As documented in the fourth extract, the hajj caravan was attacked in the wild borderland area of the two empires. The author identified as a Shia Iranian and portrayed the Sunni Ottomans as hostile, though because they held the Holy Cities and controlled the hajj pilgrimage, she and her travel companions had no choice but to continue. After fighting off the Ottomans like "fierce lions," the "heroic hajjis" descended to the Euphrates River valley, following it west on camel and horseback to Aleppo (Halab) and Damascus. Finally, they crossed the dry desert of the Hijaz to Medina and Mecca (see fig. 1.1). That there were other possible itineraries is confirmed by the widow's lament that she might have taken a less dangerous route via Mosul (now in Iraq). Still, the narrative ended rather abruptly with her setting out in the direction of Aleppo for the return journey.

Presumably composed upon her return, the widow's narrative was a verse travelogue (*safarnamah-yi manzum*) in the *masnavi* form. In rhyming couplets, it consisted of 1,200 verses—though for the ease of the reader, this long poem has been translated here into prose. The masnavi form was usually reserved for longer romantic and mystical narratives, like the story of Layla and Majnun, to which the author alluded in the opening section. But in the seventeenth century, it was particularly popular among Persian literati for travel themes in Safavid Iran and Mughal India. It may be assumed that the educated widow would have been familiar with other travelogues that narrated the hajj experience in verse. Clearly, the twelfth-century romantic poet Nizami—mentioned and cited in her *safarnamah* (see the fifth extract for an example)—was a major

Figure 1.1 The Kaaba at Mecca in the 1550s from a Persian miniature.
© Granger Historical Picture Archive / Alamy Stock Photo.

influence on the author. Her text survives in a sole manuscript that is part of an anthology (*jung, majmu'ah*) of miscellaneous writings, including poems, letters, and decrees, prepared by a scribe probably based in her family library. It thus had no original title.

The lady of Esfahan wrote in a simple but elegant style, employing established metaphorical language that is tinged with a mystical tone. For instance, much of the narrative is infused with a sense of melancholy and longing on account of the author's separation from the beloved—though there are three beloveds evoked here, with the same terms (*yar, rafiq*) used to refer to her deceased husband, her female friend, and God. There is also a sense of release, captured in the fifth extract here, when the author is unified with the divine on the fulfillment of her pilgrimage. On other occasions, the narrative breaks with mystic tropes and the language of male travelogues to share personal preferences and experiences that give it a human and often feminine character. Though the widow is frequently ill or depressed, she shows herself able to raise her spirits to admire the local landscape or bemoan the state of wayside inns. Genuine love and grief are expressed alongside moving descriptions of the hajj's religious rituals as a spiritual experience. We thus gain insight into the otherwise shadowy figure of the author as a caring, hurting, and, ultimately, reflective individual.

EXTRACTS

Commencing the Journey

Since wily fate made me suffer separation from my dear beloved, repose in bed was forbidden to me. I saw no recourse other than travel. I could neither sleep at night nor rest during the day until I would be able to circumambulate the sanctuary of the Kaaba. I prepared myself and set off with a resolve in my step. Not a single one of my family members accompanied me, so like Majnun, I headed into the wilderness alone.[1] What use is anyone's help to one when God is the friend of the hapless?—that is sufficient. When I saw the disloyalty of my loved ones, I left Esfahan like the cold wind. I washed away fear from my heart and made an auspicious augury for travel. In the litter, I breathed in the charm of the open countryside, and like a bird, I flew from the branch of sorrow. To circumambulate the house of God, I set off all alone into the wilderness.

The caravan bell melodiously called out, "Three leagues to Gaz." After I had traveled three leagues across the desert, I reached Gaz. I spent the night there in rest and at daybreak was ready to travel. The caravan bell melodiously sang out, "The garden of Khalil is here!" When we traversed the garden of my beloved, tears flooded my eyes. After we had gone five leagues, a cry rose from my bones as from a reed pipe: "Since you are fated to be with Khalil, go to his grave, nightingale." I stopped there and slept restfully all night. At dawn, when that brilliant ruby emerged from the turquoise arch, like a lamenting nightingale, weeping, I left the grave. After we had gone five leagues, suddenly a stone kiln came into view. I don't know whether it was an inn or hell. You would think it was made out of sorrow. Each chamber in it was like an ancient cave, and snakes had made a home in every corner. Its foundation had been laid without any knowledge and was detrimental to our lives. I spent a night in that house of sorrows with sadness and revulsion. At first light, I packed up my things and escaped from that place.

I traveled four leagues in a downcast state to the rhythm of the caravan bell until Momenabad suddenly appeared, which made my dejected heart joyful. It was bright as the fountainhead of the celestial bodies; the habitation was luminous like the heart of a believer (mo'men). It had good water and a fine inn, but also a bad wind. I came out of that valley in the morning as the caravan bell struck a song about the difficulties of the road. After I had traversed five leagues, I saw blossoms of all different colors there. A stream was flowing from the mountain slope, limpid as a beloved's white neck. I set up camp in that lovely land and spent the night in a grove of willows. At dawn, when the bride of the east poked its head out of the heavenly turquoise fortress, I prepared to depart for the mountains of Qahru. What mountains! Their peaks reaching up to the heavens, they were the remover of the heart's sorrows. The weather was mild like the beloved's street, fresh and happy like the face of the beloved. There were many green and lush trees. Come, listen to its rivulets!

With Relatives in Urdubad

Like an eyelash blown by the wind, we were swept into the city of Urdubad.[2] We were like ducks that fly on to land from the water. There, we unloaded our packs from the boats. When the Urdubadis became aware that a boat had come out of the water, relatives and friends, old and young, gathered on the plain. Those friends fully honored me with a welcome. They seated me on their own camel and conveyed me to safety, with a crowd of people like a wave in the ocean before my litter. With complete honor, my dear relatives carried me to the city, into the street of my kind friend. While together in Esfahan, we had been close, sincere companions in sorrow. That dear relative had been better than a sister and nicer than other family members, when suddenly cunning fate played a deceitful trick. It snatched that kind creature away from my sight just like the soul and spirit from the body. Separated by forty way stations from each other, two bodies were afflicted with parting. With no other recourse, we had both steeled our hearts to spend an age apart from each other, until at night's end the darkness of separation was transformed into the morning of union with a beloved. Alighting in that friend's street, I saw her face after thirty years. Dear ones, patience and forbearance were medicine for the incurable torment of separation. For twenty-two days, I stopped in that valley, in the street of my sympathetic friend. My Esfahani friend happily hosted me during that time. My kind friend and old beloved did not stint in taking care of me; it was as if I had dropped down from heaven. But my fortune was not favorable and did not support me for even a week. I was always tired and depressed, afflicted with fever and torment. I did not converse with her for a moment, nor did I show her any affection.

Joining a Hajj Caravan

I reached Nakhchivan.[3] Its climate was bad, and my health was affected. When I drank some water from there, it was like drinking a cup of blood. I took to my bed crying, ill, a helpless stranger. It seems that in the eight days that I was there, my troubles only increased. I couldn't pack my things to leave; it was as if I was stuck. I did not hear the sound of the caravan bell, nor did I have a moment of joy. The informed officials told me, "There are countless robbers on the road, and it would be dangerous for you to travel alone. You must wait here until you find a few companions." When I heard these words, I became sorrowful, and crying, I appealed to beneficent God, "You summoned me to your house. How do I get out of this whirlpool of sorrows? I am a helpless stranger and hapless. I am bereft of my household and possessions. Give a cure for my wounded soul. Untie the knot of my problem. Why am I stuck in this city of sorrows? Lord, free me from this sorrow." As I wept and made my plea, my heart became restless, and tears fell from my eyes and soaked my collar and skirt.

The next day, they informed me, "A caravan has arrived like a flood of rain. They have unloaded in Nakhchivan. It seems that your sleeping fortune has awakened." When I heard this news, I offered my thanks to God. The next day, they told me that the 'Ajam Aqasi[4] had arrived there. In the morning, the wise and good man came to see me in the street where I was staying and from whose cup I had drunk a draft of sorrow. The next day, my wish came true, and my time there came to an end.

Entering the Ottoman Empire

When we reached Qurkh and Kirmanlar,[5] everyone sighed deeply, for this was the boundary of Iran, and from here no one would be under the command of the shah. In one's city we are all fierce lions, but here we are oppressed by the Ottomans. We spent the night in sorrow in that valley and at dawn set off from there. Tongues stopped taking the name of Haidar,[6] and all valuables were hidden away. From the fear of the Ottomans, everyone became like mice or like a candle that is extinguished at first light. With sighs and laments, they left the land of the shah of Iran at dawn. When they had gone five leagues, they made for a safe haven, where the loads were unburdened. They spent the night in that valley. In the morning, that river wound its way to the plain to the rhythm of the bells, which rang out songs as the horses struck their hooves on stones.

When we had traversed a couple of leagues of the desert, a troop of Ottomans suddenly appeared. Having a new plan for us, they blocked our path. They said, "We want tribute. We would like ninety *tomans* from these pilgrims." Our 'Ajam Aqasi was disturbed and spoke sharply to those wretches. Their verbal exchange went on for a while, with each side making threatening faces to the other. They pulled out swords from their waists, and they let fly a volley of arrows. With firearms, guns were emptied against each other. The heroes of the caravan, like brave lions, took on those daredevils. Clashing with each other on a bridge, a lot of blood was spilled. The caravan was emptied of its men, with anyone who was a champion engaged in battle. When they saw that the caravan was without men, they rushed toward it. The heroic hajjis, like fierce lions, raced their horses swiftly and blocked their way, and they scattered helter-skelter. The hajjis drove the camels into the water, which made the Ottomans lose heart. With the blow of daggers and sharp swords, the young men caused carnage. Experiencing the onslaught of arrows and daggers, they held back from the conflict. The leader of those accursed men fell and was captured like a dog by the hajjis. They bound the hands of that fellow like game and struck him on the head and hands with a sword. Fearing the blows of the swords of those lions, the troop hid under the bridge. All at once a cry of "Allah is great" rose up from the pilgrims, like the roar of a lion. At that moment, like balls on a field, the Ottomans fled into the desert.

In the Hijaz

We traveled two leagues like the wind, not on foot but rather on our heads, until the city of Medina appeared like the bright sun behind a mountain. Calling out "God is great," we went with bare feet and heads like dervishes toward the tomb of the Prophet. I don't know how we traveled that distance. I said to my heart, "This is Medina, for which there is a permanent affection in our breast." It replied, "This is the ground of Yathrib, the home and resting place of the Prophet and king of the world and faith. Here rest sayyids and chiefs; here rests the intercessor of the day of judgment. Don't you see that Yathrib is luminous? It is pure due to the light of that tomb."[7] . . . We stayed there for two days, and on the evening of the second day, we left. Since the Amir al-Hajj had left Yathrib, the bright day appeared dark to me. In that auspicious land, we were sorrowful, not being sated with paying obeisance to the Prophet. Weeping due to the separation, I followed the others into the desert. Three leagues from Yathrib, we reached the sacred site that was called the Shajara mosque.[8] As the pilgrims made their way to the shrines, we cleansed their bodies of the dirt of sin. All the Shias put on the garb of pilgrims. With bare feet and heads, the fine-looking people set off, saying, "Here I am!" . . . .

It was the last night of separation from the beloved. My eyes were shining with the prospect of union. I washed all temptation of the devil from my heart and removed all feelings of earthly attachment. Leaving aside sorrow and grief, we made our way to the stony Kaaba. After four leagues, on the fifth of the month, the building of God became visible like the moon. They set up the tents on level ground while opening their mouths to thank God. As I had reached my destination at last, I witnessed this day with my own eyes. I remembered the famous verse that is a gem in the jewel box of Nizami: "How wonderful it is when one's hopes are attained after a long wait."[9] Since I obtained this fortune, I was beside myself. I had no words to thank God; I had no wherewithal to laugh and rejoice. I had no strength to circumambulate the Kaaba or run between Safa and Marwa.

I was dumbstruck for a while like a statue. After an hour, I came to myself but was unable to speak. At last the knot on my tongue was untied, and I spoke. I prostrated myself and said, "God, you are the adored one who is wise and incomparable. I am shamed by your unlimited kindness. How can I express gratitude for this beneficence? You have showered your grace upon me. You have given me both riches and life. You have conveyed me to my desired destination. You did not turn me away hopeless from this court. I am obliged to you that you did not resurrect me among Christians." When I had given thanks for God's kindness, I set off for his threshold. The door whose name is "Gate of Peace" is the first court of the sanctuary.[10] When I reached that lofty court, my heart did not have a care for worldly affairs, but it beat from fear of transgression. A tear streamed down my face out of shame. When my eyes fell on the house of God, my tears began to flow. How can I describe the structure? It was loftier than the way I describe it. It was peerless and seemed to be a youth with the stature of a tall cypress, clad in a dark velvet robe whose skirt was pulled from the saddle straps and tied tightly with a golden belt at the waist. The stone was the guard at the door, and its face was the place for the pilgrims to kiss. I said to myself, "Heart, where are you? Look at the sanctuary of grandeur." It replied, "Is this wakefulness or sleep? Such fortune is very rare." I said, "This is wakefulness. Don't be negligent of God's mercy." Under the load of a hundred maunds of faults and transgressions, I began to circumambulate God's lane. When I had made seven rounds of the qibla of the life and soul, the burden of sins was lifted from my back.

FURTHER READING

Rasul Jaʻfarian, ed. *Safarnamah-yi manzum-i hajj.* Tehran: Sazman-i jughrafiayi-yi niruha-yi musallah, (1386) 2007. The published versions reproduce Mss. No. 2591 in Tehran University Library.

Muzaffar Alam and Sanjay Subrahmanyam. *Indo-Persian Travels in the Age of Discoveries, 1400–1800.* Cambridge, MA: Cambridge University Press, 2007. The widow's entire text is summarized and then briefly analyzed on pages 24–44.

Kathryn Babayan. "'In Spirit We Ate Each Other's Sorrow': Female Companionship in Seventeenth-Century Safavi Isfahan." In *Islamicate Sexualities: Translations across Temporal Geographies of Desire,* edited by Kathryn Babayan and Afsaneh Najmabadi, 239–74. Cambridge, MA: Harvard Center for Middle Eastern Studies, 2008.

Suraiya Farooqhi. *Pilgrims and Sultans: The Hajj under the Ottomans 1517–1683.* London: I. B. Tauris, 1994.

NOTES

1. Majnun was the legendary madman-lover of Layla in classical Persian literature. He abandoned his family and friends and lived in the wilderness.

2. In present-day Azerbaijan.

3. This is the capital of the present-day Nakhchivan Autonomous Republic, a landlocked exclave of Azerbaijan.

4. In Safavid times, the ʻAjam Aqasi was a functionary in charge of the welfare of pilgrims from Iran. Later she also refers to the Amir al-Hajj, who was the commander of the pilgrimage.

5. Area on the western bank of the Tigris River.

6. The caliph ʻAli, who is venerated by Shias.

7. This is a reference to the tomb of the Prophet Muhammad, now known as the Green Dome.

8. The Mosque of the Tree is seven kilometers outside of Medina and one of several fixed points where pilgrims put on their special garb (ihram).

9. Nizami (d. ca. 1209) was a classical Persian poet who composed verse romances that were popular in the author's time.

10. The Gate of Peace is one of the gates of the Grand Mosque of Mecca from which pilgrims enter.

—ᴡᴡ—

NAWAB SIKANDAR BEGUM

A Queen's Impressions of Mecca

INTRODUCTION

Nawab Sikandar Begum (1816–68) (see fig. 2.1) was not the first Indian royal to make the pilgrimage to Mecca—famously, the Mughal emperor Akbar's mother, Hamida Banu, and his aunt Gulbadan had done so as early as the 1570s. She was, however, the first Indian *ruler* to fulfill this religious obligation. She was also the first ruler to publish an account of it. Her territory was the princely state of Bhopal in central India. From her husband's death in 1844, Sikandar acted as regent for their only daughter, Shah Jahan, before being named as ruler in her own right in 1860. This recognition of her sovereignty was, above all, a reward for her loyalty to the British government during the Indian rebellion of 1857. But it also acknowledged her political and administrative acumen—in particular, her reforms to Bhopal's revenue and judicial systems, military and police forces, transport, education, and civil administration. For her sagacity, Sikandar was awarded the Grand Cross of the Star of India in 1861, making her the only female knight in the British Empire besides Queen Victoria.

Sikandar set out from Bhopal on hajj late in 1863 and returned eleven months later. On her journey, she was accompanied by several relatives, including her mother, Qudsia Begum, and her uncle, Faujdar Mahomed Khan, the latter of whom is mentioned twice in the following extracts. Several of her state officers, including the chief minister and the commander-in-chief of the Bhopal army, both named in the extracts, also escorted the ruling begum, as did nearly a thousand of her subjects. From these figures, we may conjecture that the Bhopal

---

The introduction was written by Siobhan Lambert-Hurley. Extracts were selected by her and translated from the original Urdu manuscript by Daniel Majchrowicz.

Figure 2.1 Nawab Sikandar Begum of Bhopal,
from *A Pilgrimage to Mecca* (1870). Courtesy of
Siobhan Lambert-Hurley.

hajjis made up a significant proportion of the five to seven thousand estimated
to set off from India each year in the mid-nineteenth century. Though Sikandar
was fortunate in missing the devastating cholera epidemic that ravaged the hajj
just a year later in 1865, according to her own account, her party was still hit by
severe sickness, including "dysentery, fevers, and tumors in the leg." Indeed,
eight in her immediate party died on board ship or in the Hijaz, and a "great
many" more were lost from the larger caravan.

Sikandar's book, *A Pilgrimage to Mecca*, appeared in print only after her death,
first from a London-based publisher in 1870 and then in an Indian reprint from
Calcutta in 1906. That it was only published in English translation at a time when
few Indians would have been conversant in that language suggests its targeting
of a British audience. The translator, Emma Laura Willoughby-Osborne (1835–
1905), was the wife of a British army officer and civil servant who had acted as the
colonial representative, or political agent, in Bhopal at various points between
1863 and 1881. In her introduction, she claimed to have "endeavoured to adhere

to the literal meaning of the Urdú as closely as possible." While her translation is laudably faithful to the original Urdu, she frequently reorganized the text in an apparent bid to make it more coherent. These changes, along with a number of errors in the translation, have precipitated the new translation published here. This translation was made possible only by the recent discovery (in March 2020) of the original manuscript, entitled *Tarikh-i safar-i Makkah* (*An Account of a Voyage to Mecca*), whose whereabouts have long been unknown.

Apparently, the original diary in Urdu on which the published account was based was in family hands until at least the late nineteenth century. It has since been lost, but significantly, a second copy of the original Urdu was made. It was donated to the library of the School of Oriental and African Studies in London in 1970 as part of the private papers of a former colonial officer, Colonel (later Major General Sir) H. M. Durand, a foreign secretary of the government of India and previously a political agent in Bhopal. He and his wife, Lady Durand, receive mention in the opening paragraph as a specific readership for Sikandar's text, having encouraged her to prepare her narrative in the first place. Their interest in her journey may have been innocuous, but in light of British imperial interests in the region—exemplified by southern Yemen becoming a British protectorate in 1839—it might also have reflected a political imperative. Either way, the ethnographic quality of Sikandar's narrative, evident in the first, second, and fourth extracts especially, seemed to respond to the Durands' request for her "impressions of Arabia generally, and of Mecca in particular." The third extract points to how Sikandar sought to fulfill the British imagination by constructing herself as a benevolent ruler committed to financial prudency as she enforced order and introduced appropriate sanitation. Indeed, she is so scathing of the current administration of the Hijaz as to suggest that the sultan of Turkey ought to employ her to do the job instead! No wonder that other high-ranking colonial officers, like Sir William Muir, later a member of the Viceroy's Council, employed her observations as evidence in their own writings.

Overall, much of Sikandar's account is dedicated to trials and tribulations of her journey. The root of her problems appears to have been the large quantity of goods that she had brought with her from India: not only a "year's supply of grain and clothes" plus the necessary cooking vessels, but also bales of cloth, jewelry, and money to be distributed in charity. As soon as her ship docked in Jeddah and all along her route, her belongings were plundered: officially by tax collectors authorized to appropriate a quarter of all foreign goods and unofficially by Bedouin raiders. The torrent of acrimonious correspondence that this circumstance unleashed is reproduced in full in the first and third sections of Sikandar's translated account. Religious matters are relegated to a large and dry middle section that contains "notices of the names of the pilgrimage in Arabia that are visited by pilgrims and which Sikandar Begum saw or of which she heard." This section is written in the third person, suggesting that it was not composed by Sikandar Begum, who was perhaps more interested in narrating her more worldly conflicts. If one considers the scarcity of the Arabian environment in this period, it is perhaps unsurprising that a wealthy Indian ruler should have been targeted as Sikandar was, but to her, it signified a corruption that colored her assessment of the Hijaz as a whole. As the first and fourth extracts indicate, there were a few Arabian attributes that elicited admiration or at least curiosity, but on the whole, Sikandar was thoroughly unimpressed with the Hijaz's populace. Her experience of pilgrimage to the Islamic "heartlands" thus confirmed, rather than undercut, her identity as an "Indian Muslim."

EXTRACTS

On Domestic Arrangements, Women, Dress, and Religion

Houses here are badly designed, by which I mean that the toilet, the kitchen, the room where water is stored, the bedrooms, and the sitting rooms are all immediately connected to each other, such that it is not possible to prevent kitchen smoke or bathroom odors from entering the sitting room or the bedroom. That said, the houses are beautifully decorated with carpets and throw-pillows. There are few earthenware pots, glass lampshades, chandeliers, etc. but numerous containers for [objects like] rice, *missi*, and sugar. . . . The houses of the residents of Mecca Mu'azzama are built on the hills, like at Raisen.[1] The houses spread from the base of the hill to its summit. The houses do not have courtyards but have one story after another, going up and up. No house has less than three stories, nor any more than seven. Some have door frames, while others do not, but those with frames do not have doors. Where doors are used, they never have chains, locks, bolts, or hinges. They instead have a sort of wooden lock, in the shape of a cross, like those worn by Christians. I end my description of houses and toilets here. . . .

No one here knows how to sing or to dance. The women clap, snap, and whistle quite a bit. When there is a wedding, amusing dances are performed at home, that is, they dance themselves. But the dancing and singing are not good. Seeing it, one cannot help but feel disgusted and devoid of all interest. Aficionados of the type of music we listen to in Hindustan stealthily practice it in their homes. It is very common to breed camels. . . .

The manner of making and receiving visits is the same in Mecca Mu'azzama as it is in Hindustan. However, most people here are greedy and only visit the wealthy with an eye toward profiting from the meeting, never from a position of sincerity or affection. The streets of Mecca Mu'azzama are filthy and foul-smelling. A street is sometimes wide and sometimes narrow. Mecca Mu'azzama is very populous, containing about twenty thousand homes. The houses of the wealthy have an open area made of stone or brick. Outdoor areas used for eating are generally not covered, on account of the heat. . . .

Most of the bad characters who have been thrown out of Hindustan are here in Mecca. Almost anything from anywhere in the world can be found in Mecca, but for a price. The people of Mecca are well-off no matter which class they come from, and yet all miserly and greedy and do not consider it a disgrace to beg. Rich, poor, young, old, man, woman, boy, girl: all beg in a manner that accords with their rank and their intellect. No matter what you give them, they are not satisfied. Workers take a payment and then do not complete their work satisfactorily. Rather, they demand more money to complete the task and take advantage of their employer every chance they get. Everyone takes a commission for any task performed, no matter their class or background. . . . Whenever a traveler prepares to depart, the people ask them for baksheesh. . . .

The women here are more violent and outspoken than the men. Every woman gets married at least five or ten times. There are few women who have only been married once or twice. If a woman feels her husband has become feeble or weak, then the moment she takes a liking to someone else, she goes to speak with the sharif, settles the matter, and leaves her old husband for someone younger, better, and wealthier. Women typically remarry every year or two.

The people of the desert, the Bedouins, do not know how to cook. They eat their meals raw and are unable to discern good taste from bad. However, they delight in eating honey, dates, and ghee. People in the cities wear fabrics, but in the desert they only wear skins and blankets. Some of the Bedouins just wear a long shirt without any belt or tie. Most go bareheaded, though some tie a rope of palm-fiber or a similar material. As far as religious knowledge is concerned, only those in the city possess it. The people who live in the mountainous regions have no knowledge of it whatsoever. Conversations are held in Arabic. The mountain people speak proper Arabic, but those in the city do not.

Merchants operate in the following way: if the seller says that an item costs one rupee, and the prospective buyer offers half a rupee, the merchant will throw dirt at the customer and spit in their face. And once the seller has taken a payment for an item, whether that payment be a rupee or a paisa, if it is a small amount they put it in their mouth rather than in a bag or a purse. Food is never prepared with salt, which is only found in pickles and chutneys, but they know how to prepare an endless number of unique desserts. In Mecca, there are many more people from Delhi than from other regions. Liquor is sold on the sly here. The Turks drink it, as do the Hindustanis. . . . People of all classes generally move about on foot. In conversation there is always a great amount of deception and lying. There is no single type of dress in the city. The Arabs wear their clothes, while those from other regions dress according to their custom. When I visited Jabal al-Nur, I noticed that there were tiny bright stone flakes and pebbles of red, green, gold, and other colors. There is a race of people called "Java" who live in a place beyond Calcutta; they say that gold can be extracted from these stones. . . . The children of Mecca are very spoiled and disorderly and always cause a great racket. The reason for this is that there is no school or madrasa for them. The men and women are just as bad.

A Visit to the Sharif of Mecca's House

My meeting with the sharif took place as follows: I left my house and went to his on foot. Sharif sahib was sitting by himself in a room separate from the main house. Three eunuchs met me and requested that I go to the zenana. I followed them toward Sharif sahib's zenana. When I arrived, I found a few eunuchs stationed at the base of the staircase on the first floor. A few steps above them were three Georgian servants. These were followed by the Egyptian women who attended to his mother and sisters. They placed their hands under my arms and led me up the staircase. After a few steps, I encountered one of Sharif sahib's wives and behind her another wife. Beyond the door, at the place appointed for meetings such as this, in about the middle of the room, was his mother. As each of the sharif's wives greeted me, they first took my hand in theirs and then shook it. The first wife then kissed me on both sides of my neck, my cheeks, and on my lips and chin. The second wife and the mother did this as well.

Captain Muhammad Khan sahib *bahadur*, my regent Hafiz Muhammad Khan, and Captain Mittu Khan, who had come with me, were seated in the men's apartment.[2] Sharif sahib first went to meet with them. He sat with them for a full hour before a eunuch came to me and said that the sharif requested my permission to visit me in the zenana. I replied that this was his own house. I was sitting with his mother and wives. His mother spoke to me in Arabic, and her words were translated for me by Ja'far Effendi's wife.[3] She also translated my replies into Arabic. The sharif has about seven wives, of whom I met four but not the three others. Two of the four wives were Georgian. They were extremely beautiful. Wearing the finest clothing, they appeared from head to toe as brilliant as a brightest chandelier. Their heads were encircled with jeweled wreaths. Thanks to this ensemble, all that they did and said was appealing to the eye. They also wore on their heads small kerchiefs reminiscent of those that English women keep in their hands, made of the finest fabrics. These were tied in an alluring manner. The wreaths, made of flowers and diamonds, were worn above the kerchiefs. They wore similar jewelry from their neck to their waist. The faces of the Georgian wives, as well their stature and the proportion of their limbs, were as perfect as could be. One of the Georgians was wearing black satin, and the other lilac satin embroidered with stars. The third wife was an Arab with an unremarkable face. The fourth was from Abyssinia. One of the practices in the sharif's home is that only those wives who have given birth to a child will take a seat in his presence. If a wife has no offspring, she will remain standing before the sharif with her hands folded.

When the sharif came into the zenana, all four wives and his mother rose out of respect. I made a gesture of respect and then advanced a few steps to greet him. Once the sharif had taken his seat, I made an offering and then began to make conversation. After inquiring after my well-being and comfort, he asked me how far Bhopal was from this place. I replied, "Hindustan is the very reflection of paradise. You must visit it sometime."

Sharif sahib laughed and said, "My home is the Kaaba." His wives and mother then made a gesture of respect and retired to another part of the room. Out of the many Georgians and servants, some now presented us with cups of coffee, while others brought pomegranate juice, rose water, and fragrances. Just as in India it is the custom to offer rosewater or incense, here they offer you the fumes of fragrant incense. . . . After this, I returned to my house. The practice here is that whenever such a meeting occurs the women kiss each other, and men do the same.

Cause of Disagreement with the Pasha and Sharif of Mecca

To all appearances, Pasha sahib and Sharif sahib were very hospitable to me, but in actual fact, neither was very pleased with me. There appear to be two reasons for this. One was that they had heard quite a bit from the late Captain Muhammad Khan sahib *bahadur* and from those who had fled from India after the [failed] uprising [of 1857] of my support for the British during that time.[4] The second reason was that one day, astounded by the local customs and the filthiness of the homes there, I had remarked that the Ottoman sultan paid three million rupees for the upkeep of the Holy Sites [in Mecca and Medina], and yet neither was the city clean nor were proper arrangements made to staff the Holy Sites. If the sultan would give those three million rupees to me, my son-in-law and daughter could take over the running of Bhopal.[5] Then just see how clean I would make this place with all that money. I would also make proper arrangements for staffing at the Holy Sites and bring an end to the disruptions caused by the Bedouins on the roads leading to Medina Munavvara. Then the Ottoman sultan would come to know how, for generations, these traitors have been embezzling his money without making any improvements whatsoever, while I was able to set things to rights in just a few days' time. When I made this remark, Ja'far Effendi, who was the royal secretary, and a few others from Mecca Mu'azzama, were present. It seems likely that one of them went and told this to the sharif and the pasha. This is surely what happened for, one day, I detected a whiff of annoyance from the pasha's tongue during one of our conversations. During the interaction, the pasha happened to remark that many visitors to Mecca come with humility, and not arrogantly. Timur once came here with such grandeur, and just look what happened to him.[6] I surmised from this remark that he was angry about what I had said. Had he been more discerning, he might have eagerly welcomed my thoughts and asked me to describe what I had in mind.

Impressions of Mecca and Jeddah

What Sikandar Begum sahiba saw and learned in Mecca sharif and Jeddah was as follows: Jeddah is a depressing city.[7] It is filthy and fetid. Its climate is hot and humid. There are no canals, lakes, or pools. There are wells, but they do not contain abundant supplies of water, rather very little. The taste of the water is slightly sweet. The wells are more like water holes or troughs; they are not very deep, and the water is murky and often contains small insects.

Mecca is dismal and depressing. It is both wild and frightening, with its houses that climb up the mountainside. Sometimes it is cold, and sometimes it is unbearably hot. Various types of diseases, and particularly the cold, are common. The men and women alike have harsh, repellant voices, but they are also beautiful and agreeable in appearance. Beautiful from head to shoulders, with the rest of the body being ill-shaped. The women are more muscular than the men. They are corpulent and obstinate.

It occasionally rains, and sometimes green vegetables are grown here and there. Gourds and cucumbers, like those that we find in Hindustan, are not grown here. In all of the city of Mecca Mu'azzama, there are no trees, and the ground is mostly sandy with very little soil. The soil that does exist is a dark brown, almost black.

The water in Mecca is excellent, but the air is not good. What I suspect is that the air there is actually quite good, but the people of that place, by dint of their stupidity and dirty habits, have accumulated a vast amount of filth in the city, and this is why the wind no longer brings any freshness. The more detailed explanation is that the hajj brings hundreds of thousands of camels, goats, and sheep for the sacrifice. Once they are sacrificed, the meat is kept, but there is no one to remove the remaining offal from the field of Mina [where the sacrifice occurs]. Additionally, the toilets in homes are not cleaned.

The nights are pleasant and cool. The coolness is not excessive but rather quite agreeable. However, it becomes as hot as in the day when there is still an hour of darkness left. The moonlight is very clear in Mecca and not dulled by dust. There are rarely clouds in the sky and the horizon is always clear. There is little dew. The wind can be strong, and there is often lightning and thunder, but rarely rain. If it does rain, it is only intense for an hour or two. The clouds, when they appear, are light, such that there is sometimes shade, sometimes sun, though the clouds may certainly stay for a few days. . . . Fruits and vegetables of all seasonal types, particularly melons and cucumbers and pomegranates, are brought to Mecca from [the city of] Taif in great quantities and are much better and more flavorful than fruit in Hindustan. It would seem that the climate of Taif is excellent, for it manages to produce such delicious fruit all twelve months of the year.

In many of the wells in Mecca, you must dig deep underground to hit water, whereas in others you only need to dig a bit. Some wells supply brackish water, but others are a bit sweet. The men are very strong. For example, one man in Hindustan may lift three maunds, whereas there a single man will lift twelve maunds by himself and carry it to the top of a tall building. The people eat many pounds of food at once. There are also people who are tall and skinny, as well as those who are tall and fat. There are short, fat people too, but relatively few people who are both short and skinny. Most people are merciless, unskilled, clueless, stingy, surly, and rapacious. The people of Mecca sport a variety of complexions. Only a few are light-skinned. Most are darker, golden, the color of wheat, or dark brown. They eat raw meat often. The hair of their head is typically brown or golden. Only a few have black hair. They typically have small beards, not larger ones. Most have bad attitudes and dirty eating habits. They sweat a lot. These are my impressions after a four-month stay there. If I had stayed for all three seasons, then I would have learned more, to my heart's content, and recorded more about the place.

FURTHER READING

Sikandar Begum. *Tarikh-i safar-i Makkah*. Available in SOAS Library Special Collections (PP MS 55 Durand, Box 2). https://digital.soas.ac.uk/AA00001526/00001. For a blog on this discovery, see Dominique Akhoun-Schwarb, "Women's History Month 2020: Sikandar Begum, Nawab of Bhopal." https://blogs.soas.ac.uk/archives/2020/03/08 /sikandar_begum_nawab_of_bhopal.

Nawab Sikandar Begum of Bhopal. *A Pilgrimage to Mecca*. Translated by Mrs. Emma Laura Willoughby-Osborne. London: Wm H. Allen & Co., 1870; Calcutta: Thacker, Spink and Co., 1906. https://archive.org/details/APilgrimageToMecca.

Siobhan Lambert-Hurley, ed. *A Princess's Pilgrimage: Nawab Sikandar Begum's* A Pilgrimage to Mecca. Bloomington: Indiana University Press, 2008.

Shaharyar M. Khan. *The Begums of Bhopal: A Dynasty of Women Rulers in Raj India*. London: I. B. Tauris, 2000.

William Roff. "Sanitation and Security: The Imperial Powers and the Hajj in the Nineteenth Century." *Arabian Studies* 6 (1982): 143–60.

Avril A. Powell. "Indian Muslim Modernists and the Issue of Slavery in Islam." In *Slavery and South Asian History*, edited by Indrani Chatterjee and Richard Eaton, 262–86. Bloomington: Indiana University Press, 2006.

NOTES

1. A hillside town near Bhopal.

2. The men listed here all played key roles in Sikandar's administration.

3. Ja'far Effendi is first introduced as an attendant to the sharif of Mecca's family, but he later appears as an intermediary between the sharif and the nawab begum when they disagree over prandial protocols—to the point of her life being threatened! From his title and his ability to act as a Turkish interpreter, Ja'far Effendi may be presumed to be an Ottoman Turk. However, this same man's wife acted as Sikandar's interpreter in the sharif's zenana. That the couple knew "Hindustani" suggests they perhaps had some connection to India.

4. The Indian Rebellion of 1857 was termed the Sepoy Mutiny in the colonial period on account of it having begun among Indian soldiers in the East India Company's army. However, it quickly spread to other groups across the Indian subcontinent to become a large-scale civilian uprising involving many displaced or dissatisfied Indian princes. As Sikandar indicates, she was among those who remained loyal to the British government, a stance for which she was richly rewarded. Those who rebelled, on the other hand, were treated with incredible brutality by the victors, which is why many fled to Mecca.

5. The author refers to her daughter and successor, Shah Jahan, and her daughter's first husband, Baqi Muhammad Khan, who was a close ally of Sikandar. The couple remained in Bhopal during Sikandar's pilgrimage, which is why they would have been available to assume control of the state's administration.

6. This ominous reference is apparently either a fabrication or a local tradition, for there is no record of Amir Timur (or Tamerlane) ever going to Mecca.

7. The text here momentarily shifts without explanation to the third person, raising the intriguing but unanswered question of whether the text was composed (or dictated) entirely by Sikandar Begum.

THREE

—ˈ∞ˈ—

MEHRMAH KHANOM

Adventures on the Road to Iraq

INTRODUCTION

Mehrmah Khanom, titled Esmat al-Saltaneh, followed in her parents' footsteps when she set out from Iran's capital, Tehran, on hajj in 1880. Her father, Farhad Mirza Moʻtamad al-Dawleh (d. 1888), was a Qajar prince and uncle to the king, Naser al-Din Shah (r. 1848–96). During his own pilgrimage in 1875–76, he had composed a detailed travelogue entitled *Hedayat al-sabil* (*Guide for the Road*, 1877). His daughter took his example in writing a Persian travelogue preserved in manuscript as "Safarnameh-ye Makkeh" ("A Journey to Mecca"). Like several other travelogues in this anthology—including the other Qajar narratives—it was written in the form of a daily diary (*ruznameh*). It thus has a chronological form and immediacy of style that distinguishes it from more formal accounts. At the same time, it shares with many Persian travelogues from this period a focus on the danger and maltreatment experienced by Iranian pilgrims undertaking the hajj. The difficult journey Mehrmah Khanom narrates was marred by bad weather and illness that often led to death, extortion and robbery by Bedouins and local gangs, and sectarian violence directed at Shias in particular. Nevertheless, the author's appreciation of natural beauty infuses this account with an underlying delight.

In the opening passage, translated as the first excerpt here, the author recounts how she set out from Tehran in late August 1880 with two female companions also from the Qajar family (one of whom was a cousin) along with two slave girls. At the time, Mehrmah Khanom was married to her second husband

The translation was prepared by Sunil Sharma. The introduction and annotations were prepared by Siobhan Lambert-Hurley with input from Sunil Sharma.

Figure 3.1 Travelers in Iraq, like Mehrmah Khanom, typically traveled by 'arb'ana, or carts, like the one pictured here. From *National Geographic* (1914), https://www.biodiversitylibrary.org/item/96975#page/614/mode/1up.

(of three), a military official named Mirza Musa Ashtiyani, but he did not accompany her and in fact died before her return. In the second extract, she details the route taken west through Iran and into Iraq, where the travelers planned to visit the Shia shrine cities (*'atabat-e 'aliyat*). Generally, the Iranian princess seems to have traveled in a howdah, probably carried by a camel or elephant, though on occasion horseback was deemed safer (see fig. 3.1). On the move, the party stayed in tents, usually near water or gardens, or in a caravanserai, but in towns, a house was often provided in deference to their status. That the female party sometimes had to rely on helpful men for protection en route is suggested in the passages here by an officer's intercession on the road to Qasr-e Shirin and a steadying hand on the bridge to Baghdad. When they arrived in Iraq, they spent two weeks visiting holy shrines in Kazimayn, Najaf, and Karbala. Mehrmah Khanom's experience of these three holy cities is documented here in turn in the third, fourth, and fifth extracts.

From Karbala, the group joined a hajj caravan with which they traveled across the desert for an entire month before arriving in Mecca in time for the pilgrimage rites in mid-November. After three weeks, they moved on to Medina and then Jeddah, where another three weeks were spent waiting for a boat back to the port of Bushehr in Iran. On her return journey, Mehrmah Khanom spent nearly two and a half months in Shiraz before finally setting off north for Tehran via Persepolis, Esfahan, Kashan, and Qom. On the leg from Shiraz to Esfahan, she reports traveling with a larger group that included over three hundred women. The author finally arrived back in Tehran in early June 1881 after nearly nine and a half months away—only to find out that her husband had died in her absence. From her itinerary, it is clear that her route to and from Mecca from Iran was significantly different than that taken by the widow of Mirza Khalil two centuries earlier or later Qajar women, who visited some of the same places but not all, and often in a different order or by different means.

Striking in these extracts, as in the narrative as a whole, is the presence of women, many of whom are described as "hajjiyeh," denoting their own experience of the Meccan pilgrimage. This quality can be observed from the opening passage where the author writes of various female friends and companions who stayed with the traveling party at the shrine of Imamzadeh Hasan prior to their departure proper. Similarly, in the sections on Najaf and Karbala, the author recounts meeting fellow princesses and other elite Iranian women also on pilgrimage or studying abroad. Women's graves are also sought out. Little attention is given, however, to local women, or for that matter men, beyond the prevalence of crowds begging, the occasional "wretched Arab" and the inferiority of Karbala's best hammam. The general population are, in contrast, addressed in the passages on Iran, as captured in the second extract. Here, the author makes several frank remarks on local poverty—within, for example, Khanabad's crown lands and the ancient site of Bisotun—exacerbated by the mistreatment and injustice of the central government and local governors. In this candid critique of Iran's authorities, Mehrmah Khanom's work anticipates that of another Iranian traveler, Sediqeh Dowlatabadi, half a century later.

EXTRACTS

Departing from Tehran

On Tuesday, August 31, 1880, with four hours remaining until sunset, under an auspicious star we left Tehran and entered the shrine of Imamzadeh Hasan. After we entered the place, the people who had come to see us off returned to the city in their carriages. Other companions waited in the Imamzadeh until we left, at which time they would go back. We spent Tuesday night at the Imamzadeh Hasan because it is customary for the muleteer to stop on the first night. On Wednesday, Hajjiyeh Ammeh Khanom, a relation of the late Mohammad Baqer Khan, came and left after sitting with us for about two hours. Her sister and some other companions remained until sundown before returning to the city. It's a strange feeling to bid farewell to loved ones. In reality, even the doors and walls seem to be wailing. How beautifully did the poet Sa'di say, "Cries come forth from rocks on the day of parting from friends." The children of Mirza Mohammad Taqi, Mirza Mostafa, and others remained until we left before going back to the city. Five hours after nightfall on the eve of the September 2, we came out of the shrine. We sat on a platform, and Hajji Akhund recited prayers and called out the azan behind us as we set off. My companions were my cousin, who was the daughter of the late Mohammad Rahim Khan Qajar; a relative of Fath 'Ali Khan; one white slave girl; and one black.

On the Road

On Thursday, September 2, we arrived at Robat Karim. We set up camp in a garden by a canal that had very good grape vines and grapes. We asked the old gardener woman whose garden it was and whom it was entrusted to. She replied that it was the property of her lady Anis al-Dawleh and entrusted to her brother Mohammad Hasan Khan. On Thursday night, we departed from Robat Karim, and on Friday we arrived at Khanabad. On the way, we came upon a ruined village. Upon enquiring, we learned that it was crown land. It is strange that the governor does not pay proper attention to crown land! The fate of Khanabad has been that the trees are without fruit and the water is brackish. We set up a tent by a melon patch. An old woman who was a melon seller brought us a melon. Although it was not fully ripe yet, it was so good that merely with a stroke of a knife, it came apart. There is both a post office and telegraph office in Khanabad. I wrote some letters there and sent them to the city. A telegraph was also sent. On Saturday, we left Khanabad and arrived at Kushk, which is a barren village and belongs to Morad Khan Zarandi. Here too we set up our tent near a canal. The water of Kushk is sweet. On Sunday night, we left Kushk and arrived at the station of Chamran. The road was somewhat difficult because it had a lot of highs and lows. This village belongs to Ahmad Khan, son of Reza Qoli Khan. It is a very large village. Its fort has high solid walls that we didn't see elsewhere. On Sunday night, September 5, three hours after nightfall, we set off, and just at daybreak we reached Nawbaran. This too is a very large village. We received a reply from the city to our telegraph. It has become wonderfully easy due to this invention that everywhere people are informed about each other. . . .

On Sunday evening, September 6, six hours after nightfall, we left Sahneh and two hours later reached Bisotun. This mountain has a strange fame for they said that love sculpted it, but Farhad got the credit![1] It seems that there was no sculpture in ancient times; Farhad attained all the fame for polishing this slab of stone in a way that it has taken on the appearance of wood. He has attained fame for no reason, for if they were to see the sculptures at Persepolis and how the stone has been polished like a mirror, how could they have said it? There is no place like a garden or trees here. They have planted poplars in a plot that, with divine grace, will be something in five years. It is strange that the governor here has not done anything for the sake of Muslims by establishing gardens and orchards, which are both profitable and provide shade. Despite the abundance of water, they have stinted in planting gardens. With no parasols, it was very hot. This was in contrast to the previous station that had shade due to the dense greenery.

This place has strangely poor and dirty people. Large pots can be seen that, if they were to be described, no one would touch the oil from there. All the women and children in Bisotun were dirty and dark. It seems they are very poor. It would be proper if the just king were to give them a tax break and the governor would administer justly. We thanked God profusely that we are not in the same condition as these people. On Tuesday, September 14, six hours after nightfall, we left Bisotun. At the bridge of Qara Su, Heshmat al-Dowleh had sent a group of men at whose insistence we entered the garden of the late prince that is outside the city. In the andarun they treated us with great hospitality. On Tuesday, according to routine, the post went to Tehran. I wrote letters and sent them to the post office. . . .

On Monday, September 20, due to the unsafe road, we set off after the morning prayer. General Alimorad Khan accompanied us with a mounted slave and a foot soldier until we reached Qasr-e Shirin. There are remains of the ancient fort. They have done wonderful stonework. It seems like everything is of the same size. In the afternoon we went to the garden constructed at the command of the king. In the year when the king had gone on pilgrimage to the Shiite shrines, he had ordered the construction of the gardens of the Pol-e Zahab and Qasr-e Shirin. The trees in the Pol-e Zahab garden have grown better. It seems that the gardener here is more attentive. The Qasr garden was not bad either. It had lime, orange, date, and other fruit trees. The poplars had become very green, and now they grow in Shemiran. This garden had all kinds of fruit except oranges, limes, and dates because it's not the season. God grant them life, in a few years they will benefit everyone. May God protect the being of the auspicious king and not take this safety away from us, the people of Iran.

In Iraq

Five hours after nightfall, we set off for Kazimayn. We reached Baghdad before midday. Some helpful men came to us, and we crossed the bridge safely. We entered Kazimayn. . . . At last, we reached the house of the *rowzehkhan*,[2] Mulla 'Abbas. At sundown we went to the hammam to wash for the pilgrimage, and at night we went to the auspicious shrine.[3] After reciting the pilgrim's prayers, we came back. . . . A telegraph arrived from Tehran and for this reason the time was spent very pleasantly. On Tuesday night, we stopped here because of various tasks. On Wednesday, September 29, we visited the shrine and freeing ourselves from the clutches of the beggars set off. The air was very warm on the way. They had set up a tent near the river. It was not without beauty. It was close to some skiffs that plied on the water. On Wednesday evening, one hour after nightfall, some caravans were visible. We were informed that they were Yazdi merchants who trade in sugar. Tonight, two hours after nightfall, we set off again since tomorrow's station is far.

Two hours after daybreak, the auspicious dome of the children of Hazrat Muslim came into view.[4] Since the road is a bit dangerous, I alighted from the howdah and went on a horse to visit those two venerables. After an hour, some Arabs showed up and claimed they are the administrators of this place. After the visit, I returned and we entered Musayyib. Before midday, we crossed the bridge. When I was riding on the middle of the bridge, a wretched Arab suddenly appeared and startled my horse. The Lord willed that someone was on foot with me and caught the horse, otherwise I would have fallen in the water. Al-hamdu lillah, a great disaster was averted! An official government representative in Musayyib had made a garden available for us, which belongs to a dervish whose grave is right there. The nobleman Eqbal al-Dowleh has built a room with two doors there. After we had settled there, the representative of Musayyib provided the needful things and then, after an hour, sent his wife there, who sat for a while before leaving. Setting out after midnight, we reached exalted Karbala three hours after daybreak. They had vacated the house of Zeya-as-saltaneh for us.[5] After the representative arrived, sweets were sent to us. . . . Monday evening, we remained in Karbala and in the morning went to the shrine. We reached Najaf four hours after nightfall. We stayed in the tower of the caravanserai, which is quite high. The night wasn't too bad. In the morning, we said our prayers and at first light set out toward the most respected Najaf. From four leagues away, the domes were visible. We thanked praiseworthy God.

At Najaf

We entered Najaf in the afternoon. Since so many of the attendants wanted to say the pilgrimage prayers, we were not able to visit the shrine today. At night after the ablutions for the pilgrimage, in the company of my aunt Princess Hajjiyeh, we went to the entrance of the courtyard. As we got there, the many prayer-sayers for the pilgrims created such a commotion that we had no choice but to retreat to a rooftop, and we said our pilgrimage prayers facing the auspicious shrine. In the morning, we got up with the azan and went to the shrine. They read the congregational prayers. People were occupied with prayers, and finding the opportunity, we went to the threshold of the guardian angels, where we performed the proper rites, while I chanted this line the whole time: "Is this me, or am I dreaming?" May Almighty God may grant this sincere and pure chastity to all the friends of this great one that, having made a pilgrimage to this auspicious courtyard and palace, they are blessed with a visit to this threshold.

Truly, it is well said that the portico of Najaf has a particular beauty. "Haydar, look what a court it is! Kaaba, don't be proud . . ." When it was four hours until sundown, we went to the Kufa mosque. My aunt Princess Morassa Khanom was with us. How well the administrator of the Kufa mosque recited the pilgrimage prayer! We prayed in twelve stations and then visited Hazrat Muslim. Then we went into rooms, where we recited the fatiha, and then returned. Since time was short and they had mentioned that the doors close, we could not go to the al-Sahlah mosque. In any case, at night we visited the shrine. After that, we went under the eaves of the golden dome, said the pilgrimage prayers, and then came back. On the morning of Tuesday, October 5, before we left for exalted Karbala, we went to the shrine and then came back and had lunch. Afterward, we went to the shrine again, came back, and set out for Karbala. What can I say of the crowds of attendants and beggars—it is beyond description. Until the Wadi al-Salam, we had no rest from the throng. Due to the dense crowd, they hadn't put us on the howdah. When we came out from there, the plain of the Wadi al-salam was better. We searched for the grave of Hajjiyeh Baji[6] but couldn't find it. After reading the fatiha, we mounted, and around sundown, we said the noon and afternoon prayers next to the canal where the late Mohammad Esmail Khan Vakil-ol-molk left us at the water of the Euphrates and went to holy Najaf, and then we rode again. Two hours after nightfall, one league away from a caravanserai, the weather was stormy in this scary desert. It was as if one eye couldn't see another. If it hadn't been for God's grace and the attention of Hazrat 'Ali, we wouldn't have survived. With difficulty we made it to the caravanserai in a state that is beyond description. A coffee seller and a porter were missing. The torch had been with the coffee seller. With many struggles against the wind and storm, we took refuge inside and entrusted ourselves to the beneficent God. The coffee seller wasn't found. Perforce, two soldiers who were accompanying us were offered a reward and went into the desert to call out to them, the coffee seller by name. It was close to dawn when they found him and brought him. Nobody expected them to be alive. It was not God's will for them to be killed by marauding Arabs. Somehow the night passed, and at daybreak we continued on our way. At four hours to sunset on October 5, we entered Karbala.

At Karbala

We alighted at the edge of the tent city. Making our ablutions, we said our afternoon and evening prayers at the place where they have built a replica of the bridal chamber of Hazrat Qasim 'Ali,[7] near the tent city and the well where he struck his auspicious spear in the ground, and water came out with which the companions washed before going to battle. An Arab prepared to go get water from the well. As he was going down into the well, my cousin said, "I hope he doesn't fall in." From the middle of the well, the Arab said, "Strange that I would fall into the well!" As these words came out of his mouth, he suddenly fell into the well in a manner that was funny. When he emerged from the well, he said in Persian and Arabic, "By the time you said don't fall in the well, I fell, otherwise I wouldn't have fallen."

We entered the tent city, performed our pilgrimage, and then returned to the house. On Thursday morning, October 7, we went to the shrine and recited the Sura Rahman[8] and fatiha at some graves. Then I got up feeling sorrowful and wept a bit about the unreliability of this world and the vicissitudes of life and asked God for forgiveness and went on to the shrine of Hazrat 'Abbas.[9] Since the auspicious tomb was far and the weather was hot, as soon as I entered the shrine and kissed it, I was not in a condition to recite the pilgrimage prayers. I took a break in the women's mosque. The female cousin of Shaikh-or-rais's wife, who has been in Samarra for three years studying and has now come to Karbala on her way to Mecca, appeared. We conversed a little, rested from the heat, went to the shrine, recited our prayers, and came back to the house. There, I saw that some women had come to see us. After an hour of conversation, they left. I took care of some work pertaining to the people leaving for Tehran, paid them, and close to sundown went to the hammam. God, save us from this hammam, which is the respectable one in Karbala! May He reward me in the next world for this.

Two hours after nightfall on the next day, we visited Husayn's holy shrine.[10] Although it was quieter, there was a crowd, and one couldn't touch the auspicious railing. We recited our prayers and also the Kumail prayers[11] since it was Thursday evening, and then we returned to the house. On Friday morning, having taken care of some remaining tasks, all the hajj pilgrims went outside. Around midday, having done ablutions, I visited the shrine and kissing the auspicious threshold took leave. With great difficulty so that I can scarcely describe it, I got away from the crowd of beggars and attendants, safely went out, mounted, and left. In the desert, they had set up tents for the hajjis. I entered the tent tired as the post was about to leave. I began to write.

FURTHER READING

Mehrmah Khanom. "Safarnameh-ye Makkeh." MS 1225, Majles Library, Tehran. The original was edited by Rasul Ja'fariyan for publication in *Meqat-e hajj* 17 (1375/1996): 57–117. A digital version of the manuscript is available in the Women's World in Qajar Iran Digital Archive, http://www.qajarwomen.org/en/items/1018A12.html.

Morad Mirza Hosam al-Saltaneh. *Safarnameh-ye Makkeh*. Edited by Rasul Ja'fariyan. Tehran: Mash'ar, 1374 [1995/96]. It recounts a simultaneous hajj by the author's uncle. She is mentioned in his account, as he is hers.

Amineh Mahallati. "Memoirs of Iranian Women Travelers to Mecca." *Iranian Studies* 44 (2011): 831–49. This article contains some translated passages on the city of Medina and the boat ride from Jeddah to Bushehr on a British ship.

Piotr Bachtin. "Women's Writing in Action: On Female-authored Hajj Narratives in Qajar Iran." *Iranian Studies* 54, nos. 1–2 (March 2020): 67–93. https://doi.org/10.1080/00210862 .2020.1724506. Bachtin's article discusses this text.

Iraj Afshar. "Persian Travelogues: A Description and Bibliography." In *Society and Culture in Qajar Iran: Studies in Honor of Hafez Farmayan*, edited by Elton L. Daniel, 145–62. Costa Mesa, CA: Mazda, 2002.

William L. Hanaway. "Persian Travel Narratives: Notes toward the Definition of a Nineteenth-Century Genre." In *Society and Culture in Qajar Iran: Studies in Honor of Hafez Farmayan*, edited by Elton L. Daniel, 249–68. Costa Mesa, CA: Mazda, 2002.

Piotr Bachtin. "The Royal Harem of Naser al-Din Shah Qajar (r. 1848–96): The Literary Portrayal of Women's Lives by Taj al-Saltana and Anonymous 'Lady from Kerman.'" *Middle Eastern Studies* 51 (2015): 986–1009.

NOTES

1. Farhad was the legendary lover of the princess Shirin who sculpted a channel through a mountain for her. Farhad lost out to the Persian king Khosrow and killed himself.

2. A preacher and teller of religious stories.

3. This would have been the al-Kadhimiya mosque, where the tombs of the seventh and ninth Shia imams, Musa al-Kazim and Muhammad al-Taqi, respectively, are located.

4. Muhammad and Ibrahim were the sons of Muslim ibn 'Aqil al-Hashimi, a cousin of Imam Husayn.

5. Zeya-as-saltaneh (1799–1873) was the seventh daughter of Fath Ali Shah Qajar (r. 1797–1834) and an accomplished poet and calligrapher.

6. The identity of this person is not known, but it appears to have been a female relative of the author.

7. Qasim was the thirteen-year-old son of Imam Husayn who was martyred in the Battle of Karbala, fought between a small group of supporters and relatives of Husayn against the army of Yazid I, the Caliph, on October 10, 680 CE. The story of Qasim's marriage just before the battle in which he was martyred is apocryphal.

8. This is chapter 55 in the Quran, the title of which means "The Most Beneficent."

9. 'Abbas was the grandson of the Prophet Muhammad and one of the sons of Imam 'Ali who was martyred in the Battle of Karbala.

10. Husayn was another grandson of the Prophet Muhammad and the son of 'Ali. He led the Shiite forces and was also martyred during the battle. He is a revered figure among Shias.

11. Named after one of the devoted followers of Imam 'Ali, this prayer in the form of a supplication is particularly recited by Shias on Thursday evening.

FOUR

—⁓—

HAJJIYEH KHANOM ALAVIYA KERMANI

Iran to Mecca by Way of Bombay

INTRODUCTION

Hajjiyeh Khanom Alaviya Kermani is the name given by a modern editor to the anonymous author of a late-nineteenth-century Persian manuscript entitled *Ruznameh-ye safar-e hajj, 'atabat-e 'aliyat va darbar-e naseri* (*A Travel Diary of Hajj, the Sublime Thresholds and Naser's Court*). The title *hajjiyeh* distinguishes her as having performed the hajj. Her description as *Kermani* indicates her origins in the southern Iranian city of Kerman, where she hailed from a somewhat privileged background. She belonged to the Shaykhi community that was powerful in the region, maintaining distinctive practices within the wider Twelver Shiite Muslim tradition. The manuscript's title points to how the text may be divided into three main sections covering the hajj pilgrimage to Mecca, a Shia pilgrimage to Iraq's shrine cities, and an extended stay at the court of Iran's Qajar king, Naser al-Din Shah (r. 1848–96). Also indicated is the text's form as a "diary book" (*ruznameh*) with passages linked to successive dates and often written in the present tense about everyday events. Reflecting its form, the prose in this narrative is simple and colloquial, which lends it a freshness and authenticity that is not found in some scripted travel accounts.

In the *Ruznameh*, the author explains that she began her journey from Kerman in April 1892, when she set out overland for the port of Bandar Abbas on the Persian Gulf. The rulings of Shiite jurists meant that she was not required to be accompanied by a close relative as long as her safety and security was guaranteed on the journey. She thus undertook her trip with a family who may

Sunil Sharma prepared the translations from the Persian original; Siobhan Lambert-Hurley prepared the introduction and annotations with input from Sunil Sharma.

have been her friends. The male head of this family was Vali Khan, referred to by the honorific of Sarkar Khan, and his wife was Sarkar Khanom. The party was also accompanied by servants, including a maid, Taghafol, and a woman named Fatemeh. From Bandar Abbas, the group could have taken a pilgrim boat directly to Kamran island (off the coast of Yemen) to undertake the quarantine before going on hajj, but as indicated in the first extract, they instead boarded a passenger vessel for Bombay. That this detour was unwelcome is indicated by the author's preference (in the third extract) for staying aboard ship at Bombay and her "curses" (in the final extract) on the man who sent them there. In the first extract, she also expresses her anxiety on her trip being delayed further at Muscat while the ship was loaded with cargo.

Upon having completed the sea journey to and from Bombay and the required ten days of quarantine at Kamran, the travelers continued on to Jeddah and then Mecca. They finally arrived in late June 1892 in time to perform the hajj and visit Medina. While in Arabia, Vali Khan's wife succumbed to an illness that had made her unwell throughout the journey. Fatemeh, who was pregnant with Vali Khan's child, was thrown out by him, and she and the author traveled back to Iran alone. After visiting the Hijaz, the author was reluctant to travel by ship again, which she repeatedly complained was expensive and uncomfortable. Instead, she went by road to Iraq to visit the four holy shrine cities—Najaf, Karbala, Kazimayn, and Samarra—as well as Baghdad. There is little in these sections on daily life, though she does report meeting prominent notables, including Shia Islam's spiritual leader, Mirza Shirazi. She set out on the return journey for Iran in late October 1892. Upon arriving in Tehran, she would stay as a guest and attendant in the shah's harem for a year and a half, recording important observations about women's relationships within this milieu. The author finally arrived back in Kerman in mid-August 1894 after an absence of over two years.

The passages aboard ship to and from Bombay, as translated here, are revealing of the vitality of commercial travel in the Indian Ocean in this "Age of Empire." At the same time, it is clear that the author herself was not suited to sea travel: rough crossings from Muscat to Bombay and from Bombay to Aden evoked no less than the end of the world. The emphasis in these sections on hardship, fear, and suffering permeates the work as a whole. Less typical is her account of Bombay, captured in part in the third extract here, in which she reveals her surprise and wonder at this bustling and colorful city. Various locations, like the bazaar and the hammam—which she visited with Vali Khan's wife, while Vali Khan himself went elsewhere—are described in detail. She also recounts the people and their practices, including a "Hindu" wedding and a grand "celebration" held for Sultan Muhammad Shah, Aga Khan III. The latter association points to the connections made in Bombay with the Nizari Ismaili community, whose leaders had left Persia earlier in the nineteenth century after conflict with the Qajar regime. That the Nizari imams had historic links to the author's home city of Kerman—with Aga Khan I acting most recently as governor in the early 1830s—suggests a longer bond.

Also noteworthy in the extracts is the author's categorization of peoples. Men are demarcated by their skin color and dress, whereas women are defined by their mobility. Consider the juxtaposition between the author unable to remain aboard ship while anchored due to the "scandal" of men's proximity and the Hindu women selling fruit in the market while other locals travel to and fro on foot or by carriage. In the Bombay section, "Muslims" are thus distinguished from "Hindus" and "Parsis" or "Zoroastrians," as well as "Europeans." On board the pilgrim ship to Jeddah, however, Muslims themselves are disaggregated by place of origin, religious practice, sect, and wealth. Ultimately, the author's identity as a Twelver Shiite emerges most pronounced as this grouping of "twenty or thirty" is set apart from the remaining Sunnis (out of a total of "six to seven hundred" pilgrims). And yet upon arriving on the "prison" island of Kamran, all the "poor pilgrims" are united, in this lively account, in facing the inhumanity and fraudulence of quarantine procedures.

EXTRACTS

From Bandar Abbas to Muscat

Today, Friday, May 13, 1892, they informed us that we had to be ready in the boat two hours after daybreak. After having done the prayers and drunk tea, we came to the seashore in a nervous state. We recited the *kalima* and *shahada*. Two or three bare-assed black men brought chairs. I sat on one. They lifted it up and carried it to the boat. Then they brought Sarkar Khan, Sarkar Khanom, Fatemeh, and then Taghafol. Four oarsmen were also there. They began to row, and the boat set off.

My fear was completely allayed. We traveled one league in ten to twenty minutes. They came up against the ship; we stood up and went up the ladder. We were thinking of everyone back home. The cabins were clean, cleaner than our rooms at home. They had placed a mattress on two sides of a bench. One can also sit beneath the bench, but we didn't go into the cabins. I immediately went on the deck. We settled into a nice, cool place. What the hajjis say about there being lice on the ship and one being forced to sleep on top of each other is all lies. We were not in a ship for pilgrims, but on one called *Nichol*. We paid 146 tumans and 2 rials as payment for the cabins, deck, and platform for eight people, meaning that for three of us, 90 tumans, and for five others, 11 tumans and 2 rials until Jeddah. We also paid 5 tumans and 3,000 shahis for luggage, permits, and the ferry.[1] But everyone came and settled on the deck, a nice place. It is about ten or twelve meters wide and twenty or forty meters in length. Spreading a carpet, we sat down. Everyone was in quite a state except Sarkar Khanom. Our heads were spinning and our hearts were sinking, so we did not have the energy to sit. We slept. They brought lunch. I couldn't eat. I dozed off for a bit. Thank God, after sleeping everyone felt better, and we sat down to drink tea, according to custom. We walked on the deck and looked around. Even if I wanted to describe the ship, I couldn't. It cannot be put in words; one has to see it with one's own eyes. It is impossible for someone to describe everything on the ship. In short, we who had paid for the middle cabins did not go there at all, leaving them empty; everything from the people to the cargo remained on deck. They brought dinner at night. We had a stew of meat and pulses and then slept.

On the morning of Saturday, May 14, we woke up, did our prayers, and drank tea. They told us that the ship must pass between two mountains of Muscat. The sailors and ship workers were distracted. With binoculars in their hands, they stood next to the compass. They are making sure that the ship won't hit the mountains. We are all imagining the worst. Sarkar Khanom is busy with prayers. The movement of the ship does not allow me to write properly. Thank God, the ship sailed through the danger. We arrived in front of Muscat. The ship dropped anchor. Hajji Giladari, the agent of the ship, accompanied us from Bandar Abbas. He got up and got into a boat. There was a big cargo of melons, wheat, etc., which they unloaded into boats, and he went to Muscat where his family lives. He visits Muscat every three months. The captain informed us that the ship had to remain there for two or three days until they brought the cargo from Muscat. Sarkar Khanom and all of us were upset because we would lose time in reaching Jeddah. Kaikhosrow Khan is also on this ship. He calculated that we would reach Mecca in thirty-seven days. For this reason we had cause to be anxious. They brought lunch. We ate eggplants, whey, and garlic. In the evening, Sarkar Khan got into a boat and went to Muscat to see Sayyed Abd-or-Rahim, the agent of a ship that was anchored there. They discussed the delay. We would not arrive in Mecca according to schedule. What should we do? He responded, "Inshallah, early tomorrow morning, I will send the cargo to the ship, and you can start off by midday." Sarkar Khan returned at dusk. We did our prayers and ate supper, rice and eggplant stew. Then we slept. Since the ship is between two mountains, the air is very warm, and we couldn't sleep at all.

Muttrah is a village on the slope of the mountains near Muscat. From where our ship is anchored, we can hear the sound of clocks in Muscat. I can see the buildings there. Tonight there was a wedding in Muttrah. They took the bride away in the morning with instruments playing and firing of a canon. We too didn't sleep due to the heat.

Today is Sunday, May 15. We got up and did our prayers. The cargo from Muscat arrived, and from morning until now, they have been unloading it. In the morning, a steamship came to Muscat from Bombay and stopped next to us. There is a field's width distance between us. That ship is three times the size of ours and has a large number of passengers. When it came near it, set off a canon and dropped anchor. Many people got into boats and went to Muscat, and others came into the ship from Muscat. In short, whatever I would like to write about their condition and actions would not be right. We sat on the deck. About a hundred boats of all kinds ploughed the waters from this side to that, carrying cargo. It was a spectacle, and truly astonishing.

The Journey to Bombay

On Monday morning, May 16, we rose for prayers. All of us fell every which way. As it was windy since midnight, the ship was being tossed around. We were all dizzy and falling to the floor. Together we brought ourselves to the lower deck, where everybody threw up. We were tossed into the cabins, the servants in other places. We were in a bad condition. May God not let infidels suffer what we went through. Sarkar Khan and Sarkar Khanom threw up five times. All the servants, Taghafol, Fatemeh, were near to throwing up until the next day. However much I tried, I couldn't throw up. By nightfall, today everyone was in a bad state, with no medicine or food. It became dark, and with difficulty we came up to the deck. We had one or two cups of tea and slept.

On the morning of Sunday, May 22, we rose and had tea. Sahib says that the distance to Bombay is thirty leagues. The depth of the sea here is half a league. We looked, and there are a thousand boats of different kinds on the water. They were traveling all over: from Bombay to Basra, to Karachi, to Muscat, to different ports, a thousand places. Truly, until one sees it, one can't understand it. My simple mind cannot fathom the affairs of the Europeans. They load two or three thousand maunds [of cargo] in them, and three or four dark Indians sit in them. We watched until midday, and then they brought *kashk-e badenjan* [an eggplant dip] and *bereshtook* [a sweet made of chickpea flour] for lunch. Today, there was no time to sleep. Bombay is before us. About a hundred steamships were either going or dropping anchor near Bombay. Subhan Allah, a person goes crazy not knowing where to look. We reached Bombay. Boats brought us right to the shore so that we lifted our feet from the boat and stepped onto the soil of Bombay.

We arrived an hour and a half before sunset. We all stood still; astonished, we didn't know where to look, what to see. There were about a thousand people—Hindus, Europeans, Parsis, Muslims—standing on the seashore watching us. We looked back at them. Tonight, we did not disembark from the ship, nor did we go anywhere. Now two hours of the night have passed. From the time that we entered until now, about a thousand carriages, carts, and steam cars have passed before us. They brought dinner, rice and *fesenjan* [Persian pomegranate and walnut stew], and we ate. We didn't sleep all night because of the commotion of the people and carriages. All the people of this city are awake until morning and work. From one side the noise of musical instruments, from another a group of Hindus singing, and from another the whistle of ships. About thirty steamships dropped anchor around us.

In Bombay

On Friday morning, May 27, we got up. Sarkar Khan went to the hammam. Sarkar Khanom and I embarked on a trip to the bazaar. It is astonishing, and I don't know how to describe it. Seven-story-tall buildings made of stone and wood are on both sides. Carts and carriages travel in the middle of the street. Throughout the bazaar, Hindu women are seated, selling fruit. We went to the meat market. Muslims slaughter sheep and sell them. Hindu women bring fried fillets of fish, which has originally been brought from Muscat; fried prawns; and another creature similar to two big fishes. Other than these, they don't sell anything else in this bazaar.

We went to the fruit market. Hindu men sell bananas, pineapples, pomegranates, figs, tangerines, oranges, and other kinds of fruit that we did not recognize. But they are very expensive: five oranges for our one qiran, etc. We wandered around until midday. One can lose one's senses. But sleep again is on hold, with so much noise of the cargo being moved in and out of the ship, and the carts there. You would imagine they were shooting from a canon. I don't know what to write about the sound of the propellers of the boats. I am stunned.

In the evening, Sarkar Khan returned and we sat watching people. Women and men—Hindu, Zoroastrian, European—come and go, whether in carriages or on foot. It became night. They lit all the lamps in the bazaar, which didn't allow us to sleep all night.

We rose on Saturday morning and prayed. A European dentist came and left after taking the measurements of Sarkar Khan's teeth. Two carriages were brought from the house of Jangi Shah's mother.[2] We got in and went to the hammam. From Kerman to here, we hadn't visited a hammam. The hammam was clean and good. They brought lunch, and we ate it in the hammam. In the evening, we came out and we went to her bungalow, where they served tea. We wanted to stay in the ship during these few days, but they didn't allow it. They said that our staying with so many men around would cause a scandal. Our hosts took great pains to be hospitable. . . .

One day we were sitting when the sound of music rose up. They said it was a Hindu wedding. Near the bungalow where we were, the bride and groom had been seated in a carriage accompanied by a procession of drums and pipes. There were big crowds in front of and behind the carriages. In the hands of the bride and groom were all sorts of brass vessels. The Hindus got some milk, took it around the houses, and carried it to their own homes. For three days, they massaged the bride and groom with oil, turmeric, and pepper. On the fourth night, they again put the bride and groom in the carriage with the sound of flutes and lamps. There were two groups of Hindus. One group played with sticks; the other played with a large iron rod with some rings on it that were shaken accompanied by cries of congratulations. They threw flowers on the heads of the bride and groom. The furniture was made of gold. The groom was seated and had taken the bride in his lap. They waited at the foot of our bungalow. We watched.

One day we were guests of the mother of Aqa Akbar Shah for lunch.[3] One night we were the guests of Iran Khanom, daughter of Abul al-Fath Mirza, grandson of the old Zil-os-Soltan, who was the wife of the son of 'Ali Shah. Her husband died, and she has been a widow for several years. She was very hospitable to us. May God grant them a long life and good health.

Those who have surveyed the carriages of Bombay say that ten thousand of them work in Bombay day and night. In my view, perhaps there are more. From night until day and from morning until evening, there is the sound of a hundred carriages and automobiles in every street. We saw a strange thing in Bombay: a man had brought two roosters; one had four feet and the other had three. The other shriveled [feet] were hanging from under their tails.

We were invited on the twenty-seventh to a party for Sultan Muhammad Shah, who is the grandson and heir of the Aga Khan.[4] He is the son of 'Ali Shah and is eighteen years old. His mother is a princess too.[5] The daughter of Shams al-Dowleh was not in Bombay. Most of the Aga Khan's family has gone to Mahabaleshwar for a holiday.[6] They say it's a good summer place. Some were there, mostly the women of the Aga Khan's household and his daughter. In short, a celebration was held.

In the evening, we went to the house of Sultan Muhammad Khan. Around three hundred women were gathered there, but all of them were his community, and a few who were foreigners. We sat in the bungalow. First they served us sherbet, then tea. At the other end of the bungalow, there is a large wide area that has a big tank. All the Indians who were there, women and men, wore colorful clothes. They had brought many lamps, all very beautiful. They had also brought a hundred sacks of sugar and, making sherbet, drank it. Fruit sellers and bread sellers brought everything from ice cream to sweets to sell. Certainly there were ten thousand people gathered there. They were enjoying themselves, and musicians played instruments. There was noise in every corner, where people gathered and ate something. Night fell. They lit the lamps, about ten thousand ones of every kind. There were nice fireworks. We wished all our friends, acquaintances, and dear ones had been here. We watched and then left.

On Pilgrimage from Bombay

On May 28, we said goodbye [to Bombay] and came to the ship. By noon, seven hundred pilgrims—Sunni, Kabuli, and Indian Muslim—all gathered on the ship. At midday the ship set off. Since it is the beginning of monsoon season, a wind arose, and the ship started tossing around, and everyone felt seasick. Some were vomiting, some were listless, some were crying, some were praying. May God not deliver us to infidels. May God let everyone fulfil their religious obligations, but by way of dry land. We were in this condition for ten days. From morning to night, one heard *Ya Allah, Ya Muhammad, Ya 'Ali.* Everyone was united in uttering the words of faith. At one time, the ship swerved so much that we thought we would drown. The water was cresting into waves so much that it came up to the deck, and it could go no higher. Suddenly a high wave struck someone in the neck, and he fell to the ground. We who were in the cabins called out to Allah from night to day. The Sunnis made untimely calls to prayer. Herati, Kabuli, and Indian dervishes were crying out *hu hu.*[7] The Shias were beating their breasts. It was the apocalypse, Armageddon. We were all frightened and shaking. It seems that my luck was bad that the sea turned stormy. Again, al-hamdu lillah, it passed without a visitation by death. We were in this state for ten days.

We reached Aden, where the ship dropped anchor and was calm. There was a lot of cargo for Aden that was unloaded by thirty or forty men until the evening. About a 150 pilgrims came on board in Aden. Today and tonight too, we were held while the ship was being unloaded. Aden lay before us. The buildings and shops are similar to those in Bombay. When the lamps were lit at night, there was a great deal of traffic of carriages driven by horses, bullocks, and camels. There were a lot of camels and ships in Aden. Together they carried the cargo.

From Aden to the Hijaz too, they must carry the cargo on boats; some men were brought. It was not near a road. At last the ship sailed again.

On Saturday, June 11, we came to Kamran to put the wretched poor pilgrims in quarantine. Some black rogues brought a boat in which they took the pilgrims with their belongings. We too came and got into it. They took us to the "prison." The land is all soft sand, dry and empty, hot, without water or vegetation, with the sea all around. In every corner, they set up a hundred or hundred and fifty shacks made up of bamboo, wood, and reeds, for the pilgrims. They brought us prisoners and settled us in the shacks. Right now there are pilgrims from six ships. They put the people of different ships together in one corner. They don't allow anyone to mingle or go anywhere in case a pilgrim from a certain ship is sick and infects the others. They collect money by these roguish methods. Pilgrims from Bombay are in quarantine for ten days. Those from Bandar Abbas are in quarantine for twenty-four hours. Curses on the man who had us travel via Bombay. They held us there for ten days until they could collect all the pilgrims. At last, they brought groups of Sunnis, Zaidis, and various Ismailis into the ship. All beggars. About ten or fifteen children, from two to eight to ten years old. According to the arrangement, they didn't even pay their fare on the ship. They were supposed to bring us to Kamran for ten days; they kept us for fifteen. We were delayed in Aden for two days because of the severe winds and storm. All the pilgrims they brought on to the ship are beggars, naked, who beg among the other pilgrims. If you ask anyone where they are going, they say to holy Mecca. They are obviously going there to beg. In this season, pilgrims go to Mecca to beg, then return home. All the bare-assed, wretched Sunnis who don't do the ritual cleaning, they stink so that one is suffocated. In short, in our ship from Bombay, we are around six to seven hundred legal pilgrims. Twenty or thirty of us were Shia, the rest all Sunnis, etc. Each group was housed in a shack. God, may I die for the family of Hazrat 'Ali.

FURTHER READING

Hajjiyeh Khanom Alaviya Kermani. *Ruznameh-ye safar-e hajj, 'atabat-e 'aliyat va darbar-e naseri*. Edited by Rasul Ja'fariyan. Qom: Nashr-e Mo'arrekh, 2007. This is a reprint of an anonymous manuscript in Tehran University's Central Library, "Ruznameh-ye safar-e hajj, 'atabat-e aliyat, va darbar-e naseri," MS 393 Adabiyyat. A digital version of the manuscript is available in the Women's World in Qajar Iran Digital Archive. http://www.qajarwomen.org/en/items/1255A2.html.

Amineh Mahallati. "Memoirs of Iranian Women Travelers to Mecca." *Iranian Studies* 44 (2011): 831–49. This article contains a significant passage in translation from the Bombay section describing the city's botanic gardens, zoo, museum, textile factory, and water system.

Piotr Bachtin. "Women's Writing in Action: On Female-authored Hajj Narratives in Qajar Iran." *Iranian Studies* 54, nos. 1–2 (March 2020): 67–93. https://doi.org/10.1080/00210862 .2020.1724506. Bachtin's article discusses this text.

———. "The Royal Harem of Naser al-Din Shah Qajar (r. 1848–96): The Literary Portrayal of Women's Lives by Taj al-Saltana and Anonymous 'Lady from Kerman.'" *Middle Eastern Studies* 51 (2015): 986–1009.

Elton L. Daniel. "The Hajj and Qajar Travel Literature." In *Society and Culture in Qajar Iran: Studies in Honor of Hafez Farmayan*, edited by Elton L. Daniel, 215–238. Costa Mesa, CA: Mazda, 2002.

Farhad Daftary. *The Isma'ilis: Their History and Doctrines*. Cambridge, UK: Cambridge University Press, 1990.

John Slight. *The British Empire and the Hajj 1865–1965*. Cambridge, MA: Harvard University Press, 2015.

NOTES

1. Tuman, rial, and shahi were units of currency in Iran.

2. Aqa Jangi Shah was the second son of Aga Khan I, the stepbrother of Aga Khan II, and the uncle of Aga Khan III, all of whom were prominent leaders of the Nizari Ismaili community. Their hostess was thus a widow of Aga Khan I.

3. Aqa Akbar Shah was the third son of Aga Khan I. Their hostess was thus another widow of Aga Khan I.

4. Sultan Muhammad Shah, or Khan, succeeded as Aga Khan III on the death of his father, Aqa Ali Shah, in 1885.

5. As indicated here, Aga Khan III's mother, Nawab Alia Shamsul-Muluk, was a granddaughter of Fath Ali Shah, of Iran's Qajar dynasty.

6. Mahabaleshwar was a hill station that served as the summer capital of the Bombay presidency in the British colonial period.

7. *Hu* is the Arabic pronoun for *he* that was used by Sufis to refer to God.

FIVE

SAKINEH SOLTAN KHANOM ESFAHANI KUCHAK

Iraq Diary

INTRODUCTION

Sakineh Soltan Khanom Esfahani Kuchak (see fig. 5.1), who received the title Vaqar al-Dowleh (Dignity of the State), was a minor wife of the Iranian king Naser al-Din Shah (r. 1848–96). Widowed at a young age and without children, she was soon married again to Mirza Esma'il Khan Mo'tasem al-Molk Ashtiyani. Her second husband, described in the final extract here, was an agent to the provincial governor of Lorestan and Khuzestan. Both of her marriages opened up opportunities for extensive travel within the Qajar Empire. With the shah, she participated in a number of royal tours and expeditions by horseback, to which she referred later in her own travel writing. Two of these texts have been preserved in manuscript form: one describing a pilgrimage to Mecca and Iraq in 1899–1900, from which the extracts here are taken, and a second recounting a trip to Shiraz in 1905 that lasted one hundred days. On the second occasion, Sakineh Soltan traveled with her second husband on official business linked to a court marriage: to bring the cousin of his employer, bride Anis al-Dowleh, to the home of the shah's son, groom Malek-Mansur Mirza. This author also wrote poetry under the penname Vaqar.

Sakineh Soltan's interest in travel writing may have been inspired by her first husband. Having thrice undertaken official trips to Europe (in 1873, 1878, and 1889), Naser al-Din Shah wrote accounts of his travels inside and outside Iran. His son and successor, Mozaffar al-Din Shah (r. 1896–1907), also visited Europe three times and published accounts of his travels. Other women linked to the

---

The translation was prepared by Sunil Sharma. The introduction and annotations were prepared by Siobhan Lambert-Hurley with input from Sunil Sharma.

خانم شاهزاده   عجب ناز   سکینه سلطان   نوش آفرین

چهار تن از نازپروردگان حرم

Figure 5.1 Sakineh Soltan Khanom Esfahani Kuchak (*center*) and other ladies.
Courtesy of Sunil Sharma.

Qajar court, including two in this collection, preceded Sakineh Soltan in narrating local and distant travel, including the hajj. Like them, she wrote in the
form of a daily diary (*ruznameh*). Her immediate stimulus to write, however,
appears to have been a request from another widow of Naser al-Din Shah, Delbar Khanom, introduced in the first extract. In a later passage, Sakineh Soltan
records being told by this lady, "Since you are one of those who intends to go
to ziyarat"—indicating the Shia pilgrimage sites—"note all of your expenses
during this journey and acquaint us with the details [of your trip]." Accordingly,
Sakineh Soltan prepared a *safarnameh* that seems more practical guide than
spiritual reflection, though she does register her inner thoughts, emotions, and
quandaries.

Sakineh Soltan set out from Tehran for Mecca with her brother as guardian
in November 1899. The first extract is actually dated over a month before that
as she prepared for the journey by taking permission from the shah, Mozaffar
al-Din, and visiting the homes of other women of the Qajar court. Her initial
destination was Iraq to visit sites and shrines linked to Shia Islam at Kazimayn,
Karbala and Najaf. The second, third, and fourth extracts capture her sheer
delight at being present in these holy places, though rain and hospitality were
abundant in equal measure. In the fifth extract, she recounts an excursion to
Kufa marred by illness; that she rode in a howdah enabled her to keep moving.

From Iraq, Sakineh Soltan and her companions passed through Aleppo in Syria to the port of Iskanderun, now in Turkey, from where they took a boat to Jeddah. The author finally arrived in Mecca in time for the annual pilgrimage in April 1900. After visiting Medina, she began the return journey overland through the Arabian Desert, visiting Karbala and Najaf again, as well as Samarra. Upon crossing back into Qajar territory in September 1900, she went first to Borujerd in western Iran to join her husband, who was posted there "on a government assignment," before finally returning to Tehran in March 1901.

The fifth and final section of extracts includes two short passages that capture the particular qualities of this woman's travel narrative. Sakineh Soltan's writing reflects cultural expectations about women's weakness and dependence. She accepts that she must take male permission for a journey, and she defers to her brother's judgment about where to stay and when to travel. When others take on the physical demands of an arduous journey—carrying luggage or wading through rainwater—she demurs with gratitude. In the fourth extract, she relegates her inability to describe the gilded dome of Imam Ali's mosque at Najaf to feminine foibles: a weak mind, "flawed intellect," and a lack of intelligence. Yet in this same set of extracts, there is a glimpse of a less diffident figure: one who is willful enough to refuse advice against venturing out into flooded streets and, donning her chador, goes anyway. Her fortitude comes into focus in the final extracts as she responds with vigor and ferocity to her brother's seemingly capricious decision not to allow her to visit the mosque of Hazrat Zaynab at Damascus and her husband's failure to write.

EXTRACTS

Preparation for Pilgrimage

October 3, 1899: Having veiled myself, I went to see the emperor in his private quarters.[1] The treasurer informed me that His Majesty was in the bath. I waited a bit. All at once I saw the effulgence of the sun's beauty in his person as he emerged from the bath. His form was like the martyr king Husayn. I swear to God, on the five noble ones, that he preserve this great and just emperor. By God's will, his eyes fell on my lowly form. He said, "Lady, where have you been?" I said, "I have been honored to visit the Shia pilgrimage places. I seek your permission to travel." He asked whether I was thinking of Mecca. He said, "Inshallah. You will go."

I was so overjoyed by these auspicious words that there was no end to it. Since the heart of the king is in the hand of God's power, it is certain, inshallah, I will be honored by a visit to Mecca. After some formalities and niceties, he dismissed me. After wishing me well on the pilgrimage, he left for the audience hall. After conversing a bit with the treasurer and Gorji Khanom,[2] I said goodbye and came to the house of Sarkar Nur al-Dowleh.[3] I sat there for a bit visiting with Eshrat al-Saltaneh and then, saying goodbye, came out. I thought to myself that I should also visit Akhtar al-Saltaneh,[4] her close neighbor, since there wouldn't be an opportunity tomorrow. From there I went to her. She was surprised and asked, "Where have you been?" I told her I was planning to go to Karbala. She wept copiously and said, "Every year I want to go, but it is not possible." She said a long goodbye, and I came home. I saw that several thousand people were there until evening, then they bid goodbye and left.

October 2: With the goal of setting off on pilgrimage to the Shia sites, I came out of the house into the courtyard of the Sarvestan, where the princess has a house, and went to the house of Sharaf al-Saltaneh.[5] Hajjiyeh Zahra Khanom,[6] who had come to our house for a sendoff, accompanied me as far as the courtyard of the Sarvestan, sat for a bit, then went home. I spent the night there, then in the morning at the urging of the mother of Sharaf al-Saltaneh, I went to the hammam. After lunch, we bade goodbye to them and came to the house of Sarkar Delbar Khanom.[7] It had been three months since planning the trip, but because I had to do everything for myself, I still had a lot to take care of. I relaxed at Sarkar Delbar Khanom's place for a day and night from Friday to the evening, and I took care of some of the remaining tasks.

Stay in Kazimayn

November 5: A little while after we were on the road, the son of 'Abbas came. Then Hajji 'Abbas himself came and told us the amount for the viewing of the holy domes. I looked right away and saw two holy domes. How can I describe what I saw? I could call them two moons, but that would not be true. I could call them two luminous candles, but I don't know if that would be correct. May God bless everyone so that they can come and see them for themselves. Having visited the domes from afar, we expressed our thanks. We wept and prayed in turn. Inshallah, our prayers will be answered.

In half an hour, the domes were visible. Then they were not visible until we reached the great bridge, where we dismounted. They unloaded the packs, but it didn't affect us or the howdah.

We departed from this place. We thanked God that I had seen such a place. May He bless everyone with daily bread. When we entered, the maternal uncles of Mirza Ahmad Khan, who were the brothers of my brother's wife, came to receive us. They led us to their house. Some sweets, fruits, tea were all served to us. The grandmother of Mirza Ahmad also came. Her daughters-in-law came and remained until the evening. When they left, we went to the holy shrines. A hundred thanks to God that we were alive to see such a day, being honored by the auspicious threshold. We prayed for our friends—may God accept them.

During these few days that we are here, I will write a short diary because I am short on time. I want to go to the holy shrines. If something new happens, I will write about it.

November 6: I dispatched some companions for a pilgrimage to Samarra. I didn't go myself. I said, "If we are alive on the return trip, then I will go with my brother and a servant."

I handed over the letters for Tehran, which were taken to the post office. My men had gone for six nights, and they returned on the tenth. They were fortunate to visit the three imams on pilgrimage. For a few days here, I had a fever and wasn't able to visit the holy shrine. I was honored by a visit on the eve of Thursday the sixteenth.

To Karbala

On Thursday morning, we took leave and set off for a pilgrimage to sublime Karbala. Today we must reach Mahmoudiyah, which is half a league away. Being severely indisposed, I wasn't able to view the desert. All at once I saw that we had arrived, we had alighted, and accommodation had been procured. I went and slept. I couldn't even eat dinner. I was feeling very poorly. Two hours before daybreak, we mounted and were off on our way. On this leg, since we had two soldiers with us, two tribal Arabs were arrested, but they didn't tell me until the next morning. When we reached the house, they declared that, thanks to God, it had gone well.

Friday, November 17: Today, we must go to Musayyib. Again I did not feel well. Around midday, we reached the bridge at Musayyib. Our travel permits were examined, torn up, and returned to us. Before arriving at the bridge, we visited the shrines of the two children of Hazrat Muslim.[8] Then we came to the bridge. Upon seeing the bank of the Euphrates, there was a lot of weeping. We spent a night in Musayyib. Thank God that we are alive to see such a day.

Saturday, November 18, Station 29: Today, we must reach our destination. My tongue is unable to express in writing gratitude for this great bounty, and even if I had a thousand tongues, I wouldn't be able to do it. If I had a thousand hands, I wouldn't be able to write. May God answer our prayers, especially those made upon seeing the holy domes, those of the people we remembered, and those of the people who wish to make this great pilgrimage. May they be able to perform the pilgrimage and kiss the threshold of the oppressed imam very soon. I cannot describe our condition further.

Everyone knows how one feels on such a day. One is grateful. Arriving in Karbala, we went to a large nice house near the holy shrine. We had tea, performed the ritual cleaning again, and were honored by a visit to the auspicious threshold of the oppressed of Karbala. May God grant everyone pilgrimage, and accept my pilgrimage and prayers, I who am a black-faced sinful dog. May God be merciful to these oppressed ones, to the young, and the wives and children of the most noble of the martyrs. After a visit and prayers and kissing the shrine of Hazrat 'Abbas, I swear by the hands of this great one that may God accept all the pilgrimages and prayers, and with benevolence cure their pains. Since I am busy with another visit to the shrine, I will not write in this diary. I want all my thoughts to be focused on the pilgrimage. Inshallah, I will write on the day of departure. If we survive, we will be in Karbala for six nights.

To Najaf

Friday, November 24: Planning to visit the most noble Najaf today, we came out of the holy shrine, visited the shrine of Hazrat Abbas, and, taking our leave, went off.[9] The howdah was ready, and we got in. Sarkar Ghoncheh Khanom came until the door of the tent and left. We set off. With great zeal and desire for pilgrimage to Hazrat Shah Vilayat, we expressed our thanks to God a thousand times. By sundown, we reached Khan Shur, where we alighted and went to a small house that had been taken for me. After having tea and supper, we went to sleep. Our journey was six leagues daily. The next day we arose, prayed, and went on. A little rain was falling. The farther we went, the more the rain increased. According to the words of the martyred king in his travel account of the lofty Shia shrines,[10] it rained, and he said, "First be pure, then cast a glance at that pure one." He spoke the truth. May God alleviate his ranks and make the bread of his salt halal for wretched me. The pilgrimages that this black-faced one has undertaken for the king of the martyrs may help his auspicious soul. I wish we had died in his shadow. Although it is not good to utter these words on our pilgrimage, my heart burns so much for that auspicious being that I lost control of myself and said these things. I swear to God by the king of sovereignty ['Ali] that he may overlook my faults.

Indeed, the rain was so heavy that my brother said that tonight, we would remain in this caravanserai at the midway point and continue tomorrow. I saw that Mohammad Ali, cousin of our Sayyedeh Khanom, had arrived and said, "Come on, let's go. We'll reach sooner. It's not safe here." My brother told him, "Well, then, let's go and be on our way." But the more we advanced, the more the rain increased, until all of a sudden the rain was so heavy that I saw the whole plain as a sea. In some places the water was up to my waist, in some places up to the knee. In short, the rain washed us well, until an hour and a half remained to sunset when, thanks be to God, in the Wadi al-salam,[11] my eyes were illumined by the light of the holy shrine. I gave a thousand thanks to God that I didn't die and arrived at this great grace. May God improve the portion of everyone so that one day they are honored by coming to this valley and making a pilgrimage to this luminous candle.

As much as I want to describe the holy dome, it doesn't occur to me what to write. Learned men have written books. What can I, who am weak and with a flawed intellect, say that would be worthy of this great one? I, a woman, have no intelligence, the lack of which is proved by the fact that this morning, I was so afraid of the rain that I wept and, writing this entry, I forgot to mention the day of the week. . . . I know I have insulted other women, but what can I do? O God, how can my apologies be worse than my sins? Now I haven't written it, but it's Saturday.

Saturday, November 25: We entered holy Najaf in good health and stopped at the house of Hajji Sayyed Mohammad 'Ali. After taking tea, they laid out the clothes of my companions to dry, although they won't dry for another ten days. Since we just arrived, no matter how much we wanted to go to the holy shrine, they told us it was not possible today and tonight. If anyone wants to go through the streets, then either one has to go barefoot in the water or be taken on the shoulders of a porter. I went there as a guest tonight. We sat down, and in this heavy rain, these poor people had prepared such a spread for supper. Although we were no more than six persons, it seemed that preparations were made for thirty. We had supper and slept.

Sunday, November 26: Getting up in the morning, we said our prayers. After having tea, I put on a chador. No matter how much they told me to wait a bit until the streets were a bit dry, I did not agree and left. Despite everything, I went through the streets and entered a paradise on earth that was the plain of the prince of the believers ['Ali]. I rubbed the auspicious earth on my eyes and thanked God a thousand times. I prayed to God for the continuation of the life, fortune, and health of the auspicious being of his majesty. I wished for the forgiveness and first pilgrimage to the true heir of the martyr king [Husayn] and offered prayers for all the worthy ones. O God, answer the prayers of the wounded and weary.

May I be sacrificed for the prince of the believers ['Ali], and may a pilgrimage to him illumine one's soul. May God allow all my loved ones to come to this highest heaven. We stayed in Najaf for eleven nights. On the first of Sha'ban, with the permission of Hazrat, we left Najaf with a thousand sorrows.

To Kufa and Karbala

Tuesday, December 5, al-Sahlah Mosque[12]: In the morning, with a lot of weeping we came out of the holy shrine, sat in the howdah, and started for the Kufa mosque. As we left Najaf, my throat gradually became sore, and by the time we got to the Kufa mosque, I had a fever. I wasn't in good shape in the mosque. I performed the prayers for every station. When we came out, because I was not well, I forgot to visit Prophet Yunus. By the time we reached the al-Sahlah Mosque, some medication helped my throat. We spent that night there. In the morning, with the same fever and bad condition, we mounted and started on our way.

Wednesday, December 6, Khan Shur: We entered this station at three hours to sundown. By the time we reached there, they had taken a nice house. They cooked some stew, which we ate, and then slept. On the morning of the third, we got up, performed our prayers, and set out. In the excitement of seeing sublime Karbala today, my throat was somewhat better, and my fever was down too. Thanks be to God.

Thursday, December 7, Karbala: Today, I perspired a bit in the howdah. We entered Karbala three hours to sundown. During the day, because of my perspiration, I was honored by a visit to the holy shrine. At night, I was at the shrine for two hours. Thanks to God that, because of the blessing of the pilgrimage, my throat became a bit better. On Friday morning, I was sent to a physician. Now I must follow the course he has prescribed to see what happens during this time we are in Karbala, and inshallah, Aqa will come too.

The Fate of Women

Thursday, March 8, 1900, on the way to Mecca: Between last night until now, it was decided that half the pilgrims would take the road to Damascus and half to Aleppo. I said that they should take me to Damascus so that I could make a pilgrimage to Hazrat Zaynab Khatun,[13] may Allah protect her. It seems that my brother was not inclined, and the more I spoke, the less he heeded me, and they took me on the road to Aleppo. At night, I cried a lot out of unhappiness. Why would they not take me to Hazrat Zaynab at this opportune time? Whatever a woman is and whatever a man is, the poor woman is the man's slave. May God make it happen that my brother Hajji Majid, who promised, will take me there from Beirut. I don't know if he spoke the truth or not. O fate, O kismet!

Friday, August 10, Samarra: Today, after having tea and watermelon, I was honored by a visit to the shrine, where I remained until midday. Afterward, I returned to the house. Since we must leave this evening, I am in a bad state. I didn't eat lunch, nor did I sleep. I am sitting listlessly by this Arab pool of water. I won't go back to the shrine. I am thinking about not having received any letter from [my husband] Mo'tasem al-Molk. Why didn't he write? No telegram, no letter. He has tired of me very quickly. I know what I'll tell him if I remain alive. I am not a woman that he can set aside. The house of His favors is flourishing, and He will take care of us.

FURTHER READING

Sakineh Soltan Vaqar al-Dowleh. *Ruznameh-ye safar-e 'atabat va Makkeh*. Edited by Rasul Ja'fariyan and Kiyanush Kiyani Haftlang. Tehran: 'Ilm, 2010. This source contains a full reprint of the pilgrimage narrative.

———. *Safarnameh-ye Sakineh Soltan Vaqar-od-dowleh*. Edited by Kianush Kiyani Haftlang. Tehran: Taravesh-e Qalam, 2003. This source contains a second travel narrative by this author. Further translations of her travel writing can be found online at https://accessingmuslimlives.org/travel/sakineh/.

Amineh Mahallati. "Memoirs of Iranian Women Travelers to Mecca." *Iranian Studies* 44 (2011): 831–49. This article contains translated passages on the author's journeys from Damascus to Aleppo, from Aleppo to Iskandarun, and from Baghdad to Samarra.

Piotr Bachtin. "Women's Writing in Action: On Female-authored Hajj Narratives in Qajar Iran." *Iranian Studies* 54, nos. 1–2 (March 2020): 67–93. https://doi.org/10.1080/00210862.2020.1724506.

———. "The Royal Harem of Naser al-Din Shah Qajar (r. 1848–96): The Literary Portrayal of Women's Lives by Taj al-Saltana and Anonymous 'Lady from Kerman.'" *Middle Eastern Studies* 51 (2015): 986–1009.

NOTES

1. The author refers here not to her first husband, who had died in 1896, but to his successor, Mozaffar al-Din Shah Qajar (r. 1896–1907).

2. This woman was the widow of Bahman Mirza, a Qajar prince and the granduncle of the current shah, Mozaffar al-Din.

3. This woman was the wife of the current shah, Mozaffar al-Din, and the mother of Eshrat al-Saltaneh, mentioned in the next sentence.

4. This woman was, like the author, a widow of the late shah Naser al-Din.

5. This woman was the daughter of the previous shah, Naser al-Din.

6. This woman's identity is not clear.

7. This woman was, like the author, a widow of the late shah Naser al-Din.

8. Muslim ibn 'Aqil al-Hashimi was a cousin of Imam Husayn who is buried in the Grand Mosque at Kufa.

9. 'Abbas was a son of the first Shia imam, 'Ali, who was martyred at the Battle of Karbala.

10. Her late husband, Naser al-Din Shah, had authored several travelogues, one of them being a narrative to the Shia pilgrimage sites that he had visited in 1870. His account served as a model for many Iranian travel writers in the late nineteenth century.

11. This is a large cemetery in Najaf located near the shrine of Imam 'Ali that attracts many pilgrims.

12. A mosque of great significance to Shia Muslims in Kufa.

13. Zaynab was the granddaughter of the Prophet Muhammad and the daughter of 'Ali and Fatima. The Sayyidah Zaynab Mosque in Damascus contains her grave, which is a popular pilgrimage spot for Shias.

SIX

NAWAB SULTAN JAHAN BEGUM

The Long March to Medina

INTRODUCTION

A conspicuous traveler among India's colonial elite was Nawab Sultan Jahan Begum of Bhopal (1858–1930) (see fig. 6.1). The fourth in a dynasty of Muslim female rulers—her grandmother was Nawab Sikandar Begum of Bhopal (also featured in this collection)—she ruled a princely state in central India from 1901 through to her abdication in 1926. Distinguishing her reign was her determination to be an effective ruler and reformer while still maintaining strict seclusion (purdah). Not only did she introduce administrative changes intended to form an efficient and merit-based bureaucracy in her state, but she also dedicated herself to social reform. As well as founding schools, hospitals, clubs, libraries, magazines, and museums in Bhopal, she patronized Muslim education, health programs, and women's organizations throughout India as a whole. She was also a prolific author with over a dozen Urdu books to her name (some of which were made available in translation to English and other languages). Her publications included a three-volume autobiography; reformist guides on education, veiling, health, and women's rights; children's stories; and even a cookbook.

Despite appearing in public only in an all-encompassing burqa of the Afghan style, Sultan Jahan traveled widely in India and abroad, with journeys to the Middle East and Europe in 1903–4, 1911 (see the chapter on Maimoona Sultan), and 1925–26. Her first journey out of India followed the path of her esteemed grandmother on pilgrimage to Hijaz. Having made suitable arrangements for her eldest son Nasrullah to manage Bhopal's administration in her absence, she set out from Bhopal in October 1903 and returned just over five months later

---

The introduction, extracts, and annotations were prepared by Siobhan Lambert-Hurley with input from Daniel Majchrowicz.

Figure 6.1 Nawab Sultan Jahan Begum of Bhopal with her son at the Delhi Durbar, 1911. From Wikipedia Commons.

in April 1904. Accompanying the ruling begum were nearly three hundred of her subjects, over half of whom appear to have been women. Among her party was her middle son, Obaidullah, and his wife, Shaharyar Dulhan; her youngest son, Hamidullah; a British doctor, Major MacWatt, and his wife; a goodly array of state officers; and the begum's military guard. The entire party traveled by special train to Bombay, the steamship SS *Akbar*, to Yenbu (via Aden) and camel train to Medina. From Medina to Mecca, they joined the Syrian caravan to avoid further attacks by Bedouin raiders.

So many details of her journey are known because, following her grandmother's example, Sultan Jahan wrote an account of her pilgrimage. It was published first in Urdu as *Rauzat al-riyahin* (*The Fragrant Garden*, 1906–9) by a state press. The title was a chronogram intended to mark the date of the event to which it referred—here, the Islamic calendar year 1321. The text itself appears representative of an earlier era with outdated orthography, stilted language, and a page layout that was no longer current. Achieving a wide circulation was the English translation of this text, entitled *The Story of a Pilgrimage to Hijaz*, which appeared from a Calcutta-based publisher in 1909 before being reprinted in 1913. It is not clear who produced the translation—which, unlike the Urdu version, also included images—but as with Sultan Jahan's many autobiographical and reformist writings, it may have been a British colonial officer linked to Bhopal or an English-speaking state employee. The original translation is often remarkably true to the Urdu source, so it is reproduced in the extracts here.

The account begins with a substantial introduction, from which the first excerpt here is taken, outlining the necessity of the hajj pilgrimage, as well as the author's path to undertake it. Here, Sultan Jahan explains how she had yearned to visit the Kaaba since childhood but had been prevented from doing so by a series of obstacles: first, her minority, then the "domestic and official troubles" of her early adulthood, and finally her mother's death and the "arduous responsibilities" of rule. The second obstacle referred to a long-running feud with her mother, Shah Jahan, and her mother's second husband, Siddiq Hasan, as well as perhaps the birth of her five children, two of whom died prematurely. Her husband Ahmad Ali Khan's death in 1902 caused another postponement, but also a stimulus. To the British government, she justified leaving her state for the duration of the pilgrimage on the basis of grief, poor health, and religious obligation.

The main body of the text is divided into two books. The first is more guide than travelogue, including chapters on Arabia's geography, the history and upkeep of the Kaaba, and the Prophet's mosque in Medina. The factual register was maintained through two "supplements" to Book 1, one detailing Arabian currency and another offering an annotated list of Arabia's many shrines. Book 2 then shifts focus to concentrate on the "events and incidents" (*vaqi'at aur halat*) of Sultan Jahan's own pilgrimage. Much of this text reproduced lengthy correspondence with the British and Arab functionaries, state orders, speeches, and other official documents with as much attention given to preparation for and return from the pilgrimage as the actual journey. Only on occasion is this rich bureaucratic record interspersed with a narrative account of her actual journey, from which the other four extracts here are taken.

Having introduced the various shrines and outlined the necessary rituals in Book 1, Sultan Jahan gives little attention to religious activities in Book 2. Indeed, she includes just three matter-of-fact sentences on having completed the hajj rituals at Mecca. Only very occasionally—as in the fourth extract here on the party's arrival in Medina—does the reader gain any insight to the spiritual passion unleashed by the pilgrimage. Sultan Jahan's narrative also lacks the ethnographic detail present in her grandmother's account. Some landscapes are evoked and memorable meals are described (as in the third and fifth extracts), but on the whole, the people and places of Arabia remain sketchy. Of more interest to the ruling begum were the practical arrangements for her journey, particularly as a veiled woman, and the honors bestowed upon her as a traveling prince. Hence, in the second and fourth extracts, she documents in scrupulous detail the ceremonials and purdah arrangements on her departure from India and arrival in Medina.

For granting her a "reception befitting my rank," including "honors, escort and customs facilities," the Turkish government is treated to generous commendations throughout the narrative. Sultan Jahan thus makes a distinction between Turks and Arabs with the latter more often depicted, as in the fifth extract, in an Orientalist mode as greedy and corrupt. Particular venom was reserved for the sharif of Mecca—despite the begum's claim in the first extract that the hajj strengthened "fraternal bonds" among Muslims. His "unfriendliness" was routinely contrasted with the "kindly help" of a British government in India, projected as the guarantor of "freedom, liberty and security" for people of "every faith and creed." For Sultan Jahan, writing a hajj narrative offered a means to underscore her identity as an able and worthy prince and "loyal Muhammadan."

EXTRACTS

Introduction

There is a well-known Arab saying that "travel leads to success." The blessings that the civilized countries of the world have enjoyed by means of travel are everywhere manifest at the present day. The principal causes that have determined the progress of civilization resolve themselves into an exchange of ideas among the various branches of the human race and the increase of knowledge. The hajj enables Musalmans to achieve these ends in the best possible manner. Men from every corner of the habitable globe are gathered together on this occasion, and, according to their respective tastes and requirements, they can obtain information relating to the remotest parts of the world, which may thus accrue to the vast concourse of pilgrims by mutual intercourse is obvious. Moreover, the various races of mankind whom the Kaaba draws together in a spiritual bond obtain an insight into one another's social condition, and by comparing notes gather ideas for such social reforms as are necessary. The words of the holy Quran, "so that benefits may accrue to them," convey this meaning. The advantages of union are innumerable, and it is a principle that Islam has specially inculcated on its followers. In pursuance of the great Islamic doctrine that "the Faithful are brothers,"[1] all the Musalmans of the world constitute a single fraternity.

The hajj is the best means of strengthening these fraternal bonds, and the plain of Arafat is the spot where Musalmans can best cultivate one another's acquaintance. It is the place to which millions of men of all sorts and conditions resort from different parts of the world, wrapped in pieces of unsewn linen as a token of humility, with the common object of doing homage to God. It is there that Adam (Peace be upon him), after coming from Paradise into this world, first recognized his wife Eve. The spectacle is one that makes an indelible impression upon the mind. The hajj is the best means of making Musalmans realize that all are equal. In the sight of the Absolute Master of the Universe the poor and the rich, the beggar and the sovereign, are all alike, all are his servants.

Departure from India

In accordance with the arrangements previously made, my special train, which under the quarantine rules had been properly fumigated and disinfected, stood ready to receive me on the Bhopal-Ujjain Railway line toward the north of the Nishat Afza gardens, at midnight on the 6th Shaaban, 1321 Hijra, corresponding to October 28, 1903. Putting my trust in God, I got into the train. . . . Suffice it to say that it safely reached the Victoria station at Bombay at 7:00 a.m. on Friday, the 8th Shaaban, 1321 Hijra, corresponding to October 30, 1903. On the platform, I was received by Nawab Muhammad Nasrullah Khan Sahib Bahadur, Major L. Impey, the secretary to the Government of Bombay, Captain Goodridge, a number of European ladies and gentlemen, several officials of my state who had preceded me to Bombay, and certain Indian merchants. A guard of honor was also drawn up on the platform and presented arms as I alighted from the train, while a salute was fired by order of the Bombay Government. Some of the individuals presented me with garlands and bouquets. The SS *Akbar* chartered from my voyage was standing close to the platform. On alighting from the train, I and my ladies were carried in palanquins to the ship where we embarked, and then the men came on board. The [British government's] political agent [in Bhopal] and other European friends came on board to bid me farewell. . . . After 12 noon, the steamer left the wharf and anchored near the gates. At about four o'clock in the afternoon, Nawab Nasrullah Khan Sahib Bahadur came on board the ship to take leave of me. At 5:00 p.m., the vessel weighed anchor, and having chanted the verse, "In the name of God one moors it (the barge) and sets it afloat,"[2] we left the shores of India with ejaculations of Labaik (Here am I).[3] This was my first experience of a long sea voyage, and during it I had opportunity to ponder over the broad expanse of the ocean.

The March from Yanbu to Medina

The march was long, but the greater part of our route lay across a plain. Some of the plains traversed by us struck Sahibzada Muhammad Obaidullah Khan Sahib

Bahadur[4] as eminently suited for polo if he had only brought his polo sticks with him. At one place the Sahibzada, when galloping his horse, met three wild Bedouins who answered his *Salam alaikum* (Peace be to you) with *walaikumi-s-Salam* (And on you be peace) and offered him bread, onions, and cheese. The Sahibzada began to eat these, as in Arabia a refusal to accept hospitality is resented as an insult. While he was eating the bread, one of the Bedouins said, "Allahu-latifunbi-ibadihi" (God is good to his servants). The Sahibzada promptly added the remaining portion of the verse: "Yazruku man yasha wa huwa-l-Kawiyyu-l-Aziz" (He feeds whomsoever He wishes; He is the Mighty and the Great).[5] They said, "What! Are you a Hafiz" (one who can repeat the Quran by rote), and he answered, "God be praised, I am a Hafiz." His hosts then put dates before him. While the Sahibzada was there, the people wondered where he had gone, and there was much cause for anxiety till he appeared a little later. Hilmi Effendi warned him in a friendly manner that Arabia was not India, where he could wander about freely, but that there were many perils and he ought to be careful. The Sahibzada said that he had been very kindly treated by these people, but he would be cautious in the future. . . .

On the 9th Ramzan, we started in the early morning from Bir-i-Said. Our whole route lay through a hilly tract, and in front we saw high mountains. The road, however, wound so much that we escaped climbing as the mountains did not form one mass, but were separated. Before noon, after crossing a plain we saw a fertile garden of date-palms. The soil was exactly like the bed of a dried-up tank. There was also a spring of fresh water. Near sunset the caravan halted at the Ain-i-Hamra. This is a small patch of ground surrounded by hills, where there are date groves, a mosque with mud walls, and a canal. There is also a small fort with fifty Turkish troops and a little village. Here are the tombs of 'Abbas (the Prophet's cousin) and certain other holy persons, which were visited by most of the members of the caravan. When we saw how green and fresh the place looked, we thought we would halt here for a day, but at eight in the evening we heard gunshots in all directions. Sharif Ahmad-ibn-Mansur received a letter from a Bedouin Shaikh saying, "If your people are of the family of Kalb-i-Ali Khan, he promised to pay us Rs. 500 a year to keep the road clear, and on returning to India broke his word. You pay it and give a promise for the future. If you are not of his family, give us a suitable present. If not, we are assembled at the valley of Huzaifa and will not allow the caravan to proceed to Medina without a fight." A letter in similar terms was received by Abu Jud Madani, who handed it to Sahibzada Hafiz Muhammad Obaidullah Khan Sahib Bahadur. The Sahibzada spoke to me about the letter and said that he would consult Hilmi Effendi and see what he said. He consulted him accordingly and had an answer sent, but I suggested to the Sahibzada that if by paying something to these people a fight could be avoided, it would be better to pay, for "property is an atonement for life." But his manly resolution and courage objected to this. So after consulting Hilmi Effendi, he determined not to pay a price, for there are such a number of families and groups of these people that, however much we might give, their greed would never be satisfied. Apparently the emissaries of the sharif of Mecca were at the bottom of this plot. . . .

On the 10th Ramzan, the caravan left Ain-i-Hamra at 7:00 a.m. The dispositions of the Turkish military guard were changed. The immediate escort around my litter was increased, and the Turkish troops protected the caravan on all sides. The duty was performed with much bravery and intelligence. The Turkish advance guard climbed every dangerous hill, cleared the road, and signaled with flags, after which the caravan moved forward. Some of the mountains were so high that men standing at the top looked like dwarfs. . . .

At one o'clock, a number of Bedouins were seen climbing the Khif hill, and bullets began to fly from above. One bullet came quite close to Sahibzada Hafiz Muhammad Obaidullah Khan, who had a hair's-breadth escape. Behind him was the sharif's emissary's camel, which was knocked over by the bullet. A few bullets came near my litter too, but by God's mercy no one was injured. A Turkish guard at once climbed the heights, and though the Bedouins had already fled, they restored full confidence. This is the same hill on which the Bedouins frequently attacked the Prophet (Peace be upon him!). . . . As long as there was danger, the Turks maintained full precautions. When the dangerous zone had been passed, they descended from the hill singing happily, and the Sahibzada approached my litter to inform me that the Turkish troops said that there was no more cause for anxiety. I sent for Hilmi Effendi and thanked him, his soldiers, and His Majesty the Sultan, to which he replied, "Your Highness is a lady of distinction, Ruler of the Bhopal State, which is protected by the British Government. We have been repeatedly enjoined to safeguard Your Highness. Your Highness must therefore look upon us as your household servants, and the soldiers as your children. They will serve and obey Your Highness with the same zeal as your own troops."

Arriving in Medina

As we approached Bir-i-Ali, we found that from the top of the hill before us, a glimpse of the holy Medina was visible. The people of the caravan, on learning this, ran eagerly toward the mountain, and the scene was one which I shall remember as long as I live. The sight of each man hurrying toward the top of the hill in pious enthusiasm to obtain a glimpse of the city to visit which he had gone through so many difficulties, and giving vent to the rapture which filled his heart at the holy view by loudly calling out Darud (invoking peace upon the soul of the Prophet), was most exhilarating and instructive. It is worth mentioning that in the plain through which we passed, there was a very sweet smell that delighted our senses. . . .

After 9:00 a.m. I left for Medina accompanied by Sharhyar Dulhan Sahiba and the Sahibzadas Hafiz Muhammad Obaidullah Khan and Mian Muhammad Hamidullah Khan. On the way we saw large bodies of men coming from Medina. It was generally remarked that the people of Medina were not in the habit of coming out of their city to welcome anyone, and that this was a special honor done to the Begum of Bhopal. The Turks who were with me were only in attendance upon my personal procession, and over and above their band, there was also a band of slaves playing music. The procession moved on in a very stately fashion. At about 11:00 a.m., we reached the city gate, called the Bab-i-Ambariah. Outside the gate, I was received by His Excellency Izzatlu Hasn Muzaffar Pasha, Muhafiz or governor of Medina, and the treasurer-general of the Sacred Haram with troops, a band, and artillery. A salute of twenty-one guns was fired in my honor. I then entered a tent that had already been pitched to receive me and the Sahibzadas, and it was here that I received the nobles of Medina. . . .

After this, I mounted my litter and entered the city. As I reached the doorway of the Prophet's mosque, the Shaikh-ul-Haram, Izzatlu Usman Pasha, the Kazi, the Mufti, the Shaikh-ul-Aghwath (Chief of the Eunuchs), and the Shaikh-ul-Khutaba (Chief of the Preachers) came as far as the door to receive me, and they asked me whether it was my intention to present myself at the sacred shrine immediately or later on. As proper *parda* [purdah] arrangements could not be made at such short notice, and I moreover felt fatigued, I replied that I would then and there invoke peace upon the blessed Prophet and go to my house, and that I would pay a visit to the holy tomb at some other time as there was no particular hurry about the visit, for we followers of the holy Prophet invoked the blessings of heaven upon him, even from India. I then went to Sayyad Safi's house, which had been selected for my residence by the Sharif of Mecca, and stayed there.

"Our Sojourn at Medina, the Illustrious"

Sayyad Safi's house, in which I had taken up my lodgings, was situated at such a distance from the Prophet's tomb that for three whole days, I could not pay a visit to the holy shrine. On the fourth day, however, I mounted my litter and reached it. The Shaikh-ul-Haram had made excellent arrangements for the occasion so that only eunuchs were permitted to be present; there were no men inside the shrine.

The Haram is usually closed at night but is kept open at all hours during the holy month of Ramzan. I therefore experienced no difficulty in obtaining admission. The Pasha in charge of the Haram, the Kazi, the Mufti, and certain other notables stood at the doorway to receive me. I alighted from the conveyance clad in a burqa and, after exchanging salutations with these gentlemen, entered the Haram. Presently I reached the holy tomb, and my guide, Sayyad Hammad, assisted me to perform the rites of visitation.

Instead of returning to Sayyad Safi's house, I went on leaving the Haram straight to the house that had been rented in the neighborhood of the Majidi gate. This house presented the distinct advantage that I was enabled to perform the Isha (evening) service every night at the Prophet's mosque. The Pasha in charge of the Haram was good enough to provide for my personal use a separate place apart from other women, so I could spend as much time in devotion during the blessed month of Ramzan as fate had decreed for me.

On the day of our arrival in Medina, we were entertained at a dinner given by Sayyad Ali Zahid Vatri, a Bhopal State stipendiary during the rule of my late mother, who has found a seat in Paradise. . . . The dinner was after the Arab fashion and was given with all the usual Arab ceremonies.

On Thursday, the 14th Ramzan, our party was similarly entertained by Sayyad Safi. I shall describe this entertainment in detail. Two rooms had been neatly furnished. In the center of the rooms, which were elegantly carpeted, was placed a low oval table around which the guests took their seats. Half a loaf of leavened and buttered bread and a spoon were placed before each guest. Behind the guests stood servants with jars of water and a towel. A napkin was spread over the knees of each guest. The first course, according to the European custom, consisted of soup to which each guest helped himself as he liked. The used plates were then replaced by clean ones, and meat cooked with turnips, plain boiled rice, kubuli (a mess of rice and gram pulse), brinjal curry, roast meat, and similar other viands constituted the succeeding courses. The feast ended by a mouthful of plain bread to which the guests helped themselves in order to clean the mouth. When they rose from the table, they washed their hands with soap and drank coffee, and each went to his own place.

During our stay in Medina, the ladies of the household of the Shaikh-ul-Haram called on me two or three times and entertained me at dinner, to which I went with several ladies of my suite. The dinner was like that which I have just described. . . .

According to the custom here, a dinner consisting of twelve courses is regarded as a banquet, and a special delicacy is a goat roasted whole and filled with richly cooked Biryani.

FURTHER READING

Vakil Merath Nadir 'Ali. *Rauzat al-riyahin min masir al-sultan ila bilad al-amin, Madinat al-Nabi, Sayyid al-Mursalin.* Bhopal: Sultania, 1909. This manuscript was translated as *The Story of a Pilgrimage to Hijaz.* Calcutta: Thacker, Spink & Co., 1909. https://archive.org/details/thestoryofapilgroobeghuoft.

———. *Risala waqi'at-i Hijaz.* Merath: Matba' Dar al-'Ulum, n.d.

Sultan Jahan Begum. *An Account of My Life.* 3 vols. London: John Murray, 1910–1927. https://archive.org/details/accountofmylifegoosult.

Siobhan Lambert-Hurley. *Muslim Women, Reform and Princely Patronage: Nawab Sultan Jahan Begum of Bhopal.* London: Routledge, 2007.

———. "Out of India: The Journeys of the Begam of Bhopal, 1901–30." *Women's Studies' International Forum* 21, no. 3 (June 1998): 263–76.

NOTES

1. Quran 49:10.

2. Quran 11:41. This is more typically translated as "in the name of Allah is its course and its and its anchorage."

3. All Quranic verse is also contained in the original and translation.

4. The name of the author's son is transliterated as Ubaidullah in the original, but it is changed to Obaidullah here to reflect the standard spelling of his name in English.

5. Quran 42:19.

UMMAT AL-GHANI NUR AL-NISA
Notes from Mecca and the Levant

INTRODUCTION

Ummat al-Ghani Nur al-Nisa (1885–1915) was born to an upper-class family in the princely state of Hyderabad in southern India in 1885. As with all women in her family, she kept purdah throughout her life and was never a public figure. The private nature of Ummat al-Ghani's life makes her travel account, *Safarnamah-i Hijaz, Sham, o Misr* (*A Travel Account of the Hijaz,* The Levant, *and Egypt*), originally written in 1909, particularly instructive because it demonstrates how an accomplished woman of her time might have kept a journal and reflected on her travel experiences for a limited, localized audience. Although we typically think of travel writing as being published in books, in South Asia, most travel writing by women circulated locally through oral accounts, letters, and journals like this one.

What we know about Ummat al-Ghani comes from meticulous private records that trace her family's destiny across centuries and continents. These expansive archives relate the history of a clan that considered itself to be culturally and ethnically distinct from the communities in which it lived, primarily in Madras and Hyderabad. Somewhat uniquely, these records include entries on both male and female family members. From these sources, we learn that Ummat al-Ghani was a passionate and lifelong reader, and that her appreciation for poetry gave birth to a habit of collecting verse. She also took an interest in writing, to which she gave primary expression through letter writing. Some of her letters are preserved in family collections and are described as being informal, well-crafted,

Daniel Majchrowicz prepared the introduction and translation from Urdu. The original text was provided by Sylvia Vatuk.

and pleasant to read. Though women's education in India was uncommon even in the late nineteenth century, Ummat al-Ghani received a well-rounded education at home.

She likewise imbibed a passion for learning from her family, which prided itself on its intellectual accomplishments, particularly in various fields of the Islamic sciences. Her lineage linked her to ancestors of Arab descent who joined the Muslim political elite of southern India by serving as 'ulema or qazis. They first rose to prominence in the princely state of Arcot. When the dissolution of that state by the British forced their departure, the family moved to Madras in 1801, where the deposed Nawab of Arcot had taken up residence. While most of the family remained in Madras, by the mid-nineteenth century some of its members had begun to move to India's wealthiest and largest independent state, Hyderabad. It was here that Ummat al-Ghani's father, 'Abd al-Qadir (d. 1906), took up the position of city registrar. Ummat al-Ghani was the first-born daughter of his wife, Ummat al-Qadir Badr al-Nisa, who herself published a book on Sufi saints.

Even as the family moved throughout southern India in search of patronage, they maintained a strong pride in their Arab ancestry and adherence to Shafi'i law. They practiced endogamous marriage within the extended family, and Ummat al-Ghani was thus married to a cousin, Qadir Murtaza Husain, in 1902. The couple had six children. She tragically died in 1915 at the young age of thirty-one while giving birth to the sixth. As with other members of her family, she was buried in Hyderabad in the courtyard of the Yusufain shrine, which houses the remains of many notable figures.

The only instance of Ummat al-Ghani's writing publicly available today is the work translated here. *Safarnamah-i Hijaz, Sham, o Misr* recounts Ummat al-Ghani's 1909 voyage to perform the hajj and visit prominent sites of historical and religious importance in the Middle East. Her destinations included Mecca and Medina, as well as Damascus, Beirut, Palestine, the Sinai, and Cairo. She traveled with her grandmother, husband, son, brother, and two cousins, as well as two unnamed servants, over the course of approximately ten months. She began her work as a diary, but internal evidence reveals that she intended for the diary to circulate within the family. Sections detailing the cost of travel for "readers," the layout of the Holy Places, and the availability of foodstuffs suggest that the account was intended to provide knowledge to those who had not yet traveled to the region themselves. The travel account was most likely read within her family but never by the general public. She seemingly did not arrange to have her notes published in a women's magazine, which would have been feasible had she wished to do so.

Ummat al-Ghani's narrative and the details she records indicate that she was familiar with the conventions of the travelogue genre in Urdu, which was heavily dominated by men's travel writing. Her inclusion of ticket fares, sites of historic and spiritual significance, and other "useful information" were standard items in travel accounts after the turn of the twentieth century. However, her account also differs from popular travel writing of the time. In particular, her tendency to avoid elaborate description and narrative devices drawn from fiction suggest that she was more concerned with informing, or perhaps documenting, than with entertaining. Her fidelity to the often mundane nature of travel is as revealing as it is prosaic. She was sure to make an entry every day, even if only to note that she had no entry to make. The selections below are representative of her focus on the everyday aspects of the pilgrimage journey. Even the headings used in the text, which indicate only the date, underline this quotidian focus.

Ummat al-Ghani's writing employs a stream-of-consciousness approach as she notes down the various unrelated items that caught her eye during the day. Yet politics and social conditions in the ummah are never far away. Her text frequently takes up the major political topics that often proved irresistible to Muslim travelers from India to the Middle East during the heyday of Pan-Islamism. Ummat al-Ghani's text takes on a bald political stance as she reflects on the decline of Muslim power and answers back to what she perceives as European criticism of the religious community's shortcomings. Yet she is also prepared to critique Muslims who fail to live up to the religion's ideals, such as those who fail to give their servants equal respect in accordance with her understanding of Islamic guidelines, or whose dress does not conform to her conception of Islamic modesty.

EXTRACTS

Wednesday, 9 Zi al-Hijja

Today is the day of the hajj. Thousands of God's creatures are gathered here; it is a wonderful sight. Thousands upon thousands of white tents have been put up. All around are the sounds of camels calling and donkeys and mules braying. Ceremonial cannons are being fired. A delightful Turkish drum is being sounded. There are Arabs, Turks, Egyptians, Iranians, Hindustanis, Levantines, Central Asians, Chinese, Afghans, in short, people from every country and region of the world. All are wearing the same dress. Who is rich, who is poor? All wear the same two pieces of cloth. May God grant everyone a visit to this place.

The people of Europe go on and on raising cries of "Unity!" Can they present any sight such as this? Any instance where so many different people have come together as one? In fact, unity is the very inheritance of the Muslim. The bitter truth is that if Muslims could demonstrate this unity at all times, they would not be in the unfortunate situation they are today.

We remained at Arafat for the rest of the day. Some read the Quran, some were engaged in reciting the holy names of God, while still others took rest. Everyone was doing something or other. We collected small stones and pebbles here because when we return to Mina, we must perform the stoning of the devil.

Friday, 9 Muharram

There are almost no foreigners left in Mecca any longer. There are only Meccans here now. There was a wondrous atmosphere in the Haram tonight. There was not a single cloud to darken the deep blue sky. The moon glittered and shone over the azure horizon. Its pure white light pledged its life to the Haram and the Kaaba. Small, beautiful stars twinkled festively while the silverwork on the black curtains covering the Kaaba glistened. The repeated calls of Allahu Akbar added to the wondrous mood. The flickering lamps were especially pleasing to the eye against the light of the moon. White buildings, tall minarets . . . Some people performed prayers, some circled the Kaaba, some read the Quran. Others recited prayers in praise of the Prophet, while still others kissed the Black Stone. The atmosphere inside the Haram tonight filled my heart with a wonderful sense of bliss that is beyond all description, incapable of being written. Ink itself is not sufficient to record it. I pray to God that all our near and dear be given the opportunity to visit the Kaaba. Amin.

Wednesday, 4 Safar

Hajji Muhammad Ghaus Sahib has come from Medina. The hot weather has begun. The women here have taken to dressing like foreign women. They leave their necklines open like Christian women.

When infidelity arises from the Kaaba, where then is Islam safe?[1]

It is a great pity that the women of Mecca have adopted this dress.

The people of this city transcend all others in manners and morals, so much so that they consider even their slaves to be their equals. In fact, this is how it ought to be, for Islam itself commands that "all believers are brothers."[2] Among India's Muslims, it is considered a fault to treat a servant as one's equal. But those who hold this view have not reflected on Islam's position regarding the status of slaves. Do Muslims not know that Bilal was an African slave but was accorded the greatest respect by the Prophet's companions? The status of slaves was such that the Prophet's slave Zaid was married by the Prophet to his cousin Hazrat Zainab bint Jahsh. Zaid was appointed the commander of the Muslim armies on several occasions. His son Usama was appointed to lead armies that included Hazrat Abu Bakr and Hazrat 'Umar Faruq in their ranks.

In short, not even a tenth of a tenth of the status given to slaves by Islam can be found among even the most civilized nations today. Europe raises its slogans on this matter too. While they no longer have the tradition of keeping slaves, nevertheless the slaves of that time were better treated than the servants of to-day. Slaves were given a portion of the inheritance. The Prophet would give the clothes that he had worn to slaves for them to wear. He served slaves the same food he himself ate.

Monday, 9 Sha'ban

Today we left Damascus for Beirut. We boarded the train at Damascus Station and departed at 7:30 a.m. The stations are located very closely to one another. The first stop was Damascus Maidan. The second was Damascus Bramka. The sixth was 'Ain Fataha. . . . At 6:30 we arrived at the twenty-sixth station, the port of Beirut. This station is located at the very edge of the sea. It is an extremely beautiful place. We went straight to our hotel, Kaukab al-Sabah, which is in a lovely location right by the sea.

This hotel is much nicer than the Medina Hotel in Damascus. The location is perfect. Waves crash against the shore just in front of the hotel. There are thousands of little ships and boats anchored here. The railway station is right across the road. The street itself is broad and filled with hundreds of carriages drawn by Arab horses. Beautiful, elegant men, out for a stroll, walk gracefully through the streets with women at their sides.

> I have heard of wondrous Joseph and seen the beauties of the world
> But such beauty as this I have never before heard told[3]

The city is very clean and well-organized. The roads are broad. Arrangements for both the police and sanitation are excellent.

There are towns and villages the entire way between Damascus and Beirut, as I have already written. I was elated to find that the Muslims of both Damascus and Beirut are very wealthy. Christians, who are given the highest respect in our country, have absolutely no status here; it is they who drive the sanitation carts. Some perform manual labor. Ah yes, the Jews are also wealthy.

The beautiful women who visit the gardens present an absolutely stunning sight. It would be no exaggeration if I were to explain these gardens to you by comparing them to the gardens of heaven, or if I were to compare these women to the houris of paradise. Having now seen these cities, I give endless praise and thanks to God that Muslims too possess cities as wonderful and vibrant as these. That said, the population of Christians in Beirut is larger than that of Muslims. There are fewer Christians in Damascus.

Wednesday, 11 Sha'ban

In both Beirut and Jaffa, you must take a smaller boat to reach or depart from the ship. In Jaffa the seas were particularly rough, and the boats had a difficult time pulling abreast.

We went directly to Maulvi 'Abd al-Qadir Bukhari's hotel, which is located near the Jami' Mosque. The British Consul here is Hajji Darvesh. He has a number of boats at his disposal. We went in a few of these from the ship to shore.

Jaffa is a fairly small city. Fruit is very cheap here. We can see the sea from the hotel.

After noonday prayers, we took the Ottoman-built *Quds* Railway, which is a small railway, to visit the Aqsa Mosque in Jerusalem. Although there are separate cars for men and women on this line, there were men in the women's cars, and women in the men's. After some time the train began to move. Just as from Damascus to Beirut, the route to Jerusalem was lined with gardens and orchards, hills, and valleys. The train ascended the hills in the same way as the one to Beirut had. There was a gramophone playing. The cumulative effect of the train weaving through the orchards and beautiful songs playing on the gramophone created a very pleasing atmosphere.

We arrived in Jerusalem at sundown. Jerusalem Station is located outside the town itself but is surrounded by houses and shops. The houses are built in the English style. The main population of the city lives on the hill. It is densely populated. You get exhausted climbing stairs all day. There is a rest house (*tekke*) here for people from every country. People from Hindustan have their own too. It is run by Shaikh 'Abd al-Qadir Hindi. The poor are given bread and stew provided by the sultan. We are staying there. The market is somewhat far away.

Thursday, 12 Sha'ban

The roads here are cobbled, which makes it very difficult to walk. Shops are attended by Jewish and Christian girls. The man I mentioned before, the shaikh of the Hindustani guesthouse, is originally from Muthialpet in Madras. After the noon prayer, we went to the Aqsa Mosque. A Levantine man went with us. The mosque that Sulaiman [Solomon] originally built here has sunk into the earth. Another mosque was constructed over it in the Umayyad period. Lamps and torches must be lit if you wish to enter Sulaiman's mosque. It is now in ruins. It is said that Sulaiman is buried here. The Umayyad-era mosque is very large, so large that a man standing to one side appears to be a mere speck to someone standing at the other. There is no system for keeping the courtyard of the mosque clean. Grass and weeds grow freely there. There are so many shrines in the mosque that it is not possible to visit them all in a single day.

The largest object of pilgrimage of all is the *Sakhra*, or Foundation Stone, which is a large piece of rock approximately . . . [1.8] square yards in size. It hangs freely in the air. They have now constructed a dome above it and a wall beneath it. However, there is a space of five or six units between the wall and the rock where wrought paneling has been installed, but you can still see the rock hanging there. There is a well beneath it, but it has run dry. You must bring a light with you when you go. Inside the dome are the sacred spaces of Hazrat Khizr and Abraham and David. The final resting place of Solomon is located in the Aqsa Mosque. Some say that that it is inside the mosque, while others say that it is in the dome, directly beneath the rock, but only God knows best.

There are several large pools inside the mosque in which rain water collects. The entire city drinks this water.

Friday, 13 Sha'ban

Today we spent the day visiting shrines and holy places. The places we visited are as follows: The *Halqah Buraq*, that is, the ring where the Prophet tied the horse Buraq when he ascended into heaven. The Dome of the Ascension, the Dome of the Prophet, the Dome of the Soul, the Green Dome, the grave of Hazrat Da'ud [David], 'Ukashah, and other places. All of these are inside Aqsa Mosque. Then we went to the final resting place of Mary. To enter it, you must descend a staircase. The grave is an elongated box made of marble surrounded by curtains on all four sides. Like other such resting places, there are no covers over the tomb. Instead, there are only some curtains, which come from Russia, Germany, France, and Italy. The dome is decorated with candelabras of silver and gold that burn throughout the day. There were many Christians there when we visited. They all wore shoes and kept their heads uncovered inside the shrine. Some Christian women were wearing burqas too. The have soil placed on their heads, which they consider to be a blessing. On the way back, the collector of Jerusalem met with our men. He was very sincere.

According to the reckoning in Medina, today is the 13th of Sha'ban, but here it is the 14th. In the evening the mosque and minarets were illuminated. Hadith were recited. Our men participated.

15 Sha'ban

Today we took a three-horse carriage to Hebron (Mauza' Khalil al-Rahman), which is thirty-six kilometers or twenty-two and a half miles from Jerusalem. Hebron is a populated city with many gardens and mosques. Hazrat Ibrahim [Abraham] is buried here alongside his wife Sarah. The graves of Ishaq [Isaac], his wife Rebecca, Hazrat Ya'qub [Jacob], and Hazrat Yusuf are also here. We arrived at eleven and returned home later in the afternoon.

16 Sha'ban

Today we went to Bethlehem, which is the birthplace of Jesus. There are many images here of Hazrat 'Isa [Jesus] and Hazrat Maryam [Mary]. The soldiers are all Turkish here, too.

Wednesday, 19 Sha'ban

This morning we arrived at Port Said. We reached the shore by means of a small boat. The British consul examined our passports and then we went to a hotel.

Port Said is the meeting point of Asia, Africa, and Europe. Ships stop here to take on coal. The roads here are all very straight. There are many carriages, trams, and so on. The buildings are grand. The streets have electric lights. There are many shops, so many that even meat is sold in fine shops. There are also many coffee shops. The Suez Canal office is very large. There's also a shipyard where repairs can be made. The goats here are so large that they appear to be bullocks from a distance. Most of the policemen here can speak Urdu.

Thursday, 20 Sha'ban

At 8:30 this morning we boarded a train for our journey to Cairo, the capital of Egypt. The tracks run parallel to the sea and are bordered by Cyprus trees. The Suez Canal begins from this station. Ships sail into the canal one after the other. We could see the canal until the next station, after which it disappeared from view.

Ismailia Station is a junction. One branch goes to Port Suez. There are many wheat and cotton fields along the way. We reached Zagazig Station at 12:30. This is a large station—one branch goes from here to Salihiya. Next comes Banha (Naiban) Station. A line to Alexandria departs from here. We arrived in Cairo in the afternoon. This station is very large and grand.

Cairo is a massive, well-ordered city. The buildings are large and stately. The roads are broad and illuminated with electric lights. The shops are all very clean and organized, so much so that even the butcheries have marble floors. The meat is held on shelves lined with mirrors. There are electric trams and fine carriages available for the use of travelers. There are numerous mosques that are beautiful and always full. There are also many cafes. When we left the station, we headed for the hotel Dar al-Salam. The hotel is big and recently constructed. Our rooms were on the fourth floor. A movie is screened here every night. There's a large café immediately in front of the hotel with tables and chairs made of marble.

Saturday, 22 Sha'ban

Today Sahib and my brother went to Al-Azhar University.[4] They say that a huge number of students study there. The instructors teach from the pulpit while students sit in groups down below. We all went to the museum. We saw objects and bodies that were thousands of years old, plus pictures, stone idols, objects made out of stone and out of clay—in short, many thousands of things. We saw all sorts of grains, etc. From here we went to another place where live animals are kept. It is a large park. There are even mango trees there. We saw many different types of animals and birds: big, red parrots, wild asses, musk cats, white bears, zebras, etc.

From there we went to see the pyramids. There are three towers. The height of the largest one and the general quality and sturdiness of its construction make it worthy of praise. It covers eleven acres and is called the Pyramid of Giza (Jiza). . . . From here we went to see the fort. . . . There is a well in this fort that the people here call Joseph's Well. It is said that Joseph was imprisoned in this well for seven years, but this is not true. The fort was built in the year 1166 during the reign of Sultan Saladin. The prison was also constructed by him. Because his name was also Joseph, this well is now commonly known as Joseph's Well.

26 Sha'ban

Today we boarded a train for the return to Port Said. We saw a king in Port Said. His carriage was adorned with flowers. I bowed low when he passed.

28 Sha'ban

We boarded the ship and began to sail down the canal. When two ships meet one another in the canal, one of them has to stop because it is too narrow to let both pass at once. There are machines that remove silt from the canal every day. Many ships come and go every day. We reached the end of the canal at sundown. The canal is ninety-nine miles long.

18 Ramzan

A thousand thanks to God that today, after ten months and twelve days, our entire party has returned safely to the blessed city [of Hyderabad]. I thank God

for ensuring the safe return of all. I pray that all of our friends be given the opportunity to undertake the pilgrimage as well. Amen, again I say, amen

FURTHER READING

Ummat al-Ghani Nur al-Nisa. *Safarnamah-i Hijaz, Sham, o Misr.* 1909. Reprinted and
    edited by Husn-i Jahan. Hyderabad: Word Master Computer Publications Center, 1996.
    Further translated extracts are available at https://accessingmuslimlives.org/travel
    /ummat/.
M. Y. Kokan. *Khanavadah-i Qazi Badr al-Daula.* Madras: Dar al-Tasnif, 1963.
Sylvia Vatuk. "The Cultural Construction of Shared Identity: A South Indian Family
    History." *Social Analysis: International Journal of Social and Cultural Practice* 20, no. 28
    (1990): 114–31.
Saurabh Mishra. *Pilgrimage, Politics, and Pestilence: The Haj from the Indian Subcontinent,
    1860–1920.* New Delhi: Oxford University Press, 2011.

NOTES

1. A well-known line of poetry in Persian: *Chu kufr az Ka'ba bar khizad, kuja manad
musalmani.*

2. Qur'an 49:10.

3. A verse in Urdu: *Suna Yusuf ko, hasinan-i jahan bhi dekhe / husn aisa kisi ma'shuq meñ
dekha na suna.*

4. Al-Azhar is often celebrated as one of the world's oldest universities, having been
established in the tenth century. By the time of this visit, it was closely associated with
Islamic modernism.

EIGHT

BEGUM SARBULAND JANG

Seeking Sisterhood in Damascus

INTRODUCTION

Akhtar al-Nisa Begum Sarbuland Jang (1875–1956) belonged to the highest society of her time. Born into an elite family from north India, she subsequently married Hamidullah Khan Sarbuland Jang (1864–1935), the chief justice of Hyderabad, where she spent much of her adult life. Despite her proximity to the most well-known and powerful men in colonial India and her own involvement in social reform movements, she remains a shadowy figure. What is certain is that she was one of at least ten children born from the union of Nawab Agha Mirza Beg Sarvar Jang (1848–1933) with his wife Nawab Mahal Begum Sikandar Zamani, daughter of the prime minister of Alwar State. Her father became tutor, and later secretary, to Nizam Asif Jah VI, the ruler of Hyderabad. As a result, through both her lineage and upbringing, Begum Sarbuland Jang possessed an intimate familiarity with princely India.

She was also closely linked to colonial India and its intellectual life through her husband. Hamidullah Khan was the first student to be enrolled at the influential Mohammadan Anglo-Oriental College in Aligarh, which was founded by the renowned reformist Sir Sayyid Ahmad Khan. After graduating from Aligarh and Cambridge University, he served as a barrister in Allahabad before being appointed a High Court judge in Hyderabad in 1894. His own father, Sami'ullah Khan, was a dedicated benefactor and tireless advocate for Ahmad Khan and his reformist mission. Sami'ullah Khan himself wrote a travel account of a voyage to London in the late 1800s. This genealogy thus places Begum Sarbuland within a family tradition of travel writing that stemmed

---

Daniel Majchrowicz prepared the introduction and translation from Urdu.

almost from the establishment of the genre in Urdu, and which was likewise sustained by Hamidullah Khan, who wrote about the same journey as his wife in both Urdu and English.

The only extant writing by Begum Sarbuland Jang is the travel account translated here, which she wrote while traveling from her home in Hyderabad to the Middle East and Europe in 1909–10. The journey seems to have been part pilgrimage, part tourism, part family visit, and partly political. She performed a hajj in Mecca, toured the Parthenon in Athens, visited her sons and brother in London, and met with the Prince and Princess of Wales (who would become King George V and Queen Mary, respectively, only months later, shortly after which they would visit India themselves). The pair traveled over the course of five months, taking in Arabia, the Levant, Greece, France, and England, among other destinations. She kept a private journal as she traveled which was eventually published in Delhi after the passing of her husband some twenty years later under the title *Dunya 'aurat ki nazar me.ñ—mashriq o maghrib ka safarnamah* (*The World as Seen by a Woman—A Travel Account of East and West*). Though Begum Sarbuland records in a preface that she published it at the request of her children, it is possible that she took this decision herself in light of her new familial and social circumstances. For a woman to begin publishing after she has reached widowhood was not unprecedented in South Asia, particularly with regard to the genre of autobiography, though Begum Sarbuland does not reflect on the decision. She noted only that she felt her volume would be beneficial to readers by offering them the opportunity to observe and reflect on the conditions of women abroad and to meditate on these women's successes and failures. She was explicit here that her perspective was valuable in that it provided a woman's take on women's lives. Through the very title of her book, she gestured to the fact that very few travel accounts available in India at that time could provide such a perspective on these regions, setting up her own travel narrative against the more familiar corpus of travel accounts by men who not infrequently described (and on occasion prescribed) the lives of women abroad.

Begum Sarbuland kept purdah throughout her life, though she clearly felt that the proper amount of veiling or avoidance of unrelated men was highly dependent on context. She had thought deeply about the institution of purdah and followed her own version of it of her own volition. For her, purdah was both a choice and an ideal, but it should in no way limit women from engaging actively with public life. Neither did purdah prevent her from maintaining her own public career supporting the advancement and education of women. Her views on the place of women in their own society shine through clearly in her travel account.

She portrays a relationship with her husband that cedes him formal authority but is largely equal in practice. She often leaves him behind to explore on her own. Yet the pair also share experiences with one another, as in the extract detailing with the couple's brief visit to the holy sites and commercial areas of Damascus. Near the end of the translation, which includes the headings used in the original text, husband and wife worship and weep together at the shrine of Imam Husayn in Damascus. Passages like these impress upon the reader that her relationship to her husband is one of independence, mutual admiration, interdependence, and respect—albeit one in which each occupy distinct roles. At the same time, she is careful to demonstrate deference to her husband's authority, even if it appears largely symbolic.

EXTRACTS

A Visit to Damascus[1]

December 7, 1909: Today is the fourth day since we left Medina. We both woke up at dawn. Nawab sahib[2] told me that we would arrive in Damascus at three in the afternoon.

When I learned this, I told [my servant] Amina Bi to prepare our belongings, for we would be getting off the train today. Those two Turks are still with us; they've been looking after our luggage. Our train pulled to a halt at Damascus's station just after three. We have encountered many large stations throughout our journey. Each of them had good sanitary arrangements and water taps installed at regular intervals. Like these, the station in Damascus was also big and bustling.

As usual, the Cook representative[3] was waiting for us when we disembarked. But we also met someone connected with an Arab hotel. He praised his hotel extensively and suggested that we come and stay in it. "You are Muslims, and so are we. You must certainly come to our hotel." Responding to his insistence, Nawab sahib asked the man for the name of his hotel. And what a sweet name it was! "The name of my hotel is *Madina Munavvara*, Radiant Medina." The moment I heard this, I said to Nawab sahib that we *must* stay in this hotel; I like a hotel with name like that. Nawab sahib was pleased to hear the name too. The owner of the hotel picked up our luggage and placed it in a fine carriage. Arriving at the hotel, we learned that the daily rate was ten annas per person. We were both surprised to learn that the hotel was so cheap. Up until then, we had only stayed in German or English hotels, whose rates were around eight to ten rupees per night.[4] This is the first time we had encountered a Muslim hotel.

We went inside. The stairway was made of marble. We saw that each step was carpeted and were pleased that the hotel appeared to be so nice.

When we arrived upstairs, we were given a room containing six beds, but all of them were soiled, and there were cobwebs in the corners. Though the building itself was exceedingly grand and finely built, the furnishings were anything but. The table was filthy and the mirror was cracked. I had noticed that in English hotels they would put a sheet beneath the blanket so it would be kept free of sweat. After a traveler had used the sheet, it would immediately be exchanged for another one, and in this way the blanket would always remain clean and devoid of odors. Here, in place of blankets they had quilts—quilts so filthy that they reeked of perspiration. Oh, when will these people learn proper cleanliness? They don't even put a sheet beneath their quilts!

The room is very beautiful, with wonderful floors made of marble and black stone. It is a pity that the rooms are not kept clean. Typically, in an English hotel one may obtain both hot and cold water whenever one desires, but here there is no hot water. There was only one towel, and it too was dirty and smelly. I said to Sarkar: Well, now that I'm already here, I'll stay the night, but only because the name of the hotel is blessed and because it is owned by people of the faith. Otherwise, I wouldn't stay here for even a minute.

We arranged for an additional room and told Amina Bi to sleep there. That's when I noticed that the bathroom was extremely foul. It had such a stench that it set my brain to rotting. Inside there was a squat toilet. There was water everywhere. In the bathroom there was a dirty tin cup and a container filled with water. This container had a spout. Even though the bathroom floor was also made of marble, it was kept in a filthy state. I declared that I could not bring myself to use that toilet. Nawab sahib sent for a "piss-pot" to be purchased for me. The bathroom was so small that it was difficult to close the door. The owner told us that the rate of ten annas per night only included our stay—food, tea, and coffee were not available.

Once I had seen all of this, I said to Sarkar that it was only four in the afternoon, but the bathroom was not clean and that I wanted to take a bath before we went out into the city. I've heard, I told him, that the lustrous head of the Lord of Martyrs, the Oppressed of Karbala, the One Slain by Oppression and Cruelty, the grandson of the Prophet Muhammad-i Mustafa, Imam Husayn[5]—upon whom be peace—is buried here in Damascus. There are also tombs here belonging to other prophets and saints. When I had first learned of this, I was elated that we would have the honor of visiting the shrines and tombs of so many great figures. Nawab sahib replied, "All right, I will ask the man where the bathing place is." Sarkar then inquired with the owner of the hotel, who replied: "There is no hammam in the hotel, but there is one in the city."[6] When I heard this, I said that it was very inconvenient for the hammam not to be in-house, but in the city. "How am I to quickly bathe and be ready to go out now? I'm still dirty from the train, it's time for the afternoon prayer, and we are only here for one night!"

Sarkar then told me that "the way things work here is that men's and women's hammams are located in the city and everyone, both men and women, go there to bathe. It doesn't matter whether you're rich or poor, everyone goes there. The hammams are relaxing and very nice, and there are always people bathing in them." I replied that if that was what people did here, then fine, take me to the hammam. "I'll have a quick bath and then go and visit the shrines." I put a pair of clothes, some soap and flour,[7] a comb, and so forth into a small bag and left Amina Bi at the hotel to keep an eye on the luggage. Sarkar got out some clothes too, saying that he would have a bath at the hammam as well.

"Everyone's Naked in the Bath House"

The two of us set off from the hotel and found two hammams nearby, one for men, the other for women. I knocked on the door and a woman appeared from inside. When she saw me, she said, "Welcome, come in, come in." Accordingly, I went inside. Sarkar told me to bathe quickly: "I'll have a quick bath and then come out and wait for you." I agreed and went inside, where I saw thirty or forty women gathered. There were many small rooms in which rugs and carpets had been spread. In the very center of the courtyard of the hammam, there was a ceiling of translucent glass, such that sunlight could enter but the wind would stay out. In the middle of the courtyard, there was a pool filled with water. Light-skinned, rosy women who had finished with their baths were busy getting dressed. Others were taking off their clothes and heading into the hammam to bathe. All the men and women in Damascus are very light-skinned, with the exception of the Africans. I paused, thinking to myself that I was in quite the dilemma. I'll wait to begin my bath, I thought, until everyone else has finished. This being my intention, I was standing there waiting when a woman came up to me, took the bag from my hand, and began to remove my clothes. I said: "Wait, wait!" and she retorted, "No, hurry!" and said God knows what else in Arabic. I fell silent when I saw that she had no intention of listening to me. She took off all of my clothes. I wrapped myself up in a towel, and she took me by the hand and led me away. When I stepped foot into the next room, oho! my feet were immediately burned. There were vents in the ceiling above that allowed natural light to filter in and the hot steam to escape. I said, "Hey, you tyrant! Hang on, my feet are burning!" but she kept on dragging me, saying, "Come on, come inside."

In this way, we passed through three different levels of the hammam and entered into the fourth, where I saw all of the women seated barefooted before water taps, busy washing themselves. Hot water comes out of one tap and cold water from the other. There are small basins installed near the taps that fill with water when you release them. The woman began to rub my body, washing me. In fact, three or four of the women stopped bathing themselves and, coming over to me, began to scrub me as well. In Arabic, they asked me, "Who are you? Where are you from?" I said to them, "I am Indian. In India, the hammam is at home. In town, there is no hammam, but here, I saw the hammam is in the town, in the home there is none. I am astonished."

With great effort, I managed to give answers to a few of their questions. These women washed me more thoroughly than I'd ever been washed in my entire life. Here I am in this huge rush to leave, and they keep on pouring out more and more water! At last, I managed to escape them. I wrapped that same wet towel around myself so I would not be entirely naked when I exited the hammam, but all of them called out to me, saying, "Hey, sister, there are only women here." I said, "Yes, but I [still] need a towel."

I began to leave but they took hold of me, saying, "Don't go, don't go, sit, sit down for just a while more." I replied, "I don't wait, I am in a hurry, husband at door." They reluctantly released me. I exited the bathing area. When I had first entered the hammam, my feet were scorched from the heat; now, on exiting, the very same floor felt cool to the touch. I rushed to the exit and took a seat on the bench outside in the courtyard. A woman came up to me and began to dry my hair. She asked me, "Oh, Indian, are you well?" I replied, "Very well." To make a long story short, I got dressed and handed the woman a shilling. I said goodbye, picked up my bag, and went out to find Sarkar waiting for me outside. We returned to the hotel to give Amina Bi my bag and then immediately set off.

The Umayyad Mosque

First we went to the famous Ummayad Mosque. We rushed there so we would arrive in time for the sunset prayer. We passed through the Damascus bazaar on the way there. The bazaars here are roofed so the people inside them can remain protected from the rain and sun. Typically, bazaars are open air. They often have canals of flowing water. All the people of Damascus are of a white and rosy complexion. The women's manner of dress is entirely European, and even their hair is kept in the same style as that of European ladies, though they do not wear hats. Whether rich or poor, whenever these ladies go out for a walk or go shopping, they put on a simple skirt. On their heads they wear a shawl of the same color as that of their skirt. This shawl extends down to their hands. They draw a veil over their faces, wear gloves on their hands, take up their umbrellas, and then leave their houses. Often, the older women will tie a handkerchief around their heads, but their outfit is always the same, either something resembling a dressing gown, or else a skirt and blouse akin to those European ladies wear. Children wear a similar frock, and many of them tie a handkerchief over their face as high as their ears. Here, the custom is for all Muslim women to go out in the city without any big to-do. This is a great convenience for them—may God grant the women of India the same freedom from their unjust imprisonment. There was another thing here that pleased me greatly, namely, that whenever women go out in the city, the men keep their distance and treat the women with respect. This is in contrast with India, where women have no respect before men. Oh, how unfortunate are the people of India!

The Blessed Shrine of the Head of the Martyr of Karbala, Imam Husayn, Peace Be upon Him

After having seen everything here and—al-hamdu lillah!—having been blessed by our visits to these shrines, we departed in order to enter into the service of the Martyr of Tyranny and Injustice, the forbearing youngest grandson of the merciful Prophet, our dear Imam Husayn, upon whom be peace. I had heard that the head of our dear Imam (upon whom be peace) is buried here. We presented ourselves there, standing before the shrine with the greatest possible reverence. The moment we arrived, my heart was overwhelmed by a strange sensation that I am incapable of describing. Nawab sahib said, "Just look at the effect that this place has on the heart." "Yes," I replied, as tears began to fall from our eyes. It was my heartfelt desire never to part from there. A full hour passed, and yet we had not moved. Our hearts were unwilling to leave. It was only when the sound of the evening call to prayer met our ears that our hearts came to their senses. We recited the fatiha and, giving our respects once more, took our leave. Allah, Allah! Only those who have experienced the kindness and mercy that the family of the Prophet bestows on the members of this sinful community of believers may truly know the joy it brings. I am unable to describe the sense of tranquility and comfort that descended upon my heart, the extent to which I was affected by this experience.

December 8, 1909

We woke up in the morning. Al-hamdu lillah, we performed the dawn prayer and then had some breakfast. I very much wanted to go back to the hammam to bathe once more, in part because it gave relief to my body, but also because it was one of the more memorable experiences of our trip. I expressed these thoughts to Sarkar, who in turn asked the hotel owner if there were any hammams open for use in the morning, for, if so, we should like to go. He replied, "No, none are open until after noon." We were planning to catch a twelve o'clock train, so I said that it didn't matter, leave it be. But then, a short while later, the hotel manager came to us and said, "There is a hammam that will open in half an hour. My wife is coming now. She will take your wife there and point it out to her." I got my bag and put my clothes and things in it. Once I was ready to go, I sat down to wait so that moment the Arab woman arrived we would be able to set off. As I was waiting there, an Arab woman wearing a beautiful Turkish skirt and a veil over her face appeared before me and said, "Please, let's go."

Together, we departed. Sarkar went out to wait for the train. This woman took me to her house. I liked her house very much because both the house itself and the floor were cleaner than the hotel. There was a canal of water that ran through it. The house was two-storied. She showed me the first floor before we proceeded to the second. Here I found a large room with the floor covered by a beautiful carpet. There were beautiful sofas and chairs. The hotel owner's mother was seated on a raised platform upon which a soft mattress had been placed. The poor woman was very weak. When she saw me enter the room, she raised herself up with the greatest difficulty, saying, "Please, please, come in." I took her by the hand and helped her to sit down again, saying that she should not go to such trouble. Then the hotel owner's sister and daughter came in. All of these women were dressed in English clothes. The girl was wearing a frock. They were very beautiful, and their complexion was extremely fair. I don't like the style of Damascene houses. For one thing, they are all several stories high, and on top of that, the rooms are often very dark. This room, however, was very bright. Soft, cushioned seats lined the walls for people to sit on. I went and sat near to the hotel owner's mother. All of these women spoke Arabic. It was unfortunate that I could only understand them with difficulty. They were very hospitable toward me. They served me coffee. Coffee here is drunk without milk, yet it is still very delicious. It is consumed from tiny little cups that are called *finjan* here. Twenty minutes later, the hotel owner's wife got up, put on her veil, and said, "Come, sister, we must go to the hammam." "Okay," I replied. I said my goodbyes, kissed the hands of them all, and departed. The custom here is to join and kiss each other's hands at the time of departure.

The lady and I arrived at the hammam some ten minutes later. Just as before, I went inside. I had a relaxed bath, got dressed, and then left again. I gave a shilling to the attendant and eight annas to the hotel owner's wife. This made her very happy. I met Sarkar while we were still on the road. We both returned to the hotel to collect Amina Bi and the luggage. We paid the hotel owner what we owed him. The Arab woman came to me once more and said, "Come, I will show you around." I said to Sarkar that we still had a little time, and that if he so willed, that I would go with this woman for a while. Sarkar gave his permission. I went with that woman. She took me to a shop, the owner of which turned out to be English. I asked him, "*Yu ispik Inglish?*" He said, "*Yas.*" I bought a warm pair of gloves and three frocks that caught my eye and quickly returned to the hotel.

FURTHER READING

Begum Nawab Sarbuland Jang. *Dunya 'aurat ki nazar meñ—mashriq o maghrib ka safarnamah.* Delhi: Khwaja Buk Dipo, Khwaja Barqi Pres, n.d. Further translated excerpts from this text, as well as the original Urdu, are available online at https://accessingmuslimlives.org/travel/eyes/.

Nawab Muhammad Hamidullah Khan Sarbuland Jang. *Safarnamah-i Qustuntuniya.* Hyderabad: Qasim Pres, n.d.

Nawab Sarbuland Jung Bahadur Muhammad Hamidullah Khan. *A Pilgrimage to Mecca and the Near East.* Secunderabad: Bulletin Press, 1912.

Nawab Server-ul-Mulk Bahadur. *My Life: Being the Autobiography of Nawab Server-ul-Mulk Bahadur.* Translated by Nawab Jiwan Yar Jung Bahadur. London: Plymouth Press, n.d.

David Lelyveld. *Aligarh's First Generation: Muslim Solidarity in British India.* Princeton, NJ: Princeton University Press, 1978.

NOTES

1. All subheadings in this chapter come from the original text.

2. This honorific title, like sarkar in a later paragraph, refers to the author's husband. In keeping with the customary practice of her time, Begum Sarbuland does not take her husband's name in the account, nor does she offer her own.

3. This refers to the local representative of the well-known travel company Thomas Cook.

4. There are sixteen annas in a rupee.

5. Husayn was the grandson of the Prophet Muhammad. At the Battle of Karbala in 680, he was defeated by the Umayyad caliph Yazid and beheaded. His body was buried in Karbala, but his head was likely taken to Damascus and later buried there.

6. Conversations held in Arabic are typically written out in Arabic in the text without translation. Begum Sarbuland's Arabic is functional but broken, and the glosses provided here are meant to convey that sense.

7. Flour, often scented, was commonly used while bathing to facilitate scrubbing, prevent dryness, and give the bather a pleasant fragrance.

RAHIL BEGUM SHERVANIYA

Life Aboard a Pilgrim Ship

INTRODUCTION

Rahil Begum Shervaniya (1894–1983), also known as Bibi Rahila Khatun, led an active and tumultuous life defined by politics, educational reform, travel, and migration. She was born in Aligarh, India in the late nineteenth century and died in Pakistan nearly nine decades later. Raised in an influential North Indian family, she never attended public school. Nevertheless, her biographer records that she received such a fine education at home that she could "inspire jealousy in all of the women who studied in schools and colleges." She was widowed early but dedicated her subsequent life to a range of social and political projects largely connected with the All-India Muslim League and women's education. She was also the author of occasional essays, books, and poetry. The excerpts translated here are taken from her account of a journey to the Middle East entitled *Zad al-sabil, ya, rahlat al-Rahil* (*Provisions for the Journey, or, The Travels of Rahil*) composed during her trip in 1923–24 and published in 1929.

Many aspects of Rahil's life and work were defined by her prominent and famously tight-knit family, the Shervanis. The Shervani clan traced its roots to the city of Jalalabad, just beyond the Khyber Pass in present-day Afghanistan. The family would migrate to India, eventually becoming semi-independent rulers of two small states, Dataoli and Bhikampur, both near Aligarh. They practiced cousin marriage, which prevented the gradual dispersion of family property but also eventually led to later generations having health problems due to inbreeding. In the nineteenth century, the family joined other noble and well-to-do

Daniel Majchrowicz prepared the introduction and translation from Urdu.

north Indian Muslims in a range of intellectual and political movements. These included offering significant support to Sir Sayyid Ahmad Khan and his Muhammadan Anglo-Oriental College at Aligarh, as well as eventual membership in the All-India Muslim League.

Rahil Begum's family tree is laden with famous figures of modern Indian history. Even a cursory look at her immediate family members offers a sense of their accomplishments and influence. Her brother, Harun Khan (1891–1980), was a widely respected historian of South Asia and a recipient of one of independent India's highest awards, the Padma Bhushan. Her father, Nawab Musa Khan (1872–1944), was the founding secretary of the All-India Muslim League. Other close relatives were rulers or high-ranking ministers in a range of princely states across India. Women of the family were also celebrated for their accomplishments, largely achieved while in purdah and while being educated at home. These include Rahil Begum Shervaniya herself, as well as the more well-known Zahida Khatun Shervani (1894–1922), a women's rights activist and a popular poet who maintained purdah and published under the pseudonyms Nuzhat and Ze Khe Shin.

Rahil Shervaniya was thus born into an intellectually and politically vibrant home that headquartered the Muslim League in its earliest years. It is said, perhaps apocryphally, that she was admitted as a member of the Muslim League at the tender age of twelve. She saw many of northern India's most influential figures pass through her home. Her intimacy with the ruling elites of the day deepened with her marriage. She was wed, against family norms, in 1920 not to a cousin but to Yahya Beg, a north Indian aristocrat and the son of a high-ranking figure in the Hyderabad State government. Her husband's sister was Begum Sarbuland Jang (also featured in this collection), who, having traveled herself throughout the Middle East in 1909–10, helped Rahil Begum to prepare for the trip documented here. Yahya Beg died after three years, leaving Rahil Begum a young widow with two small children. She declined to remarry and, by her own account, dedicated her life to women's education and the independence cause.

After her return to India from the hajj, she served on various boards and councils for the Muslim League as a representative of Muslim women. She was a founding member of the Women's Committee of the Muslim League alongside another travel writer in this volume, Begum Habibullah. Rahil Begum also worked to promote women's education and rights in the spirit of Sir Sayyid Ahmad Khan's reformist mission, founding the Anjuman-i Dar al-Khavatin and a women's school in Aligarh. Her efforts contributed to the development of the Aligarh Muslim University Girls' College. After the Partition of India in

1947, she migrated to Karachi with her two sons, where she continued her work for social welfare and women's education.

Rahil Begum also published sporadically throughout her life. She began writing essays at the age of nine with her family's encouragement, and published her first piece, "Ms. and Mrs.," in the women's magazine 'Ismat in 1908. She continued to write various articles on issues related to women, particularly in Sharif bibi, which was edited in Lahore by Fatima Begum (who is also featured in this collection). Later in her life, she wrote poetry, newspaper articles, and at least one other book (Ta'sir-i sohbat) in addition to the travel account translated here.

After Rahil's husband tragically passed away early in their marriage, she resolved to perform the hajj to help distract herself from the pain of his loss, a fact that she emphasizes in the early pages of the account. This was no easy journey for a single woman, but she was adamant that only a visit to Medina and Mecca could give her solace. And so, she set off with a few close family members, including her brother Muhammad Shis Khan, for a nine-month journey through the Middle East in 1923–24. The account she wrote on her return and published several years later is among the most exceptional travel accounts ever written in Urdu. It is at times playful, offering a seemingly endless series of humorous stories about her fellow travelers. At other times, it employs a more serious tone, lamenting the loss of her husband and examining with concern the latest developments in political Islam. The passages taken below are drawn from the earliest pages of Rahil's travel account, just as she had set out from Bombay for Arabia. They highlight not only her sharp eye and biting satire, but also the struggles that women travelers in particular faced.

EXTRACTS

Life Aboard Ship

Tea was brought to us early this morning, even before I had finished my prayers. Leaving my cabin after tea, I saw that there were no signs of dry land in sight—all was sky and water. I'd always heard that it was terrifying to see nothing but blue in all directions, that I would feel dizzy and nauseous, that I would not be able to hold down food, much less worry about how the others were doing. But I did not find this to be the case at all. Our ship was of such a fine quality that I did not feel any kind of dizziness, nausea, distress, or fear. So I put on a burqa and took a walk around the ship to see what the state of the other passengers was. Everywhere, on both sides of the main deck as well as in first class, people were merrily eating and drinking with one another. In short, our days on the ship began with general wellness and contentment. Thanks be to God.

Our ship weighs ten thousand tons and is extremely grand, large, and of the highest quality. It previously belonged to the German navy but was purchased by Namazi sahib a year or two ago with the intention of making it the equal of every other ship in the dock. The Namazi Company has met with great success in this venture. Truly, this ship is just like the regular mail ships. Everything is of a high quality. All is orderly, clean, and punctual. All that might be required is available, and no one, whether of high status or low, could have any room for complaint. The food on board, which we were able to experience, was varied and of a high quality.[1] The ship's officers would regularly come to inquire after our needs. They treated my brother Muhammad Shis Khan with great affection and sincerity. The speed of the boat was so well managed that, sitting in our rooms, we were unable to say whether the ship was moving or stationary. It was only when you stepped outside and looked at the water that you could know if it was moving or not. In short, we were more comfortable on board than in our own homes. We had no need to open our bags, for all our requirements were met on the ship. Everything was provided: towels, bedding, sheets, and so on, so that the locks on our luggage were never once opened, and our days were spent in complete comfort.

But then, the conditions of Muslims are always deplorable. Thus, the twelve hundred pilgrims on our ship—some rich, some poor, and from all sorts of backgrounds—were ungrateful, despite all the comforts being made available to them. Every day they fought among themselves, every day stole from one another. The poor ship's officers were tired of dealing with it. Our chief officer couldn't understand much Urdu, so when a case was brought before him, he would take my brother Muhammad Shis Khan along with him to act as translator. Because of this, most of the people began to think ill of us and accused us of colluding with the crew against them. And when incidents like this occur, Muslims all stand up to bring their brothers to their own side.

And the state of these Muslim brothers is that they badly mistreat the Chinese laborers who constantly toil in the service of the passengers, who promptly and cheerfully clean up the pilgrims' filth, and whom they consider Bhangis just because they belong to the Christian faith, not even allowing them to pass by in the hallways. They fear that their clothes may come into contact with those of the Chinese and thus be defiled. And they criticize Namazi sahib, asking what kind of a Muslim would pollute his fellow Muslims by employing Chinese people. The passengers slap them on the back when they walk by, poke them with sticks, or purposefully bump into them just to bother them. They constantly complain to the officers about the Chinese. These complaints are ignored, which leads the passengers to accuse the officers of unfairly favoring "the Bhangis." The poor officers implore the passengers not to act in this way, saying that it would be a total disaster should the Chinese staff decide to go on strike. The passengers reply in turn that would be just fine, that they would be glad if they went on strike, for then the officers and Namazi sahib would get their just desserts for hiring them in the first place. One might ask these people just what they would say to Namazi sahib, when they well know what would happen should the ship come to a standstill in the middle of the ocean. I'm sick and tired of hearing these things day in and day out.

And then there are our respected sisters, who chew paan and spit its juices out. Oftentimes they spit against the wind, such that the juice is carried back into the room in a thousand different drops. Sometimes it lands on the face of a European, sometimes it ruins another's clothes. These people can't take a breath without complaining to me, but the moment I complain, I'm taken to task. My brother has become friends with the son of a trader named Mr. Headley. On one occasion, he brought his bedsheet to my brother, asking him to request them not to act in this way, but we had by this time already become infamous among the passengers, who said we were as good as infidels and would never support them. Alas, I am compelled to write that these ignorant pilgrims are more suited to rickety cargo ships where horses and goats are given the same treatment, and where they would be so thrown about that they wouldn't be able to raise their heads.

God! These people's antics nearly ruined our own trip after we told them once or twice to stop acting up. From that moment, they marked us out as enemies and accused us of being in cahoots with the English. People started to whisper among themselves, saying that we were spies or were affiliated with the secret police—otherwise, why would we act so differently from the other pilgrims? "If we say that day is night, then they should agree with us! Look at the way the English babble away with Muhammad Shis Khan from morning until night! They are definitely talking about us. They aren't here to perform the hajj—they've been sent by the English to disturb the real pilgrims. Look at the way they interact with the ship's crew! The staff are always ready to serve them. Their rooms are cleaned four whole times a day. Their chairs are brought onto the deck and returned at the appropriate times without them even saying a word. They even eat the food prepared in the ship's kitchen! The officers don't make a decision without consulting with them first. This is no secret; everyone knows it. Just wait and see what sort of mischief they get up to. We should never have boarded this ship." The people say these things to our faces, asking us if Namazi sahib is a relative of ours. Why else would the ship's officers treat us so well? In short, it was as though we were nothing but crows among a flock of swans. People only spoke to us to taunt and jab us; no one ever conversed with us normally. Then, because we acted according to the Persian aphorism "*javab-i jahilan bashad khamoshi*" [the best response to the ignorant is silence], they all assumed that we were intimidated by them.

Also in first class is a man named Hafiz Muhammad Amin sahib, who is traveling with his mother. They belong to a respected trading family of Delhi. His mother treats me with love and kindness. She is very caring and treats me as though I were family. She is always telling me to ask her for anything I might need. They are staying in the room opposite ours. Sometimes she sends over some chicken she's cooked, sometimes some fruit. I always tell her that we get everything we need in excess from the ship, but she never listens. In fact, she seems far more generous than she ought to be. She treats everyone on the ship with great kindness. Because she cares so deeply for us, she has given me friendly advice on several occasions. She suggested that I tell my brother to break off his relationships with the ship crew since it was unjustly causing strife with the other passengers. She even suggested that we stop eating food provided by the ship and eat with her instead. I did not agree—when I have not sinned in the eyes of God, why should I be afraid of His servants? She was also worried that I might—God forbid—be eating non-halal meat. She wouldn't hear a word to the contrary. She tells the others passengers that it is "their own grave, their own judgment. Even if they are secret police, or spies, or English agents, what's it to you?" But, poor thing, no one would have a word of it. There are about twenty-one people in her party here with us, but none of them are pure of heart. Of course, they all make a pretense of civility.

On Luggage

As a rule, pilgrims tend to bring with them far more luggage and supplies than they need. I suspect, though, that brother Muhammad Amin sahib has outdone everyone else in the quantity he has brought. Alongside all the other baggage, he's also brought with him three trunks of ice that have been melting throughout the sea journey. One trunk of ice lasted six days. The second lasted two. The third one produced only a small chunk of ice weighing less than half a *seer*. Now, after drinking so much ice water, how can one go back to unchilled water? These poor people are now suffering greatly without ice in their water. Shis Khan has had two bottles of ice water saved especially for them, as we would receive five bottles of ice-cold water per day. First-class passengers were not prohibited from drinking this water, but then, how could a pilgrim drink water served by Chinese hands? But when it was learned that free ice water was available, plenty of people quickly broke their vows and began to order bottles of their own. The same people who would not let the Chinese even touch their buckets now were now drinking the water served by those same hands.

One day, all the women from Delhi were sitting with me when the topic of luggage came up. They said to me, Sister, it seems as though there isn't a single piece of luggage in your room. I replied that all of our luggage was in the hold, that is, the ship's storehouse, and that I only have a few things with me in the room. Because I don't need to keep opening up my bags, I've kept the ones in my room stored under the seats. One of them asked me how much luggage I was traveling with. I replied that we had four boxes, two trunks, and a roll of bedding. "What about your cooking supplies?" she asked. They are all stored in the luggage, I said. One asked how many food stores I had brought. None whatsoever, I answered. Of course, on the advice of others, I had brought with me a can of ghee, but I've since heard that we will have to pay a tax of thirty rupee per canister in Jeddah, and now I am thinking that I should just distribute that ghee to passengers on the ship and avoid the headache of haggling over the tax. When the women heard this, they began to whisper agitatedly among themselves. One spoke up to ask if I was really so concerned about a single canister. "We alone have four canisters with us, plus two sacks of wheat flour, a sack of rice, a sack of dal, spices and seasonings, and so on." I asked her what sort of disaster she was expecting that she would bring so many supplies with her. She replied, "Sister! We wouldn't be able to bear eating Mecca sharif's stinking ghee for a single day."

"Why? Aren't the residents of Mecca human too?"

"Human or not, everyone has their own habits and tastes. We'd rather eat boiled food than their ghee. Even if we have to go without food for four days, we won't put that ghee into our mouths."

To which I replied, "Well, then you yourself should take my canister of ghee. I will eat that sticky, rotten ghee instead."

She said, "The wheat there is so bad that it clogs up your intestines," and proceeded to trash every single grain in Mecca sharif. There were about twelve women there, each of whom took a turn to sing the highest praises of the items that they had brought with them, and to try to scare me by impressing upon me my impending suffering. I replied that I was not in the habit of making my choices based on what others told me, but that I would experience it myself and then decide.

"Every struggle on this particular journey is a blessing for me. Besides, you are elegant and refined women from the city of Delhi, so how can a village person like me, who is accustomed to eating whatever comes to hand, possibly be the equal of you?"

One particularly boastful woman replied, "It's true, sister, we would sooner go hungry than eat badly."

It was during the course of this conversation that I learned that my kind benefactor, Muhammad Amin's mother, had brought forty boxes with her, not including the foodstuffs. Each person tried to outdo the next in praising the quantity of the items that they had brought with them, and each of them likewise objected to my own decisions regarding my luggage.

But there were others aboard the ship who surpassed even this group in the art of preparing for a journey. For example, those who, in addition to all of their other belongings, also brought along sheep and goats to eat on the ship itself. It was typical for people to bring baskets full of chickens, which were slaughtered every morning. Worst of all were the baskets of paan that people brought with them, their size according to the status of their owner. I learned of two people who had several large baskets of paan, each basket containing five or six thousand leaves each. They would open them and dump the contents out every day.

Arabs and Indians

There is an Arab family traveling on our ship. They are about twenty to twenty-five men and women in total, and they've occupied four or five rooms in first class. They are traders from Bahrain. Before boarding this ship, they traveled from Basra to Karachi to Bombay. Every day they slaughter a sheep and, masha Allah, every day they eat the whole thing, for they are twenty-five people, plus servants. Obviously, the number of people is immense, and their belongings innumerable. They have some fifteen or twenty travel beds with them. By my reckoning, they have enough to fill a ship on their own. I do not exaggerate when I tell you that they have two cooks who prepare food twenty-four hours a day, and masha Allah, they use the largest cooking vessels imaginable. They've definitely outdone the Indians. Given that they use two canisters of ghee a week, you can imagine how much they have brought with them. Perhaps since they themselves are Arabs, they haven't brought many foodstuffs with them, but anyhow, I can't claim to know since they seem to have some type of disgust for Indians. What's more, they don't speak Urdu, so I haven't gone to meet their women. I pass in front of their cabins often enough, but aside from finding that they are avid eaters, I haven't been able to learn much else about them. The women are somewhat ahead of the men in terms of cigarette smoking.

The general condition of our wealthier fellow passengers, who are laden with goods, is that they make fun of those of us who have little. As for the poor passengers, Namazi sahib, may God bless him, has provided them all with food and drink for the journey. Approximately six *mans* of rice and one and a half *mans* of dal are cooked twice a day and are, masha Allah, consumed entirely by the pilgrims. . . . In short, we were all very comfortable and well provided for, free from the struggles of cooking and the trouble of lugging foodstuffs about. . . .

Nor did the poor passengers have any reason to worry. Nevertheless, they constantly fought among themselves, stole from one another, and were all around ill-natured. They wouldn't allow one another to pass in the walkways, and around sunset there would be such a tumult and such cursing on the deck that you could only seek refuge in God. Not once did it occur to them that they might gather together and enjoy one another's company. Instead, they were all out for blood. . . .

The essential problem is that Indians have lost their humanity in every possible way. This is especially true of Bengalis and Biharis—may God never ask us to travel with them! They have proven to be extremely dishonest, unclean, and impolite. Their actions are nothing short of animalistic. The more you tell them the better way to do a thing, the more they knowingly insist on doing the opposite. They harbor spite and malice for the sake of it.

This was the general state of things for four days. Now it seems the passengers as a whole have become bored with the journey and are content to sit and watch the land pass by.

Quarantine on Kamran Island

We left for Kamran in the very last boat. By the time we got there, most people had already been through the sanitization process. I went straight to where the doctor was sitting and lay down on a bed by him. In the meanwhile, Muhammad Shis Khan arrived, and I asked him to inform the doctor that since I'd had a runny nose and a fever since the previous night, it would be best if I could be excused the mandatory bath. He told the lady doctor as much, but it seemed she couldn't care less.

What happened next was that I went into the room where you change your clothes for the bath. This is a large room where there are 1.5-yard towels stacked up to a height of about twelve hand widths. The women working in this room are incredibly ill-bred and rude. Their behavior is like that of wild animals. They treat the pilgrims very badly and don't say anything directly unless it's crass. When I entered, ten or twelve of the Arab women from Bahrain, the mother of Muhammad Amin, and the wife of Hafiz Hamidullah sahib Dehlavi were already there in addition to a few other foreign women. We were told to take off our clothes and tie towels around ourselves. I refused. One, because I was ill, and second, because the towels were not large enough to cover my private areas. One of the workers told me that this is all we would be allowed and then gave me a few choice words. I ripped right back into her. I told her that worthless women like her were looting the honor of noble women. "How dare you speak to me in this way? Get out of the room. We'll manage the bathing ourselves." She immediately went out and called for a nurse who did not yet know what was going on inside.

The nurse came to me and began to explain. "Sister, we have no choice; these are the government's orders."

"What kind of government is this, and who can obey such a terrible order? I'd rather die than wear this towel."

"You're getting the others excited."

"Absolutely, I am! Look at the way you are looting our honor."

"There are only women here. There are no men."

"You go and take your clothes off in front of the men. I'm not going to take my clothes off in front of women, and nor am I going to put on one of these hand-sized towels. This is un-Islamic. You ill-mannered women!"

When she heard this, she got very angry and immediately left the room. I went out behind her. She went to the doctor and complained to him in Arabic. I also went up to him and said, "Doctor, first of all, I've already had you informed that I am unwell. And even if I was well, I still wouldn't bathe with and in front of so many other people." The doctor took my pulse. Because I was so angry, my temperature was even higher than before. After taking my pulse, he told the lady doctor in English that I really did have a fever, and then, turning to me, said gently that if I did not follow the regulations, all the other women would protest as well. Again to the lady doctor, he said, "Please go with her and insist that they not pour water over her." I went back inside and asked the lady doctor to give me at least three towels. When I had removed my clothes, she gave me a few. I had no choice but to change my clothes. Back in the main room, I watched the Arab women from Bahrain wail as those terrible workers forcibly stripped off their clothing. The women from Delhi asked me where I'd been. I replied that I'd been to complain to the government. Each of the women was given but one towel.

"A poor person's anger hurts none but themselves."

We all proceeded into the bathing room together. Here we were forced to face a new calamity. Affixed to the ceiling of the bathing room were about twenty sieve-like devices from which water flowed when the handle was turned. The lady doctor put me in a corner of the room away from the others and left. The four angels of hell were posted in that room. One after the other, they dragged the women to the shower of water and forced them to stand beneath it. The room was filled with women alternately soaking in the water, shivering from having been soaked in the water, or standing in horror. It looked for all the world like the Day of Judgment. Al-hamdu lillah, I was standing far away wrapped up in three or four towels. Even so, quite a lot of water flew through the air and landed on me.

One of my towels was soaking wet. All of a sudden, one of the female servants opened a door behind me and, using gestures, told me go to through it. I went, and what did I see but dozens of women sitting there, soaked to the bone. As soon as I entered, one of them asked me, "Didn't you take a bath?" I told her that I had a fever. Another one asked me the same thing. I didn't reply. Then a third. Then a fourth. Now, I was already worked up from before, and their incessant accusations made it even worse. Finally, I became totally fed up and told them to mind their own business and not worry about what others were doing if it didn't concern them.

"It's a good thing that I didn't have to bathe, so what's it to you?"

"Well! Someone's a hothead."

"Her money's made her haughty."

"She gave a bribe, and now she shows up totally dry."

"No ma'am, she pulled a fast one to get out of it. The women with her haven't come out yet."

"Were you alone in the bathing room?"

"Yes," I replied. As this was happening, all the other women who were with me came into the room shaking and shivering. They'd just come from the steam room. All of our clothes were returned to us, now very warm. The room was extremely humid. To make a long story short, we all thanked God when we were finally released from that prison.

FURTHER READING

Rahil Shervaniya Begum. *Zad al-sabil, ya, rahlat al-Rahil*. Aligarh: Matbaʿ-i Muslim University, 1929. Additional translated extracts from this text are available online at https://accessingmuslimlives.org/travel/rahil/.

Hajji ʿAbbas Khan Shervani. *Shirvani-namah*. ʿAligarh: Shirvani Printing Pres, 1953.

Gail Minault. "Zay Khay Sheen, Aligarh's Purdah-Nashin Poet." n.d. http://www.columbia .edu/itc/mealac/pritchett/00urduhindilinks/srffest/txt_minault_zaykaysheen.pdf.

Francis Robinson. *Separatism among the Indian Muslims: The Politics of the United Provinces*. Cambridge, UK: Cambridge University Press, 2007.

NOTE

1. That she could speak to the quality of the food on the ship is noteworthy here because in this period passengers had the option of cooking for themselves rather than eating from the ship's mess. The reasons for doing so might be pecuniary or religious, because many Indian passengers felt they could not be certain that the fare provided onboard was halal.

TEN

NUR BEGUM

Poems from a Punjabi Pilgrim

INTRODUCTION

Nur Begum was not elite, urbane, or even particularly wealthy. Nevertheless, she left her village in Punjab, India, to perform the hajj in 1931.[1] The voyage lasted three months and included a journey by train to Karachi and by steamship to Jeddah. She undertook the dangerous voyage to Mecca and Medina by camel, even as her wealthier compatriots went by motorized transport. Likely the first in her family to make this journey, she traveled with a contingent from her village that included her mother and husband. After returning home, Nur wrote an account of her experience in Punjabi verse and published it in 1933 under the title *Mazahir-i Nur: safarnamah-yi Nur bara'e hajj o ziyarat-i Huzur* (*Manifestations of Celestial Light: Nur's Travel Account of the Hajj and Pilgrimage to the Exalted One*) (see fig. 10.1). It is among the earliest known travel accounts in Punjabi, and it is all the more noteworthy for the fact that she was one of the few women of her time from a rural background to publish a travel account.

The poem is divided into two sections: a travel narrative and a separate guide to the proper performance of hajj rites, with the narrative portion comprising approximately fifteen hundred lines. Her account is marked as much by intense piety as it is outspokenness, and she shifts between praising God and weighing in on all manner of social, political, and religious issues. She was particularly incensed by Wahhabi impositions at Mecca and Medina, the prohibition of certain religious practices, and the destruction of sacred sites. Her strongest words, however, are reserved for the men at home in Punjab

---

Daniel Majchrowicz prepared the introduction and translation from Punjabi.

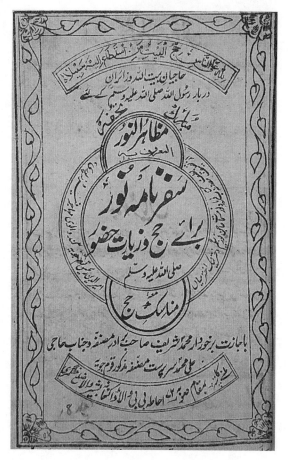

Figure 10.1 The title page of Nur Begum's
Mazahir-i Nur (1933). Courtesy of Daniel
Majchrowicz.

who degraded her for her poetry and apparently even accused her of learning
the art through illicit interactions with unrelated men. Through supplications
to God scathingly transposed into verse, Nur asks God to remind the envious
that He himself has bestowed on her these talents, and that there is no cause
for shame in a woman's poetry!

If Nur did have detractors, there were many more who relished her emotive
lines. *Mazahir-i Nur* went into at least three large print runs. Despite this, she
and her poetry are now entirely forgotten. The only information we possess
about her life is contained within the single edition of her travelogue still extant. Her nom de plume was Nur (light) and her real name was Ghulam Fatima.
She grew up in Kandhwala, a small market town near Abohar, India, one of
several children born to her father, Miyan Amiruddin Kandhvalvi. The family
belonged to the Jauiyah caste and were perhaps small *zamindars*, or members

of the land-owning gentry. At the time of her pilgrimage, she was married, but the couple may not have been able to have children, for she writes that poetry would be her only legacy.

Nur was widely read and deeply versed in the Islamic sciences at a time when the great majority of women in Punjab were illiterate. She studied both the Quran and the hadith, and her expertise in these fields is obvious: the travelogue repeatedly offers citations and commentary on classical Arabic sources alongside her own versified explication. In case her manifest erudition was insufficient attestation, the final pages of the book are filled with testimonials from religious scholars offering praise and certifying that her poetry and exegesis is informed, accurate, and edifying. These scholars, all men, recommend her book not only to women but also to all readers and would-be pilgrims.

When India was partitioned in 1947, Nur Begum and her family, who lived just a few miles from the new border, left Kandhwala for Pakistan. They probably first moved to nearby Sahiwal district, but by the early 1950s, she was living in Ichhra, Lahore, where she gave religious instruction to women. She published several books in addition to the travel account included here, all in verse. These include *Faryad-i Nur ba dargah-i Huzur* and *Nur ki pasdari ya chhatti rahdari*. Both discuss various religious matters. Promotional materials suggested that "anyone who can read Punjabi, but especially women" should learn from them. Unfortunately, both are now lost. Her choice to write in Punjabi was partly shaped by her gender, for Punjabi men often chose to write in Urdu. However, travel writing and even academic literature in Punjabi verse was remarkably popular in the Punjab during her lifetime.

Although she refers to herself as "weak, foolish Nuri," Nur Begum's verse is masterful. Her poem is written in a simple but poignant language that could be followed by any listener but at the same time celebrated by connoisseurs. Her writing, which defies any attempt at adequate translation, is deeply localized within an agrarian lifeworld. Its metaphors draw on imagery taken from everyday village life, as when she likens the color of the marble near the Kaaba to butter. She returns regularly to natural themes, using her observations of water, plants, and animals to describe her experiences and reaffirm her faith. Her palpable zeal and sincerity of devotion is omnipresent. For Nur Begum, everything related to this journey was a blessing and gift from God, hardships included. Her journey was by no means easy. Nur Begum traveled in purdah and often under grueling conditions. More than one of her companions died while en route. Even so, she remained positive and thankful. For her, this was a once-in-a-lifetime opportunity to be fully embraced. And of course, it was one to be shared with readers and listeners back home.

EXTRACTS

Departing from Home

I left my home on the Wednesday after Eid;
My father, uncles and aunts, none of them were with me.
Truly, the greatest sorrow is traveling without your loved ones!
Oh, it was death, undertaking this difficult journey alone![1]
The moment that I turned and set out for Mecca,
I felt deep sorrow, as though I had lost my own life.
I had my first taste of separation that day,
When my father and uncles seated me in the train.
But then, the happiness the kind Lord then granted me!
My entire community came to see me off with full honors.
My brothers and sisters were all there, and all my uncles, too.
They all gave this lowly, Joseph-like Nuri leave to depart,
But, like Jacob, my father would not give his permission.[2]
"It is not right that you go without me," he said repeatedly,
But his words meant nothing to this mothlike[3] heart.
"I must go, I must go!" I said, my ardor cresting ever higher,
But my father did not want me to go without him:
"No one should suffer abroad, far from their loved ones."
But whatever difficulties may befall one, all are ordained by God;
Even the cleverest person can never avert them, try as they might.
If it was fated for my dear father to accompany me,
We would have visited the Beloved's [the Prophet's] tomb together.
Since the day the Lord had me born in Kandhwala,
I had never once left it. What could I know of roads and rails?
Nor did the kind Lord ever show me a day of separation.
My family has always been near me, cooling me in the shade of their love.
My kind father has never once scolded me;
Like Jacob, he has always cared for me and loved me.
Never in life have I felt pain or suffering.
My dear family has always been near me; I have never had to seek their affection.
And yet, this mothlike heart could easily leave my dear friends behind forever!
I *must* leave them behind and depart for Medina!
For three days, I prepared for the journey as friends came to visit me.
They gave me love and shed rivers of tears at my departure.
"Oh, my dear," they said, "we cannot bear to see you go!"
But Nuri must leave soon, she can think of nothing else.
Nuri met with them and then slowly walked out the door.
As she went, every street and every lane sobbed, cries were heard all around.
She met with her brothers and sisters, then hastened on her way,
As people on every side entrusted her to God.

Friends and family accompanied her to the railway station, and,
Tears in their eyes, seated her in the train and went away weeping. . . .

Sailing from Karachi to Jeddah

When the hajjis boarded the ship, they all said bismillah.
They respectfully recited, *"Bismillah majriha wa mursaha."*[4]
Many of the passengers climbed aboard with absolute ease,
But then it was our turn, we who had never boarded a ship before.
We poor people said bismillah and placed our feet on the stairway.
Our hearts grew fearful as we saw the vessel rolling in the waves.
We were astonished, our weak hearts filled with fear,
So vexed were we that we could not utter a sound.
Then the people from Karachi came out onto the quay,
And when the ship began to move, they threw up their hands and cried.
All of the people began to wail as the anchor was weighed,
As though death had set upon the hajjis that day.
When the ship began to move, though, the hajjis fell silent;
Some lay down, others stretched out, and all drank from the cup of patience.
We went to our section, stretched out two curtains, and took our seats;
Our humble hearts felt poor and weak in this unknown place.
I hadn't realized that the ship had started to move;
I asked the people around me, "Brothers, when will we start the journey?"
They said to me, "We've already traveled twenty leagues!"
When I heard this, my humble heart was astonished,
For I was certain that when the ship began to move,
That we would all feel a jolt and be set rocking.
But there was no shudder, there was no shaking—it was completely smooth.
Finding it so, this humble one offered to sacrifice all to God.
We spent our first night there on the ship
As a corpse spends its first night in the grave—only God knew our condition!
What can I tell you? I spent the entire night fully awake;
Above, this massive ship, and below it, the fathomless sea,
And nothing at all there to support it.
These hundreds of thousands of pounds of iron afloat by God's grace alone;
Nay, not a hundred thousand pounds, but much more—its weight cannot be
    measured.
Yet it floats along, by God's grace, as though it were but a tuft of carded cotton.
Then, by His grace, Nuri heard the call to prayer just before dawn.
People stood, folded their hands in prayer, and came close to the Lord.
After the namaz, I recited more prayers and felt the fear of God.
All the hajjis were doing just as I was; none did anything else.
Everyone could be seen reading the holy Quran intently.

The poor creatures called out to God, crying, fearing for their lives.
I am a nightingale in the garden of heaven, not a fish of the sea!
Seeing the waves crashing in the ocean, I prayed to God.
All this time, I only thought of Him; nothing else entered my heart.
My blood dried up at the sight of the heaving blue ocean;
I had never even seen a swamp before, and now I was surrounded by blue water!
O Lord! Protect us! To whom can we appeal but You? . . .
We did not eat or drink. We forgot every task of this kind.
I called out repeatedly to God, for we were just like corpses.
Each of the hajjis was in exactly this state, their backs twisted with fear;
Young or old, it made no difference; no one had any enjoyment at all.
In every direction, only "Allah, Allah!" was heard, and nothing more.
The ship traveled forward smoothly, without rocking or shaking.
The ship was so large that it cannot be described;
It had all the splendor and energy of an enormous, wonderful city.
Once five pleasant days had passed, one after the other,
All the hajjis began to cry, "We're near to Aden now!"
As we neared Aden, all the hajjis had letters written up[5]
And sent their love to their families and relatives.
I too should hurry and write a letter to my dear father
And tell him about how we are faring, and relieve my restlessness,
For none of ours has performed the hajj for seven generations.
I alone have set out on this journey, leaving all behind and crying rivers of tears.
No hajji from among us has performed the hajj and returned to the village;
But the Lord has blessed us, He has worked a wonder!
What a glorious fate God bestowed on this clueless one.
I don't have the strength to praise all the sights that I have seen.
Now I will say bismillah, praise God, write a letter in verse,
And respectfully record each and every thing that I have seen:

Praise be to God, praise be to God, the Creator of the Worlds!
Without whom none in the heavens or earth could exist.
A trillion blessings and prayers upon the Pure Prophet,
And prayers for me, my grave, and for the Day of Judgment.
Prayers for the Companions, the martyrs, the *ghazis*, and the family of the Prophet!
May this lowly, useless Nuri pray for them night and day.
Having made her prayers, this lowly one seeks permission to serve
Her father, uncles, and each and every of her loved ones.
First, I respectfully send you my greetings
And then share with you, Father, how I have fared.
Praise be to God, Lord of the Worlds! He has taken care of me,
And by His grace, today this lowly one arrived in Aden.
We spent five days in the ship in complete comfort;
We have not felt any hardship, oh, my dear father!

Our ship is wonderful, it darts through the water.
We have not suffered any illness, pain, or sorrow;
Since we boarded this ship,
God ensured that we were more comfortable than even at home.
No one has gotten a headache or nausea, nor has anyone been shook about.
Subhan Allah! This great ship moves more smoothly than a buggy . . .
So far, Father, we have never been uncomfortable, and we are all very happy
May the Lord give you happiness and comfort always.
Inshallah, we will pray for your well-being;
May you please pray for ours in the mosque too.
Now I must end this letter, for we have arrived in Aden.
The ship has come to a stop and begun its activities here.
Please, take this letter to Kandhwala, let it arrive quickly!
And give my greetings to everyone, adults and children all.
I have, by the grace of God, come today to Aden;
Go quickly now, and share my news in Kandhwala!
Go and tell my father soon, lest he begin to despair;
Have this letter read aloud to everyone.

Quarantine on Kamran Island

The hajjis disembarked at Kamran and stood on the dock.
Wherever the officers told them to go, that is where they went.
"Ya hajji, ya hajji," they all called out with love,
And sent them to bathe in a strange, grand building.
The women went into a separate room to have their bath;
Each stood in line, one after the other.
This splendid, wonderful building defied description;
It had fountains built into the ceiling, water fell down like rain!
One mem and two Bedouin women led us all inside.
"Take off your clothes, and don't try to bribe us!"
When they commanded that we remove our clothing,
My weak heart became embarrassed and vexed.
It asked in shame, why should I remove my clothes?
It would be hard were only a few others present, and here there are thousands!
I folded my hands before the memsahib and gave her a signal with my eyes.
But when saw me she immediately shook her head and said:
"No one will accept gifts or bribes in this place;
Hurry up! Take off your clothes, all of you, my mothers and sisters!
We are doing what's best for you, by having you take a bath.
I don't take fees from anyone," she said, wagging her finger.
Then, pointing her finger at me, the memsahib said,
"Don't worry about being naked; I will give you some cloth."
She handed each woman two small pieces of cloth.

We wrapped one around our heads, and the other around our bodies.
Once we had put on the cloth, they lead us to the machine;
They took us to a bathing room with the showerheads.
Everyone had a precious showerhead to themselves;
Fountains of water fell on the head of every woman hajji.
Standing under the showers, all the women washed themselves;
As soon as you turned the knob, water fell down like rain.
From all directions you heard, *"Allah hu!"* so loudly nothing else could be heard.
Subhan Allah! We were surrounded by such energy,
The splendor of God's blessings on full display!
Mothers and sisters have come together from all over,
And now they are playing, laughing, and bathing together.
Once we were finished we retrieved our clothes from the steamer.[6]
When they opened the steamer, the clothes inside were warm.
The memsahib told us to pick out our own clothes ourselves:
"Take your time, make sure they are yours. Don't steal anyone else's!"
We quickly picked our clothes out and,
After putting them on, went away from there.

A Prayer in Mecca and a Defense of Poetry

The time for hajj was near, and everyone had gathered together.
There were so many people performing tawaf that it was hard to get a turn....
Women and men alike went around the Kaaba with passion and fervor:
In the court of God, no one is concerned with keeping purdah;
The Prophet himself said that women should not cover their faces during hajj;
They should tie the ihram and walk slowly around the Kaaba, never running.
The women here do not walk behind the men;
Their shoulders rub together as they walk around the Kaaba.
Crazy Nuri! Take hold of the door of the Kaaba and pray!
Inshallah all your prayers will be granted by He who hears the poor!...
O God! Your true lions never speak foolishly.
They embody the meaning of *la yuhibb ullah al-jahr.*[7]
O God! Whoever is intoxicated by *wa min al-nas yaqul*[8]
Is able to see through such foolish speech.
O God! How can those stricken with the disease of *ana khairun*[9]
Understand the meaning of *la yuhibb ullah?*
O God! I will speak the truth, and never will I fear it;
One should never fear those who accuse falsely.
O God! For as long as breath passes my lips,
I shall speak the truth, even if the whole world turns against me.
O God! Why are they so incensed when a woman writes poetry?
When they hear my cries [poems], people make a hundred thousand objections.
O God! Why do they erupt when they hear a woman's name?

Their own mothers are not donkeys either, after all!
O God! They stop at nothing to point their fingers at me.
Who else but You, Lord, will hear my unending plaints?
O God! You have given women so many blessings!
[Consider] the stories You relate in the Quran:
O God! Maryam, whose surat [chapter] is contained in the Quran
And who has been given such reverence—she too is a pure woman!
O God! And then there is the beautiful Surat Nur,
Which you sent down to defend those who are unjustly accused.[10]
O God! Beloved Aisha, who was the intimate of the Messenger of God,
Is highly regarded; she is a woman of the highest esteem.[11]
O God! And Hajira, who is close to You;
By Your grace and kindness, she too was made a woman!
O God! Where that great woman ran seven times,
Man will run in that place from now until the Day of Judgment!
O God! The practice of *sa'i* was instituted by a woman of blessed name.[12]
Those who look at me derisively are all liars and frauds.
O God! The water of the well of Zamzam is only famous because of a woman.
And then they look at Nur's books and mock them.
O God! There was in Mecca dearest Zubaida;
She too was born of a woman, she who caused a river to flow![13]
O God! This woman had been given such incredible intelligence;
Those born as men mocked her, but they could never unlock her secret.
O God! This river flows every which way;
It is no secret whence it comes, whither it goes.
O God! People benefit so much from the actions of women,
But when they read my plaints [poetry], the envious protest.
O God! The Quran bears witness that those who, like Hajira,
run the *sa'i* seven times, they will have all their sins washed away.
O God! It was *she* who came to pray, with trust and patience in God
To this uninhabited land, where there was not yet the House of God.
O God! This land was settled by that woman herself.
The House of God was built there, where *she* performed a prayer!
O God! Acting in the name of women, you have given us endless blessings.
People run here and return home fully blessed—a royal treasure open to all.
O God! Next comes Asiya bibi, who belonged to the Pharaoh;
You show in the Quran that she is close to you![14]
O God! You have bestowed on women so many honors
I ought to count out each one, so that the whole world may know.

Returning Home by Train from Bombay

Al-hamdu lillah! God brought our hajj journey to an end.
In Kandhwala, all of the women came out

To greet and congratulate this weak and useless Nuri.
After distributing gifts, prayer beads, Zamzam water,
dates, and soil from the sacred lands, I bring my hajj story to an end.

O crazed Nuri! People say that the race of women is weak and incomplete,
But everything that Nuri asked for, You gave freely!
People have forgotten the vastness of Your mercy.
They find no value in placing their trust in You.
People look at me and object; they say a man must have taught her poetry!
But they have forgotten the name of God—it is *He* who taught me!
In the time of Jesus, son of Maryam, the people began to ask:
How is it that this unmarried woman has given birth?
For so many years, no woman has ever become pregnant without a husband.
But Maryam replied: With God, everything is possible . . .
Inshallah, Nur will remain blessed by Your mercy,
And those who accuse me, saying a man has taught me, will lose their way.
Undoubtedly, I have been taught the meaning of the Quran,
And others have come to explain matters regarding the words of the Prophet,
But God has not given anyone the ability to teach the composition of poetry.
I composed these lines myself, and gave them to others to be printed.
Until today, this gift has never been stolen from a child of Adam,
Even as countless other oppressions and thefts have occurred.
Inshallah, Nuri's intentions and actions will always be proper,
And this will remain clear on the Day of Judgment.
I do not need disciples, I do not seek gifts;
I will not become a thief to gain the riches of the world.
There will be long lines at the gates [of heaven], but I will pass through easily,
And the enemies who slandered me will kindle the fires of hell.
Why should they be jealous that my Beloved has granted me a pilgrimage?
Speak badly of me as they might, they can do me no harm now.
I will keep writing books and poetry for as long as I live,
No matter how much they gossip and reproach me, I will never regret it.
I have no offspring in this world, but I do have this divine calling;
People are remembered by their children, but my legacy shall be this!
May I be remembered, through my writing, until the Day of Judgment,
And on that day, may God protect me from every hardship.

FURTHER READING

Nur Begum. *Mazahir al-Nur, al-maʻruf bih, safarnamah-i Nur baraʻe hajj o ziyarat-i Huzur.* 3rd ed. Lahore: Rahmani, [1952?]. Further translated extracts are available online at https://accessingmuslimlives.org/travel/light/.

Saurabh Mishra. *Pilgrimage, Politics, and Pestilence: The Haj from the Indian Subcontinent, 1860–1920*. Oxford: Oxford University Press, 2011.

NOTES

1. The author employs poetic license to convey the pain of separation; she in fact traveled with several friends and relatives.

2. A reference to the Quranic story of Joseph, according to which Joseph's brothers ask their father for permission to take him for an outing. Jacob hesitates, fearing for his son's safety. (Quran 12:12–13)

3. The moth, with its fatal attraction to the flame of the candle, symbolizes the crazed and devoted lover who seeks total union with God.

4. Quranic verse 11:41, "in the name of God is its course and its anchorage."

5. Many pilgrims would have been illiterate and would have dictated their letters.

6. At Kamran, clothing worn by pilgrims would be steamed to sanitize them.

7. Quran 4:148, "God does not like the mention of evil."

8. Quran 2:8, "And of the people are some who say, 'We believe in Allah and the Last Day,' but they are not believers."

9. Quran 7:12, "I am better [than he]," said boastfully by Satan in reference to Adam.

10. Quran 24:5–18 warns those who would falsely accuse a woman of immorality.

11. Aisha was one of the Prophet's wives and the daughter of the first caliph, Abu Bakr.

12. The wife of Ibrahim/Abraham is said to have run between the hills Safa and Marwah seven times in search of water for her son Isma'il. God blessed her efforts by causing a spring, called Zamzam, to appear. Every pilgrim to Mecca reenacts Hajira's search for water by performing the *sa'i*, that is, by running between Safa and Marwah seven times.

13. Zubaida was an Abbasid princess who spent vast sums of money digging wells to provide water for pilgrims, and she also built a subterranean canal to supply water to several areas visited during the hajj.

14. Asiya was the wife of the pharaoh in the time of Moses. Witnessing the miracles Moses performed in Egypt, Asiya accepted his god in secret and is held to be among the most exemplary of women. (Quran 66:11)

LADY EVELYN ZAINAB COBBOLD

At Home in the Hijaz with a British Convert

INTRODUCTION

Lady Evelyn Cobbold (1867–1963), known in later life as Zainab (see fig. 11.1), claimed to be the first European woman to complete the hajj. At the least, she was the first Englishwoman on record and the first to document her experiences. Her pilgrimage "from Mayfair to Mecca" was undertaken in 1933 to the great interest of the British press. She attracted attention as the sixty-five-year-old sister of an earl who himself had been awarded a Victoria Cross and was also lord-in-waiting to the king. Their parents were Charles Adolphus Murray, Seventh Earl of Dunmore, and Gertrude, Countess of Dunmore and daughter of the Second Earl of Leicester. After declaring bankruptcy when Evelyn was just one year old, they lived a peripatetic life between the Dunmore family estate in Scotland, the Earl of Leicester's seat at Holkham Hall in Norfolk, their villa in Cairo, and various holiday homes in North Africa.

Lady Evelyn attributed her acceptance of Islam, apparently never ratified with a formal conversion, to this North African childhood, writing, "I am often asked when and why I became a Moslem. I can only reply that I do not know the precise moment when the truth of Islam dawned on me. It seems that I have always been a Moslem." Her spiritual quest, facilitating her pilgrimage to Mecca, may have been inspired by her mother, who appears to have been attracted to a number of different sects and faiths before settling, with her husband, on Christian Science. From her father, Lady Evelyn must have inherited her wanderlust as he was a keen world traveler and later travel writer and novelist. Most celebrated was his

---

Siobhan Lambert-Hurley prepared the introductions, extracts, and annotations.

Figure 11.1 Lady Evelyn Zainab Cobbold with her grandson Toby being greeted by friends at Luxor station, Egypt, 1935. Courtesy of Angus Sladen.

epic journey through Afghanistan, Kashmir, Tibet, China, and Russian Central Asia documented in *The Pamirs* (1894). Another model for Lady Evelyn may have been her great aunt, Jane Digby, also known as Lady Ellenborough, who at the age of forty-six and after three marriages and many lovers traveled to Syria. There, she married a much younger Arab sheikh, Abdul Medjuel el Mezrab, with whom she lived until her death in Damascus in 1881.

Lady Evelyn met her own husband, John Dupuis Cobbold, the scion of a wealthy Suffolk brewing dynasty, in Cairo, where they subsequently married in 1891. The couple shared interests in travel and field sports in which they indulged from the Cobbold manor, Holywells, near Ipswich while also raising three children. But Lady Evelyn's aristocratic demeanor and Arab proclivities appear to have triggered an estrangement from her business-oriented husband and his conservative family that ultimately resulted in formal separation in 1922. Even before, Lady Evelyn had shown her independence by undertaking her first "pilgrimage" into the Egyptian desert (though she identified it as Libyan) with a female companion, Frances Gordon Alexander, around 1911. Their shared journey was documented in twin travelogues entitled *Wayfarers in the Libyan Desert* (1914), though under separate authorship with different publishers. Lady

Evelyn's version focused on her growing appreciation of Islam as a faith, even as she critiqued women's seclusion in Arab culture.

Not long after this journey, Lady Evelyn began receiving letters from Arab friends addressed for the first time to "Lady Zainab" or "our sister in Islam." At the same time, she initiated contact with Britain's growing Muslim community focused around the Woking Muslim Mission. Established in 1912, this organization sought to attract upper- and middle-class converts by showing Islam's compatibility with modern British society. A leading light was Muhammad Marmaduke Pickthall, a scholar and linguist, whom Lady Evelyn not only befriended but also quoted at length in her next travelogue, Pilgrimage to Mecca (1934), from which the extracts here are taken. Later, she also wrote a third travelogue, *Kenya: The Land of Illusion* (1935), which was more typical in focusing on landscape and wildlife.

Lady Evelyn's pilgrimage narrative was structured around the three cities in the Hijaz in which she stayed: Jeddah, Medina, and Mecca. Dated entries and use of the present tense indicate a diary format, but other sources reveal that her basic text was supplemented by long passages explicating Islam and Islamic history written under the guidance of two unnamed Muslim mentors. Her entire visit lasted about six weeks not including the lengthy journey to and from London—via Cairo and Port Said en route and Port Sudan and Marseilles on return—by train, steamship, and "air liner." Though her husband had died in 1929, Lady Evelyn still received a generous allowance negotiated at their separation that enabled her to travel in style and avoid inconveniences experienced by other pilgrims, including full quarantine, bumpy buses, and crowded lodgings. She was also the first outside King 'Abd al-'Aziz Ibn Saud's court to make the pilgrimage by car by his own permission.

Practical arrangements for a suitable vehicle and accommodation were fixed by her host in Jeddah, the explorer Harry St. John Philby, himself a convert to Islam (known as Hajji Abdullah Philby). Philby also provided Lady Evelyn with an escort, Mustapha Nazir, who appears several times in the provided extracts on the basis that he acted, in her own words, as her "shadow" while he "combined the duties of equerry and courier." Also featured are a number of other local acquaintances, including a circle of friends from Damascus and her hostesses at Medina and Mecca, with whom dialogue was facilitated by Lady Evelyn's at least rudimentary knowledge of Arabic. This element of "human interest" inspired largely complimentary reviews of her pilgrimage narrative in the contemporary press. Of particular interest to readers then as now was her nuanced depiction of Muslim women's lives in the harem that had been inaccessible to male travelers. Also appreciated was her spiritual sincerity despite her sometimes idiosyncratic approach to Islam.

EXTRACTS

Visiting in the Harem in Medina

March 17. This morning I was engaged in writing up my diary when I heard that some ladies were below waiting to see me. On being told they belonged to the family of an old friend in Damascus, I was glad to welcome them, and after unveiling and getting rid of their cloaks and hoods, they distributed themselves on the divans. There were five of them: the wife of my friend in Damascus, a very attractive personality, with a sweet expression; her sister with two young daughters; and another lady of a cheerful frame of mind, whose gay laugh infected us all. My hostess, the wife of the gentleman in whose house I was a guest, had already greeted me, and she returned to help me entertain them with tea and later with the unsweetened mocha coffee.

On removing their outer garments of the inevitable black silk or satin, these ladies were dressed in full trousers hanging in fold that fit tight below the calf of the leg and are very becoming to slim figures. They are generally made of striped silk or cotton, and a tight-fitting bodice with long sleeves is worn above, and over the whole hangs a loose transparent dress of white gauze. A piece of colored silk is wound round like a turban on the head with one end hanging down to the shoulder. Their hair hangs in two long plaits down their backs, very often twisted with gay ribbons or ropes of seed pearls. Powder and rouge is unknown, but they all have their eyes blackened with kohl, which they tell me softens the glare of the sun; as a rule, they have lovely teeth and carry themselves well.

They were very interested in hearing of my country and the lives we women live and asked me innumerable questions about our emancipation and our right to enter parliament and share in the government of our land. Also they enquire when and why I had become a Moslem, and on my admitting that I could read and write Arabic, I was taken to the texts hanging on the walls and asked to read them. Luckily I was able to do so; even the surah (chapter) "Ya Sin," which was written in the tiniest characters and embodied in the letters of Ya Sin, I could decipher as I knew that surah by heart.[1] Only two of my guests were able to read, although they all seemed very intelligent and well educated in other respects. They certainly were attractive little ladies, and I shall hope one day to meet them again, especially Fatima, the wife of Sid Ahmed as-Said, who, like her husband, was possessed with charm and sweetness of character.

When at midday I heard the Azzan [azan], I told them I was going to the mosque to pray and asked them to accompany me; they excused themselves, and on my return, I found them praying in my room. I then invited them to lunch and warned Mustapha, who occupied the room below, that the ladies were remaining and to order more food. We all sat round a large tray on which were dishes of spiced meat and vegetables, which we ate with our fingers and the aid of a spoon. Afterward a slave entered with a ewer and basin and soft towels, and we proceeded to wash our hands as she poured the water over them. The same scrupulous cleansing of the hands was done before we sat down to eat.

As I did not wish to forgo my midday sleep and the ladies showed no sign of departing, I asked their permission to rest, which was readily accorded. I lay down on my blanket and slept, to find on waking they were still there deep in conversation with my hostess, for the custom of the Arab ladies is to spend the entire day on a visit. So as the afternoon drew on, I left my guests chatting away happily with her, for I wished to explore the Sacred City.

Accompanied by Mustapha, I went on foot through the streets and bazaars with a strange feeling of exhilaration that I was the only European in the whole city.

March 21. After the siesta, I started out to return the visit of the Lady Fatima and her family, accompanied by Mustapha, as it would not have been considered correct for me to walk alone in public any more than our grandmother could have done so in the days of Queen Victoria.

The house I entered was most quaint and attractive; it was built of thick mud walls; the side facing the street was whitewashed and had no windows, save one small grille; and it felt delightfully cool on coming in from the hot street. A covered passage led at right angles into the inner apartment so that when the door opened, no curious glance could read the living-rooms. The passage opened into an oblong courtyard surrounded with colonnades, and on the south side, an open hall serves as a permanent sitting room, and it was here that my host received me. The floor of the courtyard was paved in a beautiful Arabesque design in marbles of different colors. Some orange trees in large tubs stood about, and various tropical creepers climbed the colonnade, covering it in with deep green foliage and brilliant blooms.

My host, leaving Mustapha drinking coffee in the reception room, led me up a steep, narrow staircase with painted banisters to the flat roof of the chambers that encircled the courtyard. Here were the ladies' quarters, and very charming they were, with the roof garden massed with roses and pink oleanders growing in great pots of glazed green pottery. Here Fatima welcomed me, and her husband returned below to entertain Mustapha and a few male guests who had assembled, while I made acquaintance with the ladies who had been invited to meet me.

They were a gay crowd, and we laughed and chatted over small incidents that amused us at the moment; indeed, the surroundings were so full of charm that I was prepared to laugh at any and everything that came my way, for sheer gaiety of spirit.

To my astonishment, I discovered one little Turkish lady who spoke French fluently. She told me that her father had been attached to the Turkish embassy in Paris before the war. She had married an officer in the Ottoman army, who lost his life when the railway bridge near Ma'an on the Hedjaz Railway was blown up in 1917,[2] and she was now married to a gentleman of Medina. I asked her if she ever thought with regret of the gay life of her youth in Paris and other continental cities where her father had been posted during his career, but she assured me that she was perfectly content and could not be happier than in her present home with her husband and three children, while she goes occasionally, when funds permit, to visit her family on the Bosphorus. After drinking tea and eating quantities of delicious little cakes made of honey and almonds mixed with a small amount of flour, I quite reluctantly took leave of them, as the time for the sunset prayer drew near.

With Her Hostess in Medina

March 20. Khadijah, my hostess who always comes to sit with me and share my meals, is still a young woman and would be very pretty if she did not look so ill. She tells me she has been in pain for many months, and I fear it is consumption. She has been married over ten years, but there are no children—a great grief to both of them.

I enjoy the Arab dishes and am already accustomed to their ways. Where no chairs exist, one naturally sits on the floor. I am beginning to feel at home in my Arab dress but have not discarded my stockings, and I know my feet are an object of curiosity at the mosque.

March 21. My hostess joins me for the evening meal, looking very pretty but pale and fragile, dressed entirely in pale blue. The scarf flung round her head is beautifully embroidered with tiny garlands of flowers, which she proudly exhibits as the work of her own hands, and she has every reason to be pleased with the charming result, which would require a Greuze to depict with justice.[3] She is indeed the embodiment of grace as she reclines on the divan, with one small foot tucked under her slight figure, while like all her nation she makes use of her slim hands to emphasize her words.

We sit beside the tray piled up with meat, rice, and highly spiced salads and vegetables. The meat is cooked in an earthenware jar, with a handful of herbage to close the mouth, and added to it are some peppercorns, cinnamon, and nutmeg, pounded with liquid butter, or "ghee," and by some cunning known to these people, the meat, though eaten the day it is killed, is always tender. While partaking of the really dainty feast, I tell Khadijah of the day's doings and beg her to come with me on the morrow to visit the gardens, but she declines to leave the house. I feel very sorry for her, as she is evidently suffering from homesickness in addition to other troubles, and she tells me she longs to go to her father, who lives in Damascus. . . .

We had finished our meal, had washed and dried our hands, and the slaves had removed the tray, when we were told that my two friendly sheikhs were below asking to be received.[4] Khadijah promptly left me as it was not etiquette for her to remain, even if veiled, and I sometimes wondered if these ladies ever felt a pang of envy at the freedom I was allowed.

In a Meccan Household

March 26. We stopped at the house that was to shelter me during my pilgrimage. I was received by my host and his two sons, who led me into a spacious hall, with several rooms leading out of it and up a stone staircase of fine proportions with easy shallow steps. My suite of rooms on the second floor consisted of a small anteroom opening into a very large one, furnished with the usual divans against the walls and a great bedstead that had been placed there in my honor, covered with a beautifully embroidered counterpane and a mosquito net. But alas! the bedstead spoilt the Oriental character of the room, which had the loveliest windows I had ever seen, reaching to the floor, and the lattice shutters delicately carved in a floral design in a lightish wood. The high ceiling had the same tracery round it and was domed in the center, with small windows let in, all richly carved. The stone passage on the other side of the anteroom led to the usual Arab bathroom, a stone floor with a deep hole and great jars of water standing about. On a marble ledge in the passage were porous jars with silver stoppers, and the water inside them was always cool to drink. One jar was specially filled every day with water from Zem Zem [Zamzam], the sacred spring that rises in the center of the great mosque.[5]

I was delighted with my quarters and thanked my host for providing me with such charming surroundings. When I had discarded my veil, I unpacked my portmanteau, which did not take long, as I had none of the usual impedimenta of European clothes—no hats, evening frocks, or rows of shoes. When not wearing my pilgrim dress,[6] I would change into a thin garment and my black Arab cloak and hood.

Shortly after my arrival, I was visited by the ladies of the harem. The wife of my host was a cheerful soul, mother of the two young men who helped receive me; three girls in their teens, one extremely pretty, were her nieces, and a small boy of eight was the son of a former wife who has remarried and now lives in Jeddah, where the child spends alternate months.

They bring me green caravan tea flavored with mint and a faint aroma of ambergris, which I find delicious, and we arrange that I visit the mosque and perform my 'umrah or small pilgrimage later in the evening, hoping that some of the crowd will have dispersed. Till this is done, I may not remove any of my pilgrim clothes except the veil and gloves. Presently dinner is brought in on a tray and placed on the floor before us, and my hostess shares my meal. When our hands are washed, she disappears to her own apartment to smoke her narghileh[7] while I try to rest as I have a very strenuous night before me. The mosquitoes buzz round, and I take refuge under my net, but one of the enemy has entered, and as I may not kill it, I unpack a tube of Flit that I was given on leaving Jeddah, a priceless gift. I smear myself with it, and if the mosquitoes choose to commit suicide, I feel no responsibility.

March 27. On my return from the mosque, my hostess invites me to her apartments at the top of the house, where she is entertaining several friends; the rooms are bright with Eastern rugs and divans covered in silk; a small cage holds a bulbul. The largest room opens on to a flat roof that is now a garden of flowers that, except for a few zinnias and oleanders, are unknown to me. The folded mattresses indicate that some of the ladies are sleeping outside. The sun will soon wither this garden, but in another month the family leave for their villa at Taif in the mountains, where they spend the summer. Several ladies are squatting on the divans, the older ones smoking narghilehs. Two young mothers have brought their babies, who sleep placidly through all the laughter and chatter. The visitors are evidently here for the day.

My hostess has already initiated me into the secrets of the harem or women's quarters; the bakehouse where the bread is baked to supply the needs of the large company at present inhabiting the house; the great kitchen where she, her ladies, and slaves all help in cooking and preparing the food; the laundry where more slaves are busy washing, while the three pretty nieces are ironing and folding away the household linen; and the workroom where they sit sewing and gossiping. Everything necessary for running the home is done within the harem, and the flat roofs are utilized for airing and drying, while all have their own roof to sleep on in the spring when the rooms are uncomfortably hot. Nor must we forget the goats, who also have their own roof and are plentifully fed with bunches of burseem (clover) brought from Wady Fatima, an oasis in the hills to the west. They supply the milk and butter and are not averse to devouring old papers or anything that comes within their reach.

April 1. As I have been granted the great privilege of being received as a guest in this Mecca household, I feel it is up to me to refute the false impressions that still exist in the West about the harem. Not only in this house but in every harem I have visited in Arabia, I have found my host with only one wife. Far from being a sensuous life of ease, these ladies are busy with their household duties, at the same time living a happy, even a gay, life, entertaining their friends and having their own amusements and festive occasion. There are no lonely old maids, the system being mostly of a joint family, and the joyous laughter and atmosphere of content that emanates from the harem convinces me that "all is well in the best of possible worlds."

FURTHER READING

Lady Evelyn Zainab Cobbold. *Pilgrimage to Mecca*. London: John Murray, 1934. Reprinted with an introduction by William Facey and Miranda Taylor and notes by Ahmad S. Turkistani. London: Arabian, 2008. The introduction was also reprinted with a selection of reviews from the British press in the Woking Muslim Mission's journal, *Islamic Review* 23, no. 1 (January 1935): 16–24. http://www.wokingmuslim.org/pers/ez_cobbold/isrev-jan35.htm and http://www.wokingmuslim.org/pers/ez_cobbold/isrev-jan35-r.htm.

———. *Wayfarers in the Libyan Desert*. London: Arthur L. Humphries, 1912. Also see the book by Frances Gordon Alexander of the same title (New York: Putnam, 1912). https://archive.org/details/wayfarersinlibya00alex.

———. *Kenya: The Land of Illusion*. London: John Murray, 1935.

Charles Adolphus Murray. *The Pamirs: Being a Narratives of a Year's Expedition on Horseback and on Foot through Kashmir, Western Tibet, Chinese Tartary, and Russian Central Asia*. 2 vols. London: John Murray, 1894.

Humayun Ansari. *The Infidel Within: Muslims in Britain since 1800*. London: Hurst, 2004.

NOTES

1. The author refers to the thirty-sixth chapter of the Quran. Clearly, it had been produced in a decorative fashion for display on the wall.

2. The author refers to a guerilla attack on the Ottoman-built Hedjaz Railway from Damascus to Medina during the Arab Revolt launched during the First World War with the assistance of British military officer T. E. Lawrence.

3. The author refers to the French painter Jean-Baptiste Greuze (1725–1805), known for his exquisite portraits.

4. It is indicated elsewhere in the text that her "two friendly sheikhs" were Sid Ahmed as-Said and Munshi Karamat. The first was her friend from Damascus who was husband to Fatima. The second is described as an "Indian Sheikh" who, as well as being a "very charming gentleman," "can speak a little English." Together, they had already used her car to "motor into the country" on March 10.

5. Zem Zem, usually transliterated at Zamzam, refers to the well located within the Masjid al-Haram near the Kaaba in Mecca. Its water is considered sacred on account of having sprung by divine intervention to quench the thirst of Abraham's infant son, Ismail, when he was left with his mother in the desert.

6. The author refers to the ihram dress consisting of white unstitched cloth in which she was pictured in the frontispiece to her book.

7. The narghileh is a pipe for smoking tobacco. Earlier in the narrative, Lady Evelyn refers to King Ibn Saud's enforcement of a more puritanical Islam that included a ban on smoking—with the effect that nargileh usage became a clandestine activity.

TWELVE

FATIMA BEGUM

An Indian Hajji Observes Her Fellow Pilgrims

INTRODUCTION

Fatima Begum (1890–1958) (see fig. 12.1) was a passionate activist for the Pakistan movement, rallying women's support in meetings and the streets and helping victims of violence. Her public role was enabled by her birth into a prominent family in Lahore; her father, Mahbub 'Alam, was the editor of the influential and widely read *Paisa akhbar* (*Penny Newspaper*). Following an initial education at home, she attended the Victoria Girls' High School. In 1909, when she was studying at Punjab University for the Matriculation and Munshi Fazil exams in English and Persian, respectively, her father reestablished *Sharif bibi* (*The Respectable Lady*), one of several Urdu women's magazines of the time. Fatima Begum soon became the magazine's editor—one of the first women to hold such a position in India—and continued in that post until 1919. During the 1920s, she married Raja 'Abd al-'Aziz, an aristocrat from the Northwest Frontier Provinces, and started teaching at Lady Maclagan College in Lahore. After her husband's death, she was appointed the superintendent of municipal Urdu girls' schools in Bombay in 1930. There, she founded another magazine, *Khatun* (*The Lady*), which, like *Sharif bibi*, was concerned with religious, educational, and literary matters. She also wrote several didactic novels and regularly contributed to the influential women's literary magazine *'Ismat* (*Chastity*).

Alongside her journalistic and literary activities, Fatima Begum took prominent roles in numerous social and political organizations, including the Anjuman-i Khavatin-i Islam (or All-India Muslim Ladies' Conference), the All India Women's

David Boyk prepared the introduction and translation from Urdu.

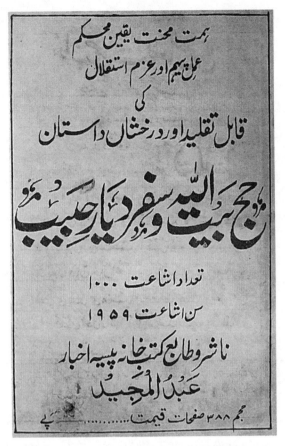

Figure 12.1 The title page of Fatima Begum's
Hajj-i Baitullah (1959). Courtesy of Daniel Majchrowicz.

Conference, the Anjuman-i Himayat-i Islam (Society for the Defense of Islam),
and most of all the All-India Muslim League. Her association with the latter
appears to date from the 1930s when, while working in Bombay, she became
involved with the provincial Muslim League Women's Sub-Committee. In 1937,
she returned from Bombay to Lahore, where she joined the Punjab and Central
Women's Muslim League Sub-Committees and founded the Jinnah Islamia
Girls' High School, inaugurated by its namesake, Muhammad Ali Jinnah. As
an educator, Fatima Begum was a founding member of the Muslim Women's
Student Federation in 1942. As communal strife became rampant in Bihar in
1946, she went there to aid the afflicted, ultimately escorting over two hundred
people to Lahore. Her close friend, Jahan Ara Shahnawaz, records in her autobiography how, in the lead-up to independence, Fatima Begum was one of a core
group of female activists teargassed and imprisoned for their civil disobedience.

After Partition, she continued to work to rehabilitate refugees and advocate for women's legal and political rights.

Hajj-i Baitullah o safar-i diyar-i Habib (*A Pilgrimage to the House of God and a Journey to the Land of the Beloved*), from which the excerpts here are translated, is a diary written by Fatima Begum during her pilgrimage to Mecca and Medina in 1934. At the beginning of her account, Fatima Begum writes that she had yearned to perform the hajj for several years and had planned to go with her father before his death in 1933. In addition, she had recently started *Khatun* and was reluctant to step away from her editorial work. Nonetheless, she pressed on, and in 1934 she left from Bombay with her mother and aunt. Their ship stopped at Karachi to pick up more passengers and eventually docked at Jeddah. From there, the pilgrims went first to Mecca, then to Medina, and finally returned to Bombay. While traveling, Fatima Begum periodically sent her diary entries to be published in *Khatun*. Shortly before the end of her life, she gathered them together as a book, which was published posthumously in 1959. In the following extracts, a note is made of where and when the entries were written, and their original titles are retained.

Religious matters are of the utmost interest to Fatima Begum, most of all those that touch on women's obligations and freedoms. While aboard ship as well as after her arrival in the Hijaz, she seems always to be engaged in discussions with both men and women regarding how women should be educated, how they should approach the hajj, and how they should balance modest dress with vigorous participation in public life. At the same time as she scrupulously patrols the boundaries of propriety, though, she clearly has little time for lectures from reactionaries. For someone like Fatima Begum, self-confident and accustomed since childhood to the company of journalists and political activists, the decision to publish her travel diary might have seemed a natural one. Throughout it, she focuses for the most part on experiences significant not only to herself and to her family but also to a wider audience. We catch glimpses here and there of her inner life—her friendships, her pleasures, and her aversions—but she devotes much more space to describing new places and customs, conversations with interesting people, and the practicalities of travel.

Upon reading Fatima Begum's travel diary, and the fond reminiscences by luminaries like Shaista Suhrawardy (also featured in this collection) and Raziq al-Khairi (the editor of '*Ismat*) that are included within, it quickly becomes apparent that she must have been an extraordinarily dynamic presence. She makes friends at every stage, among them the literary and political figures (and fellow travelogue authors) Begum Sarbuland Jang, Hasrat Mohani, and his wife, Nishat al-Nisa. Fatima Begum responds to seemingly every problem or opponent with the same confidence and composure, not to say bluntness, and her curiosity seems almost limitless. She often expresses her frustration with language barriers and especially laments her poor knowledge of Arabic. Invariably, though, she forges ahead, making do with a combination of Urdu, English, Persian, and a smattering of Arabic. Although she clearly feels a kinship with other Indians, she revels in meeting people from far-flung places, all drawn together by a common purpose. Her patrician class prejudices remain firmly intact, however.

EXTRACTS

Purdah and Muslim Women

Bombay, March 7, 1934: When I went below decks, I saw a strange spectacle. I had gone down specifically to see if I could help any of the women in purdah among the lower-class passengers, in case they were having any trouble. I was dismayed to find that an absolute prison had been constructed by tying different drapes from floor to ceiling. There already wasn't any air on this level, and now drapes had been tied so high up that the air was completely blocked. I explained that they should just set up enough of a screen so a woman wouldn't be visible while standing up, but who listened to me? They thought that if a woman caught any fresh air, it would be a catastrophe. Alas! Islam teaches nothing resembling the purdah I'm seeing these days. I was reluctant to broach this unpleasant debate at this point, but when a topic is introduced, it's necessary to express one's views.

That morning, two or three ladies belonging to the Hyderabadi aristocracy had arrived in their cars on the platform in Bombay to bid farewell to the travelers from Hyderabad. In front of thousands of men on the platform, these ladies showed their faces with bare heads and half-burqas, and there were also several adolescent girls in delicate georgette silk saris without burqas. I was anguished at this situation. I sent a message to tell these women to put coverings on their heads. Although it must have displeased them, I was obliged to. It raises my hackles to see a woman all dressed up and bareheaded. That was the situation back there, while here in the compartments, it's purdah on top of purdah, so that there's no room even to take a breath. As Hafiz says: *See the difference, from whither to whence.*

Islam teaches balance. It gives the message of *everything in moderation*; extremes in all matters are blameworthy. And both of these situations are completely against the teachings of Islam. A Muslim woman has been forbidden in clear terms from going unveiled and showing her beauty and adornment to strange men. And going among men wearing beautiful half-sleeved garments, made of delicate silk, is entirely inappropriate.

Complaints about Food

Arabian Sea, 11 March 1934: Just now we were sitting in the same place when people gathered a short distance away and raised a commotion. Several gentlemen came to me with a petition and asked me to sign it. I said, "Until I can read this thoroughly, how can I sign it?" I read the petition, in which several complaints had been made to the captain of the ship:

1. The contractor doesn't give hot water for tea, and he demands two paisas per kettle of water.
2. In the food we receive, vegetable oil is used instead of ghee, which makes us and our children sick.
3. The food is neither good nor abundant. This should be remedied.

In response, I asked them, "If we have this dispute resolved by the contractor, what objection could you have?" They said that if a decision was reached, then they would have no complaint.

I called the contractors and said that it would be best for a decision to be made regarding these three complaints. They said, "Hot water can't be given for free, because then hundreds of people would come to get it, and we wouldn't always be able to keep up with the demand."

Their response was reasonable, but I decided that the pilgrims should make their own arrangements and that the contractors would supply a samovar and fuel, and they agreed. About the ghee, they said, "Please make an inspection. We use pure ghee. There's not so much as a trace of vegetable ghee or oil. And we can't agree that the food isn't being provided in full measure. So much food is served that people eat half and throw the rest in the ocean." At this, the passengers said, "The food is unappetizing, and there's not enough of it. Four tandoori rotis per head isn't enough; some people should get five." The contractors consented, and with great difficulty this conflict was resolved.

I don't understand why people constantly fight about food, even though the food isn't so bad. Bengalis, Madrasis, people from [the United Provinces], Punjabis, Sindhis, frontier people, Bukharis—they can't all enjoy the same kind of food.

In my opinion, in the future the restaurant should arrange it so that the fees aren't paid in advance, but rather each passenger pays for each meal. Then some people would pay double while others would pay one or two annas and make do with dry roti. For those who have begged and borrowed to scrape together a hundred rupees for a ticket, and who make it through the day by chewing on a few chickpeas, paying sixteen rupees is very unpalatable.

People from Bukhara and the frontier want a sheep's meat kebab at each meal. Ultimately, they pay sixteen rupees for the round trip, so why don't they get a mutton kebab every day? In short, I don't understand what would put an end to all these complaints.

During this quarrel, the time for 'Asr prayers arrived. I said my prayers and then went up to visit Begum Sarbuland Jang.

The Women of Kashgar

Red Sea, March 16, 1934: When the men had received their pilgrimage robes, the women's turn came. It's worth seeing the state of the women of the merchants of the Kashgar valley, Turkestan, and Bukhara. If possible, I'll provide a photo. They're very tall women, who wear coarse, mud-colored tunics reaching down to their feet, and their faces and heads are wrapped up with muslin scarves. A place is left open for their eyes, and a smallish hat is perched on top of their heads, over the scarf.

It's amazing that so much care has been taken to cover the head and face, while the chest is left completely open, which is shameful to see.

Each of these women was given a scarf to wear with their pilgrimage robes, but not another tunic for them to put on instead. Clothes were requested from the ship, and a charitable and generous gentleman of Bombay donated two new tunics and two women's pajamas. As Mirza Zafar said, we'll make this army of indigents shine, and we've introduced many of the necessities for sprucing them up. And this was purely a result of his efforts.

Eight or ten children, boys and girls, are also present in this contingent. They were also given pilgrimage robes, although neither is the hajj obligatory for them nor do they understand its purpose. But they have chubby, beet-red faces, and wide, round chests, and laughing, innocent faces like red and white bowls, which the rich can't obtain even by spending thousands of rupees. Because of their ignorance and poverty, their social standing is nothing less than that of an ox or bullock. I wish that there were some way of improving their lives, but the world is a self-serving place. Everyone talks, but nobody has the courage to do anything in this empire of selfishness. After the pilgrimage robes were distributed, I came back.

An Unpleasant Conversation about Purdah

An elder who, owing to ignorance, lacked even the manners to talk with women, presented a book and said, "I'm giving this as a gift. Since you're against purdah, I was obligated to present it."

I asked him, "What led you to the conclusion that I'm against purdah according to sharia, even though I myself remain within the bounds of sharia?"

He replied, "What are your thoughts about purdah?"

I said, "According to sharia, purdah means that a woman shouldn't show her beauty, elegance, and adornment to anyone but her husband, but there's no harm if she leaves her face open to participate in worldly business. This was the purdah of the Prophet's female companions, and today it's customary in all Islamic countries. In raging against it, you have used extremely uncivilized language. Alas!" Several brothers of mine heard and stopped him in quiet tones, but the way they hushed him didn't actually work. In any case, this book has already gone on sale on the ship for two paisas. Begum Muhammadullah wanted a copy. I said, "Leave it alone. Don't even pick up this kind of foolish thing that will just make you despair." It's evident that this book is just full of obscenities, far outside the bounds of civility, and it's not worthy of being read by any lady. Girls with modern educations have, may God protect us, been given the status of prostitutes and licentious women. These kinds of books should all be gathered up and burned. If this is called Islam, then I'm fearful. Many young Muslims will bow to this. These wretched faultfinders don't know whether their actions are weakening Islam or benefiting it.

In any case, I sent that book to Begum Muhammadullah. She read it and laughed as well as cried. *We belong to God, and to Him we shall return.* May God the Highest bring Muslims to their senses, and whatever they do, may they do it within the bounds of civility. Islam never taught obscenity, and modes of argument can't be so uncivilized.

Meeting Egyptian Ladies

Mecca, March 21, 1934: In the place where I said my prayers, there were several young Egyptian ladies also praying. I tried to communicate in halting Arabic. When they heard Arabic coming from the mouth of an Indian, they were astonished.

When I asked if any of them spoke English too, they pointed to a young Egyptian lady in the row behind and said, "Munira Khanam knows English." Another young woman was with them, Husain Khatun, who could understand a little English. I spoke with Munira Khanam, and we talked about every subject.

Masha Allah, she is a very intelligent lady. We spoke for a long time about Egyptian women's schools and the state of their education, about purdah, and about domestic arrangements. As our exchange of ideas went on, it became clear that Egyptian women are progressing in every aspect of life. They're even experts in flying. Huda Shaarawi has founded an extremely influential women's organization, which is doing wonderful work.

Our Indian sisters should learn a lesson from our Egyptian sisters' progress. I asked Munira Khanam if she would send me the books that are taught in Egyptian girls' schools, and she promised that she would certainly send them.

Afterward, it became routine that when I saw her at the Haram Sharif, either I'd call her over and talk to her, or she'd call me over.

On this occasion, I very much regretted being so ignorant of Arabic that I couldn't exchange ideas with my sisters.

Mecca, March 22, 1934: Tonight I said my prayers in the Egyptian ladies' row.

The Egyptian women suspect from my burqa and pilgrimage robes that I'm not Indian. I met the wife of the Egyptian consul in Jeddah, Hafiz 'Amir. Her name was Ni'mat Khanam. She could speak English very well. At the time of 'Isha prayers, we spoke about everything related to Egypt. About the hajj, she said, "God's purpose with the hajj was not that people would just come and fulfill the requirements of the hajj by circumambulating the Kaaba, and then go home without learning any spiritual and moral lesson. God the Blessed and Exalted made it obligatory for Muslims so that every year they would gather from every part of the world. They would meet each other. They would exchange ideas. They would learn about conditions in each other's countries from the mouths of the people of those countries. They would reap commercial benefits. Political tangles would be unraveled. Mutual love would be established. Approaches to the propagation of Islam could be considered. In short, so many philosophies have been established for the benefit of Muslims in the duty to perform hajj. We should call it a great annual conference. But now, the only aspect of the hajj that remains is that it is half full of paupers, who neither have any connection with culture nor any relation with learning. And there are some clerics who have signed a contract to restrict Islam's boundaries. In this gathering, there must be very few people—wealthy and comfortable, of enlightened thought, and familiar with the needs of the age—who have come with true insight.

"Wealthy and educated people seldom think of going on hajj. If they finally take on so much trouble and come, then they end up leaving after suffering the pushing and shoving of these uncivilized, savage people, who don't even understand a woman's honor or how to let a woman pass with civility."

Mrs. Hafiz 'Amir is an exceedingly well-mannered and enlightened lady. She often stays behind after 'Asr prayers. She also invited me to come to Egypt and said, "If you come to visit Egypt's female schools, your Egyptian sisters will be very happy to see their Indian sisters."

Women with Three Scars

Today I saw a group of Sudanese women. There are huge scars from wounds on their faces. Each face bears three scars, an inch apart and about three or four inches long. They're very conspicuous.

I stopped short when I saw these scars. These women are of a black color. They have thick lips that stick out noticeably, and efforts have been made to turn these lips blue by tattooing them with black collyrium. Some have turned purple and some greenish black.

When I asked why these wounds have been made, I learned that they are there to adorn the women with beauty and splendor.

But after further inquiry, it also turned out that at some time in the past, there was great violence, together with the slave trade, and the aristocrats marked their children with wounds. And this scar was to show that these people are from elite families and they should remain protected from the slavers' plundering.

Now, most people must have forgotten the reason for these scars. They just make the wounds out of respect for custom and tradition. During the hajj, I saw hundreds of men and women adorned with these scars.

A Bukharan Merchant Persecuted by the Bolsheviks

Medina, April 15, 1934: Today, despite being extremely busy, I was obliged to attend a gathering at the house of a Bukharan merchant. . . .

The husband is from Peshawar, but the wife belongs to Bukhara. All the children speak Urdu, and they also speak exquisite Persian. . . . In Bukhara, these people were in trade. They earned lakhs of rupees and amassed a pile of money; for a time, the father was even a minister in Bukhara. But when the Russian Bolsheviks took over, they were forced to abandon the city in the span of a day, with all their possessions snatched from them.

A Living Tale of Grief

Hearing this family's story, I felt such pity that my hair stood on end. My whole conversation with this young man's mother was in Persian. When she recalled her circumstances, the woman began to cry. Her daughter and young daughter-in-law too had tears in their eyes. They had lived in such magnificent mansions, had dozens of bondswomen and slaves, had golden carpets, and ate out of silver dishes—when they were thrown out penniless from their homes. They weren't allowed to take so much as a speck of dust from their luxurious homes. They gathered their children and headed straight for Medina, the Radiant City. The husband had some property in Peshawar, and now they subsist on the three or four hundred rupees in rent that it brings in. They have bought a house in Medina.

The High-Handedness of the Bolsheviks

I kept eagerly inquiring about the situation under the Bolsheviks. By chance, I had gotten the opportunity to meet the people they had oppressed. I was told that the scoundrels had demolished mosques and propagated atheism throughout the country. God protect us, they don't acknowledge the existence of God the Highest. Ninety percent of the people have been plundered and killed, or taken out and murdered. In short, they've wrought untold cruelty and tyranny. They order people to abandon their homes and leave empty-handed, and those who refuse are punished with nothing other than death.

How could I eat when this family's story was so disturbing? And it was so fascinating to hear that, having meant to spend a few minutes, I passed a full hour. I was surprised that they had brought a wife for their son from India instead of marrying him to an Arab woman, even though there are extraordinarily beautiful girls in Medina the Radiant. But they said that an Arab woman marries often and is prepared to take a false divorce. It often happens that she'll live for several years at a time with one husband after another, and even bear a few children with each. An Indian woman would never adopt such behavior. This was these people's view, and for this reason they brought out an ordinary-looking girl from India as his bride.

FURTHER READING

Fatima Begum. *Hajj-i Baitullah o safar-i diyar-i Habib*. Lahore: Kitabkhanah-i Paisa Akhbar, 1959. Further translated excerpts from this text, as well as the original Urdu, are available online at https://accessingmuslimlives.org/travel/fatima/.

Jahan Ara Shahnawaz, *Father and Daughter: A Political Autobiography*. Karachi: Oxford University Press, 2002.

Naumana Kiran. "Fatima Begum: A Narrative of Unsung Hero of Pakistan Movement." *Journal of the Research Society of Pakistan* 54, no. 2 (December 2017): 267–80.

Gail Minault. *Secluded Scholars: Women's Education and Muslim Social Reform in Colonial India*. Delhi: Oxford University Press, 1998.

Sarfaraz Hussain Mirza. *Muslim Women's Role in the Pakistan Movement*. Lahore: Research Society of Pakistan, 1969.

QAISARI BEGUM

The Long Road to Mecca

INTRODUCTION

Qaisari Begum (1888–1976) (see fig. 13.1) was the author of a remarkable autobiography, *Kitab-i zindagi* (*The Book of Life*), recounting in Urdu her life between Delhi and Hyderabad in India with a particular focus on domestic life. Nevertheless, the volume is a wide-ranging work that also discusses family members, local celebrations and festivities, and the author's travels through India, particularly to shrines. One of its most noteworthy sections narrates Qaisari Begum's journey from Hyderabad to Mecca in 1936. It is from this section that the excerpts here are translated.

Qaisari Begum was born to an influential and well-known family in Delhi in 1888. She was the granddaughter of Deputy Nazir Ahmad (1831–1912), who is credited with being the first Urdu-language novelist. She moved with her family to the princely state of Hyderabad in southern India as a child but retained links to Delhi and traveled regularly between these two cultural and intellectual centers. Yet it was ultimately in Hyderabad that she spent most of her life. She was married to a relative in Delhi, but he too relocated to Hyderabad to take up the significant opportunities available there for educated Urdu and Persian speakers from the north. Qaisari Begum was widowed at the young age of twenty-two, by which time she had a daughter of three years. She was persuaded by her family to remarry, and she remained in Hyderabad until her passing in 1976. After Partition, she did not travel to Pakistan to be with her daughter, Muhammadi Begum, due to the state of her health. Most of her writings were done during this period, when she was confined by immobility after 1955.

Daniel Majchrowicz prepared the introduction and translation from Urdu.

بڑی امّاں(قیصری بیگم)

Figure 13.1 Qaisari Begum, from *Kitab-i zindagi*
(2018). Courtesy of Zehra Masrur Ahmad.

Throughout her long life, Qaisari Begum remained dedicated to community service and particularly to women's education. These efforts included founding and running two girls' schools in Hyderabad, one of which she called the Madrasa Tadris al-Qur'an Niswan (Women's School for Quranic Education), and composing "useful" handwritten pamphlets and booklets containing humorous jokes and anecdotes related to life in the home, tried-and-tested recipes and formulae, songs, wedding arrangements, books of sayings, ethical guidance, and collections of verses of praise for God and the Prophet. She also published a Quranic dictionary, *Lughat al-Qur'an* and a collection of answers to questions related to the Quran, *Aham masa'il al-Qur'an al-karim ma' al-javab* (Important Matters of the Holy Quran and Answers). In 1928, she was invited, as a delegate from Hyderabad, to the All-India Women's Conference in Delhi, to discuss women's rights, health, education, early marriage, and divorce, among other issues.

Today, Qaisari Begum is best remembered for her autobiography, which, ironically, she never intended to publish or even compile. The passages that make up this monumental work of over 660 printed pages were composed over a long period of time. The intended audience was primarily her family members; it was typical of the time for women to write for their relatives, and even to publish their writings in private newspapers that circulated only within the family. This also explains why many of the characters below are not introduced to the reader. The various pieces, around 260 in total, were written in seven bound notebooks and kept by her daughter Muhammadi Begum. In the 1970s, only shortly before Qaisari Begum's passing, her brother's grandson Shan-ul-Haq Haqqi (1917–2005) requested permission to publish these memoirs in installments in a literary journal, *Urdunama*. The pieces were immediately celebrated for their individualistic voice and lively style. The aging Qaisari Begum was delighted to learn that her writing had found an unexpected and appreciative audience. Unfortunately, the series came to a premature close when *Urdunama* folded in 1976. Qaisari Begum passed away soon after, but her writing found a new lease on life in the twenty-first century when her granddaughter Zehra Masroor Ahmad prepared a fully edited and published edition (2003, republished 2018).

Kitab-i zindagi is not the only source from which we may gain a picture of Qaisari Begum's life and character; she also makes several appearances in Muhammadi Begum's private travel diary (also featured in this collection). This diary reveals Qaisari Begum to be a loving mother who regularly wrote to her daughter and kept her well stocked with dried and preserved sweets, copies of the latest intellectual magazines and journals for women, and regular updates on life back home in Hyderabad. These glimpses reveal that mother and daughter shared with one another their passion for writing. Indeed, Qaisari Begum was responsible for submitting several of Muhammadi Begum's letters for publication in the journal 'Ismat.

It is also noteworthy that Muhammadi Begum and Qaisari Begum, mother and daughter, traveled at nearly the same time: Muhammadi Begum was still in England when her mother left independently to perform the hajj. We join Qaisari Begum in the first passage as she shares with the reader not only the journey itself but also the many obstacles she must overcome to perform the pilgrimage as a woman alone. The extract reveals the freshness and joy of Qaisari Begum's writing and shows, through their contrast with other writers in this book, the great diversity of approaches to writing about this sacred journey. Many wrote of the holy cities in a reverential tone, but for others like Qaisari Begum, the journey was intensely familiar and personal.

EXTRACTS

Preparing for Hajj

The pilgrims returned [to India] during the five months that I was away in Delhi. Some of them even asked me what it was that he[1] gained by preventing me from going myself. "You didn't get to go, after all." But then it was time for me to go back to Hyderabad. And so I went.

I received many pictures of the *nau maulud* ceremony[2] from England, and letters informing me that all was well there. These letters set me at ease. Muhammadi Begum sent me many fascinating letters about England that I had published in '*Ismat* magazine[3] with the intention of entertaining and informing my '*Ismati* sisters all at once. All of my sisters read the letters avidly. When a new letter was delayed in coming, the sisters grew impatient.

Last year he stopped me from going on hajj by calmly informing me that the two of us would go together the next year, but God knows that he is scared of the ocean and quakes at the very mention of going.

And then, in the blink of an eye, a year passed and the time for hajj was near once again. My heart was in such a strange place. I wanted to just fly away. I was so unsettled that no matter what task I took up, my heart was never in it. Sleep was impossible. I couldn't do anything, for what was I to do? The closer the hajj season came, the more the fire of my passion blazed. I lost all control.

My goal was to convince him to let me go. His goal was to keep me from going. He said to my brother Ihtisham al-Din sahib, "How can she make such a long journey? Please stop her. Maybe she'll listen to you."

In fact, I was willing to accept each and every word my brother told me, but when he asked me to speak my mind, I told him what I thought without any hesitation. "Brother, I'll listen to whatever you have to say, but don't try to stop me. I can't be stopped now." He reported back that I was unstoppable, that he should let me go.

I had already thought about all the preparations that would need to be made. I worried day in and day out how I would be able to pull this off without anyone else's help. I enlisted [my nephew] Na'im al-Haqq to do a few tasks for me, and he reluctantly agreed out of fear that I might become angry with him. Things like making visits to the hajj guide, Badr al-Din, gathering logistical information about the trip like when the caravan would leave and where it would halt, and so on.

And then, lost in a world of confusion and worry, what do I see in a dream but myself traveling with some eminent personage. Water and sand are commanded by the slightest movement of his finger. I am praising him to the other women, telling them how venerable he is. I couldn't stop thinking about what this dream meant. What trip was this? Who is this great person? It didn't make any sense. How could my feeble intellect make sense of all this? I would have to ask my spiritual guide and leader, *Hazrat Pir* Jama'at 'Ali Shah,[4] I thought. If one has a spiritual guide, may they be like him.

I am infinitely thankful and grateful to Allah that He always reassures his servants during times of worry. His Word tells us that *inna maʿ al-ʿusri yusra*: "Every difficulty is followed by ease."[5] Trust always in His grace and generosity. One of my most basic concerns was how I was to get the money for the trip. I had a house in Delhi sold for the purpose of funding my hajj. The money was paid in Delhi, but there were constant delays in having it transferred to Hyderabad. I feared the caravan would set off before it arrived, leaving me behind, perplexed and distressed.

Though I knew in my head and my heart that Allah is the Causer of Causes, my worry increased by the day until, suddenly, I learned that the caravan would be departing soon. Unknowing human! How can you hope to know the will of the Divine, and who and what it draws toward itself?

My days were spent thus: In the morning, I would wake up full of hope. I would pass the day waiting. There would be no news of the money. At night, I would go to bed dejected.

All of my luggage was packed and ready. I had my smallpox and cholera vaccinations. Everything was taken care of. But this one tiny snag threatened to unravel the whole plan.

Then the day of hope dawned at last. I was sitting there, lost in worry, when the son of a dear friend, *barkhurdar* Sayyid Mazhar Husain, arrived. He was elated. "My Aunty is going on hajj!"

When I told him about all the difficulties I was having in getting the money, he said without a moment's thought, "Aunty, I have some cash laying around unused. Please take it." I declined out of politeness. He refused to take no for an answer and went home to get the money. He soon returned and gave it to me without so much as asking for a promissory note or any kind of receipt. I was in a daze. God! What kind of angel have you sent me, who comes and smilingly hands me the money without even being asked?

It felt as though rain were falling on dried husks of rice. My heart swelled, my body came back to life. My courage returned to me. I wrote him a receipt and also got out some jewelry to give as collateral. He reluctantly accepted them. I told my husband to give him the money from Delhi, which would arrive any day now, inshallah, the moment it came. Then another wonderful thing happened. There was a widow in our neighborhood called Husain Bi who wore a lot of gold. She suddenly turned up looking for her hen. I said to her, "Husain Bi, what's the use in wearing all that gold jewelry. Sell it and come on the hajj."

She said, "If I go, will you come too?" I told her calmly that I was going whether she came or not. "What I am saying is that you should exchange this jewelry for the hajj." This had a profound effect on her. "All right then, sister. I'll go." She went home and declared her intention. Everyone offered their full support, telling her that such an opportunity was unlikely to come again. It's your good luck, they told her. You must go. Everything was taken care of in a flash, and she soon returned to me with banknotes in hand. "Take it. I'm coming with you."

This is the greatness of God, His divine power. He has bestowed His grace on me again and again. Rained down showers of blessings. Even that poor woman will perform the hajj and visit Medina, whose greatness she could never have imagined seeing herself. I thought to myself that if she sold her jewelry, then why shouldn't I sell some of my bangles? Thinking of the merit of such an act, I sold off a few of my gold ones. In return, I did not receive cash so much as the keys to the kingdom of the seven realms. He has showered me with His blessings.

It is the heart itself that calls you to go on the hajj and to make a pilgrimage to Medina. Once you have this desire, Allah will take care of the rest. There was a woman from Gulbarga Sharif who was going on the hajj. One of her relatives had traveled with her up to Bombay to make sure that she boarded the ship without difficulty. But then his heart would not allow him to disembark, and he remained on board until the ship had pulled away from the harbor. When the people on the ship learned of this, they began soliciting donations from the passengers until they were able to cover the cost of his passage. I saw with my own eyes that his hajj and pilgrimage to Medina were completed without him spending a single cent of his own.

Traveling from Hyderabad to Bombay

Miyan Jamil Husain's car waited at the door of the house, but by the time it arrived I had already gone to Nampally [Railway] Station in Khadija Begum's car. We went into the waiting room, where many women were waiting to say goodbye and see us off. There were tears in everyone's eyes, but as for me, I was elated that God, through His grace, was fulfilling my deepest longing.

Miyan Jamil Husain called for the station rickshaw,[6] seated me in it, and then walked alongside. There are complete arrangements at the station for women observing purdah to go from the waiting room to their train compartment without ever being exposed to public view. The other people with us . . . also came to the train. When I got to the platform, my train car was already there. But there were two European women sitting in it. The moment my rickshaw pulled up to the car, they both stood up.

To welcome me? Absolutely not! May God forgive them, they acted angry and spread their arms across the doorway to keep me from going inside! The train was to pull out at any moment. Miyan Jamil Husain only managed to get me into the car with the greatest difficulty. I was truly relieved to be inside. I took my seat. My arms were completely covered in flowers and *imam zamins.*[7] Who knows, maybe these women thought that I was a lunatic. After taking my seat, I took a good look around me. My friends and family were gazing at me with sorrow and wishing me goodbye. All of a sudden, the engine sounded its whistle, saying farewell in its own language. The train began to inch forward. The people wishing me farewell began to move forward in tandem, their handkerchiefs waving in the air. Once they were all far behind me, I took off my burqa and set the *imam zamins* and garlands to one side.

By this time the anger of my fellow passengers had cooled. They took some oranges and apples out of their food baskets and, placing them on a plate, offered them to me. I accepted with thanks. They took out their Bibles and began to recite. I remembered my own Holy Quran and began to look for it. But it wasn't there!

My heart immediately sank. I always carry my Quran with me when I travel. This trip came together so frantically that I forgot to bring the most important thing. Plus, I had placed my immunization certificates and other documents inside of it. What was I to do now? How could I get my Quran now? The train was picking up speed. It left the station behind, rushing forward with leaps and bounds.

O Allah! These worries refuse to allow me to travel to Your house in peace. I can't think of any way to fix this. Even as I was praying, the train stopped, and my nephew Na'im al-Haqq, who was traveling with me, appeared. I had decided to bring him along with me after reading a fatwa ruling that if a male relative escorted you onto the ship, then this would be sufficient to fulfill the legal requirement that a woman be appropriately accompanied on the journey. I told him that my Quran and all my important documents had been left at home.

He replied that he would get off the train here and go and get the Quran. He would board a later train and bring it to me in Bombay. Yes, son, there's no other choice. Now I was feeling at peace. But when you are traveling God's path, Satan is never content to let you be. I watched him as the train pulled forward once more. Once he was gone, I had another realization: My ticket! Oh, no! He had the tickets. This is a disaster. My heart shriveled up once more. I began to pray, O God! You are all powerful; Satan makes us forgetful.

I was surrounded by agitated thoughts. I am all alone. There is no male traveling with me. Who knows which train Miyan Na'im will board for Bombay, and when I'll see him? How exactly is he going to track me down in Bombay? I'll have to change trains at Wari in the middle of the night. They'll ask me for my ticket. God knows they'll force me to disembark. Where will I stay? Who will give me a ticket to travel on from Wari? Who will take me to the travel agent in Bombay? And so on and so on. Humans are such impatient creatures. They never seem to remember that there is nothing to worry about on the particular path that I am traveling on. Whatever He does will be for the best. Everything will be fine.

> The seven heavens turn constantly, day and night
> Something will always be happening—so why worry?[8]

Inna ma' al'usri yusra.[9] The train was dragging me forward surrounded as I was by all of these fears when it halted for a moment. A familiar voice reached my ears. Begum? I immediately looked up. Who could it be? It was [my adopted brother] Shakir 'Ali standing before me in the form an angel. "It's me. Nammi [Na'im] Miyan's gone, so I will travel with you up to Wari. I'll be so sad once you've left. I'm going to Zakir's. Zakir will be there in Wari." He said all of these things with such certainty that all my fears were put to ease. For one thing, I had found a trusted companion. And second, there would be someone in Wari to help me change trains. Now the only worry was the ticket. But Allah is all-powerful. Things happen. I need to be strong.

The train arrived in Wari at eleven that night. We had only been there a short while when I heard a voice speak to me through the window. "Is your name Qaisari Begum?" Filled with trepidation, I said it was. "What is it?"

"A telegraph has come from Hyderabad instructing us not to ask for your ticket. Your ticket is there." My strength immediately rallied. I thanked God. Then Shakir 'Ali and Zakir both appeared to help me change trains. My heart became even stronger. . . .

In this trip, and indeed in every trip, a woman is required to have a male companion with her. In Bombay, 'Abid 'Ali sahib shared with me the good news that Hazrat Pir Jama'at 'Ali Shah sahib would be traveling on the same ship as me. My heart was elated, and I suddenly remembered my dream from that night, when Allah told me that I would be traveling with a great personage whose slightest gestures command the sands and the seas. I thank God for fulfilling the joyful vision shown to me in that dream. My heart was brimming with gratitude that He resolved the issue of a male companion Himself. Now I am traveling with my spiritual advisor and guide. Our departure was scheduled for three days hence, at the crack of dawn. . . . After facing countless difficulties and challenges, Allah poured out His blessings on me so that I might see this day, that my dream might be fulfilled. He was my only hope. . . . My God-fearing sisters! If God has given you the means to perform the hajj, then you most certainly should do so, and also visit the tomb of His messenger, may peace be upon him. Make it your life's goal to attain this happiness and God's blessing.

In Mecca

Al-hamdu lillah, [after my arrival in Mecca,] I was blessed with the opportunity to offer my Friday prayers in the sacred Kaaba. May God accept them. I was also able to spend an evening there so I could see how it was at this time of day. I thought that I might be able to do my worship and circumambulations more easily at that hour. But, oh no! I ended up seeing the same multitude at night as I did in the day. I pressed my back against a wall for a moment and then stepped forward into the crowd. All my fatigue evaporated. Day no longer felt like day, night was no longer night. Every second was as luminous as though it were high noon. There is an inscription above the door by the Maqam Ibrahimi: *wa man dakhluhu kana amanan* (and whosoever enters from here shall find peace). I was constantly going in and out of that door. And when I sat by the Zamzam well, I would sit in such a way that I could see the Black Stone of the Kaaba before me.

The caravan that arrived from Medina was large, orderly, and magnificent. In it were Bedouin women who wore black-colored, blanket-like burqas. You couldn't see so much as their fingernails. They wore these burqas even while circling the Kaaba. Their beautiful faces, their moonlike visages, remained covered. As they circled, they were held by their men, who accompanied them on either side.

The cars of the Egyptian women are so splendid that they have no equal in all of Hyderabad. White cars, filled with gorgeous, healthy Egyptian women in white burqas with fair complexions and uncovered faces. It was as though the very nymphs of heaven had descended to earth. I was completely astounded. I was so struck with wonder that I was frozen to the spot, unable to move. I stood there taking in every detail like a woman mad with love.

As for the men, dressed in their ihrams, it was impossible to distinguish the rich from the poor. Everyone wore one dress: a simple belt and a broadcloth. They all moved with the same simple but intoxicated gait. If you want to see the best procession of automobiles, then have a look when you're on hajj.

The women of Palestine had their own unique grandeur. The women's bodies are so sturdy that they completely outdo their men. There wasn't a lean, weak-looking one among them. They wear massive turbans on their heads. They wrap up their real hair in these turbans and then beautify themselves by wearing wigs that look something like the black tassel on a Turkish fez. The women of Syria are also plump and fair-skinned. I saw the women from Yemen, too. They wrap a handkerchief over their mouths that spans from their noses to their chins. They wear this at all times. I saw one woman whose hand had been severed at the wrist as punishment for theft. I asked her why her hand had been cut off. How could she answer such a question, though? She said, "These people are enemies of the Yemenis."

FURTHER READING

Qaisari Begum. *Kitab-i zindagi*. Edited by Zehra Masroor Ahmad. Karachi: Fazli Sanz, 2003. Further translated extracts, as well as the original text of these selections in Urdu, are available online at https://accessingmuslimlives.org/travel/life/.

————. "Excerpts from *Kitab-i Zindagi*." Translated by Mehr Afshan Farooqi. *Annual of Urdu Studies* 20 (2005): 232–41.

Siobhan Lambert-Hurley. *Elusive Lives: Gender, Autobiography, and the Self in Muslim South Asia*. Palo Alto, CA: Stanford University Press, 2018.

NOTES

1. The author's husband, who, in keeping with convention, is not mentioned by name.

2. A ceremony in which the azan is read into the ear of a newly born child. Qaisari Begum here refers to the birth of her grandson Anwer, who was born while his mother, Muhammadi Begum, was studying at Oxford. The pictures would have been taken by her husband, Jamil, who was a keen photographer. For an account of her travels with the infant Anwer in Europe, see chapter 30.

3. One of the most famous Urdu-language journals for women.

4. Probably refers here to Amir-i Millat Jama'at 'Ali Shah (d. 1951), a famous Naqshbandi Sufi leader and a prominent supporter of the movement for Pakistan.

5. Quran 94:6.

6. A small vehicle that could transport women in purdah from their vehicle or waiting room to the train compartment without being seen publicly.

7. This is a small amount of money dedicated to a protecting figure, or imam, and tied to the arm of a departing person to protect them during their journey.

8. A verse by one of the most celebrated Urdu poets, Mirza Asadullah Ghalib (d. 1869). *Rat din gardish me haiñ sat asman, Ho rahe kuchh na kuchh ghabara'eñ kya?*

9. See note 5.

—⟳—

FOURTEEN

BEGUM HASRAT MOHANI

Letters from a Pilgrimage to Iraq

INTRODUCTION

Nishat al-Nisa Begum (1885–1937), better known as Begum Hasrat Mohani, was a prominent figure in the struggle for Indian independence (see fig14.1). She was among the first Muslim women to work publicly to bring an end to colonial rule in British India. Her political career spanned from the early 1900s until her death in 1937, during which time she became a well-known anticolonial figure. She pursued these activities alongside her husband, Hasrat Mohani, who was himself a fierce activist and advocate for independence. Both were accomplished writers. Nishat al-Nisa's writing is best known today for her letters, many of which, like the one translated here, were published by her husband.

Nishat al-Nisa was born in Mohan, near present-day Unnao in Uttar Pradesh, India, in 1885. She belonged to a land-owning (*zamindari*) family of modest means that claimed descent from migrants from Nishapur in Iran. She received a wide-ranging education that included the study of Urdu, Persian, and Arabic. She quickly passed on this education, teaching other young girls in the town how to read. In 1903 she was married to her first cousin, Sayyid Fazl al-Hasan, known today only by his pen name, Hasrat. His wife, at least in her public life, accordingly became known as Begum Hasrat Mohani. The couple had one daughter, Na'imah, to whom the letter translated here is addressed.

Nishat al-Nisa spent the first years of her marriage in purdah and within the domestic space of the household. This circumstance changed irrevocably in 1908. In that year, her husband was arrested for publishing anti-colonial material in his magazine, *Urdu-i mu'alla*. Rather than have their many projects

---

Daniel Majchrowicz prepared the introduction and translation from Urdu.

Figure 14.1 A portrait of Begum Hasrat Mohani.
Courtesy of Daniel Majchrowicz.

come to ruin by his incarceration, Nishat al-Nisa, then a mother in her early twenties, left purdah to support both her husband and the movement for independence. Thus began a career in activism that would last until her death. She immediately moved to support an array of initiatives, including the publication of *Urdu-i mu'alla* and the running of a book agency and a *swadeshi* store in support of the independence movement. Hasrat would be imprisoned twice more during her lifetime, and on both occasions she continued to manage their efforts and support herself and the couple's young daughter single-handedly. She also published her husband's poetry, which he sent her from jail, and even sent him home-cooked meals. She also maintained a correspondence with leading independence figures like Abul Kalam Azad and media outlets to keep them informed of Hasrat's condition and whereabouts during his incarceration.

While often remembered in a supporting role to her husband during the freedom struggle, Nishat al-Nisa was in fact a leading figure in her own right. She opened shops for *khadi*, or homespun cloth, to raise funds for the Indian National Congress and the Khilafat movement, even as she herself lead an austere life on the verge of poverty. She joined Sarojini Naidu, Annie Besant, and other leading women in a delegation to the Montagu-Chelmsford Commission to demand franchise for the women of India—but also, going off-script, insisted that her husband's jail conditions be improved immediately. On one occasion, she is said to have slapped the leader of the Indian National Congress and future prime minister of India, Jawaharlal Nehru, for improperly ordering a lathi charge on a protest group of which she was a member. Years later, Nehru would speak kindly of Nishat al-Nisa and send his condolences to the bereaved Hasrat at her passing.

Despite their voluminous political engagements, Nishat al-Nisa and Hasrat dedicated significant time to spiritual and religious pursuits. The couple traveled to Sufi shrines and other spiritual centers throughout their lives. Hasrat Mohani regularly attended the festival to celebrate the birth of Krishna at Mathura, and his wife may have traveled with him for these religious events as well. Yet for both husband and wife, there was no greater journey than the one to Mecca and Medina. Hasrat, who performed the hajj eleven times, completed his first hajj alone in 1932, but after this he "performed the hajj every year without fail with Begum Hasrat and [his] grandson Rizwan" until her death in 1937.

One such trip occurred in 1935, when Nishat al-Nisa traveled to Iraq and Arabia with a group of seven that included her husband; brother; two of their daughter Na'imah's children, Nafisa and Rizvan al-Haqq; a servant named Bua Kushrang; and a friend, Taslim Ahmad. The following translated extracts are from the fifth of six published letters that Nishat al-Nisa wrote to Na'imah during the journey. The writing is that of a seasoned world traveler who was deeply committed to the cause of Muslim unity and devoted to the Prophet and the saints. Her letters touch on a range of subjects, from the price of vegetables to swaddling practices to the experience of visiting the sacred shrines, but they never lose the candid and loving tone appropriate for a mother writing to her daughter.

Tragically, this journey would be the final pilgrimage that Begum Hasrat performed, for she would fall ill on the return journey from Basra and die several months later in Kanpur. The letters published here were published posthumously in *Urdu-i mu'alla*. After her passing in 1937, Begum Hasrat Mohani Nishat al-Nisa was remembered and eulogized by many, including future prime minister Jawaharlal Nehru. Yet the most poignant memorials were written by her lifelong companion, Hasrat Mohani, who composed several touching articles and poems in her memory and who personally edited and published letters that she wrote during her lifetime.

EXTRACTS

The Fifth Letter

From *Bab al-Sheikh*
Baghdad Sharif
Tuesday, 17 *Zi Qaʻdah* 1356, or, February 11th, '36

May God keep her from harm! I've finally found some time to write after several days. Every day I end up have to go somewhere or other. On Saturday morning, we went to Kazimayn Sharif.[1] There is a shrine there dedicated to Hazrat Imam Musa Kazim—God's mercy upon him. Even from a distance, you can see that the entry gate is gilded and very beautiful, with golden pillars, domes, and vast stretches of full-length wrought silver paneling. Prayers made at the shrine of Hazrat Musa carry the authority and certainty of a tried-and-tested medicine. I prayed with all my heart for your health and well-being, for your prosperity and success in the earthly and spiritual realms, and so on. May God accept my prayers.

There was a large crowd of Shia women there who were circling the silver enclosure. The Hanafi guide had us read a long prayer over the saint. We left the shrine around noon. Maulana and Taslim Ahmad went to the consulate to make the necessary legal arrangements for the onward journey.

On the way back, we happened to see a cloth market. The markets here are so vast, lively, and crowded that even if you went on walking and exploring to the point of exhaustion, you still would not have reached the end of it. Silk is sold in gigantic stores that are set up in the Meccan style. Wool and cotton fabrics are available here in great quantities. There are also plenty of goods from Japan, and food shops as well. There are toy stores and countless shops selling Japanese rubber shoes. The shoes are made here. Yesterday Maulana bought a pair in the Syrian style for his ihram; they cost one rupee and twelve annas.

Ah, yes! The first day we were here, I bought a blue, double-wool Chesterfield [coat] for four rupees. It's very long and broad. The cold is very intense, and it also rains frequently. Sometimes there's a frigid wind blowing too. The shops here sell presewn velvet coats for both men and women. There are also plenty for children on the racks. Khushrang is with me. She needs a sweater. An old coat made of velvet was bought for her, but she didn't like it. I had no choice but to take it myself. It's good, but it needs a cleaning, since it's used. God knows how

I'm going to do that. I got tired and decided to come back. There are lots and lots of meat and fruit shops here. Pomegranates sell for five annas a *ser* [two pounds]. The seeds are bright red and very sweet and juicy. Turnips, carrots, sweet lemons, sour lemons, bananas—everything, in fact, is available here. The *kampat* stores are massive and filled with countless varieties of chocolates and biscuits. From morning to afternoon, you get thick folds of cream, which is sold in great quantities. It is very good. Every day I send for a few paise's worth to eat myself. And for Rizwan too. There are chapatis made of a cornlike meal that you can get piping-hot for two paise each. There's a woman here who comes to the gate to sell chickpeas in the mornings. You get a good quantity for one paisa. They are white and large, the size of black-eyed peas. I eat some every day. There are liver kebabs and more. There are also a great many restaurants. You get every sort of food in them, and for cheap. Even milk only costs two annas a ser. I ordered some the day before yesterday. It was warm and delicious. There's also lots of beef available. And buffalo too. The cream is made from that milk. There's also meat from sheep and goats, both of which are expensive nowadays. Fat can be easily had for eight annas a ser. You can get paneer and *khoya* and every sort of vegetable.

All of the roads are wide, smooth, and sparkling, just like Thandi Road [in Kanpur], but if there's even the lightest rain, they become very slippery. Once they dry, though, they are as hard as cement.

The buggies, which are called *'arb'anas*, can seat four. The fare is incredibly cheap, and the vehicles are very large. They come with one and two decks. But the really amazing thing is that even though they are only hitched to two Iraqi horses, they still go so fast, as fast as our tiny *tangas*. Even the large goods carriages bearing the heaviest loads are drawn by horses, but the horses here are strong and powerful.

There is a bridge across the Tigris that is supported by a series of iron boats anchored to the riverbed. A long, broad bridge has been constructed across them. *'Arb'anas* are not allowed to cross the bridge. There are countless motorcars. The markets are constantly bustling and filled with great crowds of people. There are lots of sweet shops too. Everyone wears the same outfit here, no matter their class or station: a coat, pants, a tie, boots, a black Iraqi hat, and an overcoat to top it all off. Iraqis are a very fair-skinned, beautiful people. Their children are white as little balls of cotton, with wide faces. Healthy, plump, and fresh.

There is no system of purdah here. Some old-fashioned women, of course, wear a kind of Arab-style veil when they go out, but they are uncovered up to their upper calves. Their stockings are sheer, and they have ladies' shoes on their feet. The rest of the women generally, and younger women especially, are only half covered. They wear open-collared frocks and a Chesterfield coat and do their hair up. The hair falls over their cheeks to a length of eight fingers. A few of them wear long braids, while others wear a pair of braids tied at the back. But for the most part, their hair is cut short. They are extremely beautiful, with soft, tender bodies. They are fair complexioned and delicate, with fine features. They roam freely in the schoolyards and in the bazaars.

There are also a lot of cinemas here. The people are enthusiastic but also tranquil and contented. In many ways, Baghdad is just like Bombay. The bazaars are winding, as in Bombay. There's always a rush, though the stores begin to close up around sundown. By eight the entire bazaar has shut down. There are curtains that hang in the doorways of the shops such that you can pull them up or down at will. . . .

Right, so, when our fellow traveler Munavvar Raza sahib last came to Karbala, he stayed with the nawab I mentioned earlier. That afternoon, his home was nearby. Munavvar Raza went to meet with him, and his nephew called a car for us. Meanwhile, Khushrang and I were sent into the zenana of his home to wait and use the restroom. The houses here are very large, like bungalows. The nawab's personal home was two or three stories tall. There was one room for meeting callers, as well as several other large rooms. Paan leaves come here from Bombay at the rate of two rupees a bundle, but the catechu you get to accompany it is about as delicious as dirt. Begum sahiba distributed paan, but since I had my Kanpuri paan with me, I didn't take any. Khushrang did, though. Begum sahiba went on asking her about the state of things in Lucknow. She told us about herself and about the state of things in Iraq. Her two daughters and two sons were then away at school. She is middle-aged, chubby, and very fair. Anyhow, the nawab's nephew didn't have any luck finding a car either, so we all went back to Baghdad.

In the evening, two men, one Hindustani and one Punjabi, came and invited Maulana and everyone with him to the movies. We all went after sundown and found room in the women's section. The men sat in the general seats below. The show began thirty minutes later. It presented the coronation procession of the current ruler, Shah Ghazi. From beginning to end, there were countless military exercises, a rush of cars and huge crowds. Ghazi was astride a horse, inspecting the cavalry and saluting the infantry. Then the car went to the royal residence. A royal decree was read out from the balcony. Then he got back in the car and went on shaking hands with the public and receiving military salutes. This display reveals that there is a great equality between the ruler and his people here. The people went on giving handshakes, salutes, and greetings to the king without any show of formality. At the end of the reel, there were shots of the army and a horse race. Beyond that, there was no other scene or screening. My head felt dizzy. Yes, there was also a wrestling match between an Iranian and German at the very end. They were both very fair-skinned, and very strong. And that was it. Riding home, the entire bazaar was closed. So were all the restaurants. We all went to bed hungry. We managed to get only a tiny bit of oil for the lamps.

By coincidence, in the cinema I was seated next to a mother and daughter from Delhi. Her husband has been here for sixteen years. She and her elder daughter have been here for an entire year. The father married his daughter off against her mother's wishes to a man with three children whose wife had passed. She was Indian too. Her younger sons are all in India. Yesterday, the mother and daughter came to the monastery to meet with us. She told us all about her plight and asked us to pray for them in Mecca and Medina. In the cinema, she gave me a dinar, which is worth thirteen rupees and five annas, and asked me to have two goats sacrificed—one for her, and one for her deceased son—and to have the remaining funds distributed as alms in Arafat. . . .

In the evening, we were all invited to a function at the Islamic university. There was another invitation to tea at four, as well as yet another invitation that was only for Maulana and Taslim Ahmad. There was also a meeting at the Society. Well, we ended up going to the functions later in the afternoon. I wasn't planning to go, but Maulana asked me to attend the Society meeting, so I went with him. Once we were out of the house, everyone went to the meeting, but they didn't take me with them since women are not taken to the meetings. Please proceed to the women's section, they said. There was a function there. At first, I didn't know who these people were or how I was going to go in there and sit down like a total stranger. I didn't know there was a function there either, or that it was the one I'd planned to attend in the first place. The host's wife and two daughters were there. One's the same age as Anisa, and the other is bigger and healthier than your two-month-old, An'am. There was also an elderly servant.

These people are from Bareilly. The husband is either a member or the secretary of the Society. I'd seen his wife at the movies as well and had a brief chat with her at the time. I ended up having to sit there from the afternoon until well into the night. The poor wife had to help out with the arrangements for the function herself. She'd come in for a while and then go right back out again. I mostly sat there by myself with their youngest daughter, who was, in keeping with the practice here—and as I once saw done in Medina at the home of Maulana 'Abd al-Baqi sahib—tightly swaddled in a cloth and placed in a large, swinging basket made of wood. There were cushions and pillows inside. She was tucked in with a sheet and a blanket, asleep. If she wet or soiled herself, they would untie her diaper, clean it, and then tie it back tightly again. When it was time to nurse, she would open the collar of her shirt, give the child milk right in front of us, and then lay her back down again. The child just lay there, all bundled up and looking slightly dead.

There's another practice here, where the moment a child is born, they wash it thoroughly, wrap it up tightly in a cloth, and then place it in a basket to sleep all alone. The child is never made to fall asleep with its mother. It's left entirely on its own. It is unfathomable in our Hindustan that a child would be left entirely alone with its mother to sleep unencumbered on her own bed, that she would just feed it and check on its diaper from time to time. But the children here are used to this. At one point, the mother came in and changed the baby's diaper. She let the baby pee and left the diaper open for a bit. Meanwhile, the baby started bawling, but her mother was away taking care of something. I caressed her and spoke sweetly to her, but she started crying again after a short while. Her mother came back, tied her up tightly in a large piece of cloth, and returned her to the basket. She sighed, looked around for a moment or two, and then fell back asleep. The mother went on talking to me. They are good people.

There were fifteen or twenty people at the gathering. They performed the sundown and evening prayers, after which Maulana returned from the meeting and we ate. Instead of meat, they serve pulao with fried pickle and other such items. For dessert there was firni, which was excellent, and then oranges. Then came tea. After that, we returned home.

There was still no clarity regarding the issue of our passports as of yesterday, otherwise we would be leaving tomorrow, Tuesday. All our things were packed and ready so we could set off as soon as the passport issue was resolved. But it's been more of the same since morning. At night, we unpacked our things again. As of now, all of our bedding is packed up once more, and Maulana, Taslim Ahmad, and Munavvar Raza have gone back to the passport office after eating breakfast. Let's see what they find out.

Right now we are cooking alu bharta and alu-namak mirch. Rizwan, masha Allah, is constantly eating. Nasir[2] had given him a rupee. He's spending it. Maulana is constantly sending out for more cream and such.

It's very cold here. And always cloudy, though the sun comes out sometimes. First thing today we went to the market to get Rizwan's Chesterfield [coat] and some Iraqi hats. One each as a souvenir for Ahsan, Qa'im, Nasir, and Sami'. They were nine annas each. Inshallah, I'll get something for Nafisa and Anisa from Medina on the way back.

From here, the blue dome of Hazrat Ghaus-i Pak's shrine is always visible. It is inlaid with jewels and glittering stones arranged to resemble flower petals. The mosque is connected to a large hall with grand doors of engraved wood and brass locks both inside and out. After the dawn prayer, the keeper of the shrine, who is very old and frail, comes with a younger man, who is some relative of his, to remove the locks. He reads a prayer as he does so. When they are locked, the interior set of doors are covered by a green cloth with elaborate embroidery in golden thread. The keeper opens these too, after which pilgrims may enter. When they are open, you can see into the shrine from the street. Inside there is latticework of wrought silver, including a large, sloping ceiling made of lattice. Beneath it, there is a large box, or meshed metal covering—a *zarih*—that is completely covered in costly and ornately embroidered cloths bearing the kalima, the bismillah, and other Quranic verses. There are also beautiful, vibrant flowers sewn into the velvet. All of us made prayers and read the fatiha while kissing the lattice of the shrine. We also circumambulated the grave. The doors open at dawn, at noon, and again in the late afternoon.

As with the Arabs, time is kept here according to the setting of the sun. In the center of the monastery courtyard there is a large pillar with two clock faces and massive bells hanging from it. They are rung at each prayer time. Thus, the evening prayer, 'isha, is marked by two strikes of the bells (two o'clock). The dawn prayer, fajr, is at ten o'clock; next comes the zuhr prayer, at eight o'clock; and then 'asr prayers at ten o'clock. The maghrib prayer is at twelve o'clock.

Some people here wear *'abas* and turbans like the Arabs do, especially those who live in Bab al-Sheikh. This neighborhood is not unlike the Firangi Mahal area of Lucknow. The shrine of Hazrat Ghaus-i Pak is located here.

There are Shias in the other parts of the city—perhaps more even than Sunnis. In the cities of Najaf, Karbala, and Kazimayn, everyone is a Shia. There are also Christians and Jews here. There is only the tiniest difference in dress between Muslim and non-Muslim women. Muslim girls go about bareheaded with their hair in a part, wearing a frock, a gown, and socks, their calves bare. Jewish and Christian girls dress in exactly the same way, except that they also wear a small, saucer-shaped hat on their heads made of velvet or woven reeds. That's it. They look exactly the same in every other way.

FURTHER READING

Nafis Ahmad Siddiqi. *Begum Hasrat Mohani aur un ke khutut o safarnamah*. Delhi: Maulana Hasrat Mohani Foundation, 2015. A full translation of all extant letters, published in *Urdu-i mu'alla*, may be found in Daniel Majchrowicz, "Begum Hasrat Mohani's Journey to Iraq," in *Worlds of Knowledge in Women's Travel Writing*, edited by James Uden. Boston: Harvard University Press, 2022.

Muhammad Siddiq. "Hasrat Mohani." *Journal of the Pakistan Historical Society* 32, no. 1 (January 1, 1984): 31–70.

C. M. Naim. "The Maulana Who Loved Krishna." *Economic and Political Weekly* 4, no. 17 (2013): 37–44.

Gail Minault. *The Khilafat Movement. Religious Symbolism and Political Mobilization in India.* New York: Columbia University Press, 1982.

NOTES

1. This refers to the shrines of two Shia imams—Musa al-Kazim and his son, Muhammad Jawad—and the area surrounding them.

2. The author's younger brother.

FIFTEEN

—ᴂ—

MAHMOODA RIZVIA

Three Months in Iraq

INTRODUCTION

Mahmooda Rizvia was a young Urdu author from a prominent business family in the colonial Indian port city of Karachi when she published *Dunya-i Shahrazad* (*The World of Shahrazad*) in 1945. The opening chapter of this larger history of Iraq was a travel account of her three-month journey across the Arabian Sea from Karachi to Iraq undertaken the previous year. In her mid-twenties at the time, she had journeyed with her mother, brother, and sister-in-law. Rizvia's family had become important patrons of Urdu literature in Sindh in the previous decade. This familial context enabled the young Rizvia to become a well-known magazine editor and author by the time of her travels. From 1941 to 1946, she served as the coeditor of an Urdu magazine published by the Sindhi provincial branch of the Urdu literary association, the Anjuman-i Taraqqi-i Urdu (or Association for the Advancement of Urdu). *Dunya-i Shahrazad* was also published by the Anjuman (see fig. 15.1).

In the early 1940s, Mahmooda Rizvia published over a dozen Urdu books that dealt with Islam, natural history, the history of Karachi, and contemporary social ills from the perspective of Sindh. Her books were widely distributed beyond Karachi and regularly reviewed in popular Urdu periodicals in Lahore, Delhi, Lucknow, and Hyderabad. This reach reflected the unique position occupied by Rizvia in the pan–South Asian Anjuman. Not only was she one of the few women in the Anjuman's leadership, but she also was one of the most prolific authors within the Anjuman in the early 1940s. This record is all the more

Andrew Amstutz prepared the introduction and translations from Urdu.

188

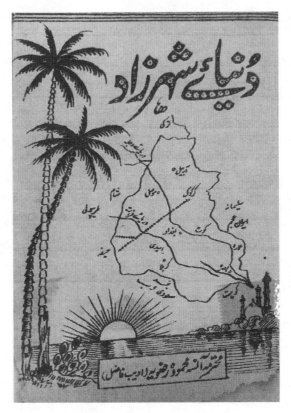

Figure 15.1 The cover of Mahmooda Rizvi's
Dunya-i Shahrazad (1945). Courtesy of Andrew
Amstutz.

remarkable if one considers that Rizvia published during the paper restrictions
and censorship of World War II. Despite her prolific publishing output in this
period, Rizvia was rapidly sidelined from the world of Urdu letters in Karachi
after the 1947 Partition of the Indian subcontinent that saw an influx of Urdu-
speaking Muslims from northern India into Pakistan. Hence, although Mahmooda Rizvia left a rich literary record covering the period from 1941 to 1946,
few details are available on her life in Karachi after the 1947 Partition.

When Mahmooda Rizvia visited Iraq in late 1944, it was a semi-independent
kingdom within the British Empire. Since 1921, Iraq had been governed by a
branch of the Hashemite family, who continued to reign until 1958. Thus, in traveling from Karachi—an increasingly important Indian Ocean port city during
World War II—to Iraq, Mahmooda Rizvia was both traversing older Islamicate
paths between the Indian subcontinent and the Middle East and moving within
a British imperial world in flux. In the introduction to *Dunya-i Shahrazad*, Afsar
Siddiqui Amrohavi, a prominent Urdu scholar in late colonial Karachi, made a

case for why Urdu readers should buy Mahmooda Rizvia's book. He insisted, "Iraq is a far off, oppressed Muslim land. Islamic India should be aware of every dimension of events there." Amrohavi endorsed Rizvia's book because "it is nothing less than a literary miracle that from the pen of a young woman of Sindh such a rare compiled text has come, from which every aspect of ancient and modern Iraq has been unveiled."

A structuring element of Mahmooda Rizvia's visit to Iraq was her pilgrimage to Muslim shrines in Karbala, Kufa, and Najaf. However, despite visiting these shrines (and the centrality of Islam to her other writings), she spent little time explicitly discussing Islam or her visits to the shrines of the Prophet's family in *Dunya-i Shahrazad*. Rizvia reasoned that it would be more helpful to write "a brief history and geographical assessment of the country of Iraq" to go along with the plethora of existing accounts of Karbala. She explained that "detailed mention of Karbala, Najaf, and Kufa are truly not necessary because every Muslim is aware of the figures and holy saints associated with these sites, and pamphlets, magazines, books, hajj guides, visitor guides, and other books have already been published about them." It seems that Rizvia pivoted away from pilgrimage in her written account in order to foreground her own historical voice and observations of the natural world.

The extracts here are taken primarily from the first chapter of *Dunya-i Shahrazad*, in which Mahmooda Rizvia recounted her journey from Karachi to Iraq and back again. Having crossed the Arabian Sea, she traveled through the Persian Gulf to coastal Iran and, finally, Iraq. Once there, she journeyed up the Shatt al-Arab River to Basra, from where she took a train to Baghdad. The first and second extracts chart how, as the days passed on the outward sea voyage, the initial appeal of the ocean's beauty faded into monotony, such that she turned her attention more to the poverty of the gulf's seafaring communities. Once she arrived at Abadan in coastal Iran, however, she returned to describing the physical beauty of the shoreline. As her boat passed through the mouth of the Karun River, Rizvia mixed poetic tropes of natural beauty with descriptions of modern oil refineries.

To give a sense of Rizvia's experiences in Iraq itself, the third extract includes descriptions of Baghdad taken from the later historical chapters, two of which are devoted to Baghdad's history. Rizvia spent an entire month in Baghdad visiting graves, touring historical sites, and connecting with business associates of her family. Her extensive writings on Baghdad reveal not only a fascination with the Abbasid past but also a willingness to celebrate contemporary Baghdad under Hashemite rule and within the British Empire. Throughout *Dunya-i Shahrazad*, Rizvia often juxtaposed Abbasid sites in the city with contemporary developments in 1940s Iraq. That Rizvia did not, in her travel writing, entirely neglect prominent Muslim graves in Baghdad is also indicated by these passages. The fourth extract, from the final page of her first chapter, points to how the author dedicated considerably less time to the return journey from Iraq to Karachi than her outward one. Still, it gives a sense of how Mahmooda Rizvia remembered her trip in retrospect.

EXTRACTS

Leaving Karachi

The Arabian Sea is that silent sign of the future and that alluring anticipation of what is to come that noisily announces its arrival with the proud and playful waves that are at every moment washing the shores of Karachi. This view of the sea comes clearly from the window in my room, and it had already become second nature for me to be absorbed by this intoxicating view in the morning and the evening. . . . I have tried to understand the sea's secrets, but until today I have not been able to grasp whether the sound of the sea comes from a lament of the destruction of Babel and Ninevah, or if the noise of the crashing waves is an elegy for the murder of [the Prophet's cousin and son-in-law] 'Ali with which the line of righteous caliphs came to an end. Or is the roar of the sea the sound of mourning for the martyrdom of Husain in the heart of Iraq? Or is the sound of the waves the mourning for the fall of Islam? Is the story of the rise of the Abbasids heard in the crashing of the waves? Or is the song of the fall of the majesty and glory of the Abbasids sung there?

Therefore, those crashing waves that were born from the Tigris and Euphrates in Iraq first passed the Arabian Peninsula to arrive at the Persian Gulf. From there, these waves crashed into the shores of Karachi, where they came to rest. From the very beginning, the sea has been the font of my imagination and a source for worthy lessons. This was the spiritual attraction that made the journey of Iraq immediately attractive to me and which, after undertaking the three-month passage, made me realize that Iraq was so much more than the *Tale of One Thousand and One Nights* or even the living tales [i.e., painted miniatures] of [the Mughal painter] Abu al-Hasan. What a silent morning it was on the twelfth of October 1944 when I left Karachi for Iraq. The universe had not yet awoken from sleep. Neither had the lovely birds begun to chirp, nor had the clatter of the start of the day's work begun. At such a moment of intense quiet, bidding farewell to my beloved homeland for some time, I left my house, as to one side the sun was busy preparing to rise above the horizon of the East.

The boat *Brala* that would take us to Iraq was awaiting us in the fog of the early morning, and the quiet waves of the ocean had fallen silent at that time. It took a half hour for the customs agents to process our luggage and the same amount of time to check the passports. By the time we arrived in our cabin after completing these initial steps, the color of the sea had become the same color as the first rays of the sun and a few fishermen were busy catching fish in the open water.

Ocean Journey to Iraq

And even the nights these days are quite dark. The sadness of those moonless, undifferentiated nights, when the trembling shadows met with the flowing waves, it was as if the waves and the shadows together were singing terrifying songs. They sang heart-rending stories of drowned souls and told tales of lost unknown ways. . . .

October 17: This evening at six o'clock, the ship arrived near a small Arab port that is called "Dubai," and we anchored about a mile from the shore. . . . On the deck some travelers are preparing to disembark. Some small boats will come out to collect them; many materials also have to be unloaded and supplies for Bahrain loaded.

October 18: The small, young Arab children, taking the smallest of boats, are circumambulating the ship. Fearless, unbowed, brave children who fought on the waves, but these children who are oppressed by poverty and whose fragile bones cry out loud the stories of their miseries in the game of life, they never get any opportunity. Destiny has been indifferent to them, and the era has rejected them outright. . . . These half-starving and naked children, who put their bodies and lives at risk in search of a few pennies. If you show them that a coin might be thrown into the ocean, they will start fighting with each other and immediately dive into the ocean to retrieve it even if the water is cold. . . .

Living in one's own country [of British India], you think to yourself, "Why did poverty tire of other countries and come to reside here [in India?]" And there is no shame in admitting that this is correct to some extent, but the situation of these innocent (children) is also lesson-worthy. They, who without any covering start their game in the cold—their entire universe is this boat as they try to avoid getting tossed out by the waves. With only their courage to call their own, these children survive on the efforts of their own sweat and, calling out, "*Rafeeq faloos! Rafeeq faloos!*" (Money, kind sir), they make many of the sensitive souls on the boat tearful. . . .

Today for the whole day, the three decks of the *Brala* are filled with the goods of merchants, but this scene of poverty was also imposed upon us again. Upon seeing the condition of the workers who were brought on board for labor, I realized that some of the conditions that we had witnessed before were also to be found in Dubai. We gave the gathered group of children biscuits, almonds, and other eatables through the porthole. These poor ones became so thrilled as if they had obtained great wealth.

I have begun to learn Arabic to pass the time. One Arab gentlemen, after seeing my attempt to comprehend a few Arabic phrases, has bestowed upon me the book *Arabic Self Taught*. However, the time eventually came to unload the goods. The terrifying Judgement Day–like sound of the crashing of the crane, the screams and cries of the workers, the Pharaoh-like orders of the owners of the goods, and the sighing of the crashing waves—all of these varied noises came together and threw me into terror for a long while. This painful image of poverty among the dock workers has had such an impact on me that until the evening, I did not go on deck, and I did not even have the heart to open the porthole, lest I see a demonstration of the impoverished Gulf laborers.

October 25: Today we will arrive in Abadan. . . . One side of the shore is under the control of Iraq and the control of the other side of the shore belongs to Iran. If it is established that the sea of the Persian Gulf is thick water, then the Shatt al-Arab River [at the confluence of the Tigris and Euphrates] is extremely clean—one is salty, the other sweet. Both waters should mix, but they cannot mix. Both stay separate. . . . People look at them with wondrous surprise and praise the workmanship of nature. . . .

Another pilot boat has come to help us reach Abadan. As we slowly made our way to the shore, night fell. Today after thirteen days, land finally came into view. The natural scenes here are extremely charming since, thanks to oil factories, this area is populated. Therefore, every evening, the port was awakened with activity, and this area was extremely lush and green to such an extent that, without exaggeration, I was reminded of heavenly Kashmir. From both sides of the [Karun] river, canals in the hundreds—no, the thousands—flowed out and at great distances watered many small gardens. . . . If, before experiencing the tales of *Alif Laila* for the first time, I had seen a magical scene such as this today, then such a gorgeous and charming scene as found in *Alif Laila* would have come into my soul. The coastal areas from Abadan all the way to Basra can, without exception, be called an earthly paradise. . . . I cannot fully express the many varied good qualities of the region here. How beautiful also are the sunrises and sunsets here?

Visit to Baghdad

Iraq's new life began with the era of the Hashemites [in 1921]. In the short period of twenty-four years of freedom, they have gained stability and educational, commercial, and agricultural advancement and are walking side by side with the cultured nations of the world. All of these are the blessings of the era of the Hashemites.... Baghdad, you are the city of peace, the neighborhood of peace, the abode of rest and relaxation, the city of peace and security, which Mansur populated and Hila Khan looted, which Harun-al Rashid raised up, and which the changing of the eras has destroyed many times over—no, more than this: destroyed countless times. In Baghdad's glory, thousands of tales have been launched to the heavens, but whose ruined condition also conceals the tears of blood that already have been spilt.... Those jewels of Islam [i.e., the Muslim scholars and saints] who are buried in your [i.e. Baghdad's] lap could have only been produced during the length of thousands of years ... Baghdad is the final resting place of Abu Hanifa. That Abu Hanifa whose holiness the angels praised. Baghdad gains prestige from possessing the final resting place of Imam Musa Kazim, whose holy existence is a mark of pride even today. The felicity of the final abode of Ibrahim and Ismail also are to be found here.... This was also the world of the heroine of *One Thousand and One Nights*, Queen Shahrazad, and the first and final abodes of her special character, Queen Zubaida Khatun. Mansur Hallaj raised the slogan "I am the Truth" here, and the beloved leader of Indians, Guru Nanak, also passed some time here in illuminating encounters with esteemed holy men....

In its era of advancement [under the Abbasids], Baghdad sat in the lap of the Tigris, where for miles and miles, ship after ship appeared, of which there were ships for war, ships for recreation, and also ships for travelers, and there were even really big ships for the Chinese who brought and took goods, and there were the small ships of the Arabs filled with silk and perfumes from China and colors and spices from India.... The story of Sinbad the Sailor from *Alif Laila*, as Professor P. K. Hitti has written, was not just a fanciful tale but rather true tales taken from the varied journeys of Muslim traders. Most Arab authors also take this point of view....

In Baghdad, there are a few remains of the period of the Abbasid caliphs. Among these, there are the Madrasa Mustansiriya, and secondly, in the Souq al-Ghazal is the minaret of a mosque, and in third place, there is the grave of the Queen Zubaida Khatun! The rest of Baghdad should be understood as *Baghdad-i jadid*, or modern Baghdad, which is in the Western style of a new city. Besides the old lanes, brand-new spacious roads, streets, and bazaars are being constructed. A number of new neighborhoods and spacious areas already have been built.... Shari' Rashid is the city's most glorious part and its most beautiful bazaar. In the place of the former boats and wooden bridges (that were used to cross) the Tigris River, now new iron, concrete, and cement bridges are constructed ... there are countless small gardens here, places for recreation, cinema theaters, a racecourse, hotels, coffee houses, etc. The quality of life is really advanced, and the city is quite large! ... The Souq al-Qamash of Baghdad is really an old-style clothing bazaar. Looking upon it, the memory of the stories of *Alif Laila* are revived anew in the hearts of men. Among the new memorials [of Baghdad] are the statues of Shah Faisal, the statue of General Maude, brand-new buildings, the new museum, and beautiful gardens. Seeing them, one is compelled to admit that in this short period of twenty-four years [during the Hashemite rule of Iraq], this city has experienced such extraordinary progress, which cannot be matched in the same amount of time anywhere else.

Return to Karachi

At twelve o'clock today, the boat dropped anchor on the shore of Karachi. Arriving back home, I came to understand that the journey to Iraq was a dream realized ... from among my limitless dreams, or even an ancient tale that had become real now that I was face-to-face with the beloved shore of my homeland and its pleasing visage.... Upon arriving at home, all were awaiting and listened to the collected news of the missing months with great impatience.

FURTHER READING

Mahmooda Rizvia. *Dunya-i Shahrazad*. Karachi: Shu'a'-i Urdu Dar-ul Isha'at, 1945.

Andrew Amstutz. "A New *Shahrazad*: The Travel Writings of Mahmooda Rizvia in India and Iraq during World War II." *Comparative Studies of South Asia, Africa and the Middle East* 40, no. 2 (2020): 372–86.

———. "Finding a Home for Urdu: Islam and Science in Modern South Asia." PhD diss., Cornell University, 2017.

Sarah Ansari. *Sufi Saints and State Power: The Pirs of Sind, 1843–1947*. Cambridge, UK: Cambridge University Press, 2003.

———. *Life after Partition: Migration, Community and Strife in Sindh: 1947–1962*. Karachi: Oxford University Press, 2005.

Michel Boivin and Matthew Cook, eds. *Interpreting the Sindhi World: Essays on Society and History*. Karachi: Oxford University Press, 2010.

Kavita Datla. "Locating Urdu: Deccani, Hindustani, and Urdu." In *The Language of Secular Islam: Urdu Nationalism and Colonial India*, 106–37. Honolulu: University of Hawai'i Press, 2013.

Shahabuddin Saqib. *Anjuman-i Taraqqi-i Urdu (Hind) ki 'ilmi aur adabi khidmat*. Aligarh: Educational Book House, 1990.

Mohammad Yunus. *Anjuman-i Taraqqi-i Urdu (Hind): Tarikh aur Khidmat 1947 tak*. Delhi: Educational Publishing House, 2008.

PART II

TRAVEL AS EMANCIPATION AND POLITICS

MANY OF THE AUTHORS IN part I sought to circulate their writings without attracting significant public attention, perhaps by sharing their accounts with readers that comprised friends and family or subscribers to magazines marketed to women. In stark contrast, the travelers in this section sought to speak to the widest possible audience and were generally explicit in their desire to introduce their experiences and ideas into the public sphere. This category of travelers is dominated by women who used their travels and writing to promote the cause of women's emancipation. These interests often intersected with other political causes, whether nationalist, internationalist, or communist. Their itineraries sometimes brought them into conversation with one another, particularly at international conferences, where activists of various stripes met with one another to discuss everything from women's enfranchisement to the veil to national liberation from colonialism. As an example, two of the authors in this section, Huda Shaarawi (from Egypt) and Shareefah Hamid Ali (from India), met with a third writer featured in part III, Iqbalunnisa Hussain (also from India), at the twelfth conference of the International Alliance of Women for Suffrage and Equal Citizenship (IAWSEC) in Istanbul, Turkey, in 1935.

Among the earliest women travelers to take up the question of religion and women's emancipation were three of the Turkish authors here: Melek Hanım, Zeyneb Hanoum, and Selma Ekrem. All three wrote autobiographical texts filled with accounts of their journeys but also Orientalist tropes such as descriptions of life in an Ottoman harem. Their books were published in Europe rather than for a Muslim audience, whereas the remaining women in this section did write for Muslims in their home countries. In most cases, those audiences were meant to be mixed gender, whether in Egypt, Turkey, India, or Indonesia. Remarkably, all of the Arabic- and Turkish-speaking authors to be found in this volume (with the singular exception of Salamah bint Said/Emily Ruete) are included in this section on emancipation and politics. Travel writing was rare in these languages, even in the modern period. It seems to have been taken up only by those who were most outspoken and willing to enter into the space of public debate. Even then, the accounts in these languages are drawn primarily from autobiographical works that did not have travel as their sole focus (with the important exception of Şükûfe Nihal Başar's Finlandiya). This observation reflects not only the relative lack of travel writing in these cultural contexts during the period but also the continuing difficulties women faced in writing and publication. Given so many of the other authors in this volume emerged from an Indo-Persianate tradition, equally notable is their comparative absence here—with only Shareefah Hamid Ali hailing from India and no authors from Iran. Still, it will be clear from other sections how political impetuses and reflections among women in these countries were woven into other travel experiences. For instance, Sughra Humayun Mirza's chapter, featured in part IV, speaks to the politics of the Caliphate shortly after its abolition. As one of the few Urdu-writing female authors to use travel writing as an explicit political platform, her work might have fit equally well here.

Also remarkable in this section is its diverse range of itineraries and destinations. It is perhaps unsurprising that so many Muslim women traveled to Arabia to complete the hajj (as in part I), or that significant numbers of women from colonized countries traveled to Europe to pursue further studies (as in part III). Here, though, feminist and anti-colonial agendas sent these authors in directions that seemingly moved outside established patterns of mobility within or between empires. Two of the Turkish authors wrote about their journeys to European locations beyond imperial metropoles: Melek Hanım to Greece in the mid-1860s and Şükûfe Nihal Başar to Finland in 1932. A shared context of nationalist and liberationist politics took another two authors from the Middle East to India in the 1930s and 1940s. While Turkish author and activist Halidé Edib mixed with India's nationalist and feminist elite throughout the length and breadth of the subcontinent, Egyptian feminist Amina Said visited the province of Sindh, now in Pakistan, to attend the All-India Women's Conference, where she spoke on the issue of Palestine. A shift in the global balance of power toward new superpowers, the United States and the Soviet Union, in the early to mid-twentieth century saw these countries become increasingly popular destinations for Muslim women travelers toward the end of our period. For communist Suharti Suwarto, a journey from newly independent Indonesia to the Soviet Union was a secular pilgrimage curiously comparable to Selma Ekrem's "American venture" from Republican Turkey to the "land of liberty." The assertive role of the United States within the new United Nations was reflected in its American headquarters visited by Indian representative Shareefah Hamid Ali in 1947. The range of destinations and political projects featured in this section thus reveal the many itineraries that Muslim women's travel writing had developed by the mid-twentieth century.

SIXTEEN

—⚬—

MELEK HANIM

An Ottoman among the Greeks

INTRODUCTION

There is some doubt as to the authorship of *Six Years in Europe* (1873). It is attributed to an Ottoman woman, Melek Hanım (1814–73). With a Greek mother and an Armenian father of French descent, she grew up in Constantinople with the name Marie Dejean. Her first husband was a European gentleman (perhaps British) with whom she traveled widely in Europe before their divorce. In Europe, she met Kıbrıslı Mehmed Emin Pasha, who was an important Ottoman administrator and statesman—a three-time grand vizier, a governor of Edirne and Aleppo, and an ambassador to London and St. Petersburg. Love inspired their marriage, at which time she converted to Islam and changed her name. In her first book, *Six Years in the Harem* (1872), Melek Hanım narrated how she accompanied her second husband to postings in Palestine and Syria, where she observed corruption and intrigue within the Ottoman administration while contributing actively to his career. The couple had three children: a daughter, Ayşe Sıdıka (introduced in the extracts here as Ayesha) and two sons, Muharrem (who died in infancy) and Mustafa Djehad.

Still, the marriage proved short-lived. When the couple's second son fell ill, Melek Hanım conspired to replace him with another child should he die. He survived, but one of her accomplices committed a murder for which she was arrested and imprisoned. The scandal resulted in a dramatic repudiation and divorce, after which she was exiled to Anatolia. The first extract here recounts her daring escape in the mid-1860s with her two surviving children aboard a mail steamer destined

---

Roberta Micallef and Siobhan Lambert-Hurley prepared the introduction, extracts, and annotations.

for the port city of Piraeus near Athens in Greece. There, they remained for around a month before continuing on to Paris. As intimated in the third extract, the rest of her life was dedicated to extracting the maintenance and property from her former husband that she deemed her due. Seeking vengeance, she even conspired with his political rivals. She learned of her husband's death in 1871 sometime after her daughter's Christian conversion and elopement. This circumstance led her to write in despair in the book's final pages: "Husband, daughter, wealth, position, prospects gone!" She committed suicide two years later.

At the end of *Six Years in Europe*, Melek Hanım recorded how her precarious financial position in exile also forced her into "supplying the necessaries of existence." Her two books—in effect, a two-part memoir—were thus written with sales figures in mind. Perhaps it is no wonder that they were melodramatic page-turners replete with Orientalist stereotypes of beautiful, childlike women (as exemplified by her description of her daughter's beauty in the first extract here), and a cruel harem full of rivalries and intrigues. Still, her text is important as an account of how misled Turkish women and young people remained about the freedoms of the West. In these extracts, representing the start of her European journey, she retains her optimism about being "Free!"—even as she critiques Greek roads, scenery, "knavery," and hospitality. But like Zeyneb Hanoum (also featured in this collection), Melek Hanım soon came to realize that she had exchanged one harem for another. Without economic freedom, there was no freedom—and yet without qualifications, a woman of her station could not earn a living without losing social footing.

In the fourth extract, the readers are exposed to the Cretan revolt (1866–69), which must have been in progress during the author's visit. The island of Crete, also known as Candia, had risen against Ottoman suzerainty during the Greek revolution launched in 1821—but when Greece received its independence in 1830, Crete was not included in the new state. A series of insurrections followed that, as the author indicates in the fourth extract, only heightened tensions between "the Greeks and the Turks." The Ottoman's economic and political difficulties led it to be identified, as the author notes, as a "sick man" by the mid-nineteenth century, ready to be dismantled by other European powers. For the British, Constantinople was important to their strategic interests in the Middle East and the protection of their trade roots from Asia to Europe. The Russian Empire, in contrast, had designs on Ottoman territory for the exit it would allow to the Aegean and Mediterranean seas. Ultimately, neither succeeded—despite the author's pessimism.

Melek Hanım's books found a ready audience in Britain, where both were published, and the first in particular went into multiple editions. Some reviewers, however, noted inaccuracies that led them to deem her work unreliable. A recent analyst, Irvin Schick, has elaborated on this theme, suggesting the considerable influence of the abolitionist editor, Louis Alexis Chamerovzow, on the text. He credits the editor's political views and affiliations with the books' success. Melek Hanım, in contrast, insisted that the sole merit of her two texts was "their truthfulness." There is no doubt that her accounts are sometimes untrustworthy, but the reader is given enough information about political events of the time to make the author appear well aware of the rhetoric of her time period. Indeed, it is this curious mixture of accuracy and inaccuracy that tempts the reader to see this text as a believable firsthand account.

EXTRACTS

Fleeing Constantinople

"Free!"—This was our first thought and exclamation on finding ourselves safely on board the *America*, the name of the mail steamer about to convey us to the Western world. "Free!"—Yet not wholly out of danger. We had fortunately evaded the police; we had obtained our passage-tickets without difficulty; but various unexpected accidents and contingencies might even now defeat our hopes. To conceal ourselves, then, until we should be well out of immediate peril, was our first impulse.

We hurried below and huddled ourselves up in a corner of the ladies' cabin, where we crouched, rather than sat, tormented with anxiety, forestalling every possible mishap, nevertheless breathing more freely, inspired with the hope of ultimately effecting our escape.

None save those who have been similarly circumstanced, who have panted between the prospect of freedom or a lifelong imprisonment, can possibly realize our emotions. Every sound, the echo of every fresh voice, the trampling of newcomers upon the deck—all these gave rise to every-changing feelings. . . .

The signal bell for departure, the revolving of the paddle wheels, the sensation of motion after what seemed an eternity of agony revived our spirits and our courage. Cramped in our cabin, longing for air—for that sunlight we felt was for us, was even exclusively our own—we at length ventured first to peep out, like mice looking if the coast is clear of cats. The noise of feet caused us to shrink back. It was only Djehad, who came to tell us we were passing Seraglio Point.[1] Thus encouraged, we came out and went on deck.

How thrilling was the sensation of freedom! To be free to move whither we liked—unveiled to breathe the air—unveiled to gaze at the sun, at the sky, at all the bright beauties of nature—at objects fast receding from view, but with which our eyes were so familiar!

As we descended the "Great Straits," every minute drawing more and more beyond danger, further and further from the immediate reach of that terrible, silent, fiery messenger, the telegraph, our spirits rose and our courage grew. To Ayesha, everything was novel, and much was startling.[2] It was odd to her to appear before everybody with her face uncovered, and she shrank from the inquisitive gaze of the menfolk on board; for to exhibit her face thus openly was so contrary to her habits, to her education, and to her belief, that to do so was not quite harmless. . . .

I might, myself, have easily passed muster in a crowd, or out of one. Ayesha, however, could not fail to challenge attention. The character of her beauty was strikingly Oriental. Her large Eastern eyes flashed with light from beneath her grand arched eyebrows and her long black eyelashes. No art could disguise the rich masses of her raven-colored hair or alter the symmetrical oval of her countenance. Her very carriage was peculiar, for let me say here no woman brought up in the harem knows how to walk. The gait is something between a waddle and a shuffle. Then, the utter freedom of her manners from the conventional restraints of what is called civilized society was of itself sufficient to attract more than passing notice.

Arriving in Greece

We arrived in Piraeus about midday, our next stage being Athens. I was rejoiced to learn that our stay at Piraeus would not exceed an hour. It is a much-frequented summer bathing place, but its general aspect disappointed me. The dwellings and the public buildings presented no striking characteristics, and the inhabitants appeared to me to be of a low type, offensively unclean in person, and uncouth in manner.

The hour proved a long one, and pleased enough were we when the carriage that was to convey us to Athens at last drew up at the door of the hotel, and we were summoned to take our places in it. . . .

From Piraeus to Athens is a two-hour ride, along a narrow, wretchedly kept-up road; if a road can be called kept up that is in a chronic condition of unrepair. The dust was fine as well as abundant, so that we seemed to be moving through a mist, and very soon became coated with a grayish white covering as though our latest employment had been grinding flour of indifferent quality. Nevertheless, our gaiety was boisterous, for we were as free as that very dust we were compelled to inhale, and for freedom's sake rather enjoyed than otherwise. The scenery was not attractive, but the sensation of perfect freedom lent it an extrinsic charm, which more than compensated for natural deficiencies. Olive tree plantations and vineyards alternated all along the road, which now ascending, brought us upon what seemed interminable plains, then dipping, plunged us into green valleys, fresh and cool, but also apparently never-ending. The fact is we were impatient to reach Athens, which at least appeared in sight. We got down at the Hôtel de la Grande Bretagne, situated immediately opposite the king's palace, and according to custom, we inscribed our names in the register kept for visitors. Little did I imagine the sensation that very simply formality would create. Kibrizli-Mehemet Pacha was a prince of Cyprus and born there; consequently his name was well-known, apart from the fact of his high official position.[3] I had never thought of this. Even if I had, I should probably not have concealed my name and quality. No sooner did these transpire than the landlord informed us, with every outward manifestation of consideration and courtesy, that our flight has been discovered, and telegrams from Constantinople had come intimating the fact to the Turkish ambassador. I received the intimation with the greatest indifference, knowing I was quite safe now, and that my presence would be rather agreeable than otherwise to the Greek party. At the table d'hôte—which I may state was in the Oriental style, most profuse and magnificent, and frequented not only by the guests staying in the hotel but also by the grandees and notabilities of the metropolis—we were the center toward which all eyes turned. The balcony of our apartments overlooked the great square, crowded by the population, who flock hither to drink coffee and to listen to the music, which every evening, as well as every morning, plays in front of the king's residence. When we came out upon the balcony, a new excitement seemed to pervade the crowd. The news of our arrival had soon spread, and our flight—probably exaggerated in its details—our rank, and our peculiar position already constituted us objects of special interest to this easily moved people.

Greek Life and Hospitality

My daughter seemed so completely happy in her novel position that I felt averse to mar her felicity by any reference to coming necessities and troubles, at least until it should be absolutely unavoidable to recall her to a sense of the realities of the house. As for plans, I had formed none very determinate, but as the days wore on, and I recovered from fatigue and the anxiety I had undergone, my spirits rose, my courage revived, and my mind recovered its elasticity and activity. Thus, from day to day, pondering over my position, I gradually came to the final determination to proceed to Paris and claim the friendly interposition of the French government to induce my husband either to allow us a fixed annual income or to give up the jewel, securities, money, and title deeds of properties settled upon myself and my daughter in our own right. I considered I had a perfect right to claim French interference in my behalf in virtue of my father's French descent.

Then, I believed in justice!

Our time in Athens, meanwhile, was passing away pleasantly enough. We went out daily to inspect the monuments and to see the sights. These latter were simply the incidents in the everyday life of the people. We made purchases, we frequented the public promenades; we contracted acquaintances, if we did not make friends. We also gained experience in numerous ways. We soon discovered the shop and stall keepers possessed a conscience of astounding elasticity in all matters of trade and would demand three and four times the worth of any article offered for sale—a price we, in our lamentable ignorance, at first paid. The value of money to us was absolutely unknown, and we did not suspect that knavery was a common element in business among these fair-spoken, smooth-tongued Greeks.

We were not long in ascertaining that hospitality does not figure among the national characteristics. In Turkey, to entertain is the rule. We found our Greek lady-acquaintances ready enough, even eager, to accept all kinds of courtesies at our hands when they visited us, but they never favored us in a similar way. The fact is pride lay at the root of their apparent churlish selfishness. In their case, the stomach suffers for the back. Their homes are not for strangers to see. Everything is sacrificed to outward show. A lady wearing gorgeous attire, and resplendent with jewels, shrinks from exposing the misery of the domestic interior, often squalid to the last degree. This absence of hospitality struck us painfully, for in Turkey even the poorest share with the stranger. Indeed, I was now prepared to find that in Europe, I must not expect to meet with hospitality upon the grand scale common in my own country. I confess that even when I discovered the cause of its absence in Athens—at least among the class I have designated—I felt disappointed, even a little mortified, interpreting it as a personal slight. I was simply oversensitive in my forlorn and peculiar position. At any rate, the prospect of being shut out from any kind of domestic intimacy with Greek female society had its influence in my deciding to make no prolonged stay where we were.

Greeks and Turks

We very frequently saw the young king on the public promenade. His countenance is intelligent, and his bearing is distinguished. He always wore a smile on his lips and saluted the multitude with the greatest affability. He struck me as being far from proud. I often thought of this young king ruling in so old a country, and I wondered whether they would grow and thrive together. He had no easy task before him, for the Greeks are a most difficult people to govern. Honesty, patriotism, public virtue, and national spirit are things unknown. Selfishness reigns paramount. In fact, the Greek element is essentially false.

Between the Greeks and the Turks, not the smallest particle of love is lost. The Turks are glad to secure the services of the Greeks because these people are so pliant, accommodating, and obsequious. In Constantinople, where the Greeks swarm and their influence makes itself felt, there is much less frankness and fair dealing than in the provinces. Self-interest is the link that brings both into association, but at bottom Greek hates Turk and Turk hates Greek. That this is the predominant popular sentiment admits of no doubt whatsoever.

The character of the people impresses itself upon the national policy, as a matter of course. Hence, that of the Greek government is sly, underhand, dark, dubious, and false. The plan of the Cretan insurrection, to wit, was known at Athens—notoriously known—long before it broke out, but the authorities, the diplomatists, knew nothing about it, or rather affected the most splendid ignorance. . . .[4]

I may say, whilst upon this subject, that I have more faith in the future of Greece than of Turkey. I regard Turkey not as a sick man, that is, a man likely to recover health and strength, but as one absolutely dying of consumption and whose last agony is a mere question of time. Turkey in Europe is an anomaly, and Constantinople is the natural geographical capital of Russia, which she will assuredly obtain someday, perhaps not so far distant. Turkey will then be thrown wholly back into Asia, upon which territory her institutions may find room and opportunity to develop among peoples of kindred religion; though it seems to me utterly impossible she can ultimately resist the inroads of Christian civilization. In contrast, Russia must grow European Turkey out of Europe. She knows how to wait, and though, when her time comes to assume possession of Constantinople, she will probably enlarge the boundaries of Greece, she was not likely, at the time of the Candian insurrection [in Crete], to take the false step of interfering in that contention, notwithstanding that her sympathies may have secretly tended that way.

Quitting Athens

I at length disclosed to my daughter my intention of quitting Athens.

This announcement suddenly aroused her to the realities of our position. We had been a month in that city; she was utterly oblivious of the past as though it were a forgotten dream. Young, entirely guileless of the world, released from the caged-up, monotonous life of the harem, with all its terrible restrains upon the mind as well as the body, she found herself all at once in a new sphere, which to her was paradise. The commonest incident of the life we were leading were to her so many new enjoyments and new sensations. It was a delight to be able to go about whither, and how, and when she listed; to speak and to be spoken to without fear. The very attempt to make herself understood—she had picked up a little French—had its charm and its amusement. Especially did she revel in the luxury of an unveiled face, of breathing the air without impediment, and in the novel indulgence of looking at those who looked at her.

So wholly was she carried away by pleasurable emotions, so absorbed was she in the luxurious felicities of her new life, that it cost me the severest pang to interrupt the current of her happiness. Had I listened to her entreaties, we should have remained in Athens. Were we not very happy? Had we not everything we needed? Were we not free? Were we not safe? Could we not communicate with her father as easily from where we were as from any other city? These and similar questions were pressed upon me, mingled with caresses and entreaties. It proved a task to convince her of the necessity of our breaking away from present temporary enjoyments in order to secure permanent prospective advantages. Then, was not Paris our destination and the haven of our hopes? There we should find the attractions and pleasures of Athens, multiplied a hundredfold. In that center of civilization, that resort of all the notabilities of the world—about to become a universal fair at which the industries of all the nations would be displayed[5]—she would enjoy the fullest opportunity of indulgence in her tastes, of augmenting her occupations, of enlarging her experience, of contracting friendships, of acquiring the education she so sorely needed to enable her to old her own among her equals; she would see the best of society in its most decorous attire, and on its foremost best behavior; she would mix with it herself, on an equality with the highest, having me constantly by, to guide and watch over her, to protect as well as love her. "And, my child," I added, "you shall then carry out your desire to embrace the Christian faith, and who knows, you may not find a new and a good husband?"

These arguments prevailed . . . we quitted Athens once more for Piraeus.

FURTHER READING

Melek Hanım. *Thirty Years in the Harem: Or, The Autobiography of Melek-Hanum Wife of H. H. Kibrizli-Mehemet-Pasha*. London: Chapman and Hall, 1872. https://archive.org/details /thirtyyearsinharoomeleuoft. Also available as a reprint with introduction by Irvin C. Schick. Piscataway, NJ: Gorgias, 2005.

Melek Hanım. *Six Years in Europe: Sequel to Thirty Years in the Harem. The Autobiographical Notes of Melek-Hanum Wife of H. H. Kibrizli-Mehemet-Pasha*, edited by L. A. Chamerovzow. London: Chapman and Hall, 1873. https://archive.org/details/sixyears ineuropeoomalirich.

Reina Lewis and Nancy Micklewright, eds. *Gender, Modernity and Liberty: Middle Eastern and Western Women's Writings: A Critical Sourcebook*, esp. 110–22. London: I. B. Tauris, 2006.

———. *Rethinking Orientalism: Women, Travel and the Ottoman Harem*. New Brunswick NJ: Rutgers University Press, 2004.

NOTES

1. Djehad was the author's youngest son. He is described elsewhere in the text as "repudiated and rejected, an outcast, and, like ourselves, a fugitive." Seraglio Point, known in Turkish as Sarayburnu, or "palace horn," is a promontory separating the Golden Horn from the Sea of Marmara. From there, the ship moved through a series of narrow waterways connecting the Black Sea to the Aegean and Mediterranean seas, or the "Great Straits."

2. Ayesha was the author's twenty-one-year-old daughter with whom she traveled.

3. The author's husband, who was, as she notes elsewhere in the text, "a member of the Council of Ministers."

4. The Cretan insurrection, or revolt, was a three-year uprising (1866–69) against Ottoman rule on the Greek island of Crete (also known as Candia). Led by Christian Cretans, it had the aim of uniting the island with independent Greece. After several more uprisings (1889, 1895, 1897), Crete was given autonomy under Ottoman suzerainty in 1898. It was recognized internationally as part of Greece in 1913.

5. The International Exposition, or *Exposition Universalle*, a world fair held in Paris in 1867.

SEVENTEEN

HUDA SHAARAWI

A European Summer on the Eve of War

INTRODUCTION

One of the most iconic episodes in Egyptian feminist history depicts Huda Shaarawi (1879–1947) (see fig. 17.1) standing on the deck of a ship and throwing her veil into the sea after attending a meeting of the International Alliance of Women in Rome in 1923. Earlier that year, she had established the Egyptian Feminist Union, seemingly in response to strained relations between male and female nationalists over women's roles in a new political system. Since 1920, she had acted as founding president of the Wafdist Women's Central Committee, the women's wing of Egypt's premier nationalist organization, forging unity between Egyptian women of different classes and religions. Under her leadership, veiled upper- and middle-class women held mass rallies and demonstrations, passed resolutions, played key diplomatic roles, facilitated communication between imprisoned and exiled male activists, and upheld morale in the face of colonial brutality. But in 1924, she resigned over the organization's lack of militancy in countering British colonialism—with women pushing for less accommodation with the colonial power than male leaders such as Saad Zaghlul. Subsequently, Huda focused her attention on feminist activism, leading the Egyptian Feminist Union until her death in 1947, while also acting as vice president of the International Alliance of Women (1935) and founding president of the Arab Feminist Union (1944). Her initiatives included two monthly journals (in Arabic and French), educational and health projects for poor women, and a number of

Siobhan Lambert-Hurley prepared the introductions, extracts, and annotations based on the English translation by Margot Badran.

Figure 17.1 A young Huda Shaarawi at her writing desk. From Wikipedia Commons.

government delegations to lobby for changes in family law, women's working conditions, and voting rights.

Huda Shaarawi's memoirs, composed in Arabic under the title *Mudhakkirati* in the final years of her life, offer an impressionistic account of her nationalist and feminist activities in the early 1920s, but not, unfortunately, her celebrated journey to Rome in 1923. Instead, they focus on her childhood and youth in the secluded environs of an upper-class harem. Her parents are introduced as Sultan Pasha, a wealthy landowner also prominent in Upper Egypt's provincial administration, and Iqbal, a Circassian beauty sent to Egypt as a child to escape war in the Caucasus. Nur al-Huda Sultan, as Huda was named at birth, was the elder of their two children, though her brother, Hasan (mentioned as a travel companion in the third extract), was favored as her father's only son from multiple marriages. Angered by this discrimination, Huda reported finding comfort from her father's elder wife, Hasiba, with whom she, her mother, and brother lived—not on her father's estate in Minya where she was born, but in his town house in a fashionable part of Cairo. When she was five years old, her father died, leaving his sister's son, Ali Shaarawi, as the trustee of his estate and his family's legal guardian. This cousin to Huda was in his forties with children older than her by a slave-concubine, but still they were wedded when she was just thirteen years old. Huda's turbulent relationship with her much older husband—indicated at the start of the first extract when he refuses to let her take their ill daughter abroad, and she in turn threatens to leave him (for a second time; they were separated from 1892 to 1900)—is a recurring theme in her memoirs. Only nationalist activism gave them a shared purpose that fortified their relationship in the final years before his death in 1922.

Also woven throughout Huda's memoirs are her accounts of travel to other parts of the Middle East and continental Europe, including Istanbul in 1905, Paris in 1908, and Europe in 1914, all three of which are extracted here. By the late nineteenth century, Egyptian royals and wealthy elites had made it a regular practice to summer abroad—meaning Huda's experiences of international travel would not have been unusual. Nevertheless, she made it clear to justify each journey on the basis of ill health with Europe constructed as a healthy place with better medical care where Egyptians could seek a "cure." In the first and third instance, the "cure" was for one of her two children, her daughter, Bathna, or her son, Muhammad, though in the second, it was for herself after her dear friend and mentor, Eugénie Le Brun, also known as Madame Rushdi, died in 1908. A Frenchwoman married to an Egyptian nobleman, Le Brun ran an intellectual salon in Cairo, where Huda may have been introduced to many of the nationalist and feminist ideals that appear in these extracts—not least France's symbolic role as a nationalist ally against British colonialism, the twinning of peace activism and women's suffrage, and the glories of former Arab rule in Europe. Earlier in her memoirs, Huda also reported meeting Marguerite Clement—the "friend" listed in the third extract—in the context of setting up a first series of lectures for women at the Egyptian University in Cairo (now Cairo University). The specific dates given in the third extract—corresponding to the first few weeks of the First World War—highlight the precariousness of traveling across Europe and the Mediterranean at this time.

EXTRACTS

A Turkish Summer

Having heard all my life how beautiful Turkey was and tales of life there, I was eager to see the country. One day at dusk, the ship glided through the Sea of Marmara. Like a bride prolonging the moment of magic, it began its slow approach into the port of Stamboul, at that fleeting moment when the sun's rays fall upon the Golden Horn, illuminating the domes and minarets of mosques around the port. The painted rooftop on the hills dotted the thick woods like roses strewn on a carpet of green. The call to prayer rose through a deep silence bespeaking the majesty of God.

On shore, we hired one of the canopy-covered carriages waiting at the water-side and began our drive up the European side of the Bosporus, toward Buyuk Deree and the *konak* [wooden house] Bashir Agha had rented for us high in the hills, in keeping with the doctor's order. We bounced along the rough cobble-stone road until it became so steep we had to get out and go the rest of the way on foot to the house. Expecting to find every comfort, especially after the arduous ride, I was stunned to see a small wooden house with a tiny courtyard lighted by a single gas lamp. Turning to the *agha*, I asked, "Weren't you able to find anything better than this? I have been noticing palatial residences all along the shore!" He answered, "This house was the best I could find and the cleanest, as well." Had I not been concerned about my mother and daughter, who were already exhausted, I would have turned around immediately. As it was, I went upstairs, hoping for something better, but the rooms had only the barest neces-sities. Deeply disappointed, I resolved to go out at dawn to find more suitable quarters.

But when the sun came up the next morning, it revealed one of the most breathtaking sights I had ever seen. The broad expanses of the Bosporus glis-tened before me, flanked on both sides by high, flower-covered hills with small, slant-roofed houses peering out. Below, the elegant residences of foreign em-bassies looked over the sea, and *yalis* [waterside mansions] sprawled gracefully to the water's edge. The panorama disarmed my annoyances with the *agha* and prevented me from looking for another house, as did the lovely garden I had just discovered. It was full of flowers and fruit trees. There were cherry trees laden with bright red clusters, and even an apricot tree, like those in my father's garden.

A Cure in Paris

Following the death of [my friend] Mme Rushdi, I became sick with grief and was advised to go abroad for a cure. My husband and I went to France. In Paris we stayed near the Champs Elysees in the Princess Hotel. I marveled at the bustling Place de la Concorde and was surprised to find an Egyptian obelisk standing in the center with its long, clean lines and handsome hieroglyphs, testi-mony to the splendor of ancient Egypt. That awesome monument of civilization symbolized a friendship between Egypt and France that had been strengthened by ties of history and cultural links. I watched the fashionably dressed women—men at their sides—promenading by the graceful fountains that sprayed water in fascinating shapes. It looked like a festival occasion, but I was told it was an everyday scene.

I liked Paris not only for its beautiful architecture, gardens and boulevards, and elegant dress and sophisticated entertainment, but because there was something to excite the imagination everywhere. Every street and square evoked the deeds of bygone heroes. Like an open book of the past, the city revealed both the prosperity enjoyed during the rule of the wise and the privation endured under the weak. The French flock to palaces, churches and museums, and historic squares. They grow up familiar with their past because of the monuments raised to honor those who have died for the freedom and independence of their country.

I liked the people, even the roughness of the common people, and admired their individualism in thinking and behavior. I believe their intense love of country, for they are French above all, is the secret of their courage and advancement.

Nevertheless, two things about Paris that I did not like were the odor of absinthe and cigarette smoke in the cafés, and the smell of the crowds leaving public places or mingling in the streets. The pushing crowds dismayed me because I thought the French were always courteous. I shall never forget the first time I entered a shop in Paris during a special sale. Seeing the crowd at the front door, I paused to let some people enter out of politeness as we do in the East, thinking someone in turn would allow me to enter. Unfortunately, not a soul was aware even of my existence. Suddenly, I was swept along by the crush of human bodies, pushed and pulled in a churning mass until I was about to cry. When I finally found myself in front of a counter and gently reached for a piece of material, as a lady would do in the East, someone snatched it from my hands. Once again I was on the verge of tears but held them back to avoid ridicule. Finally, using my arms like oars, I made my way through the human sea and escaped from the shop. Upon reaching the curb, I hailed a taxi. Before I could enter, however, a bystander jumped in without so much as a word of apology.

A European Summer on the Eve of War

The death of [of my niece Huda] profoundly affected her father, and we were all shocked, including my son, Muhammad, who was plunged into grief despite his tender age. At that time, he too had not been well and was plagued by fears. When the doctors could not determine the cause, they advised me to take to specialists in Europe and to seek the mountain air. I was forced to travel abroad. . . .

I set out burdened with sadness and worry, grieving for the death of my brother's daughter and anxious for the health of my mother and son. I had never traveled before without the company of my mother. I had the feeling I would never see her again and was about to turn back when I reach Alexandria, but my son's condition prevented me from doing so. We departed—the Pasha, my brother, his wife, and our children.

In Paris, my son was examined by doctors who advised a cure in the mountains. As my husband was in need of treatments at the mineral springs in Vittel, we decided to go there and afterward to the mountains. Hasan, his son, a student in England, as on holiday at the time and would join us.

While we were in Paris, I was invited to attend a large meeting for women who were agitating for peace and the right to vote. The meeting took place in a huge hall belonging to one of the French newspapers. Many women made speeches, including Mme Sévigné, Avril de Saint-Croix, and my friend Marguerite Clement.[1] I observed women, the youth, and even some military officers enthusiastically advocating peace. I was impressed. I began to think that Europeans had reached a high stage of advancement but was soon disabused of that idea. On the following day, I attended a lecture on psychological illnesses given by the well-known professor Père Villon, the brother of a friend of mine. When I congratulated him on the talk, he said he had heard I had attended the peace meeting the day before. "Are you a supporter of peace?"

I said, "Yes."

"How can that be when you are an Egyptian, and your country is occupied by the British army?"

I replied, "I believe in the victory of justice over force."

"Will the British leave your country peacefully? Would it be in their own interests to do so? Mlle Clement must have influenced you," he said. "I am among Frenchmen who await the day we can return the insult of the Germans."

I said I was sorry to hear him speak like that, especially after having witnessed the spirit of harmony between French and Germans at the meeting. I expressed the hope that he would change his mind.

He answered, "I hope you will come around to my way of thinking."[2]

While the Pasha was concluding his treatment at Vittel, I did some shopping in Paris. The hotels were filled up with summer visitors and had no room for Hasan and me. So we stayed with my maid, Margaret, at a flat belonging to my brother. I was surprised to find the streets of Paris quiet, the cafés closed at night, and faces sad and uneasy. I heard talk of the possibility of war between France and Germany, which I refused to believe. Europe seemed too civilized and enlightened to resort to war, the most brutal act imaginable. When my friend Marguerite Clement visited me, her face was pale, and she was bent as if carrying a heavy burden. She said that the international situation was grave and war was likely. When I asked what she and her colleagues in the peace movement would do, she said, "We will stand by our people. But, our voice is still weak." Despite these grim words, I could not believe war would come.

The train back to Vittel was uncharacteristically empty. The Pasha and children who were waiting anxiously for us at the station said that the hotel was empty and that the local inhabitants were leaving the town because it was close to the border, and they feared hostilities between the French and Germans. That was on July 29. The hotel employees were sad, especially the maids, because their husbands had been called up. The manager, preparing to deliver sacks of money to the bank, said he was ordered to close the hotel. My husband asked him to change fifty French pounds, and the manager, silent for a moment, replied, "At your service, even though this is not allowed."

We left Vittel for Switzerland the first of August. We were supposed to change trains a few hours later for one with a dining car, but the second train did not appear. When it grew late, we asked the station master what had happened, and he answered brusquely, "Is this a time for touring, especially with children?" We did not know till that moment that it was mobilization day. Trains moved past filled with soldiers waving flags and singing patriotic songs while women with tears in their eyes were bidding them farewell. Later, we were able to board another train for Switzerland.

As soon as we arrived in Basle, we headed for the nearest hotel, but the manager said he had no vacancies. I asked him if he thought I was about to take my young children and go out in to the streets at three o'clock in the morning looking for a place. When I suggested that we sleep on the couches in the lounge, which he said was forbidden, he procured rooms for us by telephone at a hotel in the old city on the other side of the Rhône and ordered taxis to take us there. It was a small, simple hotel but very clean. The maid brought us milk, cheese, and bread, and before long, we went to sleep. The next morning, we saw golden-haired and blue-eyed boys and girls playing in the street. Their gaiety lifted my fatigue and some of the melancholy that had filled me after seeing the tearful women bid their men off to war. However, even the children filled me with anguish as I thought of the young ones who would be orphaned by war.

From Basle we went to Zurich, where the train station was also filled with soldiers and their relatives, while a band played military music. Our hotel there was so crowded, we had to sleep in the reception room and take breakfast in the dining hall.

Zurich, splendidly laid out along an exquisite lake, was one of the most beautiful cities I had ever seen. On a walk with the children, I found a funicular that went to a place on the outskirts called Zurichburg. There I found a lovely hotel, and we took rooms in it on the following day. We were sorry we did not speak German and sometimes had difficulty making ourselves understood. One day, as I walked with the children in the wooded area near the hotel, a man passing by said a few words I could not understand. I was taken aback that he would speak to people he had never met. A little while later, another man on a horse with an old-fashioned saddle called out a few words of German, and again I was surprised. Afterward I learned that it is a Swiss custom to greet people on the road, especially on country lanes. That was exactly the habit of the Egyptian *fallah* [peasants].

The Pasha decided that we should leave Switzerland and return to Egypt via Italy. The train to Milan was so crowded that we were obliged to occupy a third-class carriage even though we had first-class tickets. In Milan, we stayed at a small hotel in order to economize. Our finances had begun to dwindle, especially after we had encountered a number of Egyptians who asked for help after their money had run out. Sympathetic to their plight, the Pasha gave them most of what he had, and the banks would not cash more than twenty francs a day. Our uncomfortable hotel overlooked the Piazza del Duomo, which was so crowded and noisy, mainly from the cries of newspaper vendors, that we could not rest day or night. We stayed in Milan only briefly before departing for Genoa to take a ship back to Egypt.

All ships were fully booked at that time, but we managed to get reservations from an Egyptian who had arranged passage on an Italian ship. I wanted to return to Egypt as fast as possible so my sick mother would not grow anxious over us when she learned that war had broken out. A shock might bring her closer to the grave. The SS *Oriente* departed on August 10 around midnight. Our staterooms were uninhabitable, owing to the dirt and excessive heat, and no other rooms were available. When some of the ship's officers offered their cabins at a stiff price, the Pasha gave nearly all his money to secure our comfort. Relieved, we went upstairs and found the rooms well ventilated. But no sooner had we put our heads on our pillows than we were attacked by swarms of cockroaches. We bundled the children out of the room and spent the night in chairs on the deck. The next morning, we requested the captain to have a tent set up on the deck so we could sleep there. The Pasha slept in a chair next to Muhammad while I, scarcely able to sleep for fear that one of the children would fall to the deck, occupied one next to my daughter. One night, as my weary eyes began to close, I heard what I thought was the sounds of a body hitting the deck, and I awoke screaming. Bathna had rolled over, and I could hear her saying, "Mama, don't be afraid. Nothing has happened to me."

On the fourth day out, we steamed slowly toward Naples in a dense fog, the ship's horn blowing frightening blasts. Suddenly, there was a large jolt followed by screaming from the direction of the third class. Fearing that our ship had collided with another, I ran to the railing and looked down at the sea. Hats and pieces of wood were floating on the water. I began to run in search of my children so they would be near me if we sank. Meanwhile, the captain announced that we had hit a fishing boat and that the fishermen were in the water. Officers and crew members from our ship were lowered in boats to pick up the fishermen. The sailors, dressed in white, standing erect in the boats with foghorns in their mouths, looked like phantoms in the eerie mist. For two hours they searched for the last fisherman, but he was never found. The rescue boats returned, and the fog lifted as if it had never existed. It was one of those fateful moments when the angel of death snatches up those chosen by destiny. The crew asked for donations from the passengers for the families, but pockets were empty, and only about ten pounds were collected. That evening, the ship entered the port of Naples, where it stayed loading potatoes all night. We were unable to sleep after the shock.

The next day, the ship arrived at Catania. We saw women on the beach in their national dress, which resembled Oriental clothes. They wore long, black skirts fringed with lace or a swathe of colored material and covered their heads with black shawls pinned up at the back, reminiscent of the old-fashioned *izar* [black cloak]. The ship was to stay in port all day, so we explored that fascinating town where the Arabs had once been and where there are remnants of their monuments and their customs. We visited a number of churches as well. It happened to be a saint's day, the feast of a woman saint. We watched a religious procession led by a priest in a purple robe; some people were kneeling at either side of the road while others rushed forward to kiss the hem of his robe. We were astonished at the depth of their religious feeling. Afterward, we bought the few things we were able to pay for and hurried to the ship. I was relieved when the ship pulled out because we feared that if Italy declared war, we would be forced to remain. We were sure our worst fears had been realized when we saw a small boat coming after us to guide the ship back to port, but the captain, informed of our apprehensions, said jokingly that the ship had a huge supply of potatoes that would last a good long time. I feared that the delay would be the death of my mother.

I saw other women weeping, like myself, at the unexpected delay. Their money had run out, and they were worried about how they would earn a living during the war, for most of them had no profession. As for our livelihood, I had enough jewelry and precious stones to maintain my children and myself for years. One said, "I am a good cook, and if I am detained in Italy, I can work as a chef in a pension or with a family." Another said, "I cannot sew or cook, so what shall I do?" After a pause, she continued. "Maybe I could be a nanny." When I heard that, I asked myself what I would do in their position. I could neither cook nor sew nor leave my children to work in someone's house. It was a lesson for me, and afterward I learned how to cook and sew. In later years, I admired the courage and ingenuity of the Russian women I met in Egypt after the war, some of whom were princesses, but they were not ashamed to earn honorable livelihoods after migrating from their country. One of them, whose flair for needlework I admired, told me she found consolation and satisfaction in producing work that people appreciated. She confessed she had not fully understood the meaning of life until she had begun to be creative and take on responsibilities.

After the ship anchored again at Catania, we learned that the steamship company had requested that the ship be recoaled in Alexandria. When they found it would be impossible, the ship had to turn around to take on coal for the return voyage. Our departure was delayed for another twenty-four hours, but we were greatly relieved that Italy had still not entered the war.

We docked in Alexandria on August 19.

FURTHER READING

Huda Shaarawi. *Mudhakkirat Huda Shaw'rawi ra'idat al-Mar'ah al-'Arabiyah al-ḥadithah.* Cairo: Dar al-Hilal, 1981.

Margot Badran, ed. *Harem Years: The Memoirs of an Egyptian Feminist.* London: Virago, 1986.

Leila Ahmed. "Between Two Worlds: The Formation of a Turn-of-the-Century Egyptian Feminist." In *Life/lines: Theorizing Women's Autobiography*, edited by Bella Brodzki and Celeste Schenck, 154–74. Ithaca: Cornell University Press, 1989.

S. Asha. "The Intersection of the Personal and the Political: Huda Shaarawi's Harem Years and Leila Ahmed's A Border Passage." *The IUP Journal of English Studies* 7, no. 2 (June 2012): 31–38.

Julia Lisiecka. "Re-reading Huda Shaarawi's 'Harem Years'—Bargaining with Patriarchy in Changing Egypt." *SOAS Journal of Postgraduate Research* 8 (2015): 46–58.

Sana Sharawi Lanfranchi. *Casting Off the Veil: The Life of Huda Shaarawi, Egypt's First Feminist.* London: I. B. Tauris, 2014.

NOTES

1. The most prominent of these women was Avril de Saint-Croix (1855–1939), an author and campaigner who also led prominent women's organisations, including Le Conseil Nationale de Femmes Françaises.

2. Her conciliatory tone here contrasts with her later militancy, noted in this chapter's introduction.

EIGHTEEN

ZEYNEB HANOUM

A Turkish Désenchantée in Europe

INTRODUCTION

Zeyneb Hanoum (d. ca. 1923) (see fig. 18.1) introduces herself on the title page of
A Turkish Woman's European Impressions as the "heroine of Pierre Loti's novel."
This refers to his bestseller, *Les Désenchantées*, first published in 1906. Apparently, she and her sister, Melek Hanoum—two highly educated daughters of a
prominent minister in the Sultan's government, Noury Bey, who was himself
the son of a French nobleman relocated to the Ottoman Empire—had contacted
the author two years before its publication, when he was in Istanbul gathering
material for his novels. By providing details of their segregated lives by letter,
they hoped that he would draw attention to their plight—as Turks living under
Abdul Hamid II's despotic regime and as Turkish women imprisoned within the
harem. Their fear of retaliation from the sultan—who, according to Zeyneb's
own account, was keen to bring these "dangerous women" to heel—is offered
as explanation for their flight from Turkey to Europe shortly before Loti's novel
appeared. But elsewhere, it is hinted that Zeyneb's actual motivation was an arranged marriage to her father's secretary that she could not bear. Zeyneb never
offered a detailed account of their "escape," though Melek did many years later
in an article for *The Strand Magazine*. There, she revealed how, having bribed
their Polish music teacher for passports, they traveled to France via Serbia on the
iconic Orient Express. In Belgrade, they just managed to evade arrest on false
charges, but Zeyneb's health suffered, with the effect that she was very ill with
consumption by time they landed in Nice. There are references to this "terrible

Siobhan Lambert-Hurley prepared the introduction, extracts, and annotations.

Figure 18.1 Zeyneb Hanoum in her Paris drawing room, from *A Turk-ish Woman's European Impressions* (1913). From Project Gutenberg, https://www.gutenberg.org/files/50540/50540-h/50540-h.htm.

journey" and her own poor health in the first extract, in which she records her initial impressions of arriving in Europe.

Once settled in Fontainebleau near Paris, the two sisters became a magnet for journalists eager to interview Loti's *désenchantées*: to report their experiences of Turkish life and impressions of Europe in their own words to a public already enthralled by harem literature. Zeyneb's conscious employment of this fame to further her own writing career is suggested by her adoption of Loti's pseudonyms for her and her sister: their real names were Hadjidjé Zennour and Nouryé Neyr-el Nissa. One journalist who gained their confidence on account of her sensitivity to Ottoman cultural norms was Grace Ellison (d. 1935). After meeting Zeyneb and Melek near the start of their journey in 1906, she initiated a six-year correspondence that forms the basis of *A Turkish Woman's European Impressions*. The book is thus not a continuous travelogue but is rather extracts from letters—mostly by Zeyneb, but also a few by Melek—organized into chronological chapters and framed by Ellison's dialogue on their developing friendship, including a whole chapter on their visit to the sculptor Rodin. As editor, Ellison provided an introduction to the book that vouched for Zeyneb's authenticity and provided necessary context for a Western readership. She was also responsible for at least some of the images and the chapters' alluring titles intended to entice readers with promises of Orientalist exotica while at the same time hinting at how the narrative inverted those stereotypes—in particular, through Zeyneb's critical rendering of European "freedoms." As an example, much of the longer, second extract here comes from a chapter entitled "Is This Really Freedom?"

The place and date that introduce each letter allow the reader to track Zeyneb's movements during her six years in Europe. From Fontainebleau, she and Melek traveled through France in stages to Territet and Caux in Switzerland in the hope that mountain air would improve her health. Once strong enough, they returned to France early in 1907, first spending several months in Nice before going to Paris and finally Hendaye on the Spanish border. The first extract, from this early stage of her journey, reveals Zeyneb's initial delight at being released from the harem to move about freely without a veil. But she is soon jaded by her observation of women participating in futile and arduous activities in the Alps: tennis, climbing, dancing, tobogganing, and skating. The "snobbery" that she experienced in Nice followed by the superficial socializing of a Paris season and the bloody spectacle of a Spanish bullfight made her long for greater intellectualism. When Melek married a Polish aristocrat in 1908 (after converting to Catholicism), Zeyneb traveled alone to London. The second extract, from this middle portion of her European sojourn, points to her growing disillusionment by highlighting the unfinished and often harsh realities of Western feminism. London may hold its charms—especially when compared to Paris—but in the end, Turkish women are more admired than their English counterparts. By 1911, Zeyneb was back in continental Europe, touring Italy and France before ultimately returning to Istanbul the next year. The third extract is from this final leg of her journey and reveals her disenchantment complete: the freedom she longed for had not lived up to expectation.

Shortly after Zeyneb's return to Turkey, her book appeared from a London-based publisher in 1913. Reviews were mixed, with some appreciating Zeyneb's East-West comparisons, whereas others characterized her strong opinions as a "negligible exception" rooted in "superficial" stereotypes. Her disenchantment was attributed to a youthful diet of "decadent" French literature, though in her own writing, Zeyneb also listed the *Arabian Nights* and Lady Mary Wortley Montagu's *Letters* as literary models. The same year saw her sister, Melek, publish her own book, *Abdul Hamid's Daughter: The Tragedy of an Ottoman Princess*, also with Grace Ellison. As indicated in the second extract, Ellison traveled to Turkey herself in 1908 to report on the new Young Turk government, but a longer visit in 1913–14, during which she gained privileged access to Turkish homes, led to a serialized column in the *Daily Telegraph*. It was compiled in 1915 into her best known work, *An Englishwoman in a Turkish Harem*. Clearly the relationship between Ellison and the two sisters, Zeyneb and Melek, was productive in resulting in three books. But for Zeyneb, it appears to have marked the end of her public career. In her *Telegraph* column and later books, Ellison reported that back in Turkey, Zeyneb lived a quiet existence under the close supervision of her female relations before dying, probably of consumption, in her late twenties. Still, her image of the *désenchantée* remained a potent symbol of Ottoman womanhood.

EXTRACTS

Fontainebleau, 1906

You ask me to give you my first impression of France, but it is not so much an impression of France, as the impression of being free, that I am going to write. What I would like to describe to you is the sensation of intense joy I felt as I stood for the first time before a window wide open that had neither latticework nor iron bars.

It was at Nice. We had just arrived after our terrible journey. . . . It must have been early when I awoke the next morning to find the sun forcing its way through the white curtains and flooding the whole room with gold. Ill as I was, the scene was so beautiful that I got out of bed and opened wide the window, and what was my surprise to find that there was no latticework between me and the blue sky, and the orange trees, and the hills of Nice covered with cypress and olives? The sanatorium garden was just one mass of flowers, and their sweet perfume filled the room. With my eyes I drank in the scene before me, the hills and the sea, and the sky that never seemed to end.

A short while after, my sister came in. She also from her window had been watching at the same time as I. But no explanation was necessary. For the first time in our lives, we could look freely into space—no veil, no iron bars. It was worth the price we had paid just to have the joy of being before that open window.

London, 1908–9

On those evenings when I dine at "my club" (see how English I have become!), I eat alone, studying all the time the people I see around me. What a curious harem![1] ...

The first time I dined there, I ordered the vegetarian dinner, expecting to have one of those delicious meals that you are enjoying (you lucky woman!), which consists of everything that is good.[2] But alas! the food in this harem has been a disappointment to me. Surely I must not accept this menu as a sample of what English food really is.

On a little table all to myself, I was served with, first of all, rice that was cooked not as in Turkey, and as a second course I had carrots cooked in water! After sprinkling on them quantities of salt and pepper, I could not even then swallow them, so I asked for pickles, but as there were none, that dish was sent away almost untouched to join the first. Next I was served with a compote of pears without sugar, but that also did not come up to my expectations. I ate up, however, all my bread and asked for more. Then the waiter kindly went from table to table to see how much he could collect, brought just a handful, and informed me he really could not give me any more. But I told him it was not enough. "I want a very large piece," I said, so finally he decided to consult the butler, went to the kitchen, and brought me back a loaf to myself.

All the while, the curious people around me had been staring at me devouring my loaf, but after a while they wearied at that exciting entertainment, their faces again resumed their usual calm expression, and they went on once more talking to one another. Sometimes, but not often, they almost got interested in their neighbor's remark, but as soon as the last words were uttered again, they adopted a manner that seemed to me one of absolute indifference.

As you know, I do not swear by everything Turkish, but you must now admit from experience that when once the Danube is crossed, the faces to be seen do express some emotion, either love or hate, contentment or disappointment, but not indifference. Since I left Belgrade, I have tried, almost in vain, to find in the Western faces the reflection of some personality, and so few examples have I found that their names would not certainly fill this page. Here in London, I met with the same disappointment. Have these people really lost all interest in life?

They give me the impression that they all belong to the same family, so much alike are they in appearance and in facial expression.

In the reading room, where I spent my evening, I met those same people, who spoke in whispers, wrote letters, and read the daily papers. The silence of the room was restful, there was an atmosphere almost of peace, but it is not the peace which follows strife; it is the peace of apathy. Is this, then, what the Turkish women dream of becoming one day? Is this their ideal of independence and liberty?

Were you to show my letter to one of my race, she would think that I had a distinct aversion for progress, or that I felt obliged to be in opposition to everything in the countries where I was traveling. You know enough of my life, however, to know that this is not the case. What I do feel, though, is that a *Ladies' Club* is not a big enough reward for having broken away from an Eastern harem and all the suffering that has been the consequence of that action. A club, as I said before, is after all another kind of harem, but it has none of the mystery and charm of the harem of the East.[3]

How is one to learn and teach others what might perhaps be called "the tact of evolution"—I mean the art of knowing when to stop even in the realm of progress? . . .

Do not think that this evening's pessimism is due to the fog [outside] or my poor dinner. It is the outcome of disillusions that every day become more complete. It seems to me that we Orientals are children to whom fairy tales have been told for too long—fairy tales that have every appearance of truth. You hear so much of the *mirage* of the East, but what is that compared to the *mirage* of the West, to which all Orientals are attached?

They tell you fairy tales too, you women of the West—fairy tales that, like ours, have all the appearance of truth. I wonder, when the Englishwomen have really won their vote and the right to exercise all the tiring professions of men, what they will have gained?[4] Their faces will be a little sadder, a little more weary, and they will have become wholly disillusioned.

—∞—

Since I came here, I have seen nothing but "Votes for Women" chalked all over the pavements and walls of the town. These methods of propaganda are all so new to me.

I went to a suffrage street corner meeting the other night, and I can assure you I never want to go again. The speaker carried her little stool herself, another carried a flag, and yet a third woman a bundle of leaflets and papers to distribute to the crowd. After walking for a little while, they placed the stool outside a dirty-looking public house, and the lady who carried the flag boldly got on to the stool and began to shout, not waiting till the people came to hear her, so anxious was she to begin. Although she did not look nervous in the least, she possibly was, for her speech came abruptly to an end, and my heart began to beat in sympathy with her.

When the other lady began to speak, quite a big crowd of men and women assembled: degraded-looking ruffians they were, most of them, and a class of man I had not yet seen. All the time they interrupted her, but she went bravely on, returning their rudeness with sarcasm. What an insult to womanhood it seemed to me, to have to bandy words with this vulgar mob. One man told her that "she was ugly." Another asked "if she had done her washing," but the most of their hateful remarks I could not understand, so different was their English from the English I had learned in Turkey.[5]

Yet how I admired the courage of that woman! No physical pain could be more awful to me than not to be taken for a lady, and this speaker of such remarkable eloquence and culture was not taken for a lady by the crowd, seeing she was supposed "to do her own washing" like any women of the people.

The most pitiful part of it all to me is the blind faith these women have in their cause, and the confidence they have that in explaining their policy to the street ruffians, who cannot even understand they are ladies, they will further their cause by half an inch.

I was glad when the meeting was over but sorry that such rhetoric should have been wasted on the half-intoxicated loungers who deigned to come out of the public house and listen. If this is what the women of your country have to bear in their fight for freedom, all honor to them, but I would rather groan in bondage.

—⁂—

The Englishmen remind me of the Turks. They have the same grave demeanor, the same appearance of indifference to our sex, the same look of stubborn determination, and, like the Turk, every Englishman is a sultan in his own house. Like the Turk too, he is sincere and faithful in his friendships, but Englishmen have two qualities that the Turks do not possess. They are extremely good businessmen and in social relations are extremely prudent, although it is difficult to say where prudence ends and hypocrisy begins.

But if Englishmen remind me of Turks, I can find nothing in common between English and Turkish women. They are in direct contrast to one another in everything. Perhaps it is this marked contrast that balances our friendship. A Turkish woman's life is as mysterious as an Englishwoman's life is an open book, which all can read who care. Before I met the suffragettes, I knew only sporting and society women. They were all passionately absorbed in their own amusements, which as you know do not in the least appeal to me. I suppose we Turkish women, who have so much time to devote to culture, become unreasonably exacting. But everywhere I have been—in England, Germany, France, Italy, and Spain—I have found how little and how uselessly the women read, and how society plays havoc with their taste for good books.

Englishwomen are pretty but are deficient in charm. They have no particular desire and make no effort to please. You know the charm of the Turkish woman. The Englishwoman is pigheaded, undiplomatic, brutally sincere, but a good and faithful friend. The Turkish woman—well, you must fill that in yourself! I am too near to focus on her.

But now I have seen the women of most countries, you may want to know which I most admire.

Well, I will tell you frankly, the Turkish woman. An ordinary person would answer, "Of course," but you are not an ordinary person, so I shall at once give you my reasons. It is not because I am a Turkish woman myself, but because in spite of the slavery of their existence, Turkish women have managed to keep their minds free from prejudice. With them, it is not what people think they ought to think, but what they think themselves. Nowhere else in Europe have I found women with such courage in thinking.

In every country, there are women—though they may be a mere handful—who are above classes, above nationality, and dare to be themselves. These are the people I appreciate the most. These are the people I shall always wish to know, for to them the whole world is kin.

Paris and Marseille, 1912

Do you remember the year of my arrival? Do you remember how I wanted to urge all my young friends away yonder to take their liberty as I had taken mine, so that before they died, they might have the doubtful pleasure of knowing what it was to live?

Now, I hope if ever they come to Europe, they will not come to Paris except as tourists; that they will see the beautiful things there are to be seen, the Provence with its fine cathedrals and historic surroundings; that they will amuse themselves taking motorcar trips and comparing it with their excursions on a mule's back in Asia; that they will see the light of Paris but never its shade; and that they return, as you have returned from Constantinople, with one regret, that you couldn't stay longer.

If only my experience could be of use to my compatriots who are longing as I longed six years ago for the freedom of the West, I shall never regret having suffered.

—⁂—

What heartbreaking disappointments have I not to take away with me! . . .

I do not pretend to understand the suffragettes and their "window-smashing" policy, but I must say I am even more surprised by the attitude of your government.[6] However much these ill-advised women have overstepped the boundaries of their sex privileges, however wrong they may be, surely the British government could have found some other means of dealing with them, given their cause the attention they demanded, or used some diplomatic way of keeping them quiet. I cannot tell you the horrible impression it produces on the mind of a Turkish woman to learn that England not only imprisons but tortures women; to me it is the cataclysm of all my most cherished faiths. Ever since I can remember, England had been to me a kind of Paradise on earth, the land that welcomed to its big, hospitable bosom all of Europe's political refugees. It was the land of all lands I longed to visit, and now I hear a Liberal government is torturing women. Somehow my mind will not accept this statement. . . .

Do you remember with what delight I came to France, the country of Liberté, Egalité, and Fraternité? But now I have seen those three magic words in practice, how the whole course of my ideas has changed! Not only are my theories on the nature of governments no longer the same, but my confidence in the individual happiness that each can obtain from these governments is utterly shattered.

—⁂—

Désenchantée I left Turkey, *désenchantée* I have left Europe. Is that role to be mine till the end of my days?

FURTHER READING

Zeyneb Hanoum. *A Turkish Woman's European Impressions*. Edited by Grace Ellison. London: Seely, Service & Co., 1913. https://archive.org/details/turkishwomanseuroozeyn. Also available as a reprint introduced by Reina Lewis (Piscataway, NJ: Gorgias Press, 2004).

Melek Hanoum and Grace Ellison. *Abdul Hamid's Daughter: The Tragedy of an Ottoman Princess*. London: Methuen, 1913.

Melek Hanoum. "How I Escaped from the Harem and How I Became a Dressmaker." *The Strand Magazine* (February 1926): 129–38.

Grace Ellison, *An Englishwoman in a Turkish Harem*. London: Methuen, 1915. Also available as a reprint introduced by Teresa Heffernan and Reina Lewis (Piscataway, NJ: Gorgias Press, 2007).

Grace Ellison, *Turkey Today*. London: Hutchinson, 1928.

Pierre Loti. *Les Désenchantées: Roman des Harem Turcs Contemporains*. Paris: Calmann-Levy, 1906.

Reina Lewis. "Telling Tales: Harem Literature from East to West." *Edinburgh Review*. https://edinburgh-review.com/back-issues/more/issue-125-turkey/article-reina-lewis/.

——. *Rethinking Orientalism: Women, Travel and the Ottoman Harem*. London: I. B. Tauris, 2004.

NOTES

1. Ladies' clubs had sprung up in late Victorian Britain to serve growing numbers of professional and independent women. They offered a homely refuge in London's city center, as well as the opportunity for social and political interaction with like-minded women. Zeyneb does not specify which club she attended, but some possibilities are the Lyceum Club or the Empress Club. A nearly contemporaneous Muslim woman traveler from India, Atiya Fyzee (also featured in this collection), was invited to the former and dined at the latter during her stay in London in 1906–7.

2. The author was writing to her English friend and the book's editor, Grace Ellison. At the time, she was in Constantinople for the first debate of the new Turkish parliament set up after the Young Turk Revolt of 1908.

3. Notably, Selma Ekrem (also featured in this collection) draws a similar parallel between the Turkish harem and ladies' clubs in "the West": "You here in America with your clubs reserved specially for women have better harems than we have in Turkey" (Selma Ekrem, *Unveiled: The Autobiography of a Turkish Girl*. Reprinted with an introduction by Carolyn Goffman [Piscataway, NJ: Gorgias, 2005], 312).

4. The author's question reflects her residence in London in the midst of an increasingly militant campaign for women's suffrage. As she indicated later in the same extract, it involved female activists giving speeches and holding rallies in the street, as well as more violent forms of protest. Her reference to the professions points to how recently certain occupations had been opened to British women and how others still remained closed. Though women were licensed to practice medicine from 1876, they could not qualify as a solicitor until 1922.

5. Presumably, she refers here to the cockney accents of working-class Londoners.

6. Following the defeat of the Parliamentary Franchise (Women) Bill in 1912, the Women's Social and Political Union launched a "window-smashing" campaign. It involved hammers and stones being used to smash shop windows on prominent London thoroughfares. Subsequently, large numbers of suffragettes were arrested. The "torture" to which Zeyneb refers was probably force-feeding for prisoners on hunger strike.

NINETEEN

SELMA EKREM

Alone in New York City

INTRODUCTION

Selma Ekrem (1902–86) titled her first substantive literary work *Unveiled: The Autobiography of a Turkish Girl* (see fig. 19.1). First published in 1930 by a New York–based publisher, it focused on her privileged childhood in a liberal household in the final years of the Ottoman Empire. Her father, Ali Ekrem, is repeatedly invoked as the son of Namik Kemal, the Turkish author, journalist, and playwright who played a key role in the political activities of the reformist Young Ottomans in the 1860s and 1870s. This paternal grandfather had fled to Paris in 1867 after being exiled for his criticism of the sultan's government. In contrast, Ekrem's maternal grandfather had been sent to France from his home in Egypt (then under Ottoman rule) for education at the military academy known as Saint-Cyr. After charming Napoleon III's court, he came to Istanbul—Ekrem's birthplace and sometimes childhood home—where he rose to become a decorated general in the sultan's army. That his exalted career and his son-in-law's distinguished position as one of Abdul Hamid II's secretaries could not protect the family from the ruler's spies and intrigues is indicated by the underlying current of fear in the early chapters. Ekrem's title, *Unveiled*, thus evoked a familiar image of Muslim womanhood in Europe and America while at the same time signifying that she was revealing more of what had been concealed than just women's bodies. Her unconventional perspective—as a governor's daughter raised as a Muslim in a segregated household, but inspired by her parents' liberality to question political, religious, and gender norms—made her life story irresistible to an American

Siobhan Lambert-Hurley prepared the introduction, extracts, and annotations.

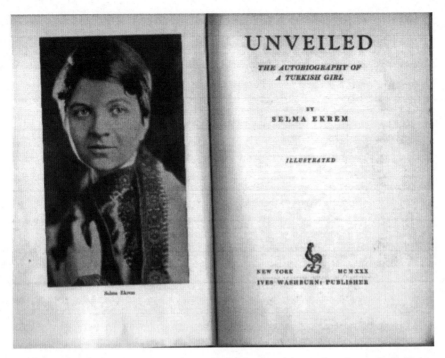

Figure 19.1 Selma Ekrem, from *Unveiled: The Autobiography of a Turkish Girl*
(1930). Courtesy of Siobhan Lambert-Hurley.

audience. By 1936, it had gone into a fourth printing after a series of approving
reviews in the mainstream press.

Ekrem's autobiography is of especial interest here because it contains four separate accounts of travel. The first and most lengthy covers the two years that she
lived in Jerusalem—between the ages of four and six—while her father acted as
governor. In exile from the imperial capital, Ekrem upholds Orientalist assumptions by projecting Jerusalem and its environs as a place of irrational passions and
fanaticism: a provincial outpost that requires "civilizing" through her father's enlightened administration. A recurrent trope is that of the "dirty" but "hospitable"
Arab who, at best, displays a noble savagery in juxtaposition to the urbanity and
cosmopolitanism of Ekrem's own family. The second recounts another year in exile, this time on the island of Rhodes, where the family lived while Ekrem's father
acted as governor-general of the Archipelago Islands (now the Aegean Islands).
The Greek inhabitants, as the Arabs, are "unruly," but her father is shown able
to win them over through a "kindness and justice" apparently not appreciated
by the new Unionist government in Constantinople. By the age of eight, Ekrem
is thus forced to leave her "carefree" life in Rhodes—a description somewhat
belied by her narrative focus on a devastating cyclone and torturous dentistry
by a barber—to return to Constantinople. The third travel section again details

Ekrem's experiences in the Archipelago Islands after her father was reposted there—specifically, to the island of Mytilene—in 1912, but as the Balkan conflict had just commenced, this section is more a narrative of war, imprisonment, and escape. Still, the itinerancy of her early years combined with a liberating education later at the American College for Girls seemed to leave Ekrem open to the "lure of adventure." With the Turkish Republic only just declared in 1924, she found herself longing to travel again—"to be a grain of sand tossed by new waves of people"—with the United States of America as her fourth destination.

The final two chapters of Ekrem's autobiography address the early days and weeks of what was to become a lifetime sojourn in the United States. The extracts here are from the first of those two chapters, "My American Venture," focusing on her departure from "old Stamboul" and her arrival in New York City. Unlike previously, Ekrem traveled alone, not even met by her one American friend until a few days into her stay. Her justification for this atypical "venture" was made in terms of the book's underlying theme: "to be able to wear a hat in peace." From early in her autobiography, Ekrem related her antipathy to women's veiling practices in Turkey as justification for wearing a European-style hat constructed as a symbol of her emancipation and modernity. For her preference, she was, according to her own telling, chastised by family and strangers alike in instances she thought unlikely to be repeated in the "land of liberty." Her ongoing investment in Orientalist stereotypes is evident in the dichotomy that she creates between a "modern," striving, technologically savvy "West" and a dreamy, plodding, lackadaisical "East." And yet she finds herself unable to escape the racialized stereotype of Turks, and Turkish women especially, that she, as a pale, blue-eyed, hat-wearing Americanophile, controverts. She thus finds her raison d'être in countering Orientalist fantasies of "daggers, veils, ephemeral silks and heavy incense" with nostalgic tales of the "real" Turk. Ultimately, Ekrem was able to sustain her life in the United States—shared with a longtime female companion—through lecture tours and journalism that traded on her positioning as an "Ottoman-Turk-in-America." Her ability to manipulate Americans' expectations of Turkey's exoticism while using language, imagery, and narrative techniques familiar to their cultural context is also evident in the extracts that follow.

EXTRACTS

Leaving Stamboul

A few years ago, a Turkish girl came from far-flung Turkey to the vastness of America and everyone asked her:

"But why did you come to the United States?"

It seems everyone comes to America with a definite aim, most to study or make money. But this young Turk had not come to imbibe American culture or to sell peanuts and popcorn and thereby return home a millionaire. This traveler from the land of incense and beauty had traveled those hazardous miles of storm to be able to wear a hat in peace.[1]

It had been a struggle. I had first to convince myself and to silence the vibrations of fear that went through me. And then I had to persuade my family. They were astonished at the news, and my father had shaken his head. What was I going to do in America? That was the question I had put to myself often while I tossed in my bed. And then America had loomed like a city of steel to which I could not find an entrance. I meant to work. Everyone found work in America, I told my parents. The world had turned its eyes to that country, and I too would do the same.

Around America I had woven a lacework of romance. She was the land of faultless people and government; she was the land of liberty, at whose every corner opportunity waited to be seized. Surely among the vast stretches of land, chance was waiting for me, and I would seize it.

I stood on the deck of the boat and saw my family disappearing one by one. Tears had crowded to their eyes and mine. It was for the first time that I was being separated from them. And then I had a wild impulse to call them back. Fear gripped me by the throat. I would acknowledge my madness and return to the safety of home. But this feeling left me when I thought of the difficulties I would have to face. Then I was alone on deck with the night closing over me and Stamboul a glitter of lights stretching to the sea.

I was really running away from uncertainty. What lay ahead of Turkish women, I could not fathom.[2] And no more could I bear the struggle for liberty, the restrictions imposed on Turkish women. All my life had grown into struggle and sorrow, and one more struggle would break my spirit.

I had rather face the uncertainty of America. This trip was a stroke of madness. I had no idea what I would do and what work I could find. I had only one friend in the United States and an implicit faith in the country, and a thirst for liberty that I believed swept through America like the Great Mississippi.

Once again Stamboul drew back and faded from my eyes, and once again the lure for adventure was throbbing in my throat. America was before me, a country as legendary as the tales my old nurse had lulled me with. To think that I had in my hands the magic key that would open up the door to the wonders that I had heard and dreamed of! I prayed that it would turn easily in the lock and that years of waiting had not rusted its powers.

Arriving in America

I woke up one morning in America. It had been like a fairy tale, this journey. I had closed my eyes and three times whispered the wish of my heart, and now I opened them in the land I had longed to see. My heart in my mouth, I ran up to the deck. But America was wearing a veil for me—when I had fled so many thousands of miles not to see one again. A tenacious cold mist held the city in a tight grip, but I felt it jerking at its bands like a trapped animal. When the mist finally cleared, the tall skyline rose before me like the walls of a fortress, formidable and foreboding. And back of that physical wall, I sensed another wall, even more stupendous, stretching its arrogant head—wealth. Here was a new world, a new people whose very thoughts were different from mine. How was I to lift that veil, tear down those walls, and come in? I had been too confident. My passport was liberty to the land of liberty, and I had thought there would be no walls to scale, no veils to tear.

Alone, I faced New York City. My one friend had telegraphed that she could not meet me. I had to tackle the city by myself. New York, I had heard, was the city of wild terror, and the thought that I would be fighting it with my two hands made my mouth dry with fear.

Forlorn, I walked by the steward carrying my luggage. The wharf was immense, and it took my breath away. How I longed then for the cramped and noisy quay of Stamboul, for the loud-voiced squabbling hamals and the red glow of fezzes. I stood before important-looking officials, and one of them lifted his head to scan me and with a smile in his voice said:

"Glad to get back, aren'tchew?"

"Back?" I echoed. "But this is the first time I'm coming to America!"

"The first time," queried the official. "But aren'tchew an American?"

"Far from it." I laughed. "I am a Turk."

The word was like a bomb. The people round me stared. I saw vague ideas of daggers, veils, ephemeral silks, and heavy incense drifting on their faces. Just then a woman whom I had never seen before touched me on the arm.

"Excuse me, my dear," she said. "Are you really a Turk?"

"Yes," said I, somewhat taken aback.

"And is your father a Turk?"

Again, I answered, "Yes."

"But," she said triumphantly, "your mother, she's not a Turk, now, is she?"

"Oh, yes," I replied. "My father is a Turk, my mother's a Turk, and so are all my sisters, and my cousins and my aunts."

"But if you have just come from Turkey," she questioned, "where did you get these clothes?"

"Strange as it may seem," I answered, "we do not go round in my country wrapped in Turkish towels." . . .

Leaving the wharf and plunging into the whirling life before me . . . I forgot about the walls that had stretched before me. I forgot the thick veil that had shrouded America from my eyes. Maybe I would strike my head on these walls, maybe I would be caught in the meshes of that tightening veil and fight in vain to find a way out. All these faded from my mind, and I turned to New York with an eagerness and joy that left no place for fear.

Walking the Streets of New York

To me, New York was the modern fairy city. There were no marble palaces, no trees laden with emerald leaves and turquoise flowers, no fairies flying in aerial chariots drawn by nightingales, no jinn brooding in underground caverns, and yet there was magic, the magic of modern inventions and the American mind, fairy lore to an Eastern eye.

One by one, I turned the leaves of this new fairy book that had been put in my hands. And this is an advantage that every foreigner has over the Americans. You have lived in this fairy land of unexpectedness and cannot realize that it is an American Thousand and One Nights Tales.

I wished then that I had a hundred pairs of eyes to look at the thousands of wonders that New York spread before me. Ahead of me was Brooklyn Bridge lying on volumes of air. This, I said to myself, is the magic carpet of old that could transport one from country to country in the days of fairy lore. We in the East dream of such wonders, and you in the West create them.

Then I was thrown in the seething bustling streets that took my breath away. I saw the people running as if their coattails were on fire, and the perpetual swift strikes made my head buzz. Where were these people running to? I craned my neck to see, but only vast streams of undulating people came to my eyes. Then I thought of the narrow streets of Stamboul and the crowd that ambles along leisurely. Often too we stop in Stamboul, right in the middle of the sidewalk, and discuss our private affairs. One can pick up the gossip of Stamboul trying to push through the crowded sidewalks.

"She had been in love with him . . ."

"Let Allah grant you long life and console you."

"I told her she was sweeping the streets too often with her skirts. But these young people . . ."

It was impossible to stop in the streets of New York. One was carried away with the flood. In America, one neither stops nor ambles; one rushes headlong onward forever. And when one stops, it is for death.

I marveled over the streets; these were so broad that one could pass a lifetime crossing to the other side. My eyes were lost in their breadth. And not the winding, cobblestoned streets of Stamboul; these were smooth as cream and walking on them was paradise to one's feet.

Crossing streets, I had thought, and now that I looked round me, I laughed. A stream of never-ending cars purred on both sides. In America one went always forward, I concluded. Then I was in a broad street, and I saw iron towers erected in the middle of it. Suddenly from all of them flashed a red light. There was a tremendous shrieking and roaring. I jumped away scared out of my head. Thousands of cars lay motionless while from the numerous side streets poured other thousands, nosing each other, honking. Big trucks rattled by. The noise was deafening. And I thought again of Stamboul, of the slow oxcarts and the donkey wagons plodding their way stubbornly and holding up the motor cars. Once more the lights changed, and the cars that had lain motionless plunged forward as if delivered from prison. It seemed to me that all the cars in the world had gathered here.

The towers drew my eyes gradually, and my head thrust sidewise; I walked and thought. How I wanted to stop and solve this mystery. What power turned these lights on and off? I could not see a soul in them, and no ladders or stairs. I wondered how the controlling powers climbed up. Perhaps they, like Douglas Fairbanks in *The Thief of Bagdad*, used the magic cord; but no, that was out of fashion now. The magic of America was even more starling. These lights, I concluded, had been trained to turn on and off by themselves. Who could bother to climb up their towers?

It was lucky that I finally met some kind person, or I would still have been wandering the streets of New York. I could not tear my eyes and feet from them. This perpetual flow and ebb fascinated me. My companion told me we were on Fifth Avenue. The name was familiar to my ears and had an enchanting sound. Still rushing at a terrific speed, I had a glimpse of enormous shops, and then I decided I would give them a look. It was not easy: each time I tried to stop, I was being swept onward. Then I managed to reach a shop window and stood spellbound. The treasures laid before me with such extravagance and taste made me catch my breath. This world of beauty was even greater than the hidden treasures of old. Shop after shop, each bigger and richer than the other. At the doors, there was a crowd flowing in and out regularly. A sea of people fighting to get in. Shopping must be difficult in America, I thought to myself. And then my companion told me:

"These are after-Christmas sales, and the people rush to buy."

I was tempted to follow this mob of shoppers. I wanted to see with my own eyes the treasures that had lain tantalizing and aloof in the shop windows. But I was swept onward, forward, onward.

We turned into another street. The scene shifted; this was another world. The clanging of a trolley reached my ears, and then I saw huge iron pillars and looked up at them. With a roar, a flash of lightning passed by. The street shook with it, and I expected to see the whole structure crash on my head. The elevated rattled away, and I felt it roar in my head. A roar above answered by a roar below. This was New York.

We took the trolley. It stopped submissively before the outstretched finger of my companion. How could we go in? I saw no steps. Probably I just stood and was transported in my magic. My companion walked to the trolley slowing up, and I followed. Suddenly steps shot out from the car, and I drew back, amazed and frightened. My companion pulled me up. I walked up those magical steps with fear. Surely they would crash under the load of people. As we entered, I saw a small box, and people dropped their coin as they entered. What a relief, I thought. In Turkey, we have the nuisance of tickets.

Imagine a trolley packed like a sardine box, where people can neither move nor breathe, and then think of a bulky ticket man walking through and collecting fares. How often I had felt like murdering the poor man, especially if he had the misfortune of stepping on my toes. But in New York, once we had fought our way in, we were saved from that nuisance. The ticket man kept pulling a cord and chewing gum. His jaws moved up and down in rhythm to the swing of the trolley.

Food and Subways

I was to have my first American meal. We entered a charming restaurant, and at first glance I noticed how attractive it was with gay colored tables and decorations. Here, I said to myself, I could sit at my ease and think about New York. Prompt as lightning, we were marshaled in. And then the charming restaurant lost its flavor. Back of us came crowds of people, and crows left in a hurry. In America one did not eat; one played a game to see who could rush in, eat first, and come out the fastest. I was not given time to think or to rest. I thought of our Turkish coffeehouses where clients pass dreamy hours over a little eggshell cup of coffee or a nargile that never ends.

I did not eat—I marveled. Everything was strange to me. The soup that was sweet, the vegetables that seemed tasteless, a salad that was made of sweetest fruits spoiled with a dash of mayonnaise. What was I to have next?

"Would you like some ice cream?" asked my companion.

It was the middle of January, the ground was covered with snow, and a terrific wind had chilled my bones all day long. I had not felt the cold in the streets because I had been lost in wonders. But soon the cold came upon me in this hot restaurant. Ice cream in the middle of winter! So this is what I would have next! But after one taste of that delicious chilliness, I could understand a story that had been told me about an American tourist. She had not stayed a day in Constantinople because she had not found ice cream in the city in winter.

The first time I took the subway, I was alone. I came upon a world built underground where people were so thick that I only saw heads moving. Here too was one big rush. I lost my head and kept wandering aimlessly terrified at every step that I took. The crowds rushed, talked; the noise and motion made me dizzy. I took my courage in hand and began to ask my way. Hurried answers drifted to me and these I could not understand. I had come to the point of tears and concluded I would spend my days in this underground prison.

Then my eyes wandered over to small boxes before which people stopped. I too stopped to look; maybe these boxes would solve the mystery and show me the way. A man was fumbling in his pockets, and I came close to him. He took a penny and dropped it in a hole. Then to my great astonishment, a package of chewing gum fell out. I forgot the subway and my fears. These boxes delighted me. Timidly I dropped a penny in the slot and almost shouted with joy when the chewing gum package fell into my hands. I tried another and then I was rewarded with chocolates. The game was entrancing, and if my pennies had not given out, I would have wandered from box to box.

Laughing to myself, I faced the crowd, and the laughter died on my lips. How was I to get out of this place? I grew afraid once more. Then I came upon an official and asked my way. He took me to a platform and told me to wait.

I waited: a tremendous roar shook me, and I opened wide my eyes. The long train crashed in excitedly. The doors were flung open, crowds rushed in. Whistles blew, doors banged, the train pulled out, and I was left on the platform.

I left New York with a sense of sorrow. The city I had barely glimpsed, and it had fascinated me.

FURTHER READING

Selma Ekrem. *Unveiled: The Autobiography of a Turkish Girl*. New York: Ives Washburn, 1930. The original text has been reprinted with an introduction by Carolyn Goffman (Piscataway, NJ: Gorgias, 2005). The chapter on Jerusalem has also been reprinted as

"Jerusalem 1908: In the Household of the Ottoman Governor." *Jerusalem Quarterly* 50 (Summer 2012): 66–88.

————. *Turkey, Old and New.* New York: Scribner's, 1947.

————. *Turkish Fairy Tales.* Illustrated by Liba Bayrak. Princeton, NJ: Von Nostrand, 1964.

Hülya Adak. "Suffragettes of the Empire, Daughters of the Republic: Women Auto/ Biographers Narrate National History (1918–35)." *New Perspectives on Turkey* 36 (2007): 27–51. http://research.sabanciuniv.edu/5287/1/adak_npt_36b.pdf.

Reina Lewis. *Rethinking Orientalism: Women, Travel, and the Ottoman Harem.* London: I. B. Tauris, 2004.

Donald Quataert. *The Ottoman Empire, 1700–1922.* Cambridge, UK: Cambridge University Press, 2000.

NOTES

1. Zeyneb Hanoum also identified the hat as a symbol of liberty for Turkish women, but in a much less favorable way. As she prepared to return to Istanbul in 1912, she wrote, "All my trunks are packed and ready, and it is with joy and not without regret that I see I have no hatbox. Not that I care for that curious and very unattractive invention, the fashionable hat, but it is the external symbol of liberty, and now I am setting aside for ever" (Zeyneb Hanoum, *A Turkish Woman's European Impressions*, edited by Grace Ellison [London: Seely, Service, & Co., 1913], 241).

2. As noted in the introduction, Ekrem left for the United States in 1924 with the Turkish Republic just declared. What that would mean for Turkey and Turkish women was thus still an "uncertainty."

TWENTY

ŞÜKÛFE NİHAL BAŞAR

Three Days in Finland

INTRODUCTION

Şükûfe Nihal Başar (1896–1973) (see fig. 20.1) is now celebrated as an "Ottoman woman of letters" on account of her career as a Turkish poet, writer, intellectual, educator, and activist. Her parents were Colonel Ahmet Abdullah Bey, a pharmacist, and Nazire Hanım, both of whom belonged to upper-class educated families that valued culture and the arts. Nihal was born in Istanbul but, due to her father's appointments, spent her childhood in various Ottoman cities, among them Damascus, Beirut, and Thessalonica. Her father took her education very seriously, sending her to private schools or, if that was not possible, engaging tutors from whom she learned French, Arabic, and Persian, among other subjects. Her father also organized gatherings of prominent intellectuals and artists in their home, during which Nihal was encouraged to interact with their guests. According to Nihal, she began writing stories at an early age but hid them as if it were a shameful act. By time she was nine or ten years old, she was experimenting with romantic fiction in the hopes of producing texts that would allow her "to live the life of an artist." Her first publication, at the age of thirteen in 1909, was an essay about girls' education, and four years later she published her first poem.

When Nihal was sixteen, she began studying at the women's university, Inas Darülfünun, in Istanbul. When her father was assigned to a new posting in Damascus, he was reticent to leave his daughter alone to continue her education and pressured her to get married instead. She attempted suicide to evade the marriage and, when it went ahead, divorced shortly after having a son. Subsequently, she continued

---

Roberta Micallef prepared the introduction and translation from Turkish.

Figure 20.1 An early photograph of Şükûfe Nihal
Başar. Courtesy of Roberta Micallef.

her education, all the while becoming increasingly involved with the nationalist
cause and the burgeoning Ottoman women's movement. In 1919, she became the first
female university graduate after sitting additional examinations previously taken
only by male students. While studying, she also married her second husband, Ahmet
Başar, with whom she remained until they were divorced in the late 1950s. In the
same year as her marriage, she solidified her role as one of the leading figures in the
women's movement by giving an electrifying speech in Fatih in which she urged men
and women to join the nationalist cause and fight for their freedom. In 1923, she also
became a founding member of the Women's People Party, which, after being denied
the status of a political party, reorganized as the Turkish Women's Union.

Nihal remained an educator throughout much of her career, teaching at various schools until 1953. She simultaneously continued her literary activities. Her
oeuvre included various genres, including poetry, travel narratives, and novels.
She held a European-style salon in her house that included all the important
literary figures of the time. She also contributed articles to all the leading journals on issues relating to women and their status in society. The final years of

Nihal's life were tragic. Not only did her beloved daughter die in childbirth, but the author herself also suffered a car accident that left her with mobility issues. Though Nihal died poor and alone, she left behind a vast collection of articles, poems, stories, and novels, as well as two travel narratives in book form. One of these, *Domaniç Dağlarının Yolcusu* (*A Traveler to the Domaniç Mountains*, 1946) has since being included in a list of "foundational books" for schoolchildren by Turkey's Ministry of Education. It narrates a trip through Anatolia in search of a woman who, according to legend, had killed her one and only son after he had inadvertently betrayed his country during the war of independence. An earlier travel narrative, *Finlandiya* (*Finland*, 1935), provides the source for the extracts translated here.

Nihal believed that travel was an important source of inspiration for artists. She also considered improving the life standards within Anatolian villages to be key to Turkey's development. For her, Finland was an excellent example of what could be achieved if development planning focused on village improvement. She first came across Finland through a book by Russian author Grigory Spiridonovich Petrov entitled *The Land of White Lilies*, first published in Serbian in 1923. Portraying Finland as a living model for other countries, it was translated into Turkish in the early years of the republic and widely distributed. It was also given as a gift to the graduates of teacher training schools and military schools. Nihal was so impressed by the high standard of living achieved despite Finland's poor climate that she decided to visit the country herself in 1932. By that time, she was in her late thirties, and though she appears to not have traveled alone, her companion is unnamed. To share her impressions with her fellow Turks, she wrote a travelogue that was published three years later in 1935.

The narrative section of *Finlandiya*, entitled "Three Days in Finland," is quite short, facilitating a full translation here. In the book, Nihal supplemented this first-person account with additional information about different aspects of Finnish culture and life such as "Turks in Finland," "Women in Finland," and "The Finnish Government." Nihal's writing style—in particular, her descriptions of the Finnish people and landscape—has a poetic and dreamlike quality that is complemented by her frequent use of ellipses. Rather than indicating an omission here, the ellipses seem to signify the trailing of thoughts about a place or a person as the train or boat moves and the author happens upon another sight worthy of comment. Also, her tenses shift between the past and present to differentiate between connections that she is making to past knowledge or information and her spontaneous, in-the-moment reactions. Taken as a whole, her travel narrative with its vivid descriptions presents Finland as a role model for the young Turkish Republic.

EXTRACTS

Three Days in Finland

Finland greeted us with a pink smile. . . . A clean, polite smile resembling a poem . . . I thought that I was before a great, quite great presence. A quivering, full of respect, began in my heart.

It was evening. . . . The sun was setting. . . . Amid an immense greenery, the horizon was on fire. We stopped in front of the charming station house with an immaculate, white facade. A group of soldiers passed in front of us; it was as if they had been cut from the same cloth or made of the same mold; slim, golden-haired youths with sun-kissed faces. . . . Their clothing was spotless. . . .

The train started to move; it's as if I am turning the pages of an album by an artist who has great aesthetic skills: to the right and left gardens, parks, houses, organized by someone with a cultivated sense of taste. . . . In the distance, a patch of pale sea reminiscent of a blue dream. . . . From a street lined with trees, pajama-clad girls as beautiful as bouquets of flowers with faces darkened by a sweet suntan are returning. They are all robust, charming, serious, fine. . . . On another road to the village, both large and small are the village children, the village girls, resembling golden balls with their blue eyes, golden hair, round cheeks. They all have traces of silent smiles on their faces. To the right and left of the train, people on bicycles are meandering.

The hours move toward night. . . . The sun, like a mischievous child who has been put to bed but refuses to sleep, keeps opening his mosquito net with his naughty hands, and once in a while, parting the clouds, smiles rosily from one end of the horizon to the other. . . .

Suddenly the redness at one corner of the pine trees expanded; I thought the sun was rising. I checked the time; it was only eleven. . . . I think the train had climbed to a higher elevation.

At a station, a beautiful young girl with a dark red velvet cap, navy uniform, and a serious demeanor: the station official . . . she is something like a figurine placed on the side of the road. . . .

The train departs: again we are passing gardens, villages, and cities. Always that same order, always that same cleanliness and beauty. . . . There is no lack of people out and about. In a colorful dusk, beautiful youths are wandering around like the lovely faeries that enter our dreams. My glances, which fly from the ground to the sky and from the sky to the ground, fear missing the tiniest bit of beauty. . . .

Dusk suddenly brightened again, as if the sun couldn't bring itself to be away from people; parting an ash-colored blanket from the edge of the dark pine groves, it sticks out its fiery tongue and jokes with the earth. . . .

There are no stars in the sky and no moon; nevertheless, I am able to read my book easily, and I am writing my notes. Oh, these fiery northern nights. . . . Under an endless sky that never ceases to smile, all the earth, meadows, bodies of water, people, laugh. . . . To live here is like a sweet dream. . . .

It's past midnight; I don't feel tired, I am not sleepy at all. If I say that I have never seen a train anywhere in Europe that had such fine, spotless, linen blankets, I won't be lying. I couldn't bring myself to sit or lie down on them. Spotless women are working in the wagons.

I dozed off for a bit; I woke up at half past three. There isn't any red left in the sky, but neither is there any darkness. There is a white night dimness. Then once again pinkness and light. . . . Here, day and night turn round and round the horizon hand in hand. While one is leaving, the other arrives.

On the roads, there isn't one stone or even a handful of soil that isn't in its place. The trees, gardens, villages, crops, they've all been put into order by an attentive person. In the cities, the villages, every house has been painted. . . . The curtains in the windows of every house have been perfectly starched. . . . Even the chicken coops sitting in a corner of the garden like a little baby palace are painted. . . . No unpainted pieces of wood can be seen anywhere! . . . Those who cannot afford good quality paint for their houses use red ochre paint because it is cheaper, and they don't leave the places where they live with a sooty, dirty face.

This place does not resemble a place where one lives, and that one wears out, but rather it looks like a living portrait that has been put together to please someone. Or else it resembles the toys belonging to a very careful child that were painstakingly organized and then enlarged and photographed. . . .

The sky is a brilliant white. . . . It is seven o'clock. We are getting closer to Helsingfors [Helsinki]. While organizing my bag, my eyes don't leave the wagon's window.

In the distance, teeny tiny lakes shivering with miniature silver waves lit by the morning sun. . . . A tiny stadium. . . . Factory pipes . . .

I descend from the train in the tremors of a happiness that cannot be described. Two cleanly dressed youths are standing in front of us; their hands and shoes are spotless. Apparently, they are porters! . . . They did not put out their hands and snatch our bags, and neither did they say anything. When I handed them our bags, I blushed a little.

We passed by a clean, large train station. Here, there are stores that sell books and newspapers; I looked; stores full of loads and loads of works to be read in many different languages. It means that in this tiny place all these books are being read. We came out to a big, clean plaza. I keep emphasizing cleanliness because I haven't seen this level of cleanliness in many of the richest countries in the world. We immediately entered the Society Hotel, which was right there; we left our things. We went to see Helsinki. One glance was enough to understand: the country's life standard, in its entirety, is at the right place. . . . Neither too much superiority, wealth, arrogance, nor backwardness, poverty, groveling! . . . In the buildings, on the roads, in the faces of the people, in the clothes, in the stores, neither the gaudiness, the excess, the arrogance, the impertinence that comes with money, and ignorance, nor the darkness, dirtiness, irritability, and shabbiness born of poverty and sadness. . . . The youths are smiling; the elderly are smiling; sun-faced people with luxurious hair are going and coming quietly with an appealing dignity just like angels.

A crowd on our route. . . . We joined it too; it turned out to be a market. It was a place full of meats, chicken coops, vegetables, flowers, birds, cages of red-eyed, white rabbits. What can I say? How can I describe it? What can I say it resembles? Here it is: Finland's, Helsinki's bazaar! . . .

On large wooden tables lies meat cut into chunks. . . . Women wearing white aprons with their heads wrapped in white are selling it. While everything exists at this bazaar, there isn't one bit of garbage on the floor. There are no bugs, no flies. The housewife, the worker, everyone coming to shop, even the poorest ones, are extremely clean. . . . There is no one you must avoid because they might brush against you. No one passes anyone by bumping into them or bothering them. There is no noise; it is a quiet, well-behaved movement.

Here, young women, young girls are all dressed with a refined, simple elegance. Not one of them has a spot of makeup on her face.

We returned to the hotel to eat. On a huge table in the dining room, there were different kinds of fish, salads, and fruit. The guests could serve themselves as much of these as they wanted. We too ate as much of what we wanted. Then the waiter came; he brought us the list of warm foods; including the wine that we drank, this lunch did not cost more than one Turkish lira.

On summer days, the sun works hard not to deprive the beautiful people of the Finnish soil of its light and warmth; however, it still sometimes appears tired. July is the hottest month here; nevertheless, patches of colorful clouds and warm raindrops are not absent. Those going out carry raincoats.

From the low-elevation green shores that curl like the lace decorating scarves, small boats leave for tiny islands about ten minutes away. Shiny, white, spotless boats are swimming above the water like white pigeons. . . . We went to one of the islands; on the boat, a fourteen-, fifteen-year-old youth is collecting tickets.

The first thing we saw on the island was a delightful café. Girls wearing local traditional clothes, colorful as flowers, were working there. Each was more beautiful than the next. A little farther down, there was a small zoo. A tiny, muddy beach in the shade of a few trees . . . under the delicate raindrops a mother was taking her child to the sea.

On the way back, a young girl was selling ice cream by the dock. When she finished her work, she sat on the bench next to her without looking in front of her or around her; she opened up the book in her hand and started to read.

We are touring Helsinki. This is not a city; it is a flower garden. . . . Houses, hotels, restaurants, stores, they are all in a green setting. There is no lack of gardens or parks. Under the trees, by the roadside, there are benches painted white, seats. Young, old, child, whoever wants to sit is here and rests, reads, sunbathes. In the gardens in the middle of the streets, there are restaurants. Food is eaten at tables placed under giant garden umbrellas at the edge of an intensely green boxwood. The young girls who work here are so elegant and clean, so well behaved that the best-raised daughters of good families couldn't be better. Even the bright white linen aprons they wear attract one to them.

A young girl comes to these restaurants, gardens by herself, drinks her beer, eats her food, opens her newspaper, her book, and no disrespectful look disturbs her.

I didn't see any police on the streets. It is evident that national civility has reached the highest level. On the edge of one of the parks, off the road one evening, a twelve-year-old shoe polish boy is sitting waiting for work. He is wearing shorts. His knees are clean, and his shoes are polished. . . . His golden hair, his azure eyes shine even more under a creamy light . . . become childlike. His head is leaning toward the book in his hand! . . .

I couldn't believe my eyes; I went and stood in front of him. I stared in disbelief; I looked at him. He looked at me; I laughed; he too laughed; for one second, we laughed from heart to heart. . . . I asked myself: I wonder if he is a revue artist who made an effort to choose this spot for his act tonight?

I looked at the dignified stance and walk of the young girls and schoolchildren with envy, and sighed. Their clothes were neat, clean, and unpretentious. Not a spot of paint on their faces or lips. In this place where their mothers don't use makeup, young girls of course won't use makeup either.

I went to the hairdresser; I noticed something; Finnish women who have their hair done neat and tidy do not paint their fingernails with dark colors; I understood that they were not trying hard to make themselves more beautiful than the way they were created. A long time ago, they moved away from these enhancements that don't add beauty to a woman. They've reached a level of higher values.

One night, passing by well-lit, tree-lined roads, golden embroidered shores where blue waters glittered, we went to Brunnspark. We ate at a hotel amid flowers. In the big garden in front of the hotel, there is a theater. An operetta named *The Desert Song* is playing. It's not bad at all. However, rather than the opera, I couldn't stop looking at a slim, golden-haired Venus standing in the middle of the garden. A fourteen-year-old living Venus who was wearing a long red velvet jacket and pants and from whose red velvet cap golden ringlets fell to her shoulders is selling cigarettes, chocolates, etc., from a small table in front of her to those coming and going. Now, whenever I think of Finnish beauties, I always visualize that feather-like Finnish girl in the midst of that green artificially-lit garden, who with her slim body, creamy velvety face, and silken hair made one feel that she might float away any second.

We got on a tram; the ticket sellers were women. They were wearing navy uniforms and caps. These too were well-mannered daughters of good homes. I looked at their hands and nails: they were very clean, there wasn't even a smidgeon of dirt or a spot to be seen. When I bought the ticket, I wasn't disgusted. I wasn't revolted. They neither spoke unnecessarily nor gossiped with the passengers.

The tram gave us a tour of distant places. We passed by Helsinki's backstreets and neighborhoods. They too were orderly and clean . . . using a wooden bridge built on a shallow, rocky waterway, we reached an island. The last raindrops from a newly ended rain were sprinkling from the fresh, green branches of trees. White-clad youths are visible at the ends of tree-lined roads that grow and extend all around us. The bird songs spreading from the gardens makes the island experience a musical dream. Colorful flowers unfold from the balconies of mansions built with the highest taste. . . . I got dizzy from the scent of the earth, flowers, colors, and sounds; I shivered as if I had reached the most real country of poetry and beauty. It was as if my soul was bathed by clean waters emptying from the skies . . . this earth belongs to everyone living in its bosom! These roads, these parks are the roads and gardens of each Finn. . . . We wandered around the entire island to its most uninhabited corners and shores; even if one searched for it, one could not find a piece of garbage, a piece of paper, or the peel of a fruit thrown on the ground.

My heart beat in the face of the politeness of brother Finns who had reached the pinnacle of civilized behavior and aesthetic feeling.

Amid the raindrops that were sprinkling again and the bird sounds that were trying to explain something secret to these polite people, our heads spinning, we left the island. . . .

In order to go to Scandinavia, we returned to the Port of Abo [Turku] with those clean trains. A small boat was waiting for us at the shore. We got on; and all the passengers boarded. Sad that we were leaving without having seen more of this country, we leaned against the railing of the deck and tried to catch as much of the scenery as possible. The boat is going to leave; the anchor is going to be pulled up. A tidy, clean youth pulled out a pair of gloves from his pocket; he quickly put them on; he bent down and untied the boats' ropes.

What's happening? A deckhand, an ordinary deckhand! . . . He's putting on gloves to pull the rope. I decided that this was not because he was a dandy. Since he could avoid it, I thought to myself, why should he get his hands dirty with this rope that is wetted by sea water and that everyone steps on? I opened my eyes wide; they could not believe what they were seeing. I looked; I looked. Who has ever seen, in what corner of the world, such a golden-haired deckhand who doesn't get his hands dirty when he doesn't have to?

The boat we boarded is like a white seagull. . . . The passengers, the cabins, the corridors, the salons, the mirrors, the working women are all spotless and smiling at us. We spent the night on the boat. In the morning, we went out on the deck; the places we had left empty at night were full of passengers. This means that the boat had stopped at various ports overnight. These were third-class passengers. . . . They've been given chaise longues, and blankets. They are sleeping. I paid attention; they were only distinguishable from other passengers because their clothes were a bit cheaper. . . . Otherwise, they were all clean people like them.

While moving farther and farther away, leaving my heart and my eyes in this land of poetry, civilization, and humanity, my greatest desire was to see it once again.

It is still so.

FURTHER READING

Şükûfe Nihal Başar. "Finladiya'da Üç Gün." In *Şükûfe Nihal Bütün Eserleri IV. Cilt: Hikâyeler, Mensureler, Gezi (1917–1973)*, edited by Yaprak Zihnioğlu, 159–65. Istanbul: Kitap Yayınevi, 2008.

Aynur Soydan Erdemir. "A Woman's Challenge: The Voice of Şuküfe Nihal in the Modernisation of Turkey." In *Women, Education, and Agency 1600–2000*, edited by Jean Spence, Sarah Jane Aiston, and Maureen M. Meikle, 125–46. London: Routledge, 2010.

Hülya Argunşah. *Bir Cumhuriyet Kadını Şükûfe Nihal.* Istanbul: Timaş, 2010.

Bahar Baskın. "II. Meşrutiyette Kadın Eğitimine Yönelik Bir Girişim İnas Darülfünunu." *İstanbul Üniversitesi Siyasal Bilgiler Fakültesi Dergisi* 38 (2008): 89–123.

Emine Hoşoğlu Doğan. "Late Ottoman Muslim Women of Letters Unsettle 'the New Ottoman Muslim Womanhood.'" PhD thesis, University of Utah, 2016.

Neriman Malkoç Öztürkmen. *Edibeler, Sefireler, Hanımefendiler: Ilk Nesil Cumhuriyet Kadınlarıyla Söyleşiler.* N.p: Kişisel Yayınlar, 1999.

—ɯ—

HALIDE ÉDIB

A Turkish Nationalist in Colonial India

INTRODUCTION

Iconic images of the Turkish war of independence often feature the diminutive, black-clad figure of Halide Édib (1884–1964) at the forefront of otherwise male groupings. The first woman to be granted a rank in the nationalist military, she worked as a translator, nurse, relief worker, orator, editor, teacher, and writer before 1923. Her participation in the nationalist movement originated in the Young Turk Revolt of 1908 when she started writing on political and cultural themes, first as a journalist and then as a novelist. Her many highly successful novels in Turkish drew on her own experience of having lived as a secluded harem lady under the old Ottoman regime before achieving "emancipation" in the new Turkey. Helping to facilitate this transition was a comprehensive education bequeathed upon her by her father, a high bureaucrat in the sultan's palace, after her mother's early death. Soon after graduation from the American College for Girls in 1901, Édib married her much older mathematics tutor, Salih Zaki Bey, with whom she bore two sons. But when he took a second wife in 1910, she sought a divorce. Her second husband, Dr. Adnan Adıvar, whom she married in 1917, shared her commitment to revolutionary nationalism as a leading figure in the Committee for Union and Progress (CUP). Édib documented this early phase of her life in her two volumes of autobiography, *Memoirs* (1926) and *The Turkish Ordeal* (1928). To reach an international readership, both were written in English, as was her later travelogue, *Inside India*, detailing a visit to the Indian subcontinent in 1935.

Siobhan Lambert-Hurley prepared the introductions, extracts, and annotations.

Figure 21.1 Halide Édib, perhaps during one of
her early sojourns in Europe. From Wikipedia
Commons.

By the time of her India tour, Édib was already a well-traveled "old woman" in
her early fifties. She had first gone to London in 1909 in fear for her life during the
counterrevolution (see fig. 21.1). In *Inside India*, she noted that this sea journey
provided her first contact with "Indians in the flesh"—not just fellow passengers
but also the "stewards and sailors" that staffed her boat. Closer acquaintances with
Indians were made from 1912 through the auspices of the Indian Red Crescent
Mission to Turkey mobilized in response to the humanitarian disaster of the
Balkan Wars. This organization was led by Dr. M. A. Ansari, a British-trained
doctor and Indian nationalist, who, many years later, was responsible for inviting
Édib to India. From 1926, Édib was in voluntary exile from Turkey after the politi-
cal faction to which she and her husband belonged was suppressed by Mustafa
Kemal. After a four-year stay in London, the couple relocated to Paris, where
Adıvar accepted a post teaching Turkish at the École Nationale des Langues Ori-
entales Vivantes. The city remained their base until they returned Turkey in 1939
after Kemal's death. It was here that Édib wrote *Inside India* for publication by a

London press in 1937. While based in Paris, Édib also traveled to the United States on a lecture tour of universities in 1929 and as a visiting professor at Columbia University in 1931–32. Her academic credentials were formalized after her return to Turkey with a professorship in the English Department of Istanbul University.

Inside India, though overtly subjective, maintained a scholarly tone through its three parts. The first, entitled "India Seen Through Salam House," documented her first two months in India as a guest at Dr. Ansari's home in Delhi. During this time, her primary occupation was delivering a series of extension lectures at a local Muslim university, the Jamia Millia Islamia, that were published soon after as *Conflict of East and West in Turkey* (1935). The novelty of her Indian experience was reflected in the first extract here in which she recorded her first impressions of Indian villages and a visit to India's most famous monument, the Taj Mahal in Agra. Also from this part is the second extract, in which Édib records a speech given at a purdah club—for Muslim women in seclusion—associated with the university to which she was attached in Delhi. The second part of the book, entitled "Indians Seen on Highways and Byways," reported Édib's subsequent tour of different Indian cities—after which chapters are named—to deliver lectures at local institutions. Her host organizations included Aligarh Muslim University, Peshawar College, Calcutta University, and Osmania University in Hyderabad, as well as smaller "associations" in Lahore, Lucknow, and Bombay. Benares, or Varanasi, was visited too for "rest and sightseeing." From this section are the third and fourth extracts, focusing on her "feminine contacts" in Lahore and her visit to a village house outside Peshawar, respectively. The third part, entitled "India in the Melting Pot," departed from the travelogue format to reflect on the different strands in contemporary Indian society and politics.

Featuring in this final section, and several chapters of part I too, was the larger-than-life figure of Mahatma Gandhi. Édib's complementary portrayal of this most important Indian nationalist was just the most extended of the many "portraits" of individual Indians that made up the bulk of her narrative. Among those featured were the great and the good of Indian nationalism and feminism, including many women. The most prominent of them was Sarojini Naidu, but a number of elite Muslim women also featured, including the All-India Muslim League politician, Begum Jahanara Shah Nawaz, who appears in the third extract here. Édib also showed a special interest in the lives of less privileged women (and men too)—for instance, along the road to Agra and in a Northwest Frontier village—and attending women's meetings, like in Delhi and Lahore. Her affiliation with India's Muslims—her "kith and kin" with whom she shared a belief in "One God"—gave her rare access to private homes and gardens, including the women's quarters. These spaces were described in detail for the "clues" they offered to "Indian character." As she wrote of a Lucknow house, "Show me the home of a person and I will tell you what kind of person he is." Yet while Édib sought to forge connections with fellow Muslims and nationalists across imperial boundaries, she still tended to depict India as timeless or backward, even compared to her native Turkey, and defined by religious identities essentialized as "Hindu" and, in her spelling, "Muslem."

EXTRACTS

A Visit to the Taj Mahal in Agra

On the way to Agra we met groups of village folk going hither and thither. We were going to see the "Taj" by moonlight. This is the proper thing for a visitor to do. Whether it is a peasant woman or a Rani, all Indian women have the grace of a picture painted on an antique jar. The villages were mostly composed of thatch-roofed mud huts, with dirty, untidy squares. Not very different from some of our own villages. The men looked less healthy than the women. Some of them lay on raised boards in the street, evidently suffering from malaria. The women are sturdier. Those who survive hardship, semistarvation, and childbirth must have unusually resistant constitutions. We also saw wells on the way: oxen draw water by a system which defies even our old ones in antiquity. "In the beginning of time," that is the pervading spirit of these village districts.

One entered Agra through miserable, dirty quarters. Such represent the worst part of the dying and stagnant East, no matter where they are found. No Eastern person will regret their passing away, though the Western writer in quest of the exotic may regret it. If native picturesqueness cannot be combined with a minimum of the decent conditions of life, let the picturesqueness pass away, and sooner the better. In justice to the Indian masses, one word must be added with regard to cleanliness. However squalid their habitation, however dirty the rags that cover them, they keep their bodies cleaner than do the poor of the West. Both Muslems and Hindus wash their bodies, all the intimate parts, even if not in very clean water. The disagreeable smell of toes and other abominations of the body of which one is conscious in a poor cinema in Europe, one does not have with the Indian masses. They have a constant habit of spitting and wiping their noses with their hands, which offends the eye. Also the lack of drainage in most parts of India, especially the village districts, is an odoriferous fact. But that does not emanate from the bodies.

As usual, the passage from the squalid to the prosperous is sudden. Speaking for the towns and cities only, there seems to be no intermediary in the economic scale. There are only the extremely poor and the extremely—shall I say shamelessly?—rich.

We were guests in an progressive Indian house, our host a prominent doctor, and his wife the first Muslim lady who had discarded the veil. At least, she was the first in Agra, for in other cities Muslim women were pointed out to me as having accomplished this feat; we could see very little of them, and that only during meals. At dinner society was mixed, English, Hindus, and Muslims being present. . . .

It was dark when we went to the "Taj." The fanciful delicacy of the decoration was hardly visible. I sat on a marble bench between two rows of black cypresses and watched the slow rise of the moon lighting the white dome. Very dramatic it was to see the moonlight slowly giving relief to the mass of whiteness, without making it too distinct. The door of the central tomb was open. An attendant passed to and fro, and a lovely lamp hanging from the veiling within lighted the interior. It had a strange poignancy, this wonder of the world, symbolizing the devotion of man to woman through the ages.[1] The supreme irony for the Westerner is that it was a Muslim who erected this eternal monument to woman! But that did not matter to me. The thing gave me restfulness and peace. I had stepped out of the range of local influence of any kind, be it of race, religion, or style in art. The spectacle defied intellectual analysis and was beyond sentimentality. What mattered if the architect was a Turk or a Florentine, or that the kind who had it built had his ancestral home in a sturdier, wilder clime? The monument was an Indian masterpiece, regardless of its style and builders. . . . At the moment, what mattered most to me with regard to "Taj" was being a leitmotiv in the great Indian symphony.

A Speech to a Purdah Club in Delhi

The first club I spoke to was composed of every class of women, Muslims in the minority. As there were no men present, all purdah women could have come, but they preferred to have their special day at their own club. . . .

In facing the purdah club audience, I was facing the Turkey of twenty-eight years ago. In dress they were not different from the emancipated clubs; their expression differed. With the others, one felt that they had decided to come out of purdah, to be part of the Indian nation in all its activities; and there were a great many professional women among them, which struck a very modern note. In the purdah club, professional women were very few. These seemed as if they were still weighing the pros and cons of emancipation before taking the final step. But no face had the passive expression of the female reconciled to being carefully hidden away behind walls because of custom or male authority. If they were there, it was from their own inclination; at least they believe it to be so. "Is the complete abolition of Purdah good or evil?" they asked me, searching my face for an answer rather than listening to my words.

Individual members of this club contributed to charities, and they helped wherever they could. In the club, their activities were limited to weekly or monthly meetings, to giving entertainments, talking among themselves and then dispersing. Naturally tea with cakes and delicacies were served at each meeting. Outside the precincts of the club, they took little interest. They were indifferent on the whole even to such Muslim institutions as the Jamia [Millia Islamia]. What a center for training women for social work the Jamia could have been if the purdah women had given some time, money, and interest to it! An Indian woman said to me: "There is a great deal of social service going on. But it is mostly done in connection with the municipalities. The natives turned Christian are in the forefront; then come the Parsees, and then the Hindus, but very few Muslims take part." I thought of this remark, and also of the number of letters I have been receiving from Muslim Indian youth. The burden of them all was: "For God's sake speak against purdah! It is this slavery of women which keeps us back. . . ." And they contained other details. But I did not mean to attack the purdah of the older generation directly. I meant rather to plead for the younger generation, though they do not seem to need help.

I remember the strange way I was drawn to this audience. I also remember the fierceness with which I spoke, as brutally frank as one can be with one's kith and kin. All the time my mind was saying: "The half of this huge hall could be made into a working room with hand looms for women who have spare hours to come and work. The garden is big enough for them to bring little ones, and the members who have leisure could take turns in looking after the children. Plenty of the poor and half-naked women would welcome such occupation, which, if it did not provide wages, would at least provide cloth to make into the dresses they so sorely need. On the terrace one could start a simple clinic where a woman doctor could receive the poor and the sick who are still too conservative to go to the municipality clinics, and one could open a practical class on the care of the child. God knows how much ignorance there is in the East about the bringing up of children. And here where I am speaking they could have day and evening classes for adult women. There were enough college-bred Muslim girls to undertake the teaching. 'What do you mean,' I thought, 'by dressing so beautifully and sitting idle instead of helping, working, teaching. . . .' And all this costly food. . . . Why, they could calculate the weekly cost, and spend it on providing meals for the poorer students of Jamia."[2]

Their native courtesy and the kinship of faith made them take my caustic talk very sweetly. They asked me for a photograph to hang on their wall. I gave them a special one with the grim look of a schoolteacher. I hope it continues telling them all that I could not say.

In Lahore

We are in Punjab, at the city of Lahore. That it is one of the principal Muslim cities, there is no doubt. The cry of "Allah Akbar" is an indication of the strength of the inter-Islamic feeling. There are several thousands to welcome a Muslim woman from a strange land.

I was the guest of a rich landowner. Luxury and beauty without end. The house built as usual round an open quadrangle. The pond in the marble hall with its lotus flowers and the fountain were worthy of an exhibition of the arts. With the hospitality and courtesy of an Indian house, it laid open its drawing room as well as its lawn for the crowds of visitors who came to see me.

The ladies of the house were behind strict Purdah. I saw them at a single meal, when there were no men present. The rest of the meals were mixed, and I was invited elsewhere for a great number of them. . . .

Feminine contacts were these: Visit to a college for young women in purdah; a tea party given by the Women's Club or Clubs. It was a sumptuous affair held under a huge silk tent beautifully embroidered in red and gold. There were about three hundred women of all races, including English. Once more I thought how much better women all over the world understood each other than men. No matter how different their loyalties, they have one loyalty in common allegiance to their sex. . . .

The dainties provided one could enjoy without a pang of conscience at Lahore; for it is the first city where there is no very sharp division between extreme misery and affluence. As a matter of fact, Lahore seemed more prosperous than the cities I had hitherto seen. Even the villages round about seem comfortably off. Though the economic crisis has affected Lahore in particular and the Punjab in general, it is still better off than other centers. Everyone looks healthy, robust, and well fed. And they are mostly fine specimens of the human race.

There was a tea party at home to which girl students came. They were all tall girls, all given to sport, and having an air of self-confidence and independence difficult to associate with purdah women. To find an assembly of such handsome lasses with such natural gaiety, one must go to an American university.

Their dress was not the sari—that is, the floating drapery of one piece wound round the figure. Beautiful as the sari is—and perhaps for that reason, it has become the national costume of the emancipated women—it always seemed to me somewhat unpractical for those who have modern professions. The Muslem girls of Lahore wear tight trousers and long silk chemises buttoned at the side, more like the Chinese woman's costume. Over their hair they have a thin floating veil, embroidered all round or at the borders. This seemed to me more practical; but I admit that women who adopt it must have the figures of Lahore women, which are not common in any nation. These girls were all daughters of the rich and their interests seemed to be confined to their own class. I have also met purdah women at the houses where I dined. Before the dinner, which was mixed, I went to the harem and had pleasant visits with the wives or mothers of my hosts. One saw three definite generations with three definite thoughts and ways of life. Grandmothers, entirely old-fashioned; mothers, though still absorbed in their homes, yet interested in women's education and proud of their English-speaking daughters who were out of purdah; such daughters who were entirely emancipated . . .

[At Shalimar Gardens], we sat in the shade with Begum Shah Nawaz, and she told me about the status of Muslim women at Lahore.[3] When she told me that the Muslems of Lahore have adopted the custom-law (old Hindu) in place of the Muslem law in regard to women's economic status and inheritance, I confess I was greatly surprised. For the Indian Muslems, on the whole, call themselves fundamentalists and are supposed to be keepers of the religious law; and the Islamic law in regard to these things is progressive and equitable, while the Hindu law does not accept woman's right to inherit at all. She told me that 170 Muslem women had become Christians in order to be able to inherit; for each religious community has its particular family law, and the individual who passes from one religion to the other also becomes subject to another inheritance law. Individuals should be free to change their faith if they find some other faith more congenial to their spiritual aspirations; but when this is done for material benefit it is ugly. And uglier still to think that men knowingly have forced women into this.

A Village House on India's Northwest Frontier

[My hosts] took me to see the Khyber Pass.[4] . . . We passed through villages on our way back. They were all Muslim villages. The sizes of the houses and the comparatively clean streets impressed me. I wanted to see the inside of one of the houses, and we stopped before the biggest of them. We went in and found ourselves in a spacious court. The owner of it received us pleasantly. He was one of the elders of the village and asked us to sit on the chairs before his house. A high wall divided this part from the women's quarters, and my companions told him that I wanted to visit the women. So we walked toward a door in the high wall, and it was already half open, a veiled face peeping out. There was some talk in Pushtu. I believe she was told that I was a Muslim woman from a far-off land who wanted to see their houses. She at once opened the door wide and asked me by a gesture to step in.

The inner court was larger, with a one-storied house on one side, all the doors of the rooms opening on a porch before them. There were two young women and an elderly one, who was evidently their mother. It was a perfect pandemonium which we all enjoyed, talking to each other by gestures and sounds. I marveled at how much one could express oneself without words. I made them understand that I wanted to see their rooms and all that was in them. And they at once took me into the rooms, showing me everything, even the inside of cupboards. They neither questioned the reason nor seemed to resent the unseemly curiosity. It was enough to be a Muslim and believe in the One God. You were one of them. Never in my life had I such a clear perception of the freemasonic spirit of my religion.

The last room I visited was the kitchen, and an old, toothless woman was squatting and cleaning some vegetables. She looked up and smiled very winningly, and they all talked and patted my shoulder, highly pleased with their visitor, as if she were a whimsical but harmless child instead of an old woman. The whole interior was pleasant and showed a comfortable, even prosperous, standard for a village. There was even a Singer sewing machine.

My hostesses rubbed their hands together and indicated that there was nothing more to see. Then one of them brought a chair and sat on it; another pretended to bring her something on a tray; all three pretended to sip something, smacking their lips; and all of them said, "Chai." It meant that I must sit there and drink tea with them, and perchance eat something. I know how particular villagers are about offering something to drink and eat to their visitors. But I looked at my watch and felt that I must fly. . . . They all stood under the massive door opening to the men's court and waved me goodbye.

FURTHER READING

Halide Édib. *Inside India*. London: George Allen & Unwin, 1937. https://archive.org/details /in.ernet.dli.2015.53724. An Urdu translation by Maulvi Syed Hashimi appeared soon after as *Andarun-i Hind* (New Delhi: Anjuman-i Taraqqi-i Urdu, 1939). The original English version was republished with an introduction and notes by Mushirul Hasan (New Delhi: Oxford University Press, 2002; also published to Oxford Scholarship Online, 2012). A Turkish version, originally serialized in the daily newspaper, *Yeni Sabah*, in

1940–41, was republished with an afterword by Hülya Adak as *Hindistan'a Dair* (Istanbul: Can Yayınları, 2014).

———. *Conflict of East and West in Turkey*. Delhi: Maktaba Jamia Millia Islamia, 1935. https://archive.org/details/conflictofeastan030796mbp.

———. *Memoirs of Halidé Edib*. London: John Murray, 1926. https://archive.org/details/in .ernet.dli.2015.175589.

———. *The Turkish Ordeal: Being the Further Memoirs of Halidé Edib*. London: John Murray, 1928. https://archive.org/details/in.ernet.dli.2015.499070.

Reina Lewis. *Rethinking Orientalism: Women, Travel and the Ottoman Harem*. London: I. B. Tauris, 2004, esp. 36–42.

Mushirul Hasan. *Between Modernity and Nationalism: Halide Edip's Encounter with Gandhi's India*. New Delhi: Oxford University Press, 2010.

Roberta Micallef. "From the *House with Wisteria* to *Inside India*: Halide Edib's Journey to the Symbolic." In *On the Wonders of Land and Sea: Persianate Travel Writing*, edited by Roberta Micallef and Sunil Sharma, 151–70. Boston: Ilex, 2013.

NOTES

1. As the author indicates, the Taj Mahal was commissioned by the Mughal emperor Shah Jahan to house the tomb of his favorite wife, Mumtaz Mahal, after she died in childbirth in 1631.

2. The author's ideal was reality in purdah women's clubs elsewhere in India at this time—for instance, the Princess of Wales Ladies' Club in Bhopal established by Nawab Sultan Jahan Begum (also featured in this collection) in 1909.

3. Begum Jahanara Shah Nawaz (1896–1979) was a women's rights activist, author, and politician connected with the All-India Muslim League.

4. The author refers to the mountain pass that connected India's Northwest Frontier Province (now Pakistan's Khyber Pakhtunkhwa) with Afghanistan.

TWENTY-TWO

—ᴡᴡ—

AMINA SAID

An Egyptian Feminist at an Indian Conference

INTRODUCTION

Amina Said (1914–95) (see fig. 22.1) was one of the most prominent Egyptian journalists and advocates for women's rights of the twentieth century. At just fourteen years of age, she joined the youth section of the Egyptian Feminist Union led by Huda Shaarawi (also featured in this collection). From a young age, she thus recognized the importance of women's rights, a cause to which she dedicated much of her life's work. In 1935, she became one of the first women graduates of the King Fouad I University of Cairo (now Cairo University). This education enabled her to found in 1954 Egypt's widely read women's magazine *Hawwa* (*Eve*), which published articles and essays advocating women's rights throughout the Arab world. Soon after, she became secretary-general of both the Pan-Arab League Women's Union and the Egyptian Union of Journalists. She also served as Egypt's representative at a number of international conferences, including the eighteenth session of the All-India Women's Conference (AIWC) in Hyderabad, Sindh, in December 1945–January 1946. This conference had emerged as India's leading women's organization after being established in 1927 to promote female education. Said's experience was described at some length in her travelogue *Mushahadat fi'l-Hind* (*Observations from India*, 1946), originally published in Arabic, from which the extracts below are translated.

As a journalist with global interests, Amina Said was used to traveling extensively, visiting and reporting on the United States, the Soviet Union, and India,

---

C. Ceyhun Arslan and Greg Halaby prepared the introduction and translation from Arabic. Siobhan Lambert-Hurley added material on the All-India Women's Conference and the Indian context to the introduction and annotations.

259

Figure 22.1 Amina Said visiting London's Scotland Yard in 1955. © Keystone
Pictures USA / Alamy Stock Photo.

among other countries. Her professional life and writings show the extent to
which she viewed women's rights advocacy as a crucial pan-Arab as well as a
global issue. She belonged to a generation of women's rights activists, including
Nawal El Saadawi and Fathiya al-Assal, whose condemnation of sexist practices
sparked controversy. In particular, they drew sharp criticism from some conservative Egyptians who considered them pawns of Western imperialist values.
Against such criticisms, Said continually denounced any religious establishment
that promoted a patriarchal interpretation of Islam—though not Islam itself,

which she viewed as a religion "flexible enough" to respond to societal and life changes. Although she approved and defended many "Western" values, she did not have an unbridled fascination for "the West," which had, according to her, exacerbated unequal power hierarchies in the world. In spite of her contentious viewpoints, she garnered respect from much of Egyptian society, including its leaders, some of whom were the object of her censure. For her wide-ranging accomplishments, the Egyptian state granted her numerous awards, including the First Order of the Republic (1975) and the National Arts Award (1982).

Said's Indian travelogue, *Mushahadat fi'l-Hind*, was one of a growing number of early twentieth-century Arabic travelogues that focused on India, though its predecessors, including Athnasiyus Ighnatiyus Nuri's *Rihla ila al-Hind* (*Journey to India*, 1899–1900) and Yusuf Kamal's *Siyahati fi bilad al-hind al-injiliziyya wa kashmir* (*My Journey to British India and Kashmir*, 1913–14), were male authored. In the main, Said offered her observations of India's largest cities, including Delhi, Karachi, and Hyderabad in the Deccan. Her travelogue also reflected consciously on the similarities and differences between Muslims in Egypt and India, as well as Hindu-Muslim relations in India, which were deteriorating at the time of her visit on account of widespread communal violence associated with the creation of independent India and Pakistan. Key figures from India's main political parties were also introduced—notably, Jawaharlal Nehru, the leader of the Indian National Congress who was to become India's first prime minister, and Muhammad Ali Jinnah, the leader of the All-India Muslim League and Pakistan's first governor-general. Emerging from a political landscape marked by rising Egyptian nationalism and growing engagement with the Soviet Union, Said criticized European imperialism while showing her sensitivity to economic inequalities that, in her view, also contributed to patriarchy.

As indicated, *Mushahadat fi'l-Hind* was written at a crucial moment in South Asian and Middle Eastern history: on the eve of India's independence and Partition (1947) and shortly before the establishment of the Israeli state (1948). Said's observations of the AIWC, as contained in the extracts, draw attention to political and social opinions circulating in India at this transitional moment. Clearly, Said viewed women's rights, economic inequality, the Palestinian cause, and India's independence as interrelated issues. Like many other participants in the conference—including the president, Hansa Mehta—Said considered herself an important agent of political change on issues not traditionally associated with women's rights. Her speech on the Palestinian cause, for example, seems to have influenced the perceptions of many Hindus and Muslims in India regarding Palestine and Zionism. Said also expressed a strong desire to reinforce cultural and political ties between India and the

Arab world—in particular, by introducing India's influential poet and activist Sarojini Naidu to her readership. Recognizing that Arabs' perceptions of India were colored by exoticized tales and legends, she encouraged her readers to be more engaged with political and social affairs in India. As she discovered, Indian participants at the conference were already well informed about political transformations in the Arab world. Older links through travel and Pan-Islamism fostered this familiarity while also shaping Said's reception; according to AIWC proceedings, her "striking and passionate patriotism" had "evoked warm sympathy" among Indian women.

EXTRACTS

Arriving in Sindh

I went to Hyderabad in the Sindh region to attend the All-India Women's Conference, not previously knowing much about the value of this conference or the potential of its success. Neither did I know anything about Indian women and the extent of their interest in affairs of politics and society, and therefore I did not set a specific agenda, nor did I decide the type of topics about which I would speak. I left these matters to the moment of my arrival and examination of the actual circumstances there.

I was quite astonished when I observed in Karachi that conversations in India were all revolving around this conference, especially in light of the fact that many Western countries participated in it. I came across delegations from the United States of America, England, New Zealand, Australia, Sweden, Egypt, and Lebanon. This is a novel occurrence because never before had all of these countries participated together in an Indian women's conference.[1]

Maybe this phenomenon is due to the expansion of political horizons during the war, such that other countries could set their minds to the necessity of cooperation in order to support the pillars of much-desired world peace.

I became more content upon reading the agenda of the conference, finding that educated Indian women would address all the political, economic, and social problems of their country. I accordingly simplified my message and devised my agenda. I decided that the Palestinian issue would be the entire focus of my effort, because it is a unique opportunity to expose the Palestinian cause to Western delegations and to have them hear the Arab perspective that rarely reached their countries.

My task was not simple or easy, given the strong enmity between Hindus and Muslims that motivates each group to abandon the cause that the other group is defending. Luck would have it that Palestine was among those issues that did not get the support of both sides. Muslims declare that it is purely an Islamic issue that they ought to defend with the support of Arabs, and to establish their legitimate right to the Holy Land. Indeed, they exerted a noble effort, and Muhammad Ali Jinnah, the leader of the Muslim League, delivered a speech to the viceroy asking about the British political position in regard to Palestine. The viceroy answered with an official reply that promised that its government would not adopt a resolution without first returning to the Arabs to consult with them and obtain their agreement.[2]

When Hindus heard of this issue, they completely abandoned the Palestinian cause, showing no interest in it. The Zionist perspectives infiltrated them, and the Hindus considered them more acceptable and appealing.

When I observed this situation upon my arrival, I was concerned that I would be unsuccessful in delivering my message, for most of the members of the conference were Hindus. The Muslim women left it years ago when all Muslims were separated from the conference. Only a small number remained, not exceeding the fingers of one hand. These Muslim women who remained do not follow the platform of the Muslim League.[3] When I noticed that, I decided to undertake a wide-ranging preliminary initiative to convince the Hindus of their mistaken position and to make them understand that the Palestinian issue is a national cause, not a religious one. Everyone who calls for justice should support it and demand the freedom of the weak.

I seized the opportunity of the gatherings that were held for me and the various press organizations to speak about Palestine and about the legitimate right of Arabs to it. I refuted the widespread Zionist claims there, and my speeches had a clear effect that appeared on the pages of newspapers in the form of articles summarizing my statements. People eagerly sought to read my articles, and they welcomed the Arab perspective. Only a handful of days passed until Indians, regardless of their creed, were speaking about Palestine with evident fervor.

Here, I criticize Arabs for their shameful disregard for propagating their just cause, and for confining their speeches and writings to their own countries, never reaching out to the West. As for the Zionists, they only gave a few speeches, instead exerting their entire effort and vast wealth in something more beneficial than rhetoric. They undertook extensive propaganda and spread their claims all over the world. People supported them without even knowing anything about the claims and arguments of the other side. I remember that after I gave speeches at the conference and sent the texts of the ones about Palestine to the newspapers, I approached some of the delegations from the West, and they showed extreme affinity for our cause. They asserted their belief in the legitimacy of the demands that I mentioned as well as the strength of the arguments I put forth. They asked me with surprise how it is that the Arabs are so quiet, not reaching out to the whole world or sending out people to advocate for them in the rest of the world. They prepared me to demand that the leaders, upon my return to Egypt, show interest in external propaganda. They said that if their people heard these arguments, they would be convinced of them and would support the Arabs and force their governments to take a just stance.

Besides the Palestinian cause, there were other complicated issues. Despite the fact that they went beyond the program's scope, I considered it my duty to explain them to the public and show people the reality of these issues. Accusations reached India that defame our political positions and cast a dusty halo around some of the honorable figures of our country.

I performed my duty in this respect, explaining our position to the journalists and establishing its validity. I enumerated for them the achievements of these honorable figures whom the journalists had misjudged, as well as the legacy of those achievements in the development and rise of Egypt. The newspapers published some of my clarifications while refraining from referring to many others to avoid the burden of censorship that was still prevalent.

The Inauguration and a Resolution on Palestine

The inauguration of the Women's Conference was grand and majestic. The pavilions that were set up in the garden of N. A. Academy were full with no less than five thousand people, men and women, coming from all corners of India to participate in the success of the women's conference.

The highest honor belonged to Sarojini Naidu, the world-famous poet, or "the nightingale of India," as they call her there. Her English poetry compilations attained global fame, and her writings varied between premodern and modern, and the "fever of Naidu" struck the world of European and American readers. They were interested in perusing what she wrote with interest and wonder. Later, this fever declined gradually just as happened before with the poet Tagore.[4]

Sarojini Naidu is still the first lady of India because she does not confine her efforts to poetry alone but also participates in the politics of the country and leads nationalist movements, drawing people to her and granting her high esteem to the hearts of leaders.

This creative poet spontaneously delivered a speech in English at the inauguration that shook the audience's emotions and awoke happiness and optimism in their souls. Thus she garnered a great welcoming. Gradually the flower-braided necklaces increased around her neck so that her short, plump body almost disappeared under its weight. Wearing necklaces is a common practice in India. People offer them as a token of appreciation, commemoration, and hospitality. Naidu was braided with flowers and elegant roses, connected with delicate metals of silver and gold, resembling the *thaali*[5] that was common among brides of past generations.

Mrs. Hansa Mehta was the current president of the conference and delivered the inauguration speech in elegant English in which she addressed political, economic, social, and national problems of India.[6] She treated all of them with intelligence and wide-ranging erudition.

I would like to mention at this point that the most important speeches of the conference were delivered in English because this language is widely spoken in India and understood by almost everyone. As for the rest of speeches, they were delivered in Hindi. We could not understand them due to the lack of translators to interpret these speeches for us. After Mrs. Hansa Mehta, delegations of foreign countries came one after another to present short reports on the efforts of women in their country and their urgent demands for the present and future. When my turn came, I spoke about Egypt at length and concluded the speech with the issue of Palestine.[7] I found that there was general interest in the Palestinian cause. Applause grew louder for the Arabs, and the following day, the newspapers published signs of encouragement, which confirmed to me that the conference would adopt a clear-cut resolution on this particular issue.

After several days, hope was lost, as I sensed that some of the few regressive contingents fought the idea of adopting the resolution out of concern that there might be support for it among Indian Muslims. The resolution would be unattainable due to the existing enmity.

These contingents at their peak had powerful influence. I feared my plan would fail; therefore, I redoubled my efforts and addressed various committees with extensive speeches that explained the Palestinian cause from top to bottom. God granted success to my efforts. The conference adopted a firm resolution, which says:

> Due to the fact that this conference is established for the sake of peace and renounces imposing the will of strong nations upon the weak, it watches with extreme concern the situation in Palestine. It has been the cradle of the Arab people for centuries, where they built their civilization, and lived always in safety, peace, and tolerance for different creeds. For this reason, the conference expresses the utmost heartfelt empathy and its complete support for the request of Arab Women's Union to nullify the Balfour Declaration that promised Jews a national homeland in Palestine against the will of the Arabs, the indigenous and legitimate inhabitants of the land. It demands the US and Great Britain to eliminate this injustice immediately.[8]

Some copies of this resolution were sent to the great powers and to the Arab League.

Women leaders of India came up one after another to the podium; each one delivered an eloquent speech in support of the resolution. When the turn came for Lady Rama Rau, one of the esteemed women of India, she stood before the microphone and announced that she asks me to deliver a message from the women of India to their Arab sisters. In essence, the message stated that Indian women, who now know the reality of the Palestinian cause, will pursue the issue with the same interest that they follow the issues of their own country. They will fight for the cause with their blood, to the very last drop if necessary.

When the votes were cast for the Palestinian resolution, the attendees approved it unanimously, without any dissent.

Cooperation with Indian Women

The Palestinian resolution was one of the thirty-six resolutions that the conference issued regarding the various problems in India. In truth, the women of India filled my heart with wonder. Enlivened with wisdom, intelligence, and open-mindedness, they came one after another to the podium each morning and evening to discuss the most pressing issues. I felt at times that I was in front of people endowed with sound strong minds, set unfailingly on achieving their goals in the near future.

The most important issues discussed at the conference included adopting firm resolutions on the need for Indian independence and turning over the reins of power to its people so that the country can rise upon firm foundations of freedom, progress, and reform.

The conference discussed freedoms of weaker countries. It supported Indonesia, from which it demanded the withdrawal of British Indian forces.[9] The Indian National Army attained full support and assistance. Indian women demanded halting the prosecution of the army's three officers and freeing its imprisoned soldiers.[10]

The conference demanded the elimination of prevalent censorship, the freedom of press and publishing, as well as the release of political captives.

Indian women castigated the mismanagement and the abject neglect in guarding against the harm caused by Bengal's floods, which led to a famine that took the lives of millions.[11]

Women addressed the lack of garments and the paucity of textiles in the markets, especially in rural areas, which resulted in the suicide of some women due to inaccessibility of proper clothing. They demanded the government make more factories and fix the prices so that the people's needs are met and the merchants' greed is curtailed.[12]

I spoke for quite a while at the conference but emphasized two key points: The first one is affirming the noble Indian character as well as the grave problems in society. These problems do not lessen the intensity of its feelings of camaraderie toward Easterners generally and Arabs specifically. The Hindus consider us close brothers and sisters. They regard our problems with concern and follow news about us with deep interest. The second point is to provide an accurate depiction of educated Indian women, as well as of what women can accomplish if given the opportunity for education. Without a doubt, the Indian woman could accomplish a great deal given her distinguished character, sharp perception, and sound logic with which she cautiously examines her country's problems. She reveals the cause of these problems to her fellow citizens, striving to resolve them in ways that are in harmony with the modern world as well as with a firm attachment to a healthy nationalism, which does not clash with the spirit of the modern age.

I believe firmly that the grave problems of India deplete the energy of men and preoccupy their minds with issues of the homeland. If they do not engage with these problems and instead entrust them to women, these women would find a suitable solution, and India would be at its highest stature. This is because Indian women are more refined than their fellow male citizens with respect to character, will, wisdom, and vitality. This is an observation that captured my attention and captures that of every foreigner who visits this country.

Cooperation with educated Indian women brings about general good, but we, as a group of Egyptian women, cannot take a step like this at the present time. Nevertheless, I gave a passionately written letter to the president of the Egyptian Feminist Union, in which women leaders of India requested the formation of a coalition between them and us. However, existing religious conflict there in India prevents us from taking the side of one group over another. Until Muslims and Hindus treat each other fairly, we will not accept under any circumstance the formation of the requested coalition so that hostility does not become further aggravated and our country, Egypt, does not become enmeshed in the existing religious enmity in India.

Here, I wish to criticize the Arabs for their neglect of their Indian brothers and sisters, as well as their grave ignorance of Indian affairs. If we mention India, our minds think of its sundry wonders and rarities, as though this vast country consists of nothing more. At the same time, they know a great deal about us, supporting us with affection, respect, and admiration, in addition to following our political issues passionately. This affinity and familial affection do not find an echo in our hearts, despite the fact that various connections bind us together, including complexion, Easternness, some customs, and hardships, past and present.

FURTHER READING

Amina Said. *Mushahadat fi'l-Hind*. Cairo: Dar al-Ma'arif, 1946.

The Proceedings of the Eighteenth Session of the All-India Women's Conference in Hyderabad, Sindh (December 28, 1945–January 1, 1946). This contains Amina Said's opening speech, as well as the resolution and related discussion on Palestine. http://dspace.gipe.ac.in/xmlui/handle/10973/39934.

Margot Badran and Miriam Cooke. *Opening the Gates: A Century of Arab Feminist Writing*. Bloomington: Indiana University Press, 1990. This source contains two of Amina Said's later writings in translation, "Feast of Unveiling" (1973) and "Why, Reverent Shaikh?" (1976).

Mohamed Younis. "The Daughters of the Nile: The Evolution of Feminism in Egypt." *Washington and Lee Journal of Civil Rights and Social Justice* 13, no. 2 (2007): 463–90.

NOTES

1. According to the AIWC's own report, this meeting was labeled in the press as the "All-India Women's International Conference" on the basis of the "large and representative" cohort of foreign delegates.

2. Notably, Jinnah often expressed his support for the Palestinian cause, including in resolutions "from the chair" made at several sessions of the All-India Muslim League in the early 1940s.

3. As the author indicates, Indian Muslim women did not participate in mainstream women's associations, like the AIWC, in large numbers by the 1940s, instead favoring separate Muslim organizations. However, Shareefah Hamid Ali (also featured in this collection) remained a patron and a member of the standing committee—though she did not attend this meeting.

4. The author refers to two collections of poetry, *The Golden Threshold* (1905) and *The Bird of Time: Songs of Life, Death and the Spring* (1912).

5. *Thaali*, also known as *mangala sutra*, is a necklace that a groom ties around a bride's neck during a traditional Hindu marriage ceremony.

6. Hansa Mehta (1897–1995) organized the AIWC's Bombay branch and acted as vice president of the conference several times before being elected president in 1945–46. She was also an educationalist and politician involved with the Indian National Congress.

7. This speech is recorded in the AIWC's proceedings (pp. 28–32).

8. This resolution and related discussion are recorded in the AIWC proceedings (pp. 77–82).

9. This sympathy with Indonesia's freedom struggle meant Herawati Diah (also featured in this collection) was invited to participate in the AIWC in Madras in December 1947 as part of an Indonesian delegation. In her memoirs, she reports how her group was hailed as "true freedom fighters" by conference participants (Herawati Diah, *An Endless*

Journey: Reflections of an Indonesian Journalist. Translated by Heather Waugh [Jakarta: Equinox, 2005]).

10. The Indian National Army (INA) was an armed force of Indian nationalists formed in 1942 to fight in alliance with imperial Japan during the Second World War against British colonial rule. At the time of the AIWC conference, INA soldiers were court-martialed in public trials at the Red Fort in Delhi. Though intended to turn the public against the INA, the joint trial of the first three soldiers—Prem Sahgal, Gurubaksh Singh Dhillon, and Shah Nawaz Khan—resulted in them being celebrated as patriots with the support of the Indian National Congress and All-India Muslim League. Ultimately, the three defendants and their fellow INA soldiers were released.

11. The author refers to widespread flooding in coastal Bengal resulting from a devastating cyclone in the Bay of Bengal in October 1942. This natural disaster triggered the catastrophic Bengal famine in which, exacerbated by colonial management, as many as three million people are estimated to have died.

12. These observations point to the economic crisis in India during the Second World War that led to high inflation, shortages of food and—as indicated here—cloth, and soaring prices on essential commodities that hit the rural poor especially.

TWENTY-THREE

SHAREEFAH HAMID ALI

Representing India at the United Nations

INTRODUCTION

Shareefah Hamid Ali (1883–1947) took up travel writing after being appointed India's representative to the first session of the Commission on the Status of Women at the newly formed United Nations in New York in 1947 (see fig 23.1). Her high-profile appointment recognized her many years of social service, as well as her family's nationalist pedigree. Her father, Abbas, was part of Bombay's influential Tyabji clan and spent his career in the judicial service of the princely state of Baroda, but after retirement, he became a close associate of Gandhi. Her mother, Amina, was the eldest daughter of the esteemed jurist, reformer, and nationalist Badruddin Tyabji. After traveling to Europe with the maharani of Baroda in 1893–94, she became involved with various social, educational, and political projects linked to Muslim girls' education and the Indian National Congress. Shareefah's childhood in a liberal household within a "progressive" princely state meant that she never observed purdah, and with her two sisters, she attended school. Subsequently, she married her cousin Hamid Ali, who had studied in England before entering the Indian Civil Service. The couple moved between postings in Sindh and Bombay presidency, but Hamid never rose above collector and district magistrate before his retirement around 1934—probably on account of his family's nationalist leanings. Unable to bear children, Shareefah dedicated herself to social work related to girls' education, nursing centers, and "uplift" for village women within her husband's districts. After attending a controversial session of the Indian National Congress in Surat in 1907, she also began advocating the use of Indian-made, or *swadeshi*, goods

---

Siobhan Lambert-Hurley prepared the introduction, extracts, and annotations.

Figure 23.1 Shareefah Hamid Ali representing India at the first session of the Commission on the Status of Women at the United Nations in 1947. © United Nations.

and later became interested in eradicating untouchability—a concern also revealed in the extracts here.

Shareefah's involvement with a national women's movement was sparked by the establishment of the All-India Women's Conference (AIWC) in 1927. At the inaugural meeting in Poona (now Pune), she not only proposed the first president, Maharani Chimnabai Gaekwad of Baroda, but also tabled a resolution in favor of "proper facilities for the education of women in purdah." As chairperson at the AIWC's second meeting in Delhi in 1928, she began a sustained campaign to lobby for legislation—in the form of the Child Marriage Restraint Act, or Sarda Act, of 1929—to end the custom of child marriage in India. Notably, this meeting was presided over by Nawab Sultan Jahan Begum of Bhopal, who also appears in this collection. From 1931, Shareefah shifted her attention to representing the AIWC on Indian franchise and women's suffrage, for which she even traveled to London in 1933 to give evidence before the joint parliamentary committee on Indian constitutional reform. Rejecting women's seats and separate electorates, she argued for universal adult suffrage within mixed general electorates. In the 1930s, Shareefah also represented the AIWC at a number of international women's meetings, including the first and only All-Asian Women's Conference in Lahore in 1931; the twelfth conference of the International Alliance of Women for Suffrage and Equal Citizenship (IAWSEC) in Istanbul, Turkey, in 1935; and the ninth congress of the Women's International League for Peace and Freedom in Lahočovice, Czechoslovakia, in 1937. At IAWSEC, she spoke alongside Iqbal-unnisa Hussain, another Muslim woman traveler from India featured in this collection, on "East and West in Cooperation." Shareefah's many contributions were recognized with important posts within the AIWC, including honorary treasurer, vice president and (in 1940) president.

This level of experience with national and international organizations must have made Shareefah a natural choice for government appointments to the United Nations and, after India's independence in 1947, the women's subcommittee of the National Planning Committee and the Hindustan Textbook Committee. Formed in 1946, the UN Commission on the Status of Women had, as Shareefah recorded, "no limit to its terms of reference"; it would have to "embrace every single problem which deals in any way with woman." In the opening paragraph of her travelogue, Shareefah detailed how she was selected as one of fifteen representatives to this commission by the government of India for a period of two years in September 1946. However, she found herself unable to book a passage by ship to New York with the effect that, after a two-month wait—and with only a week left before the first session began at Lake Success, New York, in early February—she decided to "risk" the three-day air journey. Commercial air travel had been introduced before the First World War with regular services to India from the 1920s. However, because the planes were small (often with fewer than twenty passengers) and the costs were high, it is unsurprising that Shareefah and her readers would have been unfamiliar with this mode of transport by the late 1940s. The first extract here reveals her wonder at so many aspects of air travel now taken for granted by the modern reader. At the same time, it points to the additional discomforts resulting from the many stops necessary before the jet age. When Shareefah and her husband had to return to India abruptly after Partition violence erupted in the hill station of Mussoorie—their home since Hamid's retirement—they chose to travel by sea.

Shareefah published her travel narrative as a series of four articles in the AIWC's Delhi-based journal *Roshni* between July and November 1947. An editor's note indicated that the series would have been longer had her appointment not been interrupted by her impromptu midterm return to India. The four articles that made it to press varied widely in content and style. The first article, most of which is reproduced here in the first extract, was a chatty account of the author's "extraordinary" three-day plane journey from Bombay to New York. The second article, not included in the extracts, was a more formal report of discussions held at the first session of the Commission on the Status of Women in mid-February 1947. The third article, entitled "Washington Diary," began with a date ("First March, 1947"), suggesting its origin in a diary that may have been the basis for all four articles. The third and fourth articles, from which the second and third extracts here are taken, were perhaps the most typical fare for a travelogue: recounting a visit to Washington, DC, for an embassy reception and a day of sightseeing and, from there, an outing to the former home of George and Martha Washington at Mount Vernon in Virginia. Throughout the series, the author's tone is frank and often judgmental, making it easy to discern her strong feelings against social discrimination of all types—gender, race, caste—that inspired her nationalist and feminist politics.

EXTRACTS

A Journey to America by Air

After waiting in vain in Bombay for two and a half months to get passages by ship to the USA, I decided to risk an air journey and reach New York to attend the first sessions of the Commission on the Status of Women, UNO, to which I have been appointed a delegate and representative of India for two years by the government of India. . . .

I shall deal with the air journey only for the present and the extraordinary experience my husband (who could luckily accompany me) and I gained by living in an aeroplane for three days. . . .

When I got into the plane and climbed the last step in Bombay, I felt I was saying goodbye to the world! There were about forty seats, and every seat was occupied. Luckily, we had Mr. B. R. Sen of the Indian embassy as a fellow passenger, who proved a very good friend indeed and was helpful in every way.[1]

As soon as we got into our seats, the air hostess, a very charming and very efficient person, came round, tidied our luggage, gave us chewing gum, and advised us to start chewing it as it relieves the pressure from the ears, which hurt otherwise, and offered us books and magazines and papers to read.

The chairs were comfortable and adjustable. We could tilt them backward and forward, and with extra pillows and rugs, [we] were made as comfortable as possible for resting in the day. The nighttime was a different matter altogether; we got cramps and were most uncomfortable confined in such a small space. Soon a sign became visible that warned us our plane was starting, and we had to fix our safety belts. This became a regular routine throughout the journey at the time of ascending and descending and rough weather. Our pilot was extremely careful, and all through the journey we never had a jar or an untoward incident.

We were lucky in this, but most unlucky in the weather. We went through wind and snowstorms right up to New York. We had to break our journey every few hours, which was a great trial to us. Each time our passports and papers and hand luggage had to be taken down, and an incredible amount of fuss and inefficiency and loss of time endured before we were to have some food and rest. Our vaccination and inoculation papers were always looked into—and they were quite numerous! Our first stop was "Zahran" [Dhahran] in Saudi Arabia, a very bare, uninviting place where we had coffee and extremely unwieldy sandwiches, the largest I have seen in my life.

It was a good thing that we had a tasty lunch given to us on the plane, served daintily on small trays placed on pillows in our laps—with everything necessary in miniature and handily placed.

It was also interesting to watch the deftness and agility with which the air hostess served forty people, all in a few minutes. Our fellow passengers were from all countries and of all ages. One was a baby a few months old; one large party consisted of seven members of a family including big and small children. There were quite a number of Jews obviously going to Palestine.[2] We reached Lydda (Palestine) [Lod] at 9:00 p.m. and had an awful dinner after many custom formalities at eleven o'clock at night.

Lydda seemed to be a large town, from the lights we saw shining at a distance.

One of the tantalizing and disagreeable conditions of air travel is that you see practically nothing of the people in the country through which you are passing.

The transport company makes fairly efficient arrangements for food and lodging but never takes the least trouble to allow passengers to see anything of the cities through which the air route takes them. This was especially regretted by the three of us, Mr. Sen and ourselves, when we flew over Cairo, Athens, Rome, and had no opportunity of sightseeing although we had very many hours to spend in each place. We just waited about for transport and were barred from excursions by restrictions that the carrying company enforced. We were lodged in quite good hotels, but when we boarded our plane again, we found that new passengers had coolly appropriated our seats, and we were left to find anything we could get—a curious and unseemly arrangement very forcibly and vocally resented by all the passengers except the newcomers! . . . At Athens, we had to find a hotel in a village miles away from the aerodrome. I liked the Greek hotel with its Greek food and the nice, friendly people in it. My husband was dressed in Indian clothes as always, so of course he had to be taken for a "Maharaja"! . . . Any man who wears Indian clothes is supposed to be a Maharaja, but the same does not hold good for a woman dressed in Indian clothes. Sad, isn't it? I don't think that sex discrimination like this should be tolerated.

The chief inconvenience of air travel is that you can never hope to have a decent wash, let alone a bath, on the plane. There is only one wash room for women and one for men. The quantity of water is extremely limited and gets finished up in the first two or three hours. Sometimes we had to get down from the plane when it was raining or when there is a snowstorm on.

We reached Shannon in Eire after a brief stay in Paris, at two o'clock at night. It was terribly cold with snow on the ground. All the people we met at the airport were so friendly and smiling—the typical Irish men and women we read in books. I felt a great desire to visit and know that hospitable land and its people.

We flew straight over the Atlantic for over three thousand miles and reached a desolate-looking place called Gander in Newfoundland. The whole land was covered with snow; it looked quite pretty occasionally when we got glimpses of pine forests. We then reached Boston and later New York after ten hours' flight. . . .

The weather had been so stormy that sometimes we were flying above snow clouds—much higher than was good for many of us. We thus had to be given oxygen from a small oxygen apparatus attached to each chair. An amusing incident in life in the air is that it is always time for breakfast and seldom lunch! The reason is that one is continually putting back the clock by a few hours.

I was so glad to get down at last at New York. We were thoroughly exhausted and longing for a bath and a comfortable bed. We had to go through unbelievable delay and formalities at the New York airport. Even Mr. Sen, who is a minister at Washington, could not be saved from inconveniences with his diplomatic visa.

It was nice to see our liaison people in America, who took complete charge of us and our luggage and housed us safely in one of New York's largest hotels. We stayed in this hotel for nearly two months. I had work to do most of the time excepting a tenday's pleasant visit to Washington. I saw practically nothing of America but just New York.

The outside of New York is neither attractive nor artistic. It is a new town and has few historical associations. I hear it is a great center for music, drama, cinema, art, and literary activities with universities and college and famous medical institutions. As I had no opportunity of seeing this side of life in America, I should not venture to speak about it.

Visiting Washington, DC

It is three days since we came to Washington, but we have already seen a good deal of the city and have shaken hands with about a thousand of its citizens! The chief reason for our coming to Washington is to greet our newly appointed ambassador for India and to join in a reception given to his honor by the India League.[3]

The reception was held in a large Hotel drawing room at 5:30 p.m., where about a thousand guests came to meet and welcome Mr. Asaf Ali.[4] The ambassador stood at the entrance of the reception room, and all the guests came in a file, spoke their own names, shook hands, and passed on. After we had greeted him, our hosts made us stand near Mr. Asaf Ali and receive the guests. So we also had the privilege of shaking hands so hard that we felt quite limp! We slipped away for a few minutes every now and then so as to have breathing time and also to greet old and new friends. Poor Mr. Asaf Ali! he was so tired at the end. Even when he sat down for a quiet cup of tea, photographer and people who wanted to be included in his pictures didn't give him any rest but continued to hover around him all the time.

Mr. Asaf Ali was very pleasant and cordial to everyone, especially so to all his old friends. . . .

Next day, we had lunch at the [Indian] embassy. The house is well situated, looks very imposing and spacious, and has fine grounds. Mr. Asaf Ali is keen to furnish it entirely with Indian material and to make it look like an Indian home. He had not been a week in the house when we saw it. He was just beginning to settle in.

We have already seen a good deal of the city. It is a beautiful and impressive place, very much more interesting than New York. Here, the historical life of America lies before one's eyes like an open book. Each stage of its freedom can be seen at a glance. Glimpses of culture and the influence of the older civilization of England are manifest among the people.

There are still scions of the old well-known families of Britain established in Washington who are very proud of their connections and their heritage. . . .

Now I unfold the tale of yesterday: Our good friend Mrs. Eldridge took us out for a long drive in her car, and we had a good look at the whole town and got an idea of its layout. We visited the monuments of Lincoln, Washington, and Jefferson. They are most impressive and add to the grandeur and beauty of the city. . . . Later, we crossed the large bridge over the River Potomac and drove straight into the state of Virginia, which is just across the river. The first thing to be seen is Lee House (Arlington House) situated on the top of a small hill.[5] It is an old-fashioned house belonging to Mrs. Washington's people. . . . This house is kept just as it was in its historical setting and is therefore extremely interesting. We were especially interested in the children's room and study; there was an old-fashioned spinning wheel in a corner, and the first map of America and also the first magnifying glass. The living rooms are good, but we were extraordinarily

interested to see the Negro servants' (or "slaves'") comfortable rooms.[6] The garden belonging to the house is very large. The government converted a good part
of it into a military cemetery during World War I. There is also the Grave of the
Unknown Soldier, which, situated in such a place and creating an atmosphere
of loneliness, touches one's heart (yet the care of the government is manifest)
as the whole place was covered by snow. The snow-white ground in the forest
of trees looked very pretty. Our hostess expressed regret at every turn that we
were "not seeing the garden and the grounds at their best—no flowers, no green
lawns," but in reality seeing every tree and every inch of ground covered with
soft white snow looked so enchanting to us, and so novel, we did not regret much
the change for once. From there, we came to the other side of the hill and saw
the much talked of "Pentagon," which is a very curious and unusual building.[7] It
houses forty thousand military personnel. Their offices; their arrangements for
food, shopping, recreation; and every conceivable necessity are housed in that
building. It is simply colossal. It may be my ignorance, but I refuse to think it wise
to put all one's eggs in one basket in this manner! In these days of aeroplanes
and atomic bombs and now—Heaven help us!—curious flying discs roaming
about the skies![8] The Pentagon is certainly a tour de force, but in no way does
it beautify the world. As there are long corridors and much walking to do, I felt
pretty tired and was glad to seek a chair and, later, to go on to lunch as guests of
Mr. and Mrs. Eldridge.... After lunch, we went to see the congressional library
[Library of Congress]. It is one of the places every visitor to America must make
a point of visiting. It gives one an inside view of the extraordinary capacity for
organization possessed by the Americans, and there are many rare treasures
housed in that library. One of them is one of the original copies of the Magna
Carta, which is on loan for two years....

We also saw the American Charter of Independence, and a little thrill of emotion went through our hearts. We put up a silent prayer that, God granted, the
time should soon come when our own country also would be writing its Charter
of Independence in letters of gold.

Excursion to Mount Vernon

It had been arranged by our embassy friends in Washington that we should visit
Mt. Vernon, the home of Martha and George Washington, on a Sunday, but the
day turned out to be damp and unsuitable—it was snowing all the time. We gave
up our outing on Sunday and did the trip in an excursion bus later. Luckily, it
was a warm and sunny day, and we got tickets without difficulty. We had an early
meal and got ready to start. The time for meals here are different from what we

are accustomed to in India. Everyone rises early, and the night, for ordinary people, begins early also. In most places, the lunch hour begins from 12:00 or 12:30 while dinner is ordinarily obtainable from 6:00 to 8:00 p.m. No afternoon tea. We have not yet got accustomed to this privation and usually grumble over it!

To come back to my story. We left in a large roomy bus with thirty passengers and spent four hours roaming about and sightseeing. We saw many interesting and lovely sights, but the most lovely one was the River Potomac. All the surrounding country was still white with snow, and so were all the trees and branches and leaves, giving an impression that we were looking at the conventional Christmas cards. . . .

Our guide was a very humorous person (like one of Mark Twain's creations). He kept us amused and laughing all the time. As I was too tired to get down at all the "sights," I kept sitting in the bus and had long talks with the driver. He said he was of mixed blood, half American Indian.[9] He described many of the hardships Negroes and his people had to suffer on account of race discrimination. According to him, the colored people are "segregated" practically in the same manner as our ill-treated Harijans were in the past. I was greatly pained to hear him, and over and over again I regretted bitterly when I remembered that our poor, long-suffering "bhangis" and depressed class people were ostracized in almost the same manner that he was describing. Thank God, those days are passing away for us in India. But for the American Indians, the Indian camps and reserved areas and, for the Negroes, the "Jim Crow" laws still exist. Alas, for humanity.[10] What unforgivable sins are committed to uphold this worthless thing called "race prestige"!

FURTHER READING

Shareefah Hamid Ali. "My Journey to American by Air." *Roshni* 2, no. 6 (July 1947): 23–28. "My Visit to America. II." *Roshni* 2, no. 7 (August 1947): 16–22. "Washington Diary III." *Roshni* 2, no. 8 (October 1947): 23–6. "Excursion to Mount Vernon." *Roshni* 2, no. 9 (November 1947): 5–7.

———. "East and West in Cooperation" (1935). International Alliance of Women Papers, Sophia Smith Collection, Smith College, Northampton MA. Reprinted in *The Essential Feminist Reader*, edited by Estelle Freedman, 217–19 (New York: Random House, 2007).

———. "Presidential Address of Begum Hamid Ali." *Bulletin of Indian Women's Movement* no. 23 (March 1940), I VII, MSS.Eur.F.165/172.

Sálim Ali. *The Fall of a Sparrow*. New Delhi: Oxford University Press, 1985.

Aparna Basu and Bharati Ray. *Women's Struggle: A History of the All India Women's Conference 1927–1990*. New Delhi: Manohar, 1990.

"Short History of the Commission on the Status of Women." http://www.un.org/womenwatch /daw/CSW6oYRS/CSWbriefhistory.pdf.

Gordon Pirie. "Incidental Tourism: British Imperial Air Travel in the 1930s." *Journal of Tourism History* 1, no. 1 (March 2009): 49–66.

NOTES

1. As the author indicates, Binay Ranjan Sen (1898–1993) was a civil servant and diplomat who, at this point, formed part of India's first delegation to the United Nations.

2. A ban on mass Jewish immigration to Palestine was maintained by the British administration after the Second World War, despite large numbers of refugees in Europe. Around the time of the author's journey, a Zionist uprising within Palestine coupled with international pressure led Britain to announce its intention to terminate its mandate and hand the Palestine question over the United Nations for resolution.

3. The India League of America, led by Indian businessmen and intellectuals in the eastern United States, had sought to galvanize American support for the Indian National Congress during India's nationalist struggle.

4. Asaf Ali (1888–1953) was a lawyer and politician prominent in the Indian nationalist movement before he was appointed India's first ambassador to the United States from February 1947 to April 1948.

5. Arlington House was built in Greek revival-style under the direction of G. W. P. Custis in 1802. The author connects it to Martha Washington rather than her second husband, George Washington, on the basis that Custis was born to a son from her first marriage, John Parke Custis. The mansion was subsequently renamed after a later resident, Confederate general Robert E. Lee.

6. Her language here reflects the changing nomenclature of the time.

7. As the author indicates, the Pentagon is the headquarters of the United States Department of Defense. Her concerns about its vulnerability seem oddly prescient in light of the attacks on September 11, 2001.

8. The author appears to refer to a number of highly publicized sightings of "flying saucers" around this time.

9. Her labels—"American Indian," "Negroes," "Harijans," "bhangis"—reflect the nomenclature of the time.

10. The author refers here first to Indian Reservations formed by the US government in the nineteenth century to contain native American tribes apart from European populations. She then references state and local laws introduced from 1890—and still in force up to 1965—that enforced racial segregation in the southern United States.

TWENTY-FOUR

SUHARTI SUWARTO

Ten Indonesian Women in the Soviet Union

INTRODUCTION

Suharti Suwarto (1935–?) was known as a communist "hardliner" within the women's organization affiliated with the Communist Party of Indonesia (PKI) called Gerwani (short for Gerakan Wanita Indonesia, or Indonesian Women's Movement). In 1954, she traveled with a group of ten Indonesian women on a delegation to the Soviet Union organized by Gerwani. Invited by the Anti-Fascist Committee, they intended to witness the development taking place in the Soviet Union. Their trip involved a complicated plane journey from Jakarta to Moscow via the Netherlands followed by a three-week tour taking in the Republic of Uzbekistan, the Republic of Georgia, and the city of Leningrad. As well as visiting monuments and universities, they met with various government agencies and cultural organizations, including the Ministry of Social Affairs, the Ministry of Justice, and the Labor Union of the Soviet Union. Their collected travel writings were published in 1956 in a volume entitled *Kumpulan Kesan-Kesan Sepuluh Wanita Indonesia ke Sovjet Uni* (*Collection of Impressions from Ten Indonesian Women in the Soviet Union*), from which the extracts in this chapter are taken (see fig. 24.1). These writings offer a window into the activities of women's organizations and the landscape of political expression in Indonesia in the early 1950s while also pointing to the new doors opened by communism for international travel.

Featured in the text are women's interactions with international women's organizations in the Soviet Union, as well as their aspirations to cultivate

Megan Hewitt prepared the introduction and translation from Indonesian with input from Siobhan Lambert-Hurley and Daniel Majchrowicz.

Kumpulan kesan-kesan
sepuluh wanita Indonesia
ke Sovjet Uni

Figure 24.1 Suharti Suwarto's delegation of Indonesian women during their visit to the Soviet
Union in 1954. Courtesy of Daniel Majchrowicz.

international friendship for global peace at the start of the Cold War. This emphasis on international friendship is highlighted by the frequent use of *saudara*,
meaning sister, brother, or family member in Indonesian, as a gender-neutral
honorific for comrades among socialist organizations. The collection was thus
written against the backdrop of growing Cold War sentiments as new political divisions and alliances were forming around the world. Communism had
existed in the Indonesian archipelago from the late 1920s, connected with the
growth of such organizations as Sarekat Islam (the Islamic Union). A failed
communist coup in 1926 in Batavia (present-day Jakarta) resulted in the brief
dissolution of communist presence by the Dutch colonial rulers. However,
communist organizations reemerged after the Japanese surrender at the end of
the Second World War, joining the struggle for Indonesia's independence declared on August 17, 1945. Communism was confirmed as one of many options
for political and cultural expression in the new nation state of Indonesia—such
that in 1955, the PKI came fourth in the Indonesia's first national elections with

16 percent of the votes. In total, there were twenty-eight parties in the new parliament.

The broad spectrum of party alliances available in the landscape of early Indonesian politics is reflected in the diversity of political and social interests represented by the delegates invited to visit the Soviet Union. They included members of nationalist (Perwari), communist (Gerwani), Islamic (Muslimaat), and Christian (PMI) women's organizations, as well as youth, student, labor, and other educational (Taman Siswa) associations. Many of the women participating in this delegation were also involved in the 1952 Indonesian Women's Congress (Kowani), a mass women's civil society organization started in 1928 that continues to work in the fields of education, health, social welfare (including economic and labor interests), development, and electoral politics.

Fittingly, the authors contributing to the collection offered their impressions of education, culture, social affairs, industrialization, farming, mechanization and economics, many highlighting features of progress (*kemajuan*), and development (*pembangunan*) witnessed in the Soviet Union. Amazed by the postwar recovery achieved since the October 1917 Revolution, they reflected on the ways in which Indonesia could learn from the Soviet Union. Progress was described in terms of the role the Soviet government played in creating legal and practical protections for women and children (including free daycare and health clinics), lowering prices of goods, raising wage standards of labor, advancing mechanical production capabilities, providing free education for men and women in cities and rural areas as well as scholarships for college students, and eradicating illiteracy and child mortality. There were also notes about how women were no longer forced to prostitute themselves to make a living and that women were now able to hold local and national government office.

The first extract, summarizing the delegation's journey from Jakarta and initial experiences in Moscow, is taken from the uncredited introduction to the collection. The other three, presented under their original titles in translation, were all written by Suharti Suwarto. At the time of her travels to the Soviet Union, she was vice president of Gerwani and a member of the PKI Central Committee. During the revolutionary and early independence periods, she had been active in a variety of women's youth organizations, serving as president of the Putri Pemuda Indonesia (PPI, Young Women of Indonesia) and secretary of Kowani. She was also one of nine female representatives on Indonesia's earliest government body, the Majelis Permusyawaratan Rakyat Sementara (or Provisional Parliament of the Republic of Indonesia). Later, she served in the first Parliament of the Republic of Indonesia as one of six PKI representatives.

Suharti's experience in the struggles of Indonesian women toward national independence and gender equality resonate in her recounting of the history of Soviet women's liberation. She writes a great deal about women's and children's issues, establishing for her audience in Indonesia a comparative understanding of their own history in relation to Soviet history. Throughout her writing, Suharti uses the informal personal pronoun *aku* (rather than the more formal *saya*), indicating her voice and audience in that her writing is personal and unguarded. She writes in a style intended to "raise the consciousness" of her Indonesian sisters. In the small details of her descriptions—for example, of flower arrangements within hotels during their travels—she is speaking to an audience of her peers in Indonesia: women active in the women's movements for whom flower arranging was a common social activity. Observations are combined with an engagement with early feminist discourse on the "fractured souls of women that references Simone De Beauvoir's writing." Though Islam is rarely discussed in the work as a whole, Suharti does make some brief references to God (*Tuhan*), indicating that it was not incompatible to be both communist and religious in the 1950s.

EXTRACTS

From the Introduction

On August 1, 1954, we left the Kemayoran airfield [outside Jakarta]. At 10:00 a.m., we landed in Singapore and a few minutes later our airplane left Singapore for Bangkok. The natural beauty reminded us of the fertile nature of Indonesia, with green rice fields stretching far, lush valleys, and dense mountains. We were not able to enjoy the natural beauty of Bangkok for long because our airplane brought us into the heavy heat of Karachi. For a while we were able to rest on the airfield. Our journey by airplane was very satisfying; words of praise cannot describe how great the flight was. Several hours later we arrived in Calcutta, but only briefly. Not long after, we landed at the airport in Cairo in the state of Egypt, which only recently has undergone a change in its form of government. These changes have brought all manner of consequence as well as progress after overturning the negligence and oppression of Farouk's group.[1] A few of us bought handicrafts modeled on ancient Egyptian art. Then we continued our journey to Geneva, admiring the natural beauty of Europe along the way. The beauty, freshness, and tranquility of its mountains and wide, green valleys gave us no hint of all the problems Europe is facing these days. We witnessed the beauty of the Alps after departing Geneva for Amsterdam. This unbroken mountain range, peaks covered in snow, was like a symbol of the strength and greatness of Europe. The expanses of fertile beauty and natural serenity, however, do not reveal the difficulties facing Europe today. We stayed one night in Amsterdam and the following night in Prague. From Prague we continued our journey toward Moscow. As we arrived in the airfield of this big and beautiful Soviet capital city, we were greeted by dozens of women. Among them were the administrators of *Wanita Anti Fascist* [Anti-Fascist Women] and several leaders of large factories, including a watch factory, etc. The atmosphere was very joyful and culminated in a reception. Several strings of flowers were hung around our necks, accompanied by warm greetings from a female representative who spoke fluent Indonesian. The opportunity to shake hands with the others was testing because there were so many people there to welcome us. We were escorted toward a place to rest. In their enthusiasm, they practically picked us up. We, who had yet to shake off the calm atmosphere of the airplane, were nonetheless moved by their greeting.

We were in this festive state for one hour. We responded to the welcome speeches with our own, to express our happiness. Once finished, we were brought to a hotel that was quite far from the air field. On the way into the city, we saw expansive views of beautiful nature. Houses were not yet visible. The road we traveled was big and wide; it took fifteen minutes to reach the city. Just before we arrived at the hotel, all along the city streets we saw big buildings, more buildings next to those; there were buildings that were about to be constructed, and those already under construction. We also passed by the big university building that is the pride of the Soviet people.

We stayed in a place located in the center of the city of Moscow. We saw many vehicles, among them buses, trams, and many kinds of cars that looked very different from anything we had ever seen. Not far from our hotel, we caught the metro, a train station below ground. It was as beautiful as a palace. Surrounding us at the hotel were foreign workers and visitors. The hotel is very beautiful, the same as first-class in Europe with one shortfall, that is, the flower arrangements are not as appealing. Waking in the morning, we were able to see the street cleaner completing his job with a street-sweeping vehicle. After the streets that already looked clean were hosed down, the cars began to sweep up the dust. There is almost no trash; people along the street throw their trash in provided trash cans. The food is much the same as most European food, but they provided rice for us.

While visiting the city, we had the opportunity to see the Kremlin, which is home to the highest levels of the Soviet government. It looks like a strong fort with a big square inside it. Around it, within the walls, we could see former churches containing the graves of kings from the czarist era. Next to the Kremlin is a Mausoleum for the remains of Lenin and Stalin, their bodies encased in glass. Thousands of people make a pilgrimage to this place every day. We had to go downstairs before arriving where the bodies lay. It was dark; there was only light around the bodies. None of the visitors spoke or made noise. It was quiet. With Mrs. Soebandrio we laid a bouquet of flowers on the grave of Lenin and Stalin.[2] Next to the mausoleum was Red Square.

Next we drove around by car, seeing the beauty of Moscow. There are many types of buildings, from modern ones to those that retain the appearance of churches or mosques with an Arab style.

The reception at the Indonesian embassy in Moscow was very agreeable. Ambassador Soebandrio and his wife greeted us in a friendly manner. The atmosphere of Mrs. Soebandrio's home was like in Indonesia. The embassy building was multi-storied, with the office below and residence above. The building was not very large but pleasant. The domestic help were two Soviet people, and the head of the household was Mrs. Ida from Indonesia. Mrs. Soebandrio's son was very funny and always entertained us when we were fatigued. He is a very good pianist. We met many other Indonesian families in Moscow, all of whom were diplomats.

We observed the celebration of Indonesia's independence in Moscow the first time that it was observed there. We helped with the preparations. Among those present was Mr. Semun, who spoke to us without losing any of his Javanese accent. His family was out of town at the time.

After one day at the home of Ambassador Soebandrio, we returned to our lodgings. On the way we saw many ice vendors provided by the government for the public. We saw an ice seller every fifty meters. It is funny that they cleaned the glasses automatically with hot water.

We were all pleased to visit the Lenin Library, the largest in Moscow. The building has eighteen floors and over seventeen million books from authors from all over the world. There are also books from the eleventh century. For example, the works of Ivan Fyodorov, who wrote about religion.[3] Centuries-old books are kept in a temperature-controlled room so as to prevent damage.

It can serve as many as five thousand visitors each day. Visitors range from small children to adults who fill the reading and borrowing rooms. The space is made up of fourteen rooms. There are also many varieties of newspapers in ten world languages. There is also a newspaper from 1703 that we saw there.[4]

Seeing Women's and Social Life in the Soviet Union

In Russia, people build peaceful lives.
The people are polite and always happy.

I was very moved by their friendly and polite behavior, which perfectly illustrates the refined character [of people] in the Soviet Union. We never heard an arrogant word, even though their society appeared to me as a blend of greatness, grandeur, and beauty. We were brought from great cities full of skyscrapers to faraway corners. Apart from the skyscrapers, in every corner of every village, the ruins of old homes wrecked in the war were scattered here and there. Homes destroyed, roads widened, machines of development everywhere, as though saying that the Soviet Union is creating the kind of life that is good for mankind, and that it will continue to grow. The rubble of houses, churches, and schools throughout the Soviet Union tell me there has been incomparable suffering in this territory as a result of the Second World War.

Now? Gardens are full of beautiful flowers. I saw mothers and their babies sitting happily and affectionately. Young men and women read and chat in the gardens. Grandfathers and grandmothers are reading novels, apparently remembering the bitterness of the war that has passed. I could see the beaming, gentle smiles of people who fill the big streets in Moscow, Leningrad, etc. Every person seems to look joyful, the picture of a happy and satisfying life. There was no trace of revenge illustrated in those thousands of people.

There was no sense of preparation for war in the country. They were eager to say that they hate war. They know the meaning of war because of the war that wrecked everything valuable to humanity: children, husbands, loved ones, and property. Now in this peaceful atmosphere, they feel the pleasure of life, because with peace, people have the opportunity to build something that is valuable for humanity.

In the countries that did not experience total destruction in the last war, the screams of the people calling for peace could be considered "nonsense" by small-minded people. Several residents of a village we visited told me: "We want peace forever, just as now, and every day and night we pray for a world which is eternally at peace."

> *Bread and art are of equal importance in the Soviet Union,*
> *individuality develops without restriction.*

Only after seeing their beautiful artistic creations could I understand the individuality of people in the Soviet Union. Calm, friendly, and polite. Here, the soul of art flows as strongly as red blood in their veins! Bread and art are of equal importance to the people here; one is not separated from the other. The hustle and bustle of life could be witnessed in every beautiful theater. Ballet, opera, and drama quench the thirsty souls of the growing masses. Ballet and opera are a fusion of humanity and beauty. The beauty of the Soviet Union is reflected in the harmony of their way of life.

"Ever expanding, soaring into the distant sky"—this is the motto of individuality in the Soviet Union. There was no trace or indication that the government of the Soviet Union limits the development of human individuality. Since art here is the creation and property of the people, it is thus closely intertwined with the aspirations, joys, sorrows, and philosophy that live in the hearts of the people. Because art and the people here are one, actors and actresses are valued and fully guaranteed their livelihoods. During the time of the czars, however, they were only considered clowns and beggars covered in fancy clothes. Dances in restaurants were limited to very polite and refined events. The joy of life in the Soviet Union includes all aspects of life. That the system of Soviet government in no way represses a person's spiritual growth and individuality seems to be proven by the grandeur of architecture, mechanization, and original creations of the sons and daughters of the original Soviet Union! If the future is promised to every child, and protected by detailed and assertive state regulations, then how could the Soviet Union not become a store of knowledge? By protecting and cultivating the best in each Soviet child, they deserve to hope for a better and brighter future for humanity.

Indonesian Women See Their Aspirations Implemented in the Soviet Union

If many visitors to the Soviet Union are amazed, then the group of Indonesian women were possibly the most amazed to witness the greatness of development in the Soviet Union. This is because, for over twenty-five years, Indonesian women have been organizing and working together for the betterment of social conditions, especially for female laborers, for mandatory education and scholarships for college students and children, for improved marriage laws, for the eradication of human trafficking in children, women, and others. All of this has been championed by the women's movement for over twenty-five years. Today we see this being implemented in the Soviet Union, down to the smallest detail. In fact, there are many social guarantees that Indonesian women never dreamed of.

The fate of every baby in the Soviet Union is the same, without exception. The future of every baby is guaranteed, no matter their situation. I'll start with orphaned children: there are places especially for orphaned babies. Children up until the age of two and a half are cared for in a "crèche." Children three to six years old are cared for in "kindergarten."

"Kindergartens/*frobelschools*" are near the orphanages. Beginning from the age of about six, children in the cities and industrial centers must attend school for ten years. In our country they are commonly named *sekolah rendah* and *menengah* [elementary and secondary school]. School attendance for ten years is mandatory in the Soviet Union. Those who do not fulfill this can be prosecuted. Child labor is strictly prohibited because of this.

The Unbreakable Soul of Women

In many ways, women laborers have more guarantees than men.

Every factory or facility has its own "crèche" childcare, kindergarten, sanatorium, hospital, and more. Every Sunday and in the summer, women are given vacation, with the transport expenses for themselves, their children, and their families provided free of cost. Thus, every woman, if necessary, is able to work alongside her husband without any worry [for her children]. The Soviet woman does not have a fractured soul in facing the responsibilities of home and society outside of the home. Their souls don't need to be divided, half for home and half for society, as is common in the souls of women from countries formerly colonized or half-colonized!

In the Soviet Union, complex issues have long been eliminated because of social guarantees. Every man in the Soviet Union holds fast to the teachings of Lenin. My friend, a Soviet woman, told me: "Every woman who is a hero in the kitchen must also become a hero for society and country."

I was frankly amazed to witness the lives of men in the Soviet Union in relation to their wives and mothers of their children. I understand and am sure that at some time in the future, the Indonesian men and women's outlook on life will be as equal as that of the people of the Soviet Union, if only the circumstances in our country will allow it. I increasingly understand the words of Rousseau, that humankind was born good from God, but the bad arrangement of society makes him bad too.[5]

The faces of women looked radiant everywhere, in the factory, in the stores, and in the streets. In schools and in shops, there were no toys that would plant a seed or enrich an instinct to fight or go to war. The army built great buildings. Everything gives the impression of the development of a peaceful society and brings peace to the hearts of those that witness it. There is no sign or emergent feeling that there are any small preparations being made for war, like has been reported in the news, especially in our country.

After witnessing with my own eyes how people in the Soviet Union enjoy lives like kings, it was not my heart's desire to be dazzled by this but rather to be more aware of the call of my people and my homeland in Indonesia, which I love deeply.

FURTHER READING

Kumpulan Kesan-Kesan Sepuluh Wanita Indonesia ke Sovjet Uni. Jakarta: Panitia Penerbit Rombongan Wanita, 1956.

Suharti Suwarto. "Indonesian Women Struggle for Peace and Their Rights." *For a Lasting Peace, for a People's Democracy* (March 9, 1956): 4. This article appears in the journal of the Cominform.

Donald Hinley. *The Communist Party of Indonesia 1951–63.* Berkeley: University of California Press, 1966.

Susan Blackburn. *Women and the State in Modern Indonesia.* Cambridge, UK: Cambridge University Press, 2004.

Elizabeth Martyn. *The Women's Movement in Post-Colonial Indonesia: Gender and Nation in a New Democracy.* London: Routledge Curzon, 2005.

Kathryn May Robinson. *Gender, Islam, and Democracy in Indonesia.* London: Routledge, 2009.

Saskia Wieringa. *Sexual Politics in Indonesia.* New York: Palgrave Macmillan, 2002.

NOTES

1. Farouk I (1920–65) was the tenth ruler of Egypt and Sudan from Muhammad Ali's dynasty. He came to power in 1936 but, following a military coup in 1952, abdicated the throne to his infant son, Ahmad Fuad.

2. As indicated in the next paragraph, Mrs. Soebandrio was the wife of Indonesia's ambassador to the Soviet Union. The couple remained in Moscow from 1954 to 1956.

3. Ivan Fyodorov was a printer responsible for producing, among other religious books, the Ostrog Bible (1581). It is celebrated as the first complete printed edition of the Bible in a Slavic language.

4. The author must refer to Russia's first printed newspaper, *Vedemosti* (*News*, 1703–27).

5. The author appears to be summarizing Rousseau's ideas on humanity's shift from a state of nature to one of civil society in *Discourse on the Origin of Inequality among Men* (1755).

PART III

TRAVEL AS EDUCATION

AROUND THE WORLD, ACCESS TO education witnessed broad expansion in the nineteenth century. Women, who had not always been privy to formal schooling, often faced additional barriers to entry—much as they do in many parts of the world today where women's literacy continues to lag behind those of men. In some Muslim societies, how and to what extent to provide women's education was a hotly debated topic in the late nineteenth and early twentieth centuries, and one that inflamed passions. While some denied women any education at all beyond a basic grounding in religion and household management delivered at home, others advocated the establishment of dedicated girls' schools as a prerequisite to the advancement of Muslim civilization as a whole. Most of the female authors included in these pages were part of the reformist camp advocating the latter, though they often differed over whether this schooling should feature a syllabus focused on "feminine occupations" or a more comprehensive curriculum to the primary, secondary, or higher standard in local or European languages. Still, through their efforts, women's education became increasingly typical. Only a select few were able to study at the university level, and fewer still were able to travel away from their homes in the pursuit of higher education. The chapters in this section tell the story of those women who did.

Generally, the authors here all came from privileged backgrounds, and more often than not, their families were also famed for their advocacy of social reform. The earliest travelers came from the wealthiest and most influential families of their times: Bombay's renowned Tyabji clan in the case of Atiya Fyzee (and her sister Nazli Begum and cousins Safia Jabir Ali and Shareefah Hamid Ali, featured in parts II and IV, respectively) and Bhopal's princely dynasty in the case of Maimoona Sultan (and her mother-in-law Nawab Sultan Jahan Begum and husband's great-grandmother Nawab Sikandar Begum, featured in part I). However, as women's travel and education became increasingly socially accepted, women from less remarkable backgrounds also began to leave their homes in Iran, South Asia, or Indonesia for education. All of the women here traveled to Europe or, by the latest decade, the United States. These locations not only represented the colonial metropole; they were also considered to have the best universities and training colleges run on a Western model. Sometimes these educational institutions also taught methodologies or offered programs not available elsewhere at the time. There are no accounts of women traveling to other Muslim polities for an Islamic education because these institutions were not open to women in this period. However, women did sometimes study Islamic themes while in Europe, such as Muhammadi Begum (whose mother Qaisari Begum is featured in part I writing about hajj), took up Arabic and wrote at length about her engagement with university debates on religion. Most women here undertaking formal education took up practical subjects such as education or medicine. Others did not study formally themselves at all but instead visited their children at boarding schools abroad or simply attempted to learn about the world through travel. Some aimed to become scholars, and others were clearly motivated to establish themselves as paid practitioners in their respective fields. Though the motives, experiences, and results of these educational journeys varied greatly, education nevertheless remains a central theme in the history of Muslim women's travel writing.

ATIYA FYZEE

Living and Learning in London

INTRODUCTION

Atiya Fyzee (1877–1967) achieved notoriety in her own time and after for her friendships with prominent male Muslim intellectuals in her native India— notably, Maulana Shibli Numani and Muhammad Iqbal. Yet her own cultural and literary achievements are as worthy of recognition. She belonged to the Tyabji clan at the forefront of Bombay's Sulaimani Bohra community. But she was born in Ottoman Istanbul, where her father, Hasanally Feyzhyder, was a merchant. In time, her mother, Amirunnisa, returned to Bombay with her seven children, of whom Atiya was the fifth, so that they may be educated under the influence of their esteemed relative, Badruddin Tyabji. Following his example, Atiya and her two elder sisters, Zehra and Nazli (also featured in this collection), were prominent in reformist activities for Indian Muslim women in the early years of the twentieth century. As well as contributing to Urdu journalism by writing on education, health, marriage, language, and travel, they also partici- pated in some of the first Muslim women's associations in India.

In 1912 (at the mature age of thirty-five), Atiya married established artist and writer Samuel Rahamin after his conversion from Judaism to Islam. Over the next three decades, they traveled widely in India, Europe, and North America pursuing and patronizing the arts, including painting, music, dance, literature, and the theater. Perhaps their most successful collaboration was a popular book on Indian music (first published in 1914) that combined Atiya's text with

---

Sunil Sharma prepared the translations from the Urdu original, and Siobhan Lambert-Hurley prepared the annotations, originally for their coauthored book, *Atiya's Journeys: A Muslim Woman from Colonial Bombay to Edwardian Britain*. Siobhan Lambert-Hurley also prepared the introduction.

Figure 25.1 Atiya Fyzee (*seated in the front row, third from right*) with the students and staff at Maria Grey Training College, Brondesbury, London, 1905–7. Courtesy of Brunel University Archives.

Samuel's illustrations. Later, Atiya also published a widely circulated book of correspondence, *Iqbal* (1947), and an illustrated pamphlet on Mughal gardens. The latter was completed in Karachi after she, Samuel, and Nazli migrated there in 1948 shortly after Indian independence and Partition.

The extracts here come from an earlier publication known by its book title, *Zamana-i tahsil* (*A Time of Education*). As the title suggests, it focused on Atiya's experience of studying in London in 1906–7 before returning to India after thirteen months via France and Germany. Her travel account began as letters to her family in Bombay that were then edited by her eldest sister, Zehra, for publication in an Urdu-language women's magazine, *Tahzib al-niswan* (*Women's Culture*). This journal had been established in Lahore a few years before in 1898 by the esteemed reformer Sayyid Mumtaz Ali and his wife, Muhammadi Begum, who also acted as the magazine's editor. The diary format, with its short entries in a chatty and colloquial Bombay Urdu and identified by a specific date, was well suited to serialization in a monthly journal.

That Atiya was aware of her larger audience, even as she wrote the original letters, was evident from her direct address to her *Tahzibi* "sisters"—by which she meant the community of subscribers to the journal—including in two of the entries below. Undoubtedly, their specific interest in reformist topics like female education, household management, and veiling practices shaped her subject matter. But the extracts here also reflect many of Atiya's own preoccupations in her travel diary, among them, food, domestic interiors, gardens, dress, comparative religion, cooking and cleanliness, transportation, and the weather. According to Atiya's own account, her journal articles were read with such "great enthusiasm" that ultimately she agreed to print them as a collection with a north Indian publisher of Urdu books, Mufid-i 'Am, in 1921.

As Atiya noted in her preface to the book edition, she traveled to London in 1906 after being awarded one of two scholarships from the Bengal government to complete a two-year teacher training program in Britain—though she only managed one year due to ill health. The scholarship's intention was to educate two Indian women, "one a Hindu, one Mahomedan," so that they may boost numbers of qualified female staff in local girls' schools. The other recipient was a widowed Bengali Hindu named Sarala Bala Mitter. Their shared destination was Maria Grey Training College (see fig. 25.1), an institution for female education in northwest London renowned for its innovative methods. According to Atiya, a third Indian woman, Sarojini Das, also from Bengal, studied here at the same time. The burgeoning numbers of Indian women studying in Britain in this period led Atiya to record in the summer of 1907, "Whichever educational institution I go to, I always find some or other Indian girl."

On her journey to Europe by P&O steamship, Atiya traveled with her two classmates plus two of her male relatives: her third brother, Dr. Ali Azhar Beg, and her nephew, Tyab Ali Akbar. Both of them also came to Britain for education, the former to complete a higher medical degree and the latter to complete his schooling before studying law. Upon arrival in London, the whole party was received by representatives from the National Indian Association assigned by the India Office to greet and integrate Indian students, as well as another of Atiya's relatives, Camruddin Abdul Latif. Already settled in London with his wife and children, the Latif home provided a hub for Atiya to meet many of her male and female Tyabji relatives who were visiting or studying in Britain in the Edwardian era.

A feature of Atiya's narrative is the candid descriptions that she provides of the many different individuals she met over the course of her year abroad. Some are represented in the extracts here: Maria Grey's teachers, staff and students, journalists from the *Lady's Pictorial*, international performers such as Clara Butt, Indians residing in Britain (including new acquaintances and her old friend Navajbai Tata), and British aristocrats at Henley Regatta. Others included former colonial officers and their wives, nationalist and loyalist politicians, wealthy merchants and industrialists, local professionals, Indian royalty and suffragettes, Muslim reformers, and a host of international students (though rarely Muhammad Iqbal, whom she seems to have edited out of her narrative for propriety reasons). In her assessment of these people and the contexts in which she met them, Atiya gave a sense of her growing ambivalence to British society and norms. Surely there was much to be admired, but in recounting the most everyday of activities while a student in London, this traveler also offered a frank critique of imperial culture as an Indian Muslim and as a woman.

EXTRACTS

Arriving in London

September 17, 1906: How can London be described, and how can it be imagined without seeing it! Such streets and what a grand city, and the shops! It appears very nice when it is lit up at night. The way each shop is decorated—it's truly a skill. How much can a person see? People are models of fashion and getup. As we neared our residence, the quiet shops and people began to appear in their true forms.

September 18, 1906: There are thirty-five rooms in my hall. Miss Case is a warden in this place. She is an extremely balanced and capable old woman. God knows how these people are so accomplished. The college, which is near this hall, opens tomorrow. . . .

All day girls of utterly pleasing manners kept arriving, and with respect to education, many have degrees from Cambridge or London.[1] Due to their education, the level of conversation has reached such a height that in India one cannot even imagine this. If only the men of our country were like these women. No girl under nineteen years is admitted to the training college. And they all study different things—some high school training, some art, some teaching kindergarten—education is provided to whoever has ability, interest, and understanding for something. This is truly wonderful. . . .

The windows in all the passages are open. This is among the ways of the house. No one has even tasted alcohol here; they only drink water, and eat very little meat; in fact, most of them do not eat it. They eat very little. In comparison to them, it seems that I can be reckoned as someone who eats well. How these people take care and how tasteful they are. Upper-class English people are something else. Truly, I have landed in a different world.

On Education

September 24, 1906: We have to be present at college at ten minutes to ten. At ten o'clock exactly, the lady teachers arrive, and different subjects are taught. Accordingly they taught physical education today, but in what a manner! The body and limbs of the lady teacher are worth seeing. She told us that in the future for this lesson we should wear rubber-soled shoes and loose clothing. And you should know that whatever is taught to us is done in a way that we can teach it to children. That is why we are receiving this education. We were also taught botany, to draw on the blackboard, i.e., to remember to draw enough so that what we teach will settle in the minds of the children. At one o'clock we came to the hall, ate lunch, and made notes on the botany lecture.

At five minutes to two, we were again in our places. First there was a lecture on all kinds of small matters, then on geometry. . . . Then from three to four, there was a lecture on physical geography—it is amazing. I only took two or three pages of notes on the subjects of botany, astronomy, history, geology, which were all explained so well. Then many other things, and ten or twelve books written on these subjects, were shown to us.

October 11, 1906: Our lady teachers who lecture are each more capable and outstanding than the other, and their headmistress is Miss Woods. All the lecturers meet me one after another to converse and ask about India. They give me advice on how to provide education and what must be done. But they lead the conversation in such a way and acquire the information that I am under the impression that they are only questioning me. In fact, the truth is that they are very knowledgeable about India, so what can I say? When I sometimes express my thoughts and make a mistake, they tactfully refute it in the course of the discussion to show me the error. Conversation and discussion with them lays the foundation of learning.

May 25, 1907: Sisters, for your information, I will describe the situation here in terms of what kind of education is imparted for different professions in order for people to become professionals. If someone wants to be a wrestler, then it is necessary to study anatomy; if he wants to be a gardener, then botany is taught; if the work is with animals, then she must study zoology. Thus, it seems that it is necessary to know everything deeply, otherwise a person is never considered qualified for his job. In the nursery of Sutton, the famous sellers of flower and vegetable seeds, where there is a storehouse of plants, even the lowliest worker is an expert in botany. If you go by rail, then the flowers they have planted can be seen for miles. These people grow flowers and plants from every country and climate and prepare seeds from them. Their skillfulness is mind-boggling. Truly, if this nation did not have these virtues, then half the world wouldn't be in their control. They are really accomplished people.

On Christian Festivals

September 30, 1906: I went with some girls to the church of Saint [John the] Baptist, which is decorated very finely. The building is made with such skill that, if you say something, it echoes in the whole room. There is an excellent organ and a moving, sad melody is sung in a low voice. On the pulpit was a heap of flowers that seemed to have been put there not in a special way but carelessly, but if you looked carefully, every flower was in its proper place, and underneath this a heap of flowers. There were loaves of bread as big as small babies, and the shape of the loaves was such as if it was a mound of wheat in somebody's hand. There were breads of other shapes, but I liked the one like a mound of wheat most of all.[2] Then melodies were sung in God's praise. In other words, everything was presented with moving and winsome cunning so as to incline and attract unknowing hearts. . . . Then there was a sermon; many good things were said, with a trembling voice in appropriate places. Truly they are an extraordinary people.

December 21, 2006: Truly the Christian religion is not bad, but the fuss these people make—God help! One is amazed by it. There is worship at midnight, for which an invitation has arrived. It means that everyone stays up to see the passing of the old year, the beginning of the new one and how it will turn out.[3]

December 25, 2006: Today the entire city appears to be joyful and spirited. Everyone has tried to wear something new and appear to be hale and hearty. The way the children are decked up like angels—how lovely and innocent! . . .

We are going to celebrate Christmas at home. . . . This is the general custom of Christmas: keep eating until one gets sick!!

On Cooking and Cleanliness

October 30, 1906: I have written before regarding cooking, but I feel like writing about it again in greater detail. I hope that my sisters will not be weary of it. Pots and pans are placed on a gas stove, i.e., iron *chulha*, at whatever temperature is desired. Food is prepared with such speed, cleanliness, and low lost. Cleanliness is to the highest degree—the hand hardly touches anything. Vegetables are cut by a machine. There are special kinds of tools for mixing and stirring them. Everything is done in a novel way. There is no doubt that everything is of the highest quality. These people are experts in the art of cleaning things by scrubbing them. All things connected to cooking, e.g., trays, tables, etc., are washed every day with high-pressured water and then cleaned with soda. These people are so conscious of cleanliness. There is no trouble for them to observe the cleaning rules of us Muslims. To accept English ways in a Muslim manner is a simple, easy, and effortless task. Then an excellent state of affairs can be achieved.

On Dress

October 1, 1906: The lady editor and a woman photographer-artist from the *Lady's Pictorial*[4] met me. . . . They were both amazed by the artistry and suitability of my clothes. Until now they had ungainly thoughts regarding Indians. If they meet an Indian who does not meet their stereotypical views, they are totally flabbergasted. I don't know at which level they place Indians in their minds that everything about them is surprising!

October 6, 1906: I have become extremely disgusted by the decking up of the ladies here, especially what I have seen on Regent Street and Bond Street. Why do they like to make themselves up in this way? I am at a loss. In London . . . the shops are filled with choice goods that are so enticing that these women make themselves paupers in the mania for clothes. Every day new things are produced that are better than the previous day.

October 13, 1906: We went to the Albert Hall. . . . Many famous singers performed, among whom Clara Butt seemed to be just as we always see her in her picture in the newspapers.[5] She is a very ugly woman. Her clothes were delicate, pistachio-colored, shiny, on which here and there was black glitter and diamonds in places. Her hair was black. Regarding her waist, I remembered this line of poetry:

> I left a blank spot in my book of poetry,
> When I created an image of your delicate waist.

God knows how she can bind herself and sing in such a constricted state, and that too with a smile. These people bear all kinds of tortures for the sake of appearance.

November 10, 1906: I have been meaning to write for a while that I have continued wearing my Indian clothes and do not intend to ever give them up. When I go out, I cover my head, etc., with a gauze cloth. Everything is covered except my face. And our Fyzee charshaf[6] on our body, gloved hands, umbrella, good walking shoes on our feet—altogether it seems to be a complete simple outfit. And everyone appreciates the fact greatly that I have kept my ways in the English world and am setting a good example. Of course, I have modified the Fyzee charshaf a bit, which serves well instead of an English cloak.

November 21, 2006: I happened to meet an Indian gentleman and his wife. The man has invented a new kind of device, and they earn well from it. It is not easy to earn a living from something scientific in London; one must have a great mind. They have been living here for seven years, but God help them with their English pronunciation. His wife has been here for two years. Her English too seems to be hopeless. This lady is pretty, but unfortunately she wears badly tailored and tasteless, gaudy English clothes, with a wig or coiffed hair on her head in which there are strings of fake diamonds and pearls! And a big colorful hat, two or three artificial black beauty marks on her face, which is painted red and white. I felt great distress at seeing her. God has given her a pretty face, so why make herself an object of ridicule? I explained to her delicately that we can continue wearing our clothes in this country without any problems. After a lot of explaining, thankfully she understood that this was possible! And she promised solemnly that she would come wearing her own clothes. Why Indians make a spectacle of themselves in this way, I don't know.

On Local Transport

December 1, 1906: [My brother Ali Azhar] took me . . . in something new, which is called the Tube.[7] I boarded it for the first time. From the street, you go down a few steps by way of a tunnel and sit in a lift, which goes a far distance underground. Then the train comes there, which you immediately board, and that's all. "When there is even a moment's delay, Praise be to God, thine is the glory!" *Whrrrrrr*—and you are at your destination. Before you can think, it's all over. Speed and efficiency have reached perfection with this invention. This small railway comes and goes continuously, and people stand ready to board. If you delay, it's gone, to appear again in a few moments. It's the working of a jinn.[8]

Meeting the Tatas

June 1, 1907: My dear friend Navajbai Tata had invited me to stay with her [at York House] from Saturday to Monday. . . . The house and garden are extremely fine.[9] The entrance is so nice! My friend was in the drawing room. We were so happy to see each other—it is indescribable. After embracing each other properly, we were calmed. To meet that sincere, nice, and true friend in this artificial world is a blessing. She also said warmly, "Darling Atiya, how can this happy meeting be described!"

The entire drawing room was decorated in pink, and she was wearing matching clothes. Right now they have twenty-one servants. A haughty and cunning doorman of long service—how many revolutions he must have seen—opened the door; the well-built and tall gardeners; the boys serving at the table with such well-bred manners, dressed in dark blue and gold uniforms; the cook's manner is unique; and there are four maids. I don't know how many guest rooms there are. This mansion has been renovated and is almost ready. There are such old things here. There are Louis XV and XVI rooms that are as pretty as a picture. The sensibility, politeness, and propriety of the servants are perfect. None of them is visible, but whenever one is needed, they are present. Their system of appearing is beyond my comprehension. Navajbai's hand is hardly on the bell before a servant appears quietly from a corner. I have never seen them making a sound or talking. I don't know where the maids hide, for if you go in your room ten times and mess everything up, even then everything is always in its place. It is not possible to see anything just lying around. I had decided that I must see how these people serve so energetically, but it was not possible to see any maid. Indeed, it seems that they work like clockwork. After coming here, I have been refreshed. It is as if I am at a loved one's place. God bless her—she is so kind and gracious.

At Henley Royal Regatta

July 4, 1907: Mrs. Crisp[10] was standing on a high landing welcoming everybody. This place, called a boathouse, was packed with over a hundred people. There was not an inch of free space. Most of the guests were from the aristocracy as was clear from their appearance, jewelry, and clothes. It rained continuously— God help us. A sharp wind was also blowing and it seemed as if it would enter one's body. Crouching, I went and sat in a corner because the boathouse was completely open, the rain was blinding, and the air humid. I began to feel sick due to the cold. In the end, I went and wore my cloak.

The whole time, there was a continuous to and fro in the boats. One group would return from a boat tour and do justice to the refreshments set out. On the table there were grapes, apricots, and strawberries from this garden, and Mr. Crisp was present the whole time, making everyone eat. Truly he has a humble nature. The English ate so much that God protect us. Their ignorance reminded me of this line of poetry: "You believe that living is for eating." The boats on the river, the houseboat, etc., on which dainty women clad in colorful, fine dresses with full adornment were seen moving around; loads of flowers were set up here and there; music was playing; there was a lot of tea-drinking. All in all, a joyous spectacle, but some behavior was very unacceptable.[11] I pray that the influence of culture in our country is not of this type.

FURTHER READING

Atiya Fyzee-Rahamin. *Zamana-i tahsil.* Agra: Mufid-i 'Am, 1921. For examples of the author's original contributions to *Tahzib al-niswan,* see issues dated January 26, 1907– November 30, 1907.

——. *Indian Music.* London: W. Marchant, 1914. Reprinted as *The Music of India.* London: Luzac, 1925; and *Sangīt of India.* Bombay: n.p., 1942.

——. *Iqbal.* Bombay: Victory Printing Press, 1947.

————. *Gardens*. Karachi: Ameen Art Press, n.d.

Siobhan Lambert-Hurley and Sunil Sharma, *Atiya's Journeys: A Muslim Woman from Colonial Bombay to Edwardian Britain*. Delhi: Oxford University Press, 2010.

Siobhan Lambert-Hurley. "Fyzee, Atiya (1877–1967)." *Oxford Dictionary of National Biography*. http://www.oxforddnb.com/index/101102459/Fyzee.

NOTES

1. The author's observation reflected the high graduate intake to Maria Grey College in this period, with nearly half of students coming with an undergraduate degree.

2. The flowers and bread on the altar suggest that it was Harvest Festival.

3. The author may have confused the Christmas Eve service with a New Year's Eve celebration.

4. The *Lady's Pictorial* was a newspaper for primarily middle-class women featuring columns on court and society news, fashion, sport, plays and musicals, cookery, and books.

5. Clara Butt (1872–1936) was a singer renowned for her concert performances of popular ballads.

6. The charshaf (often transliterated in Turkish as *tcharchaff*) was a type of veil worn by Turkish women outside their homes. It consisted of a thick black piece of sewn cloth covering the head, face, shoulders, and bosom that was usually worn with a long cloak and gloves. Atiya's elder sister, Nazli, had introduced this style to India after visiting their father in Turkey in the early 1890s—though Atiya's addition of "Fyzee" as a descriptor suggests that the style had been altered to suit the family's needs.

7. The author refers here to a new type of train introduced to London in 1906 that moved through deep, circular tunnels, or "tubes," rather than the "cut and cover" tunnels that had been used previously.

8. Jinn are spirit beings made from fire that are imperceptible to humans and usually malevolent, though not exclusively so. It is notable here that Selma Ekrem also referred to jinn, but in terms of their absence: "modern inventions," like she observed in New York, were "magic," but not in an "Eastern" sense (see chapter 19).

9. York House was a stately home in Twickenham, now in the London borough of Richmond upon Thames. It had been purchased by the Indian industrialist Ratan Tata and his wife, Navajbai, in 1906. As the author suggests, she and Navajbai had been friends since childhood.

10. Mrs. Catherine Crisp was the wife of reputed barrister Mr. (later Sir) Frank Crisp, introduced in the next paragraph. They owned a mansion, Friar Park, in Henley-on-Thames, from which they offered the lavish hospitality described here during Henley Royal Regatta.

11. The author appears to refer to Henley's legendary drunkenness.

TWENTY-SIX

—ɯ—

MAIMOONA SULTAN

To Turkey by Train through a Child's Eyes

INTRODUCTION

Maimoona Sultan (1900–82), also known as Shah Bano Begum, was a child
of only eleven years old when she first traveled from India to Britain, Europe,
and the Middle East in 1911. Yet she had already undertaken an epic journey
six years before when, in 1905, she had moved with her immediate family from
Peshawar on British India's Northwest Frontier to the princely state of Bhopal
in central India. The five-year-old Maimoona was to marry Nawab Sultan Jahan Begum's youngest son, Hamidullah Khan, then eleven years old. She had
been chosen as his child-bride on the basis of her aristocratic Afghan lineage
traced to the eighteenth-century king Ahmad Shah Abdali. Though the nawab
begum was opposed ostensibly to early marriage, she justified the union on the
basis that female education was neglected among Indian Muslims: to provide
an educated wife for her educated son, she would need to raise the girl herself.
Accordingly, Maimoona was given a comprehensive education under the ruling
Begum's watchful eye intended to craft her into what her eldest daughter, Abida
Sultaan, described later as "the epitome of a modern Muslim princess." Alongside a "traditional grounding" in Islamic law, history, calligraphy, and languages
were lessons in "Western mores," including European languages, music, and
sports. This training allowed Maimoona to participate alongside her esteemed
mother-in-law in various reformist activities for women at the local and national
level, including clubs and organizations, art exhibitions, and maternity and child
welfare events. She also gave birth to three daughters in her early to midteens.

Daniel Majchrowicz prepared the translations from Urdu; Siobhan Lambert-Hurley prepared the
introduction and annotations.

Figure 26.1 Maimoona Sultan (*second from left*) with her husband, Nawab
Hamidullah Khan; three daughters; and a Claridges' footman, London, 1932.
From Wikipedia Commons.

The 1911 trip was another educational opportunity. Sultan Jahan Begum (also
featured in this collection) traveled with two specific aims: first, to take her
middle son, Obaidullah, to consult medical specialists in England and Germany,
and second, to attend the coronation of the new king-emperor, George V. But she
also hoped, in Maimoona's words, to learn "new things" that would help in "advancing the welfare of her people." To that end, the itinerary included a six-week
stay in Redhill near London and a month at the spa in Bad Nauheim in Germany
on top of short visits to a number of European and Middle Eastern cities, including Paris, Geneva, Constantinople, Budapest, Venice, Florence, and Cairo.
The extracts cover part of the journey's final leg, from London to Budapest. In
total, the nawab begum traveled for just over six months with a party of around
twenty-five people. From her own family were Maimoona and Hamidullah, as
well as Obaidullah; his wife, Shaharyar Dulhan; and their two eldest children,
Birjis Jahan and Wahid-uz-zafar. The ruler was also accompanied by at least
three of her ministers and state employees, her British "lady doctor," and several
maidservants. Not accompanying the party was Maimoona's own mother and
sisters. At first, this separation triggered homesickness in the young traveler to
which her guardian's stern response was not to "waste time in fretting": "keep

in view the great object of all travels"—education—"and endeavor to derive profit thereby."

To further distract the young girl, Sultan Jahan Begum (referred to in the extracts as Her Highness or Sarkar) encouraged Maimoona to keep a diary of her travels that could be later strung into a narrative and published as a book for presentation to her sisters upon her return. Convinced that her writing would make "useful reading for girls of my age," Maimoona proceeded with a readership of "Bhopal girls" in mind—few of whom had, in her assessment, "traveled at all." Her effort was published first in Urdu as *Siyahat-i Sultani* (1913) before appearing in English translation as *A Trip to Europe* (1914). The first translator was Mrs. G. Baksh, the "lady superintendent" of one of Bhopal's girls' schools, who had also been part of the traveling party. In a short introduction, she professed to provide an "almost literal translation," but as this claim is not sustained, a new translation is offered here. Baksh also praised the "young writer" for "the modesty with which the story is told." This "modesty" was exemplified in Maimoona's constant deference to her great mother-in-law's version of events and opinion in the Constantinople and Budapest sections included here.

In large part, Maimoona's dependence on Sultan Jahan Begum was necessitated by her specific travel experience as part of a "zenana party." In strict seclusion, Maimoona spent much of her first trip to Europe and the Middle East confined to "special" travel compartments, hotel suites, or their rented house in Redhill with its garden "screened from public view." Her mother-in-law, in contrast, moved about fairly freely in an all-encompassing burqa, or veil. At an audience with Queen Alexandra, the nawab begum explained her purdah arrangements to be different from those of her daughters-in-law, Maimoona and Shaharyar, on the basis that she was a "ruling chief"—but in reality, their marital status seemed key. Only a bit younger than Maimoona but still unmarried, Birjis often left her playmate at home to accompany her widowed grandmother on public outings in London. Maimoona, in contrast, had to rely—as in the extracts here—on descriptions provided mainly by her mother-in-law, brother-in-law, and husband, or sometimes what she could glean from the newspapers. This complex relationship between purdah and travel resurfaced when Maimoona visited Britain five more times in the 1920s and 1930s. She traveled with Sultan Jahan again in 1925–26, and she remained in purdah but surreptitiously began to move about unveiled with her husband's blessing. Hamidullah then used a trip in 1928—after his ascension to Bhopal's throne—to officially take his wife out of purdah. On three more visits in the 1930s, Maimoona traveled without a burqa but always with her head modesty covered (see fig. 26.1).

EXTRACTS

London to Geneva, Geneva to Istanbul

We departed from London on July 16 after a stay of a month and a half [in England]. Dr. Mackenzie had told my brother [Obaidullah] that he should continue on to Geneva as the weather there was more suitable to his convalescence. . . . We then decided that from here we would continue on to Jerusalem via Istanbul. This was because, first, the heat [in Geneva] did not agree with Her Highness. Second, we were planning to return home in October but also fervently wished to make a pilgrimage to Jerusalem first.

And so we set off for Istanbul. As we moved farther from Geneva, climactic and conditional changes became increasingly apparent. The civilization and grand sights that we saw while traveling between France and England began to fall away, and the farther we went, the more stark the differences became. After Vienna, it was as though we were back in Hindustan. The plains of Budapest, Serbia, and Bulgaria were exactly like the plains in Hindustan. Even the construction of the buildings was in the Hindustani style, right down to the tiled roofs. There were waving fields of corn and millet. We also saw buffalo and camels. There were even bullock carts and bullock plows. In short, by the time we reached the borders of Turkey, we had the pleasure of seeing a bit of Bhopal, Gwalior, Indore, Punjab, Mussoorie, and Shimla. But when we reached the limits of the Ottoman capital, the scene was the spitting image of Rajputana.[1]

My brother had disembarked at Vienna to visit the city.

Arrival in Turkey and Entering Istanbul

After we entered Turkey, we no longer saw flowers, greenery, towns, or villages. The train carried us through a wilderness for two days. In the place of roses and lilacs, we saw red Turkish caps here and there, and also a few rickety customs check-posts manned by the odd soldier. Otherwise, there was nothing but grass in every direction. The railway stations en route were in a bad way, the lights barely on. Our stations in Hindustan are much better. This was an unbroken wilderness, with desolate plains distinguished only by the mountain streams running through them. We did see, on occasion, the shimmer of a weapon brandished by one of the villagers or the Turkish nomads tending to their flocks. It was, altogether, a strange and frightening scene. And then, after a long and arduous journey, Istanbul at last came into view, spreading a breathtaking vista before our eyes. My heart was thrilled to see light glinting off the golden spires atop the minarets of the mosques. Five months had passed since my eyes last saw a Muslim city, minarets, or mosques.

But as the train pulled into the city, the vision that it presented from afar could not be sustained. Inside, it was revealed to be dirty and poorly maintained. Her Highness had sent word ahead of time that her arrival was to be entirely private. Despite this, Sultan *al-Muʿazzam* sent His Excellency Raghib Bey and one of his aides-de-camp to the station to receive us.[2] A buggy from the royal stable was on hand as well. The British ambassador sent his secretary. It was here that we began to encounter Eastern hospitality. On our arrival, the officers of rank asked after our well-being according to protocol.

We, the ladies, were sitting to one side in purdah. After a brief conversation, Her Highness descended from the train and got into Sultan *al-Muʿazzam*'s carriage and departed for [the hotel] Pera Palace. This carriage was open, for all the women here ride in open carriages. For this reason, a Victoria was sent for Sarkar as well. For our use, a Landau carriage had been arranged by an agent of [travel agency] Thomas Cook.[3] We got in and drove to the Pera, where Sarkar dismissed Raghib Bey. . . .

They say that Ahmad Rıza Bey, the head of parliament, is a clever and well-known person.[4] He was a persona non grata during the rule of Sultan Abdul Hamid Khan. He spent twenty years in Paris, which experience made him all the more capable. He was at the time of our visit busy establishing a school for girls. Her Highness went to have a look at the building that will house the school. It is located on the Asian side of the Bosporus. She went there on one of the sultan's boats. She told me that the building, while still incomplete, is beautiful and placed in an ideal location with a connecting garden. She met with two of the bey's sisters while there. Both sisters were very welcoming and respectful. Of them, Sulaiman Hanım, who stayed with her brother for many years in Paris, is highly educated. Coffee was brought to the building, which they all had together.

The sisters also invited Her Highness to their home. Sarkar found an appropriate way to delay this engagement, reasoning that were she to accept it she would receive more invitations from other women, and that any later invitation would be all the more difficult to decline. However, she did pay them a visit during our last days in Istanbul to gain a closer look at Turkish society. Sarkar told me that the society here is similar to European society, though somewhat unique owing to the institution of purdah. Suleiman Hanım was not present when she went for her visit, so she came to say her farewells at the Pera. I met her too. I also met the other respected women who came to visit. In Turkey, it is still considered a disgrace for a woman to visit a hotel, but out of respect for Her Highness, several women still came to visit.

Meeting the Sultan and Sultana

A meeting with Sultan *al-Mu'azzam* was organized through the British ambassador. But at that time, the ambassador still had not met with Sultan *al-
Mu'azzam*. It was thus determined that the British ambassador would first have
the honor of meeting with Sultan *al-Mu'azzam*, and he would then formally
introduce Her Highness. Accordingly, the ambassador met him and then fixed
a date and time for a meeting with Sarkar. Although Sarkar has had a royal carriage at her disposal since the day that she arrived in Constantinople, on the
appointed day she was sent a Landau from the royal garage in keeping with the
formal nature of the proceedings. A Victoria was also sent for my brother and
Hamid Sultan [Hamidullah].

His Excellency Raghib Pasha first came to the hotel to receive Sarkar. She
left at 4:00 p.m. for the royal palace. She told me later that some of the journey
from the hotel to the palace reminded her of Goharganj in Bhopal,[5] and that
from this familiarity she surmised that she had entered the administrative area
of the city. Soon after this, they came onto a clear road lined on either side by
trees reminiscent of British army cantonments [in India].

The carriage arrived at the palace a few minutes later. The enclosure, with its
golden gate and marble staircase, presented a beautiful sight nestled among the
verdant trees. The garden itself was extremely fine, as though it had come from
some other world entirely. All of this is the master work of French craftsmen.[6]

Turkish officers were standing at attention to receive her. The carriage stopped
in front of the staircase at the palace entrance, and an officer stepped forward.
He salaamed in the Turkish way, kissed her hand, and then, taking on the role
of vanguard, advanced before her. After a lengthy climb they reached a grand,
carpeted hall with a red fabric laid across it. This was lined on either side by African servants. After passing through this lengthy hall, they came to a smaller
staircase. They crossed this too and, following several twists and turns, came
to the reception room. This was formally arranged, with fine furniture and silk
chair covers embroidered with arboreal patterns.

Her Highness, my brother, and Hamid Sultan sat to wait for Sultan *al-
Mu'azzam*. A *khwajasara* presented them with a tray bearing glasses of sherbet
with the utmost ceremony. Sarkar returned it with thanks. Likewise, another
eunuch presented several glasses before my brother and Hamid Sultan. The
two of them drank. A few moments later, that same eunuch then returned bearing coffee in jeweled cups. Sarkar had some, while my brother and Hamid Sultan declined with thanks. While all of this was happening, a Turkish officer
came to inform them that Sultan *al-Mu'azzam* was conversing with the British

ambassador and that the ambassador would introduce them once that meeting had concluded.

The summons came after five minutes. Sarkar, my brother, and Hamid Sultan went into the reception room and made their greetings in the Turkish style. My brother and Hamid Sultan kissed the hand of Sultan *al-Mu'azzam*, who was standing. Then all took their seats on chairs. Sultan *al-Mu'azzam* has a very humble and affable personality. He was wearing a long black coat, striped trousers, and a fez. After a few minutes of conversation, Sultan *al-Mu'azzam* himself took Sarkar into the harem to meet with the sultana.

Sarkar told me that they passed through a number of long galleries until, as they neared the women's gallery, she saw a line of eunuchs standing in formation. This indicated that they had reached the point beyond which men's feathers are burned.[7] When they reached the end of this gallery, there was yet another beyond it. Here, there were only women servants standing guard; even the eunuchs were nowhere to be seen.

Thus, the King of Islam, who shared his name with the Lord of the Universe, served as Sarkar's guide. After passing through all of these galleries, they came to a room where he asked her to wait. The sultana and one of her servants emerged from the gallery. They too salaamed one another and kissed each other's hands. Sultan *al-Mu'azzam* was fluent in Persian, and he served as translator between Her Highness and the sultana. Each of the women shared their thoughts with one another, Sarkar speaking in Persian and the sultana in Turkish. After a short while, the sultan said [in Persian] before taking his leave, "You two continue your conversation here, and I will take my leave so that I might offer coffee to the British ambassador and the princes."

Sarkar then took off her veil, and the sultana embraced her as one might a sister. The two began to converse. Sarkar, for her part, now spoke in English, and the daughter of one of Sultan *al-Mu'azzam*'s secretaries translated her words into Turkish. This continued as tea was brought and served.

Once this meeting had concluded, Sarkar had returned, and Sir Lutfi Bey, who was appointed to Lord Chamberlain's office, gave them a tour of Dolmabahçe Palace, in which Sultan *al-Mu'azzam* lives.

On Turkish Women, Education, and Islam

Turkish women wear English clothes, and society is also generally European, but they still have a very close relationship with their religion. Nevertheless, the waves of freedom grow taller by the day. The practice of purdah is becoming less common. If matters continue at this pace, Turkey will soon be like Egypt. As far as education goes, it is not quite so advanced as we had heard, but the indications [that it is on the rise] are all there. . . .

Her Highness said that compared to the advances and boldness of Europe, when one looks at Turkey, one has no choice but to conclude that they still have much to learn, much to do. They lag behind Europe by every metric.

She also said that while the country certainly displays an Islamic morality and a tradition of hospitality that are the result of religious education, it is unfortunately weak when it comes to religion itself. This is not true of everyone, of course, but there is a general negligence toward religion that surpasses even that found among the Muslims of Hindustan. The mosques are filled with theologians, but here, as in Hindustan, they are the subject of much mockery. The Turks, like the people of Afghanistan, are little influenced by them. This is largely the fault of the theologians themselves, for they are far more given to prejudice than to emulating the good actions of the Prophet.

As a rule, until one speaks from the heart, one cannot reach the heart of another. How can the people heed the theologians when they are caught up in worldly issues even more than the people themselves are? As a matter of fact, they actually have a negative influence on the nature of the people, for when people see their actions, their minds become poisoned toward religion. And thus, they become less and less dedicated to its exhortations and limitations. This is one of the primary causes of Muslims' communal and moral decline. In His sacred Word, God on high has said of these very theologians: "Do you order righteousness of the people and forget yourselves while you recite the Scripture? Then will you not reason?"[8] Rather than make difficult matters easy, our theologians make easy matters and tasks hard.

Departure from Constantinople and Arrival in Budapest

We were unfortunately not able to stay [in Istanbul] until the blessed month of Ramadan. My brother left and returned to Bad Nauheim. As for us, after learning that this was not the right time to visit Jerusalem—it would be very hot, and the weather would not be salubrious—we decided to cancel our plans to go. We asked Sultan *al-Mu'azzam* for his permission to depart and then made our way to Budapest. . . .

Budapest is a fine city. Though it is nominally under the control of the King of Austria, it has its own parliament and government.[9] It is feared that after the death of the king, it might become entirely independent.

Budapest is the capital of the country of Hungary. It was conquered by Turkey once too. They even sieged Vienna, though it has long since slipped from their hands. Nevertheless, there are still many visible reminders of these Islamic conquests, just as in Spain. Even mosques are to be seen here, and it is only natural that one would be sorrowful on seeing the decline of Muslim influence evidenced by these places.

But then, when Muslims no longer have their morals or courage; when their sense of justice and compassion has vanished; when their stores of knowledge and skill have become depleted, then this disobedience toward God and his Prophet could not but result in their destruction. They lose their ability to rule, and the world begins to look at them with hate and disgust. Some people say that this was their destiny, and resigning themselves to this fate, they sit with their hands folded. But they have failed to understand the meaning of the word destiny. The Quran in several places tells us that forethought and effort are the surest means to success. This is a world of causes, and "destiny" is precisely the result of deliberate action and courage. This is an extremely complex subject, such that I am incapable of writing competently on it. . . . Perhaps on reading the thoughts shared in the preceding pages my sisters will think to themselves, "She is so young, and yet she wishes to talk about such issues as these!" Many will say to themselves, "Big words, tiny mouth." Most people will think that this is unjustifiable verbosity and pedantry. In truth, this is all the result of Her Highness's efforts to educate me. These words are an overview of Her Highness's thoughts on the subject that I have recorded here, and that have had a deep effect on me. The method that Her Highness has adopted to educate and fashion me is as follows: Whenever she sees something or takes note of an interesting matter or situation, she explains them to me in various ways in order to give me the firmest grasp over them. She later asks me questions about them in order to evaluate my understanding of them.

Likewise, my heart has been greatly influenced by simply remaining always within the folds of Her Highness's garment of affection and benevolence. I try, through my own initiative, to understand and enquire after such issues. And *this* is the true lesson that creates the successful family, and thence the nation, and thence the country. If children were explained and taught such useful things from the earliest age in order to strengthen their courage, self-respect, compassion, and understanding of their own condition in life, then you may be sure that all our national misfortunes would quickly become distant memories.

FURTHER READING

Maimoona Sultan Shah Bano Begum. *Siyahat-i Sultani*. Agra: Muhammad Qadir 'Ali Khan, 1913. It was translated in full by Mrs. G. Baksh as *A Trip to Europe* (Calcutta: Thacker, Spink & Co., 1914). https://archive.org/details/triptoeuropetranoomaimuoft.

More recently, the Urdu version was reprinted with its original title (Karachi: Oxford University Press, 2008).

A Brief Decennial Report of "The Princess of Wales Ladies' Club," Bhopal. Calcutta: Thacker, Spink & Co., 1922. The report contains a number of Maimoona's speeches in English translation.

Abida Sultaan. *Memoirs of a Rebel Princess*. Karachi: Oxford University Press, 2004. It includes descriptions of Maimoona Sultan by her eldest daughter.

Siobhan Lambert-Hurley. *Muslim Women, Reform and Princely Patronage: Nawab Sultan Jahan Begam of Bhopal*. London: Routledge, 2007.

Shaharyar M. Khan. *The Begums of Bhopal: A Dynasty of Women Rulers in Raj India*. London: I. B. Tauris, 2000.

Claire Chambers. *Britain through Muslim Eyes: Literary Representations, 1780–1988*. Basingstoke, UK: PalgraveMacmillan, 2015.

Douglas Scott Brookes, ed. and trans. *On the Sultan's Service: Halid Ziya Uşaklıgil's Memoir of the Ottoman Palace, 1909–1912*. Bloomington: Indiana University Press, 2020.

NOTES

1. The author refers to a number of princely states, provinces, and cities in colonial India exemplified by different types of terrain. Mussoorie and Shimla, for example, are located in the foothills of the Himalaya, whereas Rajputana was defined by an arid terrain.

2. Sultan *al-Mu'azzam* is an honorific title here referring to Ottoman Sultan Mehmed-i Khamis or Mehmet Reşat (1844–1918), who was the penultimate sultan of the Ottoman Empire.

3. The Landau carriage, though convertible, must have had its top up to maintain purdah in contrast to the unenclosed Victoria.

4. Ahmet Rıza (1858–1930) was an Ottoman politician and leading member of the nationalist Young Turks who brought multiparty democracy to the Ottoman Empire.

5. A footnote in the 2008 edition (see Further Reading for this chapter) specifies that Goharganj was "an administrative area of Bhopal with uneven and poorly-maintained streets."

6. Dolmabahçe Palace then served as the administrative center of the Ottoman Empire. Situated along the Bosporus, the palace is a unique architectural blend of European and Ottoman styles, offering a largely European façade but an interior designed to maintain functions and practices sustained by the Ottoman royal family.

7. That is, they had reached the point beyond which men other than the sultan were not allowed to proceed.

8. Surah al-Baqra, verse 44. Translation from Sahih International.

9. In 1911, Budapest was in fact a part of the Austro-Hungarian Empire but retained some local autonomy under the empire's administrative structure.

SEDIQEH DOWLATABADI

An Iranian Feminist Travels to France

INTRODUCTION

Sediqeh Dowlatabadi (1882–1961) (see fig. 27.1) is an icon of Iranian feminism. Born in Esfahan, she received a liberal education at home encouraged by her father, Mirza Hadi Dowlatabadi. A scholar of Islamic law, or *mojtahed*, he was also a leading figure in the Azali-Babi community. Persecution led the family to move to Tehran when Sediqeh was still a child, and she and her brothers, Yahya and 'Ali Mohammad, later became involved in the constitutionalist movement leading to Iran's 1906 revolution. A brief and childless marriage at the age of twenty ended in divorce, after which around 1908, Sediqeh made plans to travel to Europe for higher education. Her father's death in that same year meant that she instead took over care for her two very young half sisters, Fakhr-e Taj and Qamar-e Taj. Subsequently, Sediqeh returned to Esfahan where, between 1915 and 1917, she founded two girls' schools and a women's business cooperative. The schools were soon closed due to conservative opposition, but the cooperative was more successful. Around that same time, she again considered a sojourn in Europe only to be discouraged by members of her own family, who thought her two young charges were too young to travel.

Sediqeh's career as a journalist, for which she is best known, was launched in 1919 when she began publishing a daring and controversial newspaper entitled *Zaban-e zanan* or, in her translation, "The voice of the women." Other women's periodicals were already in publication in Iran's capital by this time, but Sediqeh's newspaper was pioneering in featuring the word *women* (*zanan*) in

Siobhan Lambert-Hurley prepared the introduction, and Sunil Sharma prepared the translation from Persian.

Figure 27.1 A photographic postcard of Sediqeh
Dowlatabadi (*left*) with two other women at a
party in Paris in the late 1920s. From Women's
World's in Qajar Iran, http://www.qajarwomen
.org/en/items/906A3.html.

its title and accepting only women's contributions. Garnering criticism from the
clergy and the government was, first, her strident advocacy of female education
that brought her into direct conflict with the Ministry of Education, and second,
her nationalist opposition to the Anglo-Persian Agreement of 1919 that would
have allowed Britain to dominate Iran's financial and military affairs. *Zaban-e
zanan* was thus banned in early 1921, forcing Sediqeh to return to Tehran, where
she persisted in publishing the magazine until 1922, though without its political
overtones. Much later, from 1942 until 1945, the newspaper was revived as the organ of an educational institution known as Kanun-e Banuvan (Ladies' Society).
Sediqeh was made director of this state-run women's center in 1935—a position
she maintained until her death—after her uncompromising views on female
education, unveiling, the age of marriage, and patriotic motherhood found favor
with Iran's autocratic ruler, modernist Reza Shah Pahlavi (r. 1925–41).

Sediqeh traveled out of Iran for the first time in 1923, by which time she was in her early forties. Her trip by land and sea took her to Baghdad, Aleppo, Beirut, Marseilles, Bern, Berlin, and finally Paris. She justified her journey on the basis of poor health for which a cure could only be found in Europe, but as she did not return to Iran until 1927 after studying for a teacher's diploma at Sorbonne University in Paris, education may have been an ulterior motive. This intention was also revealed in a reply to the Iranian ambassador in Paris, Momtaz-os-saltaneh, contained in the fourth extract here. While in Europe, Sediqeh also delivered lectures and wrote for local periodicals, including the nationalist *Iranshahr* (Berlin) and *L'Asie française* (Paris). In 1926, she represented Iran at the Tenth Congress of the International Woman Suffrage Alliance in Paris. As indicated in the fifth extract, her engagement with European feminists was often charged on the basis of their ignorance, in her view, of Iran and Iranian women, but still she made a second visit to Paris for an international conference in 1947. About her first European sojourn, Sediqeh did not compose a travelogue in the form of a book but rather published a series of articles and letters in various Persian newspapers. She also wrote letters to her adopted half sisters that described her travel experiences and impressions.

Sediqeh's first article on travel, from which the first extract here is taken, was published contemporaneously as a letter to the editor of a daily newspaper in Tehran, the *Mihan-e yaumiyeh*. Entitled "From Iran to Switzerland," it detailed the first leg of her journey to Bern, during which she was accompanied not by a male relative but instead by a family friend, the French physician Dr. Roland, who also provided medical treatment en route. In a letter about the journey, Sediqeh suggested that many of the difficulties she experienced leaving Iran, including harassment, arrest, and confiscation of her travel documents, were the effect of gender discrimination against a single woman traveling with a foreign man. But in the newspaper article, she neutralized her gender, signing the letter simply as "traveler" (*mosafer*), perhaps to add authority to her concerns. The emphasis was on the ignorance and corruption of Iran's border guards and official representatives—like the consul general in Baghdad, Mo'taman-os-saltaneh—rather than the local people or sights. The contrast between an "old" outmoded Iran represented by the officials and a "new" modern one with which Sadiqeh identified was made even more stark through the introduction of the deposed consul in Beirut, the "young" and "worthy" Mirza Mohammad Khan.

The second and fourth extracts were, according to Sediqeh's preface, written during her stay in France but only published many years later in 1945 in the resuscitated *Zaban-e zanan*. Her long exchange with the French immigration officer and the shorter one with the last Qajar ruler, Ahmad Shah, at a party for Iranian New Year (*Nowruz*) offer examples of her talent in various kinds of narrative, including dialogue. The extract on arriving in Europe also points to the exceptionality of an Iranian Muslim woman, like Sediqeh, traveling alone to Europe at this time, as well as the treatment of other Iranian female travelers who had made the journey before her. Clearly, Sediqeh's knowledge of the French language facilitated her access to local French society, even if, as documented in the third extract on her train journey from Berlin to Paris, it isolated her in Germany. From this letter to her half sister Qamar, there is also a sense of Sediqeh's ambivalence to Europe: not living up to expectation, yet still a model for a future Iran. Her commitment to that "brilliant new era" seems summed up by her dress on the Paris Nowruz. Although the "old-fashioned" Shah wished to see her in a chador, or veil, she chose an elegant dress and fashionable turban that remained her style even after returning to Iran.

EXTRACTS

From Iran to Switzerland

Since I intend to present things worth hearing to my fellow compatriots by means of newspapers until the end of my trip, and now that I have been in Switzerland for several days and am presently in Bern, I am presenting to the national newspaper *Mihan* without delay an important piece related to our officials. In my view, everyone who loves the country should pay attention to these points at an opportune moment.

From what I observed, central bureaucrats are very negligent and completely unaware of the behavior of officials outside the capital. Although much of what we who have traveled say truly has no effect, I will not hold my pen back so that the objective truth can be known and perhaps make some difference.

My main reason for traveling via Baghdad was to see part of a large Islamic country under the rule of foreigners, and especially to pay full attention during the course of my trip to the behavior of officials inside and outside Iran, seeing if they acted according to the laws of the constitution and customs of the land or not. If only I had not resolved on this and not made an investigation, then certainly countless troubles would not have been added to my pain. A wise person told me when I was leaving Tehran, "Now that you are going to travel abroad, consider Iran dead so that you may be at ease." But this idea is impossible for a sensitive person.

Indeed, until Hamadan I was faced with the bad quality of the road and getting stuck in floods and ditches, an account of which (until Qazvin) the newspaper *Iran* has published. I saw normal conditions up to Kermanshah and did not witness anything contrary to my expectations. But from outside Kermanshah until the frontier, an area that is under the control of the army, everything was contrary to my expectations.

I am convinced that the minister of war is unaware of and would not be happy with the situation. In order that he may hear about it and pay attention to improving the situation, I am recording the words of one decent army official and two other underlings as I myself witnessed.

One soldier said, "When I was stationed at the frontier from Kermanshah, I passed through Karand, and ʿAli Akbar Khan, brother of the commander-in-chief of the west, kept me for three days to do things that were not my official duties."

Another soldier asked me for a fee. When I objected, he said, "What can we poor folk do? Four months pass, and they hold on to our salaries. If respected people like you don't help us out, then we have to steal. Isn't this better than stealing?" I was moved by his words, which were obviously uttered in a truthful and sincere manner, and I helped him out. But again, the situation of the departments of the army was more hopeful and respectable than other offices.

I bid farewell to the land of Iran with a heart full of regret and sorrow and my eyes full of tears. My consolation in being far from home was in the fact that I wouldn't see those who were treacherous to it for a long time. I passed on to foreign soil with the hope that when I returned, an invisible hand would have made Iran flourish.

I entered Baghdad, and after a stop of two or three days, I set off for Aleppo. It was apparent that my passport had to be signed at the consulate of Iran. I was forced to get information from an Arab person who had a two-day acquaintance with me. He said, "Your consul general is Moʿtaman-os-saltaneh, but he is seldom at the consulate. He usually goes to Kazimayn for pilgrimage and to meet the ʿulema. But Merʾat-od-dowleh, director of passports, is always in the consulate and is truly a good man. If he too isn't there, then the consulate should be called a house of disgrace."

I met Merʾat-od-dowleh and made investigations after leaving. Truly, he is a man who knows his duty and to an extent also sorts the problems that Moʿtaman-os-saltaneh creates. Moʿtaman-os-saltaneh is an ill old man with old-fashioned and egotistical ideas who is in a position of power, loves money, and is ignorant of politics. Why does the government appoint such a man as consul general in an important place like Baghdad? Since I am disheartened by the answer to that question, I won't say more!

I left Baghdad and arrived in Aleppo. I stayed for two days and on the third left for . . . Beirut. Because I was ill, I changed my mind about going to Damascus to avoid encountering any problems. In Beirut, I took lodgings for ten days because I wanted to see it well and become informed of its antiquities and natural sights. With respect to nature, I can say that I have not seen a city like Beirut until now (as far as I have traveled).

I went from Beirut to Marseilles, and from there I came to Bern.

Entering Europe

Dear readers, don't expect to read an organized travelogue with regular dated entries. Rather, these are instructional memoirs about whatever I thought would be useful to my fellow compatriots that were recorded during a six-year period of education (from Farvardin 1301 to Farvardin 1306)[1] as the opportunity arose and delayed in being published at the proper time. It is a fortunate moment that after a gap of twenty years, the journal *Zaban-e zanan* has given me the chance to publish bits of those memoirs in consecutive issues. Although the subject matter and report are over twenty years old, there are some things worthy of being said and read that have not become old.

"Here is my passport."

"Are you Iranian? You must certainly be Armenian Iranian, isn't it?"

"I am Iranian but not Armenian."

"You can't be Muslim. Perhaps you are Jewish?"

"No, sir. I am not Jewish. Not only have my ancestors been of Muslim and Iranian origin for generations, but my father was one of the Muslim *mojtaheds* of his time."

"I can't believe that I am facing a Muslim and Iranian woman. Now tell me, with whom have you come all the way here? I mean, who has brought you?"

"I traveled alone. God was with me everywhere."

The official made a gesture of surprise. "My god! A Muslim Iranian woman has traveled alone from Tehran to France. How did your government permit you to leave? Where did you get this passport?"

"Our Minister of External Affairs is Mr. Forughi. I obtained the passport through a personal introduction to him. This paper is also a document of recommendation to the governors of provinces and border officials so that I can travel easily. These signatures are of the foreign embassies located in Tehran, through whose lands I have passed. If in all of Europe they view Iranians through your eyes, it would be good for me to turn back from here."

The director looked at me in amazement. "Describe the route you have traveled."

"Tehran, Qazvin, Hamadan, Kermanshah, Khanaqin, Baghdad, Aleppo, Beirut, Marseilles."

"Where did you learn French?"

"In my country. Excuse me, sir. It should be made clear to me whether I have entered France, a friendly country, or I am being cross-examined in a time of war on enemy soil."

"Oh, excuse me. Madam, I too, like you, am confused. Should I believe your words or the behavior of your male countrymen toward their women? Actually, if one out of a hundred Iranian travelers had a woman with them, not only would he watch over that poor woman like his luggage so that nobody sees her or steals her, but he would even strive that the woman not see or speak to anyone. He would leave the poor woman in a room with a locked door so that for long hours, there would be no sign of her. Truly, from where in your country are those kinds of men?"

"I don't know any men of that kind, but I seek permission to ask a question. I heard that in Europe time is like gold. Then why are you holding up yourself and me so much?"

"Madam, I have been in the customs office for thirty years, but only today have I seen a Muslim Iranian woman who has come here alone. This is the only thing that is the cause of my curiosity. Perhaps to some extent it is within the purview of my duties."

"It's well that I remembered. I have a letter from your ambassador in Baghdad. Read it to remove any error on your part."

"Very good. I no longer have any doubt, especially since you are a journalist. Please tell me where you are going from here so that I can help with your travels."

"I am going to Bern, the capital of Switzerland, to see my friend, the wife of Zoka-od-dowleh, who is the ambassador of Iran there."

"If you wish, come with me so that your passport can be stamped, and I can order them not to open your suitcases, and the transit people can put them in the luggage storage of the train. Your embassy can get them in Bern."

While walking, he asked, "Where will you go from Switzerland? Be assured that you will have plenty of help from the sponsor in France."

"Thank you, but I don't need help because I will study at my own expense."

"Excuse me. It's not monetary help, but all students are entitled to certain benefits. That's the law. For example, the train companies give a 2 percent discount to students."

By this time, we had reached the customs area, and orders were necessary. They gave me a bill of landing and stamped my passport. They even bought the train ticket to Bern for me. That man respectfully said goodbye and left, and I went to the train station.

Letter to Qamar, August 5, 1923

I will now write to you about my travels and Paris. From Berlin I arrived in Cologne by train. A ten-hour trip took six hours. I rested in Cologne, then again got a ticket for Paris. I was very comfortable there due to the French language. Ah! Saved from Germany and their harsh language, of which not one word is understandable. But until the last point at the border, I was harassed by German. Two unfriendly girls came into the train. Seeing that a group of us were all speaking French, they scowled and stood like that in front of us. No matter how much I tried to make space for them and asked them to sit, they shrugged and stood for thirty leagues. Germans are very bad-tempered. But I didn't see the things I had heard about in Paris. For example, it is the bride of cities and a city of love, etc. I didn't see any of this. Yes, it is very beautiful and prosperous, but the people exaggerate much. All the cities of Europe that I have seen so far are pretty and prosperous, but at first sight due to so much soot, they are like the doors and walls of the traditional kitchens in Iran. The reason is the great number of factories, and to make up for this they have large mirrors in their toilets. They made me wish that our country would be prosperous and sooty in this same way with many industries and factories.

Nowruz in Paris

On Nowruz 1924, the late Ahmad Shah, while still the ruler of Iran, had traveled to Europe. Mr. Momtaz-os-saltaneh, the ambassador of Iran in Paris, had hosted a New Year's event for him. He invited all the Iranians. I too was among the invitees. On that day, our ancient Nowruz festival was absolutely dull and did not even resemble a simple party.

Firstly, other than me there was no woman at the party, and they seated me all alone in a room. Secondly, the formalities consisted of a tray with tea and biscuits. There were even very few flowers, which are common in the salons and parties of Europe, to be seen in the Iranian embassy, which is the private house of Momtaz-os-saltaneh.

I had a dark-colored, simple, long dress. My hat was of the same fabric as the dress in the shape of a turban. Upon the entry of the shah, in the salon, they expelled me. I left. The shah was in front and a row of the grandees of the state and courtiers were standing behind him. Some of those men are still around and certainly remember that day. The ambassador of Iran introduced me to the shah, who extended his hand and asked, "Madam, what are you doing here?"

"I came for education."

"In which field are you studying?"

"Pedagogy."

"Wonderful! You have chosen an appropriate field of study. But wouldn't it have been better if you had put on some sort of chador like Turkish and Arab women?"

"My educational life is very simple and monotonous. Don't you think that if they saw a foreign face, they wouldn't pay attention?"

"You are right, madam. But what can I do? I am old-fashioned."

"But the young women of Iran are hopeful that under the benevolence of a young emperor, old-fashionedness will be removed from the country, and they will see a brilliant new era. Now Your Majesty is saying that he is old-fashioned?"

The men standing behind the shah silently applauded me, but the shah did not respond and in a forced way said, "Very good. Good luck. Goodbye."

Letter to Qamar, June 9, 1926

My dear lass, Iran was the most renowned country of the world, and now it is the most obscure. If you had been with me on the day I entered the Congress [of the International Woman Suffrage Alliance] and registered my name as the representative of the women of Iran, you would have seen the feelings of the American women toward me and wept. On the surface, there was unimaginable joy. The connotation of each word of theirs was harsher than two thousand curses. For example, one said, "When your letter arrived that an Iranian woman is present as the representative, we, the special members of the Congress, were dancing. This medal and these articles that we are presenting to you, this is the fifth time that we have taken them with us to every country we visited, waiting for a representative from Iran but ultimately bringing them back with no result. Thank God they have found their proper place." They invited me to lunch. I arrived five minutes late because the train was delayed. I apologized to them; they said, "Seeing that we were waiting a long time for a woman from your country, waiting five minutes is nothing." At a general gathering, all the representatives were introduced. When they saw me with an Iranian flag, they would ask me whether I was Italian since the colors of the Italian flag are similar to ours. When I would say that I was Iranian, they would think that I was a European woman who was representing the women of Iran. I was forced to give a long-winded explanation to each one that Iran has educated and intelligent women, etc. At last, an unpleasant Englishwoman asked me, "Where are you from? We know Iranians well. Their men are not into these things yet. You are surely married to an Iranian?" I was stunned, and for half an hour I spoke about the progress of Iranian women and the new schools, etc. Now do you understand what I am saying? Indeed, my dear, one must work in the world, gain benefit, and share it. I hope that the day comes again when we can eat together and, God willing, I can help you in your maternal tasks. Don't neglect your own education.

FURTHER READING

Mahdokht Sanati and Afsaneh Najmabadi, eds. *Sédighé Dolatabadi: Letters, Writings, and Remembrances*. 3 vols. Chicago: Midland Press, 1998. The extracts here are translated from vol. 1, p. 111; vol. 2, pp. 405–407, 420–421; and vol. 3, pp. 526–531, 570.

Lloyd Ridgeon, ed. *Religion and Politics in Modern Iran: A Reader*. London: I. B. Tauris, 2005, ch. 5: "Sediqeh Dowlatabadi: An Iranian Feminist (1882–1961)." This chapter contains several examples of Sediqeh's writings on female education, veiling and politics, translated and introduced by Mansoureh Ettehadieh.

Jasmin Khosravie. "Iranian Women on the Road: The Case of Sadiqe Doulatabadi in Europe, 1923–27." In *Venturing beyond Borders: Reflections on Genre, Function and Boundaries in Middle Eastern Travel Writing*, edited by Bekim Agai, Olcay Akyıldız, and Caspar Hillebrand, 131–74. Würzburg: Ergon, 2013.

———. *Zaban-i zanan, Die Stimme der Frauen: Leben und Werk von Sadiqa Doulatabadi (1882–1961)*. Berlin: EB-Verlag, 2012.

NOTE

1. These dates are given in the Persian calendar, but they correspond to March 1922 to March 1927.

—⟶—

BEGUM INAM HABIBULLAH

With Three Boys at an English Boarding School

INTRODUCTION

Begum Inam Habibullah (1883–1975) (see fig. 28.1) was born to the Alavi family in Kakori in northern India, a town with close links to a prominent local shrine. She was educated at home, learning Urdu, Persian, poetry, and the Quran, though she also studied English later in life. Family memory recounts that she inherited an interest in community service and humanitarian work from her mother, who observed purdah yet remained in Kakori during a cholera outbreak to aid the ill. In 1905, Begum Habibullah was married to Sheikh Muhammad Habibullah (d. 1948), a member of the landholding class from nearby Saidanpur. Muhammad Habibullah graduated from Canning College, which would later be named Lucknow University. After serving for a period in the colonial administration, he became the university's vice chancellor and was ultimately awarded an Order of the British Empire. Both he and wife became closely involved with the All-India Muslim League later in life.

The couple had four children, all of whom were given an English education, initially with an English governess. The family spent their summers in the relative cool of hill stations like Nainital, a retreat popular with British soldiers and colonial officials. Meanwhile, Muhammad Habibullah encouraged his wife to abandon purdah and introduced her into British Indian social circles. In 1920, the couple's three sons were sent to England to attend boarding school, though it is unclear whether or not Begum Habibullah supported this decision. Unlike her brothers, their only daughter, Tazeen, was

---

Daniel Majchrowicz prepared the introduction and translation from the original Urdu with input from Siobhan Lambert-Hurley.

Figure 28.1 Begum Inam Habibullah (*seated, left*) with her three sons, daughter, and husband during their stay in England in the 1920s. Courtesy of Muneeza Shamsie.

educated at a school in Lucknow at the insistence of her mother—and against the wishes of her father, who preferred for her to be educated at home. Their father had no such misgivings about sending his sons away for their education. Tazeen's brothers remained in England for sixteen years, during which time their mother and sister were only able to visit once, in 1924. The travel account translated here, *Ta'ssurat-i safar-i Yurap* (Impressions of a Journey to Europe), records this visit. Begum Habibullah abandoned purdah on this trip, for which she was ostracized on her return to India, so much that many refused to allow her to enter their homes.

Soon after her return to India, Begum Habibullah turned her attention increasingly to social and political work. Beginning in the late 1920s, she led a number of committees and organizations, including, most prominently, the Muslim League's Women's League, which she helped to establish. In 1936, she was elected a member of the United Provinces Legislative Assembly on a Muslim League ticket. Throughout her political career, she was a vociferous supporter of women's rights. She was a particularly staunch advocate for banning child marriage, improving educational standards for women, and encouraging women to leave purdah and engage with the world outside the home. She argued that Islam itself offered women a range of rights that had been systematically stolen from them. "Islam leads and is far ahead of all creeds in the recognition and safeguarding of the rights of women," she said on one occasion, clarifying on another that "the rights the Muslim women enjoy have been usurped by their men by introducing customs against such rights."

Begum Habibullah was also connected with an international network of Muslim women working for similar causes. She maintained correspondence with feminists in Egypt and also met the renowned Turkish feminist Halidé Edib (also featured in this volume) in 1935. At home, she assisted in the founding of several colleges, including the Avadh Degree College and the Talimgah-i Niswan in Lucknow, and Lady Irwin College, now part of University of Delhi. She also published at least two small books in addition to her travelogue, *Nazr-i 'aqidat* (1955) and *Namaz ka tarjama* (n.d.), which were written with the intention of giving instruction and guidance to her grandchildren, by then dispersed across India, Pakistan, and Britain.

When India and Pakistan attained independence in 1947, upper-class Muslims in the United Upper Provinces were faced with a choice: remain in their ancestral homelands or leave to start new lives in cities like Karachi and Lahore. Although Begum Habibullah represented the party that had demanded Pakistan's creation, she was already nearly sixty-five years old and felt that Pakistan was a country for the young. She and her husband accordingly remained in India. Two of her children, Isha'at (1911–91) and Begum Tazeen Faridi (1918–2010), moved to Pakistan, and Ali Bahadur (1909–82), who was posted at the Indian High Commission in London in 1947, elected to stay permanently in Britain. Only Enaith ('Inayat; 1911–91) remained in India.

Impressions of a Journey to Europe was likely published in 1937, more than a decade after Begum Habibullah's return from Europe. The preface to the text notes that she originally kept a journal to pass the time and to share impressions about life in Europe with her "sisters" back home. The volume was published, however, only after she had entered public life. The volume offers a candid look at everyday life in England, where she remained for several months while visiting her children. She is particularly careful to note how her children had changed as a result of their time abroad, but she also reveals how a small but tight-knit community of Indians could offer the warmth of home even in chilly England. The excerpts given here are from an early passage, beginning with Begum Habibullah, her husband, and her daughter reaching the end of the long journey from Lucknow to Dorset and being moments away from being reunited with her sons after four long years apart.

EXTRACTS

The Family Reunited

April 10, 1924: The train pulled away from the station [in London] at half past
ten. It had been cloudy, and it soon began to rain. After some time it began to
appear, if you looked closely, that little white droplets were falling from the sky
like pieces of cotton. Sahib[1] told me that this was snow. Having never seen snow
fall, I watched with fascination. After some time, the balls of cotton began to
stick to the ground and blanket the roofs. Fields and squares were enrobed in
white garments. How beautiful it was. Subhan Allah.

Look there! A pedestrian passes by coated in snow from head to toe. The
people here pay little attention to snowfall. As a rule, they simply go about their
business, even when it's snowing. This state of affairs persisted for about an hour.
By the end, the trees, the gardens, and hillocks had all turned white. . . .

Today, the train happened to arrive a half hour behind schedule. I was constantly checking my watch, willing the time to pass quickly. At long last, the
train pulled into Dorchester Station at two. The boys were there waiting for
me with their guardian, Mr. Harrison. They threw their arms around me the
moment the spotted me and swept their sister into their laps and showered her
with love. She had only been two and a half years old when they left Hindustan
for England.

The boys only returned from school to celebrate the Easter holidays yesterday.
Thanks be to God, I found them all to be happy and in the best of health. I'll
never forget what they said to me then: "Dearest Mummy, you had become a
dream for us." Ali Bahadur has grown so much since I last saw him, masha Allah. I also detect some changes in his face. Enaith and Isha'at have both grown
for sure, but they don't look any different from before. Last year, a dear friend
who visited the boys while on a trip to England told me that they had completely
forgotten how to speak Urdu. For this reason, I determined that I would speak
to them only in Urdu for the entirety of my stay in England. But we didn't have
much time to chat at the station. After ages, I was once again taking my dear
children with me to the car.

Mr. Harrison had arranged a house for our stay. The boys live in Dorset, which
is not far from here.[2] From the station we went directly to the house he arranged.
The [cooks] had prepared food for us, but at that moment I was neither hungry
nor thirsty. I was seeing my darlings after an eternity. Tears of joy spilled from
my eyes. God! With what words can I express my thanks to you for allowing me
to reach my children safely and rest my eyes upon them again? You alone were

their protector during these years abroad. I entrusted all my hope for their well-being to you when I was separated from them. You continuously reassured me [during moments of doubt].

I was happy to see that, [in fact,] the boys spoke Urdu just as well as they had when they went abroad. They told me that they had seen a fair bit of England during their time here, but that this country had not been blessed with the beauty that one encounters in Hindustan. Everything here is so uniform, they complained, that viewing it gives no pleasure. Person by person, they asked after each of their friends and relatives. They had not forgotten a single lane in all of Lucknow! By God's grace, their religious beliefs are intact, as well. They want to understand their prayers when they say them. I explained the meaning of the prayers to them in Urdu. I will write to the mosque in Woking[3] to ask them to send me a copy of the English translation of the holy Quran, since I believe that it is *bid'at* [reprehensible innovation] to simply go through the motions of praying and reciting God's word without understanding it. This book [the Quran] was sent down with clear instructions to guide mankind. If we do not understand its meaning, how can we obtain guidance? It is because of this lack of understanding that Muslims today lag behind others. . . .

It is unfortunate that I haven't been able to make daily entries to my journal, but I am busy with the children all day long. Anyhow, even though the houses are built right up against one another, it is impossible to know if any given house is inhabited or not. There is a constant stillness. The doors are always closed. Dear God, what kind of life the people here must live! Our landlord says that people know nothing about one another's personal lives. She conjectured that she might have been to one of her neighbor's houses only once, and that too only because she was living entirely alone. Vendors selling milk, butter, bread, fish, meat, and so on bring their goods on carts. They ring the bell. The door opens. Items are bought, and the doors are closed anew.

Our routine here is as follows: my three children come at nine in the morning and spend the entire day with me. In the evening they go back to Dorchester, which is a mile and a half from here. This is the small village of fifty or sixty houses where their guardian lives.[4] There is a broad, green field in front of Mr. Harrison's house. After four years of spending their holidays here, the children have become accustomed to it. The open, fresh air makes it a salubrious place to stay. Once, Mr. Harrison invited us to tea. His daughter [June] is a little younger than Tazeen, but, masha Allah, is so fat that when I tried to pick her up and put her in my lap, I was not able to. It felt like someone had filled up her entire body with mercury. Mr. Harrison showed us the house, the gardens, and the two rooms my boys stay in. He decorated it himself. All the family pictures that they had requested we send were on display. . . . As we were leaving, Mrs. Harrison plucked a bouquet of flowers from her garden to give us. Their garden has many varieties of narcissus.

One day, we took a trip to Weymouth, a beautiful town by the sea that is surrounded on three sides by hills. The sea lies before you, while grand buildings press up against the hills. Someone has fashioned stone horses and other animals in such a way that the grass does not grow on those parts of the hill. It appears as though they are really there. The sunset is beautiful here. The fish, particularly the sole, is famous. It is eight miles from Dorset.[5] Mr. Harrison's family was with us. Tazeen and June spent a long time playing in the sand. There are lots of small children here. Some of them swung on the swings, while others walked about the beach barefoot. Where we live, playing in the dirt and walking barefoot are considered bad habits. But here, children are built to be strong and sturdy. Just as a child is to be given food, water, and a place to sleep, it is also considered necessary for them to play in this way. This is why the children here are so strong and healthy. We went out onto the beach to watch the children play.

There is a restaurant here called Trocadero. The boys told me that they serve a "gravy," or sauce, that is better than the ones you get in Hindustan. We went there for lunch. The poor boys haven't had a Hindustani meal in such a long time that they were thrilled to eat there. I thought it was terrible.

We went shopping afterward. One of the items on my list was an overcoat. We visited several shops, but I didn't find the color I was looking for. The workers here are called "shop girls." They are all very proper and eager to assist, and are far more well-mannered and cultured than the English shop girls that work at stores in Hindustan. One shop had hundreds of coats, and they kept bringing out more in an effort to find just the color I was looking for. This was a lot of work, but they were cheerful from first to last.

At the station, there was a ten- or twelve-year-old girl who had the strangest hairstyle. Her hair was combed and treated so that it stood on end, like a peacock. I don't think she'll ever be able to wear a hat. I found it to be very unbecoming. She could only turn her head with the utmost care for fear that her hair would fall out of place. Mrs. Harrison was surprised too. "What beautiful effect is this supposed to convey that she should find it necessary to adopt such a troublesome style?"

The boys accompanied us home as far as Dorchester. Mahmud miyan[6] will come for the Easter holidays. He's just bought a motorbike for himself, on which he loves to travel. He wrote to say that he won't be taking the train. This being the holiday season, I was worried that the roads would be packed. The newspapers are always reporting car accidents. He shouldn't have traveled so far on a motorbike, but thanks be to God, he arrived safely at our home on the eighteenth of April. The boys were elated to see him after such a long time. Mahmood miyan stayed with us for eight happy days.

Everyone, including the children, is excited to celebrate Eid and to offer their prayers at the mosque in Woking. I checked with Sadruddin, who informed me that Mahmud miyan's school will resume during the Eid holidays. We were very disappointed.

The children spend their days playing and laughing. Sometimes they play golf, sometimes they go for a visit to Weymouth or Bournemouth. Other times, they go to their friends' for tea. . . . Mrs. Harrison has invited us to visit on the twenty-eighth. It is Juney's birthday, and the boys insisted that I dress Tazeen in Hindustani clothes for the occasion. Ali Bahadur himself sat down to do her hair and put on her jewelry. Seeing his sister in a sari made him puff up with pride. "Mummy," he said, "she looks so beautiful. You should always dress her up like this."

We took a car to Monkton.[7] A large number of guests had gathered for the event. Tazeen's clothing and jewelry became a spectacle for them all. One memsahib told me, "Your daughter has found a place in my heart. I can't keep my eyes off of her. And she speaks English with such a fine accent!" May God keep her safe from the jealous, she wins the affections of all around her wherever she goes.

After tea, there were songs and children's games. Both the old and young took part. The people here are so cheerful and lighthearted! We returned home at seven. It was late, so the children did not come back to the house with us.

Celebrating Eid in London

Lady Imam[8] invited us to celebrate Eid at her home in London on May 2. Eid will be on May 4. The children are excited to get new clothes stitched for Eid. They came first thing in the morning to go shopping and select the fabric. We asked for the clothes to be prepared quickly. The poor things, this is the first Eid that they have spent with us in a long time. In happy spirits, we left Dorchester at 9:00 a.m. on the appointed date. The last time we traveled this path there was snow everywhere, but now it is all gone. . . .

The train pulled into Victoria Station at noon. We found Sir Ali Imam's secretary waiting for us there. We went with him to 93 Chatham Place. The doors were shut, as is the custom here. We rang the bell. A butler came to open the door. Sir Ali Imam met us with warmth and enthusiasm. He was on his way somewhere. He said he had to leave on urgent business but that we should feel ourselves at home. "Your [figurative] sister-in-law is here." I was very happy to meet Lady Imam. I hadn't met a close friend or relative from India in a long time. She took us upstairs to show us our rooms, and then we left for lunch with Sir Krishna Gupta,[9] Sir Ali Imam's two sons, and a number of other people. His sons have been here to study for the last fourteen years.

The elder son has completed his education. He went back to India for one year and then returned to England. Talking to him, I realized that those who return to England from India prefer an English lifestyle. He told me that the heat in India is unbearable. What's more, he added, it is unbecoming for an insightful individual to believe that one particular place is their homeland. The world has been created for humanity. Thus, the entire world is their homeland. If God willed all people to think in this way, then perhaps the struggles between different communities, and people of different backgrounds, would come to an end. These power struggles happen every day and frequently lead to bloodshed but are never resolved.

I replied to him that it was true that the heat of India is unbearable to people who live in Europe, but the wonderful thing [about India] is that you can always find a climate that is pleasing to you. You might, for instance, spend your summers in the mountains. If you require a moderate climate, then there are many places for you to choose from, such as Srinagar in Kashmir. You can go wherever you need to. But he did not see eye to eye with me on the issue.

On the other hand, Sir [Ali] Imam's second son, who is still studying, sang India's praises. When we had finished eating and moved to the drawing room, he asked a number of questions about India's culture, festivals, and practices. He then reminisced happily about getting to wear shiny, colorful clothes during his childhood in India. Then we turned to the topic of Hindustani festivals. He said that he did not understand England's tradition of Easter eggs. "Even if," he said, "all of my brother's complaints about Hindustan are true, it is nevertheless also a fact that we cannot ever live comfortably in this land. The reason for this is that we will always remain foreigners, strangers, here, and the proof of this is the way that people here interact with us." We discussed issues such as these at great length. Eventually, Lady sahiba suggested we get some rest.

She took us to her own room, where the sister of one of her relatives was busy with some household task. This woman was full of complaints about life in England. She said that it was difficult and alienating to keep the fast, perform prayers, and remain ritually clean. The poor woman seemed very simple and likeable. Since coming to this house, I've completely forgotten that I am living in England. There are dozens of Hindustani servants, Hindustani foods, fun and games, and a comfortable informality. Even the house is vast, like a palace, with twenty-two bedrooms, not to mention the drawing room, etc. We stayed here for four wonderful days. "Though it was only four days, we stayed among the roses."

I was happy to hear that my friend the princess[10] was staying somewhere nearby. I thought to myself that I would go to visit her tomorrow. I spoke with Sahib and Sir [Ali] Imam about bringing the children for Eid. Sir [Ali] Imam said that he did not think it a good idea for the children to go to Woking, as Khwaja Kamaluddin was not there.[11] I had no reply to this, but it was certainly a blow. Who knows if I will ever get to spend an Eid with them again. The children were so happy to get their Eid clothes stitched, and so excited to go with me to offer Eid prayers at Woking. Sahib says that though it is not advisable, if this is what I want, then he will send for the children to be brought to London. How can I tell them not to go for Eid prayers? "Enabling a sin is worse than the sin." Though it weighed heavily on me, I kept my silence. . . .

If you want to take a walk or have a bit of fresh air here, you must go to the public gardens. The houses do not have even the smallest courtyard. In fact, the comforts that we acquire for just a few rupees cannot be purchased here for even hundreds. And the food, I think, can't but taste bad to a Hindustani. I can make this conjecture, for when I was in India, I was accustomed to eating English food regularly. But to be honest, since coming here, I've grown to detest it. Most of the time, the food here is only nominally put before a flame. You'll often cut into a piece of meat and watch blood begin to ooze out. The people here declare it "juicy" and gobble it up.

Anyhow, we all went to eat in the restaurant. There were many tables put out, but thus far, only a few people were present. All of these began to look in astonishment at the Hindustani party. I hated the feeling of their gazes on us. Perhaps they were staring so intently because they saw us as some sort of wonder. Otherwise, it is considered very bad manners in England to stare at someone like this.

FURTHER READING

Begum In'am Habibullah. *Ta'ssurat-i safar-i Yurap.* Lucknow: n.p., 1937(?). https://www
.rekhta.org/ebooks/taassurat-e-safar-e-europe-ebooks/. Further extracts and the Urdu
text of the passages published here are available online at https://accessingmuslimlives
.org/travel/impressions/.
Karin Anne Deutsch. "*Marriage in Islam* by Begum Habibullah (1883–1975)." *Indian Journal of Gender Studies* 4, no. 2 (1997): 269–73.
Muneeza Shamsie. "Imperial Shadows: A Tale of Two Childhoods, Colonial and Postcolonial." *Journal of Commonwealth and Postcolonial Studies* 16, no. 1 (2009): 114–32.
———. "Discovering the Matrix." *Critical Muslim* 4, no. 3 (2012): 165–76.

Karin Anne Deutsch. *Muslim Women in Colonial North India circa 1920–1947: Politics, Law and Community Identity.* PhD thesis, University of Cambridge, 1998.

NOTES

1. Like others in this collection, the author uses an honorific to refer to her husband.

2. The local geography described in this text, particularly the location of Dorchester and Dorset, appears to be confused. She writes "Dorset" here, which is a county, but appears to mean the county town of Dorchester.

3. The author refers to the Shah Jahan Mosque in Woking, England, which was constructed in 1889 and was the first to be purpose-built in the United Kingdom. The mosque published Maulana Muhammad Ali's well-known English translation of the Quran in 1917.

4. See note 2.

5. See note 2. Dorchester is approximately eight miles from Weymouth; both are located in Dorset.

6. Mahmuduzzafar Khan (1908–54) was a nationalist and a Marxist best remembered for helping to establish the Progressive Writers' Association, a group of left-leaning, anti-imperialist writers that had a profound effect on Indian literature and social reform movements.

7. See note 3. She seems to mean the village of Winterborne Monkton, between Dorchester and Weymouth.

8. Anees Fatimah née Karim (1901–79), a wealthy politician. She was the first female member of the Legislative Council of Bihar and the third wife of barrister Sir Saiyid Ali Imam (1869–1932), prime minister of Hyderabad from 1919 to 1922.

9. The barrister Sir Krishna Govinda Gupta (1851–1926).

10. This likely refers to Princess Bhuban, the daughter of the prime minister of Nepal, Chandra Shamsher Jang Bahadur Rana.

11. Khwaja Kamaluddin was the leading figure at the Woking mosque.

TWENTY-NINE

—⟨⟨⟨—

IQBALUNNISA HUSSAIN

At the University of Leeds

INTRODUCTION

Iqbalunnisa Hussain (1897–1954) was an Indian educationalist and activist who composed two major, if largely forgotten, literary works in English. The first was a collection of essays and speeches entitled *Changing India: A Muslim Woman Speaks* that was published in her native Bangalore in 1940. The second was a novel, *Purdah and Polygamy: Life in an Indian Muslim Household*, that appeared four years later. By the time they were published, the author was already a mature woman in her forties who had borne seven children after being married at the age of fifteen to Syed Ghulam Hussain, a government official in the Indian princely state of Mysore. She came from an impressive lineage. Her father, Ghulam Mohiuddin, was a superintendent in the colonial police force who claimed direct descent from Mysore's most famous king, Tipu Sultan. Tipu Sultan is best known for his fierce defense of Mysore state against expanding East India Company rule in south India in the late eighteenth century. Iqbalunnisa's father also bequeathed her an education at home in Urdu, Persian, and Arabic that may have stimulated her own interest in teaching. By the early 1930s, she had founded a number of educational institutions, including a girls' middle school, a vocational training institute for women, and a teachers' association in Bangalore. She was also an active member of the All-India Women's Conference (AIWC), acting as Mysore's delegate to annual meetings in Lahore (1931), Madras (1931–32) and Lucknow (1932–33).

Siobhan Lambert-Hurley prepared the introductions, extracts, and annotations.

Figure 29.1 Iqbalunnisa Hussain (*standing in second row, fifth from left*) with her class at Leeds University. Courtesy of Leeds University and Arif Zaman.

Iqbalunnisa's decision to travel to Britain in 1933 was, as highlighted in the first extract, a follow-on to completing her bachelor of arts at Maharani College in Mysore three years before. She made the trip with her eldest son, Bashir al-Zaman, and both aimed to study: Bashir was to prepare in London for the entrance examinations for the Indian Civil Service (ICS), and Iqbalunnisa was to complete a diploma in education from the University of Leeds (see fig. 29.1). In doing so, they followed generations of Indian students—the first had come for ICS training in the early 1860s—in seeking the prestige and opportunities opened up by a British education within a hierarchical imperial system. The significant costs involved, both emotionally and financially, are intimated by Iqbalunnisa's sad allusion to the "depressed condition" of her "little ones," as well as her own pursuit of a scholarship and, when that was unsuccessful, cheaper travel and lodgings. The example of Atiya Fyzee (in chapter 25) points to the growing, if still comparatively small, number of South Asian female students in Britain in the early twentieth century, some of whom did receive the government or private scholarships denied to Iqbalunnisa to complete teacher training or other programs of study, including medicine and law. Having resolved to come in a private capacity, Iqbalunnisa highlights the ample assistance received on arrival from the National Indian Association (NIA)—the philanthropic organization charged by the India Office in London with receiving and settling newly arrived Indian students—and her chosen institution, the University of Leeds.

On her return to India, Iqbalunnisa Hussain gave two lectures on her experience of living and studying in Britain. The first, from which the two extracts here are taken, was entitled: "My Experience in an English University." It was delivered as an extension lecture, presumably to a mixed audience of men and women, under the auspices of Mysore University on November 29, 1935. In tone, it divided into two halves, also reflected in the two extracts. The first half, from which a longer selection is taken, offers a chatty account of the author's arrival and reception in Britain: the perils of the sea voyage, her awkward first days in Leeds, welcome receptions at the university. The second half is a less personal discussion, though still based on her own experience, of the comparative value of university education in India and England. It is not clear to whom the second lecture, entitled "Impressions of a Visit to Europe," was directed, but a passing reference to the "present war" suggests that it was delivered sometime later. In contrast to the first lecture, it is shorter and more formal in tone throughout. A main aim was to pay tribute to illustrious individuals who befriended her in England or who aided her studies by arranging school visits in Egypt and Turkey—among them, parliamentarians Eleanor Rathbone and Viscountess Astor and Chief Girl Guide Lady Baden Powell. It then summarized a number of positive points about English education made in the first lecture to justify a less antagonistic approach to "Western civilization" than was prevalent at the time under India's nationalist ferment. Iqbalunnisa's personal commitment to this stance was evident in her later decision to move to the United Kingdom in 1951 to join two of her sons, Wahid al-Zaman and Rafi al-Zaman, already resident there. She died in London in 1954.

Both lectures on Iqbalunnisa's first trip to Europe were published in *Changing India* alongside a number of other speeches and articles, some of which had, according to the foreword, been published previously in English-language newspapers in India and Ceylon. Other lectures reprinted here point to Iqbalunnisa's activities or interests fostered during her time in Europe. Her commitment to women's internationalism and female citizenship was reflected in her report on the Girl Guide movement in India to the eighth world conference of the International Girl Guide and Girl Scouts in Switzerland in 1934. She also delivered two speeches—one on "Women of East and West in Cooperation" and another, not reproduced in *Changing India*, on "Women's Rights and Duties as Citizen"—at the twelfth conference of the International Alliance of Women for Suffrage and

Equal Citizenship (IAWSEC) in Istanbul, Turkey in 1935. Here, she met two other authors featured in this collection, Shareefah Hamid Ali from India and Huda Shaarawi from Egypt. Shortly before her departure from Britain in 1935, Iqbalunnisa was also invited to speak before the Muslim Society of Great Britain in London. This organization was closely associated with the Woking Muslim Mission of whom the primary benefactor was another Muslim female traveler from India, Nawab Sultan Jahan Begum of Bhopal. In her speech, Iqbalunnisa emphasized the importance of women's education in light of the essential sameness of men and women—thus articulating a focus on "woman as an individual" within the abstract category of "humanity" that permeated much of her writing and activism.

EXTRACTS

Arrival and Reception at an English University

I have been asked to speak to you tonight about "My Experience in an English University." I do know I am not competent to speak authoritatively on the aims and working of English universities during my short stay in England for two years. Fortunately for me I am asked to speak on my experiences, and if what I may say tonight does not meet with your approval, I may be kindly excused on the plea that they are my experiences. Our experiences in life are more often bitter than pleasant, and I will be failing in my duty if I do not narrate all my experiences during my short stay in England.

The thought of going to an English university entered my mind immediately after I got my degree at Mysore in 1930. But what with the disability of my sex and of leaving my six children, the youngest of whom was only five years old—often I thought it was a mad idea and an idle dream, but sometime the dream came true. For a period of two years, it was occupying my mind, increasing gradually in its complexity and force until during the summer of 1933, it became an accomplished fact. My eldest son, who graduated from the Madras University in 1933, was determined to proceed to England for higher studies and ICS training. This was a driving force to accomplish my own strong desire, which I had cherished for over two years in my mind. It will be out of place in this lecture if I proceed to narrate the difficulties we had to encounter in the matter of arrangement for our departure. I applied to our government for the award of a scholarship to me, but unfortunately it was not given, and I was told that scholarships for education were not given, as if the education of our country, especially that of women, had come of age, and hence it needed no further attention or encouragement. This refusal was a bombshell, but the desire in me was so deep-rooted that I determined to proceed against all odds. On the tenth [of] September, I left Bangalore for Colombo with my son. The depressed condition of my little ones needs no description. We took a Japanese ship from Colombo that was supposed to be the cheapest of all others. It took twenty-five days to reach England. Both of us are poor sailors, but I proved to be the worst, and for seventeen days I was in bed and lived only on water and fruits. We reached London the eighth of October.... As my financial condition could not permit me to stay in the university halls, I decided to live in the private lodging where boarding and lodging were given at comparatively less cost. A lady was in charge of the halls for ladies who was careful to see that no lady student coming to study in the university from outside stayed in private lodging. . . .[1] [A] room in one of the nearest halls to the University of Leeds ha[d] been reserved for me by Miss Hibgame,[2] but I requested them to recommend me to some lodging. I reached Leeds at 5:30 in the evening. It was very dark and raining, and I stayed for the night in a registered lodging.

Next morning at nine o'clock Mr. Ghose, the secretary of the Indian Association[,] came to take me to the university.[3] We first went to the Education House to see Miss Blackburn, the principal of the women's section. The secretary knocked at the door and went in to inform the authorities about my arrival. To my surprise the principal came herself to welcome me, saying that she was anxiously waiting for me. One never finds servants sitting idly in front of doors as we see here. She herself brought a chair and made me sit down. She questioned me on various topics ranging from the weather, convenient journey on the sea to conditions in India. The conversation then turned to the university, the subjects taught there, and other things relating to my purpose. She also asked me about my school, the subjects I was interested in. I was then introduced to Professor Smith, the head of the Department of Education, who happened to meet us.

It was ten o'clock, and Miss Blackburn had a lecture. She asked me if I would go with her to the lecture theater. On my agreeing to do so, she took a big attaché case containing books, pictures, and papers and asked me to accompany her. Thought old, bordering on sixty years of age, she was more energetic and active than a normal Indian of half her age. We had to get down the steps, and to my surprise before I got down two of them, she was down on the floor waiting for me. We walked to the university and had to pass long corridors. When we were still half the way to the lecture theater, the bell had gone. She seemed excited and extended her arm perhaps to take mine in hers. But as I was not used to this kind of familiarity in Indian universities, I offered my notebook to her thinking that was what she wanted. She just took it, turned it this way and that way, and returned it to me. Evidently, she did not want to embarrass me by saying that she did not want the book. We climbed up to the lecture theater, which was on the third floor, and before I was comfortably seated, Miss Blackburn had already removed her coat, hat, and gloves and was taking the attendance. How ashamed I was of my wonderful impracticability! She called my name, and as I could not understand her pronunciation, I did not answer. I thought she was calling the name of some Mrs. Hoozan, though I came to know afterward that in a class of eighty students there was no "Mrs."! After the lecture was over, she joined me again and took me to a secluded place and asked me to pronounce my name. After I did it, she repeated it twice and told me she would not forget it. The other lecturers too did the same thing.

She then directed one of the students to take me to Miss Hibgame, the secretary of the halls. The latter welcomed me heartily and began to ask me about my lodging, saying that she had already reserved a room for me in the Lyddon Hall. We decided to go to the Lyddon Hall, and it was another trial for me to walk with one whose steps seemed so light that they hardly touched the ground. We went to the warden, a nice old lady who, on seeing me, approached me with a smiling face and hands outstretched to welcome me. I was then taken to my room, which I must call a blue room where everything, including the bed, curtains, carpet, and vase with lovely blue flowers was all blue. There was a lovely fire burning, and a bedstead was spread near it, so that it might be warm. My things were ordered to be brought from the lodging, and I became an inmate of the hall against my previous determination.

The dinner hour came, and as the bell was heard, a beautiful girl came to my room to take me to the common room where all the students and wardens meet and where they choose their partners for their dinner. As soon as I entered the hall, I saw the principal, who came to me and asked me whether I would like to be her partner. It puzzled me, and I only said yes. She at once took my arm in hers and stood majestically talking to me and to the other students of the hall. Meanwhile, I very keenly watched the other people accepting such offers. The acceptance was in the following terms—"I would love to be," or "With great pleasure," "Yes, thank you," and so on. The second gong was heard. Miss Blackburn led me first, and the rest followed us. We went to a table where the warden, with her partners and the executive members of the Hostel Committee, also joined us. After a small prayer by the warden, we sat down to dinner. All the time my partner had an eye on me inquiring about my needs. What a contrast with the kind of airs we are accustomed to see in our professors here. She was trying to find out my aptitude and interests. The more shy a girl was the more was she free with her to make her shake off her shyness. After dinner we went back to the common room in the same grand procession and had a hearty talk, as all the students began to put questions on India and social customs, etc. Then the girls danced, and the warden played on the piano. My partner asked me whether I knew dancing. I have been dwelling upon these details just to impress upon you the kind of relationship that exists between students and professors in England. In all cases the initiative of forwardness originates from the professors. How I wish the same atmosphere prevailed over here.

Every year when the term begins, the vice chancellor's reception in honor of the freshers to the university is a grand function. Shortly after I entered the university, I had the pleasure of an invitation from the vice chancellor to this annual function. The staff are also invited. There were three thousand students and seventy-five members of the staff. The vice chancellor and his wife received every one of us during this function, and one could see professors and students playing indoor games as equals. Some teachers took it as a great pleasure to serve tea and other refreshments to students. The vice chancellor and his wife would be seen on this occasion moving about and talking to every one of the invitees.

Another striking instance was the reception given to students and the staff by the public of the place. I was pleased to find that they had developed a sense of internationalism. They were posted with the most up-to-date information relating to the different countries from which students had come. The public get from the university a list of students with their nationality and country noted against each and invite them to tea and for the weekend. Lest the invitees should find it inconvenient to find out their residence, they send them the maps and plans of their houses, or sometimes they personally take them to their house. This shows the keen interest that the public and the parents take in the cause of education, which is so woefully absent in India. We in India do not treat the members of this noblest but sorriest of professions—I mean the teaching profession—with that respect which its workers so richly deserve.

Comparing University Education in Britain and India

You may be interested to know something about the course of training given to students in an English university. What I am going to say is the practice in the Leeds University, and it is much the same in any other English university. You will see how it radically differs from the training given to students here in India. In India intellectual work is the dominant if not the only factor that is kept in view. Students sit in their classes from 11:00 a.m. to 5:00 p.m. and receive all information that is given to them by the several teachers. We are all familiar with the examination bogey. There are examinations in all countries in the world, but the evil of making much of the results of examination is peculiar to India. This is because an average Indian parent regards the education of his son or daughter as a financial investment capable of fetching a high price in the market. Education therefore is desired not for acquisition of culture but of gain and a good job in service. On account of this worship of results, the poor students are crammed, notes are dictated, and all possible questions are answered, so that anything important from the examination point of view is stuffed into the students, and anything unimportant from *that* viewpoint, even though of high educational value, is rejected. The result is that there is only time for cramming and cramming alone, and absolutely no time for education and culture. You are all familiar with the statement "A sound mind in a sound body." Unfortunately in India, the latter is given little or no attention. It is only nowadays we see students—a small portion of them—playing in fields. It is no matter for surprise that we see in India that the intellectual giants are physical dwarfs. . . .

The aim of the University of Leeds, as of the others in European countries, is not to send out students with swollen heads stuffed with all kinds of information but to develop their powers of mind and body and to fit them for their duties in after life, to give them a practical knowledge of life as fit citizens. They rightly understood that such a knowledge of life and men cannot be had within classrooms but by association with fellow students and participation in the social and athletic fields of activity.

You may ask me how the universities in England achieve this aim. As soon as a student joins the university, he is given the following hints for his conduct in the university.

1. He is told that he is not going to be taught everything. He is asked to have his eyes open and learn things by himself. The university handbook and the notice boards are his only guides.
2. He is taught the value of societies and told that societies do not require sleeping partners. He is asked to take an active interest in the conduct of these societies with determination and enthusiasm.
3. He is taught to take an active part in all athletic activities of the university and also in public activities. The value of exercises and the cooperation involved in them is clearly impressed on his mind.

—⁂—

Such in brief is the training that is given to students in England. You will see how it is opposed to the system of education that prevails in India. In India, students are trained to develop only one side, the intellectual side. The education given to our students is thus defective, narrow, and one-sided. The aim of Indian education is not to fit students to circumstance of the ever-changing environment of the world, nor to enable them to contribute toward the world, nor to enable them to contribute toward the progress and prosperity of their country, so the training pays no attention to achieve the ideal. I don't mean to say that the system prevailing in England is perfect, but there is an honest attempt toward giving the right sort of training to students. Students in England are made to develop not only the intellectual faculty but also the social, physical, moral, and aesthetical senses. The educationalists in India must put their heads together to devise a common system of training for our students with a view to turn out fit citizens after their career and to fuse a link between the school and the university life, and the life after the completion of education. Reduction of too many subjects and specialization in one at the university is indispensable. The present Indian system has made the students beginners in all subjects and master of none.

More freedom to the students to mix with their teachers should be given so that this sense of inferiority could be replaced by power, expression, assertion, and independent thinking among them. In England a student does not feel a sense of inferiority in the company of teachers. They are made to feel that the university is a spacious garden which every student is expected to dress and take care of. The main aim of the university in England is not to teach but to open the vision of the students to the conditions and needs of men, to enable them to think and act independently, and to be guided by their own convictions. The subjects taught are not treated as ends but as tools for a larger purpose. An English university serves as a guide to the life of man and, unlike [in] India, prevents the terrible waste of labor and talent.

FURTHER READING

Iqbalunnisa Hussain. *Changing India: A Moslem Woman Speaks.* Bangalore: Hosali, 1940. Also available as a reprint with an introduction by Asiya Alam (Karachi: Oxford University Press, 2015).

———. *Purdah and Polygamy: Life in an Indian Muslim Household.* Bangalore: Hosali, 1944. Chaps. 2, 4, and 9 are reprinted in Eunice de Souza and Lindsay Pereira, eds. *Women's Voices: Selections from Nineteenth and Early-Twentieth Century Indian Writings in English.* New Delhi: Oxford University Press, 2002.

Shompa Lahiri. *Indians in Britain: Anglo-Indian Encounters, Race and Identity, 1880–1930.* London: Frank Cass, 2000.

A. Martin Wainwright. *'The Better Class' of Indians: Social Rank, Imperial Identity, and South Asians in Britain 1858–1914*. Manchester, UK: Manchester University Press, 2008.
Kristine Alexander. "The Girl Guide Movement and Imperial Internationalism in the 1920s and the 1930s." *Journal of the History of Childhood and Youth* 2, no. 1 (Winter 2009): 39–63.
Leila J. Rupp. *Worlds of Women: The Making of an International Women's Movement*. Princeton, NJ: Princeton University Press, 1997.

NOTES

1. As indicated here, the author was far from the only international student, male or female, at the University of Leeds. Indeed, a number of provincial British universities recorded a small but significant body of primarily male Indian students in this period.

2. The author notes below that Miss Hibgame was "the secretary of the halls."

3. The author refers here to a representative of the National Indian Association who was deputed to assist her and other Indian students upon arrival in Britain.

THIRTY

MUHAMMADI BEGUM

Oxford Diary

INTRODUCTION

The vast majority of what Muhammadi Begum (1911–90) wrote was in the form of personal correspondence that was never published. Nevertheless, she is still widely remembered among her family and friends for the quality of her writing. She was born in Hyderabad—then a large princely state in southern India—to a family that had migrated from Delhi a decade earlier. Though she and her family continued to visit Delhi regularly and maintained both relatives and property there, Muhammadi Begum grew up and pursued her studies in Hyderabad. She began her formal education at the age of nine and rapidly became an avid reader. She was an exceptionally brilliant student, and by her mid-twenties she was comfortable in Urdu, Persian, Arabic, English, and French. In 1932 she completed her BA at Osmania University. At this time, the university, and indeed Hyderabad itself, was enjoying an intellectual renaissance as scholars and activists came from all over India and beyond to fashion a modern but distinctly Muslim institution. They sought to reform Islamic education and develop India's vernacular languages, particularly Urdu, as vehicles of higher learning. Within this spirited milieu, Muhammadi Begum received the highest marks in her exams and was offered a scholarship by the Nizam's government to pursue postgraduate studies at the University of Oxford (see fig. 30.1). In the same year, she was married to Syed Jamil Husain (Jamil in the extracts), who was employed in the administrative service of the state of Hyderabad.

Daniel Majchrowicz prepared the introduction and translation from Urdu. A copy of the diary was provided by Zehra Masrur Ahmad.

Figure 30.1 Muhammadi Begum with her husband and baby son while studying at Oxford in the mid-1930s. Courtesy of Zehra Masrur Ahmad.

In September 1934, the pair traveled together to England to pursue their respective interests. Husain studied development at the Institute of Rural Economy at Oxford, while Muhammadi Begum joined St. Hugh's College to study
French, Arabic, and English. Her experiences abroad are recorded in an Urdu-
language diary that she kept while living as a student in Britain and traveling in
Europe. Like much of what she wrote, this rare source has been preserved by her
daughter, Zehra Ahmad, and it is from the original that the extracts in this chapter are translated. During Muhammadi Begum's time at Oxford, she made many
friends and kept a wide social circle, although she often struggled to reconcile
herself to the more cloistered style of living in England. She met with many of
England's most prominent literary figures: an autograph book she kept contains
signatures from H. G. Wells, Bernard Shaw, and Julian Huxley, alongside that
of Muhammad Ali Jinnah. Despite the difficulties of pursuing higher education
full-time in an unfamiliar environment, Muhammadi Begum gave birth to two
children while in Britain. Her first son, Anwer, is introduced in the following
passages. She also had her first daughter, Zehra, during this period.

The family, now doubled in size, returned to Hyderabad in January 1937, where
Muhammadi Begum would eventually give birth to seven more children. Husain began his work for the state government serving as deputy commissioner
for two districts, Gulbarga and Karimnagar, and also subedar for two more,
Warangal and Medak. He remained in the state until 1948, in which year Indian

troops invaded, forcibly terminated the independent rule of the nizam, and integrated the state into India. That year, Husain left Hyderabad for Lahore in the newly created Pakistan, where he found new employment as the deputy rehabilitation commissioner for Lahore and Lyallpur tasked with accommodating newly arrived refugees from India. In 1950 he brought Muhammadi Begum and their children from Hyderabad, now in India. After moving to Karachi to work for the provincial governments of Sindh and Balochistan, he went to retrieve his family from Lahore in 1951. That year he developed a heart condition and passed away in 1957.

With her husband unable to work, Muhammadi Begum sought to support her large family in a number of ways. She remained in Karachi from 1951 to 1957 before returning to Lahore to take a position at the Office of Press and Publishing as a censor, particularly for religious publications. She also hosted paying guests in her home, including Iranians who had come to study in Lahore. Previous to this, she worked in the tourism section of the Punjab Secretariat. Despite the challenges that she must have faced during these years, she regularly visited her extended family in Karachi and Hyderabad, India, and continued to look after relatives in need. She passed away in Lahore in 1990, only a few years after her mother, Qaisari Begum (also featured in this collection).

Muhammadi Begum came from a family of distinguished writers, and thus she may have received her passion for literature as an inheritance. Qaisari Begum's memoir, *The Book of Life*, is a masterpiece of autobiographical writing in Urdu (see chapter 13). The two women had a deep bond that was often maintained by means of the mail, and it is thus likely that Muhammadi Begum developed her own voice and epistolary style in dialogue with her mother. Furthermore, her maternal great-grandfather was one of Urdu's first "best-selling" authors, Deputy Nazir Ahmad (1831–1912). He is widely regarded as the father of the Urdu novel, although he thought of himself primarily as an educator and an advocate for women's education. Although Nazir Ahmad and Muhammadi Begum, separated by three generations, differed in their reformist ideals—she actively opposed the institution of purdah, for instance—refractions of his progressivist thought are easily discerned in Muhammadi Begum's own writing.

Reflecting her deep interest in language and literature, Muhammadi Begum's collected works reveal a talented and erudite author with a frank voice and insightful perspective. Her succinct prose is peppered with verses and aphorisms drawn from several languages. This easy erudition is on full display in the excerpts from her private travel diary included here. In the first ones, we encounter her in London, which she is visiting from Oxford for the winter holidays. In the last she describes the experience of hosting American friends for dinner and teaching them basic Islamic principles. Muhammadi Begum was only twenty-four years old when she moved to Britain to pursue higher education. And yet her youth belies the maturity and confidence shown in her writing, even in these private musings. Her daily entries are disarmingly candid and often introspective.

EXTRACTS

Writing Letters Home

January 3, 1935: Since I went to sleep at two last night, when Annie came to give me tea, I managed to wake up, but I was very tired and feeling a little weak. I went back to sleep and didn't come to again until noon. I quickly performed my morning routine, got ready, and ate some fruit. The bell for lunch rang around 4:30. I went downstairs to eat. Today is the day for sea mail, and there were so many letters I was supposed to write. I am so afflicted with the disease of detail that few of my letters are ever brief. I wrote long, thorough letters to [my mother] Amma jaan and to [my brother] Muhammad miyan. Muhammad miyan specifically asked that I write detailed letters. I also wrote to [my cousin-in-law] Tasneem and Miss Pope.[1] Three days of every week are taken up with writing letters.

The sea mail leaves for Hindustan on Thursday. Airmail is on Friday and Saturday. The wait for letters begins on Saturday evening. In other words, the entire week is spent either in writing letters or waiting for them. Most people find it a taxing exercise to read and write so many. I should really write fewer letters, or at least be more concise. But I just can't write a short letter. Amma jaan and most of the others are excited to read them. Plus, if they collect all these letters together, then I will have a complete set of my impressions. Otherwise, who can write so many minute details day after day? And finally, I do not want my friends and family to remain unaware of our experiences or the life that we are living here. I want to keep them informed about what we are doing.

I often end up writing a long letter just answering all of the questions that are sent to me about this place. At any rate, I cannot write them as quickly as I ought to. I scribble them out and don't even have time to read them over. The moment I have finished, Jamil[2] must take them and sprint over to the post office. Otherwise, the mail would go out, and my letters would be left behind. On more than one occasion, he has had to run so fast that he became dizzy. He's even gotten sick. Of course, another reason that I write lengthy letters is so that I get lengthy replies in return that keep me informed about what's happening at home, in my extended family in Hyderabad, and in Hindustan. All things that we are constantly thirsting for here. If I don't write a long letter, then others won't either.

At four in the afternoon, Jamil broke his fast with a date. Then we had tea downstairs. Parathas were cooked at madam's request. After eating, we walked over to Swiss Cottage. There is a shop here that sells sweaters, cardigans, and jumpers made by the blind. Khala said that they were cheap and well made. And they really are great. There are also beautiful and elegant baskets of willow or recycled paper woven by the blind. There were also vases, chairs, and more.

After having a look around, we took a bus to Baker Street. From there, we went [window shopping] until we reached Oxford Street. I walked a lot today, so much that I was exhausted, even a little ill. . . . Everywhere we went, the stores were advertising New Year's discounts. Everything was on sale. We have already got just about all we needed, and that too from Harrod's, which is considered a very expensive store.

When I got home I had Ovaltine and regained my bearings. I prayed the morning and midday namaz together, and, later, the afternoon, sundown and evening namaz together. Then I read a *vazifa* prayer. Jamil will fast tomorrow. By God's grace, we are both now saying our prayers regularly. I am going to sleep late again tonight. It must be one in the morning by now.

Eid in England

January 6, 1935: Jamil wasn't able to sleep last night, perhaps because of the excitement of Eid and because he was thinking about all the preparations that needed to be taken care of in the morning. I woke up at six but decided to stay in bed until Annie brought tea on account of the cold and the fact that there was still a while before prayer time. But as it turns out, the clock had stopped working. I thought it was only seven, but it was in fact already eight.

Jamil was completely ready by the time I got up. He didn't have an *ara pajama* or a Turkish hat (fez), so he wore a black shervani over white pants. In place of a fez, he kept with him a *kasani* cap with two folds, a Gandhi cap, for namaz. I washed up in the room at Jamil's insistence, and with his help I put on an ochre *kadmani* sari with a solid white *sadri* blouse. I read my prayers and was ready to go. We both also applied just a tiny amount of the rosewater perfume that we had brought from Hindustan specifically for Eid, since this is a Hindustani tradition. We had some of last night's reheated *sheer khurma* and then went to [our friend] Rasheed sahib's. He was already ready when we arrived, since we had called him in the morning and let him know when we would be arriving. The three of us took the Tube from Baker Street to Waterloo.

The station at Waterloo is large and grand. It feels airy and vast. We could see Hindustanis standing there on the platform under the open sky. Puri sahib and Sheikh Jalal were there too. We learned from Puri sahib that prayers would be held in the West End too, and that many people were going there because it was closer. My heart sunk seeing that small group of Hindustanis standing there. London is such a large city. There are so many Muslims. So many students. And yet only this tiny handful of people has come for Eid prayers! Hindustani students come all the way from Liverpool, Birmingham, Sheffield, Leeds, Cambridge, etc. just to get measured for a suit, to buy clothes, to see a movie, to drink tea at someone's house, to eat some food, to meet with someone—even to wash their hands after a meal, if they think they need to. And then they can't manage to come to the house of God even once or twice a year to celebrate Eid. If London is all foreignness and exile, then Woking [Mosque] should be the homeland.

The train arrived a short while later. The three of us started rushing from one end of the train to the other along with everyone else, inspecting the carriages to see which would be the most comfortable and least crowded. While we were doing this, I realized that the carriages were full of dark-complexioned people. I immediately realized my mistake. I had completely forgotten that Hindustanis could take the train from any station in London, not just Waterloo, and that they could come from anywhere in England, not just London. When I saw those few people at Waterloo station, I thought they were the only ones going on this line. Masha Allah! My heart swelled with happiness and pride. I was deeply touched to see so many Muslims in a town such as this, and realizing that every one of them has the same objective, that they all recite the kalima—*There is no God but God*—and are all believers in this simple and straightforward religion.

We found space in one of the carriages. There were two Egyptians already sitting there. They were speaking to one another in Arabic. I tried to follow their conversation, but they were sitting too far away and were speaking so fast that I couldn't get a single word of it. Still, it gave me a sort of happiness to hear the Arabic language after so long. I was even happier to think that although we come from places thousands of miles apart and are completely different from one another in terms of traditions and other aspects, the very fact that we were coreligionists joined in the same purpose made these men seem a little less like strangers to me. In fact, I watched them with interest. After a while, they began to make the call for the *takbir* [Allahu Akbar, "God is great"] and to read prayers and Quranic verses out loud. Their prayers inspired me, and I too began to recite the kalima and who knows what under my breath. I looked over at Jamil and saw that he was reciting something quietly too. I am very happy with Jamil's devotion to religion. He has a true fervor for Islam. I thank God for this.

Along with us five Muslims, there was another passenger in the carriage, an Englishman. He was busy reading his newspaper. Every once in a while, he would raise his eyes to have a look at the Egyptians. The Egyptians were speaking freely to one another in loud voices. This was the first time I had heard someone speaking in a loud voice in the train, which is usually quiet. Even the newspaper vendors and cleaners do their work as quietly as possible.

A Discussion on Indian Students in England

January 8, 1935: The new year has begun, but I have made no improvements to myself, except that by the grace of God, I have started saying my prayers—even if they tend to be late.

By the time I got up, it was noon. Annie brought me 'Uruj Ahmad Khan sahib's card. Our room was all topsy-turvy, so I had them seated in the drawing room downstairs, which was, despite the gas, quite cold. He and I discussed various things, but eventually the conversation turned once more toward a comparison of Hindustani and English culture and society. Nearly every Hindustani student who comes to study in England feels these cultural and societal differences. And everyone has a different perspective. Many of them are swallow-like humans who are in absolute awe of English culture. They praise every little thing the English do, professing their total devotion and disowning their own. To them, England is like a paradise on earth, etc. etc. They see nothing that is good in their own culture. Decrying their own culture and society, they are thus base in their own eyes. And as such, they make themselves ignoble in the eyes of the locals. The people here value self-respect, and they surely think that these Hindustanis who imitate them are like the crow that fancies itself a swan.

Some of these Hindustani gentleman are believers in the verse "Oh ascetics! Eat, be debauched, and be happy but" don't think about the sorrows of yesterday or the concerns of tomorrow.[3] They think that they should enjoy this place as much as they possibly can. And beyond that, they don't have to worry or think about a thing. True, there are a precious few who look closely and think deeply about their own culture and society and the culture and society of this place. They don't want to go home and flip all the tables over. Rather they act here according to the principle "Adopt that which is good, and reject that which is not."[4] And they want to use the same principles to effect reform back home. 'Uruj sahib and we discussed why we need reforms, and precisely what type of reform is necessary. The flood of Western culture will come to Hindustan accompanied by all of its good values and ills. If all of the evils of this place reach Hindustan (for example, the extreme freedom which is lamented even by people here), what effect will it have there? Will this effect be lasting or temporary? How can this flood of evils be halted?

'Uruj sahib and we tried to untangle the complicated knot of these issues for quite some time. There is no doubt that bringing about reform is hard work. May God give us the courage to go [to Hindustan] and work to fulfill our purpose. The good qualities of this society, such as punctuality, conscientiousness, hard work and dynamism, diligence, etc. cannot be learned in just a handful of days. For this it would be necessary that, instead of just a couple of individuals, an entire group come every year so that they may all learn at the same time before returning home. See and learn from all the same sources. Study and reflect, share and improve their ideas with one another. And only then return and, together, completely overhaul the machine. This is what they have attempted to do in Afghanistan, and in Japan as well.[5] Otherwise, one [student] will come and go, and then another, and so on, and there will be no chance for real change.... after he goes back 'Uruj sahib plans to bring about the societal reform of women by working through his sisters.

A Mixed Marriage

March 7, 1935: We still hadn't finished breakfast when Shamim sahib came bringing Fazl al-Rahman sahib with him. Fazl al-Rahman sahib of Delhi is the son of Sir 'Abd al-Rahman Ra'is, vice chancellor of Delhi University. They have a deep connection to the "khari baoli family."[6] He came here four years ago after finishing his BS Hons in Delhi. Then he did a BA Hons in law here. Now he's doing a bachelor's in civil law. The course isn't an easy one, but he says that he will try to finish in the next year. He's also studying to become a barrister at the same time.

Last June, he married a student from St. Hughes who belonged to a respected family from Derby.... Everyone is talking about their civil marriage here. They got married last June. And everyone is talking about it because, first, their marriage has taken a toll on her studies. She only had four terms left. Second, when they had a civil marriage, they also performed a *nikah*.... Fazl al-Rahman said that he wasn't interested in marrying a Hindustani girl because their mixed English and Hindustani manners and ways have made them "half a partridge, half a quail."[7] Neither English nor Hindustani. "It would be better for her to be completely Hindustani. I don't see anything wrong with being completely Eastern. Otherwise, she should adopt English ways completely." This statement really touched a nerve. I do not like it at all. He also said that they don't have any opportunities to meet or interact with women in Hindustan. "We have no way of knowing how or what they think. Their knowledge is so limited that we cannot have debates with them. We can't exchange opinions with them. And so they can't possibly be companions in the proper sense." Shamim sahib agreed with him. My opinion is that the demands and complaints the Hindustani boys make are not misguided. They are kept away from Hindustani women in so many ways. Sometimes through their niqab, sometimes through the domestic and outside environment.

Entertaining American Friends

July 30, 1935: Today we hosted Mr. and Mrs. Brodhead for dinner. Everything needed to be arranged—I couldn't entrust the arrangements to Mrs. Reza. There was also quite a bit to do beside this. I had to prepare my tutorial lessons for M. F. and Ms. S. and then go to both places for the tutorials. Then I gave the baby a bath and started cooking for Suzanne and Charles's dinner.[8] I had to cook everything in a rush but, thank God, it all turned out well. . . . I made vegetables and rice (*tarkari pulao),* shami kebab, and almond kheer. The almond kheer was no good. Just almonds, milk, and sugar. But Suzanne and Charles ate the food with obvious relish.

Suzanne very much wanted to try on Indian clothes. She has been asking me when I would dress her up in one of my saris, and I promised to do it today. So I dressed her up in my *karchobi* sari and kurta.[9] My bangles didn't fit her. Instead I had her wear the loose brass bangles that Mrs. Aishi had sent me. I also gave her Jamil's shoes to wear. Charles put on Jamil's gold-embroidered wedding shervani. It was dark by then, but we took pictures anyway. Hopefully they will come out well.

Suzanne wore my clothes until it was time to leave. She was very happy and said that once she went back to America, she would host a party for her friends. "I'll put on a sari and make pulao and feed it to everyone!" She asked the measurements for a sari. Everyone here is crazy about Hindustani clothes. Ever since the Jubilee in London this has become the latest fashion trend. . . . I gave her a small piece of cloth that could be [tied to an evening gown and] brought over the head like an *anchal,* like with a sari. Mrs. Aishi was crazy about this kind of outfit, too. . . . Jamil says that if you go to Lady Margaret Hall,[10] then you should dress all of your girlfriends in these clothes, and get them to fold them up again too, since folding them is such a pain. I said, Forgive me, sir, but my clothes are not meant to be worn by everyone until they're in tatters. And my saris get spoiled when they wear them. Even though I hardly wear them myself.

Suzanne and Charles are both very good people. We showed them a translation from the Quran and read to them a passage from Surat Fatiha and told them that this is recited in every prayer. Charles wrote down several passage from the Quran, especially those related to "guidance." For example, *ahdina al-sirat al-mustaqim.* "Guide us properly."[11]

Charles told Jamil that they should travel to Denmark. But Jamil wouldn't agree to go. May Allah keep him on the straight path. Both of us have strayed.

Our hearts have become rusted. There are just so many worries and misfortunes. May God on high have mercy.

FURTHER READING

Muhammadi Begum. "Personal Diary for the Year 1935." Original copy in the private collection of Zehra Masroor Ahmad. Further translated excerpts from this text are available online at https://accessingmuslimlives.org/uncategorized/personal-diary-1935/. For a full translation by the author's daughter, see Kulsoom Husein, ed. *A Long Way from Hyderabad: Diary of a Young Muslim Woman in 1930s Britain.* Translated by Zehra Ahmad and Zainab Masud. Delhi: Primus Books, 2022.

Muhammadi Begum. "Haidarabad se Inglistan." *'Ismat* 55, no. 2 (August 1935): 160–62.

Muhammadi Begum. "Oxford se khat." *'Ismat* 55, no. 3 (September 1935): 256–59.

Kavita Saraswathi Datla. *The Language of Secular Islam: Urdu Nationalism and Colonial India.* Honolulu: University of Hawai'i Press, 2013.

Shompa Lahiri. *Indians in Britain: Anglo-Indian Encounters, Race and Identity, 1880–1930.* London: Frank Cass, 2000.

NOTES

1. Miss Amina Pope, a Canadian convert to Islam, was the principal of Osmania University College for Women in Hyderabad. She had encouraged the author to pursue further studies at Oxford.

2. In this period, it was atypical for wives to record their husband's names. Writing in a private journal, however, Muhammadi Begum seems not to have felt a need to adhere to this practice.

3. The beginning of a verse by the Persian-language poet Hafiz.

4. An old Arabic proverb: *khudh ma sala, wada' ma kadura.* Notably, this same proverb was employed by another traveler in this collection, Nawab Sultan Jahan Begum, to justify her own approach to European customs.

5. Muhammadi Begum here likely refers to the modernization project on a Western model pursued in the 1920s by Amir Amanullah Khan in Afghanistan and the Meiji reforms in Japan, both of which attracted significant interest in India.

6. Author and educationalist Nazir Ahmad and his family lived at Khari Baoli in Delhi. Nazir Ahmad was instrumental in the education of Sir 'Abd al-Rahman.

7. An Urdu saying that suggests that they have lost their own identities by copying that of another.

8. Muhammadi Begum gave birth to this child several months prior.

9. *Karchobi* is elaborate embroidery of silver thread on silk, sometimes so dense the silk is no longer visible. The sari mentioned here was that worn by Muhammadi Begum at her wedding.

10. A constituent college of the University of Oxford for women.

11. Quran 1:6. The English translation is given in the diary.

THIRTY-ONE

—ɷ—

HERAWATI DIAH

A Journalist in the Making

INTRODUCTION

In 1941, Herawati Latip (later Diah) (1917–2016) became the first Indonesian woman to graduate from an American university when she received a BA in sociology from Barnard College at Columbia University in New York. On returning to Java in 1942, Herawati began a career in journalism with United Press International, witnessing firsthand the late Dutch colonial period, the Japanese occupation, and the establishment of the Indonesian nation in 1945. Together with her husband, B. M. Diah, she founded the daily newspaper *Harian Merdeka* (The Daily Independent), in 1945 and then, in 1955, the first English language newspaper in Indonesia, *The Indonesian Observer*. Hence, she was among the first generation of modern Indonesian women to travel extensively outside of the archipelago, and one of the first female journalists in the newly independent nation of Indonesia.

With a career in journalism that spans the length of contemporary Indonesian history, her extant works of English and Indonesian language news, essays, editorials, and memoirs of her life traveling as an international journalist are extensive. The travel writings selected here are among her earliest published writings, letters first written to her mother while living in the United States in the late 1930s. Published under her maiden name, Herawati Latip, "The American Letters" (*Amerikaansche Brieven*) first appeared in the Malay and Dutch language women's magazine, *Doenia Kita* (Our World), founded by her mother, Siti Almiah. Published serially from 1941 to 1942, these letters offer a firsthand account of a young woman traveling and studying abroad in the United States, and a window into the shifting political and social landscape of her time.

Megan Hewitt worked with Siobhan Lambert-Hurley to prepare the introduction and extracts.

Figure 31.1 Herawati Latip (later Diah) (*second from right*) with her fellow
delegates at the second World Youth Congress at Vassar College in 1938.
Courtesy of Megan Hewitt.

Herawati was born in Tanjung Pandan, Belitung, near Sumatra, and raised in
the Dutch colonial city of Batavia (now Jakarta), the capital of the Dutch East
Indies in present-day Indonesia. She was born into a highly educated and well-
traveled family of the time; her grandfather had traveled to the Netherlands in
1863 to live for two years before returning to Java. Herawati's own educational experiences represent a new kind of internationalism for women of her generation
in Java. She attended European elementary schools (*Europeeche Lagere School*) in
Jakarta and studied for two years at an American high school in Japan. As Diah
describes early in her memoir, her mother encouraged all of her children to travel
and study abroad from an early age: "It was [my mother] who insisted we follow
a Western lifestyle. The pressure of colonialism had made her determined to see
her children advance so that they were on the same level as the colonizers. For
her, we would only be able to advance if we embraced Western culture. So we
were like the Dutch, the only difference being the color of our skin."

Herawati thus attended college in the United States from 1937 to 1941, studying in New York first at Elmira College followed by Barnard College (see fig.
31.1). The choice to study in the United States was "revolutionary" at the time,
reflecting her mother's determination that she "study in a country that does not

have colonies." It was while abroad that Herawati became more seriously interested in journalism, driving from New York to California by car to attend a
summer school at Stanford University.

Herawati composed "The American Letters" originally in English even
though the magazine in which her mother published them—notably, without
her daughter's express permission—was predominantly in the Dutch and Malay
languages. Here, they were presented as an opportunity for readers to practice
their English skills while learning about America. Many include the following introduction in Dutch: "We think we should do well by incorporating the
words of Miss Herawati uninterruptedly in order to allow readers to read English
letters written by an Indonesian young lady who visits an American school."
Magazines such as *Doenia Kita* circulated among a growing readership of local
educated women in the Dutch colony. The establishment of an educated middle-
class in Java, as in many other late colonial contexts, facilitated the growth of
nationalist sentiment in the early twentieth century.

The significance of education for social and political mobility was also a feature of
the women's movement at the time. This trend can be seen in what are regarded as
the earliest feminist writings in Indonesia, the works of R. A. Kartini (1879–1904).
She stands as one of Herawati's primary influences for writing "The American Letters." Kartini had been born into the Javanese aristocracy, and, rare for women at
the time, she was educated in Dutch, Javanese, and Malay language schools. She
wrote letters to a Dutch woman living in the Netherlands reflecting on the condition of native women in colonial Java. She critiqued the social and cultural limits
placed on women in Javanese society and appealed to the Dutch to implement
educational reforms and widening access for the underclasses in Java. Published
posthumously in Dutch as *Door Duisternis tot Licht* (From Out of Dark Comes
Light, 1911), and in English as *Letters of a Javanese Princess* (1921), Kartini's works
circulated widely during Diah's time. Diah's aunt, Siti Khadija (later known as Siti
Abdurachman), even founded one of the first Kartini schools in Jakarta in 1907.

In writing these letters to her mother in the late thirties, Herawati was also
conscious of joining a growing movement of women writing and publishing
their personal experiences more publicly. In her memoir, she recorded how her
favorite reading in the United States was a "daily column" called "My Day"
written by First Lady Eleanor Roosevelt—who notably had also written the
preface for the American edition of Kartini's letters. Herawati's letters thus offer
contemporary readers a look at the intersections of global women's and student
movements of the early twentieth century. The young Herawati reflects on the
growing sense of internationalism she experienced among students studying

abroad in the United States, and she infuses her narrative with an excitement and enthusiasm—but also the occasional note of caution—in response to American education, culture, and society.

EXTRACTS

Across the Pacific

Heian Maru. August 19, 1937: Here she is, the American adventurer. I boarded the ship today with the needed money in traveler's checks and a heart heavy of loneliness but brave for the future.

It is certainly quite an undertaking to travel alone if you take into account the hundred and one responsibilities resting upon your shoulders. You know what I missed today while departing from Japan and friends? The traditional "slamets"[1] and "take good care of yourself." It just happened that the people who saw me off were not of the "slamet" kind.

It was really terribly lonesome when I had left the Japanese coast behind me. Not a single soul on the boat whom I knew, until I met a girl who already graduated from the American school last year. And now I finally feel that I am going to America, the much promising country!

The boat is full of ladies, a few men compared to the amazing number of the female sex. You see, there has been a world conference in Japan this summer, and the ladies are in an overwhelming majority. My cabin mate is also a member of that group—a typical American lady, kindhearted in a business way. We don't care much about each other's doings.

My cabin is not very nice, very hot and narrow. But they say that in a few days the trip will become quite cool.

Elmira College, New York

October 2, 1937: We are in the swings of college life, and I admit that I like college a lot.

The atmosphere of Elmira is so friendly, everywhere you find a welcoming face, and although you don't know the girls, you just say hello and you feel yourself just one among them. Gradually we choose friends, and among them one hundred freshmen groups are being formed. It is not easy to make good friends, but I can tell you more or less by the outward appearances whom I like and whom I don't. But if you treat people nicely, they usually react the same. The college spirit is excellent, and we have a marvelous time.

Now about American girls in general. I am absolutely surprised about the freedom and independency [*sic*] they possess. The majority of the girls drive their own motorcars; even the oldest women professors are not afraid to drive with a 90 Km speed. One of my classmates came all the way from California with her mother in her motor car without a chauffeur. I was perplexed when she told me that, but it seems to be very common to them.

I also noticed that American girls get mature at an early stage. And this of course is the result of the movies. All children can go to the movies whether mind-spoiling or not: there are special prices for children.

It is also amazing to hear about the hundreds of cases of illegitimate children here. I am glad, therefore, that the college girls are chosen from the best families. Before entering college, they ask from you a whole list of questions to be answered, and they are strict upon the point of medical and physical examinations.

Judged by the conversations, the college girls are mostly conscious of this evil, and a great majority are studying sociology. They think it is a national disgrace on the country, but what can you do in a country of such an immense population? But let's not pay much attention to the disgrace of a country in which I have to reside for a period of four years. I have decided to grasp all the good virtues of America and to take them with me. But I cannot close my eyes [to] the less valuable characteristics of this country.

Summer in Niagara Falls

June 13, 1938: My summer is going to be an interesting one, I think. Here I sit on my college friend's bed. Five hours ago we were still in Elmira, but now the place of action has changed to Niagara Falls. I am so fortunate as to have a friend who lives in Niagara Falls, and who was so kind as to invite me to spend the three first weeks of the summer with her. After that I must go to New York City, where I planned to attend the summer session at Columbia University....

The days I spent in Niagara Falls went by like the wind. For me it was a pleasant experience to see the everyday life of an American family. This family happens to be a very kindhearted and hospitable one. They furthermore treat me as if I were one of them. The life that this family is leading doesn't come anywhere near the glamorized American movie phantasies. I would not be surprised, however, if there ever really existed families in this country who live in "Hollywood style," but my experience so far has convinced me that not everything the movies show has to be accepted as a general conception of the whole nation. Let me tell you more about this family. It happens to be a doctor's family. They live in a nice house that has all the conveniences every housewife ever dreams of. At first

I was surprised to hear that there were no servants in the house, and that only once a week a man came to clean the garden. But now I understand why they can get along without a maid just as well. In the first place, the servant problem is a difficult one in America; in the second place, all the household facilities make the existence of a maid not absolutely necessary. An American kitchen does not seem complete if it does not possess a Frigidaire and an electric oven. A busy or a lazy housewife sometimes has an electric dishwasher, so that she does not need to dirty her hands. These electric facilities are of course much more reasonably priced here, where they are manufactured.

Acceptance at Barnard College

July, 1938: I am in a hurry to tell you the wonderful news that I have been accepted at Barnard College, the women's department of Columbia University. I am so glad, gladder than when I was accepted at Elmira College. Just think that in September I am going to attend one of America's biggest outstanding universities. . . . I sang loud in the park today; people thought I was being optimistic because the weather was far from sunny.

Talking about the weather, we had depressing days with showers. They do cool the New York temperature somehow, but I love the sun. My room does not look out on the Hudson River. Those rooms along the Hudson are for plutocrats (people with a lot of money; $7.50 a week). No, I decided to sacrifice a good room—however, I should not use the word sacrifice for a student should never live in luxury—and for most of the time I am not in my room anyway. It is rather hard to study in the room because the ever-running subway makes an unearthly noise day in, day out, night in, night out. That is New York City for you! But I quiet myself by saying that soon I shall get used to the noises of the city. I do most of the studying in the afternoon in the library where it is nice and quiet. My classes are over in the morning at 11:30 so that I have a whole afternoon all to myself. Often I lunch [by] myself. There are very nice eating places around the university; most of them are air-cooled. My lunch consists of a glass of chocolate milk and a good-sized sandwich. You don't like eating much in the summertime. I can eat breakfast for fifteen cents. . . . It really is lots of fun to be so independent of routine meal hours and of a special eating place.

I was invited to New Rochelle, a suburb of New York City on the seashore, for the weekend by the family Doom. . . . They really are wonderful people, very hospitable and good-hearted. They met me at the station in their nice sedan car and drove me around the city. It made me feel so good to see the sea again. Then I had dinner at their home. The cooking was à la southern style, which reminds me very much of our Javanese cooking. Lots of sauce and delicious chicken. You really appreciate a home meal after restaurant food so much. After dinner the family drove me all the way back to the International House, which I thought was awfully nice of them. Mrs. Doom did not say goodbye without extending the wish that I should feel free to visit them anytime I want to, whenever I get tired of city life. Wasn't that a sweet thing to do?

This morning we had our first psychology examination. There was so much to study for it, because in two weeks we covered one-third of the whole summer material. I could not tell you how I made out, but I hope that I will get a good mark on it. The introduction to psychology is rather hard, the first part is over however. There is lots of reading to do for my school work. And once you start reading about an interesting topic, it is hard to stop.

Meanwhile the time for the World Youth Peace Congress is not far off. One more month, and then I shall be busy attending discussion groups at Vassar College. I am really anxious to go, especially now I hear from other delegates what it is going to be like. The delegates from Europe are going to stay in the International House for nothing. They will [only] have about three days before the congress really starts. I expect to go to the harbor with other delegates in order to welcome them.

A Letter from New York

June, 1939: While my liberal education is progressing quite satisfactorily, a curious notion has grown up in my mind. I have grown like a stranger toward Indonesian women. What do they think nowadays? How progressive are the women? I wish I knew. There are things like Oriental Workers' Mass Meetings, which I am invited to as the only woman. Five hundred men and I, the only woman. I would rather refuse, but no, I must be brave. One experience makes life richer yet.

In a profession that of doctor or lawyer, for women I do not believe anymore.

Unless a woman thinks it her Vocation (with a capital letter) to be a doctor, dentist, lawyer—then I would not object. But a woman can be educated without becoming a doctor etc. Such professions are men professions; a woman is too soft of nature to indulge in a thing like that. There are other fields that need the mind of a woman much more. I am thinking of humanistic sciences or arts such as literature, music (history of it included), or nursing, or social service (service of mankind literally). In these fields women could be—in my opinion—much happier, and besides the job in the home, where she actually belongs, she could at the same time be engaged in this sort of things. We need intelligent, educated women more than professional women. Let us leave it up to the men to cure sickness and to decide law cases, our task is to help the men and to educate the nation. Of course I do not wish to go back to the Dark Ages, where woman's place was in the home and in the home only. I still think that woman's place is in the home, but her place is much more important now, and is of ever increasing social importance. She should not lead a life of leisure, no, she should be awake and ready to give her services for the nation. I hope that I am able to realize my ideas when time comes, but what do you think about it?

In America, woman has struggled so much in order to be equal to man in all sorts of respects, woman's suffrage, etc. that it has become a problem—"the woman's problem" it is called. And this problem has to do with unemployment for men (caused by woman invasion into the field of men) and unmarried women; furthermore the problem of divorce, "broken homes" are connected with [unreadable] I advocate a nonprofessional field for Indonesian women?

Yes indeed, women can contribute in many other ways toward the advancement of the nation. But first we need schools in order to see our ideas realized. Sometimes I think that we could do much more if we were independent. But independence has to be acquired slowly, and not rashly. Education first and the rest follows gradually. Today I saw a movie picture in which a few Malayan women played; I felt rather homesick. From American friends and friends among other nationalities, I do not have to complain; they are all sweet and good to me.

How Does the Foreign Student Like America?

November, 1939: Once I overheard the best conversation I had heard in weeks. There was an unusual combination of students sitting in a secluded corner of the International House the other day. Five nationalities were represented; one could tell that the girl with the beautiful sari came from India, that the cute "ooh la la" accent belonged to a Parisienne, that the exotic-looking girl came from China, that the fourth one was unmistakably South American, and that the fifth looked either Turkish or Persian. They all had so much to say.

The New York World's Fair started the conversation; Pygmalion was thoroughly criticized, and the newest decision in the Supreme Court even was not forgotten. And then Vivera from South America remarked in apropos fashion:

"It's not the laziness I object, but living like country [*sic*]. Only upon me it has the wrong effect. I have become terribly lazy, you know. Everything is so convenient here. If I want to have hot or cold water, I just need to turn the water on. I never suffer from the cold inside the buildings, radiators all over the place. Plenty of motorcars, and if you own one yourself, you're a mile ahead of the rest of them. You should see us slave at home!"

"It's not the laziness I object, but living like a machine," the girl from France contributed to the conversation. "Maybe it is just New York that is to be blamed for it, but in the mornings—strange as it may sound—when I get up, I pinch myself hard to see whether there is still flesh and blood in me. It is a silly conception, I know, but I do want to remain myself instead of becoming a machine. But perhaps," she pensively continued, "the people in the backwards of America are different from the New Yorkers. It must be pleasant to be in these regions. And after all, New York alone is not America."

The Turkish or Persian girl who had been rather silent all this while slowly said, "I like this country. I feel just like a new being here. I admire the independent spirit with which everybody seems to have been born. The American girls are so energetic and so free. We Mohammedan women may certainly envy them. They are not restricted in their actions as we are. Look at the numbers of women shopping alone in the streets, holding public meetings, and being active in all sorts of human endeavors. It is America that breeds women of this sort. On the other hand, there are also certain things in American, just like in any other country, which are less admirable, and which we foreign students must learn to criticize. But oh, it is such a wonderful experience to be here."

The Kwie Lin felt that she had to contribute something to the conversation too, and in her sweet voice she spoke: "I like America mostly because it has taught me to be free and to think for myself. It has made me realize that I have my own will, free from customs, tradition, and family influence. This is why I like America."

The conversation must have lasted longer, but I had to go on my way. But from these few bits of conversation, one might gather that customarily foreign students like America, that being in this country enables them to evaluate their own customs and culture much better, and that there is much in America that they want to learn.

FURTHER READING

Herawati Latip. "Amerikaansche Brieven." *Doenia Kita* (Jakarta) 1, no. 2 (December 1937)–3, no.1 (November 1939). Additional extracts from this text are available online at https://accessingmuslimlives.org/travel/brieven/.

Herawati Diah. *An Endless Journey: Reflections of an Indonesian Journalist.* Translated by Heather Waugh. Jakarta: Equinox, 2005.

Herawati Diah. *Kembara Tiada Berakhir.* Edited by Debra H. Yatim. Jakarta: Yayasan Keluarga, 1993.

R. A. Kartini. *Letters of a Javanese Princess.* Translated by Hildred Geertz, with preface by Eleanor Roosevelt. New York: University Press of America, 1985.

Cora Vreede-de Stuers. *The Indonesian Woman: Struggles and Achievements.* The Hague: Mouton & Co., 1960.

Kathryn May Robinson. *Gender, Islam, and Democracy in Indonesia.* London: Routledge, 2009.

NOTE

1. "Slamets" or "slametan" are Javanese communal events. As a cultural practice, they can range from very informal gatherings, such as going-away parties or birthday celebrations, to more formal occasions, such as circumcision, marriage, or funerals.

THIRTY-TWO

—ᴍᴍ—

MEHR AL-NISA

An Indian Nurse in Ohio

INTRODUCTION

Mehr al-Nisa (ca. 1936–?) was seventeen years old when, in 1953, she departed from Hyderabad in newly independent India to travel, first to the United Kingdom and then to the United States (see fig. 32.1). Shortly before her departure, she had married her first cousin Aftab Husain, six years her senior, who had gone through medical school at Hyderabad's Osmania University. Together, they would spend nearly two years abroad studying and working in the medical field. About their experiences, Mehr al-Nisa wrote *Hamara safar o sarguzasht: Hindustan se Landan o Amrika, 1953 ta 1955* (*Our Journey and Memoir: From India to London and America, 1953–55*), which was published shortly after her return. Although the book's title could also be translated as *My Journey and Memoir*, Mehr al-Nisa makes clear that she and her husband shared an affectionate relationship and regarded their travels as a joint endeavor.

The young couple's shared paternal grandfather, Abdul Husain, better known by the title Arastu Yar Jung, was a prominent allopathic doctor whose patients included the sixth nizam of Hyderabad, and many of his descendants followed him into medicine. Soon after their wedding, Aftab Husain—whom Mehr al-Nisa calls "Doctor sahib"—was accepted for further training at Mercy Hospital in Canton, Ohio, while Mehr al-Nisa was admitted into nursing schools in London and Edinburgh. Following relatives' advice, she changed her plans and decided to accompany her husband and study nursing at the same hospital. She would go on to become an X-ray nurse, while her husband worked as a urologist;

David Boyk prepared the introduction and translation from Urdu.

363

Figure 32.1 Mehr al-Nisa in her nurse's uniform during her stay in the United States in the mid-1950s, from *Hamara safar o sarguzasht* (1956). Courtesy of Daniel Majchrowicz.

later, he would take a position in Bayonne, New Jersey, while she continued her training in nearby Jersey City. At the same time, Aftab Husain's younger brother Siraj was also a medical resident, first at Aultman Hospital, also in Canton, and later in Reading, Pennsylvania. Throughout *Hamara safar o sarguzasht*, other family members appear constantly—some of the many who were, and still are, scattered throughout the United Kingdom and North America.

Throughout her narrative, Mehr al-Nisa's tone is chatty and genial. Because she and her husband were abroad for an extended period, she had plenty of time to move beyond discussions of travel and tourism to describe more thoroughly her experiences of living and working in the United States. She devoted a few pages at the beginning to their departure from Hyderabad to Bombay and subsequent voyage by ship through the Suez Canal and on to London. Once in London, the couple spent nearly three months traveling around England and Scotland, during which time they visited relatives, did the usual tourist rounds, and joined the crowds watching the coronation of Queen Elizabeth II. They then took a decommissioned troopship to New York, where they saw the sights before taking a Greyhound bus to Canton, Ohio, from which point the extracts here begin. Eventually, the couple shifted to New Jersey, where their daughter Nora Najma was born. Mehr al-Nisa ultimately flew home with her baby, while her husband stayed on in New Jersey for some time.

As she recounts all of these peregrinations, Mehr al-Nisa displays a sprightly interest in the places where she finds herself. In the extracts here, she enthusiastically celebrates the prosperity of 1950s America, delighting in its roller coasters, supermarkets, and vending machines, and in the locals' friendly hospitality. At the same time, she criticizes what she sees as Americans' loose sexual mores. Otherwise, though, she is largely silent about politics, either American or Indian, and although racism exists in the background, she says little about it directly. She and her husband, who often lived separately for practical reasons, developed friendships with American colleagues and neighbors and took special pleasure in meeting and comforting homesick compatriots. At the outset, Mehr al-Nisa dedicates her book to her fellow young Indian women and notes that she has written it in a mix of Urdu and English. Indeed, her writing is generously peppered with English words written in the Roman script. Misspellings have been fixed and a few terms changed here and there; for instance, "suitcase" is given for "attachy" when it was clear that Mehr al-Nisa was not referring to a briefcase. However, a few obsolete racial terms are left as written.

EXTRACTS

Arriving in Canton

On June 26th, 1953, we arrived in Canton and put our luggage in lockers. When we asked our fellow travelers, they said that Mercy Hospital was very close by. When we heard this, Siraj bhai got a taxi, put his luggage in it, and left for his hospital. His Aultman Hospital was relatively far away. Then the two of us walked over to our hospital, said bismillah, and entered. It was built on Market Avenue, which is the main street here—what better location could there be? It was quite a nice building, and including the basement, it was six stories tall. This hospital belonged to the nuns, and they ran it themselves. When we asked to meet the head nurse, Sister Henrietta, we had to wait a little bit, and then we were called into her office. We were greeted very warmly. Doctor sahib was in a suit, so what could she say to him! But when she saw my sari, she started asking, "Do people over there wear this kind of clothing? It's decent, but if you want to work in the hospital, you'll have to wear the usual local clothing of skirts and so forth."

I was willing to change my clothing, and the head nurse explained some things to Doctor sahib about starting work in the hospital and asked a few routine questions, like "When did you arrive? How was the journey?"

An important question was that of our accommodation. Newcomers were given so much consideration that in the nursing home, there was a room set aside for short-term residence, where the student nurses stayed. In the same way, Doctor sahib got a room in the patient clinic.... Visiting Doctor sahib's room wasn't hard for me to do, but I had to return to my room before eleven o'clock because the door to the nurses' home was locked then. The first day, I ended up going to my room and falling asleep. When day broke the following morning, I got ready and went out to meet the nurses. I visited their rooms, and we laughed and chatted together. They liked my long hair, and they praised my sari too. Seeing that they were all ready to go to work, I went downstairs and sat down in the library. Right then, Doctor sahib arrived, and we went outside together. After having breakfast in a hotel, we headed to the stores. Ladies' clothing was on the second floor, and we picked out a couple of skirts. Here, everything is grouped by size, and prices are fixed. I figured out my size, looked at the right set of items, and bought the ones I liked. If you want, you can also try on clothes to see how they look. Little rooms have been set aside for the purpose, where you can put things on and make sure you're satisfied with them. I didn't know my size, so I had to figure it out from square one. Since this was the first time we'd tried this kind of shopping, it took us a while, but at any rate, we bought some other essentials and went back.

The next day, I put on a skirt and got ready and waited for Doctor sahib downstairs. As soon as he appeared, I got up, and we went over together. He was already used to wearing a suit, but I was feeling awkward in my skirt. He already understood the philosophy of "different countries, different customs," and now I started to grasp the saying "When in Rome, do as the Romans do." When I abandoned Indian clothes, the Americans stopped staring at me in surprise. It was as though I'd blended in with them in terms of clothing. The first day that I changed my attire is unforgettable—I'll always remember not just my gray skirt but my white blouse too. So that issue had been taken care of, but there was still the question of where I'd live.... After staying at the nurses' home for four days, I took all my belongings and went straight to the Association. After arriving there, it turned out that this was a residence specifically for colored girls, and only Negro girls lived here.[1] Should I stay? We were seeking a room, and we'd found one, and very cheap too. On top of this, we'd given our word, so I had to stay there. Whenever Doctor sahib came to visit, he'd sit a little while and then leave, because it wasn't permitted for men to stay here. But for the time being,

I was staying in the guest room, so according to the rules, he could come. The administrators were very obliging to us. We could talk as long as we wanted, and they never even said a word.

Fun with the Patients

As I kept working, I developed a sense of how things operated. I had become an old fixture here, but new patients were always arriving, and I was completely new for them. Every patient I encountered would talk with great interest about India and would ask me questions about it. I enjoyed talking to them too. They always tried to remember my name, but none of them managed to get it right. They called me by different names; a few that I remember are Husain, Maggie, Mary, Susie, Susan, and so on and so forth. Each patient would call me by whatever name they liked and whatever was convenient for them. When one patient found out that I had come from India and that I knew Urdu, he was overjoyed. He'd spent a year in India, and he loved Urdu, but since he didn't get the chance to practice speaking, he'd forgotten everything he'd learned. When I paid close attention to his broken Urdu, I was startled by his enthusiasm. Whenever I came by, he would say, *"Namaste, mem sahib ji! Kaise ho?"* ("Hello, ma'am! How are you?") He also remembered a poem, and when he was in a good mood, he'd energetically sing, *"Bhes to badla magar dil ko badalna chahiye"* ("I've changed my appearance, but I should change my heart").[2]

When we chatted, all the patients in the ward would listen to us, and a few of them would ask jokingly if we were slandering them behind their backs—"We have no idea what you're talking about!" Then they'd turn the situation around on us and say, "Friends! We know French and Spanish—let's talk so they can't understand us!" Miss Campbell, who worked on this floor, would say to the other girls, "Go listen! Who's Husain talking to, and what's she talking about?" The other girls would come and say, "Hey, say this! Say that!" When I showed them my Urdu writing, they laughed and said, "Wow, it's shorthand!"

In this way, we had some fun, and the patients benefited by forgetting their illnesses for a little while. If this kind of pleasant diversion weren't good for one's health, then every hospital wouldn't have a nursing home as an integral element. This department offers patients both care and delight, and its founder was truly a great philosopher. What I mean is that when I talked to patients, a beautiful light came into my mind. As I cared for them, each service I performed made every corner of my heart glitter, and as a result of my sincere ministrations, the patients loved me. When they recovered and were discharged from the hospital, they would ask me to write down my address so they could keep in touch. They'd give me presents, and I would always come away from visiting each patient with a piece of candy.

A Day at the Fair

Dr. Anson, Dr. Freites, and the two of us went in Dr. Freites's car to see Meyers Lake. This is an amusement park where there's a fair set up for a whole month. Wherever you go, there are throngs of people strolling around; wherever you look, there are crowds of spectators who have come to gawk at the spectacles and marvel at the wonders on display. We rode a train called the Comet—it would put lightning to shame, and a mirage would be embarrassed before it, it was so incredibly fast. In just three minutes, it went all the way around, climbed to the highest heights, and swooped to the lowest depths. It wasn't afraid to soar, and it didn't shrink from falling—it was as if the peaks and drops were all the same to it. When it plunged from the ferocious heights to the terrifying depths, the riders screamed helplessly. Still today, the memory of its perilous rounds makes my heart tremble. Not just this train but everything there astonished us. The Americans have come up with dozens, scores, hundreds of inventions, and it's impossible to describe them all in detail. Lots of things are automatic; you just put in a nickel or a dime and see all kinds of new spectacles. They have the same kinds of machines for food. We put in some money, and out came whatever we wanted, and it worked the same for different games and rides. Every day, visitors here come face to face with wonders straight out of the *Tilism-i hoshruba*.[3] The most amazing thing is that these magical enchantments aren't uncommon, but abundant. There are fun houses over here and thoroughfares over there, and the whole day passes so quickly you don't even feel the time passing. As we watched, it went from morning to evening, but the enticing sights never ended. After spending the whole day there, we went back, but we still weren't sated after one day's trip, so we returned one or two more times.

A Baby on the Way

Doctor sahib had a farewell gathering with his hospital colleagues on June 28, and then Doctor sahib, Badr bhai, and I all went to the bus station. Doctor sahib departed Canton on a bus, and Badr bhai dropped me at my room. This was the first time that I had ever been apart from my husband. I felt miserable, and my heart was dejected, but what could I do? It was my time to learn how to do my job. So I would start my routine work, I'd finish my domestic tasks, I'd eat, the Association residents would visit me in my room, and that's how my days passed. Up to this point, no one knew I was pregnant. Every morning, I'd have

morning sickness. I told my friends the reason myself. They congratulated me
delightedly and started taking good care of me in every way possible. But when
people at the hospital asked, I fell silent, only because I thought they wouldn't
give me any work to do and my goal of admission in a training program would
remain unfulfilled. Since I still had a long time to work there, though, in the end
I told the people at the hospital why I was feeling nauseous. Now they started
giving me more time to rest and started to be even more affectionate toward
me. Whenever I heard anyone say anything, it was, "Name it after me!" By saying this, they were expressing their intense happiness. Often, the nursing girls
would ask, "Have you bought this? Have you gotten that ready for the baby?
What other preparations will you make? Such a wonderful time is on the way!
I wish I were in your shoes!" In this way, they'd encourage me, and they'd also
throw me little parties.

I was going to leave Canton soon, so everyone got together and decided that
rather than throwing me a party here, it would be even better to have a picnic
party. They collected donations, and on July 15, we went to a park that they'd
previously picked out. Everyone brought their favorite dish, and I brought a few
papadums. The papadums were fried and other things heated up, and we all ate
together. We had a lot of fun talking and laughing, and took some pictures, and
when evening fell, we went back. This was my last week working at the hospital.
As long as I was there, Badr bhai came to visit me at the Association every day.
I'd already told him my plans. When my last day at work came, I had a farewell
gathering with the whole staff and the patients. The girls who worked on my
floor gave me goodbye presents, and I gave them gifts too. After thanking them
all one by one, I returned to the Association.

An Indian Gathering in Philadelphia

Doctor sahib would constantly talk to me and ask how I was doing. One day he
said, "Siraj bhai wrote to invite me to join him in Philadelphia this weekend.
I'll get to see my brother and visit a new city besides. These days, you're not in
a condition to tolerate the discomfort of travel, so I want to go alone." At first, I
agreed to this, but then when his departure date grew close, I realized I wanted
to go with him, because if I didn't go now, then God knows when another chance
would come. I called him and said, "I'm coming with you too."

My life partner didn't try to deter me. When the day came, I had breakfast at
dawn and packed my camera and a few things in a little bag. I was all ready when
Doctor sahib appeared. We left the YWCA, got to the bus on time, and arrived at
Journal Square, where the Philadelphia bus was about to leave. We waved to the

bus driver, bought a ticket, climbed aboard, and chatted cheerfully the whole way. At the station, you can wash up for five cents, and they even give you a towel and soap. Everything is very neat and clean; the bathing arrangements seemed excellent. There's a machine on the washroom door, and if you put in a nickel, the door will open up, and then when you leave, it'll close automatically. It was a huge station, and everything in it was modern. After we'd washed our hands and faces, we tucked into a big lunch because we were famished. We took a moment, freshened up, and then went looking for the International House, because Siraj bhai was supposed to arrive there at four in the afternoon. This was a smallish building, and the manager said there would be an Indian students' meeting at 6:00 p.m. Giving us the program, the woman said, "You're very welcome if you'd like to attend. If other people weren't staying in the guest room, then you could have stayed there. Nevertheless, I'll try to find a room here and let you know what happens."

We told her our plans and asked her to let Siraj bhai know we'd arrived whenever he showed up. Then we went out to roam around, and by chance we met a local professor who volunteered to give us a personal tour of the university. Then, because it was getting close to Siraj bhai's arrival time, we thanked the professor and went back to the International House. Not even a moment had passed before Siraj bhai appeared, smiling. We talked, ate and drank something, and then went out for a tour in his car. We'd left our bag in a locker at the station, so we asked around for the station, ate dinner, and then picked up the bag and headed back to the International House. Here the meeting had begun; there were introductions, then votes were taken for who would become president and so forth. Next, all the members started talking to their friends. On account of all the noise, we didn't like this meeting much. We met a student there whose name was 'Inayat 'Ali Khan sahib and who knew Father. He was a very genuine, friendly man, and we quickly dropped all formality. When he found out we were only planning to spend a day here, and that we'd arranged a room, he announced, "Come on, I'll introduce you to the president of the Indian Students' Committee, and you can stay comfortably with him. He loves to be able to say he's hosting Indian guests." Khan sahib took us and introduced us to the distinguished president. I'll briefly describe his circumstances to the extent of my knowledge.

This Dr. Bhatta is Indian, but he adopted the American way of life forty years ago. We found Dr. Bhatta and his American wife to have very fine characters. Their children now have children, but in accordance with the custom here, their children live apart from them. We were very happy to have met them. They invited us to their home, and we were happy to go with them. They drove in their car, and we went in Siraj bhai's car.

Dr. Bhatta lives in prosperous style, with his office and house separate from each other. He also has a country house, and on the weekend, they go out to the countryside to stay there. He first showed us his office and house, and then he took us to his country house. This was such a nice house that I wished we could live there. It was such an open place, and such a pleasant environment, that if a person couldn't be happy here, then where could they? By the time we got there, dusk had fallen, so dinner was prepared. After finishing our meal, a room was given to the two of us and another one to Siraj bhai and 'Inayat sahib. Everyone was tired, so we all went to sleep. Our room was upstairs, and when morning came, we contentedly went downstairs. When we'd said the customary good mornings and started to get breakfast ready, Mrs. Bhatta said, "Go outside and have a look at our garden." We all went outside and saw a huge garden, teeming with flowers. In one direction, all different kinds of roses were showing off their splendor, with rose beds stretching out into the distance. In the other direction, flowers were laughing together. It was a wondrous scene. Whenever there is a flower show, their flowers win certificates from the judges; we were shown quite a collection of these. When we advanced a bit past the landscaping, then the apple trees drew our attention. It was a delight to see the trees laden with apples, and with a carpet of them laid out below. We had fun eating lots of apples, strolled around a bit more, and then went back inside. Breakfast was ready, and very good too, and we ate our fill. Everyone washed the dishes together and put them all back neatly. We joked around merrily while we worked and then went back out to the garden to take photos. This time, Dr. Bhatta was with us. He told us all about his garden, which truly brought to mind our toddy palm garden. He also plucked a few flowers for us. Since it had gotten very late, we asked his leave to depart, but he kept on talking. Maybe he didn't want us to go yet. It was evident that his heart was brimming with love for India and Indians, because he also loved 'Inayat sahib like his own children and always called him "son." Finally, we profusely thanked this gentleman of many virtues and got into Siraj bhai's car. On our way back from there, we visited all the historical places, including Independence Hall, where there is an enormous bell, as well as a pen and inkstand.

FURTHER READING

Mehr al-Nisa. *Hamara safar o sarguzasht: Hindustan se Landan o Amrika, 1953 ta 1955.* Hyderabad: Arastu Academy, 1956. Additional translations from this work may be found at https://accessingmuslimlives.org/travel/mehr/.

Karen Isaksen Leonard. *Locating Home: India's Hyderabadis Abroad*. New Delhi: Oxford University Press, 2008.

Liping Bu. *Making the World like Us: Education, Cultural Expansion, and the American Century*. Westport, CT: Praeger, 2004.

NOTES

1. The author writes these terms in English. The association in question is the Phillis Wheatley Association.

2. The reference is to a Christian hymn.

3. The author refers to a fantastical epic of magic and adventure.

THIRTY-THREE

ZAIB-UN-NISSA HAMIDULLAH

Sixty Days in America

INTRODUCTION

Zaib-un-nissa Hamidullah (1918–2000) was a pioneer of Pakistani journalism. She was born in Calcutta, which was then in colonial Bengal. Her father, S. Wajid Ali, was a Cambridge-educated barrister and magistrate who also translated prominent Urdu writings into Bengali, edited literary magazines in Bengali and in English, and hosted intellectual gatherings of well-known Bengali writers and thinkers at his home. Her English mother, Eleanor Saxby, had moved to India after marrying Wajid Ali during his student days. The couple separated in 1928 after the birth of two sons and their one daughter, Zaib-un-nissa. Subsequently, Zaib-un-nissa studied at Loreto House, an elite convent school in Calcutta, during which time she took to writing poetry. When one of her poems was published in a student magazine with a picture alongside, she drew the attention of a Punjabi student in Calcutta, Khalifa Muhammad Hamidullah, to whom she was introduced by a mutual friend. They married out of love—rather than arrangement as would have been the norm—in 1940. Soon after, the young couple moved to the very different environs of rural Punjab for Hamidullah to take a job at the headquarters of multinational shoe manufacturers, Bata. Their two daughters, Nilofer and Yasmine, were born in 1943 and 1949, respectively.

Through marriage and motherhood, Begum Hamidullah continued to write poetry in English. Her first collection, *Indian Bouquet*, receiving a warm reception when it was published at her father's initiative in 1943. She thus followed it up

---

Siobhan Lambert-Hurley prepared the introductions, extracts, and annotations.

Figure 33.1 Zaib-un-nissa Hamidullah meeting
President Eisenhower's press secretary, James
C. Haggerty, during a party in her honor at the
Pakistan Embassy in Washington, DC, May 15,
1956. Courtesy of Yasmine Ahmed and Akbar
Shahid Ahmed.

with three more collections, *Lotus Leaves* (1946), *The Flute of Memory* (1964), and
Poems (1970), as well as a book of short stories, *The Young Wife and Other Stories*
(1958). Her journalistic career began in earnest after the formation of Pakistan in
1947, and shortly after, the family moved to Karachi. A weekly column started in
late 1947 for the English-language newspaper, *Dawn*, came to an end in 1951 when
she refused to limit her subject matter to "feminine matters," instead addressing
various political developments in the new state. At a time when Pakistan still had
few professional female journalists, Begum Hamidullah turned to publishing
her own magazine, a glossy pictorial entitled *The Mirror*. It became known for her
outspoken editorials in which she often criticized the government—leading the
publication to be banned several times in the late 1950s and 1960s before closing
down in 1971 when she and her husband moved to Ireland for his career. Among
her targets was Prime Minister Mohammad Ali Bogra for his much-criticized
polygamous second marriage in 1955, seemingly referred to in the opening lines
of the fifth extract in this chapter.

Begum Hamidullah's high profile meant that despite controversy, she was included in many of Pakistan's press delegations abroad in the 1950s. She was also invited to take part in the Foreign Leader Exchange Programme supported by US Department of State (see fig. 33.1). It enabled her and her husband to spend two months touring the United States to, in her own words, "see this mightiest democracy of all at work." No requirements were placed on her itinerary, nor arrangements made for internal travel; instead, she was given a return ticket for first-class air travel, a frugal allowance of twelve dollars a day, and "carte blanche" on her program. Her experiences provided the material for a daily column in *The Times of Karachi* encompassing forty-four short articles. Soon after her return, the full set was pulled together for a book entitled *Sixty Days in America* for publication by her own press in 1956. It is from this source that the following extracts are taken using her original chapter titles.

A unique feature of Begum Hamidullah's tour was her desire to cross the United States by car; she was the first in the Leadership program to do so. She and her husband thus purchased a secondhand vehicle in which they undertook the eight-thousand-mile round trip journey from Washington, DC, to Los Angeles, taking in small towns, bustling cities, and iconic tourist spots as they went. The extracts here point to stops in Cincinnati, Sacramento, Salt Lake City, and Chicago, but the couple also visited Kansas City, Lamar (in Colorado), Santa Fe, the Grand Canyon, Las Vegas, Beverly Hills, San Francisco, the Niagara Falls, and New York City. Nights in roadside motels and drive-in meals provide a backdrop to some rare encounters—not least a press conference with President Eisenhower at the White House, a party attended by film star Henry Fonda in Hollywood, and an appearance on talk show host Art Linkletter's *House Party* (with an audience of nine million viewers). Also in the itinerary were embassy functions, Eid celebrations, private dinners, and public functions at women's clubs—the latter representing the All Pakistan Women's Association or the Business and Professional Women's Club of Karachi, of which Begum Hamidullah was founding president.

The author's tone throughout *Sixty Days in America* is chatty, informal, self-deprecating, and often idealistic. While attentive to grand monuments and glorious scenery, she is most keen to record her interactions with curious and welcoming Americans—as in the third extract here on an informal dinner with a "typical" young American family. An eye for women's quotidian experience is reflected in her attention to the weekly shop, housewifery, white goods, polygamy, and personal grooming in the selected passages. In the full text, these less formal observations are complemented by chapters dedicated to American women's working practices, politics, and organizations. Clearly,

Begum Hamidullah's own colorful saris and unusual shoes ("Pakistani *joo-tees*") drew attention, particularly in small-town America, where she expresses a certain glee at the possibility of being mistaken for a "Red Indian" or a "mad Mexican." While discrimination against African Americans is noted at points, race is more often treated to gentle irony, as in the final extract. Truly defining throughout is her strong and synonymous identification with Islam and the new Pakistan—even as she is not uncritical of her country's cultural practices and government. Hence, "Pakistani begums" could be chided for their indolence at home, while Muslims in Sacramento who migrated from colonial India to the United States nearly half a century before independence are claimed as "Pakistani Americans."

EXTRACTS

In a Supermarket

This is the place where the housewife shops. It is the place from where she purchases all the requirements for the household. Since time is a most precious factor, the average American housewife does not come daily to do her shopping but does it all together once or maybe twice a week. To do it she comes to the supermarket, and if she has a small child, well, junior also comes along with her. At the supermarket, everything is done to make shopping as easy and as pleasant as possible.

Each customer takes a kind of trolly, which she wheels around the various stalls where almost every household item one can think of is displayed. Whatever she requires, she takes and places in her trolly. Thus she will go from stall to stall, taking her time over her selection or hurrying if she has to. Meanwhile, what does she do with junior, you might be wondering? Well, junior's having a wonderful time. He's sitting right up in his mother's trolly in a little place specially provided, and enjoying the ride while pointing out to his mother any little thing that takes his fancy.

Here at the supermarket are purchased the week's provisions. You can buy meat here, you can buy chicken, you can buy fish. If you want only half a chicken, well you just go and take the packet marked "half." Or perhaps you're the kind who only enjoys the legs of a chicken. Don't worry, you're catered for, there in that corner are parcels made up only of chicken's legs. And so it goes on and almost every individual want is satisfied. You can also select the type of meat most suitable for the dish you have in mind. They're specially marked for roasting, stewing, frying, or boiling. But so cleanly are they cut up and so attractively displayed in transparent paper packages that you never once feel that you're in a meat market.

For those too lazy or too busy to prepare a meal for themselves, there are ready-cooked dishes wrapped up in tin foil. All you have to do is to take them home and warm them up, and you have a delicious dinner. If you prefer tinned foods, well then, take tin foods. They're there by the dozens and of every variety. Want butter, want bread, want cheese, want jam, want potatoes, want onions, want carrots, want cauliflower? Just go ahead and take your choice; they're all there. And after you've finished your shopping and your trolly is full, you wheel it to the cash counter, where they check each item, giving you a bill, which you pay, and go out to get your car, leaving the trolly in the shop. From the shop, it is wheeled out by one of the shop assistants and taken to a side door, where you come in your car and have everything put in it.

Sounds a simply, perfectly enjoyable way to do shopping, doesn't it? And it is.

Pakistani Begums in the US

Strange though it may appear, coming to America has made good cooks of our Pakistani begums. What's more, it's made them most energetic. So much so, that the majority of them are doing the jobs of ayahs, bearers, cooks, drivers, and cleaners combined and at the same time managing to look more attractive and self-assured than they did in Pakistan.

Quite an achievement this, you'll agree. And maybe agree with me too when I state, not without a little legitimate pride, that our begums are as good or as bad as any in the world, and if in Pakistan they tend at times to become slothful, self-centered, and intellectually sleepy, it's not so much they themselves who are to blame as our whole way of life.

Here in America, they're doing all that an American housewife does, and doing it as well. I've had an opportunity to see this for myself at the number of dinners and luncheons to which I've been invited. The meals served up at them have been delicious and all cooked by the hostesses themselves. This, in view of the fact that guests numbered from twenty to thirty at a time, is, you'll understand, no mean achievement. Nor is that all. The house has been cleaned, the children washed and clothes, the shopping done and dishes washed, all by the self-same begum, who would, in Pakistan, have just sat back in streamlined comfort and ordered half a dozen servants to do exactly the same things.

It's an education in itself for our begums to come here, and I do wish more and more of my sex had the opportunity to do so. For once having come to America and lived here for a considerable period of time, no Pakistani begum can ever be quite the same. Her whole outlook will have widened and her horizon become much wider than the narrow four walls of the home. What's more important, she will have learned, by watching the average American housewife, that is possible to be a good wife and mother while at the same time being a good citizen. For she will have seen how eager an interest the American woman takes in the affairs of her district and state and how she has her say in almost all matters of local importance.

Quite a few Pakistani girls are working here. They are the daughters of Pakistani officials and come from families where careers for girls would normally have been frowned upon. But in the independent atmosphere of America, these girls have won their independence without even having to fight for it. And such is the climate around them that their parents take great pride in the fact that their girls are working. Let's hope this modern outlook continues and that, on their return, these Pakistani parents will not retire into their shell of convention and frown upon all those who, believing in the dignity of labor, are what is termed as "working women."

With a Family in Cincinnati

In Cincinnati, an appointment for dinner awaited us with a typical young American couple. After a quick look around the city, therefore, and after getting the direction to our host's house explained by telephone, we were on our way. It was a delightful evening that we spent with "Dick and Betsy," as they insisted we call them. The atmosphere was delightfully informal, and within a few minutes, the four of us were chatting away like old friends. Dick is working in an important soap factory here, and Betsy is content (for the time being) in being nothing more or less than a housewife. And at that she has her hands full, for she is the mother of two darling little children, one two years and the other just nine months old. Dick and Betsy McKinney have been married three years and are, like all young couples throughout the world, full of plans for the future.

One of their plans, which Dick hopes will materialize pretty soon, is to have a house of their own instead of living in the rented apartment where they do now. The apartment is a neat, prettily situated one with just enough accommodation for a small family to live in ease and comfort. Dick showed off his home proudly to us while Betsy was busy with giving the kids their dinner. He even took us to the basement and showed me where they have stored their numerous wedding presents in barrels and where they will safely stay until they have the house to display them in.

Among the time-saving devices that Betsy has to help her run her home is a washing machine, and I was given an interesting demonstration of how it worked. "What about the ironing?" I questioned her. "That's still a bit of a nuisance," she admitted, "but many of the new fabrics don't require any ironing at all, and so I buy that kind for the children's clothes and for mine." Their home has also a lovely Frigidaire, well-stocked with the week's provisions, and a freezer where meat, fruit, and vegetables can be stored for months at a time.

Betsy served up a delicious dinner of steak and topped it with a desert of ice cream and strawberries. After dinner, we sat and chatted for quite a while. Dick was very interested in everything Pakistani, and I on my part in everything American, so you can realize that the time passed quickly. In fact, it was much, much too quick. But we had to leave as we wanted to get out of the city before it grew too dark. And so, after a while we said farewell and were on our way again after spending one of the friendliest, most enjoyable evenings in America.

Pakistanis in America

It's rather a sad tale I have to relate today. But sad though it may be, it is nonetheless an inspiring one. It is the story of Pakistanis in America. Pakistanis who came over to this young and growing country decades ago. Muslims who worked here with dogged grit and determination until, out of nothing, they created for themselves flourishing farms, business houses, and most admirable of all a respectable position in society.

Most of them live in the rich agriculture country in and around Sacramento (California). And tonight I'm at Butte City, in the lovely guest house of Mr. Fazal Mohammad Khan and Mr. Named Khan, well-to-do landowners and farmers. Before this, we dined at Mr. Kaloo Khan's and met there many other American Pakistanis and talked with them on almost every topic under the sun.

Most of these men come originally from the fertile land of the former Punjab, and almost all of them were ignorant and uneducated. And today, even though they have been in America for nearly fifty years, most of them still are, and all the English they know are a few broken sentences. Yet it's inspiring to find that in spite of these handicaps, these men earned an honest living for themselves all these years and never forgot to send some money back every month to their relations in Pakistan.

Fifty to sixty years ago, they first set foot in this "new world." They were young then. Young, full of energy, and eager with the spirit of enterprise and adventure that filled the hearts of all the people from many lands who had flocked to this new country. They came by diverse different means, but came they did, and once arrived in America, it was America that they made their home and where they have lived ever since. Two world wars came and went, bringing in their wake much changes. In the First World War, when feeling against Japan and China ran high in America, these Muslims were deprived with them of all their civil rights. This was a terrible tough time for them. Not being allowed to own property in their own right or do any business, they would have starved. But though the law of the land had turned unkind, the people had not. An even today these Pakistani Americans speak in glowing terms of the friendliness of their neighbors and of how they helped them. Helped them even by hoodwinking the law. This they did by allowing the Pakistanis to transfer their property into the names of full American citizens and work it under these names. And, may it be said to the eternal credit of these Americans of old, in not one single instance did they take advantage of the Pakistanis helplessness and defraud them of their property. All they did was to make life easier and, as soon as law permitted it, gave the title to the property back into the hands of their rightful owners. . . .

Of that brave band of youths who came over fifty or sixty years ago, a meager three hundred or so Muslims are left. The others have passed on to the land of shadows, passed without even once setting eyes again on the haunts of their childhood or seeing the beloved, well-remembered faces of fathers, mothers, sisters, brothers, or even wives. Of those that remain, many have now grown too old to travel. Their hands tremble and their eyes are weak, for most of them are over sixty years of age and some are in their seventies. Yet still do they continue to work, still do they do their share and refuse to admit the all too apparent fact that the years have got the better of them. . . .

Have they not married? Have they no children? You might ask, even as I asked them. In those bright days when they were young, color prejudice in America was strong, and no woman wanted a "colored" man. Later on, when they grew rich and prosperous, they grew afraid too. Afraid of the independence and ambitiousness of the American women and did not wish to marry them. As one of them told me a little sadly, "American women want only money. They would never give us love and affection, and what use of marriage without love?" Perhaps they were a little too sweeping in their condemnation. But later I learned that they speak from bitter experience, for many had married, and the wife asked for a divorce soon after and made them pay alimony ever afterward.

Be that as it may, the fact is that these Pakistanis here in America are lonely old men.

Polygamy in the USA: Mormons

Polygamy is a practice that, most unfortunately, Pakistan has come to be connected with in recent years the wide world over. Among the countries that seemed the most scandalized and horrified at the practice of it by prominent modern Pakistanis was America. This is understandable, you'll think, since the USA is such a progressive country that the very thought of polygamy must shock them, let alone its practice. When I tell, therefore, that until only a few years ago, polygamy was practiced in America, I doubt whether you'll believe me. And if I go further and inform you that a man who had not four but twenty-eight wives, is honored as an American prophet, and has even today millions of followers, I'm sure you'll feel inclined to consider me a liar.

But I'm very definitely telling you the truth. What's more, I've just returned from a visit to the church of this prophet. Of course, in all fairness let me tell you that the practice of polygamy is no longer allowed in America. In fact it is illegal. Yet the religion that encouraged it is flourishing, and the followers of it, while obeying the law, still accept plural marriages as an article of their faith. . . .

Since I realize how curious you must be getting, I'll go right ahead and tell you the name of the American prophet of whom I'm speaking. He is Joseph Smith, a man who, at the young age of twenty-four, published a book that, he stated, had been revealed to him on a mountaintop by a person clothed in white who announced himself as Moroni, a resurrected being. . . . Thus, Joseph Smith's book was named the Book of Mormon, and his followers are called the Mormons. They are a cult of Christianity since they believe in all the Christian beliefs and are known as the Church of Jesus Christ of Latter-day Saints. Joseph Smith was killed by a mob in Carthage, Illinois, on June 27, 1844, at the age of thirty-nine. His followers, however, continued to increase and multiply and today number millions and are to be found in almost all parts of the world.

It was in Salt Lake City, Utah, that I learned all this. For this is the center of the Mormon world, and its Temple Square attracts travelers from all over the world.

Chicago

Seems as though we human beings are never satisfied. Here in Chicago, upon the beaches on Lake Shore Drive, Americans sit long, hot hours through sunning themselves. They do this not so much because they love the sun, but because they love a brown skin. Tan, is what they call it. And they love it so much that they'll put up with any inconvenience so that they turn brown.

Toasting themselves, that's what it looks like, though I must confess they do it in a most attractive manner, especially the thousands of pretty girls. Some of them even go to the extent of buttering themselves as well. Strictly speaking, I should say, oiling. This they do so that the tan is more even and, more important, so that they do not dry their skins too much in the process of tanning.

How they love to become brown, and how we brown races would love to become white, or at any rate, fairer than we are now. I'm sure the average Pakistani Begum, who stays indoors as much as possible during the summer months so that the hot sun has not the slightest excuse to turn her even half a shade darker than she actually is, would never be able either to understand or appreciate the anxiety of her American brothers and sisters to turn themselves as dark as they possibly can. Perhaps the reason is, as I said before, that we humans are seldom satisfied with things as they are. And there is another little thing I've noticed that makes this statement still stronger, which this time concerns the hair. Here in America, the ladies love curly hair and visit their hairdresser regularly to have a "perm" and keep their waves trim. Whereas the American Negro, who has been endowed by nature with tight, natural waves, will give anything to have straight hair. In fact they even go to the extent of going to a hairdresser to have their curls straightened out by a process that is the reversal of that used to curl straight hair!

FURTHER READING

Zaib-un-nissa Hamidullah. *Sixty Days in America*. Karachi: Mirror Publications, 1956.
———. *The Young Wife and Other Stories*. Karachi: Oxford University Press, 2008. This is a reprint of her volume of short stories first published in 1958.
Muneeza Shamsie. *Hybrid Tapestries: The Development of Pakistani Literature in English*. Karachi: Oxford University Press, 2017. It includes a chapter on this "pioneering writer."
K. I. Leonard. *Making Ethnic Choices: California's Punjabi Mexican Americans*. Philadelphia, PA: Temple University Press, 1995.
M. Ramnath. *Haj to Utopia: How the Ghadar Movement Charted Global Radicalism and Attempted to Overthrow the British Empire*. Berkeley: University of California Press, 2011.

PART IV

TRAVEL AS OBLIGATION AND PLEASURE

WHILE THE IDEA OF TRAVEL as a pleasurable undertaking has long been a part of the human experience, a new mode of pleasure travel, labeled "tourism," is thought to have emerged in seventeenth-century Europe with the institution of the Grand Tour. An integral part of elite, male education, it saw young noblemen touring the continent with the intention of imbibing culture, history, and art. Having become well established among the wealthiest classes by the eighteenth century, modern tourism was embraced by those from other social groups and parts of the world too. Improvements in transportation technology dated to the nineteenth century, including railway networks and passenger steamships, facilitated travel as a leisure activity alongside other entertainments. One of the first travel agencies easing the process of travel by offering transportation, accommodation, and food as a package was Thomas Cook & Son, established in 1841. By the 1880s, the company had offices from Leicester to Auckland expediting pleasure travel to Europe, the Middle East, South Asia, and elsewhere. Several authors in this collection report employing the company's services for journeys to the Ottoman Empire in particular, where, upon arrival in each city, they would have the reassurance of being met by a "Cook representative." The proliferation of cars, buses, and, from the 1930s, air travel enabled a tourism industry to literally take flight.

For most women into the twentieth century, there were only limited options to travel for enjoyment according to their own whim. Neither of the earliest examples here, Jahanara and Dilshad, though at opposite ends of the social hierarchy, were mobile out of choice. The former was committed to accompanying the royal household as it processed through India's imperial territories, while the latter experienced forced migration as a prisoner of the khan of Khoqand. Socioreligious reformers sought to open up educational opportunities to women from the late nineteenth century, with travel as an integral part for some. They did so, however, while emphasizing the centrality of women's roles as wives and mothers, often within a colonial paradigm of companionate marriage. Obligations to one's family, articulated as Islamic duty intersecting with Victorian ideals (particularly in South Asia and Egypt), could thus enable Muslim women's travel. Women were required to accompany their male relatives to offer crucial support and care, and thus reconstruct the much vaunted "stable" and patriarchal family unit in foreign lands. In short, many women traveled because their menfolk traveled: an appendage while fathers, brothers, husbands, and sons undertook education, pursued occupations, or experienced exile. For her German lover, Sayyida Salamah bint Said even risked elopement and apostasy.

Even if family travel is construed as an obligation, this is not to say that many of the authors included here did not take full advantage of it to travel to pursue their own, often pleasurable ends. Jahanara, for instance, was clearly delighted to find herself in the scenic and temperate Kashmir valley with the opportunity to meet her Sufi master. For Dilshad, her experience as an "immigrant" enabled a new identity as a poet. By the early twentieth century, a sojourn abroad with a working husband or an exiled father could provide a chance to sightsee, attend cultural events, write, or study. Shaista Suhrawardy Ikramullah even managed a coveted PhD thanks to hired help with her three young children. Required travel might thus offer a chance to escape, if only temporarily, the mundanity of everyday life—perhaps the domestic chores and childcare responsibilities that plagued most women then, as now—in favor of enjoyment and edification. Of course, while "pleasure" finds its own articulations here, nearly all the women in this book engaged with travel as pleasure in some way. Students in England certainly took side trips, and women performing the hajj frequently included that journey within a larger sightseeing tour if they had the financial means. What this final section highlights, however, is that travel need not be subordinated to larger concerns. Widowhood especially seemed to open doors to travel for travel's sake. Some of the most enjoyable pieces in this section are those that narrate the beauty of nature or the wonders of human civilization without any broader purpose.

PRINCESS JAHANARA

Mystical Meetings in Kashmir

INTRODUCTION

Jahanara (1614–81) (see fig. 34.1) was the eldest surviving child of India's powerful Mughal emperor Shah Jahan (r. 1628–58) and his wife Mumtaz Mahal. Famously, the latter died in childbirth in 1631, after which Shah Jahan commissioned the iconic Taj Mahal at Agra as her tomb. In her youth, Jahanara received an education at court encompassing religious knowledge, Persian literature, and etiquette. After her mother's death, she took over management of the imperial household in preference to her father's three other wives. One of her first major responsibilities was to prepare for the wedding of her adored younger brother, Muhammad Dara Shikoh (1615–59), who was the emperor's eldest son and heir apparent. In recognition of her status, Shah Jahan entrusted Jahanara with the imperial seal and bestowed her with the title of *Sahibat al-Zamani* (Lady of the Age). Mughal sources also refer to her as Begum Sahib or Padshah Begum, indicating her political power and influence over the ruler.

In addition, the Mughal princess controlled great wealth, having been granted a personal fortune, an annual grant from the privy purse, and half her mother's estate by her father. Jahanara also received revenue from a number of land grants (*jagirs*), including, from 1644, the prosperous port city of Surat on India's western coast. She owned several ships involved in the Indian Ocean trade, among them the *Sahibi* that transported grain to Mecca's poor and destitute on an annual basis. Other charitable pursuits included sponsorship for pilgrimages to Mecca, as well as patronage of learning and the arts. Jahanara also funded

Sunil Sharma prepared the translations from Persian; Siobhan Lambert-Hurley prepared the introduction with input from Sunil Sharma.

Figure 34.1 Princess Jahanara, attributed to Lalchand, ca. 1631–33. © British Library, London.

the construction of several monumental buildings such as the Friday mosque in Agra, the Mulla Shah mosque in Srinagar, a garden in Kashmir, and caravanserai for travelers. She never married and, after the war of succession between her four brothers, looked after her father, who was incarcerated by the winner, Aurangzeb, in the Agra fort for the last eight years of his life.

In the war of succession, Jahanara backed Dara Shikoh, who, as if to undergird his claim to the throne, is mentioned several times in the selected extracts as "exalted" or "wise." The siblings Jahanara and Dara were extremely close, and she followed her brother in his mystical pursuits, first within the widespread Chishti Sufi order and then within the Qadiri Sufi order. While the Chishtis had been associated with the Mughal dynasty since the time of Jahanara's great-grandfather, the emperor Akbar (r. 1556–1605), the Qadiris were favored for the first time during Shah Jahan's reign. For Jahanara, the linkage may have been a product of convenience. As she notes in the first extract, she was seeking a master from the "family of Chisht," but, as she was in Lahore where the Qadiri order was based, its guides may have been more accessible. Political considerations also appear as a factor: Qadiri networks stretched into Badakhshan where, at this time, Shah Jahan was seeking to establish imperial power over ancestral lands.

Jahanara composed two works in Persian on mystical themes. Both underline the Mughal dynasty's religiosity in a way that helped to sustain its political sovereignty. *Munis al-arvah* (*Confidant of the Spirits*) is a history of the Chishti Sufis with a hagiographical account of the major spiritual masters (*sheikhs*) of the order. Appended to this work is an account of Jahanara's visit to the shrine of the thirteenth-century mystic Mu'inuddin Chishti in Ajmer with her father. *Sahibiya* (*The Lady's Treatise*), from which the extracts here are taken, is a shorter work on Jahanara's initiation into the Qadiri order in Lahore. It details her interaction with the Sufi Mulla Shah (d. 1661), who was originally from Badakhshan in Central Asia but settled in Kashmir, and who was the spiritual successor of Sufi saint Miyan Mir (d. 1635). There are no surviving manuscripts of the latter work today, but fortunately the text is still available after a scholar transcribed and published it in a journal in 1979–80, having consulted a manuscript that was available then.

Before the war of succession, Jahanara frequently traveled to various parts of the empire with her father and brother. In the selected extracts, she describes a trip to the picturesque Kashmir Valley, which was a popular retreat for the imperial family during the summer months on account of its cool climate. Her narrative is as much about a personal spiritual journey on the path of Sufism as about a physical trip, thus combining two established genres in classical Persian literature. Writing about Kashmir in particular was a literary fad among Mughal poets and historians during the seventeenth century, though most focused exclusively on the gardens and landscape of the valley. In her narrative, Jahanara describes her service to her Sufi master, whom she calls Hazrat to denote his esteemed status, and the spiritual reward she gained from the experience of travel. These highly personal and engaging reflections contrast with the more factual compendiums of imperial events and deeds composed by her male predecessors.

Search for a Sufi Master in Lahore

My esteemed and kind father set off from Kabul for Lahore and, on November 19, 1639, entered that city. My zeal in the pursuit of acquiring truth and gnosis had increased because many sheikhs and great personages resided in Lahore, and I went about seeking a master who would guide me on the right path. I decided that I would not receive instruction until I had encountered a master who was a perfect sage and had attained a lofty state, and my exalted brother, who was both a sibling and confidant, became acquainted with that great one and sent me to him. I especially strove in my search among the masters of the family of Chisht. Any place where I heard about an ascetic and saint, I sent someone to investigate the circumstances of that great one, became informed about him, sent him offerings and prayers, and requested a task or chant from him. I received a task and chant from some great ones of various orders. But none appealed to me, and I did not see any use in it until I got news from many of the disciples and associates of Hazrat Miyan Mir (may God be pleased with him).

I especially beseeched Mulla Khvaja Bihari, who is among the chief companions and disciples of Hazrat Miyan Jiv. He has not accepted any disciple, nor will he, and he did not accept me. But since he was a kind and benevolent *faqir,* I sometimes got news about him. Some time passed in this search and discussion, but I did not find a master whose precept and instruction would provide a complete remedy and reassurance for my mind. My lack of success was not because this age and world are devoid of the existence of saints of God. The world was never, is not, and will not be devoid of this exalted class, and it is stable due to their existence. If, for example, one day at a certain hour, the world would become empty of the presence of the saints of God who are leaders, noble, upright, pious, grand, substitutes, poles, and redressers (may God be pleased with them all), the earth will not stay on its axis, and it, along with everything in it, would fall apart. In any case, seeking a perfect master is the essential duty and essence of the obligation of a novice.

I always used to keep my ears open for such a great one and be on the lookout for a sage. If the disciple and seeker of the true path places the hand of intention on the skirt of the perfect master with sincerity and trust, it is impossible that she not find the true path and become close to the truth of truths. Although my wish was to find a sheikh of this kind in the respected Chishti order, that would be better and more appropriate, for in this time there will be many perfect, wise, and accomplished sheikhs in this exalted order, and the high-ranking and heavenly masters of this great order are beyond praise and description, but since many of them are in a secluded state and keep themselves away from the general populace, I could not easily gather information about them.

My honorable life—every breath of which is dear and enriched, and since whatever passes cannot be obtained again—was wasted in nothingness and uselessness. My age was twenty-seven. Perforce I turned my attention to the real matter of reaching God and desired to attach myself to a perfect master who was accessible, of whatever order he may be. Since I was sincere in my quest, almighty God, who is worshipped, in truth would make this lowly one at his threshold benefit from his eternal felicity and undying fortune in understanding the truth of truths and finding the way to the lord of unity.

Traveling to Kashmir

During this time of auspicious beginning and end, my great father set out for Kashmir, the peerless and charming place that does not need any praise or description. I reached Kashmir with him on March 31, 1640, of the same year. Since I had no knowledge of the reality of the felicitous lives of the saints there, when I first arrived, I heard from many that the land of Kashmir today is adorned by the grace of the felicitous presence of that refuge of sainthood, guide on the path, chosen of the Prophet's family, Hazrat Mulla Shah (may God keep him in permanence). From the auspiciousness of his blessed feet, this land has become heaven's partner, but rather it makes a higher claim than that. In the great and exalted Qadiri order, from the magnificence of companions and most virtuous disciples, Hazrat Miyan Mir (may God sanctify his secret) is the possessor of saintly virtues, first in the list of great sheikhs, leader of the renowned saints, seeing one of the knower of consciences, superior of minds, informed of the esoteric and exoteric, leader of things paltry and great.

My successful brother, of lofty nature and exalted rank, who is a knower of God and my master in truth and guidance, is also devoted to Hazrat Miyan Jiv. In those auspicious days, he would go to Hazrat, and occupying himself in acquiring the unending graces, he had become the master of the higher states and stations, reaching the upper levels of oneness and lofty ranks of unity, he had attained a perfect level and degree of closeness to Hazrat. I heard such praise of the virtues of the guiding Hazrat from his sincere tongue that from my heart and soul, I became devoted to him out of perfect sincerity, belief, and extreme purity of obedience. And I became successful in my search and goal as stated in the meaning of the prophetic hadith, "Whoever seeks something will find it." Boldly I wrote two or three petitions full of extreme sincerity and expression of total belief in his service: "If that sunlike visage becomes accessible to me / I will make a claim of lordship, not just of kingship."

Knowing the sending of gifts to be a breach of form, for the first time I sent *nan* and *sag* cooked with my own hands along with a note through my chamberlain Gharib. At first for about a month he did not respond and, in keeping with his independence, showed great detachment. But he read the notes and said what did he have to do with worldly people and kings. But I did not desist from sending notes, expressing my sincerity and servitude and showing all kinds of service. My brother who traversed the path of truth also was in his service continuously and spoke about my sincerity and belief. Later by his discovery and inner light, he found me to be sincere in my quest and need and knew that my true intention was nothing but searching for the path of God. Out of kindness, he answered my notes bit by bit, and the scent of perfect hope that he would guide me reached the olfactory part of my soul. When I came to know the truth about the life, stations, lofty rank, and heavenly station of Hazrat through my wise brother's sincere words, no doubt remained in my heart. I saw his great beauty from another place when, according to an overwhelming desire, my great father summoned him, and he in keeping with the verse "Obey God and obey the Prophet . . ." came to his house. From the shining light that emanated from his clear forehead, the discerning eye and eye of belief were dazzled. From the auspiciousness of seeing him, my belief and sincerity increased a thousandfold, and the conditions I had made with myself that until I would see such a great man with my own eyes and learn his true story from my wise brother, I would not take a master were all met. By means of the lofty notable, I myself touched his skirt of felicity with my hand of devotion, and he too with the utmost kindness and affection that a perfect master has for his sincere disciples, suggested and kept me occupied with duties and chants of remembrance that are common in this loftiest of lofty and regal Qadiri order.

Before I could see the perfect beauty of my Hazrat physically, my exalted brother had given me his portrait that a master painter had painted on paper. I continuously studied that noble portrait with the glance of sincerity and eye of belief, and at special times I imagined and contemplated his auspicious form. On the first day that my wise brother kept me occupied according to the command of Hazrat in the path of the honorable Qadiri order and fixed in my mind the way to meditate on and imagine the portrait of the pir, the Prophet, and his four great Companions and other saints, that same day I bathed and, wearing clean clothes, kept a fast and in the evening broke it with the quince that Hazrat had kindly sent. I ate a little of the dervish's meal that had come from the home of Mulla

Muhammad Sa'id, one of the wise and accomplished disciples of Hazrat, who also partakes of the food from his house. Then I sat in the mosque that is in my house until midnight and said the night prayers, then returning to my chamber, I sat facing the qibla and focusing my attention on the portrait of Hazrat and occupied myself by imaging the company of the Prophet (peace be upon him, his chosen Companions, the *sahaba*, and saints).

It occurred to me that I was a disciple of the Chishti order, but now that I was entering the Qadiri order, would there be a conflict in me? Is there benefit from the guidance and instruction of Hazrat Shah or not? As soon as I became aware, I was overtaken by a state where I was neither asleep nor awake, and I witnessed the holy assembly of the Prophet (may peace be upon him), his Companions, and great saints (may God be pleased with them). The Prophet was seated there, and the four great friends and a group of elder companions were present. Hazrat Akhund sahib was also near that leader in the bounteous assembly and had placed his head on the auspicious feet of the Prophet. The Prophet said, "O Mulla Shah! You have lighted the lamp of the Timurids."[1] When I came to from this state, my heart was overjoyed with these tidings, and I prostrated myself in gratitude before the absolute God and had this quatrain on my tongue:

> O King, you are the one who saves through purity.
> By God, your glance is a grace for the seekers.
> Whoever you look at reaches his goal.
> The light of your glance is perhaps the light of God.

I expressed a thousand thanks because I had been honored by the blessing of the Prophet and the great Companions, and because I had heard the words "You have lighted the lamp of the Timurids" from the miraculous tongue of that leader. Further, I knew that he said that to expel the doubt in my mind, and since only we, brother and sister from the family of Timur, Lord of Two Conjunctions, had set upon the path of God and extended the hand of devotion to the skirt of Hazrat, no one from the nobility had been honored by this felicity or placed their foot on the path of seeking God and the truth. I didn't know what to do for the passionate joy I experienced. My belief was strengthened a thousandfold because I had tied the girdle of sincerity in ten places around my waist, put the ring of servitude to Hazrat in the ear of my soul, made him my master from the bottom of my heart, and chosen to follow him as leader in this world and the next. For the comprehension of this immense honor, I gave thanks at the court of the merciful God and said to myself in my heart that what is this great fortune that happened to a lowly person like me, and what is this felicity that came to a helpless one. My wise brother had experienced this felicity one day, and by the auspicious attention of that brother reached me too and not anyone else from the lineage of Timur.

For a period of six months less two days, we stayed in the land of Kashmir, and during this time I myself wrote petitions to the Hazrat with sincerity and belief. Often he replied out of kindness, and although he has achieved perfection without need from the temporary pleasures of the world and those of the next, by way of obtaining felicity, I presented him with varieties of scents and different kinds of dishes that I cooked with my own hands. Although I refrained from those customs that are prohibited in the law of Muhammad, from the felicitous time that I saw the luminousness of Hazrat Mulla sahib, I illumined my eyes with the cascading light of the complete beauty of the perfect master.

Departure from Kashmir

When two or three days remained for our departure from Kashmir, on Thursday evening after the evening prayer, I became absorbed in contemplating his auspicious form and witnessed his presence. In that state, I prayed that he bestow on me the sash (*dupatta*) that was on his auspicious shoulders. In the morning, I wanted to make a request in the form of a written petition covered with a sash. In the meantime, my chamberlain Puran, who always went back and forth in his felicitous service, came and said, "Last evening I had gone to the service of the refuge of sainthood. After the evening prayer, he took off the sash that was over his shoulders and gave it to me to carry to someone." I took the auspicious sash and rubbed it over my eyes and placed it on my head. I experienced immense joy and presence and benefice. It was a manifestly wondrous miracle, but what wonder from him! Today with the power that almighty God has gifted him, and with the rank of sainthood and station of kindness, he can do whatever he wants....

I was blessed with two felicitous and beneficent meetings with Hazrat and illumined the vision of my heart and eyes by the light of the beauty of his rank and glory. Once with my aforementioned brother, the second time on the day when we were coming out from Lahore, I made a written petition that since we were on the way, he may in his generosity be kind as to grace me with a meeting so I could derive complete enjoyment and benefit from the blessings of his sight. Hazrat, may my soul follow the dust on the hoof of his horse, agreed to my request and felicitously came on a mount to where my path lay, and sat under a mulberry tree with a red shawl thrown over him. I was in an elephant howdah desirous for beauty, and when I arrived before that tree, I stopped the elephant near him. I saw with the desire of my sincere soul and wish of belief that was connected to the world-adorning beauty of that kind master who was like the full moon in heaven and brilliant and bounteous sun. I reached that spot with myriad blessings and auspiciousness, and a total dread of his loftiness filled my heart, and from the shining light that shone from his clear forehead, my eyes were dazzled and the hair on my body stood up from overpowering zeal....

Bidding farewell, I set off from the external and internal world of service to that Hazrat with tearful eyes and a heavy heart. And Hazrat, the kind and perfect master, also got on his mount in felicity and left for his auspicious abode.

FURTHER READING

Jahanara. "Risala-i Sahibiya." Edited by Muhammad Aslam. *Journal of the Research Society of Pakistan* 16 (1979): 78–110; 17 (1980): 69–107.

Carl Ernst. "A Princess of Piety." In *Women of Sufism, A Hidden Treasure: Writings and Stories of Mystic Poets, Scholars & Saints*, edited by Camille Adams Helminski, 128–131. Boston: Shambhala, 2003. This chapter includes a translation of Jahanara's account of her Ajmer visit from *Munis al-arvah*.

Qamar Jahan Ali. *Princess Jahan Ara Begam: Her Life and Works*. Karachi: S. M. Hamid, 1991.

Afshan Bokhari. "The 'Light' of the Timuria: Jahan Ara Begum's Patronage, Piety, and Poetry in 17th-Century Mughal India." *Marg* 60 (2008): 53–61.

———. "Masculine Modes of Female Subjectivity: The Case of Jahanara Begam." In *Speaking of the Self: Gender, Performance, and Autobiography in South Asia*, edited by Anshu Malhotra and Siobhan Lambert-Hurley, 165–204. Durham, NC: Duke University Press, 2015.

Sunil Sharma. *Mughal Arcadia: Persian Poetry in an Indian Court*. Cambridge, MA: Harvard University Press, 2017.

NOTE

1. This is an allusion to the ancestors of the Mughals, the Timurid dynasty founded by Timur or Tamerlane (1335–1405). The Timurids were great patrons of the arts and Sufis at their court centered in Herat, Afghanistan.

—w—

DILSHAD

A Prisoner Is Taken to Khoqand

INTRODUCTION

Dilshad (1800–1900?) was a poet, historian, and teacher from Central Asia. She is perhaps one of the very few women from a nonelite background who wrote not only poetry but also an autobiographical historical text in nineteenth-century Central Asia. She was born in Ura-tepe, now in Tajikistan, into a modest Persian-speaking family. Ura-tepe, a major agriculturally productive town connecting the Ferghana Valley and Mawarannahr, was an autonomous city-state on the borders of two warring Uzbek polities, the Bukharan Amirate and the Khoqand Khanate. At the age of seventeen, Dilshad was among several thousand Ura-tepen immigrants who were forcibly deported and settled in Khoqand during the capture of her hometown by the forces of the Amir Omar Khan. She spent most of her life, which spanned more than a century, in that city. She not only wrote poetry in both Chaghatai Turki and Persian but also produced a fascinating first-person history, *Tarikh-i muhajiran* (*The History of Immigrants*) (see fig. 35.1), in which she describes her forced migration and her transition to a new environment and the formation of her new identity as a poet in the context of other "immigrants" or "prisoners of war," who like her were deported to Khoqand. Throughout the text, which was written late in her life, she seamlessly weaves her personal story into the narrative of other immigrants as well as larger political and cultural history of the region. As such, her text transcends existing conventions of writing.

Nurten Kilic-Schubel prepared the introductions, annotations, and translations from Chagatai Turki and Persian.

Figure 35.1 A sample page from Dilshad's *Tarikh-i muhajiran*. Courtesy of
Nurten Kilic-Schubel.

Much of what we know about Dilshad comes from her poetry collections
and her two autobiographical and historical texts: the aforementioned *Tarikh-i
muhajiran*, written in Persian, and *Sebat al-besher ma' Tarikh-i muhajiran* (*Tra-
vails of Humanity and History of Immigrants*), written in Turki. Both texts exist
in manuscript forms written on the margins of her poetry collections. Several
pages, including the beginnings, are missing from both versions. Neither text
contains dates, but both seem to have been written in the late nineteenth century. She lived in a city with a strong bilingual literary tradition, so she makes
literary and cultural observations by writing her poetry and history in both
languages. Though there is quite a bit of overlap between the two versions, it
is clear that one is not the translation of the other; they are two separate texts.
While the Persian text includes occasional sentences in Chaghatai Turki, the
Turki version is laden with Persian vocabulary. The selected excerpts are taken
from the Persian version.

   In these excerpts and throughout the text, language and sounds provide a
connecting thread of her life narrative. She frequently points out her inability to
understand Turki in her first days in the city of Khoqand. Indeed, her struggle
to ultimately master the Turki language in order to be able to write and teach
in both languages is her subtle way of showing how she overcame enormous

challenges. While not knowing the language was initially disorienting for her, as she tells us, the language and sounds of poetry and poets themselves ultimately become a source of familiarity. It is poetry and the poets that allows her to establish affective connections with her new city. Interestingly, she does not provide physical descriptions of her now adopted town of Khoqand. Instead, she provides a literary landscape of it. Neighborhoods are described in terms of poets living there. She makes sure to include the names of those students whom she taught and trained and others with whom she shared and developed her poetic talents.

Dilshad frequently refers to herself as "a humbled one," adopting a self-effacing interlocutor voice. This was not merely rhetorical device or a convention of authorial humility for her. She was indeed from a humble and modest background. Although she was not from an elite family or renowned literary circle, nonetheless in her narrative, Dilshad emerges as a hero. As she tells us, her early childhood was a time of constant military conflicts and familial and personal tragedy. By the time she was fourteen, she had been orphaned—her father died during one of these conflicts, and her mother died of plague. After that, she was raised by her elderly grandmother, who made a living by spinning. Following the siege of Ura-tepe by Amir Omar Khan in late 1816–17, she was taken prisoner and brought to Khoqand along with thousands of other prisoners from Ura-tepe. However, her story takes a markedly different path from that of the other forced migrants. Along with two other girls, she was separated from rest of the migrants. Due to her beauty and poetic talents, she was then presented to Omar Khan, who was himself a well-known poet and patron of poets.

As the excerpt reveals, her poetic encounter with Omar Khan emerges as one of the key moments in her life. In this encounter, she defies the power of the khan through her poetry. She was then given to one of the khan's subordinates, who happened to be a young man of Ura-tepen origin, who set her free. She then found herself wandering destitute in the streets of Khoqand at night not knowing where to go. Eventually, she finds herself in front of a small dervish lodge associated with the Sufi mystic order, the Qalandariyya. They take her in and become, as she tells us, her lifelong companions and friends. The leader of these *qalandars* entrusts her to a Turki-speaking female teacher and poet who lived with her aging bachelor son, an imam in the local mosque. Ultimately, Dilshad marries the son, and her mother-in-law teaches her Turki language and, along with it, the profession of teaching girls.

Dilshad presents *Tarikh-i muhajiran* as a history rather than as a memoir or travel account, though it may be read as one. She self-consciously presents her text as a historiographical intervention providing the legitimate account of the events of the war of Ura-tepe in 1816. As her title, *The History of Immigrants*, suggests, she explicitly portrays herself as a historian, one writing as a first-person narrator, who is both a witness and survivor of the "wondrous and strange" events described in her historical account of the experience of the captives and forced migrants of Ura-tepe. Here, the individual author herself is the primary source for her history, and her history takes the form of personal testimony. She confidently makes an authorial claim on her right to tell this history. Furthermore, she claims her voice as that of the common and ordinary people and seeks to register their lives in her work.

EXTRACTS

My account of the history of the invasion of Ura-tepe has dragged on. Still, so many astonishing tales remain to be told. Although I am just one humble narrator among many, I am the one who can best recall these events, especially with regard to this history, because I saw them with my own tearful eyes and witnessed them with my own tormented heart. The title of this narrative is *The History of Immigrants*. None of the events I recall in this strange and wondrous history have been related by previous authors. . . .

In the autumn of year 1816, at the time when ordinary people were returning to the city from their orchards and were busy repairing and fortifying their houses, the battle of Amir Umar Khan began. It was reported that the invading army had surrounded the city from the north, west, and south, and that they had set up their camp in the locality of Kalla Minaret, and were waiting for the people of Ura-tepe to surrender. . . . The rumors about the city's siege; the plunder of the amir's soldiers; the destruction of villages, buildings, and bridges; and the burning of trees, especially outside the city wall, had created fear and panic among the people.

My mother had died three years earlier during the plague, and as for my father, he had died in battle. His head was decapitated, and his body was left to rot in the locality of Kalla Minaret. From our household, only I and my ninety-year-old grandmother were left alive, making a living by spinning.

In this six-day-long battle, all the men of the city were busy waging war in the streets and the city square, while the elderly and the women and children were in hiding in their homes or in large cauldrons. . . . The horror of the war spread everywhere. Suddenly, the invading army, after launching another attack, entered the city. The invading soldiers, along with the guards and intimates of the amir, went from house to house, looting and plundering people's goods and possessions, and [taking] their daughters. . . .

Prisoners of war had been herded together in the square of Chor-su. I still don't know what happened to my poor grandmother.[1] I did not hear a single report about her after I was captured on that day. It was rumored that 13,400 people had been taken as prisoners and gathered into a square, which is now known as the Ibret Square [Square of Admonition]. Amir Umar Khan was renowned for being a scholar and a great poet. Yet he did not show the slightest compassion to a single scholar or poet of this innocent city.[2]

At dawn, countless cavalrymen came from the city's southern direction known as the "Bazaar-e Goze" and marched toward the square where the prisoners were gathered. . . . After the massacre, the remaining three thousand prisoners were dragged in front of their oppressors. Pushed, shoved, and crying, they walked barefoot through the steppes of Navganda, Bekat, Kurkat, and Mahram. The names of those steppe regions, which I learned from other prisoners, are still in my memory. Out on these steppes, like the other prisoners on the road, my feet were cut by sharp rocks and thorns, and like the other prisoners, the soles of my feet became swollen; my toenails blistered and bled. I became too exhausted and weak to take another step.

When all of us prisoners were standing in Khoqand's large, open square, trembling with pain, the people of this city, with regret, stared in the direction of the khan's military encampment [orda] filled with grief, agony, and hatred.[3] The men were brought in through the eastern gate, while the women were brought in via gardens by the southern gate. After we entered the citadel, some women came and separated three girls from among the prisoners and took them to the khan's harem. I still remember the names of those girls. One was Izzatay, another was Huremetay, and the third was me, Dilshad. The three of us were kept in one cell. . . . You already know the description of these three cellmates.[4] During those days, I heard about the conditions of the other Uratepen prisoners and what fate the winds of time had brought upon them. It became known that that some of the prisoners later received an order of emigration and settled in a place named Ottuz Adir by the Andijan water canal. I used to think about the wide landscape of the Bekat desert and dream about these unlucky and resilient prisoners and what conditions they were in now.

It was later heard that the prisoners were given the order of "ak üylük" in the steppe and were sentenced to become tent-dwellers in the steppe for seven years, forbidden to build houses.[5] Years later, I again heard that the immigrants had petitioned the khan, requesting permission to build houses. After seven years, they were given permission to build houses and establish a city. This city was known as the city of Amir Omar Khan and is now called Shahrikhan. This is the second city of the people of Ura-tepe.

Let me now turn to tell you the story of my own circumstances. I was brought to a room in the presence of the khan by a woman. In this room, the amir was sitting in his nightgown. Between him and me was a low black table, and on it was a cup of water, a knife, and a pomegranate. The khan was tall in stature, with black eyes, eyebrows, a beard, and a broad face. After responding to my greeting, he treated me well with kind words. Despite his fine treatment of me, he was, in my eyes, the king of oppressors who had shed blood in the square of massacre. He said to me, "Come here, you, the poet girl of the Tajiks . . ."[6]

After querying me about my name and family, the amir showed me a pomegranate and requested that I compose a ghazal about it. I recited the following ghazal at that time:

> I saw the heavenly dome in which everything was filled with pain.
> Silken veil covered their faces. I saw their eyes wet and hearts bleeding.
> I saw that every beauty's heart was torn by the sword of the oppressive rule of Omar Khan.

When these lines were completed, the amir struck me twice, and one of his subordinates entered the room. The amir said to him, "Take this guilty one to the prison." He signaled to him with his eyes, but I did not understand what he meant.

Later, when we were passing together by the gate by the citadel, this subordinate told me, "Little daughter, did you know that the amir had bestowed you to me? But I did not know your situation, whether you already had a beloved or not. I hoped that you would tell me whether you have a loved one."

I said, "The love of a young man from my hometown has found a place in my heart."

He then said, "Hey, girl, do you want me to set you free?"

I said, "Yes."

He said, "I set you free, then."

I said, "I am an oppressed guest [misafir], where could I go?"

He said, "Daughter, do you see over there where the forty soldiers sitting in the barracks on the two wings of the gate are now sleeping?"

After expressing my gratitude to this compassionate young man from Ura-tepe, I followed after him. At that time, this youth showed great intrepidity and opened the gate for me. I went outside, walking toward a light coming from afar. As I got closer to the source of that light, I saw that it was a hammam [public bath]. Fearing the bath stokers sleeping in the ashes, I took another path. To the north, I saw a black shed where drunken qalandars [Sufi mystics] were busy drinking *boza*.[7] After leaning over its slightly opened door, I collapsed! I don't remember what happened to me afterward. When I came to myself, I saw that I was lying on the floor with a piece of cloth covering my face.

I heard all kinds of sounds and voices that I could not understand, as I did not know a word of the Turki language at that time. Suddenly, I heard Persian. I rose up from my place and saw that those Persian words were uttered by the leader of the qalandars. He was a man of short stature with a long beard and wore a frayed cap. He asked me about my name, family, and place of origin. I gave succinct answers, and it was then and there that I recited the ghazal with the refrain *"amadaem"* ["I came"]. Afterward, he gave a signal to one of the qalandars that I did not understand. He then spoke to me in Persian, "You, the unfortunate one, accompany this man. He will take you to a place. Hurry up—it is late. If you dawdle, once the mullah recites the call to prayer, it would be hard for a woman to walk outside on the streets."

I quickly rose up and expressed my gratitude to this leader. Following the qalandar, I set out on the path of my future destiny. We finally arrived at the house where I now live. I saw that the gate was not locked, and at a signal from the qalandar, I went inside, and he departed.

The courtyard extended from east to west, and there were two old rooms facing toward the gate of the courtyard. One could see the light of a candle coming through the thresholds of both rooms. As I walked closer to the rooms, I heard a male voice reciting the Quran from the room on the left, and a voice of an old woman reciting a ghazal from the room on the right.

With confidence, I finally entered that room pronouncing a greeting. I saw an old woman, probably eighty years old. She rose up and greeted me with an honest and sincere face. Showing great hospitality, she spoke to me of many things, but I did not understand the meaning of any of what she said. Once she realized that I was a Farsi speaker, she started to speak in eloquent Persian. When morning came, and the voice of the call to prayer was heard, we were both awoken at that time and went outside to do our ablutions. After the morning prayers, during breakfast we began to converse. After hearing my perfect answers to her questions in Persian, she too began to talk about her own life circumstances. The man who had been reciting the Quran was her fifty-year-old son.[8]

After staying twelve days in this house, following destiny and my own volition, I married this old woman's son, Tash Muhammad. At that time, Tash Muhammad was an imam in the neighborhood mosque, and his mother was a teacher to girls.[9]

I served the mother for thirteen years, and through her I learned the Turkic language perfectly, and took the profession of teaching as my inheritance. In those days, my mother-in-law was ninety-two years old, but she was still giving lessons to girls and sewing without the help of eyeglasses.

After seven more years, my mother-in-law passed away. At that time I was thirty-seven years old. I had eight children from Mahmud, but only two of them survived.[10] Mahmud outlived his mother for another twenty years, and he too died at the age of ninety. At that time, I was fifty-seven years old, I did not want to marry a second time even though I still had a youthful and elegant stature. Until I was eighty-eight years old, I could write and sew without eyeglasses. . . .

My confidants and close companions were girls of great intellect and poetic talent. I have been a teacher to girls for fifty-one years. At the school, from high to middle levels, twenty to thirty students received education from me in any given year. Altogether I educated and graduated 891 girls. Among these, close to one-third of them were learned sages of their times, and gifted poets. . . .

Furthermore, two years after I left the khan's orda, broken and injured, I found out that the queen of Ferghana, the master of poetry and prominent poet of her time, i.e., Nadira-i Devran, was living there. I made several attempts to meet with her, but I was unsuccessful.[11]

I did not always have the skills to compose ghazals or eloquent speech. Nonetheless, out of necessity, and because of the destiny of Khoqand and Ura-tepe in the field of literature, it would not leave me in peace; I could not escape from being a poet. Because of the pain of separation from my homeland; the grief for my mother and father, and my grandmother, who showed tremendous affection toward me, and who was the only friend to this hapless one (*natevan*); and because the pain of separation from my first love made my heart melancholy and my tears abundant, for these reasons I made poetry my great profession and major occupation.

FURTHER READING

Dilshad. *Sebat al-besher ma' Tarikh-i muhajiran*. Tashkent Abu Rayhan Beruni Oriental Institute, Ms.1207. This source is the Turki version.

A. Mukhtarov. *Dilshod and Her Place in the Social Thought of the Tadjik People*. Dushanbe: Danish, 1969. This is a study of the author in Russia. This book includes a facsimile of Persian version of *Tarikh-i muhajiran*.

Nurten Kilic-Schubel. "Writing Women: Women's Poetry and Literary Networks in Nineteenth-Century Central Asia." In *Horizons of the World: Festschrift for İsenbike Togan*, edited by Nurten Kilic-Schubel and Evrim Binbaş, 405–40. Istanbul: Ithaki Press, 2011.

Nurten Kilic-Schubel. "Arts: Poets and Poetry: Central Asia." In *Encyclopedia of Women and Islamic Cultures*, vol. 5, edited by Suad Joseph. Leiden: Brill, 2007. https://referenceworks .brillonline.com/browse/encyclopedia-of-women-and-islamic-cultures.

Mahmuba Qodirova. *Dilshad*. Tashkent: Fan, 1972. This is a biography of the author in Uzbek.

NOTES

1. In the Turkic version of her account, Dilshad tells her readers that she was hidden by her grandmother in her house, but the soldiers found her and took her away, leaving the grandmother behind (*Tarikh-i muhajiran*, 4).

2. Amir Omar Khan (d. 1822) was an established poet and patron of art and literature who himself wrote a diwan under the pen name of Amiri.

3. Orda is a politico-military institution in Mongol and post-Mongol empires. Here, she uses the term to refer to the khan's royal military encampment and place of residence.

4. The Persian text is missing pages here. In her Turki text, she mentions they spent three days in the harem and that she was then separated from the other two girls and was given a bath and clean clothes before being taken to the khan.

5. "Ay üylük" is literally "white house." Here, she refers to those who were made dwellers of the steppe or nomadic tents, which were often white.

6. She offers a somewhat different version in her autobiographical verse. In her verse version of the encounter, the khan says, "What do you say of this pomegranate?" She said, "You filled it with the blood of young girls."

7. Boza is an alcoholic beverage made from fermented millet, wheat, or maize. It has a low alcohol content.

8. In the Turkic version of the text, she tells us that he was a bachelor due to poverty.

9. Interestingly, within the text, she writes this sentence in Turki language and then provides Persian translation.

10. In the Turkic version, she provides the names of her surviving children. These include Sayyid 'Azim, Sayyid Mahmud, and Mehrinisa.

11. Nadira, the pen name (*makhlas*) of Mahlar Ayim (d. 1842), was the wife of Omar Khan of Khoqand (d. 1822) and the mother of another Khoqand Khan, Madali Khan (d. 1842). She was a prominent poet on her own. Her poems in Turkic and Persian were collected in two divans. She was executed along with her sons and grandsons by the amir of Bukhara, Nasralladin, during the invasion of the city of Khoqand by the forces of Bukharan Amirate in 1842. Interestingly, Dilshad does not mention this dramatic event.

THIRTY-SIX

SAYYIDA SALAMAH BINT SAID / EMILY RUETE

A Lover's Flight from Zanzibar

INTRODUCTION

Sayyida Salamah bint Said (1844–1924), later known as Emily Ruete, was styled in her own time as a princess of Oman and Zanzibar. Her father, Sayyid Said, bore the title of sultan of Zanzibar and imam of Muscat. Her mother, Djilfidan, was a Circassian slave who lived in the royal household with her only daughter, Salamah, alongside seventy-five co-wives and their thirty-five children. Salamah's highly privileged childhood is documented in her memoirs as a series of relaxed social engagements, lavish meals, meticulous life-cycle rituals, colorful religious festivals, and childhood pranks. However, it began to unravel when her father died in 1856, leading to factional fighting among his many offspring. Though Salamah's favored brother Majid succeeded to the throne, she soon became embroiled in an unsuccessful rebellion on the side of another brother, Barghash. Salamah was, according to her own account, subsequently reconciled to Majid (who ruled Zanzibar until his death in 1870, when Bargash returned from exile in Bombay to be enthroned), but she still found herself ostracized by family and friends. In this uncomfortable circumstance, she struck up an uncommon friendship that matured to love with a German neighbor, Rudolph Heinrich Ruete. Ruete was employed in Zanzibar with a Hamburg-based trading firm, Oswald & Co. When the illicit relationship became public in 1866, Salamah obtained the assistance of the British consul to escape Zanzibar for Aden, where she gave birth to their first son.

This first journey, from Zanzibar to Aden, initiated an itinerancy that characterized the rest of Salamah's life. Once reunited with her lover in Aden in 1867,

Siobhan Lambert-Hurley prepared the introduction and extracts.

Figure 36.1 Salamah bint Said, also known as Emily Ruete, with her husband and two children in Hamburg, ca. 1869–70. From Wikipedia Commons.

she converted to Christianity, taking the name Emily, so they could marry in an Anglican chapel and set sail for Europe the same day. The next three years were spent in her husband's native Hamburg, where she gave birth to two daughters while seeking to adapt to a new life in Germany (see fig. 36.1). When her husband died in a tragic tram accident in 1870, she respected his wish to raise their three children as Christians in Europe. Seeking to provide for them through Arabic and Swahili language tuition, she moved to Dresden, then Berlin, and finally Cologne. She traveled to London in 1875 in the failed hope of meeting her brother Barghash, then on a state visit from Zanzibar. After nineteen years abroad, she returned to Zanzibar with her children in 1885 and again in 1888 in an attempt to reconcile with her siblings and claim her inheritance denied due to her elopement and apostasy. Unsuccessful, she settled first in Jaffa in the Levant and then in Beirut in Lebanon. She remained in the Middle East until war broke out in 1914, at which point she returned to Germany, where she died of pneumonia in 1924.

So much is known of Ruete's peripatetic life because she documented it meticulously in letters, memoir, and ethnography—all three genres of which are represented in the extracts here. The first extract, detailing her sea voyage from Aden and arrival in Europe in June 1867, is taken from her *Letters Home* (*Briefe nach der Heimat*). Though unpublished until fairly recently, this set of letters appears to have been composed sometime after 1888 for the benefit of a "dear friend" in Zanzibar whose identity remains unknown. In her memoirs, Ruete projects her acculturation to European society as fairly straightforward, but these letters suggest a more tortured process. Of particular note was her struggle with the European climate and social customs, the German language, and the Christian religion—the latter to which she never seems to have been entirely reconciled.

The second and third extracts come from her first volume of memoirs, originally entitled *Memoiren einer Arabischen Prinzessin*. According to the author's preface, prepared in Berlin in May 1886, Ruete began penning her life story nine years before "for the information of my children," who, she projected, knew little of her origins, youth, or "the course of my fate." A general audience was not envisaged in her telling until, "upon urgent persuasion," she agreed for the memoirs to be published. More recent commentators have suggested that raising money for her impoverished family after her husband's death was a more significant factor in publication, an interpretation supported by her writing's orientation to a broad German readership. Throughout her memoirs, Ruete made direct comparisons between her life in Zanzibar and what readers would know "here in Germany," often projecting civilizational differences in bounded and oppositional terms: between "Western" and "Eastern" countries, "Europeans" and "Orientals," "Christians" and "Mahometans," or as she constructs it in the second extract, "Northerners" and "Southerners." Raised in "the East" but conversant with "the West," Ruete was in a unique position to provide a firsthand account of the inner workings of the sultan's harem—a topic eagerly consumed by European audiences. At the same time, she hoped to disavow them of their "erroneous views" on Arab women and gender relations. This latter aim gave her memoirs a critical edge by which, as seen in the second and third extracts, European mores and practices were assessed as wanting against an "East" idealized after her many difficult years in Europe.

Ruete's intended audience was also evident in her use of German for the original composition, though the memoirs were soon translated into a variety of other European languages to widespread and enthusiastic acclaim. The first English translation appeared in 1888, soon after the original publication, under the title *Memoirs of an Arabian Princess: An Autobiography*, but the second edition, published in 1907 and from which the extracts here are taken, has proved more enduring. Lavishly illustrated, it appeared in a series of "Memoirs of Charming Women." In a short introduction, translator Lionel Strachey attributed renewed interest in Ruete's memoirs to the fulfillment of Europe's colonial ambitions in eastern and southern Africa only in their infancy when she first wrote. The fourth extract is taken from another short book, *Syrian Customs and Usages* (*Syrische Sitten und Gebräuche*), in which Ruete again sought to make "the East" intelligible to a European audience. Written upon her return to Arab lands later in life (though, again, not published until fairly recently), it offers observations of Beirut's streets, homes, social customs, and dress. In melding "old and new," Arab and European, it seemed to offer Ruete a place where, after all of her travels, she could finally be at ease.

EXTRACTS

A New Life: From *Letters Home*

How often have you asked me, dear friend, to report to you more in detail about my experiences in the North? The main reason why this was not done to your satisfaction so far is that I was almost afraid of reliving everything in detail once again in my mind. Nor am I not at all sure that I am able to do justice to your wish in general, and to your satisfaction in particular, because life, manners, customs, and perceptions of the people of the North are so totally different from ours, that I fear that much will appear exaggerated to you, perhaps even impossible. Was it any different for me in the beginning, when I was transposed in person into their midst? I needed years to get out of the quiet astonishment about everything which surrounded me and which, in the course of time, I came to watch and hear. . . .

Our journey on the Red Sea [in June 1870] was indescribably hot. Around midday nobody would dare to stay under the awnings, and all passengers had to remain in the saloon until the sun declined toward the West. Meals with so many gentlemen and ladies who were completely unknown to me were very unpleasant, and I was always happy when these sessions came to an end, the more so because I suspected pork and also lard in every dish. So it was that I declined everything which my senses considered not to be free of pork. Therefore, I lived in the beginning mostly on biscuits, boiled eggs, tea, and fruits alone. False shame prevented me from telling my husband about my fear of these unclean and with us strictly forbidden animals, for with Christians, everything is permitted and the words "clean" and "unclean" with regard to food are unknown. I therefore pretended lack of appetite in most cases and put my hopes on the future, which so often works wonders. If there was anything that seemed to mock my former seclusion from the world of men, it was these few nights here on board the ship. For during the last few nights, all the first-class passengers—man, woman, and child—slept together on their mattresses in the saloon. I was not very pleased with this new kind of freedom, but as a prospective civilized person, I had to comply. When I told my husband that I preferred to sleep in the stiflingly hot cabin rather than upstairs in the saloon, as he proposed, he told this to Mrs. C, a most amiable lady from Mauritius, French by birth. This lady did not rest before she had wormed out of me the difficult promise to sleep upstairs with the other passengers. In appreciation for my giving in, she promised to always sleep next to me in the saloon. Most amusing was the sight next morning when waking up! All the gentlemen in nightshirts and thin white underpants, but nothing else. The ladies all in long English nightgowns with a thin white skirt over it. No one of course was wearing stockings, and only a few people had a woolen blanket to cover themselves. Every sleeper who woke up tried to leave his resting place as soon as possible so that no one might see him in his scanty dress.

The first European town I ever entered was Marseille. Though we arrived in June, I was so numb with cold that the gentle Mrs. C was friendly enough to wrap me up in her shawl. . . .

While we were driving from our hotel to the railway station, I was seized by such a fear, otherwise unknown to me, that I would have preferred to cry aloud. It seemed to me as if from now on, my homeland would be removed from me more and more and that all bridges had collapsed behind me. My soul was crying out for all of you and seemed to blend with a thousand voices from my beloved island, calling me back with one warning: "Go no further! Instead come back!" I fought a terrible fight with myself. Mechanically I mounted the train whose purpose it was to bring me as quickly as possible to an unknown country, to perfect strangers, as if I too were in the greatest hurry to reach my future destination as soon as possible—and so we drove on and on toward the North. . . .

You will of course want to know how I felt and thought on European soil during this short time, or not? There were extremely strange sensations indeed which dominated me completely. Everything taken together—and this I frankly admit—I felt continuously afraid. Only in my husband's presence was I able to free myself from this feeling, which tormented me day and night. For everything was so strange to me, so completely different from what I had known and had been accustomed to until now. That one voice only, which I believe to hear continuously—for I had no understanding of all the rest—still rang in my soul: "And here you wish to pass the rest of your life?" It would have been easier to give my life than to be able to answer this dreadful question with an honest "Yes." In addition, there was, externally, the Christian name, whereas internally I was as good a Muslim woman as you yourself are. I appeared to myself so utterly despicable for posing differently from what I in reality was. This I tell you quite frankly: beware of changing your religion without true conviction. . . .

The first period in Europe passed almost as in a dream. . . . Imagine yourself surrounded by your household without being able to speak with your servants. You must go to strangers and pay visits while your conversation with them consists exclusively in shaking hands. The same is repeated when you repay the unavoidable return visits. You are invited to a great party, where the eyes of all the guests are turned to you but in whose glances you read only inquisitiveness. Gentlemen and ladies observe you from head to foot until you, for decorum's sake, have to lower your astonished eyes. You need something and would like to have it, but you cannot possibly obtain it during your husband's absence because it is he who has to translate your various wishes and needs to the servants. Every day, except on Sunday, it was completely impossible for me to speak, and from half past nine till four o'clock, I had as a rule to be silent, because my husband during that time was in his office. As you see, all this was nothing but unpleasantness for me, and so nothing was left to me but to learn the language. . . . I wanted to do anything in my power to learn as quickly as possible the manners and customs of the land in which I now live lest our education, considered by many as primitive, be branded as an object of universal pity.

The Vaunted Activity of Northern Peoples: From *Memoirs*

Over and over again, I have been asked: "How on earth do the people manage to exist in your country without anything to do?" And the question is justifiable enough from the point of view of the Northerner, who simply cannot imagine life without work, and who is convinced the Oriental never stirs her little finger but dreams away most of her time in the seclusion of the harem. Of course, natural conditions vary throughout the world, and it is they that govern our ideas, our habits, and our customs. In the North, one is compelled to exert oneself in order to live at all, and very hard too, if one wishes to enjoy life, but the Southern races are greatly favored. I repeat the word "favored" because the frugality of a people is an inestimable blessing; the Arabs, who are often described in books as exceedingly idle, are remarkably frugal, more so perhaps than any but the Chinese. Nature herself has ordained that the Southerner can work, while the Northerner must. The Northern nations seem to be very conceited and look down with pride and contempt upon the people of the tropics—not a laudable state of mind. At the same time, they are blind to the fact, in Europe, that their activity is absolutely compulsory to prevent them from perishing by the hundred thousand. The European is obliged to work—that is all; hence he has no right to make such a great virtue of sheer necessity. Are not Italians, Spaniards, and Portuguese less industrious than Germans and Englishmen? And what may the reason be? Merely that the former have more summer than winter, and consequently, they have less of a struggle for existence. A cold climate implies the providing and securing oneself against all sorts of contingencies and actualities quite unknown in Southern lands.

Luxury plays the same part everywhere. Who has the money and the inclination will find opportunity to gratify his fancies, whatever quarter of the globe he may inhabit. So let us leave this subject untouched and confine ourselves to the real necessities of life. If in this country the newborn infant requires a quantity of things to protect its frail existence against the perversities of a changeable climate, the little brown-skinned Southerner lies almost naked, slumbering easily while fanned by a perpetual current of warm air. If in Germany a two-year-old child needs shoes, stockings, pantalettes, a couple of petticoats, a dress, an overcoat, gloves, scarf, gaiters, muff, and a fur cap, whether it belongs to a banker or a laborer—the quality being all that differs—in Zanzibar the costume of a royal prince of the same age comprises two articles, shirt and cap. Then why should an Arabian mother, whose demands for herself and child are so small, work as hard as a German housewife? She has never heard of darning gloves and stockings, of performing the sundry labors done for a European child once a week. . . . All these, and several other considerations, help to make the Oriental woman's lot more bearable and comfortable than the European's, without particular regard to social station.

Defects of European Civilization: From Memoirs

It is inevitable that, having been brought up where I was, I should make comparisons with the European system, of which my children enjoyed the privileges. There certainly is a great disparity between German overeducation and Arabian ignorance; too much is exacted on the one side, too little demanded on the other. But I suppose such sharp differences will never cease but will persist to the end of the world, as no race appears capable of settling upon a golden mean. Here, at all events, the children have their minds stuffed with a great deal more than they can possibly absorb. Their schooldays once begun, the parents see very little of them. Owing to the sundry tasks that have to be prepared for the next day, true family life is out of the question, and with this loss a steady, telling influence upon the juvenile character must in many cases be forfeited. All day long it is not living, but hurry and scramble, scramble and hurry, from one lesson to another. What a lot of time they waste too in arduously gaining facts destined to prove utterly useless, inasmuch as they seem to be imparted for the sole purpose of being forgotten! How to approve a method by which the young are robbed of time that were much better spent at home?

Besides, the poor things are confined every day for five or more hours in a prisonlike space called a "schoolroom," hot and stuffy beyond description. Four tumblers to drink water out of allowed by an institution harboring two hundred children! Would this not disgust a mother who wanted to kiss her child upon its return from that place? And why express surprise if under such conditions the little ones fall ill? Do for them what one may at home to keep them in health, the foul air of the schoolhouse must frustrate all one's efforts. How wretched many of the scholars look in this country, and how your heart bleeds for their deplorable state! Give me that open, airy veranda of ours. What profits the highest education so the body be ruined in the struggle to possess it?

I notice little here of that respect which we all, my brothers, sisters, and self, accorded to our parents and teachers, in fact, to age generally. Neither does the religious instruction given at the schools seem to be as effective as it ought, and no wonder, since it takes a purely mechanical form; endless lists of dates pertaining to ecclesiastical history are the children compelled to learn by heart, instead of being urged to observe a regular attendance at church, where a good sermon would inspire them far more than those barren historical facts. We had to memorize lessons too, but not to the entire neglect of the soul, which here suffers at the expense of the brain. Book learning is overdone here—that is my opinion. Everybody wants to rise up and up so high through education that finally manual labor becomes a disgrace; too much importance is attached to knowledge and culture. Therefore, it is not surprising if deference, honesty, piety, and contentment yield to appalling ungodliness, scorn for everything sacred and established, and the unscrupulous pursuit of worldly advantages. With their outward education people's necessities increase and their demands upon life, hence the severity and the bitterness of competition among them. Yes, the mind is cultivated, to be sure, but the heart is left untilled. One should study the word of God and His holy commandments first, speculating upon "force and matter" last. . . .

European culture offends the [Muslim]'s religious views in countless ways. They often ridicule the Turkish half-education, yet the Turks have done more than is good for them to become civilized, if only superficially. The Turks have weakened themselves by those endeavors, in spite of which they have still remained uncivilized, because European civilization contradicts and opposes all their fundamental axioms. You cannot produce civilization by force, and you should allow other nations the right to follow their own ideas and traditions—which must have developed as the result of mature experience and practical wisdom—in seeking enlightenment after their own fashion. A pious Arab would feel deeply affronted were one to attempt beginning his illumination by inculcating science, without which there can be no question of higher culture in Europe. It would give him a terrible shock, it would convulse his mentality, if one spoke to him of "natural laws" to him who, in the whole life of the universe, down to the smallest details, through the eyes of his immutable faith, sees only one thing—the all-guiding, all-governing hand of God!

The City of Beirut: From *Syrian Customs and Usages*

The city of Beirut is very picturesquely situated. Surrounded by the high Lebanon and splashed by the Mediterranean, it makes a very pleasant impression upon the newcomer. Ships coming from the north or the south arrive here mostly at sunrise. The reason is that traffic takes place only during daylight; the customhouse and the offices close at sunset. From afar the arriving seafarer sees the high Lebanon veiled in morning twilight; in winter, snow covers the slopes. . . .

The streets of Beirut are generally wide but very badly kept because the honorable municipality prefers to line its own pockets instead of using the local rates for the benefit of the community, as should be the case. Therefore, dust in summer and mud in winter are permanent guests on the streets. But as soon as one enters the houses, almost without exception constructed very airily and massively, the dirty streets are quickly forgotten. Here everything is neat and clean, even with the poorest people. The more elegant houses are in general paved with a marble floor, while red-polished tiles are sometimes chosen for the bedrooms. The design of the houses is very simple but corresponds to the climate and is very pleasant. One enters directly into a very large hall paved with marble, about eleven meters long and seven meters wide. Into this emerge the doors of all the rooms, which are situated eastward, southward, and westward. On the northern side, the house is walled in by high windows and a door that leads to a balcony. The room on the northern side is mostly used as a living room, being always cool in summer since it is not exposed to the sun. The favored rooms are those that lie westward, because a refreshing wind usually blows from that direction, thus making them particularly suitable as bedrooms. Almost all houses have small gardens, frequently tended and cultivated by the ladies themselves. . . .

Well-to-do people live completely "alla franca," that is to say in the European way. They eat with knives and forks at a laid table, sleep in European beds, and make use of every item that offers them ease. This brings about great contrasts. The same people who are surrounded by all imaginable ease often have their parents, brothers, sisters, and close relatives with them, who live as their ancestors did a thousand years ago, and to whom the use of beds and dining tables has remained completely alien. It looks very strange to see a Syrian lady dashing forward in her carriage, dressed from head to foot after the latest French fashion, with her mother or aunt next to her, still dressed after the old fashion: a black mantilla on the head instead of a mighty Parisian hat. The same is true for the modern gentlemen, who wear European hats while their relatives stick to the old headgear. The contrasts between old and new make a remarkable impression upon the observer. There they sit on their divans, the respectable old people, drinking black coffee and smoking their narghile (waterpipe), as it has been done for immemorial times, watching and meditating; next to them sit their progeny on modern European seats, dressed in the latest Parisian fashion, speaking French with their contemporaries.

FURTHER READING

Sayyida Salamah bint Said. *Memoiren einer Arabischen Prinzessin*. Berlin: Verlag von Friedrich Ludhardt, 1886. http://digital.staatsbibliothek-berlin.de/werkansicht?PPN=PP N655943161&PHYSID=PHYS_0009&DMDID=DMDLOG_0001. English translations appeared under the title of *Memoirs of an Arabian Princess* (New York: D. Appleton, 1888), https://archive.org/details/memoirsofarabianooruetuoft, and in a translation by Lionel Strachey (New York: Doubleday, Page, 1907), http://digital.library.upenn.edu/women /ruete/arabian/arabian.html. For a recent reprint, see *Memoirs of an Arabian Princess from Zanzibar* (Mineola, NY: Dover, 2009).

Emily Ruete. *Briefe nach der Heimat*. Edited by Heinz Schnepen. Berlin: Philo, 1999.

Sayyida Salme (Emily Ruete). *An Arabian Princess between Two Worlds: Memoirs, Letters Home, Sequels to the Memoirs, Syrian Customs and Usages*. Edited by E. J. van Donzel. Leiden: Brill, 1992.

Jeremy Prestholdt. "From Zanzibar to Beirut: Sayyida Salme bint Said and the Tensions of Cosmopolitanism." In *Global Muslims in the Age of Steam and Print*, edited by James L. Gelvin and Nile Green, 204–26. Berkeley: University of California Press, 2014.

THIRTY-SEVEN

TAJ AL-SALTANAH

Life and Death in Qajar Iran

INTRODUCTION

Taj al-Saltanah (1883–1936) (see fig. 37.1) achieved notoriety in late Qajar Iran for a rebellious lifestyle documented in her memoir. Written sometime around 1914, this unfinished and untitled Persian text charts thirty years of her life, from pampered princess in the royal harem through a troubled marriage to unconventional independence. The author's father was the great Naser al-Din Shah (r. 1848–96), and her mother was a minor princess titled Turan al-Saltanah. The latter was one of approximately eighty women wedded to the shah in the course of his reign. Taj thus grew up alongside around seven hundred of the shah's wives and dependents in the Golestan Palace within the Royal Citadel (Arg-e Soltani) in Tehran. In her memoir, she recounts vividly how any maternal warmth came not from her mother but from her "black nanny"—on whom she modeled her own hands-on and affectionate motherhood displayed in the extracts here. Her informal education in the harem may have been marred by, in her own words, her own "perversity and willfulness and disobedience," but still it provided enough mastery of Persian literature and language to enable her to write with precision and eloquence later in life.

Three extracts from Taj's memoirs relating to travel are produced in translation here. As a set, they all relate to a fairly narrow period during her marriage. A year after her half brother Mozaffar al-Din Shah (r. 1896–1906) ascended to the throne, Taj's wedding festivities were celebrated—having been arranged three years previously for the political and economic benefits that would accrue.

Siobhan Lambert-Hurley prepared the introduction and worked with Sunil Sharma to prepare the extracts and annotations from Anna Vanzan and Amin Neshati's translation.

Figure 37.1 Taj al-Saltanah, attributed to the stu-
dio of Monsieur Roussie-Khan in Tehran, 1909.
From Women's Worlds in Qajar Iran, http://
www.qajarwomen.org/en/items/15155A10.html.

The chosen husband, Hasan, belonged to an established military family; his father, Mohammad Baqer Khan Sardar Akram, was at the time head of the royal
guards. The latter is introduced in less-than-exemplary terms in the first extract
for appropriating Taj's substantial royal pension. That the couple were roughly
the same age—around thirteen years old—and not separated by decades suggests changing norms in Iran's royal household around this time. However, the
marriage was clearly not a happy one. In the first extract, on the family's move
to Azerbaijan around 1900, Hasan's proclivities for violence, infidelity, animals
(including, oddly, mules), and lavish expenditure are revealed—as is the author's
own willingness to seek comfort elsewhere. Though Taj bore four children, her
husband's venereal disease may have contributed to miscarriage, birth defects,
and infant death.

Also threatening the family's health and, in turn, inspiring travel documented
in the second extract was a cholera epidemic around 1904. This and the third
extract, narrating a pilgrimage to the shrine of Fatima Ma'suma at Qom soon
after, point to how, for women in Qajar Iran, travel was most often undertaken

within the bounds of the Persian Empire. During Naser al-Din's time, a ban had been maintained on European travel except for diplomacy to discourage liberal dissent. The shah himself undertook three separate journeys to Europe (in 1873, 1878, and 1889), during which he kept travel diaries that became available in print. These publications would have allowed royal women like Taj to visit Europe vicariously through his simple, if rather dry, prose. Only one of his many wives was ever permitted to accompany him on these journeys—and even then, in complete concealment to receive medical treatment. Mozaffar al-Din Shah followed his father's footsteps in making three trips to Europe (in 1900, 1902, and 1905), of which the first receives mention in the extracts here. Taj's willingness to mock the tedium of her brother's European diary elsewhere in her memoir suggests his travel writing could not have provided a model for her own imaginative and frank prose. At the same time, her emphasis on the difficulties and strains of travel evokes older models of Persianate travel writing.

Literate in French as well as Persian by her twenties—and thus able to access foreign news and literature—Taj was clearly well-informed about Europe and North America, including women's activism there. Indeed, in her memoir she expressed her desire to "travel to Europe and meet those freedom-seeking ladies!" Her purpose, she explained, would be to draw their attention to the "continent of Asia" where, behind high walls, women languished as "a mass of oppressed cripples" caught in the "chains of captivity and the resistless weight of subjugation." Her commitment to addressing women's grievances linked, in particular, to veiling, education, work, and arranged marriage led her to participate much later, in the late 1910s, in the founding of the Anjoman-e Horriyat-e Nesvan (Society for the Emancipation of Women). There is no indication, however, that she ever fulfilled her desire for European travel. Instead, Taj's sister, Eftekhar al-Saltanah was one of the first elite Persian women to tour Europe in 1911.

The selections here point to the revealing quality of Taj's memoir. As Abbas Amanat, editor of the English translation from which these extracts are taken, observes, "she narrates the story of her life with the lucidity of an intimate conversation" reflecting the "candid language of the womenfolk." Not only does she write about her husband's shortcomings, their financial instability, and the failures of the Qajar regime and the brutality of death, as seen in the passages here, but subsequently she also narrates the breakdown of her marriage. By 1906, the couple had separated, with Taj using the sale of her jewelry to fund what she called a "liberated life." Contemporary descriptions corroborate her own account of an unveiled princess living lavishly without male guardianship, but certainly not without male company, in a sumptuous villa frequented by poets, musicians, and a dissolute nobility. By the time she finished penning her life story, she may have been experiencing a personal and religious crisis that even led her to attempt suicide. But still she kept sight of her longing to travel with the mantra "The world is not confined to Tehran!"

EXTRACTS

Moving to Azerbaijan

Prior to [my brother Mozaffar al-Din Shah's first] European trip [in 1900], my father-in-law was appointed officer of finances to Azerbaijan, where the crown prince [Mohammad Ali Shah] lived; as he left for his post, he took me along. Before setting out, however, something farcical happened. Two months after I was married, my father-in-law said to me, "Why not put me in charge of your finances? I will manage them for you and hand them over whenever you ask." I had agreed, thinking that I would thereby have some savings. For two or three years, he had received my income. On the day that we were due to depart for Azerbaijan, Sayyid Ebrahim, the silk merchant who had outfitted me for the past couple of years, came to me and said, "You owe me two thousand eight hundred *tomans*. Unless you pay, I won't let you go." I sent a message to my father-in-law: "What is this sayyid saying? Have I been responsible for my own expenses all this time?"

He replied, "I took a princess for a daughter-in-law so that she would manage her own expenses."

"Very well," I said. "If you hand over all my money which is in your keeping, totaling nine thousand *tomans*, I'll pay the sayyid his money."

He replied, "I don't have any money of yours."

I complained to my mother about the situation. Her talking to him, however, proved to no avail, and it became apparent that he intended to keep my money. My mother agreed to pay my debt to the sayyid, and I left her in charge of my income.

In view of this problem and a thousand other family vexations, I was unwilling to go on this trip, but my mother forced me. My grandfather came along to take over governorship of Orumiyya. The journey was very unpleasant and difficult; everyone was hostile and unfriendly to one another. Poor me! Fallen amidst this band of travelers, friendless, alone, and heartsick, I could hardly draw an easy breath. My one son having died, I now had two daughters, who were the only joy of my life. After traveling for a month, we arrived in Azarbaijan, and I was freed from the hardships of the trip and the sight of insincere faces.

My house was apart and at a great distance from that of my father-in-law, who was now Amir Nezam.[1] The crown prince and [his wife] Malekeh-ye Jahan were very kind to me, but my inner turmoil kept me from outdoor activity. Grief-stricken and melancholy, I spent most of my time alone. My husband was the commander of the armed forces in Azarbaijan and should have sought to benefit from his new job. But he had discovered an intense zeal for collecting horses and mules; in short time, he had amassed ten mules at government expense. All his own income went into the purchase of straw and barley. Another activity that he was inordinately fond of was beating people. Every day he would beat up a few people, then give them new clothes. This was repeated every day. Sometimes this commander of the troops, with all the dignity and stateliness that went with his rank, was reduced to a sergeant's uniform. When he gave that away as well, he perforce had to stay home for a couple of days until he got his new clothes.

This beloved husband of mine was a devotee of the god of hedonism. He derived enormous pleasure from being with simple youths. There was a dancer named Tayhu, almost twenty years old; my husband was beside himself, enthralled by this dancer, on whom he spent a fortune.[2] I no longer turned to my father-in-law for any favors, having seen how base and niggardly he was. My husband was engrossed in his pleasures and his collection of mules. So I was left with no recourse but to sell my jewelry in order to provide for my expenses. The chief goldsmith bought everything very cheaply. Quietly, I was managing my own finances.

In this land of strangers, my sole companion and friend was an Armenian girl named Anna, and her story follows.

She was eighteen years old, pretty, with beautiful dark eyes, and made her living as a seamstress. A month after we arrived, when I needed to have a new dress made, this girl was sent for. Little by little, I became close to her. She bore an equally sincere love for me and was often in my house. In the corners of her large, dark eyes, there were often teardrops that sparkled like diamonds. With a pleasant voice she would say, "I love you!" Her voice penetrated to the core of my being, and I listened for it with eagerness. . . .

During my stay in Tabriz, I was constantly preoccupied and weary. It was also here that God bestowed a son on me, at which my delight was boundless. I loved my children very much, spending my time on nothing and nobody else.

Sometime later we got news of the Shah's return from Europe. It was decided that Amir Nezam would go to Tehran to receive him and arrange for me to go separately. I was delighted to hear this, for I would be leaving behind my life of loneliness in a strange land and returning home. We set out for the capital. My husband, having quarreled with his father, joined me on the trip, which proved to be very difficult. My dear friend and charming traveling companion, Amir Nezam's wife, heard of someone's death whom she loved very much. This much-loved friend was one of her servants who tutored her sons. Her husband had sensed her love for the servant, whom he sent on a mission, dispatching another servant to kill him. As a result, the young man was murdered after we had departed. His daughter met us along the way and filled our desert lives with sorrow and regret.

I was overjoyed to arrive in Tehran and see my relatives. This joy, however, proved to be short-lived. My husband went to receive the monarch via Qazvin, and I was left alone in Tehran. His time away lasted six months because, after passing through Rasht to join the royal reception, he was taken to Azarbaijan by his father. After some time he sent for me, but I refused to go. After my father-in-law's family had left Tehran to join him, he sent my husband back.

Escaping Cholera

Summer came, and we moved to our summer resort. Before our departure, the death of the Imam Jum'a, my sister's husband, had stirred a minor scare among the people. It was said he had died of cholera. However, not one in hundred paid heed. In order to hearten themselves, people refused to believe it. Two or three others died in a similar fashion. Still, people were not wary enough of the disease. In the summer it assumed major proportions, and it became clear there was an epidemic. Between eighty and a hundred people died every day. Two months into the summer, I was still unaware of it, because all references to the subject had been forbidden in the vicinity of the Sahebqaraniyya, lest the shah should be afraid. Once it intensified, we learned of it. I was terribly anxious and panic-stricken, not for myself—having never feared death from the time I was a child—but for my relatives and children. Summoning the family physician, I asked him, "Where can we go to get away from this disease?"

He replied, "Stay right here and don't leave the house at all. Be very careful of your health and watch your food and water."

After the physician had left, we, husband and wife, were so terrified we could not remain at home. Unmindful of the fact that heat and travel would increase chances of contamination, we decided to go to Posht-e Kuh.[3] Forming a large caravan with others, we set out from Shemiran [just north of Tehran]. Our traveling companions—men, women, and children—numbered eighty-six. Our first two stops were very pleasant. But for the remainder of the trip, we saw sick and dead people everywhere. Most of the contaminated ones had been thrown out of the villages, and these unfortunates were suffering the agonies of death under the hot sun.

The man who had taught me as a child, and who now taught my children, went with us. Despite all this poor man's insistence that we go back, we persisted in moving on. At every stop we made, the disease had ravaged the area like a tongue of fire. One morning I woke up to find that all our fellow travelers had fled. The only ones left were my husband, me, and the women and children. The women too were setting off into the desert. On asking, we found out that the bodies of the dead were washed for burial in the very same river on whose bank we had camped. From a very little, ramshackle village nearby, ten or twelve dead were carried away that night, which is why our companions had fled in terror.

With infinite care we gathered everyone together and decided to go back. We departed at once. That night, at our next stop, one of our servants who had caught the disease died in a matter of minutes. He died so quickly that the doctor who was with us did not have the time to give the poor youth any medicine. When we awoke the next day, the desert was wrapped in stillness. Not a sound could be heard, except a plaintive, pitiful moaning from the unfortunate youth's mother. The color fled from our faces, and we began to succumb to a ghastly terror and a sense of absolute despair. The poor young victim was laid in a tent near a large stream. I was overcome with horror but realized that, if I betrayed the slightest fear, all my companions would run away and I would be lost in the desert. Quickly I began to talk, threatening some of the travelers and comforting the others, and we set off. . . .

Traveling with speed, we returned to our residential garden. There also we found that two of the people left behind had died: a very handsome, strapping young Caucasian who had been my husband's coachman, and a poor, unknown Turkish soldier. All the people had resigned themselves to their fate, living in imminent expectation of death. The shah lived in the Sahebqaraniyya, terribly rattled. All traffic around the royal mansion, even in the village, was forbidden. . . . Persia was an unremitting graveyard and her people the dead. . . .

In any case, that sweltering summer was ushered out, leaving several thousand dead in its wake. In a month or two, everyone returned to his former condition and resumed his prior activities. It is a noteworthy aspect of the Persian character to suddenly take up a pursuit for a while and follow it to its extremity. But by the same token, as quickly as they erupt, Persians are liable to simmer down and forget. Everything about them is superficial, impromptu, and lacking a sound foundation. I swear to you that between morning and bedtime, every Persian spins dreams of the common weal; the profitable business ventures he will launch; the fallow, despoiled lands he will make fertile and prosperous; the beautiful aqueducts he will construct. But these are all dreams with no basis in reality. Europeans say, "There are two people who are never capable of accomplishing any work: he who thinks too much and he who thinks not at all." When our ideas prove futile, we comfort ourselves with the thought that God is great, that the Lord of the Age himself will come to our aid.

Having been assured that the epidemic had ended, we came into the city, which we found ravaged and its people utterly transformed. Though this epidemic was a sign of divine wrath and chastisement, we can still say that it was engendered by an inattention to hygiene and the contamination of the water. Every government's first duty is to see to the cleanliness of the streets and the water, as well as the tranquility of the people. There was a municipality in name, but, like other arms of the government, none in actual fact—and yet the employees felt entitled to their undeserved salaries. Throughout the year in Persia, and particularly in Tehran, several fatal, infectious diseases rage because of unhygienic conditions. The streets are all filthy—in winter covered in mud and sludge, and in the summer dusty and dirt-encrusted. The watercourses are open, and the filth from the houses is washed away into them. This water circulates through the town, and people drink it and fall prey to all manner of maladies. . . . If every resident of Tehran kept only the doorway to his house clean and saw to the cleanliness of his own street, undoubtedly the number of fatalities would be reduced by half each year.

Pilgrimage to Qom

Two or three months after his return from Shemiran, the shah departed on a pilgrimage to the shrine of Ma'suma.[4] In thanksgiving for our health and deliverance during that frightful year, we accompanied him. We hired an omnibus for twelve, formed a little caravan, and set out. My husband, a doctor, and a renowned musician traveled with us in a separate carriage. A wagon carried the servants and supplies; another brought our baggage and belongings. We rode in the omnibus. Although traveling in Persia is never without its fair share of hardship and terror, we enjoyed ourselves on the road. We stayed at the shrine of Ma'suma for ten days before going back. Nothing new happened on this trip for me to report, other than pilgrimage and sightseeing. I tended to participate very little in either of these activities, because I had to walk through a graveyard. Inevitably, every time I stepped outside, I saw many corpses being buried—corpses with ghastly faces and hideous figures.

This trip was a very humbling experience. Seeing the corpses—the way all of us would end up—was a great lesson for me and held in check my youthful pride, my vivacity and self-centeredness. Although like the rest of humanity, I am forgetful, and the vivid impressions from this trip did not leave any lasting results, yet now that several years have passed, I shudder as I write this, as if I can see our end with my eyes.

These corpses were laid in coffins, wrapped in felt, brought there by mule from faraway places. At every stop, when the mules were to be rested or fed, the ropes were untied, and the two coffins came crashing down to the ground, mangling the corpses. By the time they reached the shrine of Ma'suma, the coffins were in pieces, the shrouds ripped to shreds, and the corpses' heads and limbs broken. Then the corpses were carried around the shrine in circumambulation and brought to the graveyard. There were so many corpses piled atop one another in the graves that there were no room for others. So they had to open other graves and lay the new corpse on the others and cover them all with a little dirt. When graves were reopened, the corpses appeared in varying degrees of decay: on some the flesh had rotted away and turned black, on others a part of it had separated from the bones while the rest hung loosely. Such eerie shapes, such horrid faces! May God preserve us all from such sights! Severed hands, severed legs, wild and disordered hair that had fallen, rotting shrouds.

Oh, my teacher! Oblivious to such an end, what lofty hopes we cherish, what unbearable suffering we inflict on our own kind, what corrupt deeds and intrigues we devise to destroy the good fortune of someone we consider happy! What agonies of greed and avarice we suffer night and day! Oh, alas! Negligence, man's greatest enemy, is closer to him than any friend. . . .

As much as I had enjoyed the trip out, I had a miserable time going back, haunted by thoughts of despair. Not a day passed without my sighing fifty times and my eyes tearing up, as I thought of man's helpless plight. From then on, I renounced my haughtiness and ostentation, and my aristocratic pride abated. Although I nursed an extreme fear of death, there never passed a day but that I longed for it. In order to win a measure of release from my various tiresome, oppressing occupations, I hung my head down in thought most of the time.

FURTHER READING

Taj al-Saltana. *Crowning Anguish: Memoirs of a Persian Princess from the Harem to Modernity, 1884–1914.* Edited by Abbas Amanat, translated by Anna Vanzan and Amin Neshati. Washington, DC: Mage, 2003. The selections here may be found on pp. 267–74, 278–83, 294–301.

S. Mahdavi. "Taj al-Saltanah, an Emancipated Qajar Princess." *Middle Eastern Studies* 23 (1987): 188–93.

Afsaneh Najmabadi. "A Different Voice: Taj os-Saltaneh." In *Women's Autobiographies in Contemporary Iran,* edited by A. Najmabadi, 17–31. Cambridge, MA: Center for Middle Eastern Studies, Harvard University, 1990.

James W. Redhouse. *The Diary of H. M. the Shah of Persia during His Tour through Europe in A.D. 1873*. London: John Murray, 1874. This is a contemporary translation of Naser al-Din Shah's *Ruznameh-ye Safar-e Farangistan*. https://archive.org/details /diaryofhmshahofpoonasiuoft/page/n12.

Naghmeh Sohrabi. *Taken for Wonder: Nineteenth Century Travel Accounts from Iran to Europe*. New York: Oxford University Press, 2012.

NOTES

1. A highly responsible post within the Qajar regime that seems to have involved supervising military and administrative affairs in Azerbaijan, where the crown prince and his retinue also resided.

2. It may be clarified that Tayhu was a male lover. From Taj's account, Hasan emerges as bisexual, enjoying first female and later male partners.

3. Posht-e Kuh, literally "behind the mountain," was a tribal area near Iran's coast.

4. The shrine of Fatema Ma'suma is located in Iran's sacred city of Qom. It is dedicated to a female saint celebrated as the sister of the eighth Twelver Shia imam Reza and the daughter of the seventh Twelver Shia imam Musa al-Kadhim.

THIRTY-EIGHT

ROKEYA SAKHAWAT HOSSAIN

A Pleasure Trip to the Himalaya

INTRODUCTION

Rokeya Sakhawat Hossain (sometimes Hossein), or Begum Rokeya (1880–1932), is celebrated as a path-breaking feminist writer and educationist from eastern India. As the founder of several girls' schools in Bihar and Bengal and an author of an impressive body of prose fiction, poetry, and essays, Begum Rokeya became a highly visible activist for the education of women and their greater representation in the public sphere. She is perhaps best known for founding the Sakhawat Memorial Girls School in Bhagalpur and, in 1911, its equivalent in Calcutta. Later, she acquired donations from authorities as famous as the Agha Khan, founded associations, participated and spoke at public meetings, and lectured on topics connected with women's education and role in Indian society. These activities enabled her to assume an important role in the public representation of Muslim women and women in general. Hers has been the most prominent voice among first-generation Bengali feminists, and her works remain popular with general readers and scholars to this day. The short Bengali-language travel article included here, entitled "Kupamanduker Himalaydarshan" (A Frog in a Well Seeing the Himalaya), is less known.

Born in a village in Rangpur in northern Bengal (today's northwestern Bangladesh) and brought to Calcutta by her mother, Rahatunnessa Sabera Chowdhurani, early in her life, Begum Rokeya experienced the excesses of female seclusion firsthand. Neither her mother nor her father, Zahiruddin Mohammad Abu Ali Saber, a large landholder (zamindar), sanctioned her interest in Bengali

Hans Harder prepared the introduction and translation from Bengali.

Figure 38.1 Rokeya Sakhawat Hossain with her
husband, ca. 1898. From Wikipedia Commons.

or English, and she was not sent to school outside the home, like her two brothers. Instead, she relied first on the help of her elder sister Karimunnessa and
then her eldest brother Ibrahim to educate herself. At the age of sixteen, she
was married to a much older widower, Syed Sakhawat Hossain, then in his late
thirties (see fig. 38.1). He was a civil servant educated in India and England, and
he was liberal-minded and supportive of her struggle for female emancipation.
He is almost certain to be the unnamed companion referred to by the occasional
"we" in the text translated here.

Begum Rokeya herself credited her husband for encouraging her to write and
publish. Her literary output is overwhelmingly in Bengali. But her most famous
piece in Bengal and beyond—in part because it is one of the very few texts she
wrote originally in English—is "Sultana's Dream" (1905). In this short story,
Begum Rokeya describes a feminist utopia in which men have been put into
purdah, while women run the country efficiently and peacefully with the help
of advanced technology. Sunlight is processed into mighty weaponry to ward
off enemies, and flying carriages are used for transportation.

The piece here, "Kupamanduker Himalaydarshan," predates "Sultana's Dream"
by a year and was one of a number of early articles published by Begum Rokeya in
Calcutta-based journals in 1903–4. The first of a handful of travel accounts by the

author, it describes a leisure trip to Kurseong in the eastern Himalaya with her husband. The specific periodical for this output was the very one mentioned in the text itself: *Mahila* (*Lady*). This magazine was one of around a dozen Bengali women's periodicals that appeared mostly from Calcutta in the colonial period. While there were already female editors and even a periodical entirely prepared by women for women (*Antahpur*), *Mahila* was brought out by two male editors, Girishchandra Sen and Brajagopal Niyogi, between 1897 and 1915 with the aim to educate women morally and spiritually. The article appeared in a section of this magazine called *Mahilar rachana,* or "works by women"—a rubric introduced by the earliest Bengali women's periodical *Bamabodhini patrika* in 1863 and common in many early Bengali women's journals until the beginning of the twentieth century. Such textual segregation clearly signals that at that time, the majority of those who contributed to women's periodicals were still male. Begum Rokeya's text is also included in her collected works. Interestingly, it is not the only testimony of her travels in the Himalaya, for she had already published two poems, both titled "Kanchanjangha," the same year.

Other travel accounts by Begum Rokeya appeared decades later and do not fit into the category of travelogue as neatly as this one. One is a short hajj account called "Hajjver maydane" (On the Hajj Field, 1931) that says nothing about her own experiences but schematically reports on the various elements the pilgrimage to Mecca entails. The other, "Bayuyane panchash mail" (Fifty Miles in an Airplane), depicts a flight in 1930 that she published in 1932. Interestingly, it bears the subtitle "Saphal svapna" (A Dream Fulfilled) that refers directly to the feminist utopia she had written more than twenty-five years previously. Aviation, she claims, was a thing entirely imagined and unknown to her in 1905 when she wrote "Sultana's Dream," and the actual experience of flying around Calcutta for half an hour in late 1930 utterly electrified her.

In all of these travel texts, we encounter Begum Rokeya as a sensitive writer and privileged individual. She seems to recall her travels in a spirit of gratitude, but also with a full consciousness of (and a certain pride in) being privileged. To connect these texts with her general thoughts on women's role in society, we only need to think of her famous writings in the volume *Abarodhbasini* (*The Secluded Ones*, 1931). As noted in this volume's introduction, a number of these essays speak in drastic terms about the extremely denigrating conditions in which women were moved from one place to another when the circumstances made it unavoidable. They thus provide the reader with quite a different perspective on women's, and particularly Muslim women's, mobility in eastern India. Customs and fear of social visibility literally suffocated them so much that mobility, or rather being moved around, became at times a threat to their health and even lives. It is against the background of such circumstances that Begum Rokeya's travels gain an additional nimbus of personal liberation with the image of the "frog in the well" attaining its immediate relevance.

It is interesting to note that this text, which is otherwise entirely scripted in Bengali letters—including a concluding indication of place and month of composition (Kurseong, *Ashvin*)—is signed in Roman script as "(Mrs.) R S Hossein." This use of two scripts in a single text is very uncommon in the women's writing section of *Mahila* and awaits explanation. Beyond this, "Kupamanduker Himalaydarshan" is translated in its entirety here. We thus have Begum Rokeya's full commentary on Bhutanese women's dress and workload, her reflections on civilization and purdah, her remarks on Himalayan landscape and fauna, and her invocations of God as the Creator of such beauty. Even though the last line may seem to announce a sequel, the text was apparently never continued and is complete as it is.

EXTRACTS

A Frog in a Well Seeing the Himalaya

Now we are in the Himalayas. An old wish fulfilled: I have seen the mountains. The Himalayas may be nothing new for our female readers, but for me it was an entirely novel experience. My desire to see the Himalayas had been awakened by reading in books about its lakes, mountains, springs, and so on. With a silent sigh, I used to think that it would be impossible for me to see all that. What increased my pain was the thought that people from faraway Europe visit our Himalayas, but we do not get to see it! But finally, by the grace of God, we have also seen the Himalayas.

Traveling on time, we reached Siliguri Station. The Himalayan Rail Road starts from Siliguri. The eastern Bengal trains are smaller than the East India trains, and the Himalayan train is even smaller than the former. These small trains are as beautiful as toy trains. And the wagons are very low, so much so that the passengers, if they like, can effortlessly get on and off while the train is in motion.

Our train went upward very slowly, covering a long, winding path. The wagons made rumbling sounds as they loop south or north again. There were amazing sights on both sides of the rails: in some places deep lowlands, in others extremely steep summits, and in yet others dense forests.

At times I saw refreshment rooms and stations. There was a ladies' waiting room in almost all those places. The rooms were well furnished. Our European cotraveling sisters got off at most stations to take rest. In the waiting rooms, there were many vessels for washing one's face, and four ladies could wash their hands and faces at the same time. Whether the ladies bring luggage with them or not, they most certainly have with them a comb, a brush, and powder. Bengali women do not manage to order their thick hair in such a short time! But however that may be, the diligence of the European sisters is most laudable. In the waiting rooms, there are ayahs from Bhutan.

Gradually we have come up to three thousand feet above sea level. There is no cold yet, but we have moved through the clouds! I suddenly began to mistake the clean white fog in the deep valley for a river. The trees, creepers, grass, and leaves—all are amazing. Such big grass I have never seen before. Even the green tea fields have enhanced the natural beauty a hundred times. The lines and rows of bushes look very beautiful from afar. The occasional narrow walking path look like a parting on the head of the earth! The dense, dark green woods are the thick hair of the earth, and the paths her bending part.

Many waterfalls or springs came into view while on the railroad. Their beauty is beyond description. They emerge from somewhere with incredible speed and disappear elsewhere, constantly splitting the stony heart of the snowy mountains. Who would believe that one of these is the source of the mighty Ganges? The train stopped by a large creek, and we thought it did so that we might behold the water stream to our hearts' content. (In reality, however, the real reason was something else: the water was exchanged there.) But for whatever reason, the train stopped and our hearts' desire was fulfilled.

Now we have ascended to four thousand feet. I don't feel cold yet, but I was released from the terror of the heat that had by then almost exhausted our life-breath. A light wind was blowing smoothly. Here, at 4,120 feet's height, is Maha-nadi Station. I couldn't read the station's name very well, but from what I saw it seems to be Mahanadi indeed. However, if the name of the station is erroneous, it is not my fault but that of the distance between my wagon and the station!

Finally we arrived at Kurseong Station, at a height of 4,864 feet. Upon seeing the crowd at the station, I sat down for a while in the ladies' waiting room and watched the face-washing and hairdressing of the European sisters. One had a little boy with her. She ordered the ayah to wash his face and got on the train. The ayah cared little about making the boy wash his face. She wiped the boy's face with the lady's leftover towel and ran to the train approximately ten seconds later. This is what happens when you rely on servants. It became less crowded when the train left, so we left the waiting room.

Our place was not far from the station, so we got there quickly. Some of our trunks had erroneously been booked to Darjeeling. We arrived (before dark), but lacking our things, we couldn't make ourselves quite at home. Our trunks came back with the evening train. Before we could go to Darjeeling ourselves, our belongings had succeeded in breathing in its air! From the very next day, we felt absolutely at home. Therefore I say that it isn't enough to find refuge in order to feel at home; you also need the necessary furniture and equipment!

Here it hasn't yet started to get cold, but it isn't warm either. How about calling this the mountainous springtime? The sun rays are very sharp. Since we came, it has only once rained a little. The air is very healthy, though the water is reportedly not good. We filter our drinking water. But the water looks very clear and clean. There are no wells, nor rivers or ponds—it is genuine spring water. Looking at the pure cool water soothes the eyes, its touch soothes the hands, and the cool air or thick fog all around it soothe the heart!

The air here is clean and light. Watching the hide and seek of wind and cloud is fabulous! At one moment the cloud is on one side, then the wind comes from the other and drives the cloud away. Every day the setting sun creates a kingdom of amazing beauty with the wind and the clouds. Liquid gold is poured on the mountains in the western sky. Thereafter many youthful clouds smear gold on their bodies and start running from here to there with the wind. Looking at their spectacle, I pass my time; I lose myself and cannot do anything else.

I remember that I once read in *Mahila* magazine about [a particular type of] fern. I had taken this fern for some tiny shrub. It was only from a geology book that I had learned that in the carboniferous age, there were huge fern trees. Now I saw these fern trees with my own eyes. I was full of joy. I broke a branch and measured it to be twelve feet long. The whole tree would be twenty to twenty-five feet high.

In some places the woods are very dense. The good thing is that there are no tigers, so you can walk around without fear. We love it to stroll around on lonely, wild paths. There are snakes and leeches. So far we haven't come across any snakes, and leeches have sucked our blood only two or three times.

The women of this place are not afraid of leeches. Bhalu, our servant from Bhutan, says: "What harm do leeches do? When they have sucked enough blood they go away by themselves." The Bhutanese women wear a seven-yard-long piece of cloth like a skirt. Another piece of cloth is bound around the waist, which they top with a jacket and cover the head with a foreign shawl. They climb some stony, disheveled path with one or two *maunds* [i.e., roughly 37–74 kg] of load on their backs without hesitation, and walk down again the same way! With this weight they playfully walk up a path, the sight of which makes all our courage disappear!

The editor of the *Mahila* magazine once wrote about us that "the female sex is weak, therefore they are called *abala*, those without strength." I ask whether these Bhutanese women are also a part of this weak sex. They do not depend on men for their food but earn it themselves. I even see more women than men carrying stones: the men don't carry more than they do! The *abalas*, those without strength, carry stones away. The *sabals*, those with strength, spread the stones on the path to build streets, and both boys and girls join in this work. So "those with strength" here seem to include both boys and girls.

The Bhutanese women introduce themselves as *paharni*, or mountain women, and they call us *niche ka admi*, people from below. As if, in their opinion, the "people from below" were uncivilized! They are by nature diligent, fond of work, courageous, and sincere. But living in touch with the "people from below," they are by and by losing their virtues. They learn faults like stealing little amounts of money in the market, mixing water into the milk, etc. They even marry "people from below"! In this way they are getting mixed with various peoples.

Many don't understand how one can travel to different countries while observing the purdah system ordained by the Muslim scriptures. So they feel in danger when they have to leave the house to go somewhere. The current purdah system is harsher even than the few strict rules concerning purdah in the scriptures! However, if you just obey the scriptures, you don't face too many difficulties. In my view, the one who considers brothers and sisters the same is the true guardian of purdah.

Almost a mile away from our habitation flows a huge creek; one can see that water stream with its milky foam from here. Hearing the song of its waves day and night, the intensity of devotion to God flows twice or thrice as much. Why, I ask, doesn't the heart too, like this creek, flow and fall below the feet of the highest Lord?

What else shall I say? Here in the mountains, I am extremely happy and grateful to God. I have seen a humble sample of the ocean, that is, the Bay of Bengal; what remained to be seen was a sample of the mountains. Now this wish has also been fulfilled.

But no, it hasn't been fulfilled, for the more I see, the more my thirst for seeing grows! But God has given me only two eyes; how much can I see with them? Why hasn't He given me many eyes? I am not able to express in words all that I see and think!

Each high summit, each creek first seems to say, "Look at me, look at me!" When I behold it with eyes wide open from astonishment, they seem to smile and say with a frown, "Are you looking at *me*? Remember my Creator!" They are right. Looking at a painting, one can understand the skill of the painter. Or does anybody know anyone only by name? How huge, how extended, how great are these foothills of the Himalayas for us! And how humble is the Himalayas' place in the world created by that Great Artist! Even calling it a grain of sand would make it too big!

Does it now amount to treason if we don't sing the praise of the Creator's qualities with these beautiful eyes, ears, and this mind of ours? Only if we worship with our mind, brain, and heart do we attain satisfaction. Worship is not achieved, in my opinion at least, by just pronouncing some words that one has learnt by heart like a parrot. Where is the heart's emotion in such worship? Where is the enthusiasm? When looking at the beauty of nature, mind and heart break out in unison, "Only God is worthy of praise! Only He is laudable!" Then there is no need to voice all these words.

"A Frog in a Well Seeing the Himalaya" is today herewith concluded.

FURTHER READINGS

R. S. Hossein. "Kupamanduker himalaydarshan." *Mahila* 10, no. 4 (Karttik 1311 BE/1904): 108–12. See *Begum Rokeya rachana samagra*, edited by Tapan Rudra (Dhaka: Salma Book Depot, 2007), 277–79, for a recent reprint of the original journal article.

Roushan Jahan and Hanna Papanek, eds. *Sultana's Dream: A Feminist Utopia, and Selections from* The Secluded Ones. New York: Feminist, 1988.

Mohammad A. Quayum, ed. and trans. *The Essential Rokeya: Selected Works of Rokeya Sakhawat Hossain (1880–1932)*. Leiden: Brill, 2013.

Barnita Bagchi. "Towards Ladyland: Rokeya Sakhawat Hossain and the Movement for Women's Education in Bengal, c. 1900–c. 1932." *Paedagogica Historica* 45, no. 6 (2009): 743–55.

Barnita Bagchi. "Ramabai and Rokeya: The History of Gendered Social Capital in India." In *Women, Education, and Agency, 1600–2000*, edited by Jean Spence, Sarah Aiston, and Maureen M. Meikle, 66–82. London: Routledge, 2010.

Barnita Bagchi. *The Politics of the (Im)possible: Utopia and Dystopia Reconsidered*. Thousand Oaks, CA: Sage, 2012.

Sonia Nishat Amin. *The World of Muslim Women in Colonial Bengal 1876–1939*. Leiden: Brill, 1996.

NAZLI BEGUM

On Grand Tour with the Nawab of Janjira

INTRODUCTION

H. H. Nazli Rafia Sultan Nawab Begum Sahiba (1874–1968) derived her status from her husband, Sidi Ahmad Khan Sidi Ibrahim Khan. He was the ruler of a small princely state on India's west coast, usually known as Janjira but also as Jazira or Habshan. Born in Istanbul, Nazli was the second daughter (of three girls and four boys) of an Indian merchant, Hasanally Feyzhyder, and his first wife (of two), Amirunissa. They belonged to the prominent Tyabji clan associated with Muslim reformism and Indian nationalism that was at the forefront of Bombay's Sulaimani Bohra community by the early twentieth century. Though Nazli's father remained in Istanbul until his death, her mother returned to Bombay with her children to live among her extended family (among whom were several travelers featured in this collection, including Shareefah Hamid Ali and Safia Jabir Ali). In Bombay, Nazli was educated alongside her sisters and cousins at a local convent school while also receiving supplementary tutoring at home in Urdu, Persian, and the Quran. Nazli's education and good looks appear to have attracted the attention of Bombay's colonial governor, Lord Reay, who made the suggestion of an unorthodox match with the Janjira royals. The nawab, then in his early twenties, had already taken a bride from another Sunni Muslim princely state, but she had died without issue after just three years of marriage. In 1886, Nazli became his new queen at just twelve years old. Their marriage lasted until 1913, when the childless Nazli was separated from the nawab after he took a third wife in the hopes of bearing an heir.

Sunil Sharma prepared the translations from Urdu; Siobhan Lambert-Hurley prepared the introduction and annotations.

Figure 39.1 Nazli Begum with her husband,
the nawab of Janjira, in London, 1908.
© Chris Hellier / Alamy Stock Photo.

As well as playing a key role in Janjira's administration, Nazli was a patron of
Muslim education and a participant in some of the earliest women's organizations in India, alongside her sisters Atiya and Zehra Fyzee (the former is also
featured in this collection). Notable was her presidency of the Bharat Stree Ma-
hamandal (the Large Circle of Indian Women) at its first session in Allahabad
in 1910, as well as her attendance at the inaugural Anjuman-i Khavatin-i Islam
(or All-India Muslim Ladies' Conference) in Aligarh in 1914 and the All India
Ladies' Association in Bhopal in 1918. These occasions and others offered Nazli
opportunities to travel within India, usually without her husband, though often
with her sisters. In 1908, she came out of purdah to undertake a formal tour of
Britain, Europe, and the Ottoman Empire with the nawab (see fig. 39.1), during
which they were received by the king-emperor Edward VII and awarded med-
als of honor by the Turkish sultan Abdülhamid II. On their six-month journey,
the Janjira royals were accompanied by Nazli's youngest sister, Atiya, and her
brother (or "Bhai"), Ali Asghar, along with two state officials, a doctor, and a servant each. That there were several other princely travelers on their steamship, the

Macedonia, from Bombay to Marseilles points to how fashionable it had become for Indian royalty to spend time in Europe by the first decade of the twentieth century. Later, Nazli traveled to the United States in 1918 and to England for a second time in 1936.

Many princes also documented their journeys in order to affirm their status as modern, sovereign rulers who traveled for learning and improvement. Nazli too kept a record in Urdu of her movements, encounters, and impressions in the form of dated entries resembling a *roznamchah*, or daily diary. The preface to the book version published soon after her return points to how Nazli's travelogue began life as letters to her relatives in India before being published in a Delhi women's magazine, 'Ismat, as serialized entries. Founded in 1908, this magazine routinely carried short or serialized travelogues written by Muslim women visiting other cities in India, the Hijaz, or Europe. That Nazli always intended publication is clear from her references to a future "book" and "readers" from the outset. The "Behen" (sister) to whom she addressed some of her comments must have been Zehra, who, having remained in India, was ultimately responsible for editing the travelogue for publication. Nazli's model seems to have been her sister Atiya's travel diary written just a couple of years before in 1906–7. However, the texts are very different in style, with Nazli's *Sair* displaying a formality in its structure and language not present in the shorter entries in colloquial Urdu in Atiya's *Zamana-i tahsil*, and the use of Persian and Arabic expressions (in italics below).

In the introduction, Nazli introduces her travelogue in terms of its style, content, and approach. Notable in this extract is her internalization of Orientalist perceptions of Asian and Muslim decline, but also her reformist evocation of female education as the antidote. Her stance is tempered in the second extract, in which she expresses her amazement at how the British live so differently in their own country than in colonial India. Clearly, the experience of travel had led Nazli to be more cautious of British values and habits while also encouraging a greater appreciation of Indian culture. Her protonationalism is expressed even more clearly in the third and fourth extracts, in which she recounts a chance encounter with an American tourist at the Paris opera before turning to the embarrassing conduct of Indians in Paris. For this reforming princess, only female education could turn the tide of India's ruination. The two extracts from the Istanbul section of Nazli's narrative reveal, in turn, her disappointment with the facilities, hospitality, and customs that she encountered in the Ottoman Empire just weeks after the Young Turk Revolution. So committed to fulfilling colonial standards of good government in Janjira, she recoiled from the lack of cleanliness in her city of birth that was also meaningful to Indian Muslims as home to the Islamic caliphate. Particularly difficult to fathom was how Turkish women had, in her view, abandoned their culture for European clothes, ways, and manner-isms while remaining so curtailed by "old" restrictions. Perceptions of "center" and "periphery" within the Islamic world are thus shown to be undermined by Nazli's visit to this Muslim "heartland."

EXTRACTS

Introduction to the Text

When I compare Europe and Asia, I am diminished in my own eyes. Sadly, Asia has become the way Europe was a thousand or twelve hundred years ago. For people of this age, it would be wishful thinking for Asia to become equal to Europe, let alone surpass it. Yes, if Asians would provide for female education, then in a hundred or two hundred years, they would catch up. I am so wistful when I see the decline and bad condition of the people of Islam after a deluge of progress and the Noah's flood–like spread of Muslims. Unfortunately, we our-selves don't know who our great Muslim writers were and what they wrote on which subject. One feels endless shame and envy in seeing the libraries of Paris and London. We might protest that we have no money. The reply would be that we appropriated it for ourselves.

English Society in London

June 10, 1908: It is a pity that one cannot do anything here in the morning. Noth-ing opens before eleven o'clock. The shops, etc. are all shut. Therefore, one has to go out after eleven o'clock. After strolling about, it was lunchtime, and we ate somewhere. At teatime we had tea somewhere. Sometimes I like this practice, but at other times it irks me. How can one enjoy eating and drinking and doing everything in public? In England there is an indiscriminate increase in eating out at hotels and such establishments. People are getting fed up with domestic problems and dealing with servants and prefer this way of life. No one has time to run a household. What in English is called "home life" is especially rare in London. But it is found in the countryside. The people of London have become very independent. They send their children to boarding schools and themselves eat and drink in any which way. . . . There are many in India who must have no idea at all about the lifestyle of the nobles of the city here: eating and drinking sumptuously, going to playhouses, and holding parties. They are so busy taking part in festivities and having fun gambling that they don't have a moment's free time. Even then men act wisely, otherwise how could England have become so wealthy and flourishing. . . . It is an excellent practice among the people of

London that anything that is invented to provide comfort is found in every house. An example of this is electric lights. Now they are found in almost all houses, boarding houses, and hotels. . . . The more I travel through developed countries, the more I remember the virtues of my homeland, although it is still in the dark ages and years behind.

A Conversation at the Paris Opera

July 3, 1908: To my left [at the Grand Opera], an elderly American woman was seated. While passing near her, my foot touched hers, and I excused myself. It seems as if she was looking for an opportunity to ask questions. She kept apologizing that she wasn't asking just out of inquisitiveness, but she was very interested in Indians and had a lot of sympathy for them. She enquired about my name, address, religion, nationality, everything, and didn't leave anything unasked. I explained everything and said, "I am a Muslim. Do you know what that is?" She said, "Yes, your God is Confucius (the name of a Chinese sage), isn't he?" I said, "No, no. He is the God of the Chinese. There is not a hair's difference between our God and yours. We worship the same God that you do. Lord Jesus is also our prophet. In the same way, we also accept Moses, David, etc. as prophets." Upon hearing this, there was no end to the questions. Then she asked about Hindus. I answered that there were so many types of Hindus that you cannot imagine. They cannot intermarry or eat each other's food.

Then she asked about India, whether Indians wanted to become independent and under self-rule. Do they approve of democratic rule or not? I answered that this was not their original aim, but when the government kindly enabled them to enjoy the fruits of knowledge, then their eyes were opened, and they now feel that they are capable of doing those things that the British do. And my view is that if the government pays more attention to their rights, the Indians are so poor that they won't rise up. There are certainly many benefits of British rule, but there is also no doubt that the eyes of Indians have been opened. Indian minds are very sharp. With full education and training, they are not inferior to any nation.

Indians in Europe

July 20, 1908: One hears strange stories about Indians. In London, perhaps they show restraint, but in a paradisial place like Paris, they lose control of themselves. It is sad and regretful that they are infected by every kind of Western influence that is very injurious and harmful for their beings. They are forced to come to Europe to acquire knowledge and skills. When it comes to company, if they are fortunate, then they meet good people, otherwise God help them.

The biggest and real cause for this is connected to the education of women. Thinking about the matter on this line, if places of education for women in India were to be built, the thoughts of men wouldn't be scattered to this degree, for the sincere attachment to the home along with good thoughts would bring them back to their homeland. They wouldn't be tempted to fall into any evil. Those parents who think their daughters' education is not a worthy thing are ruining the foundation of India with the thorns they have sown. When a boy returns from Europe under its influence, what does he see in his house? Complete disorder and stark ignorance; then why would his heart be attached to such a home? And how would he blindly feel affection for his own people? It is impossible, rather, it is clear that he becomes more contemptuous and falls into excesses. The parents are ready to cry and also to curse Europe. But they remain ignorant of the real cause of the ruin. Boys from noble families are reduced to nothing and the reason is only the inattention to women's education and nothing else. Each girl who is ruined is the weakening of India's stability, not just the loss of her family. Today Europe is the center of education, and not sending a young man there is also not possible. Then it is better that cultured partners for them are born in India so that his life can pass with propriety and attachment. "*We gave appropriate advice.*" Dear Behen jan, I cannot express how such matters cause sorrow to the heart. May God effect that a better system be there for this. Otherwise in the future, ruination will show an even more horrifying aspect.

First Impressions of Istanbul

August, 31 1908: We are resident in the Palace Hotel in Pera[1] since yesterday. It is the best hotel here. It is so dirty and old, not to speak of the food! The tariff is so high that one wouldn't pay so much in Paris or London. We will certainly have to change hotels. . . . We slept comfortably all night and in the morning set out to see the city. The roads are extremely rough and uneven. Truly, I was so shocked to see the condition of the city. It is astonishing that we are in Europe— or have we come to a five-hundred-year-old dirty town. Alas. Since the time we disembarked at the jetty, there was the hope that better streets and roads would appear ahead, but it was the same condition until the hotel. Today too we saw the same conditions. And on top of everything, the fighting of large dogs is a great problem. When all the trash is thrown on the street, there will naturally be poison and filthiness. If one sits in a carriage, it is so bumpy that God help you. What else can one expect from uneven roads. It is not strange that the new party is upset and seeks constitutional rule.[2] It is quite a trial for a newcomer, especially those who have come from special places or Europe. It is better not to discuss this experience.

We crossed a bridge whose every plank was loose, like the teeth of an old person that are about to fall out. I hear that this bridge is repaired regularly. When one plank becomes loose and falls off, a new one is put in so that people don't fall in the water. Truly I feel like crying. God has bestowed a beauty on it that no other city has the good fortune to possess, but the ignorance of people and their carelessness is worth contemplating.

The citizens here appear big, large-boned, healthy, and strong, as well as handsome. In manners, the influence of France is evident. In some places, the smell of bread and kebabs, and various other delicacies, is very fine. Passing over good and bad streets and lanes, at last we reached the Grand Bazaar. There are some five to six thousand shops there, some small, some big, some not so clean, and others so-so. This bazaar is roofed, and light comes through ventilators. There are scores of winding ways where one has to go around as in a maze. Here too there is no cleanliness. Rare and expensive things are also sold here, although the condition of the shops is nothing at all. We were walking around in a daze. In some places women were walking slowly, huffing and puffing, while some were bargaining with the shopkeepers. Some had their entire family with them; others were lording it alone. The *charshafs* we were wearing are not quite in fashion anymore, but we saw that some form of the *naqab* still survives.[3] Seeing all this, the stories of the Thousand and One Nights came to mind. It is such an interesting and charming country. If the city were a bit cleaner, it would be a wonderfully delightful place.

Meeting Women in Istanbul

September 7, 1908: There is a strange mixture of old and new customs here that our defective intellects cannot comprehend. Today, we went and visited Büyükdere in the carriage. It is about half an hour to forty-five minutes from here, but the town is the same, strange and dull. We were invited somewhere and boarded a launch, because to get to a place, one has to do that on this shore. The sea was rough, and I began to feel sick. The boat was so packed that there was no place to sit. I was standing holding on to a pole. Not one woman felt sorry enough for me to shift and make room for me to sit, but all of them stared pointedly at me and some told their children to come closer and not to look in my direction. As if looking at me would have a bad effect on their children. I am amazed that these women are devoid of normal Muslim hospitality. And the one who felt sorry for me was a God-fearing, kindhearted Greek woman who moved her children to make room for me. I was praying that I wouldn't vomit and become a full spectacle for those women. This happened while going there, but on the return God provided a change—"*After banishment comes joy.*"

While returning, we saw Madam Adham Beg on the boat.[4] . . . She is courageous since she lived in Egypt, where women are very independent-minded, but
she was not willing to be that way here since there is no freedom in Turkey. This
lady is brimming with good taste, education, and has a charming and refined
bearing. Her face is nice too, with kohl in her eyes and curls on her forehead. Her
clothes were completely European. Her charshaf seemed to be part of her clothing, and the portion that was unsuccessfully attempting to cover her head with
pretty pins was cleverly kept in place with a thick naqab, leaving the charming
curls to one side. The only jewelry she wore were small earrings, a pocket watch
chain, and a ring. There was no doubt that it was a smart outfit but completely
European, which was the only displeasing thing. The conversation flowed on
about education, upbringing, customs, and traditions. A discussion was held on
clothing. I told her about the Aligarh and Karachi exhibitions, and Behen jan,
you were mentioned a lot too. She liked the idea of the exhibitions very much.
That's why we said that by doing this, you will help national arts and crafts. Now
that we have freedom, we will definitely make an effort. We spoke a lot about
clothing, and she was very happy seeing that we have maintained our clothes
by modifying them according to the requirements of our own times. If she had
her way, she would modify the old clothing and choose to wear it again. But this
is almost impossible here because even old ladies would hardly remember the
real Turkish clothing. It was given up so long ago that it would be difficult to
find a sample. But it seems that here gentlemen with the most modern thoughts
would not approve of women participating in men's gatherings without any veil.
I also do not approve of this. Rather, it should be that separate gatherings in the
women's quarters be organized to increase closeness and affection, and they find
their own topics which would provide them enjoyment. Then there would be no
need felt to participate in men's gatherings.

Then I told her that we wanted to acquire good Muslim customs from you
people, but we saw such strictness and restriction here that we were stunned.
Then regarding the charshaf also I said that my elder sister Zehra Begum Fyzee
had come here fifteen or seventeen years ago. She approved of it and chose to
wear it, and it was she who made it prevalent in India. Although before this,
perhaps some men had approved of the charshaf and taken it to India, but they
merely collected them and did not make it prevalent. Only exhibition dolls were
dressed in the charshaf as an example and sent here and there. But now hundreds
of women are wearing it. However, the difference between you all and us is that
we wear it to protect our clothes and as a veil, and you all have made it part of
your clothing. Then I said that my elder sister approves of Turkish customs.

In the same way, my respected mother, who has lived in Constantinople, used various small and big objects picked from here. And there are some customs and ways so fixed among us that it seems that no one can distinguish whether they are genuine or not. We are so used to these customs. It is possible that some things of this period, which are still with us, have disappeared from you all due to French influence. . . . Another lady spoke to us too. Both welcomed us and asked how we like Constantinople. We said we liked it very much but that the condition of the city is unfortunate, and I was truly disappointed. These ladies were also respectable.

In the evening, we went to Madam Adham Beg's place, which was decorated completely in European style but not so tastefully. If we didn't know her nationality, we would have been deceived. Uncovered head, short hair, fashionable clothes, manner of speech—everything was like the Europeans. There is no hint of anything Eastern. She did have kohl in her eyes, and her hair was hennaed. Two Greek ladies were sitting there to whom we were introduced. . . . They liked our clothes very much and praised the fact that we have made adjustments while keeping our own. One of the Greek ladies was well informed about the situation in India because she had read a lot about the country. She was very interested in fakirs and kept asking us whether they still performed miracles. We were served tea in the French manner and homemade cake. After a while, her Egyptian sister, who also had the same French style, arrived. I had taken some aloeswood for Madam Adham Beg, but these people don't know about these Eastern things anymore. These people are very desirous of visiting India. I gave them my address, but who knows whether they will be free to travel. If only Turkish women could visit India, it would be so nice. Madam has one son and one daughter who are very sweet. In their room, there was a framed reproduction of a Raphael painting of Mary and Jesus. I was a bit surprised to see this and wondered what its purpose was. But perhaps it was only there for decoration. These people were astonished that we wear jewelry on the feet. We returned having had a good time.

FURTHER READING

H. H. Nazli Rafia Sultan Nawab Begum Sahiba of the State of Jazira. *Sair-i Yurap.* Edited by Zehra Begum Fyzee sahiba. Lahore: Union Steam, 1909?. Individual entries were also published in '*Ismat* (Delhi). A translation of the full text by Sunil Sharma with an introduction by Siobhan Lambert-Hurley is in progress.

S. Fyzee-Rahamin. *Gilded India.* London: Herbert Joseph, 1938.

Siobhan Lambert-Hurley. "Fyzee, Atiya (1877–1967)." *Oxford Dictionary of National Biography.* http://www.oxforddnb.com/index/101102459/Fyzee.

Sunil Sharma. "Delight and Disgust: Gendered Encounters in the Travelogues of the Fyzee Sisters." In *On the Wonders of Land and Sea: Persianate Travel Writing*, edited by Roberta Micallef and Sunil Sharma, 119–31. Boston: Ilex, 2013.

Salima Tyabji. *The Changing World of a Bombay Muslim Community, 1870–1945*. Margao: Cinnamon Teal, 2013.

Daniel Majchrowicz. "Travel, Travel Writing and the 'Means to Victory' in Modern South Asia." Unpublished PhD thesis, Harvard University, 2015. Chapter 3, "Strategy, Legitimacy and Travel Writing in the Princely States."

NOTES

1. Today, the area is called Beyoğlu; often Nazli uses the Greek forms of names of neighborhood that were current then. Notably, Bhopal's princely party had stayed at this same hotel in 1911.

2. The author refers here to the Young Turks who had sought the restoration of the 1876 constitution.

3. The Fyzee sisters had begun wearing an adapted version of the charshaf after Nazli's elder sister, Zehra, had visited Turkey in the early 1890s—which may account for their unfashionable attire.

4. This woman's identity is unclear.

SAFIA JABIR ALI

Touring Europe on Business

INTRODUCTION

Safia Jabir Ali (1893–1962) had multiple experiences of travel about which she wrote in manuscript form. The second youngest of eighteen children born to esteemed jurist Badruddin Tyabji and his wife, Rahat un-Nafs, she grew up at the heart of Bombay's Tyabji clan within India's Sulaimani Bohra community. From a young age, she was inculcated with her father's ideals linked to Muslim reformism and Indian nationalism. As well as attending an English-medium school, she and her twelve sisters received lessons at home in Urdu, the Quran, music, art, and sport. Two of her elder sisters, Nasima and Rafia, were also sent abroad to finish their education at a girls' boarding school in England. Safia's idyllic childhood was interrupted by her parents' deaths in quick succession in 1905 and 1906, after which she lived with her much older sister Sakina and her young family. A flirtatious courtship with a cousin, Jabir Ali, led to marriage in 1915, after which the couple relocated to Burma (now Myanmar), where Jabir was engaged in business ventures linked to wolfram mining and hardware with a cousin and brother. Safia and Jabir lived first in Tavoy (now Dawei) and then, from 1919, in Rangoon (now Yangon) (see fig. 40.1). From there, they traveled to Europe shortly after the First World War for Jabir to establish business contacts for the Rangoon branch of the family's hardware business in Burma.

Jabir had studied for a diploma in agriculture at the University of Cambridge but, upon returning to India in 1910, was unable to secure a suitable appointment. His business ventures were also unsuccessful with the effect that after several

Siobhan Lambert-Hurley prepared the introductions, extracts, and annotations.

Figure 40.1 Safia Jabir Ali (*seated, right*) with
family in Burma. Her husband, Jabir, stands to
her left. Courtesy of Salima Tyabji.

years in Burma, the couple returned to Bombay in 1924. Struggling with debt,
they decided to revive Jabir's agricultural dream by farming an isolated patch of
family land cleared from the jungle then surrounding Bombay. To capture their
unique experience, Safia decided to keep a diary in Urdu, now referred to her as
her "memoirs," that was started in 1926 but only continued in the early 1940s. The
long break was probably enforced by the birth of her only natural son, Amiruddin, in 1928 (after the loss of two infant girls in Burma), plus the couple's active
participation in the Indian national movement—for which Jabir was jailed for
nearly five years in three spells between 1929 and 1935. As well as attending meetings of the Indian National Congress (INC) in Karachi in 1930 and Ahmedabad
in 1931, the couple also participated in nonviolent protests connected with Gandhi's salt satyagraha, picketed liquor shops, and sold khadi (homespun) cloth.
Later, Jabir continued as a leading figure in the INC, acting as president of his
local committee for many years. In the second, longer phase of her diary, Safia

wrote about politics alongside more quotidian matters while also reflecting back on her family history, childhood, marriage, and life in Burma.

The extracts here come not from Safia's diary but from an unpublished speech about her journey to Europe written around 1920. According to her diary, this speech was read out to a group of women in Rangoon—the "sisters" of her opening address—within a year of her return. She claimed at the outset to be speaking before an audience for the first time, but perhaps she meant a public audience because it seems likely that she, like other members of her family, would have presented before the Tyabji family ladies' club, Akdé Suraya, at some point in her youth. She certainly did later, providing copies of her speeches to her son Amiruddin—from whom this manuscript was recovered—so that he may "learn about [his] mother's views." Other female relatives used the club to give speeches on travel from at least the 1890s that may have provided a model to Safia. A likely example was her eldest sister, Amina (mother of Shareefah Hamid Ali, who is also featured in this collection). Amina gave a brief and impressionistic account to the club in Urdu about her journey to Europe in accompaniment of the maharani of Baroda shortly after her return in 1894. Subsequently, she was also pressed into writing two short travel pieces in Urdu on her experience of visiting Britain, France, Switzerland, and Italy in a set of family diaries known as the *akhbar*, or news, books. As Safia was an avid contributor to these books from a young age, it seems likely that she would have read her sister's entries before writing her own travel account, even if she was too young to hear the original speech delivered in person.

Typewritten in English, the script for Safia's own speech was just eight pages in total, meaning that most of it is reproduced here. The language of composition must reflect her mixed audience—of Indians and Burmese from different regions and religious communities—because she generally wrote in Urdu, not English. In the opening passage, Safia recounts how she traveled alone from Bombay to London by steamship and train via Marseilles, Paris, Boulogne, and Folkestone. According to her brother-in-law Sálim Ali's memoirs, her husband had traveled to Europe ahead of her accompanied by a new business partner, Yusuf Khan of Osman Mustikhan & Co., but when the latter died suddenly of a heart attack, Jabir was left alone. Presumably, this unfortunate turn of events occasioned Safia's own journey to join her husband. Once reunited, the couple spent six weeks in the imperial capital of London before touring many towns and cities in England, Scotland, and Germany in pursuit of Jabir's business interests—among them Bournemouth, Cambridge, Birmingham, Manchester, Liverpool, Sheffield, Edinburgh, Glasgow, Rosyth, Hamburg, and Leipzig. About each town or city, Safia recorded what had left the "best most vivid impression," whether it be a place, activity, or an encounter, after her often solitary sightseeing. The result— despite an opening gambit of modesty—was a rather bold and uninhibited account: Safia's candid impressions of the local people and the local people of her set against a backdrop of picturesque land-scapes, industrial gloom, and postwar decay.

EXTRACTS

Introduction

Sisters: This is the first time in my life that I am standing to speak a few words before an audience—indeed, I feel very diffident about interesting you suffi-ciently, but what cannot be cured must be endured, so I hope you will have the patience to bear with me!

I want to tell you of our trip to Europe last year. Most people in Burma and India were under the impression that people who traveled in Europe then—so shortly after the war—had a great many hardships to endure, and many friends advised me not to go then—however I was not to be dissuaded.

From Bombay to London

I had to travel by myself from Bombay to Marseilles, and that was the first time I had occasion to depend so entirely on myself and spend more than three weeks among entire strangers. However, as probably some of you know by experience, on board the steamer, one gets to know people very soon. I was lucky in being able to travel on the *Loyalty*, the steamer of an Indian Company,[1] where there were a good many Indian passengers, and some of us soon became great friends. As it was the month of June, the Indian Ocean was very rough, and we pitched and rolled terribly—many travelers confined themselves to their bunks. And could neither eat nor drink, but fortunately for me, I am a good sailor and was able to spend most of the time on the deck—even slept on deck, one side of the deck having been reserved for ladies. It was beautiful to watch the ocean under every shade of light, and the waves splashing and spraying, and hear it roaring.

Great excitement prevailed whenever we neared land—and people with bin-oculars filled the decks. It broke the monotony of life on a steamer. The first piece of land we passed was Arabia and Africa. The Suez Canal is very narrow, and it created a magical sensation to see before you, on one side Asia and on the other Africa. As the steamer took us slowly through, we watched the houses and the people in the streets, on camels and horses, and children playing, and as a picture and not as reality! We all landed at Port Said and wandered through the little town, saw the quarters where are the European shops and the Arab-quarters as well. It was gladdening to meet some Indian friends there, by chance, and to be invited to their home and fed on delicious Indian food. The Arab hawkers and street sellers are so full of spirit and so independent and cheeky. They also can pester your life!

Shoeblacks actually get hold of your feet, before you are aware of their presence and tell you some sweet things when you insist on being left alone! We thought them such a contrast to the meek Indian boys who can be frightened away so easily. Another thing that caused a pleasant surprise was to find a good many Sindhi shops there, well-kept and inviting to the view.

It is wonderful how on board the ship, you only eat and drink, talk and read and sleep. Of course there are games of bridge and quoits and draughts and suchlike, but a great many go without even these amusements, and yet time passes pleasantly enough. Now and again we feel a little impatient to get our destination, and a little tired of the life. But on the whole it was very enjoyable and gave us perfect peace. I felt perfectly content to gaze on the deep sea and think my thoughts.

Our steamer took us through the straits of Messina in the evening when the moon was shining beautifully and the hilly coasts of Italy and Sicily looked lovelier with the glitter of thousands of lights from the populated towns than I can well describe. We looked at it with wonder, as if we were getting a vision of a fairyland. We see beauty as great in our own land when the sun rises or sets, or the moon shines down up on us—but this was a different kind of scenery to any I had seen before, and after days and days of voyaging on the sea, with only water, water everywhere, the beauty of the lighted coasts on the moonlit sea inspired even the most unpoetic.

We reached Marseilles at last, but as it was evening, past the hour when the ship could get into harbor, we had to anchor at a little distance. Marseilles looked very picturesque with the glow of the setting sun, but the town itself is not at all like the first impression I had of it from the ship, and distance had indeed lent enchantment to the scene. . . .

From Marseilles, after a whole night's journey in the train, we got to Paris; after staying the day there, the next morning saw us off by train to Boulogne, and from Boulogne by a very comfortable and fast boat to Folkestone, thence on to London. It is not possible in a talk like this to describe to you the different scenes through which we passed, the beautiful orchards and fields of France, the villages and towns, however interesting and new they seemed to me. Marseilles,

Paris, and London! My mind was whirling with emotion and excitement, and I could hardly realize that what was before me, I actually saw with my bodily eyes, and that we were so many thousands of miles away from our dear native land!

Visiting England

We lived in Maida Vale in London. I had never thought much as I had read and heard of the greatest of cities that one could live so peacefully and quietly in it, but no noise or smoke troubled us there, and there were green trees and lawns and flowers round us. The English certainly know how to make their homes beautiful, and each house had such a well-kept garden—so neat, and full of flowers—it was summer—that it gladdened one's heart. Almost the first thing that struck me on getting out of the train in London was the hurry people seemed to be in; everyone was rushing—no one walked leisurely as we do here—and the funny part of it was that I too got the injection from them and could not walk at the same pace that I am accustomed to here—but adopted a pace between walking and running. Again, the bustling, rushing crowds were composed largely of women, a great many well-to-do and well educated.

The tube is the most convenient way of going about in the city, and though at first it was very, very bewildering, in a day or two only I had gone backward and forward so often that I was emboldened to travel in it by myself—especially when I found how considerate and kind the English people were to foreigners. The orderly way in which people got into the trains was also very surprising. Every two minutes there was a train, and crowds of passengers to get in, but the firstcomers stood first, and there was never any pushing or jostling. My experience of the English, in their own country, is all that is praiseworthy. In the streets, shops, etc., they were always polite, and without in any way interfering in other people's business, they came forward immediately to your aid when you needed it. Very often when I lost my way and was looking for directions, a kind lady would help me, going out of her way to do so.

The landlady of our boarding house was all kindness, so willing to oblige us, and did not mind if we gave her trouble by not keeping to fixed hours for meals.

The friends we called on, or were invited to stay with, were not less hospitable and kind than Indians—and having known my father,[2] they treated us very affectionately, which was more than I had expected and which touched me very much, being so far away from all my relatives.

In London and elsewhere on the continent, it made me feel quite envious to see the women being able to work so hard—their robust constitutions made me wish we could become like them in this respect. In India one finds the women so frail and sickly—it is a fair thing to find a middle-class woman capable of real hard-work, being herself in perfect health. The climate as well as their energetic outdoor life gives them this health, which is so necessary for all of us, if we would do anything in this world, and not become a burden to others.

One thing that surprised me was the ignorance even educated people showed toward India. One would naturally expect them to know a good deal about us. We read so much about them, and have adopted so many of their customs, and are so familiar with their literature, thought, art, and ways of living that it is quite easy for us to live with them there without having to learn anything extraordinary about them. But they, on the contrary, seem to be ignorant of everything connected with us! There were many who were awfully surprised to find an Indian women of a good, well-to-do family, being able to walk about and go about in their moving staircases and lifts, etc. without being scared to death! Also they are under the impression that Indian ladies generally lie on durwans [divans] in gorgeous apparel, waited on by women, and dream away their days surrounded by wealth and luxury! I had to tell them that though we did not work half as hard as they did, still we were not anything like what they imagined!

As to the city of London, you have all heard and read of it, I am sure, so I shall not weary you with descriptions all the wonderful things I saw there. . . .

We toured a little in England—in fact, we traveled from the southernmost town right up to the north but unfortunately were forced to stay only in the large towns: Birmingham, Manchester, Liverpool, and Sheffield. The journey from one town to another gave us a very good opportunity of seeing the country. I shall pass these towns on with only this remark: that after having been in London, they all seemed to a foreigner like me, a poor imitation of it, on a small scale, besides being smoky and gloomy most days.

Touring Scotland

The train journey from Manchester to Glasgow was especially enjoyable, as it took us through the most beautiful scenery. It was interesting when, at one point north of Carlisle, we left England and entered Scotland.

Glasgow can boast of some fairly interesting sights, besides the fact of the Highlands of Scotland being within an easy distance; but after London, the town in itself suffers in the visitor's estimation.

It was amusing to note the difference in the manners and speech of the Scotch from the English; the waiters and maids at the hotels spoke with an unmistakable accent of their own.

The thing that has left the best most vivid impression on my mind of Glasgow is our attempt to get to Loch Lomond.[3] . . . Although we were not able to reach our destination, and in spite of the trouble we had to undergo, I am glad we attempted it because we got a vision of one of the loveliest sunsets I have ever seen. The place we saw it from was lonely country—the purple highlands mountains, and old historical Dumbarton Castle[4] formed the background, and nearer us were some green mountains, and the River Clyde in which were cast the reflections of the setting sun—the sky seemed to be in flames, so rich were the colors.

We had licenses to visit Rosyth,[5] a place about three hours' run in a fast train from Glasgow. It is one of the biggest naval houses of England, and although it is very instructive to see the huge works, tanks, and machinery, I am afraid, not being especially interested in things of that sort, what I enjoyed most was the day's outing in the meadows and the collecting of different flowers—the whole place was one mass of bluebells, daisies, thistles, buttercups, and ever so many other wildflowers, and I lost my head when I found myself in the midst of such profusion.

I must tell you of an incident that amused us very much. When we were waiting at the little Rosyth tramway station, near which were a number of cottages, we noticed a group of chubby little children playing about; but I was fairly taken by surprise, and very agreeable surprise too, when one of them came up to me shyly with a few flowers plucked from his garden and, addressing me as "Lady," presented me with them. I thought how considerate and kind it was of him, and I thanked him and said so. A little later, two or three others came along, and then some more, and I had to repeat my thanks and accept their offerings. Turning round, I saw these children run with smiles on their lips to a group collected not far from us and, by the eager way in which they immediately began to talk, and the interest of their listeners, together with the curious glances they shot at us, I was able to guess all that lay behind their minds! They had wanted to know what a colored lady would do when she was given flowers, for instance. Would she speak? And if she did, in what language? Also I suppose they desired to get a nearer view of the strange specimen of humanity before them. Anyway, we had a good laugh over it and enjoyed their little enterprise very much.

Talking of children, and of the curiosity they showed to us, I will tell you of how when we visited the London Zoo, children, merely to look us, would pass us and repass us, whispering and discussing us. I once overheard them wondering to what nationality we belonged, and when one was able to decide the matter definitely and finally and said we were Indians, she commanded great respect for her superior knowledge. It made us feel we were also a part of the zoo for them!

I consider it lucky that were able to pay a flying visit to Edinburgh. It is a town really worth going to, even if one had seen other Western towns. It has a picturesqueness peculiar to itself and has an atmosphere of the old romantic days round it, which one feels as soon as one gets off the train. . . . I liked the town so much. I wished our visit could have been longer.

On to Germany

After a stay of a few more days in London, we said goodbye to our friends there, very sorry to go away from a place which had given us so much pleasure, and crossed over to Germany from Whitby in Yorkshire. We passed a very disagreeable day and night on the steamer, the sea being awfully choppy, and were heartily glad to land in Hamburg.

It was a gray, drizzling, gloomy day, and we could immediately tell effects of the war among the Germans. In England, there seemed no change—everything was very much the same to the outward view, at least—but here, the effects were terribly visible even to a stranger visiting the country for the first time as I was doing, and much more assuredly to person who had been there before, as my husband had been.[6]

Roads were unrepaired, houses in dilapidated conditions, parks and gardens unkempt and overgrown with weeds; animals at the zoo were destroyed during the war, and never replaced—how could they afford to feed dumb beasts and birds when men were starving? Of the world famous zoo of Hagenbeck, nothing now remains to speak of.[7]

The municipal buildings are covered with bullet marks and are surrounded by barricades of barbed wire as there are frequent rebellions—the poor, not getting sufficient food, resort on the authorities in this way.

The hotel we stopped at—one of the best in Hamburg—had nothing of the luxury of the English hotels. Food control was much stricter, although we always were able to get good food because we did not mind paying in marks. The value of marks was extremely low—so that what was cheap for a foreigner was awfully expensive for the natives of the country. Some articles of food like sugar and bread were difficult to obtain and sometimes could not be had at all.

The Germans are much more sociable than the English. They do not wait for introductions but start to converse quite unreservedly even with strangers. My husband's knowledge of German stood us in good stead, and as a number of Germans know English, so I too could talk to them. We soon came to know a few very well. In Leipzig, two ladies were particularly kind—I had never met them before, but being introduced to them, they took me under their wing and would come for me (my husband being engaged in business of his own) and take me sightseeing. Through them, we were able to see and hear many things which otherwise would have been impossible.

FURTHER READING

Safia Jabir Ali. "Address by Mrs. Safia Jabir Ali." A typewritten transcript of speech was consulted in the private collection of her son Amiruddin Jabir Ali in Mumbai. Additional extracts from this text are available online at https://accessingmuslimlives.org/travel /address/. The speech of her sister, Amina Tyabji, handwritten in Urdu for presentation on August 22, 1894, was consulted in the private collection of Rafia Abdul Ali in Mumbai.

Safia Jabir Ali. "Manuscript Memoirs of Mrs. Safia Jabir Ali." Badruddin Tyabji Family Papers VI, Nehru Memorial Museum and Library, New Delhi, India.

Salima Tyabji. *The Changing World of a Bombay Muslim Community, 1870–1945*. Margao: CinnamonTeal, 2013.

Sálim Ali. *The Fall of a Sparrow*. Delhi: Oxford University Press, 1985.

NOTES

1. As the author indicates, the SS *Loyalty* was owned by the Scindia Steam Navigation Company. It was the first wholly Indian-owned ship traversing from India to the United Kingdom. Safia may even have sailed on its maiden voyage in this capacity that launched on April 5, 1919—now celebrated as India's National Maritime Day.

2. The author refers here to her famous father, Badruddin Tyabji, who was a frequent visitor to England after first studying there in the 1860s. He died there in 1906.

3. The author refers to a large and very picturesque lake north of Glasgow.

4. Dumbarton Castle is described as "historical" because it has the longest recorded history of any stronghold in Scotland. It sits on an outcrop of volcanic rock on the banks of the River Clyde.

5. As the author indicates, Rosyth Dockyard on the Firth of Forth in Fife was a very large naval complex, having been expanded significantly during the First World War.

6. It is not clear when the author's husband, Jabir Ali, had visited Germany previously— perhaps during his studies in England (1906–10). Maybe it was during that visit that, as she notes below, he learned some of the language too.

7. The author refers to a highly successful private zoo, renowned for its open viewing enclosures, established by Carl Hagenbeck in Hamburg's Stellingen district in 1907.

FORTY-ONE

SUGHRA HUMAYUN MIRZA

Meeting the Caliph in Switzerland

INTRODUCTION

Sughra Humayun Mirza "Haya" (1884–1958) (see fig. 41.1) was among the most prolific women writers in early twentieth-century India, despite the fact that she was not, primarily, an author. Rather, she was a reformist who harnessed the power of the press and rising rates of women's literacy to bring about social change. She was born in the south Indian city of Hyderabad, then the capital of a semi-independent state at the center of an intellectual renaissance that flowered largely in Urdu. Her father was Captain Hajji Safdar ʿAli Mirza, a surgeon in the Hyderabad state army. Her mother, Mariam Begum, was herself a recognized scholar of Arabic and Persian. Their daughter was educated, as was common among the Muslim elite, at home by private tutors. At the age of sixteen, Sughra was married to Humayun Mirza, a well-to-do lawyer from Patna who had recently relocated to Hyderabad and, enraptured, sought her hand. He became an ardent supporter of his wife's reformist cause. Indeed, in her European travelogue *Safarnamah-i Yurap* (*A Tour of Europe*), excerpted here, the couple appear to be in total consonance, making decisions about where to go and what to see together.

Mirza's writing, all in Urdu, spanned a number of genres and countless publications, including standalone books and journal articles. Yet, as indicated, this was not art for art's sake. Mirza was above all a tireless activist for women's rights, occupying leadership roles in a number of social reform organizations, including the Anjuman-i Khavatin-i Islam (or All-India Muslim Ladies' Conference). It was this cause that both inspired and guided her writing, which was

Daniel Majchrowicz prepared the introduction and translation from Urdu.

Figure 41.1 Sughra Humayun Mirza, 1934. Courtesy of Gail Minault.

unapologetically didactic. Mirza condemned the oppression of women and the
imposition of purdah. She advocated for the rehabilitation of and right of divorce
for women in abusive marriages and for widow remarriage. Perhaps because she
took up these controversial causes by writing entertaining novels and addressing
her women readers in a friendly, familiar voice, she attained wide recognition
and a faithful readership.

Mirza wrote at least five travel accounts in addition to fourteen novels. Three
of these accounts detail her travels to various regions in India (1914, and two in
1918), and two others cover journeys to Iraq (1915) and to Europe (1924). These
travel narratives were often first serialized in influential women's journals, like
al-Nisa (Hyderabad) and *Zeb al-Nisa* (Lahore), of which Mirza was the editor
and primarily contributor. As her travels in India stemmed largely from her efforts to promote social reform, these travel texts give little attention to touristic
sites but instead focus on meetings and reformist activities. Her international
accounts, however, are more conventional, providing a generalized view of the
countries that she visited—though with the topic of women's rights and Islamic
rejuvenation never far away. *Safarnamah-i Yurap*, for instance, is meticulous
in describing the main points of attraction in the regions that she toured with

her husband (who appears here as "Barrister sahib"). At the same time, it often returns to the subject of women, as Mirza observes their lives and records her interactions with them.

By the time she began her account of Europe, Sughra Humayun Mirza was a widely recognized figure, and Urdu-reading women amenable to her message would likely have been familiar with her work. As a result, *Safarnamah-i Yurap* is conversational from the outset, as though resuming a dialogue with a female friend or updating an old acquaintance after a stint away. The text is explicit in addressing the female reader. This friendly, relaxed approach is maintained throughout several hundred pages, as Mirza describes her journey and the major sights while drawing the reader's attention to the dynamics of everyday life in England, France, Germany, and Switzerland. She also details the speeches she made and her observations on the quality of life abroad versus that at home. Like other Indian authors of her day, she was acutely aware of the state of Muslims outside India, and she frequently returns to the topic of reform and advancement in her travel accounts, often with a comparative gaze.

The passages below reflect this concern for the well-being of the Muslim world. While visiting Switzerland, Mirza and her husband traveled from Zurich to a small town on the shores of Lake Geneva to visit Abdülmecid II, who as the nominal head of the Ottoman imperial household was the last caliph of Islam, a position that commanded immense respect and interest among Indian Muslims. For many years in the 1910s and 1920s, the fate of the Ottoman Empire and the position of the caliphate was followed closely in South Asia. Across the subcontinent, both Hindus and Muslims united in lobbying for the preservation of this position, and the movement is widely credited with substantively advancing the cause for India's own independence. Despite years of agitation in India, the caliphate was abolished by Turkey's national leader, Mustafa Kemal Ataturk, in 1924. Abdülmecid II was deposed and expelled from the country. He left for Europe in March of the same year.

The following September, only a few months after his exile, Sughra Humayun Mirza and her husband went to visit him. This visit would have been one of the first by any Indian to the figure whose position had transfixed India for the better part of a decade. Indeed, there was such devotion to the caliph that in his exile he was at least partially supported by stipends contributed by various Indian rulers and princes. By her own account, Mirza was the first Indian woman to meet the deposed Ottomans in their exile—though other women travelers, including Begum Sarbuland Jang and Sultan Jahan in this volume, had met the family at their previous residence, the Dolmabahçe, in Istanbul. On those occasions, female visitors might have only a brief audience with the caliph before being whisked to the women's quarters to interact with the queen and princesses. Mirza's meeting was starkly different, with the two couples spending a quiet evening conversing and dining together. Although Mirza points out that the women at this meeting were modestly dressed, purdah was not practiced and gender spaces were not demarcated. She is patently pleased with what she describes as the "true Islamic spirit" of this arrangement, signaling her own vision for Muslims in India.

EXTRACTS

At Territet in Switzerland

September 5, 1924: We were so exhausted when we went to bed last night that we woke up very late. In the morning we had a bath, got dressed, and ate breakfast. We boarded the twelve o'clock train with the intention of going to meet with His Noble Highness Abdülmecid II. The name of this station is Zürich Bahnhof. The trains here have a unique design. The carriages are very long, and the seating arrangement is such that two people may sit on either side of the carriage. There is also a restaurant car in the train. We had lunch at one o'clock. The food was excellent and very delicious. The grapes were outstanding and the pears (a kind of *nashpati* [pear]) without equal. A meal for two cost fifteen Swiss francs. Twenty-two francs are equivalent to one English pound, or fifteen rupees.

Oh, how beautiful and lush the meadows of Switzerland are! Here a chain of mountains stretches away before you, while there a river meanders and flows. Here a waterfall tumbles, while there a village clings to the mountain. The train continues on its merry way while my eyes struggle to decide which of these sights to take in, which to praise next. I was lost in wonder and astonishment. Even the land that lies at the foot of the mountains is of the same wondrous quality, with a garden here, a field there. The luxuriant verdure of the grass was oppressively beautiful. The forests are all cleared by horse carts.

We had to change stations at Bern. Here we boarded another train. Along the way, we passed the cities of Vevey and Montreux. These cities are also worth seeing, but we did not stop to visit them. They are very beautiful. At 5:00 p.m. Lake Geneva came into view. This is a strange, wonderful lake. Water flows from the mountains into this lake. It is considered to be the best lake in the world. To one side are mountains whose peaks rend the sky. These mountains are even higher than those in Iran. There were clouds when we passed, clouds that appeared to be snow on the mountain. We saw a number of snow-clad mountains too. There is a chain of mountains on one side of the lake, and houses on the other. Lake Geneva is captivating, and I am incapable of describing its beauty. It simply has to be seen.

Our train arrived at Dimli station at six. We alighted from the train and got into a tram, which we rode for half an hour. To one side was Lake Geneva, and an expanse of human habitation to the other. There were villages on the mountain and others at its foot. Between the two was a road for trams, cars, and carriages.

Then we arrived at the Hôtel des Alpes. This is an extremely luxurious hotel. In fact, it is fit for a king. The drawing room of the hotel is approximately thirty yards long. The dining room is also large and magnificent. There is an enormous space in front of the hotel filled with gardens, orchards and a tennis court. As it is located on the shores of Lake Geneva, the hotel has boats as well. Anyone who so desires may take a boat and go out on the lake. This is not a hotel; it is a small piece of heaven itself. It is grand and beautiful.

Watches of the highest quality are made in Geneva. Each watch we saw was even more wonderful than the last. The people of Switzerland are very polite and friendly. Their facial structure is oval. The facial features of each region of Europe differ from one another. Their complexions are all white, but their features vary.

The language spoken here is Swiss. They are very reliant on the ox. The carts are drawn by oxen, as are the plows. The style of houses is not beautiful; most are them are tiled. The buildings in the cities are also typically tiled. The people are of average beauty, but the landscape is unrivaled no matter which direction you look.

The Honor of a Visit to Caliph Abdülmecid II

When we arrived at the Grand Hôtel des Alpes that evening, the manager said that he had been expecting us. Using a telephone (there is a telephone in every room of the hotel), he informed the caliph's private secretary of our arrival. The private secretary took us into the drawing room and offered us a seat. He then left, saying that he would inform His Majesty that we had come. He returned a few moments later and asked us to follow him, for His Majesty was then free. Accordingly, we proceeded to the second floor. There, in a small room, was the caliph, seated resplendently in a large chair upholstered in red velvet. In front of him was a round table upon which a few books and newspapers were spread.

When [his secretary?] Mr. Karamat Bey brought us into the room, His Highness stood up and, placing his right hand to his heart, bowed to us in greeting.

We each kissed his hand one after the other. Making a gesture with his hand, he indicated that I should sit in the chair that had been placed in front of his own. Barrister sahib took a seat in the chair to the left. The private secretary placed his right hand on his heart and greeted the caliph before sitting down himself.

We were asking after one other's well-being when Her Highness, Queen Şehsuvar Hanım[1]—may God grant her prosperity—entered the room. We each kissed her hand. She took her seat to the right of the caliph in another large velvet chair. Her outfit, which was white in color, was modest. Not a single hair on her head could be seen; only her face remained uncovered. She respects and keeps the true Islamic purdah. I had brought a few gifts with me, among which was a copy of one of my own books. Her Highness asked me to dedicate the book to her in my own hand. It was only when I asked the private secretary for Her Highness's name that I came to know that she was Queen Şehsuvar Hanım. We spoke together for a long time about a great many topics. The queen's blessed eyes welled up with tears when she told me that I was the first Muslim woman since the time of their exile to have traveled so far just to visit her and her husband and to express sympathy for their plight.

A little while later, both the caliph and Her Highness expressed a desire that we should stay to dine with them as their guests. We thanked them and accepted their invitation. She then said to me: "You, an Indian Muslim, will be the first woman to dine with me since I left Turkey. I will never forget this kindness of yours for as long as I live."

The queen then said: "You look very similar to Turkish women. Do all women in Hyderabad look this way, or is it that you have Turkish roots?" I was astonished to hear this and replied that my grandfather was from Turkey, and the family on my maternal side was from Iran, but that now we are Hyderabadi.

At 8:00 p.m. we all proceeded to the dining room. This was not the regular public dining room; rather, it was a small room with a single table and five chairs arranged around it. His Noble Highness took his seat at the head of the table. To his right was Her Highness. Across from her and to the left of His Noble Highness sat the barrister. Karamat Bey sat across the table from His Noble Highness.

While we were eating dinner, Her Highness took my hand over and over to tell me that this meeting and our kindness and affection would remain a cherished memory forever. "You are my Islamic sister," she would say. Her Highness's deeply sorrowful words tore my heart to pieces. Meanwhile, His Highness the caliph, who was engrossed in his conversation with Barrister sahib, began to say: "I have absolutely no interest in dwelling on the treatment that has been meted out to me. My only consideration, my only worry, is that Islam is ringed by its enemies on all sides. In circumstances such as these, the destruction of the caliphate has placed Islam in an even greater danger."

We returned to the sitting room at the end of the meal. His Noble Highness does not smoke himself, but he told Barrister sahib that he would send for some cigarettes. In keeping with the dictates of proper etiquette in such a situation, Barrister sahib thanked the caliph but declined to smoke. The conversation continued until very late. Around midnight our hosts remarked that after a journey of six or seven hours, we must be very tired and in need of rest. "We will meet again in the morning, inshallah."

Mr. Karamat Bey led us to a large bedroom that was very finely furnished. The room must have been reserved for us ahead of time. In the morning, we met with Mr. Karamat Bey after breakfast and tea. We told him that we intended to return via the 9:00 a.m. train. He replied, "Last evening, His Noble Highness said that you should have lunch with him and then depart on the 1:00 p.m. train. The Commander of the Faithful will join you with Her Highness the queen at eleven, leaving you free to take the train at one." We agreed to stay, and then the three of us went out to visit the town of Territet.

Switzerland is a mountainous country. Its beauty is unparalleled anywhere in the world. It is often said that Kashmir is the Switzerland of Asia, but in truth the two cannot be compared. Switzerland, which is a land extremely rich in mountains and hills, is also a land of lakes. Lake Geneva, which is a very famous lake, is lined with towns perched on the hills. These towns extend down the hills to the shores of the lake: for instance, Vevey, Geneva, Lausanne (where the war's final conference was held), Montreaux, and Territet are all charming, beautiful, salubrious, and lively. The mountains here range from two thousand to four thousand feet above sea level. The slopes are verdant, with waterfalls and houses small and large nestled among the hills. These are ringed by lovely gardens bursting with all types of beautiful flowers. They are a wonder to behold. There are also shops to be found in these hills that provide everything one might need to live here. There are also many hotels, some small, some large. Churches too.

The roads are tortuous. There are several that will take you up into the hills; eight, perhaps. There is a separate route for train locomotives, that is, engines.... There is also a large vehicle called a funicular that consists of a single large compartment. Running on water and electricity, the funicular rises two thousand feet straight up. One goes up and another comes down every hour. It is a strange, astonishing thing. We rode the funicular all the way to the top, where there were views to be had in every direction. It was a true testament to the glory of God's creation. In this place, the hand of God and the handiwork of man have joined together to create a wondrous miracle. There is also a snow-covered mountain in the Alps. It was very near to where we were, and it could be seen easily. There is also an old fort in Territet that is said to be six hundred years old.

We returned to the hotel at eleven. At twelve, we went to have lunch in the same room in we had dined the previous night. The chairs were arranged in the same way as before. His Noble Highness told us that this Friday was, for them, particularly blessed as they were dining in the company of a Muslim brother and a Muslim sister. I submitted in reply that my own emotions were simultaneously of joy and sorrow. Joy, that I had the honor and blessing to dine with His Highness, the caliph. And sorrow, at seeing His Noble Highness in such a situation. When we had finished eating and were returning to the sitting room, His Highness quickened his pace, moved ahead of the group, and went to hold the door for us. I wanted to enter the room quickly, but Her Highness, who had placed her hand in my own, was walking slowly. Barrister sahib and Karamat Bey were conversing as they walked behind us. The scene before me at that moment, with His Highness the caliph holding the door and waiting for us to reach him, had a profound effect on me. Allahu akbar! The caliph of the Ottoman line, whose forefathers had adorned the throne of the caliphate in Europe for five hundred years, who had brought turmoil and chaos to Christian Europe for centuries— today, he stands holding open the door for me!

As I was leaving, Her Highness the queen embraced me and said many prayers and wishes for my well-being. As she was doing this, the embroidered lining of my sari got caught on Her Highness's clothes. Seeing this, she said: "Now the love between us has become permanent. Inshallah, it will never wane. Even our clothing has joined together." She then called her daughter to introduce us. The princess greeted me before I was able to do so. I returned her salaam lovingly and prayed for her well-being.

After taking our leave from His Highness the caliph and Her Highness the queen, we went to the railway station. The private secretary escorted us all the way there. His Highness has only one wife, one son, one daughter, and one granddaughter. His son was then away in France on important business. His Highness Abdülmecid II is the son of the deceased Sultan Abdülaziz, who was the caliph until 1875, before the start of the Russo-Turkish War.[2] His conversation and manner are dignified, considerate, and profound. His face radiates majesty. His Highness is approximately sixty years old, but he remains healthy and strong. He cares deeply for, and loves, Islam. I found him to be very well informed on matters of European politics. Seeing him pass the remainder of his days there in the Alpes Hotel with but just a few other souls brought to mind the absolute power of God. Waves of sorrow and melancholy crashed in the sea of my heart. This man, who was raised in the palace of Dolmabahçe[3] and who, until only recently, was called the "Leader of the Faithful" throughout the Islamic World, was now counting out his final breaths in this way. This man, whose forefathers had ruled over Europe and Asia with glory, honor, and dignity and humbled all of Christian Europe for six hundred years, was today reduced to relying on the aid of others. "Therefore take warning, oh those who see."[4]

May God above give just recompense to their highnesses the nizam of the Deccan and the ruler of Bhopal, both of whom have proven their devotion to and empathy for Islam by giving assistance to His Noble Highness during this moment of tribulation and helplessness. The amount allotted by these rulers was an unanticipated blessing for His Noble Highness at this precarious moment. If the Turks, for their own expediency, have decided to eject His Highness the caliph and all the members of the Ottoman line (who are said to be 115 in number) from the country, then they might at the very least have made arrangements for their sustenance going forward. What kind of Islam is this, what kind of humanity? If the Turks have no need for the caliphate, then that is one thing, but the Islamic world still needs it. Even stripped of all the trappings of worldly power, the caliphate is nevertheless still a vital religious and spiritual institution—though these elements have not been found in the caliphs for some time now. Now, all that we can do is wait until next year and see what decisions are made regarding the caliphate at the conference in Egypt.[5]

FURTHER READING

Sughra Humayun Mirza. *Safarnamah-i Yurap*. Hyderabad: A'zam Stim Pres, 1926. Further translated extracts, as well as the original Urdu text translated here, are available at https://accessingmuslimlives.org/uncategorized/sughra/.

———. *Roznamchah-i Safar-i Bhopal aur Agra aur Dilli ke halat*. Hyderabad: Matba' Nizam-i Dakkan, 1918. This is an example of the author's Indian travel writing.

Margrit Pernau. "Female Voices: Women Writers in Hyderabad at the Beginning of the Twentieth Century." *Annual of Urdu Studies* 17 (2002): 36–54.

Gail Minault. *Secluded Scholars: Women's Education and Muslim Social Reform in Colonial India*. Delhi: Oxford University Press, 1998.

———. *The Khilafat Movement: Religious Symbolism and Political Mobilization in India*. New York: Columbia University Press, 1982.

NOTES

1. The text erroneously refers to the caliph's wife as Şehvar Hanım throughout. These, and other errors in foreign names and places (such as Tirāte for Territet), have been corrected in the translation.

2. In actuality, Abdülaziz reigned until 1876.

3. A palace located in Istanbul on the shores of the Bosporus that served as the administrative center of the Ottoman Empire in the early twentieth century.

4. Quran 59:2.

5. This is a reference to what would become the Cairo Caliphate Conference of 1926, which was intended to resolve the crisis occasioned by the abolition of the caliphate in 1924. The conference was not held in 1925, as Mirza anticipates, due to criticism of certain aspects of the proposed conference within Egypt.

FORTY-TWO

SUGHRA SABZVARI

An Indian Family in Iran

INTRODUCTION

Sughra Sabzvari (1911–97), also known as S. K. Sughra and Begum Rezwi (see fig. 42.1), first drew public attention as an author when she wrote an account of her journey from eastern India to Iran entitled "*Safarnamah-i Iran*" (Travelogue of Iran), which was serialized in the Urdu journal *'Ismat* in 1935. At the time, she was a wife and mother in her early twenties who hailed from an Indo-Persian family of traders and merchants in Calcutta (now Kolkata). Her father, Syed Ghulam Mahdi, came from the town of Sabzevar in the Khorasan province of Iran and sold Persian goods to Indian elites and royal households, like those of the nizam of Hyderabad, the nawab of Murshidabad, and the nawab of Rampur. After his father Syed Ghulam Rasul Sabzvari's death, Syed Ghulam Mahdi married Rabia Begum from a Murshidabad family and settled in Calcutta. At that time, the city served as a crucial port in the trading networks of the Indian Ocean linking Southeast Asia, Africa, and the Persian Gulf. The couple's daughter, Sughra, received her primary education at home and later developed an interest in literature, journalism, and history. She went on to publish in Urdu women's magazines like *'Ismat* and *Khatun-i mashriq*, as well as English newspapers like *The Statesman*.

Around 1930, Sughra Sabzvari married Syed Muhammad Taher Rezwi (1905–47), a scholar of Persian history and literature originally from Bihar. Rezwi had received his higher education at Islamia College in Calcutta. He later completed his master's degree in Urdu and Persian from Calcutta University and, in 1928,

Asiya Alam prepared the translations from Urdu and worked with Siobhan Lambert-Hurley to prepare the introductions and annotations.

Figure 42.1 A portrait of Sughra Sabzvari late in
her life. Courtesy of Azra Rezwi.

joined Presidency College (now University) as a professor of Persian—which
accounts for why, in the extracts below translated from his wife's travelogue, he
features as "Professor sahib" or, in a sign of respect from others, "Agha-yi Ta-
hir." Taher Rezwi regularly published articles on the history of ancient Persia,
Islam, and Persian literature in journals such as *Iran League Quarterly*, *Nadeem*,
and *Mashriq*. In 1928, he also published a book on the history of Zoroastrianism
entitled *Parsis: A People of the Book* that proclaimed to offer a "brief survey" of
that religion "in light of Biblical and Quranic teachings."

In acknowledgment of his expertise, Taher Rezwi and his wife Sughra were,
in 1934, invited by the government of Iran—then led by modernizing emperor Reza Shah Pahlavi—to attend celebrations marking the thousandth an-
niversary of the birth of Persian poet Ferdowsi. Held in Tehran, Mashhad,
and Tus, these events also underscored the impact of the poet's famous poem
"Shahnameh" (Book of Kings) on Persian and Islamic history. Participants
included scholars from Europe, the Middle East, and Asia, among them at
least seven from India, including Taher Rezwi and Dr. Muhammad Nizamuddin, who appears in the excerpts here with his wife. In her travelogue, Sughra

Sabzvari details how she and her husband traveled with their young children and Sughra's mother, first by train from Calcutta to Delhi and then on to Quetta in Balochistan, from where they continued overland to Iran. Their first and lengthiest stop was Mashhad in Khorasan, where they attended the Ferdowsi Festival before moving on to Tehran for the Millennial Congress in early October 1934. The four passages below recount their time in Tehran after the Congress when they met acquaintances, went sightseeing, visited a hammam, and toured holy sites.

Shortly before her journey abroad, Sughra Sabzvari had begun teaching at the pioneering Sakhawat Memorial Girls' School in Calcutta while still a student herself in the women's section of Asutosh College at the University of Calcutta. Upon her return, she gave a lecture at her place of work on the conditions of women in Iran that was covered in *The Statesman* and the *Star of India*. News reports highlighted her focus on Iranian women's freedom of movement enabled by the chador, their high levels of education, and the prevalence of monogamy in Iranian families—all themes that resonate with her descriptions below. Subsequently, the Rezwi's own family continued to grow—Sughra ultimately gave birth to nine children, two of whom died in infancy—even as she remained dedicated to her educational career. After the Partition of the Indian subcontinent in 1947, Taher Rezwi moved to East Pakistan (later Bangladesh) to become president of Rajshahi College, where he would also oversee Arabic and Persian instruction. At this crucial juncture, Sughra Sabzvari made the bold decision to stay in Calcutta. Just a few months later, Taher Rezwi died of a heart attack.

After her husband's death, Sughra Sabzvari raised her children on her own and participated in community organizations (notably, the Young Women's Christian Association) while continuing to travel widely, including to the Middle East, North America, and East Asia. In later years, she also pursued a literary career. After independence, she focused particularly on retaining Urdu as a crucial component in the school curriculum, authoring two school textbooks, *Qaumi qisse* (*Stories of the Community*) and *Hamari tarikhi hikayateñ* (*Our Historical Teachings*). She also published short stories, novels, and poetry and translated Bengali works of Rabindranath Tagore and Bankim Chandra Chatterjee into Urdu. Among her best-known works are a collection of short stories, *Navratan* (*Nine Jewels*), and three novels, *Khwab o bedari* (*Sleep and Wakefulness*, 1967), *Maut ka saya* (*The Shadow of Death*), and *Gumnam hamsafar* (*Anonymous Fellow Traveler*, 1976). Her early travel writing was the harbinger of this later creativity.

Introducing Tehran

Tehran is an expansive and magnificent city, the capital of the Sultanate of Iran. It has a population of 3.25 lakhs. It has been repaired and cleaned recently; old buildings and bazaars have been replaced with new styles of shops and residential houses. The roads are also beautiful with a park and flowerbeds in the middle of each intersection. There are also big lampposts in the middle of each intersection. There is a huge open field in the middle of the city called *Maidan-i Topkhanah*, around which are built majestic government buildings like the head office of the police, of the city, and the suburbs; head office of municipal government; the office of the parliament; post and telegraph office; royal national and cooperative banks; etc.[1] There are parking spaces for cars at the four corners of the maidan where vans and lorries are always available for rent. All the bazaars and the roads of the city terminate at this maidan. There are royal mansions and royal offices on the southern side of the maidan, which are surrounded by eye-catching gardens and other buildings. On the same side is located the Golestan Palace, which was opened to guests in October. On the northern side of the maidan, there is a road lined with foreign embassies. Amongst the embassy buildings, the largest belong to the British and the Germans. There are beautiful gardens in the enclosure of these two buildings. The national park of the city is also worth seeing.

At any rate, the house we arrived at was not so comfortable. The next morning, we rented a second house in the Mashin Street quarter. I suggested to Professor sahib that we could stay at Itela al-Daulah sahib's place. During our stay in holy Mashhad, I had met his wife and daughter, and they had insisted that I should stay with them when I was in Tehran. They are government employees, and Itela al-Daulah is on pension. His eldest son is an assistant in the office of the *vazir*. But the professor did not think it wise to trouble anybody.

Meeting Acquaintances

The following day, when Professor sahib was to leave for Lalezar [street], I thought I should meet Mrs. Dr. Nizamuddin sahiba since she was planning to leave in a day or two and for this reason was staying in the hotel.[2] Professor sahib had said I could go the next day, and then he went on his own. When he returned, he said that the editor of *Iran Pastan*, Agha Saif Azad, has invited us for tea. Thus, the following afternoon, we got ready, sent our children out for a walk, and left for Agha Saif Azad's home. Agha's house was magnificent and looked like the palace of some nawab, with beautiful tile work surrounded by a huge enclosure full of flowerbeds. The trees were indescribably beautiful. We were led to and seated in an extremely beautiful room. After a few moments, his daughter came. She was very cultured and a good manager of the house despite her young age. We were happy to meet her and had a long conversation with her. She took us to another room, which was also decorated with expensive pieces of art, in the middle of which was a full-size picture of Emperor Reza Shah Pahlavi covered in velvet as a mark of respect.

After a while, Agha Saif Azad joined us carrying a big bouquet of roses in his hand (Iran's flowers are famous). He handed these flowers to his daughter and instructed her to present them to us, which she did. She gave one to me and another to Professor sahib. After some time, a domestic servant appeared who could easily have been confused for the lady of the house. She came with a tray of snacks. As a norm, snacks must include grapes and muskmelon. Here, they do not peel the muskmelon and slice it into pieces. Instead, they cut it into two parts and take out the seeds. It is then eaten with a fork, which they call *changal*. In brief, at eight in the evening, they wished us goodbye, accompanying us to the door as we thanked them for their unforgettable hospitality and love. We took a carriage and went to the Lalezar Hotel, where it had been arranged that the guests would stay. We met Mr. and Mrs. Nizamuddin sahiba; they were still in the same room where we had stayed when we first arrived. We also met an Iranian lady, Fatima Khanom, who was associated with the Ministry of Education. We had a long conversation with them and then returned home. The next morning, on October 22, Mrs. Nizam[uddin] was to leave for India via Esfahan. I didn't go anywhere on October 22 and sent the children for a walk. I stayed at home in consideration of my mother's loneliness.

Visiting the Hammam and Shah 'Abd al-'Azim Shrine

On October 23, Professor sahib left to meet the people of Kunjuro after breakfast, and I left with the children for the famous hammam of Tehran. There are hammams all over Iran, but none of them compares to the one in Tehran. Very likely, our sisters in India may not be familiar with the nature of a hammam because women in India do not go there these days. In Iran, on the contrary, there is no arrangement for bathing at home, with the possible exception of a wealthy man at a very fine house who might love baths and comfort and thus would have constructed a hammam inside the house. The poor and middle-class people cannot afford to have a hammam in their house. This would be very expensive. Thus in each neighborhood, there is at least one hammam where women and children go for bathing. The rate for using the hammam is one qiran or half a qiran for elders, that is, ten paisa or five paisa, and for children, it is either five or two paisa. There is separate arrangement for men.

The hammam is like a deep basement reached by descending a set of steps. First, one comes to a room with a fountain or a *hauz*, which isn't higher than the ground but of the same height and is surrounded by embankments with mats on them. There is also a pitcher for drinking water and a *samovar* for tea, with cups and one hookah. There is a woman to attend to these things. This is the place where women change clothes before and after their bath. The woman attendant collects money and takes care of the clothes. After that, there is a door that takes you to a magnificent room inside, where there are tanks that are two and half yards long and one and half yards deep. One tank contains hot water and the other cold water. Thirty or forty women and children can bathe together at the same time in these tanks. You will see some cleaning themselves, some sitting with *henna* [drying] on their hands and others combing their hair. If someone feels hungry while bathing, they will cut one of the melons that are placed along the tank and start eating. All in all, it is an interesting place where you can easily spend three or four hours. There is no discomfort inside the hammam, no matter how cold it is outside.

We returned from the hammam and had lunch in the afternoon. After some discussion, we decided to go visit Shahzadah 'Abd al-'Azim.[3] We started by car at five. When we arrived there, it was raining heavily. This caused us considerable inconvenience. This is a small town of four miles to the south of Tehran with a population of three thousand people. It is full of gardens and rich land; it has water and mountains and is a beautiful town. It has a big bazaar with shops of high quality. The evening in particular is lively. In the middle is the grand mausoleum of Shah 'Abd al-'Azim, son of Imam Reza. There is also the grave of Sultan Nasiruddin Qajar, the former king of Iran, over which stands a marble statue of him as if the king is lying in his crown and military gear. There is also a meter gauge train that runs between Tehran and Shah 'Abd al-'Azim. We could not buy anything here because of the rain even though things are cheaper here than in Tehran. We returned home early. The following day, on October 24, we slept late in the morning because we were tired and [planned to] stay at home. Our neighbor was very good, and women often met [at her home] to chat. Time passes but memories remain.

Guests in an Iranian Home

We had no intention of going anywhere on October 25 either, but incidentally Professor sahib met the younger son of Itela al-Daulah. He complained and reminded the professor of the promise that we had made in Khorasan—that when we were in Tehran, we would stay with them. He said that he was surprised that we hadn't kept our word and that they had been waiting for us since they had read about our arrival in the newspapers. Professor sahib could not refuse him, and he took him to his house at that moment and only let him go on the promise that he would return with his wife and children in the evening. When Professor sahib returned, he related the whole incident to me and told us that we must go to visit them in the evening as he had promised them.

Early in the evening, I got ready, said my prayers, and left for their house, which was far from ours. We were staying at a distance from the city, and their house was in the middle of the city on Amin al-Daulah Street. As soon as they heard of our arrival, they warmly welcomed us and seated us in a room, which was extremely clean and simple. After I was seated, they brought a small box, inside of which were several chadors. I wasn't familiar with this practice but understood that we should remove our veils and put on the chador. I took off my veil and put on the chador. They folded my veil and placed it inside the box. After this, the maid brought cake and some fine cookies. They insisted that we eat them, and then we started conversing. We faced strong complaints for not staying with them. I had no idea that they would show so much love for us after staying together for just a few days in Khorasan. It was soon ten, and I asked for their leave to return home. But then, we knew that we couldn't leave without having dinner. Eventually, we had to eat, although there was nothing formal about it, and the food was delicious and tasty. After dinner, we were allowed to leave on the condition that the following morning, we would return with our luggage and stay with them until we left Tehran. Eventually, we agreed to do this and returned home at eleven.

On October 26, I prepared to go to their place. I thought I would leave our luggage behind and pick it up when we left Tehran. Itela al-Daulah's young son had come with the complaint that his family was waiting for us, but we had not yet left our home. When we hurriedly got ready, they insisted that we also take our luggage with us, and so we did. We saw that his two brothers, the elder and middle, were waiting for us outside the door of their house. They hadn't eaten anything. As before, when I entered their house, the same box appeared. This is a custom there, for when they go outside, they only wear their clothing, which resemble an English style frock, and wear over it veil, rather than a dupatta. When they take off this veil, they replace it with a long scarf. They don't carry a long scarf with them when meeting others, so the hostess usually keeps chadors like this for the use of guests. The female guest takes off her veil and puts on a chador. Otherwise, they would have to sit with their veil on. I told them that this wasn't necessary for us, as our dress is such that a chador isn't required. I then took off my veil, and they were surprised at [the nature of] my dress and praised it greatly. When asked what it was, I replied that it was "a sari. This is an Indian outfit." After this, the table was set, and we ate. By evening, a room had been prepared for us on the second floor. It was quite comfortable. There was a separate bed for each of us. The time was spent chatting, and then we went upstairs after dinner. The whole floor was reserved for us. In the morning, the domestic servant came with the samovar, milk, sugar, bread, and cheese shortly after I finished my prayer. We had tea and then went downstairs.

October 27 was also spent in their delightful company. On October 28, I had intended to go to the mountain of Bibi Shahar Bano, and on the same day, we had planned to leave Tehran.[4] But in consideration of the love they had shown us, we were compelled to stay for one more day. A special Iranian dish was prepared for us that day, called *ash-i arad*. In the late afternoon, we left with his younger son, Mirza Abu'l Qasim, for Bibi Shaher Bano, which is situated on a mountain peak at a distance of three miles from the northeast of Shah 'Abd al-'Azim. It is commonly held that the grave of Bibi Shaher Bano, the wife of Imam Husain, is located on the peak of that mountain. It is reached by a climb of half a mile. The shrine has white dome. There is also a small mosque. A road has been made to the top of the mountain. There is also a water tank. The land at the foot of the mountain is surrounded by gardens, and there is also a coffeehouse and an inn. The climb to the mountain was difficult, mostly because of the children. It took about half an hour. When we arrived, we washed our faces, did our ablutions, and read our prayers. The dome, which looked small from the ground, was actually very big. Going down was easy; in fact, due to the slope, it seemed as if someone was pushing us down. By the time we came down, our host sister had come to meet us. We were happy to see each other. We had a conversation about the Indian style of living, which they listened to with curiosity. She cooked the food for us herself. I stayed for one more day because of them.

We stayed there for four days, and she treated us with such care and hospitality that I was humbled. It felt like home. I will never forget the love and affection of their younger daughter, Najm al-Muluk. The elder daughter, Badr al-Muluk, was also very kind. Iran's hospitality is famous. Professor sahib also enjoyed the same hospitality among the male members of the house. We were to leave on October 29; the Iranian government arranged the transport. I came downstairs after finishing breakfast. They were all sad at our departure. Najm al-Muluk gave us as a souvenir a handkerchief that she had made herself and a purse. They gifted the children doll's clothes. I also gifted a souvenir to everyone from whatever

I could manage to obtain during my travels. After this, the middle daughter, Fakhr al-Muluk, accompanied us to the bazaar, and I bought a samovar and the famous sweet dish *gaz*. At five, the cars came and we loaded our luggage into them. Their entire family, including children and elders, were so sad, as though one of their own relatives were departing. Though we had just met their sister, she was also very sad. The domestic servants were also sad. I cannot describe the condition of Najma Khanom. They bid us adieu under the Quran.[5] Outside, Itela al-Daulah and their three sons were interacting with Professor sahib as though they were seeing off their own son. They said to him, "Agha-yi Taher, do not forget us." They did not reenter their house until the car had disappeared from view. We did not stay in Tehran as long as we did in Khorasan, but I still nurse their unforgettable love in my heart, although we are now separated by thousands of miles. We set off at sunset. We arrived in a small town at 8:00 p.m., stayed there, drank tea, prayed, and again started, finally arriving in Qom at 11:00 p.m. The entire city was silent; shops were closed; people were asleep. We also slept. Early in the morning, we woke up and had tea. Since the bridge had been broken, it was difficult to take the car, so we rented a cart to go along the river. We went around the city in this cart.

FURTHER READING

S. K. Sughra [Sughra Sabzvari]. "Safarnamah-i Iran." *'Ismat* 56, no. 2 (February 1936): 111–15. There are further articles in this serialized account from January 1935 onwards.

"Modern Iran: Lecture on Condition of Women." *The Statesman* (Calcutta), March 22, 1935. This source covers the speech given by Sughra Sabzvari on her return from Iran.

"Present-day Iran: Begum Sughra Rezwi's Interesting Lecture." *Star of India* (Calcutta), March 23, 1935. This source covers the speech given by Sughra Sabzvari on her return from Iran.

Shahid Iqbal. *Sughra Sabzvari*. Kolkata: Maghribi Bengal Urdu Academy, 2013. This is a biography of the author in Urdu.

Syed Muhammad Taher Rezwi. *Parsis: A People of the Book*. Calcutta: S. M. Taher Rezwi, 1928. This was republished by the World Zoroastrian Organisation in 2014. For a preview, see https://www.w-z-o.org/dmdocuments/Hamazor%2014-3Preview.pdf.

A. Shahpur Shahzadi. "Ferdowsi, Abu'l-Qāsem iv. Millenary Celebration." *Encyclopaedia Iranica*. http://www.iranicaonline.org/articles/ferdowsi-iv.

NOTES

1. The author refers to an important town square in Tehran. After the Iranian Revolution, it was renamed Ayatollah Khomeini Square.

2. Lalezar was Tehran's first major boulevard and the center of the city's culture.

3. The author refers to the shrine of Shah 'Abd al-'Azim, who is revered in Shia Islam as a descendent of 'Ali's eldest son, Hasan. He was buried here in the ninth century after being sent to the area by the eighth Shia Imam, Imam Reza—who, contrary to the author's description, was not his father—to escape persecution.

4. As noted later in the chapter, Bibi Shaher Bano is the wife of Imam Husain in Shia belief.

5. To bid someone adieu under the Quran is the gesture of holding the Quran over their heads as they leave. It is a gesture of love and is meant to guarantee a safe journey.

FORTY-THREE

SHAISTA SUHRAWARDY IKRAMULLAH
Life in England on the Brink of War

INTRODUCTION

When Pakistan's constituent assembly sat for the first time in 1948, Shaista Suhrawardy Ikramullah (1915–2000) was one of just two women members alongside seventy-nine men. Her involvement with the All-India Muslim League in the 1940s had seen her elected to India's constituent assembly in 1946, but in the political turmoil before India's independence and Partition in 1947, she never took her seat. Elected again in Pakistan, she remained in parliament for seven years, during which time she gained a reputation as a maverick for opposing the government. She also acted as Pakistan's delegate to a number of international organizations. Foremost among them was the third session of the United Nations in Paris in 1948, at which she served on the committee drafting the Universal Declaration of Human Rights (1948). After resigning from parliament in 1953 in protest to the delay in framing Pakistan's constitution, Shaista continued as a diplomat. As well as representing her country at the tumultuous session of the United Nations in 1956, she was appointed Pakistan's ambassador to Morocco (1964–67).

Shaista Suhrawardy Ikramullah's political and diplomatic career challenges stereotypes around Muslim women and domesticity, but it seems more predictable if one considers her family and upbringing. According to her autobiography, she was born Shaista Akhtar Banu Suhrawardy in the "old-fashioned house" of her mother Shaherbano's aristocratic family in Calcutta. But her father, Lt. Gen. Dr. Hassan Suhrawardy, was a "modern" man. After completing postgraduate

Asiya Alam prepared the translations from Urdu, and Siobhan Lambert-Hurley prepared the introduction and annotations.

Figure 43.1 Shaista Suhrawardy Ikramullah with her children. Courtesy of Ghulam Nabi Kazi.

qualifications in England, he had a highly distinguished medical career while also engaging in public service and politics. Among his appointments were chief medical and health officer of East India Railway, vice chancellor and dean of the Faculty of Medicine at Calcutta University, and advisor to the secretary of state for India. In recognition, he received many imperial honors, including a knighthood in 1932. Shaista's uncle, Sir Abdullah Suhrawardy, was also a key actor in imperial and Muslim politics, as was her cousin, Huseyn Suhrawardy—most notably as the last premier of colonial Bengal and, later, prime minister of Pakistan. Another influential figure was her father's sister, Khujista Akhtar Bano, a pioneer of female education in Bengal as well as an Urdu litterateur and Persian scholar.

Her father's employment with East India Railway meant that Shaista grew up in what she called "pseudo-English railway colonies" where the interior décor, gardens, school curriculum, clothes, language, and even diet were all "essentially

English." At the same time, she was taught Urdu, Arabic, and the Quran at home while maintaining strict purdah. At the age of twelve, her father enrolled her at the prestigious convent school and college Loreto House in Calcutta. Because it was affiliated with Calcutta University, she graduated with a BA Hons in 1933. The same year, she was married to an officer in the Indian Civil Service, Mohammad Ikramullah. Shortly after their wedding, he was posted to New Delhi, where he encouraged his wife to come out of purdah so she could accompany him to official events. Having adjusted to "mixed" company, Shaista visited Britain for the first time with her father in 1936. In her autobiography, she described her first experience of England as being "at once familiar and strange" after her "Westernized" childhood. An idyllic holiday was spent in part in an "unspoilt" English village and for the remainder at Newnham College, where she received a "taste" of a privileged university education.

Only a year later, in 1937, Mohammad Ikramullah was posted to England. The "charm" of Shaista's first visit meant that she was glad to be given this opportunity to live in London's affluent neighborhood of Chelsea for three years. On arrival, her eldest son, Inam, was three years old; a daughter, Salma, and a son, Naz, were born in quick succession in London (a fourth child, Sarvath, arrived a decade later) (see fig. 43.1). Still, with the help of a Swedish nurse and an English nanny, Shaista used her time abroad to complete a PhD at the University of London in Urdu literature. This thesis was published a few years later as *A Critical Survey of the Development of the Urdu Novel and Short Story* (1945). With fewer social commitments than in New Delhi, Shaista also indulged in new pursuits that demonstrated her artistic temperament, including theater and ballet. From London, she also accompanied her husband on an official visit to Holland in 1939, during which she toured Amsterdam's art museums, the International Court of Justice at The Hague, and picturesque villages.

A chapter on these years in England was published in her autobiography, *From Purdah to Parliament*, by the Cresset Press in London in 1963. It offers a cursory overview of her "formative" experience from the coronation of George VI in 1937 to Britain's preparations for war in 1939. At the time, she also wrote a series of articles in Urdu for a Delhi women's magazine, 'Ismat, from which two extracts are translated here. Shaista reflected the magazine's privileged readership and reformist bent by focusing on servants and education in England against a backdrop of international politics and war. The first extract, from an article written soon after her arrival in 1937, focused on the system for hiring domestic help in England. The second, written soon after her departure in 1940, recounted the outbreak of the Second World War. That she and her family were on holiday at the Devonshire seaside in September 1939 suggests how they had adopted travel for the purpose of leisure and recreation in imitation of their English hosts while living in Britain. Subsequently, Shaista wrote several more travel pieces for 'Ismat in the 1940s on pleasure travel within India. Evident throughout is her effusive admiration for British women—whether for completing their own household chores or remaining calm in the face of danger—from whom she took important lessons for Indian women.

EXTRACTS

Finding Servants in England

When I heard from the mems in Hindustan that finding servants in England is difficult, I did not pay any attention to it. But now that I have come to live in London for three years, I feel that it is true. There is hardly any culture of keeping servants here. In Hindustan, middle-class people keep two or three servants, and even those who only earn fifty rupees have one boy as a servant. But here, even those who have a monthly income of seven or eight hundred rupees do not keep any servants other than a "cook general." Here, "cook general" refers to the woman who comes around eight or eight thirty in the morning and leaves around seven in the evening. Some only stay until two. They are tasked with cleaning the house (here, there is no [Indian-style] brush but only a "broom," which is a kind of brush that can be used to sweep while standing. The floor is cleaned using this, and those who have carpets clean their floor using a "vacuum cleaner"), cooking meals for the day, or cooking vegetables for the evening. Then they leave. We have to do all the minor tasks that we ask servants to do in Hindustan ourselves because, first, there is hardly any custom of keeping servants, and second, even if there are one or two servants present, they don't do anything but their specific, appointed tasks. Our middle-class women can really take a lesson from the women here. The wives of Hindustani officers in particular should definitely learn from the lives of women of their class here. In Hindustan, what do wives of those officers whose income is 1,000–1,500 [rupees] do but give orders to cooks and ayahs? They consider doing any work on their own contrary to their pride. Here, the wives of officers with the same income wash their clothes, water their plants, and take care of the garden, if they have one. Spreading the mattress, cleaning the shoes, washing the tea utensils, laying out the dining table: they do every task themselves. The housewife goes to the bazaar and does all of the shopping herself.

The income of a maid here is more than that of one of our clerks, that is, twenty-five shillings a week or seventy-five rupees per month. A children's maid makes thirty shillings per week, the cook three shillings per week and, if they cook very well, then two pounds a week. For male cooks, the salary is at least four pounds a week. The income of an attendant or guard etc. is more than our revenue collectors, inspectors, and school masters, that is, three to five hundred rupees per month. This is why no one thinks of keeping an attendant except for very rich people. Nor is there any culture of keeping a male cook. We keep a washer man and a gardener in our homes; here, doing this is almost impossible. Almost no one keeps a washer man. Perhaps in some very old-fashioned, rich homes, there might be a maid or a female servant who's solely responsible for washing clothes. The same is true of gardeners. Only dukes and lords with huge mansions and large gardens keep gardeners, or can keep them. But in Hindustan, except for the poorest people, everyone gives their clothes to a washer man. Here, though, they wash their clothes at home and wear them after ironing them. No one gives "women's underwear," that is, a petticoat, undergarments, etc. to the washer man. Dresses and big things like sheets and curtains are given to the washer man, but even then, restraint is observed. One dress is ironed and worn several times before being given to the washer man. Some even wash their sheets at home. Similarly, those who have a small courtyard (and here, homes with gardens are becoming fewer and fewer by the day) water and take care of the plants themselves. The men here also take part in household tasks on nonworking days alongside the women. For example, tending to the garden is always the responsibility of the husband.

As I wrote above, most people here have only one "cook general," and she goes home in the evening. Women often cook meals and wash the utensils themselves in the evening. It is not considered inappropriate or bad for husbands to help in washing the utensils. Twelve- to fourteen-year-olds, even eight- to ten-year-olds, often help in household tasks like spreading sheets, washing utensils, etc. when they come back from school.

There is no servant here at the level of a bhangi, although a "charwoman" can be called this place's bhangi. They work in two or three homes at the rate of ten or twenty [shillings]. Their task is to sweep the house and do any other work related to dirt such as cleaning the kitchen floor and the bathrooms, washing the tubs, and cleaning the gas stoves—in other words, doing all the work that requires a lot of effort. Some people call a "char" for just an hour in a day or call them once or twice a week for a day to get the house cleaned properly. Except for a "char," one can get servants for two to four hours a day. So some people call one "cook general" for two hours in the evening instead of have them stay from morning to afternoon. This depends on the routine of one's home and who has to work at what part of the day. People like actors or newspaper reporters, who have to work during the night, keep servants only during the evening, not during the day.

The culture of keeping very few servants exists here because the pay of servants is very high. In addition, you must also feed them from what you yourself eat. Except for the "cook general," servants also need separate living quarters, not the kind of small huts that we give our servants. Homes here are very expensive, and no one takes a house with more than two or three rooms. So why would you keep three or four servants when you will need rooms for them? . . .

Thus, finding a servant here is not easy. Generally, everyone complains that servants are proud and arrogant.

The Initial Weeks of War

In September of 1938, the agreement that took place between Hitler and Chamberlain in Munich kept the political atmosphere clear for only a few weeks; from Christmas onward, international relations started deteriorating again. Mussolini started threatening France and, in April 1939, conquered Albania. After this, things went from bad to worse, and finally by July, war clouds started looming over Europe once again. . . .

August is the month for school holidays, but given the political conditions, all teachers had returned to school and were waiting for government instructions. At the same time, hope persisted that God would save them from this disaster.

Even though instructions to take children out of cities had not yet been given, many people had left cities on their own or were making preparations to leave. On August 22, we also thought it wise to leave London. Luckily, we had already made hotel bookings as we were planning to take the children to the beach around the same time. We saw fit to leave a few days early . . . and the hotel manager agreed to allow us to arrive two days early.

We left the next day by the twelve o'clock train. The station that day looked as though the apocalypse had arrived. Neither porters nor carts were to be found. Thousands upon thousands of people were fleeing the city. Every cabin of the train was packed. We entered a cabin in desperation where there were already three children and four women. There wasn't even a place to stand. We placed our coat on the floor and seated the children in the corridor, that is, in a place connecting two cabins. There wasn't a place to keep luggage either, neither in the corridor nor in the guard's van. Sahib[1] was forced to stay and bring the luggage on the next train.

Thankfully, that day the restaurant car that accompanies the train cars wasn't shut down, and the train reached Compton, where we were going, on time—in four and a half hours. Just a few days later, the restaurant car was shut down, and the journey started to last nine or ten hours instead of four and a half. Instead of several trains, as usual, there was now only one train running on this line, and it would stop at every station. After a few days, it got better, but the first few days were spent in panic.

August, as I have said before, is the month of vacation in England. During this month, everyone, whether rich or poor, goes to spend their vacation at the seaside or in the mountains. Many people had come to spend their vacations at the hotel that we booked. At this point, the anxiety and worry that had spread in London wasn't present here.

I reached Compton, which is a small town in England's most beautiful county, Devonshire, one week before the start of war. In that one week, my respect for English men and women increased in my heart after I saw their attitude, and I understood the reasons for the success of this community. If [this country] is so forbearing and stoic today, when it is considered weaker than before, then what courage and gall must it have had in their days of glory and domination.

War clouds were hovering over our heads. Though conditions were deteriorating, not just day by day but moment by moment, people were not at all worried. Those who had come to spend their vacation did not want it to be sullied. Their approach was to handle any worries or tensions when they came. As much as possible, time was to be spent happily—yet *our* temperaments have developed in such a way that we start making a fuss even before it is appropriate to do so.

Even as people played and enjoyed themselves, they were also following the news. During tennis, ping-pong, and swimming, the radio news bulletins were followed regularly. Sometimes there would be a ray of hope, but then it would be dimmed, and the future appeared dark once more. Those days were a cause of great concern for everyone.

On Thursday, August 30, there was supposed to be a dance at the hotel. It was not postponed, even though conditions were bad, and people danced happily. I sat amazed at their stoicism, which had reached a level where conditions didn't affect or influence them. At eleven o'clock, the news on the radio was very disturbing. After presenting his conditions for conciliation with Poland, Hitler himself announced that they were no longer valid. The [new] conditions were now being announced on the radio. In other words, they were announcing the beginning of the war. After listening to this news, there was tension on everyone's face—but only for a few minutes. Then they got up and began dancing once more. The news was read again at twelve. They reported that there would be an announcement tomorrow about children being outside and gave the names of battalions that were being called for war. This news destroyed whatever dim hopes were left. The gathering ended after the national anthem and much cursing of Hitler. Some people sat down with upset faces. Someone's son, someone's son-in-law, someone's brother, or someone's fiancé was old enough to be sent to war. Everyone was sick with worry, wondering when their loved ones would be called. They returned sad-faced to their rooms around two in the morning.

In the morning, we received news that Germany had invaded Poland. By afternoon, the news was confirmed. That day, instructions went out for blackout and dimming the lights. The hotel managers put up black drapes in the dining and sitting rooms. For the bedrooms, we were given candles because it was difficult to put curtains in so many rooms in one day. The news on the radio that night gave a full account of the war's events that day. It was heard that Britain had given an ultimatum to Germany. At this point, the war between Germany and Britain had not yet started. There were even a few people who still harbored some hope. Saturday ended in this uncertainty. The hotel emptied out the very same day. Everyone returned to their homes. War was now certain, and it was therefore necessary to stay at home. A few people had come from the city with their children, and only they now remained at the hotel. At eleven, it was broadcast that everyone should assemble, as they would soon announce important news. Everyone crowded around the radio with pounding hearts. The announcer said that the prime minister would speak from Downing Street. [Prime Minister] Neville Chamberlain's voice was extremely somber, and the radio offered up a deeply sorrowful tone. He announced with a heavy heart that no response was received to the ultimatum given to Germany. Therefore, at eleven that day, war between Britain and Germany would recommence after twenty-two years. He requested the people to deal with the coming war with courage and stoicism and to have faith in God. After that, the national anthem was sung. All remaining hope was destroyed. The fears that had hovered for two and a half years came true. The flame of war was rekindled. Now we could only wait to see what the future would bring.

There was a lot of panic in England in the initial weeks after the start of the war. Though conditions were bad and many preparations had been made, not everyone was ready for war. The first difficulty people had involved blackouts and evacuations.

Even though there had been counsel for months that arrangements be made for dimming the lights, very few people had paid attention to it. Black curtains, black paper, glue, etc. were not available at home. People suddenly stormed the stores; sometimes it was difficult to find these items at the stores. Curtains stitched hastily were often not correct, and light could be seen from the outside. The wardens, that is, those responsible for managing the people in days of war, insisted that light should not be visible at all. Black shades were being put up in every home. The other difficulty was that children brought from the cities were dispersed across various houses, four in one, two elsewhere, and yet another somewhere else. Depending on how much room people had in their homes, the elderly and the sick were taken out of the city and were put up in people's homes. Those who were kind and generous or who had unexpectedly received good-natured guests welcomed them, but homeowners often had no choice. Relations between guests and hosts were difficult. . . .

By November, most people had returned to their homes, and preparations for the blackout had also been made. Trains had also started running smoothly, though not like before. Instead of going all the way to the villages, people began to settle near London so that men could reach their offices and avoid having to keep two homes, a capacity very few people had. We had come from Compton and had started living in Cambridge. By Christmas, people had become accustomed to the war, and business ran as usual. Stores were decorated as before. Special Christmas foods, toys, and decorations were seen in every store. There was the same merriment, the same theater, and the same fun. In short, all the recreations of Western life had begun again. Airstrikes had not yet begun after the unexpected start of war, and there was no maritime or land damage that anyone might notice. This was the reason that people had become relaxed. Many times air strikes were announced, but these announcements proved to be wrong. . . . When I left England, there was no fear at all, though there was certainly danger.

Before finishing this article, I would like to write a few sentences about the Indian women living in England during the war. I say with great sadness that most among them showed a lot of fear and weakness. They approached the difficulties that were created early on due to war with apathy. They troubled their husbands with endless complaints. They worried in such a way that they tired those who were with them. They showed no courage or strength. They displayed no stoicism or fortitude. There were some among them who had come to England for a visit, and no arrangements could now be made for their immediate return due to the outbreak of war. So many people were reporting that it was difficult to get a booking on a ship. But these women wanted the government to abandon everything and arrange for them to go home. They paid no attention to why there was a delay and why there was difficulty. It never struck them that the biggest war in world history had broken out. Thousands were dying, and hundreds of thousands would die. People were suffering huge ordeals, and to worry about minor problems is inappropriate. Those women who were living in England—and their number is large—were unaffected by such problems. For instance, it was a problem to leave one's own home and eat in hotels instead. Or there were problems faced by those living in villages, especially in circumstances where the village administration was disturbed. It was these minor problems that Indian women could not tolerate. The women showing this weakness were old-fashioned, and their ignorance can explain this. These were supposedly educated women. I felt shame to see their fear in front of brave English women. There were, however, a few who did deal with the situation with stoicism and bravery, especially those Indian women who were in Italy and Germany and who had come to London without any resources.

FURTHER READING

Shaista Suhrawardy Ikramullah. "Inglistan meñ naukaroñ ke halat." 'Ismat 59, no. 5 (November 1937): 355–58; and "Inglistan meñ jang ke ibtida'i hafte." 'Ismat 64, no. 6 (June 1940): 408–12. Shaista Suhrawardy Ikramullah's other travel articles in 'Ismat from this period include "Holland ki sair," 62, no. 5 (May 1939): 345–48, translation available at https://accessingmuslimlives.org/travel/shaista1/; and "Dauran-i jang meñ samundar ka safar," 64, no. 6 (Jun. 1940): 465, translation available at https://accessingmuslimlives .org/travel/shaista2/. Additional travel pieces by this author are cited on the website.
———. From Purdah to Parliament. London: Cresset Press, 1963; Reprinted Karachi: Oxford University Press, 1998.
Shaista Akhtar Banu Suhrawardy. A Critical Survey of the Development of the Urdu Novel and Short Story. London: Longmans Green, 1945; Reprinted Karachi: Oxford University Press, 2007. http://www.columbia.edu/itc/mealac/pritchett/00urduhindilinks/suhrawardy /suhrawardy.html.
Gail Minault. Women's Education and Muslim Social Reform in Colonial India. Delhi: Oxford University Press, 1998.

NOTE

1. The author's husband.

FORTY-FOUR

SHAMS PAHLAVI

A Shah's Daughter in Exile

INTRODUCTION

Shams Pahlavi (1917–96) (see fig. 44.1) was the daughter of one king of Iran and the sister of another. Yet she had none of the public profile of her younger twin siblings, Mohammad Reza Pahlavi and Ashraf Pahlavi, or even her youngest brother, Ali Reza Pahlavi. All four were the children of the first Pahlavi ruler, Reza Khan, and his second of four wives, Taj-ol-Moluk. Reza Khan had assumed the crown as shah of a new dynasty in 1925 after, first taking part in a British-supported coup d'état as an officer in the Iranian army in 1921 and then being chosen as prime minister in 1923. As king, Reza Shah sought to reform Iranian state and society through a comprehensive modernization program enforced through authoritarian rule. His family moved into an annex of the Golestan Palace in Tehran, where his sons and daughters received a formal education from private tutors that included instruction in the French language. Many years later, Ashraf penned a memoir, *Faces in a Mirror*, in which she offered a rare depiction of her elder sister as a child, foreshadowing a later life: "Shams was, like my mother, small and delicate and fair, very feminine and comfortable in the traditional female role, which was centered completely on marriage and homemaking. She loved to play with her hundreds of dolls and always looked forward to the day when she would have a husband or children of her own."

A visit to the crown prince, Mohammad Reza Pahlavi, at his exclusive school in Switzerland provided a first opportunity for Shams to travel outside Iran with her mother and sister in 1933. From Tehran, the royal party took a car to

The translation from Persian was prepared by Sunil Sharma. The introduction and annotations were prepared by Siobhan Lambert-Hurley with input from Sunil Sharma.

Figure 44.1 Princess Shams Pahlavi, ca. 1950.
From Wikipedia Commons.

the port of Bandar Pahlavi (previously and once more named Bandar Anzali) on the Caspian Sea, where they boarded a Russian ship to Baku. From there, they journeyed by train to Switzerland through the Soviet Union, Poland, and Germany with only a two-day stopover in Berlin—where, according to Ashraf's memoir, they received flowers from the new German chancellor, Adolf Hitler. Upon their return, Reza Shah decided that "in interest of bringing progress to his country," his wife and daughters would appear unveiled for the first time at a public function in Tehran in 1934. Shams thus led the way for one of her father's most controversial acts: the banning of the veil, or hijab, in 1936. Yet she and Ashraf were still expected to fulfil more traditional functions, entering into arranged marriages with sons of their father's political allies in 1937. For Shams, it meant an unhappy marriage to a young army officer, Fereydoun Djam, whose father, Mahmoud Djam—named in the fourth extract—was then Iran's prime minister.

Alongside internal reforms, Reza Shah also moved to minimize foreign influence in Iran from Britain and the Soviet Union. As a counterbalance, he courted

German commercial interests while also declaring Iran's neutrality in the Second World War. His policy came unstuck when, after the Anglo-Soviet Agreement in 1941, Britain and the Soviet Union united to invade and occupy Iran. On a pretext of the shah having Nazi sympathies, they secured access to Iranian oil and supply lines to the Eastern Front. Reza Shah was forced to abdicate in favor of his eldest son, Mohammad Reza Pahlavi—thus described by Shams in the first extract here as her "crowned brother"—before going into exile. Among the exiled royal party, destined for Argentina according to Ashraf's account, were Shams, her stepmother, and her youngest brother; the twins remained together in Tehran. En route to his destination, the former shah was also accompanied by a British civil servant, Claremont Skrine, who according to Shams was their "companion and guide." Shams documented this journey into exile in her native Persian for eventual publication in installments in the monthly magazine of a major national newspaper in Iran, *Ettela'at*, in 1948. On the basis of its circulation, we may presume that her readership would have been very large.

As indicated in the first extract, the royal party's first destination was not Argentina but India via a ship from the port city of Bandar Abbas to Bombay. However, having arrived in Bombay on October 1, 1941, the Pahlavis were not allowed to go on shore because the British rulers feared that their Indian subjects would rise up in support of Reza Shah. Instead, the party were forced to remain on board the *Bandra* for five days until they moved to a larger vessel, the *Burma*. By that time, British officials had decided to send the former shah and his family to Mauritius, where they spent a few months. Shams's telling suggests that they saw little here on account of being in "absolute seclusion" without any contact with local people. Although he was not permitted to return home, Reza Shah wanted his children to be back in Iran. It was thus decided that Shams, her stepmother, and her brother would go to Cairo in Egypt via Durban in South Africa and Mombasa in Kenya, and from there make their way to Tehran. Shams documented how, from Durban, she also took a day trip to Johannesburg. It proved prescient as, a couple of years later in 1944, her father died there while still a British captive exiled from his family and home.

Shams's account of her months of exile with her family is, as one might expect, focused largely on her father's emotions and physical state. The extracts translated here are the sections where she writes about herself, especially with reference to travel on different ships on the Arabian Sea and the Indian Ocean at the height of the Second World War. Shams's style of writing is simple and elegant, and even where she narrates her emotional state—on being parted from her father and, while ill in a Mombasa hotel during festivities for the Persian

New Year (Nowruz), her mother and brother too—it is done with a quiet dignity. Her narrative ends with a sense of resolution: her return to Iran to be reunited with her homeland, brother, and mother. But in fact it marked a new beginning in her life. Soon after her father's death, she divorced her first husband to marry her music teacher, Mehrdad Pahlbod, with whom she had three children. She also embraced Roman Catholicism. While her sister Ashraf engaged in politics with her twin brother, Shams dedicated her life to her family and managing a vast fortune inherited from her father. Ultimately, the Iranian Revolution forced the Pahlavis into exile again, with Shams living out her days in the United States. After the shah's fall, her twinned brother and sister both wrote a memoir, as did her brother's wife, Farah. But from Shams, only this travelogue offers unique insight into her emotions and personality at a pivotal moment in Iranian and global history.

EXTRACTS

Moored outside Bombay

Every day in the evenings, from the ship we observed a scene with a great storm, thunder and lightning, in the city of Bombay. In the roar of the thunder and the astonishing brightness of the lightning, Bombay had a special brilliance. I asked myself whether a day would arrive when a ray of hope would shine in our hearts.

After five days of not moving on the sea, every hour seemed like a year to us. It became dull and difficult to pass the time until the arrival of the ocean-navigating ship that had been requested for the continuation of our trip to the island of Mauritius. We were compelled to leave the *Bandra* that had brought us from Bandar Abbas to the waters of Bombay, and by means of a boat, we transferred to the new ship. This ship, the *Burma*, was also a small naval vessel with capacity of eleven tons. It was a vessel of an Indian shipping company, and on the whole, its condition was much better than that of the *Bandra*.

When everything was loaded, the voice of the ship captain announced its departure, and it didn't take long until the *Burma* was tearing through the shoreless breast of the ocean, heading for the hot tropical waters and areas. At that dark and scary moment, which I don't know how to describe, I thought to myself: What will be the end of this unknown trip? Would the day of freedom and release follow this imprisonment, and would the conclusion of this trip be a return? Would we see our dear homeland again, and my crowned brother, our home, and friends? Unfortunately, I did not find hopeful answers to these questions, and it was only divine grace that shone a ray of hope on my dejected state, giving me tidings of life.

On the Burma

On this ship too, our life was the same as on the *Bandra*. His Majesty my father generally paced the deck of the ship during day hours, lost in distant thoughts. Every hour and moment that he saw us, he said, "Try to keep up your spirits. Be strong. Don't let despair get the better of you." He was most concerned that we not lose our confidence in the face of difficulties and succumb to grief and sorrow. He preferred to eat his meals alone in his room, but as we traveled farther and neared the equator, the weather became warmer, and he would relax on deck. The weather was not agreeable to most of us, and we were uncomfortable and lethargic most hours of the day and night. . . .

On the *Burma*, as on the *Bandra*, we were without news about Tehran and generally about the world. Several times we wanted to send a telegram to Tehran from the ship. They accepted our telegrams but explained that we shouldn't expect an answer. Mr. Skrine[1] was our companion and guide on this ship. He remained with us until Mauritius, and once there, he was our guest for a week or two.

Our trip from the waters of Bombay to the island of Mauritius lasted ten days. During this time, our fatigue and boredom was so extreme that we all wanted to reach dry land as soon as possible and be freed from the hardship of travel and the sea. Early morning on October 15, the island of Mauritius became visible. From afar it appeared paradisial, like a thicket of flowers and greenery. The sight of this lovely lush place caused us all to be joyful. That day, after twenty days of suffering and searing heat, we felt happiness in our hearts.

The ship halted near the island and gave a signal to the lighthouse, which was returned. One of the Indian functionaries was a man named Sohrab whose mother was an Iranian from Kerman. Since he knew Persian well, we asked when we would disembark on the island. He said 4:00 p.m. We were of course disheartened by the idea of staying on the ship until 4:00 p.m., but we took it in stride. At four o'clock, the British governor of the island, Sir Bede Clifford,[2] and a group of men from the city, all dressed in uniforms, arrived on a boat to welcome us. They greeted His Majesty officially and took us to the port. Several city taxis for hire, bigger than the ones in Tehran, were waiting for us. My father and I sat in the first taxi, while the others got into the other ones, and right away we were taken to a building with a garden in a nice part of the city that had been chosen for our residence. That day the local newspapers briefly wrote about the arrival of His Majesty and us in the daily news section.

I imagine it would be fitting that, before I write about our lives and living quarters in Mauritius, I briefly describe here the geographical location and the condition of the inhabitants for my fellow countrymen. Indeed, since we did not have contact with them and remained in absolute seclusion, my information about the island is cursory.

From Mauritius to Durban

The passenger ship on which we traveled from Mauritius was a Dutch grand luxury ship that came from the East Indies. The passengers were generally women and children, and old men and women, who were being removed from the war zone in the Dutch Indies to a safe place. Despite the shortage of space on the ship, they were fully cooperative and kind to us, giving each one of us a proper room. In addition, since the ship was passing through dangerous areas where at any moment it could be the target of Japanese submarine attacks, they gave a life vest to each one of us, instructed us how to use it and how to board a lifeboat, and blew an emergency whistle a few times. We practiced these actions several times.

I think that the date of our departure from Mauritius was March 8 or 9. The duration of our trip, the only time that one could say we were comfortable on this Dutch ship, was four days. After four days, we dropped anchor at Durban, which is a port on the shore of Natal, one of the united provinces of South Africa. We embarked and went to a hotel in the city to wait for another ship on which we would continue our journey.

Durban too, like all parts of Africa, is full of trees and greenery. Many trees were visible on the roads and lanes. They said that this is among the most important summering places of South Africa, but to my mind the climate was hot and humid. Since we had a couple of free days, I decided that I would use them to see Johannesburg, which is reckoned the biggest city of South Africa and is 482 miles from Durban. Certainly, on that day I did not know that the city I was going to visit would be the one where fate would bring my father to spend the rest of his weary days. Until now, no discussion had taken place about Johannesburg being the city of his residence after Mauritius, and such a thought had not passed my mind either. The reason for going to Johannesburg was only because I had heard about its beauty and importance in Africa, and since I was forced to stop in Durban, I wanted to spend a day seeing it. But perhaps God's will and fate were such that before I returned to my homeland, I should see the city where my father would spend the last days of his life. In any case, I had a great desire to see this city, and although I was exhausted from the inconveniences of travel, I was resolved and set off with one of my companions.

From Durban to Mombasa

Compared to the Dutch ship on which we had traveled from Mauritius, the ship that was to carry us from Durban was old and dilapidated and full of soldiers.

It was originally French, and the sailors were mostly French too. I don't know what had happened, but it had fallen into the hands of the British, perhaps as a result of the conflict between the supporters of the Vichy government and the British. Since it was run-down, the British planned to take it to Bombay and turn it into a hospital. The French sailors were opposed to the British plan, and therefore every day they had a conflict with the British on board and sometimes, if the opportunity presented itself, did not hold back from further destroying the ship. Incidentally, this old and decrepit ship had to pass through dangerous waters in the route of Japanese submarines. Around this time the Japanese submarines had torpedoed a commercial vessel, so you can imagine how our morale was. Unfortunately, the slowness of the ship, which had a speed of less than ten kilometers per hour and frequently stopped for repairs, doubled our agitation and worry, and we passed some very bitter and disturbing days.

Another sorrowful incident that affected our weary minds was that one of the French sailors, who like the other sailors was unhappy with the course of events, one day threw himself into the water and drowned. They said that this person had thrown himself into the sea several times before, and they had rescued him, but this time they could not succeed in saving him.

In this way, for ten days we were on the water, anxious and confused, beset with great sorrow and sadness, until the ship reached Mombasa, the chief port of Kenya in East Africa and 150 miles from Zanzibar. After the ship arrived, first they had the soldiers disembark but did not give us permission to leave because of the extraordinary war and military situation of Mombasa. At that time Mombasa was considered the biggest center and base for the British naval forces in their fight against Japanese submarines and protection of the Indian Ocean. In fact, three areas were important in this regard. One was Ceylon [Sri Lanka], which was practically threatened by the Japanese and had lost its importance; the other was Madagascar, which was in the hands of the French and where there was the fear of a revolution. Therefore, the only important base of the British navy and army was Mombasa. The warm and debilitating sea climate at the time the ship was docked also became the reason for my illness, and a high fever caused me to be laid up. Although this became a cause of worry for my fellow travelers, and even the British doctor on the ship advised that unless I was moved to the shore to rest, I was in danger, the strict war rules did not allow them to be lenient with me. Eventually, after my illness continued for a few days, due to the insistence and recommendation of the doctor, they agreed that only I and one of my companions could leave, while the ship was being repaired until it was ready to depart, and stay in one of the hotels in the city. Meanwhile by chance, the *Burma,* the same ship that had brought us to Mauritius, dropped anchor in

Mombasa, and seeing it awakened all the old memories for me, and I recalled the troubles that we experienced from the day we boarded it until today. When the captain and workers of the *Burma* saw us in that situation, they were kind, and the captain found us a hotel in Mombasa for a few days.

For a short while, as we rode from the ship to the hotel, I managed to see Mombasa, whose people are mostly black, and which at that time was full of British soldiers. Later I heard that in the eleventh century, our ancestors and Arabs had also come to Mombasa, and Ibn Battuta mentioned it in his travelogue.[3]

We spent the first day in the hotel and the next day wanted to go and see the city for an hour, when they informed us from the hotel's office that a British officer had said, "The princess should not leave the hotel and should wait for me at four o'clock." I was forced to change my plans and sat down to wait for four o'clock, not knowing whether someone would come to see me and whether the news would be good or bad. He came at four o'clock sharp and in an official and dry tone told me, "I have the responsibility to inform you that you do not have permission to leave the hotel." After that, they appointed a soldier to watch over me, who was changed every two hours. These officers sat outside the door of my room. I was extremely depressed by this, in my condition of illness, and said that if you won't give me permission to leave the hotel, give me permission to return to the ship. At least on the ship, I have more freedom, and at night the warmth of the sea breeze is lessened. But they did not grant permission for me to go to the ship and said that for now I should stay in the hotel. Earlier I had arranged for the rest of my traveling companions who had remained on the ship to be allowed to come to the city and not suffer my fate, but now I tried to find a way to send them a message to not come to the city and to stay on the ship. But before I could do anything, they arrived there and shared in my bitter fate. The last resort that occurred to me was that through His Majesty King Faroruk of Egypt I would send a telegram to inform Mr. Djam,[4] the ambassador of Iran in Cairo, and ask to be rescued. Immediately I prepared the text of the telegram and gave it to my guard to send to Egypt.

It was the evening of the festival of Nowruz,[5] and I was alone in my room, lost in my disturbed thoughts and so affected that I couldn't control my tears. I thought to myself that it was the evening of Nowruz and my whole family should be gathered together, but I was neither with my father nor with my mother and brother. I wondered if anyone was remembering me as the year changed and whether anyone except almighty God was thinking of me. That night I was not able to sleep and spent a night so bitter that I will never forget it all my life.

The sad thoughts of that night had scarcely left me the day after Nowruz when the appointed British officer knocked on my door and informed me that the commander of the British forces would come to see me at eleven o'clock. Since I had become accustomed to wait daily for a new development, at hearing this, I became anxious and waited to see what the officer's intention was in meeting with me. At last, eleven o'clock arrived, and the British commander, who was an old officer and had an aristocratic and gentlemanly appearance, came through the door. First of all, he expressed regret about the state of affairs and explained that the strict war agreements necessitated some inconvenience for His Majesty. Then he said, "They have commanded us from Cairo that we should get two seats ready on the first airplane that will fly from here to Cairo, one for Your Highness and the other for one of your companions. Since the plane leaves in two days, prepare yourself for the trip." I asked, "What should the others do?" He replied, "The others have no choice but to go to Bombay on a ship, which is being repaired now, and from there to Iran by train or ship."

Although this news was an end to my troubles, I was worried about the others, especially my siblings. My wish was that if there was a way out, it would be for all of us, and I wouldn't be separated from them. But since I had no choice, I accepted the situation and requested the commander that I be allowed to go out of the hotel for some personal tasks. He agreed on the condition that a guard would accompany me. Two days later, I flew to Cairo, where I spent a few days in the Iranian embassy, and from there I left for Iran. After a period of sorrowful parting and separation from my friends and country, I was rewarded with the sight of my dear homeland, my brother the king, and my respected mother.

FURTHER READING

Shams Pahlavi's text was published as a series of essays in 1948 in the magazine *Ettela'at-e mahyaneh*. They were reprinted in their entirety in *Reza Shah: Khaterat-e Solayman Behbodi, Shams Pahlavi, 'Ali Ezadi*. Edited by Gholamhosayn Mirza Saleh, 401–47. Tehran: Tarh-i Naw, 1993.

Ashraf Pahlavi. *Faces in a Mirror: Memoirs from Exile*. Englewood Cliffs NJ: Prentice-Hall, 1980.

Mohammad Reza Pahlavi. *The Shah's Story*. London: Michael Joseph, 1980.

Farah Pahlavi. *An Enduring Love: My Life with the Shah—A Memoir*. New York: Miramax Books, 2005.

Clarmont Skrine. *World War in Iran*. London: Constable, 1962.

Touraj Atabaki and Erik J. Zürcher, eds. *Men of Order: Authoritarian Modernization under Atatürk and Reza Shah*. London: I. B. Tauris, 2017.

NOTES

1. Sir Clarmont Percival Skrine (1888–1974) was a British civil servant who at this time was serving as counselor for Indian affairs in Tehran, Iran.

2. Sir Bede Edmund Hugh Clifford (1890–1969), governor of Mauritius from 1937 to 1941, also held high administrative positions in other parts of the British Empire.

3. Ibn Battuta was a famous fourteenth-century Muslim traveler from Morocco who described his extensive travels from North Africa over land and sea all the way to China and back in his *Rihla*.

4. Shams had an arranged marriage with the ambassador's son, Fereydoun Djam, that lasted only until after her father's death in 1944.

5. This important family holiday is the Persian new year that falls on the spring equinox.

FORTY-FIVE

—⚬—

NYONYA AULIA-SALIM

An Indonesian Tours America by Motor

INTRODUCTION

In the early 1950s, Nyonya Aulia-Salim left her native Indonesia to accompany her husband on a momentous ten-month journey across the United States (see fig. 45.1). As head of the Department of Internal Medicine at the University of Indonesia, Professor Aulia had been invited to tour medical facilities across the country. The couple began their journey in New York City before traveling west to California through New Orleans and Birmingham in the American South and concluding in Washington, DC. Professor Aulia's time was often occupied with working in one hospital or another—and because his wife was not used to going out unaccompanied, she spent long days in hotel rooms, passing the hours with reading or writing. By the end, Nyonya Aulia-Salim had produced a large collection of letters that, on her return, were preserved as a book with the title *Melawat ke Amerika* (*A Journey to America*, 1954).

Nyonya Aulia-Salim's own interest in their American journey was a reflection of her family background, marital status, and public activities. She was born in the late colonial period in Tanjung Pinang, the capital of the Riau Islands in the South China Sea. She belonged to the extended family of Haji Agus Salim, renowned as one of the forefathers of Indonesian independence and the architects of the Indonesian constitution, as well as foreign minister in the late 1940s. Access to higher education and travel during the late colonial and early independence periods was reserved primarily for men, but after Indonesia gained independence in 1949, a growing number of women from the upper classes

---

Megan Hewitt prepared the introduction and translations from Indonesian with input from Siobhan Lambert-Hurley and Daniel Majchrowicz.

nj. N. Aulia-Salim beserta Prof. Aulia dengan seorang
Pemuda Indonesia di San Francisco.

Figure 45.1 Nyonya Aulia-Salim with her husband in San Francisco's Union
Square, 1951. Courtesy of Daniel Majchrowicz.

experienced greater social and physical mobility. Being the wife of a prominent
Indonesian leader—diplomat, doctor, politician, or journalist—was an important category for social and political organization in the new nation-state. Many
of the earliest women's organizations in Indonesia were formed alongside major
national organizations, often by wives of politicians and leaders of their time.

Living in Jakarta, Nyonya Aulia-Salim was embedded within a community
of women working to foster cultural dialogue between Indonesian and Western
women in the country. To this end, she was a member of the Women's International Club (WIC), an organization founded in 1950s with the following aims:
"To foster friendship and mutual understanding between women of different
nationalities; to contribute to the cultural development of women in general,
and to promote the cause of education and social reform in the interest and
welfare of women and children." As part of her involvement with this organization, Nyonya Aulia-Salim published monthly Indonesian language lessons in
the WIC's journal. These contributions inspired the publication of a second
book just one year after the publication of *Melawat ke America*. What began as
a monthly language lesson in the WIC periodical culminated, at the urging of
her readers, in a textbook, *Indonesian Language* (1955).

Melawat ke America began life as letters to a female companion in Indonesia addressed as *adinda*, or sister—though the exact relationship is unclear. According to the book's preface, this relative had solicited the letters on the basis that she wanted "stories of our adventures." Nyonya Aulia-Salim explained that they had similar tastes and interests—and so she had found it easy to craft the content on the basis of what would interest her reader. Only later did she consider publication when "several friends in the Netherlands" suggested that this large collection of letters be printed. The title is an allusion to another popular work of travel writing, *Melawat ke Barat* (*A Journey to the West*), written by one of the pioneers of the Indonesian press, Djamaluddin Adinegoro, while studying in Germany and the Netherlands between 1926 and 1930. Though his book was first published in 1930, it was reissued in 1950 due to its popularity. Much like Adinegoro's work, Nyonya Aulia-Salim reflects on the world in terms of a growing sense of Indonesian national consciousness. Written in the immediate postindependence era, her travel writing is also infused with the pride of newly acquired nationhood.

The extracts here—linked to specific locations across the United States—are representative of the book as a whole in that they capture the sights, sounds, and feelings of travel. Nyonya Aulia-Salim's style of writing is very personal as she reflects on her excitement, nervousness, and frustrations with travel. Throughout, the reader is given a sense of the limitations of traveling as a Malay Muslim woman from an upper-class background and the difficulties that diplomats' wives faced in supporting the work (and travel) of their husbands. At the same time, the work is very meticulous as she records the precise details of logistical minutia, from specific costs and timings of hotels and transportation to exact names and dates of people and places visited. The book thus offers a window into 1950s America from the rare perspective of an Indonesian woman—with descriptions of American society and bureaucracy, race relations, the women's movement, and Eleanor Roosevelt.

EXTRACTS

New York City

We sat in our small room, reflecting for a moment. Looking out the window, nothing was visible except tall stone buildings. We were surrounded only by stones. Our chests tightened at the sight of it, the feeling of being crushed by those stones. The stone buildings are all full of small windows. The city feels like a beehive made of stone, and we humans are the bees, without any power.

After reflecting for a while, my husband picked up the telephone book to find the number for the consulate office. Oh, my, the thickness of that book is no joke. No less than eight fingers wide, and long too. Heavy to lift. But for more than eleven million residents, of course the telephone book would need to be that thick. Even if not every person has a telephone, there are certainly many people who have two or three telephones in their homes.

Happiness fills the heart, thinking of our people who are free and able to become representatives for our new nation in America.

Since the next day we would be taken to Washington, that night a young man took us to see the city of New York. For hours we were taken around by car. We went to see places that were very crowded and full of people having fun.

Wah, this is what New York is like, a giant city in the country where "possibilities are endless!" We were surprised and full of awe. By car we passed by several skyscrapers, each tens of stories high. The iron bridges surprised us the most; layered, hundreds of meters long, illuminated by tens of thousands of electric lamps, shimmering and shining brilliantly. Some were like necklaces with pendants, others like a crown studded with diamonds and precious gems, or angelic pavilions. Not a human creation, but something made by jinns and sprites. Not a place for humans to live, but the abode of gods in heaven!

Lastly, we were brought to Times Square, the busiest part of New York City. It is the main place for entertainment. Big-name film stars in a race of beauty and brains to capture hearts. The movie theater is a popular place to gather there. The place is full of theaters, nightclubs, dancing, and all manner of enjoyment.

It is also a place where the rich go to empty their pockets, destroy their health, and wreck their homes. Times Square is bright and boisterous until morning. There are many stores open day and night, never closing, especially the places for entertainment.

But the law of life cannot be denied. Wherever wealth has reached its peak, there will also be many impoverished people. In the middle of the electric lights that shine like the sun, in the middle of all these people having fun and wearing beautiful clothes, we saw a beggar. A large body with blind eyes, singing sad songs, trying to inspire pity in the hearts of people around him, whom he could hear laughing and chatting nearby. It broke our hearts to see another human being forced to humiliate themselves in trying simply to stay alive. Each time and place we saw this, we wondered how it was appropriate for the government to leave them in this condition? If in times of war all youth are mobilized to sacrifice their lives to defend the country, if every person capable of working is obliged to surrender part of their income to the state, should not that government be responsible for guaranteeing the lives of those people? Especially when they are no longer able to work?

We sat for a while at a restaurant in Times Square. We drank iced drinks and watch hundreds of people cross the street on foot. After that we were brought back to the hotel. It was very late, and we felt very tired. It was enough to see and experience for one day.

On Eleanor Roosevelt

Mrs. Roosevelt is popular here, and because of it, with just one word, she opened the doors to the women's movement and [gatherings for] children's education for us. It is unfortunate that we are not part of the movement. It would yield great results if we were champions of the women's movement. Escorted by Mrs. Roosevelt's secretary, we met with a member of the governing body of the women's movement in New York.

We explained to them that we are not part of a movement, nor were we sent by any group. We only want to know about the progress women have made in America, and what kinds of work are available to them.

We went on to explain that we were actually quite excited about our movement [in Indonesia], but as the wives of public servants during the Dutch colonial period, we were blocked from entering any nationalist gatherings. They strictly guarded these gatherings, and even reciting the smallest bit of poetry without intending to incite, we were nonetheless called in front of the police on two separate occasions. The first time in Semarang because of a poem, and another time in Jakarta because of another poem that had already been published in Semarang and was not seen as having anything wrong with it at the time!

After these two times, "snap," we stopped reciting poetry. We thought, what's the use of endangering the position of our husbands, especially when these compositions were not yet useful?

We explained all of this to the women that we met from the movement. They really wanted to introduce us to their group, but since it was summer, schools were closed, their meetings were less active, and most of their members were out of town. We really would have liked to have seen one of their meetings and their work. They are reportedly very progressive and well organized. We were also given several brochures about their inner workings.

We did not forget to tell them that in our country, the women's movement has progressed. We were pleased to explain how "votes for women" is not an issue in our country. As long as our people are free, women have their own "voice." It was reportedly only after a fierce battle in 1920 that women gained their voice [i.e., the right to vote] here.

In short, they tried very hard to convince us to return before winter in order to see everything they described. We parted in hopes of meeting again. We understand that their movement was made possible by the influence of Mrs. Roosevelt, who is very popular among progressive people here.

Berkeley

On Sunday, we were picked up in a car by a professor from the medical school at the "University of California." Professor R. had already visited our country and our home to have a meeting with several of our professors.

We drove through San Francisco and across the Oakland Bay Bridge. Professor R. brought us to his home to meet his wife and children. Beforehand, we were driven around the Berkeley Hills for hours. The hills were truly beautiful, with their pools and valleys. The road wound around up and down like in Puncak and Bandung. It reminded us of all of those places: Sindanlaya, Megamendung, Tjibodas, etc. Though at that time we could see how difficult it was to compare our country to this place. Many places in our mountain regions are more beautiful than the hills and mountains we saw here.

It was of course great to travel by car. The roads were slippery and wide, traversing through mountains and over bridges. Our nation may lose [in terms of infrastructure], but in the beauty of our nature and glimmering sun that rises and sets, that is where we win.

Professor R. brought us around town by car for a while. After we were satisfied with what we had seen, he brought us to his home.

For hours we sat drinking tea and eating cakes with his wife, who was very friendly and sweet. They seemed so happy to meet with us, people who are rarely seen in the United States.

Many people here do not know where Indonesia is located; there are also those who think we are from India. In Indonesia we know much about America and other large nations, so we were surprised to think that the people of this educated nation could know so little about other nations.

New Orleans

On our journey from New York to Los Angeles, we have not seen anything offensive from white-skinned people toward Negro people or their descendants.[1] Reportedly, even if someone has white skin, if they have any Negro blood in their ancestry, they still suffer from "segregation." In this situation, women are especially affected, as far as we have heard. . . .

Our airplane flew us to Dallas, a small city not far from New Orleans. Here we saw with our own eyes the separation of Negro people, "Segregation." Several places displayed signs, "For white only," "For black only." Reading this, our blood pounded. We were reminded of our own country, where we are still colonized by the Netherlands. Truly surprising! This is the form of all white-skinned people! The Americans toward Negro people; the Dutch people toward us; the English toward Indians; the French toward all of their colonies. They're all the same!

Their thoughts fall far from the truth. Do they not understand that while they are satisfied, there are those that will resist? After hundreds of years sowing hate and revenge, is not a disaster going to grow?

They don't believe that at some point retaliation will come. They are convinced that colored peoples will never have another chance for freedom and strength. They are truly arrogant! . . .

One day we were walking down "Canal Street." Cheerfully we looked at all of the beautiful things. We were suddenly startled and stopped in our tracks. At a "candy shop," there was a large statue, as big as a person, stuck in the front of the door. The store was called "Aunt Sally." The statue was of a Negro woman with a cloth on her head and a layered dress like we see in films. The neck of the statue was tied with a rope that was nailed to the doorway, looking as though the person was being hung. The eyes "glared," bright for a moment and then dark, like a person being choked, nearly dead.

Breathless, we could feel the dark eyes we were looking at, and several of us stopped, pensive. We could not believe our own eyes. How could this be possible in this age of progress, in the year 1951? While the United States government is working to foster friendship with all nations, while thousands of dollars are spent to solidify the United Nations, the people of the United States are still doing this? It's truly difficult to understand.

We have already been in the United States for months. We have not met anyone unkind. Everyone has been courteous, helpful, and curious to know us. It's not possible that American people, who are so advanced and educated, would allow something as barbaric as that!

Our cheerfulness vanished, and with a feeling of shock, we continued walking. Not far from there was another statue at the front of a store, also of a Negro woman. Both of her hands were tied tightly with a rope!

Our shock could not be exhausted, we thought. What could they mean? Is there not one among the white people here who would advise the owner of the store to remove these offensive statues? Can it not be understood by the shop owner that an action like that in this era is truly dangerous?

Negro people, who they say have already reached fourteen million in the United States, will be easily incited by communists if they continue to be hurt in this way. The American people, who are not stupid, still continue to sow the seeds of communism.

We are not political experts, and we don't really understand all of the ins and outs, but we are sure that people who feel hurt will certainly become our enemies. What's more: wrongdoings will not generate good results!

Not just Negro people, but all peoples with colored skin would feel hurt by seeing these offenses!

But in the South, the kindness and courtesy of white people is very different from this disheartening situation. There is no limit to their friendliness and eagerness to help when compared to people in the North, who are called "Yankees" here. Every person here looks as though they really like getting to know us. Whatever we ask about, they happily give their time to completely explain everything.

Birmingham, Alabama

While in Birmingham, we did not see anything insulting toward Negro people, not like the very offensive statues in New Orleans. Here, "Segregation" is not as strong.

In several places we read the signs, "For black only" and "For white only" [sic]. Different churches, different schools, different hospitals, or separate rooms within larger hospitals; in short, the Negro people are strictly excluded from all fields. Even taxi drivers are not allowed to drive Negro passengers.

The first time my husband went to the hospital, he suffered from this segregation. When he wanted to take a taxi, the driver looked somewhat stunned before opening the automobile door. With a doubtful gaze he looked closely at my husband's face before proceeding to invite him into the car, saying, "Get in."

Indeed, his actions were very rude, but my husband did not pay much mind. Once he'd arrived at the hospital but before paying for the ride, he asked, "Why were you so doubtful earlier, before opening the automobile door?" The taxi driver replied, "At first I thought you were a Negro person. We're not allowed to drive Negro people." With a patient voice, as though explaining to a student, my husband replied, "Is that how American people are? Who pride themselves on democracy, to treat Negro people who have already lived and died together for hundreds of years? Are you not afraid that this could sow the seeds of communism?" "Yeah," replied the driver. "It's true what you say, but I didn't make the rule."

This must happen often to foreign visitors with colored skin. How would most people know that we are not the descendants of Negro people? Does this not complicate the relationship between nationalities? Because of this, the government of the United States should truly work to obliterate these cruel customs. Only contemptible people like to offend!

Washington, DC

The State Department covered the cost of travel throughout the United States for the husbands. But we, the wives, had to pay for ourselves. No matter how much we save, it's just not possible to cover all of our daily expenses. It would also cost a lot if we stayed in New York while our husbands traveled to all of the places described.

We explained this situation at the State Department office in Washington, DC, and asked for a responsible clerk to ask their government to request to borrow money from Jakarta that could be paid back to their office in Washington, DC.

As you already know, while we needed the money here, our husbands' salaries were paid in Jakarta. This is government regulation. The wives of civil servants are considered silent. More than that! Other than those that work as civil servants for the state, it can be said that the wives of civil servants are seen as obstacles in the affairs of sending civil servants abroad. Troublesome affairs, only spending their money!

It's often forgotten that many wives suffer the same misery as their husbands while traveling, and for many years after. They are no less brave in opposing danger and persevering in the face of misery. Would there be victory if they were not just as fully committed in the struggle? Now, only the civil servants are awarded!

After struggling together, after attaining victory, the time has come when we can harvest the fruits of our struggle, but wives must always stay behind. She can only accompany her husband if he gets permission to bring his wife! Wow, it is truly miserable being a wife! What's bitter at first is sweet in the end . . . we must wait!

We are lucky to be able to accompany our husbands traveling for over six months. There is another regulation that gives wives permission to join only if the journey is longer than one or two years. If less than that, the wives must be left behind. This is very dangerous for the safety of a household, it cannot be denied. The strength of the state is dependent on the safety and stability of the households of the people. But this does not seem to be one of the beliefs of our government. But what more is there to say? We are "only" women, and "what do women know?"

The State Department clerk just smiled while listening to our suggestions, and we did not push it any further.

A few days later, we came back to the office for other business. Cheerfully the clerk gave us a letter stating that all of the expenses from our travels in the United States would be covered by the State Department. I'm sure this happened because of the work of the clerk helping us. Our hearts were filled with gratitude. Just like that, all of our previous concerns about travel vanished. We would not be happy leaving the United States without apologizing to the State Department office clerk.

FURTHER READING

Nyonya Aulia-Salim. *Melawat ke Amerika*. Djakarta: Saksama, 1954. Additional translated extracts from this text are available online at: https://accessingmuslimlives.org/travel/aulia/.

——. *Indonesian Language (Bahasa Indonesia)*. Djakarta: Tintamas, 1955.

——. "Apakah Poligami Semata-Mata Soal Wanita?" *Suara Perwari* 6, no. 3 (1956): 12–13.

——. "The Matriarchal System." *Women's International Club Journal* 7, no. 4 (1959): 128–31.

Elizabeth Martyn. *The Women's Movement in Post-Colonial Indonesia: Gender and Nation in a New Democracy*. London: Routledge Curzon, 2005.

Kathryn May Robinson and Sharon Bessell, eds. *Women in Indonesia: Gender, Equity and Development*. Singapore: Institute of Southeast Asian Studies, 2002.

NOTE

1. The author uses the phrase "*bangsa Negro*." *Bangsa* is a distinction that can be used in Indonesian to mean ethnicity, nationality, or any shared identity of a group of people. For Nyonya Aulia-Salim, the term *bangsa* carried a great resonance within the context of a newly independent Indonesia, and the sense of a shared identity solidified by nationalism.

GLOSSARY

Allahu akbar A common interjection used in many settings; it means "God is great."

amin Amen.

andarun Literally, "that which is inside." It often refers to those parts of the house that are occupied by women and not accessible to unrelated male visitors.

azan The call to prayer; also spelled adhan.

barkhurdar In South Asia, a term of address for a young man.

begum/begam Historically, a royal or aristocratic title in Central Asia. It is now widely used to denote any Muslim woman of high rank, particularly in South Asia. It may also denote a married woman.

Bhangi A member of the sweeper-class in South Asia; formerly referred to as the "untouchable" caste.

bismillah A common Arabic phrase that means "In the name of God." It is typically invoked at the start of an activity.

burqa One of many types of outer garments worn by women that covers both the body and face. Its style and coverage vary.

chador A large, sheetlike cloth worn by women, particularly in Iran and Iraq, as an outer cloak and held in place by hand.

charshaf Often transliterated in Turkish as *tcharchaff*, this was a type of veil worn by Turkish women. It consisted of a thick black piece of sewn cloth covering the head, face, shoulders, and bosom that was usually worn with a long cloak and gloves.

dupatta A long scarf or shawl used in many South Asian styles of women's dress. It is typically draped over the head and chest.

durud Prayers or blessings said for the Prophet Muhammad.

Eid May refer to either of two major Muslim holidays: Eid al-Fitr, which occurs at the end of the fasting month of Ramadan, or Eid al-Adha, which marks Abraham's sacrifice.

Emamzadeh The descendent of a Shia imam.

faqir A poor or destitute person; frequently used to refer to mendicants, ascetics, or other figures who have turned away from worldly affairs.

Fatiha The first chapter of the Quran. It is commonly recited over graves.

ghazi A title given to successful Muslim warriors or conquerors.

ghee A type of clarified butter used particularly in South Asian cooking.

hadith The sayings of the Prophet Muhammad, as recalled by his companions and later recorded by religious scholars.

hajji An honorific for one who has completed the hajj pilgrimage or is in the process of doing so.

Al-Hajr al-Aswad A black stone set into one corner of the Kaaba that is an object of reverence.

Al-Hamdu lillah "Praise be to God." An Arabic phrase that is used widely by Muslims of all backgrounds.

hammam A bathhouse, the popularity and form of which varies widely.

haram An Arabic word that literally means "sanctuary" or "holy space." It is most often used to describe the precincts of the main mosque in Mecca and the mosque in Medina that contains the tomb of the Prophet. When used to refer to the women's quarter of a house, it is spelled *harem*, in keeping with common usage.

harijan Literally "children of God," a now-dated term for dalits, also formerly known as "untouchables"; the term was advocated by Gandhi.

Hatim Also known as the Hajr Isma'il, this is a small wall opposite the Kaaba that lies within the circular space around which pilgrims walk while performing the tawaf, or ritual circumambulation.

hijab A broad term that may refer to any type of covering worn by a woman for the purpose of modesty in front of unrelated men. It typically refers to covering the head and chest, and sometimes the face. The word may also be used to refer to modesty before men generally.

ihram The clothing worn while performing the hajj or 'umrah pilgrimages. Men typically wear two white, unstitched cloths. Women's clothing may vary, but often do not include a veil or face covering.

imam In Shiism, descendants of the Prophet Muhammad who are his rightful, designated successors to both spiritual and worldly leadership.

inshallah Literally, "If God wills it." A phrase applied to any future plan or to denote uncertainty.

jan Literally, "life." A term of endearment and an intimate honorific suffix.

jinn In Islamic theology, the jinn are a class of supernatural creatures created from fire who are credited with varying types and levels of superhuman abilities.

Kaaba The most sacred place in Islam, it is a small building located at the center of the Haram Mosque in Mecca. Muslims face it when performing prayers. It is circumambulated during pilgrimage.

kalima See shahada.

Kamran An island in the Red Sea that now belongs to Yemen. In the nineteenth and early twentieth centuries, it housed a large quarantine station that was managed by the Ottoman Turkish and, later, British governments.

kazi See qazi.

Labbaik The Arabic call of the pilgrim evoking an intention to perform the pilgrimage only for God's glory.

lakh A number corresponding to one hundred thousand.

Maqam Ibrahimi A stone located in the Kaaba that is associated with the prophet Abraham, or Ibrahim in the Islamic tradition.

Masha Allah "God has willed it." A widely used Arabic phrase that conveys a range of
meanings, including happiness and thankfulness. It is the past tense form of inshallah,
"If God wills it."

maund A unit of measurement in India. Its weight varies but is generally about eighty
pounds.

mem/memsahib A South Asian term used to refer to European, and particularly English,
women. It derives from the word "madame."

miyan A term used after someone's name to denote respect, particularly in
South Asia.

mu'allim A guide that leads pilgrims through various ritual actions and prayers, and who
might also be tasked with arranging accommodation and transportation.

mu'azzama "Great" or "Honored." An Arabic term often appended to the name of the city
Mecca.

mufti Interpreters of religious law; authorized to issue fatwas or legal opinions.

mujtahid/mojtahed One who is qualified to practice ijtihad, or using reason and logic
to formulate solutions to religious issues in accordance with sources such as the
Quran and hadith.

munawwara "Luminous." A term often appended to the name of the city of Medina.

namaz A Persian-language term for the five daily prayers stipulated in Islam. Corresponds
to the Arabic term *salat*.

naqab/niqab A type of face covering or mask worn by some Muslim women.

navab/nawab A title imbued with various meanings in Mughal and British India, but
which generally referred to individuals who ruled over a territory, often in the name
of a higher power. English nabob.

pir A title for a Sufi spiritual guide.

paan A preparation with a base consisting of a betel leaf and areca nut; it is a mild stimulant
and is widely consumed, particularly in South Asia.

purdah A general term, typically South Asian in usage, that refers to any form of seclusion
practiced by women from unrelated men, whether through dress or through physical
separation; for example, separate seating or travel arrangements.

qazi A judge in the Islamic legal tradition. Also spelled qadi.

qibla The direction or object toward which Muslims turn when performing prayers, that is,
the Kaaba in Mecca. Also used as a suffix to denote respect.

Quran The primary religious text in Islam, it is believed to be the word of God as revealed
to the Prophet Muhammad over a period of many years. It is divided into chapters
(surahs) and verses (ayahs).

Safa and Marwa Two hills now located within the precincts of the Great Mosque of Mecca
between which pilgrims are expected to run seven times.

sahib An honorific, typically affixed to the end of a name. In South Asia, where women
sometimes avoid uttering the name of their spouse, it may also be used to refer to one's
husband.

sahiba The female form of sahib.

sarkar An honorific that may be used to refer to an official, or simply to denote respect.
Like the term sahib, it may also be used by women to refer to their husband in
South Asia.

shahada The Islamic profession of faith ("There is no god but God; Muhammad is the messenger of God.")

shahi "Royal."

sharif "Noble." A term typically appended to the names of places, including tombs, shrines, and cities, deemed holy. As a noun, it may refer to the political leader of the sharifate of Mecca.

sheikh An Arabic term that refers to a respected elder or tribal leader, but it is used in a range of languages and contexts to refer to an official, an expert in a field, an instructor, or simply to any Arab.

Subhan Allah "God be praised." A widely used Arabic phrase intended to glorify God that is used in several contexts but frequently expresses wonder, happiness, or astonishment.

Takbir To recite the phrase Allahu Akbar, "God is great."

tawaf The act of circumambulation, typically of the Kaaba.

'umrah Refers to the "minor" or "lesser" pilgrimage, involving circumambulation of the Kaaba, that may be completed at any time of the year. It is contrasted with the "major" pilgrimage, the hajj, which may only be completed at a specified time and takes more time as it consists of more rituals.

wudu'/vuzu' Ritual ablution, or the act of washing to purify oneself before prayer or handling the Quran, typically according to a set order.

Young Turk Revolution A 1908 revolution in the Ottoman Empire that reinstituted a short-lived constitution that stipulated a multiparty political system in the Ottoman parliament.

zenana Literally, "the women's area." It is used to refer to those parts of the house that are occupied by women and are thus not accessible to unrelated male visitors. Also called andarun and haram or harem.

CONTRIBUTORS

SIOBHAN LAMBERT-HURLEY is Professor of Global History at the University of Sheffield. She is author of *Elusive Lives: Gender, Autobiography, and the Self in Muslim South Asia*; (with Sunil Sharma) of *Atiya's Journeys: A Muslim Woman from Colonial Bombay to Edwardian Britain*; and of *Muslim Women, Reform and Princely Patronage: Nawab Sultan Jahan Begam of Bhopal*. She is editor (with Anshu Malhotra) of *Speaking of the Self: Gender, Performance, and Autobiography in South Asia* and of *A Princess's Pilgrimage: Nawab Sikandar Begum's* A Pilgrimage to Mecca.

DANIEL MAJCHROWICZ is Assistant Professor of South Asian Literature and Culture at Northwestern University. He is author of a book on South Asian travel writing, *The World in Words: Travel Writing and the Global Imagination in Muslim South Asia*. His work also appears in a number of edited volumes and journals, including *South Asia: Journal of South Asian Studies* and *Journal of Urdu Studies*.

SUNIL SHARMA is Professor of Persianate and Comparative Literature at Boston University. He is author of *Mughal Arcadia: Persian Literature in an Indian Court*; of *Amir Khusraw: The Poet of Sultans and Sufis*; of *Persian Poetry at the Indian Frontier: Mas'ud Sa'd Salman of Lahore*; and (with Siobhan Lambert-Hurley) of *Atiya's Journeys: A Muslim Woman from Colonial Bombay to Edwardian Britain*. He is editor (with Roberta Micallef) of *On the Wonders of Land and Sea: Persianate Travel Writing* and (with Siobhan Lambert-Hurley) of *Atiya's Journeys: A Muslim Woman from Colonial Bombay to Edwardian Britain*.

ASIYA ALAM is Associate Professor in the Department of History at Louisiana State University. She is author of *Women, Islam and Familial Intimacy in Colonial South Asia*.

ANDREW AMSTUTZ is Assistant Professor of History at the University of Arkansas at Little Rock. His work appears in various journals, including *South Asia: Journal of South Asian Studies* and *Comparative Studies of South Asia, Africa and the Middle East*.

C. CEYHUN ARSLAN is Assistant Professor of Comparative Literature at Koç University. His work appears in various journals, including *Comparative Literature Studies* and *Journal of Arabic Literature*.

DAVID BOYK is Assistant Professor of Instruction in the Department of Asian Languages and Cultures at Northwestern University. His work appears in *South Asia: Journal of South Asian Studies* and *Comparative Studies of South Asia, Africa and the Middle East*.

GREG HALABY teaches Arabic at Harvard University.

HANS HARDER is Professor and Head of the Department of Modern South Asian Languages and Literatures at Heidelberg University. He is author of *Sufism and Saint Veneration in Contemporary Bangladesh: The Maijbhandaris of Chittagong*. He is editor of *Literature and Nationalist Ideology: Writing Histories of Modern Indian Languages* and (with Beate Eschment) of *Looking at the Coloniser: Cross-Cultural Perceptions in Central Asia and the Caucasus, Bengal, and Related Areas*.

MEGAN ROBIN HEWITT is a professional Indonesian/Malay language translator and a documentary filmmaker with a PhD from the Department of South and Southeast Asian Studies at the University of California, Berkeley. Her research interests include cultural studies, comparative literature, performing arts, emancipatory pedagogies, agrarian history, and grassroots activism in Southeast Asia with a focus on Indonesia.

NURTEN KILIC-SCHUBEL is Associate Professor of History at Kenyon College. Her research focuses on political culture, state-building, and gender in medieval and early modern Central Eurasia.

ROBERTA MICALLEF is Professor of the Practice in Middle Eastern Literatures at Boston University. She is editor of *Illusion and Disillusionment: Travel Writing in the Modern Age* and (with Sunil Sharma) of *On the Wonders of Land and Sea: Persianate Travel Writing*.

INDEX